S0-AZA-893

THE US WAR MACHINE

WAR MACHINE

An illustrated encyclopedia of American military equipment and strategy

THE US

WAR MACHINE

An illustrated encyclopedia of American military equipment and strategy

Consultant: Dr. James E. Dornan, Jr.

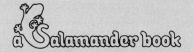

a Salamander book

Published by Crown Publishers, Inc.
NEW YORK

A Salamander Book

First published in 1978 in the United States by Crown Publishers Inc., One Park Avenue, New York, New York 10016, United States of America.

All rights reserved. Except for use in a review, no part of this book may be utilized or reproduced in any form or by any means, electronic or mechanical, including photocopying, recording, or by any information storage and retrieval system, without the permission in writing from the publisher.

First published in the United Kingdom in 1978 by Salamander Books Limited.

Library of Congress Cataloging in Publication Data
  Main entry under title:

The US war machine.

  Includes index.
  1. United States—Armed Forces. 2. United States—Military policy. 3. Munitions—United States. I. Dornan, James E.
UA23.U55   355'.00973   78-9071

© Salamander Books Ltd. 1978, Salamander House, 27 Old Gloucester Street, London WC1N 3AF, United Kingdom.

ISBN 0-517-53543-2

Second Impression 1979

All correspondence concerning the content of this volume should be addressed to Salamander Books Ltd.

This book is not to be sold outside the United States of America and Canada.

Published in Canada by General Publishing Company Ltd.

Credits

Editor: Ray Bonds

Designer: Steve Henderson

Color drawings: (aircraft) © Pilot Press, and Keith Fretwell (© Salamander Books Ltd.); (armored vehicles) Gordon Davies and Terry Hadler (© Salamander Books Ltd.) and © Profile Publications.

Line drawings: (aircraft 3-views and cutaways) © Pilot Press, except FB-111H (Paul Morris © Salamander Books Ltd.); (warships, except *Ohio* class submarine) A. D. Baker, with kind permission of Jane's *Fighting Ships*.

Filmset by SX Composing Ltd., England.

Color reproduction: Colourcraftsmen Ltd., and Metric Reproductions Ltd., England.

Monotone, two-tone and tri-tone reproduction: Tenreck Ltd., England.

Printed in Belgium by Henri Proost & Cie, Turnhout.

Editor's Acknowledgments

In the process of preparing this unique volume for publication I have been fortunate in having received the help and advice of so many people and organizations that it is impossible to acknowledge them all individually here. But I do thank them all for their assistance and their patience in the face of my persistent requests for information and illustrations. In particular, while co-ordinating the efforts of all concerned, I have been extremely grateful to have been able to call upon the unstinting energy and great depth of knowledge of United States (and worldwide) military/political affairs exercised by the consultant, the late Dr. James E. Dornan, Jr. With his guidance, an authoritative team of commentators was forged together whose contributions, combined with those of British technical specialists, will I am sure become standard works of reference (and food for thought). Dr. Dornan died tragically in January 1979. Each of the US Services has been extremely helpful, and I accordingly thank the offices of information of the Department of Defense, the Army, Navy, Air Force and Marine Corps, the Defense Intelligence Agency and other government organizations and agencies in the United States and in Europe.

I sincerely thank *Air Force Magazine* and *Army* for their cooperation in allowing us to reproduce or use as references some of their tables, diagrams and charts, and thank also all of the manufacturers of weapons and systems for making available many excellent photographs and useful information.

Ray Bonds

Contents

Foreword 8

The History of the
US Armed Forces 10

The US Concept
of National Interest 20

The US Defense
Organization 32

The US Intelligence
Machine 46

The US Strategic
Triad 58

The United States
Army 68

US Ground Forces
Weapons 86

The United States
Navy 102

US Warships 118

The United States
Air Force 146

US Combat Aircraft 160

The United States
Marine Corps 208

US Rockets and
Missiles 218

US Reserves and
National Guard 242

The War Machine
Evaluated 252

Appendices 264

Index 268

The Consultant

Dr. James E. Dornan, Jr., was Associate Professor and Chairman of the Department of Politics at the Catholic University of America, and Senior Political Science Scientist at the Strategic Studies Center of Stanford Research Institute International, Washington D.C. He received a B.A. (magna cum laude) from Le Moyne College and the Ph.D. from the Johns Hopkins University, both in Political Science. He also taught at Johns Hopkins University, lectured at numerous colleges and universities, and contributed articles to many professional journals, including *Political Science Reviewer, the Journal of Politics, Armed Forces Journal, Intercollegiate Review* (of which he was contributing editor), *Modern Age, Sea Power* and *Brassey's Annual.* He also contributed chapters to many books and monographs, including Salamander's *The Soviet War Machine,* and was the editor and co-author of the forthcoming volume, *US National Security Policy in the Decade Ahead* (Crane Russak). Dr. Dornan received research grants from NATO and the Earheart Foundation for the study of US–NATO military policy, and made study-visits to and attended conferences in both Europe and Asia a number of times in recent years. He was also a contributing editor of the *Journal of International Relations* and a member of the Editorial Board of *Orbis,* the Journal of the Foreign Policy Research Institute, University of Pennsylvania.

The Authors

Lt. Col. John R. Angolia, USA, JCOS, DUCO, is Instructor/Author at the US Army Command and General Staff College, Fort Leavenworth, Kansas. He received the B.A. in History from the Virginia Military Institute, is the author of seven books dealing with the history of Nazi Germany and its militaria, and has contributed numerous articles to professional journals on military subjects.

Dr. William R. Van Cleave is Professor of International Relations and Director of the Defense and Strategic Studies Program at the University of Southern California. He is a Consultant to the Office of the Secretary of Defense; was a member of the "B Team" (Presidential Panel to Review National Intelligence on USSR, 1976–77); was Special Assistant, Strategic Policy, NSC Affairs, and SALT, Office of the Secretary of Defense (ASD/ISA, 1969–71); was a member of the US Delegation to the Strategic Arms Limitation Talks (SALT) 1969–1971. Dr. Van Cleave is also a consultant to the Central Intelligence Agency, the US Energy Research and Development Agency and to many non-Governmental research institutes and agencies. He has contributed to very many professional journals and other publications, has testified to the US Senate, Committee on Armed Services, and is on the Board of Editors of *Orbis, Strategic Review* and the *Journal of International Relations.*

Dr. Ray S. Cline is Executive Director at Georgetown University Center for Strategic and International Studies, Washington D.C. Before assuming this position in 1974 Dr. Cline served for more than 30 years in several US Government agencies. He was Deputy Director for Intelligence in the Central Intelligence Agency (1962–66) and Director of the Bureau of Intelligence and Research in the Department of State (1969–73), a position equivalent to Assistant Secretary of State. Dr. Cline holds A.B., M.A. and Ph.D. degrees from Harvard University; he also studied at Balliol College, Oxford University, as a Henry Prize Fellow,

and later was a member of the Society of Fellows at Harvard. Dr. Cline is author of *Washington Command Post US Army in World War II,* a book on US military planning during World War II which is a standard reference on the subject; *Policy Without Intelligence, Foreign Policy* No. 17; *Secrets, Spies and Scholars: A Blueprint of the Essential CIA;* and *World Power Assessment.*

Christopher F. Foss is recognised as a leading authority on the world's armored fighting vehicles and allied subjects. He is editor of Jane's *World Armoured Fighting Vehicles,* author of two Jane's pocketbooks on modern AFV's and towed artillery, besides contributing annually to Jane's *Weapon Systems* and to *Infantry Weapons.* He is weapons correspondent to *Defence* magazine, and contributor to many professional journals. Mr. Foss is author and co-author of many other books on ground forces weapons, and was consultant and chief author of Salamander's *The Illustrated Encyclopedia of the World's Tanks and Fighting Vehicles.*

Stephen P. Gibert is Professor of Government and Director of the National Security Studies Program at Georgetown University, Washington D.C. Dr. Gibert has served as an advisor to the Asia Foundation and the Government of the Union of Burma, and has been a visiting Professor at the University of Rangoon and the US Naval War College. He has contributed a number of articles on foreign policy and international security affairs to leading professional journals and is co-author of the book, *Arms for the Third World: Soviet Military Aid Diplomacy.* His most recent work is *Soviet Images of America.*

Maj. Gen. Robert N. Ginsburgh, USAF (ret.) has served in numerous important posts in the US Air Force command, including Deputy Director of the Joint Staff, Organization of the Joint Chiefs of Staff; Air Force Member, Chair-

man's Staff Group, Office of the Chairman, Joint Chiefs of Staff; Commander of the Aerospace Studies Institute; Chief, Office of Air Force History; Director of Information, Office of the Secretary of the Air Force. Maj. Gen. Ginsburgh also served as senior staff member, National Security Council Staff, and was the Armed Forces Aide to the President (1968). He graduated from Phillips Academy, Andover, Mass., Harvard University, the US Military Academy at West Point, the Air Command and Staff School at Maxwell AFB, and the National War College. His military decorations and awards include the Distinguished Service Medal, Silver Star, Legion of Merit with one oak leaf cluster, Joint Service Commendation Medal, Army Commendation Medal, and Purple Heart.

Bill Gunston is an advisor to several major aviation companies. He is a noted writer on aviation and technical affairs, being former technical editor of *Flight International*, and technology editor of *Science Journal*. He is a contributor to Jane's *All The World's Aircraft* and to many authoritative international military journals. Mr. Gunston is author of the Salamander book, *The Illustrated Encyclopedia of the World's Modern Military Aircraft*, and contributed to Salamander's *The Soviet War Machine*.

Lawrence J. Korb is Professor of Management, US Naval War College, and Adjunct Scholar of the American Enterprise Institute for federal budgetary analysis and national security policy. He served as consultant to the Office of the Secretary of Defense, the National Security Council and the Office of Education. He is the author of *The Joint Chiefs of Staff: The First Twenty Years; The Price of Preparedness, The FY 1978-82 Defense Program;* and has co-authored *Public Claims on US Output: Federal Budget Options for the Last Half of the Decade.* In addition he has edited and contributed articles on military affairs to several books and journals.

Hugh Lyon is former Research Officer of the Shipbuilding Record Survey, London. He is founder-member of Warship Society, a contributor to several international technical journals on naval affairs, and author of technical books, including Salamander's *The Encyclopedia of the World's Warships*. He holds a B.A. (Hons) in History from Durham University.

Bruce F. Powers is Director of (Research) Planning and Director of a Study of Sea-Based Aircraft at the University of Rochester's Center for Naval Analyses, Arlington, Virginia. He has been with the University for over 17 years, and his career has alternated between studies in Washington and one-year assignments with admirals who were in command of fleets. The most recent of these was in London, with CinCUSNavEur; the one before that was at sea with the Sixth Fleet Commander in the Mediterranean. He holds degrees in Operational Research (Illinois Institute of Technology), Physical Chemistry (University of Chicago) and Chemistry (University of Illinois).

Alan Ned Sabrosky, Ph. D. (University of Michigan) is Assistant Professor of Politics at the Catholic University of America, and Research Associate at the Foreign Policy Research Institute, Philadelphia. A specialist in international security affairs and civil-military relations, he has contributed to numerous military anthologies and professional journals, including *Asian Affairs, South-East Asian Spectrum* and the *Journal of Conflict Resolution.* He is editor of *Blue-Collar Soldiers? —Unionization and the US Military;* author of *Defense Manpower Policy: A Critical Reappraisal;* and co-author of *The Conventional-Revisionist Controversy and the US Role in World Affairs.*

Lt. Col Donald B. Vought, USA (Ret.) retired from service with the US Army after 23 years of service which included three years with NATO, one year in Vietnam and one year in Iran as advisor to the Imperial Armor School. He was for seven years on the faculty of the US Army Command and General Staff College at Fort Leavenworth, Kansas, where he specialized in low-intensity warfare, intercultural communications and the study of national development as a multidisciplinary phenomenon. He is a graduate of Norwich University with M.A.s in Political Science (University of Louisville) and International Relations (Boston University). Lt. Col. Vought has been a frequent contributor to professional conferences and publications.

Roy A. Werner is on the staff of the US Senate Foreign Relations Committee and has previously served as a Foreign Affairs Officer in the US Federal Energy Administration. He has been Task Force Director and Associate Director, Programs, White House Conference on Youth, consultant to Senator Philip Hart, Legislative Assistant to Senator John Glenn, an analyst at the Office of the Secretary of the Army, and Secretary (Executive Director), Oxford University Strategic Studies Group. He received a D.Phil. and B.Phil. from Oxford University, his B.A. (magna cum laude) from Florida Technological University, and a Diploma from the Industrial College of the Armed Forces.

Russell F. Weigley is professor of history at Temple University, Philadelphia. He has taught also at the University of Pennsylvania, Drexel University, and Dartmouth College, and in 1973–74 he was US Army Visiting Professor of Military History Research at the US Army Military History Institute and the Army War College. He is president of the Pennsylvania Historical Association and has been president of the American Military Institute. His books include *Towards an American Army: Military Thought from Washington to Marshall; History of the United States Army;* and *The American Way of War: A History of United States Military Strategy and Policy.*

Foreword

by General Richard G. Stilwell,
US Army (Ret.), former Commander,
Eighth Army and United Nations
Command, Korea

Throughout the 1970s, the foreign and defense policies of the United States have been the subject of deepening controversey. And since policies and power are closely interrelated, the primary focus of debate has been the posture of the American military establishment. Issues of deterrent and war fighting concepts, of force structure and force balance, of tactical doctrine, of weaponry, of deployments, readiness and staying power have all come under intense scrutiny and critique. While the great bulk of analyses and commentary has originated in American circles and been addressed to the domestic body politics, interest in these vital matters has been international in scope. The debates have commanded high and sustained attention among the allies of the United States, within much of the balance of the free world and in the Peoples Republic of China. The reason needs no elaboration. In varying degrees, all of these nations are dependent on the will and ability of the United States—and principally through the medium of its armed forces—to help them deal with extant and perceived future threats to their security and well-being. Hence, the timeliness and importance of this comprehensive and objective profile of the American military machine.

As detailed in the pages of this volume, the United States armed forces are impressive for their size, power, and versatility. Their reach is global. They possess the means for, and are geared to conduct, military operations throughout the entire spectrum of conflict from strategic nuclear exchange to high intensity conventional combat to sub-limited warfare to projection of power in support of political initiative. Backing these forces are enormous demographic resources, unsurpassed industrial capability and a pre-eminent scientific base. In the aggregate, these formidable strengths are proof positive that the United States is a military superpower. However, these strengths alone do not gauge the adequacy of the defense posture of the nation or, pertinently, of the free

world. That assessment involves consideration of numerous other factors, some quantifiable and some not. Principal among these factors are the range and nature of missions assigned and the capabilities of potential adversaries.

In the years since World War II the United States military establishment has shouldered responsibilities of unprecedented magnitude and diversity. Its supreme mission—akin to that of the armed forces of any nation which acts responsibly—is to protect the American people, institutions and territory from direct and indirect attack. Beyond that, it is tasked with the contingent defense of Western Europe, Japan and numerous other nations persuant to multi-lateral and bi-lateral security arrangements to which the United States is party; all of these commitments, incidentally, involve extensive preparations for the orchestration of US and allied forces under varying coalition modes. Moreover, since the United States exercises leadership of what is, in essence, a maritime alliance its military establishment bears primary responsibility for ensuring that member states have uninterrupted use of international waters and air space and access to markets, raw materials and energy sources. Overall, those armed forces have had the generic task of preventing the threat of use of naked military force—particularly nuclear—for purpose of political or economic coercion of the nations of the free world community. Though this complex of missions has generated exceedingly heavy demands and the United States military resources have been spread correspondingly thin, the record of the last twenty years and more has been quite creditable. All major tasks have been successfully discharged. Vietnam, of course, was a conspicuous failure, albeit one due, in the main, to collapse of national will rather than inadequate military performance. In any case, past achievements are not a harbinger of the future. For one thing, the United States and her allies were spared multiple concurrent crises. For another, the United States enjoyed, for most of the period, both actual and perceived superiority in the strategic nuclear dimension, reasonably assured command of the seas and a decided edge in capability to project force to areas outside the Eurasian land mass. These favorable differentials counterbalanced weaknesses in other segments of the overall defense posture. However, these differentials are not likely to persist, given the prodigious Soviet efforts to overcome the United States' lead in precisely these areas.

To be sure, the lengthening shadow cast by the Soviet military machine is not the only threat that needs to be reckoned with. But it is certainly the most ominous. The last ten years have been witness to extraordinary increases in Soviet nuclear and conventional forces. As the build-up continues unabated all evidence points to Soviet intent to achieve dominance in every dimension of military power. Though prepared for the eventuality of armed conflict at any level and at any time, the Soviets have studied Clausewitz with consummate care. They thus aspire to advance, step by step, toward world hegemony employing every strategem short of unambiguous war. By consequence, the principal role of the Soviet armed forces is to undergird political and economical moves to disrupt the free world alliance system, sap the vitality of the free enterprise area and isolate the United States and China. Thus, the Soviet armed forces constitute a many faceted threat.

Over two centuries, the US military has been tested, retested, and never found wanting, but its supreme challenge lies ahead. With the quantitative military balance (not only in the ground components, where Soviet advantages have been long standing, but in nuclear, naval and air dimensions as well, given the respective military trend lines) decidedly adverse and with the former qualitative edge increasingly in doubt, we can assume a favorable outcome in the event of war only by superior concepts, tactics and leadership. We are desperately in need of a strategy —not only for war-fighting, but for winning without war.

For the first time since the War of Independence, the United States forces are destined to be the under-dog. These predictable developments are cause for concern but they by no means portend unfavorable outcomes either in war or in military confrontation in crisis scenarios short of war. In the long history of warfare numerical advantage has rarely been the decisive factor. Nor have perceptions of relative power in crisis situations been primarily shaped by size alone. Most frequently, the major determinents of favorable issue—in campaign or in confrontation— have been superior strategy, tactical concepts, leadership, audacity and discipline. Naturally the United States and its allies cannot afford to let the quantitative gap widen appreciably more or, worse yet, accept technological inferiority. As an example, the Soviets must not be permitted to attain a politically exploitable superiority in strategic nuclear systems. Nor can the Soviets be allowed to inhibit free world projection of power or untrammelled use of the high seas. But, in the last analysis, the United States armed forces will measure up to their manifold tasks to the extent —and only to the extent—that they are able to devise the better strategy and carry out that strategy with unexcelled professionalism.

The History of the US Armed Forces

Russell F. Weigley, Professor of History at Temple University, Philadelphia; past-president, American Military Institute.

The famous martial pageantry of the US Military Academy at West Point is that of a bygone era. The close-order drill of the Corps of Cadets has its roots in the discipline taught by Baron von Steuben to General George Washington's Continental Army at Valley Forge in 1778, and beyond that in the necessity of eighteenth-century armies to maneuver on the battlefield as though the soldiers were automatons on parade, to maintain the line in the face of the enemy's volley firing and bayonet charge. The cadets' gray uniforms memorialize Winfield Scott's and Eleazar Wheelock Ripley's brigades of United States Regulars who charged the British at Chippewa and Lundy's Lane in Upper Canada in 1814, the first battles in which American troops were able to hold their own against approximately equal numbers of British veterans in stand-up combat throughout the battle. Scott's and Ripley's men happened to be clothed in gray, because the quartermaster had run out of regulation United States Army blue.

For the United States, the perpetuating of ancient military memories and rituals is much more paradoxical than it is for other nations such as Britain, because for Great Britain the remote past is for the most part the nation's militarily prominent past. For the United States, in contrast, as General Maxwell D. Taylor remarked in a West Point commencement address in 1963 in the very midst of the antique pageantry, it is only since World War II that the nation has assuredly attained a special eminence among the military powers of the world. It did so with abrupt suddenness. Through most of the American past, the United States was in military tutelage to Europe, almost in a colonial relationship militarily. Since 1945, military officers from all countries friendly to the United States have attended military schools in America; but until the abrupt change of World War II, Americans learned their military lessons from Europe.

The principal reason for this history of recent and rapid transition from military obscurity to military prominence is simply that until World War I, or at least until the American War with Spain in 1898, the United States was an isolated power not participating in world military events or the world diplomacy of the military great powers. The oceans, not American ships or forts, were the source of American security. The American army was less an army of the European type than a constabulary for the patrolling of the Indian country in the West. By European standards, the American armed forces are almost armed forces without a history—which is no doubt one reason why Americans cling all the more tightly to the thin historical military tradition that does exist, as in the West Point parades.

After so rapid a rise to first-rank power, the American forces in the twentieth century have displayed a sensitivity about their status as newcomers. For a century, from the close of the 1775–1783 and 1812–1815 conflicts with Great Britain until World War I, the military forces of United States did not have to test themselves against any first-rate foreign foe. Under these circumstances, General John J. Pershing, the commander of the 1917–1918 American Expedi-

tionary Force, was exceedingly conscious that his army was meeting first-division opponents on the first modern occasion, and that he must take care to make a good impression from the very beginning, for the sake of his own army's morale as well as to uphold America's weight in Allied councils. Many American soldiers themselves had come to doubt, as Lieutenant Colonel James S. Pettit had put it in a prize-winning essay in the *Journal* of the United States Military Service Institution in 1906, whether the American democracy could "maintain an organization or discipline comparable to that of little Japan", let alone the Continental powers.

General Pershing himself sufficiently doubted American readiness for European military competition that, if he had been able to have his way, he would have put every American division through nearly a year-long training regimen in France under French and British instructors, as he did the 1st Division, before committing his troops to the front in carefully planned set-piece battles, as he did with the 1st Division in a small offensive at Cantigny on May 28, 1918. The great German offensives of 1918 washed away Pershing's painstaking plans, obliging him to commit his troops to battle with much less preparation than he would have liked. Their performance was considerably better than their own officers anticipated, but sensitivity to the feeling — and reality — of being newcomers lingered on. In their final campaign of the war, the Meuse–Argonne Offensive of September 26–November 11, 1918, American troops were still suffering the disproportionately high casualties that fall to soldiers who are not battle-wise and battle-wary.

As late as World War II, the US Navy still displayed an acute and no doubt excessive consciousness of the fact that it was the only great navy that had never fought a full-scale fleet action. Because the Navy had no Tsushima and no Jutland in its past, in the Pacific Ocean war in 1941–1945 it pursued a super-Jutland—a grand, climactic battle against the Japanese fleet—with zeal beyond the boundaries of strategic good sense. The pursuit almost produced disaster when Admiral William F. Halsey followed a Japanese decoy fleet and thus exposed the Philippine Islands invasion force at Leyte Gulf to the main Japanese fleet in October, 1944. Fortunately, by this time the skill as well as the bravery of the crews of the smaller and older American warships guarding the invasion beaches was enough to discourage Japanese admirals who enjoyed material superiority.

The recency of America's emergence as a world military power has shaped the American armed forces also in matters more profound than an acute sensitivity about the thinness of the country's past military tradition. Having fought few wars against major foreign powers, at least until the recent past, Americans still tend to regard foreign war as an extraordinary occasion. Their military history combines with the national ideology, which is derived from the liberalism of the eighteenth and nineteenth centuries, to assure them that war is an abnormal state of affairs, that it can be accounted for only in terms of an uncommon eruption of evil into the world, and that the appropriate response is to extirpate the evil by means of an

In comparison with human history the life-span of the United States is but the blink of an eyelid. But these two centuries have seen the US involved in military actions of every kind. Gettysburg, 1-3 July 1864 (below) is remembered for its intensity of casualties, among other things, whereas the favorite heroic image is the raising of the Old Glory over Iwo Jima on 26 March 1944 by four Marines, subject of the Marine Corps Memorial at Arlington (far left). Controversy reached its peak in the "involvement" in Southeast Asia, though it was muted in 1965 when the F-4B Phantom of Navy squadron VF-21 dropped its bombs on the Viet Cong (left).

all-out military assault upon it. Thus the American propensity for demanding "unconditional surrender" of their country's enemies in war. To the argument that Americans may have grown more sophisticated in the use of military force to serve their national interests during their exercise of world power since 1945, it is necessary to respond with partial agreement, but also to point to the popular dissatisfaction in America during both the Korean and the Vietnam wars over the fact that in those conflicts military force was applied in limited, measured dosage, not hurled all-out against the enemy to compel his complete capitulation.

Indeed, the American tendency to regard war as demanding unlimited force in pursuit of the unlimited subjugation of the enemy has still deeper roots than those provided by inexperience in world affairs and by the national ideology, with still deeper consequences in shaping the American armed forces. Though American wars against European military powers have been few, the American past includes much experience of war with the North American Indians—almost continuous experience from 1607 to 1890. The military struggles against the Indians were of course the first wars fought in their new homes by Europeans who emigrated to the New World, the first wars to form a distinctive part of the American national memory.

From a very early juncture, the Indian wars took a different line of development from that which warfare in Europe was following in the seventeenth and eighteenth centuries. European war was becoming limited war, an enterprise of statecraft waged for dynastic, boundary, and colonial advantages but not for the very survival of the major states, in an era when monarchs recognized their common European and monarchical interests as well as their mutual rivalry and thus did not seek to eliminate each other altogether. In the same era, between

the Peace of Westphalia in 1648 and the onset of the French Revolution, when European war developed strict limitations, war in America grew decidedly unlimited. War in America became war for survival.

As early as 1643, for example, the Pequot War between the Connecticut and Massachusetts settlements on the one hand and the Pequot tribe on the other ended in the white men's complete destruction of the Pequots as an identifiable tribe. In King Philip's War, fought by a confederation of Wampanoags, Narragansetts, Nipmucks, and Abenaki under a chieftain the English called King Philip against the New England colonies in 1675–1676, the Indians in turn came dangerously close to throwing the still-youthful New England settlements back into the sea. The Americans' experience of war against the Indians became an experience of war aimed at total results, the extermination of the enemy as a military power, even as a society. Because the wars were frequently fought by what a later generation would call guerrilla methods, and since the Indians did not observe European rules for the conduct of the fighting, the wars aimed at total results seemed often to be waged with total ferocity.

In the War of the American Revolution, the Americans again displayed the conviction nourished by their Indian wars that only total solutions would suffice. First the Indians had to be removed completely from the neighborhood of the white Americans' settlements; then the French had to decamp from North America; now it was the British whose presence could in no way be endured. Not satisfied to expel the British from those colonies that had spontaneously risen in rebellion, the American rebels promptly in 1775 mounted expeditions to drive the British from Canada, which had not joined the rebellion. Though the conquest of

Canada proved beyond the rebels' strength, the idea of again attempting it persisted throughout the war.

Furthermore, the American desire for total solutions made itself felt once more in the new Treaty of Paris of 1783, ending the War of the Revolution, just as it had shaped the older Treaty of Paris of 1763. Having tried and failed to conquer Canada, the new United States could hardly demand its cession. But the presumptuousness of the infant Republic was considerable nevertheless. With only the most tenuous of military claims to the vast area extending west from the Appalachian Mountains to the Mississippi River, and with the British still in effective control of much of the area, the United States insisted that the British should not only recognize the independence of the thirteen rebellious colonies, but should cede to them the whole trans-Appalachian region. Once again furthermore, the American preference for unlimited solutions to the issues of war converged with a British desire to placate —this time to wean the United States from its 1778 alliance with France by means of British generosity. The United States received the Mississippi River as its western frontier.

It might be argued that the limitations of American military power during the Republic's early years soon curbed the tendency to seek total results from war. In the War of 1812–1815 with Great Britain, after all, the United States eventually settled for a peace reverting to the status quo ante bellum. In the War with Mexico in 1846–1848, the Yankees did not totally exterminate Mexican military power or sov-

Below: A stylized yet possibly truthful painting (by Chappel, 1828-87) of the Wyoming massacre of July 1778, one of a series in which settlers in the Susquehanna valley were murdered by Tories and Indians.

ereignty, but rather made do with the limited territorial acquisitions of the former Republic of Texas plus everything west from Texas to the Pacific Ocean—present New Mexico, Arizona, Utah, Nevada, and California, along with parts of Colorado and Wyoming (which might lead to the exclamation, "Some limits!"). But caution is necessary in ascribing even to the early, and militarily weak, American Republic any limited conception of the proper results of war. Though the actual peace terms of the War of 1812 were modest, they had been preceded by plenty of American talk about the annexation of all of Canada; it was not the will that was lacking, but the means. In regard to Mexico in 1848, by which time American military means were more ample, President James K. Polk rushed through the Senate a peace treaty negotiated by an emissary whom he had already repudiated before the terms were arranged, in part because the President thought he must hurry lest public sentiment for the annexation of all of Mexico get out of hand.

Nor did the military power of the American Republic remain at all feeble for very long. As early as the War with Mexico, the United States had the military capacity to conquer another American republic having to travel thousands of miles from the economic and population centers of the United States in order to do so. By the 1680s, the United States could mobilize against a domestic rebellion, taking the form of the secession of eleven of its sourthern states, great armies and navies that made it 'y 1865 the foremost military nation in the world—for a brief moment at least, until, characteristically, with the extermination of the evils that had caused the war the country hastily demobilized.

Meanwhile, for four years the American Civil War pitted armies of hundreds of thousands against each other in an arena that was continental in extent—one of the major wars of world history, and even though viewed legalistically it involved "only" a domestic rebellion, by far the greatest American war until World War II, and thus a war that confirmed American conceptions about the nature

of war and military power all the way to World War II, at the least. Once more, the United States sought a total resolution of all the issues of the war, particularly the total extermination of all of the rebellious Southern Confederacy's pretensions to sovereignty. If this absolute result was largely implicit in the fact that the contest originated in a rebellion, nevertheless American preconceptions about war made the Union government all the more ready to assume, without examining the issue, that the outcome could be nothing else but total elimination of the enemy as a political and military force. Furthermore, the means of pursuing this end still more explicitly reflected the combination of American military experience in the Indian wars and the plenitude of United States military power by the 1860s. The means of securing the Confederacy's unconditional surrender was to be the total destruction of the Confederate armies.

When U. S. Grant moved from triumphs in the western theater of war to become Commanding General of all the Armies of the United States at the beginning of 1864, he instructed each of the commanders of major army groups and field armies under him that their objective was the destruction of the enemy armies contending against them. Thus to Major General George G. Meade, commanding the Army of the Potomac, the principal Union army in the eastern theater, Grant wrote: "Lee's army will be your objective point. Wherever Lee goes, there you will go also." To Major General William Tecumseh Sherman, commanding a group of three Union armies in the West, Grant gave similar instructions to grasp in battle and destroy the Confederate forces led by General Joseph E. Johnston. When the Confederates formed a new army later in the year to operate in the Shenandoah Valley of Virginia, Grant again similarly told the War Department: ". . . I want Sheridan put in command of all the troops in the field, with instructions to put himself south of the enemy and follow him to the death. Wherever the enemy goes let our troops go also."

Sherman advancing out of the western theater toward the Atlantic coast and Major General

Above: President Lincoln conferring with McClellan and staff officers after the Battle of Antietam in September 1862. This removed the threat to Washington and drove the South from Northern soil.

Philip Sheridan in the Shenandoah carried still further the totalization of the means by which total submission was to be imposed upon the enemy. With Grant's advice and encouragement, Sherman and Sheridan attempted to destroy not only the enemy armies, but also the Confederacy's economic ability to sustain the war, and the will of the southern people to persevere in the war. Grant instructed Sheridan: "If the war is to last another year, we want the Shenandoah Valley to remain a barren waste." Sherman's avowed purpose was not only to deprive the Confederacy of economic resources, but to break the morale of the people by terrorizing them: ". . . we are not only fighting hostile armies," he wrote, "but a hostile people, and must make old and young, rich and poor, feel the hard hand of war, as well as the organized armies."

After the utter destruction of the Confederate armies and the ruination of the Confederate economy produced the desired complete abandonment of Confederate claims to sovereignty, the United States returned with renewed vigor to fight the last of the wars against the Indians and rid the continental domain of Indian military power—and any vital Indian culture— once and for all. As the attitudes formed from the beginning of the Indian wars helped lead the United States to conduct the Civil War as a total war, so the experience of the Civil War diluted any humane compunctions that hitherto restrained the United States Army in dealing with the Indians. Specifically, the Army now applied the strategy of Sherman and Sheridan to the Indian wars, aiming its blows not only at the Indians' fighting power but at their fragile economy and their ability to maintain any existence at all independent of the white men.

An American historical tradition at least as strong as the compulsion to pursue war to total

victory—the fear of entanglement in Europe—
served to keep the war with Spain in 1898 a
relatively limited conflict. The Americans were
content to destroy all the remnants of the
Spanish Empire in the western hemisphere and
the Pacific, without carrying the war to Spain
itself. In World War I, the American participation came too late and was relatively too small
for the American attitudes toward war to have
much impact on the peace. Indeed, American
emotional involvement was limited enough that
President Woodrow Wilson could appear
especially generous in his peacemaking policies
toward Germany. At that, Wilson did not
necessarily reflect American public opinion,
and General Pershing was probably closer to
the views of most of his countrymen in his
urging that the Allies should punish Germany
by marching all the way to Berlin.

In World War II, the United States participated much longer and made a much larger
contribution to the eventual Allied victory, with
a consequently larger impact on the shape of
the war and the peace terms that followed it.
The United States emerged from the war at its

**Right: American "doughboys" in World
War I made up in spirit for their lack of
experience. This is the 43rd Balloon
Company USA on the march near
Bertrance Farm shortly before the
Armistice.**

**Below: In World War II American
industrial might was crucial to Allied
victory. Here, supplies and troops pour
onto Normandy beaches just after D-Day,
supporting the ousting of German forces
from France.**

military high tide, unquestionably the greatest military power in the world of 1945. The war was a climax of American military history also in the sense that the American past fitted the United States so well to wage its part in it. Adolf Hitler's Nazi regime and its partners and accessories in international crime appeared throughout the Allied world to be enemies so villainous that there could be almost universal agreement on the American prescription of "unconditional surrender" as the only appropriate peace terms for such a crew. If a characteristically American peace of total victory over altogether submissive enemies won assent as the objective of all the Allies, then a characteristically American military strategy became a suitable means of pursuing the objective, though on this point agreement proved less universal.

Nevertheless, the American strategists persuaded their somewhat reluctant British partners that the principal Anglo-American military effort of the war in Europe must be a cross-Channel invasion of Europe, to take on the German armies in western Europe not where they were weak but where their strength was greatest, to confront the enemy's strength and annihilate it in the manner of U. S. Grant facing Robert E. Lee. The American emphasis on the simultaneous strategy of the Combined Bomber Offensive against Germany meanwhile echoed Sherman's and Sheridan's extension of Grant's strategy of annihilation from the enemy armed forces to the enemy economy. In the Pacific Ocean war, the US Navy similarly sought to annihilate the principal enemy armed force in the theater of war, in this instance the Japanese battle fleet, drawing on the strategic precepts not only of the American Civil War but of the Navy's own great strategic

thinker, the turn-of-the-century American prophet of sea power, Rear Admiral Alfred Thayer Mahan. From the air, the Americans wracked Japan not only with a bomber offensive comparable to the one waged against Germany, but eventually with the weapon representing the apotheosis of the Sherman-Sheridan manner of war. Meanwhile the tremendous wealth of the United States, as developed in the midtwentieth century, and its large population, afforded it ample resources to wage a war seeking unconditional surrender through unconditional means. So well did the circumstances of World War II fit American capacities and methods in the waging of war, that it was with this war that the United States became abruptly transformed from pupil to tutor in its relations with most of the other military powers.

It will have become apparent by now, furthermore, that however recent the emergence of the United States as a major actor on the world military stage, the Americans historically have not been altogether a peaceful, unmilitary people. Yet they have also drawn from their history strong prejudices regarding the military. The Americans, like the British, have usually been loath to apply military conscription in peacetime. The desire to escape compulsory military service was among the motives that propelled many of their immigrant ancestors to the New World. The United States also inherited from its British antecedents the British suspicion of standing, professional military forces. When the victors of the American Revolution wrote the United States Constitution in 1787, the military dictatorship of Cromwell was recent enough to be a vivid part of their historical memories, and still more recently Great Britain's threat to maintain a large standing army in her American colonies

had reacted upon inherited fears of military usurpation of power to serve as one of the major causes of the Revolution. Therefore the United States Constitution contains elaborate safeguards against military despotism, such as guarantees of the existence of armed citizens' militias in the various states to offset the federal military forces, and division of control over the federal military between the President and Congress.

At that, fear that the Constitution went too far toward encouraging a powerful military helped make its ratification a near thing, and throughout the nineteenth century Americans persisted in viewing the small Regular Army acting as a constabulary on the Indian frontier as though it were a potential praetorian guard that might bar the doors of Congress and create an emperor.

Thus the Americans have waged war zestfully when war has engulfed them; but in addition to regarding war as an abnormal condition, they have distrusted the professional soldiers whom they need to lead them in war. One effect of a widespread civilian distrust of the military has been a reciprocated military of American society, politics, and even democracy, on the part of the professional soldiers. The American army's leading writer and intellectual in the nineteenth century, Brevet Major General Emory Upton, capitalized upon his Civil War record of heroism to spread through the army after the war a gospel of military reforms along German lines to im-

Below: The US Army is back in the Philippines and a 37mm anti-tank gun of the 129th Regiment, 37th Division, opens up on Japanese positions on the west wall of the Intramuros, Manila.

prove the efficiency of the army, coupled with a pessimism that democratic America would ever reorganize its military in the proper German manner, or that therefore the United States could ever compete militarily with the great powers. Upton's doleful influence was a principal ingredient in the self-doubt already alluded to as part of the American forces' belated plunge into the mainstream of military history.

The means on which Americans have historically preferred to rely to reconcile their distrust of professional soldiers and standing armies with their penchant for ferocity in war has been some form of people's army. Before the Revolution, every British colony had maintained a citizens' militia of part-time soldiers, who left their plows and workshops to take up muskets whenever they were needed for defense against the Indians and the French. The Continental Army of the Revolution sprang forth from these citizens' militias, and the Continental Army's eventual success against the British army, despite the military deficiencies of the Continentals' militia origins, lent substance to the belief of the writers of the Constitution that state militias could fend off the potential military tyranny of a federal army. The citizens' militias maintained by the states indeed gave each of the member states of the American Union enough military power of its own, and thus a large enough measure of sovereignty, that the states had the capacity to go to war against one another in 1861. The Southern Confederacy began life with an army already in being, because it had the militia forces of the seceded states. Just as the colonial militia had formed the core of the Continental Army in the Revolution, so now in the Civil War it was the militia forces of the states—not the Regular Army, so tiny as to be insignificant —around which both the Union and the Confederate armies took shape.

With such a military tradition as this, it is not remarkable that well into the twentieth century opponents of Emory Upton's ideas of reforming the American military on the German model argued for reorganization upon the Swiss model instead. The latter would have reduced the professional cadre to the slimmest of skeletons and made almost the whole of the American army a citizens' militia. Paradoxically in view of the historic American dislike of conscription, the means of recruitment for this democratized army would have been universal military training.

Taking on the military responsibilities of a great power ruled out, if nothing else did, America's emulating the Swiss army. Nevertheless, we have now surveyed a complex of deeply engrained American attitudes toward the military and war, all of which enhance the difficulties of maintaining American armed forces suitable to the responsibilities of the United States in the late 20th century. The introduction in 1945 of nuclear weapons made the absolute destruction of both enemy armed forces and enemy resources and population all too literally possible. Despite the nation's past military history, Americans still nourish a sense of guilt over having dropped two atomic bombs on Japanese cities; American military power had to be used henceforth with uncharacteristic limitations and restraint.

Yet the Korean and Vietnam wars indicate how quickly the American public become impatient with a restrained application of military power—with a so-called "no win" war—and these wars cast doubt on the future availability of limited war as a tool of American statecraft. The historic American suspicion of the military remains alive, furthermore, to aggravate public discontent whenever the United States attempts to use military force as an instrument of policy.

Because few Americans trust the military in any event, during an unpopular limited war the military can be equally accused of bloodthirsty militarism for waging the war at all, and of pusillanimity for not waging it in the historic American mode with all available means employed! During the Vietnam crisis, the American military were thus assailed at home from right and left simultaneously, and much of the public apparently believed both lines of criticism simultaneously, however contradictory they were. Meanwhile, with the United States since World War II maintaining by far the largest peacetime armed forces in its history —about two and a half million men and women even after the close of the Vietnam War—and at immense cost, traditional fears of military influence upon government have been aroused as never since the eighteenth century. Occasionally the old fear of a military *coup d'état*— Oliver Cromwell updated—surfaces again, as in the novel *Seven Days in May.*

More realistically, the fear is that military forces so consistently large and expensive, with much of the economy at least partially dependent on their remaining large, have created a military-industrial complex whose influence on national policy is everywhere and inescapable. There is also public apprehension that having immense military power at their disposal will make Presidents excessively willing to seek a military route out of every otherwise intractable international crisis—though what happened at home during the Korean and Vietnam wars

Below: In the closing stages of the Pacific war every ounce of firepower was needed to reduce fanatical defenders of even small islands and atolls. Here a BB— possibly the Missouri, "Mighty Mo", on which the Japanese surrender was signed —pounds Okinawa in April 1945.

should have considerably undercut this ground for concern.

Altogether, the persistent American suspicion of the military and its place in American life did much to end conscription and cause the United States to revert in 1974 to all-volunteer armed forces. Another paradox is involved here, for just as the pre-World-War-II proponents of a Swiss-style army recognized the implicitly democratic character of a universal obligation to military service, so in assisting the return to all-volunteer forces, the opponents of military influence in American life have helped increase the separation of the military from civilian contributions to their attitudes and values.

These unsettling and destabilizing historical tendencies and conditions affecting the American war machine ought to be pondered by all those states and those millions of the world's people who rely on American military power as the principal counterweight to the might of the Soviet Union. With the Americans carrying the military leadership of the non-Communist world, a still relatively inexperienced military hand is at the throttle, and one not accustomed to measured, patient applications of military force adjusted to complex situations. Furthermore, the American military have to contend

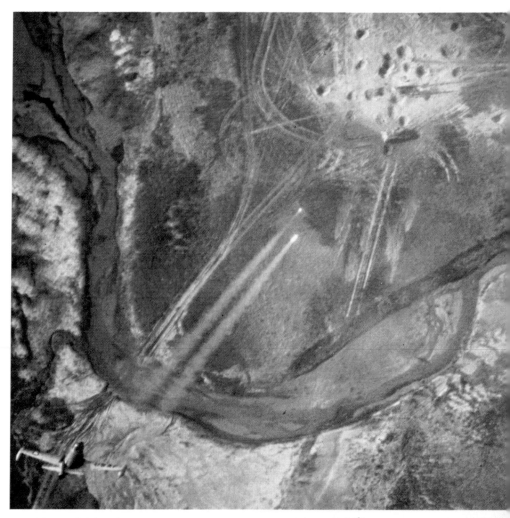

Right: Korea caught Western allies off-balance. Even shiny new jets, such as this F-80C Shooting Star rocketing North Korean tanks, were ill-adapted to harsh and distant land campaigns.

Below: September 1951 and men of the 1st Marine Division advance warily on the suspected hideout of a sniper who had been holding up the US advance. Advanced technology was often little help, to the slogging foot-soldier.

Above: Trying to climb up Mutters Ridge near the DMZ (Demilitarized Zone) north of Dong Ha, Vietnam, in 1968, Marines of the 2nd Battalion, 3rd Division throw grenades.

Below: Early in the American involvement, on 8 January 1966, M48A3 battle tanks of the 1st Infantry Division trundle slowly behind a rice-laden bullock cart heading for Trung Lap northwest of Saigon.

with all the international military menaces of a perilous world while also fending off constant suspicion at home.

The problems arising out of the history of the American armed forces ought to be pondered, and have been emphasized here, because so much depends on American strength. Rising above their problems, however, the American armed forces have served their country and the the rest of the world's democracies far from badly since 1941, and it would be a distortion to paint a historical survey in wholly gloomy colors. Because offsetting the Soviet war machine does so much depend on the United States, the large size and the cost of American military power are obviously not merely a problem. The very fact that Americans can still contemplate warfare in terms of complete victories bespeaks, beyond a disconcerting immoderation, the deep reservoirs of economic strength, skilled manpower, and technological leadership they can mobilize for military purposes.

In past wars, furthermore, Americans have overcome their enemies with more than sheer material power; they have not simply transformed their gross national product into munitions and thrown it at their enemies. The Americans may have been historically an unmilitary people, but American fighting men have consistently displayed a considerable aptitude for battle. It was that aptitude, and much more than simply the material resources of the United States, that led Winston Churchill to remark of his hearing the news of Pearl Harbor and the American entry into World War II: "I had studied the American Civil War, fought out to the last desperate inch. . . . I went to bed and slept the sleep of the saved and the thankful."

Beyond the aptitude for battle, there has also been the heartening American aptitude for military leadership—which brings us back to West Point, where we began. The antique military ritual of the Point symbolizes a tradition that, though a thin current usually well separated from the mainstream of American life, and though only recently brought to the attention of the world at large, has maintained a remarkable continuity in an often inhospitable environment: the tradition of military professionalism, and of professional excellence, in the American officer corps.

Founded under President Thomas Jefferson in 1802, vitalized by Superintendent Sylvanus Thayer in 1817–1833, the United States Military Academy early began to transform military officership in America from a gentlemen's avocation to a profession. Though of course West Point is an undergraduate school, and graduate-level professional education for American officers mainly had to wait until after the Civil War, the Military Academy even before the Civil War nourished professional military attainments and study all out of proportion to the tiny size of the American army, in the teaching and writing of its Professor Dennis Hart Mahan—father of the naval strategist Alfred Thayer Mahan—and in the writing of such pupils as Henry Wager Halleck and George B. McClellan. Professional studies nourished in turn professional standards of military skill and performance. In these areas, the American officer corps of the nineteenth century was scarcely the Prussian officer corps; but because it was unhampered by the class barriers that plagued British officership, or by the political feuds of the French, the American officer corps often surpassed any Europeans except the Prussians in the early development of professional standards of military administration and command. Contrast, for example, the staff and logistical performance that sustained the Union armies over distances of thousands of miles in the Civil War with the staff and logistical work that failed to sustain a small British army in the Crimea.

Furthermore, while the actual duties of the nineteenth-century American army were largely those of policing the Indian tribes, the United

Active Duty Military Personnel, Selected Periods 1918 to 1976

Year	Army	Air Force	Navy	Marine Corps	Totals
30 June 1918	2,395,742	—	448,606	52,819	2,897,167
30 June 1939	189,839	—	125,202	19,432	334,473
31 May 1945 [2]	5,983,330	2,310,436	3,359,283 [1]	471,369	12,124,418
30 April 1952 [3]	1,658,084	971,017	813,936 [1]	242,017	3,685,054
30 June 1968 [4]	1,570,343	904,850	765,457 [1]	307,252	3,547,902
31 December 1976 [5]	775,051	579,864	528,578	188,506	2,071,999

1. Excluding Coast Guard.   3. Korean War peak.   5. Financial Year 1977.   All information from US Department of Defense publication,
2. World War II peak.   4. Vietnam Conflict peak.   "Selected Manpower Statistics" May 1977.

States Army always directed its education and preparation toward eventual participation in the European military arena. When America made its debut as a world military power in the world wars, the rank and file may have performed at first with a lack of battlefield skill and wariness that produced high casualties and had to be compensated for in courage and élan. The American officer corps, in contrast, performed almost immediately at a European level of professional skill: witness as early as September 1918 the Americans' secret, concealed movement of about a million men in a three-week period, at night and over inadequate roads and railways, from the area of their St. Mihiel offensive to the concentration area for their coming Meuse-Argonne offensive, while the St. Mihiel battle was in progress. This feat was mainly the work of the young operations officer of 4th American First Army, Colonel George C. Marshall, Jr.

After a twenty-year interval spent in the scarcely larger than the old Indian wars constabulary—plus, importantly, more study and teaching in the army's schools—this same Marshall with apparently equal ease assumed the principal strategic and administrative leadership of the Anglo-American coalition's far-flung military forces in World War II, and carried them through to almost universal admiration. General Marshall was perhaps the best product of the American officer corps' tradition of professional excellence in the twentieth century, but he was also representative of the remarkably widespread ability of that officer corps to readjust almost overnight to command responsibilities over hundreds of thousands of their own and Allied forces in global war. Dwight D. Eisenhower, Douglas MacArthur, Omar N. Bradley, Carl A. Spaatz, and in the navy Ernest J. King and Chester A. Nimitz, all showed similar capacities.

Perhaps the mushroom expansion of the American armed forces has diluted the standards that in the past permitted the officers of small forces to take on large tasks so well; it is surely an understatement to say that American military leadership in the Vietnam War did not produce a George C. Marshall. Nevertheless, the quality of the American professional officer corps has remained so high through so many generations that there is good reason to hope that the tradition of excellence still persists. The democracies owe much to the American professional soldiers who led in the world wars. On their professional heirs rest many hopes for the future.

Below: Though hated by the Viet Cong, the B-52 was designed for work utterly unlike the Vietnam war. This Loran-guided B-52F is sending down 750lb bombs on what may well be empty forest.

The US Concept of National Security

Dr. Stephen P. Gibert, Professor of Government and Director of the National Security Studies Program, Georgetown University, Washington D.C.

In early 1977 Vice President Mondale arrived in Tokyo to inform the Japanese government that the US had decided to remove its ground forces from Korea over the next several years, where they had been stationed since the end of the Korean War in 1953. In August Secretary of State Vance went to Peking, supposedly to begin the process of negotiating the "transferring" of US formal diplomatic relations from the Republic of China on Taiwan to the Peoples Republic of China in Peking. The Secretary did not have much time to spend in Peking, however, for he had to hurry back to testify on Capitol Hill about the new treaty being prepared to replace American control over the Panama Canal with that of the Republic of Panama.

With regard to the Korean case, the US Joint Chiefs of Staff recommended against the decision; as for "abandoning" Taiwan, a number of pressure groups are currently mobilizing in an attempt to get the Administration to change its mind on this question or, at the minimum, to provide safeguards for the Republic of China to help secure it against future attack from the mainland. And as for the Panama Canal treaty, even before it has been submitted—reminiscent of the case with the League of Nations treaty in 1919—several senators have announced their intention to attempt to secure the necessary 34 senatorial votes to block consent to ratification.

These events serve to once again remind us that the US President, his circle of advisors, and the professional foreign policy and national security bureaucracy will confront bitter opposition if the policies they pursue do not, in the eyes of "attentive elites" involved in international affairs, further American national interests. Unfortunately, however, it is not possible to define the concept of national interest with sufficient precision that it may have relevance for policy choices and command wide support for the courses of action chosen. Nevertheless, at the present time there is widespread agreement that three policy areas are most important to US national security in that all three involve the possibility of military conflict: the American–Soviet relationship; Korean–American relations and US force presence in Northeast Asia; and American security concerns in the Middle East.

American–Soviet Relations

It is appropriate to begin with American–Soviet relations since the Soviet "threat" and what to do about it have preoccupied American policymakers from the enunciation of the Truman Doctrine in March, 1947, until recent times. This is not surprising, since in the early postwar years American leaders were convinced that the Soviet Union was bent upon expansion, certainly in Europe, probably in the Middle East, and perhaps in Asia as well. This perception was the dominant one, leading to the establishment of NATO and a more or less permanent American military presence in Western Europe, despite the fact that the USSR was significantly weaker than the United States in strategic power and had, in fact, behaved with prudence and restraint when confrontations, such as occurred in Berlin in 1948 and 1961 and Cuba in 1962 occurred between the two superpowers.

The containment school of thought dominated American discussions of superpower and East–West relationships for most of the period between 1947 and 1972. However, as early as the 1948 presidential election, a new interpretation of the Cold War—later referred to as "revisionism"—arose in the left end of the political spectrum. Bolting the Democratic Party, Roosevelt's former Vice President, Henry Wallace, campaigned in 1948 on the basis that the United States was overreacting to what were essentially Soviet defensive moves in world politics. This position did not command much support at the time and Wallace did not carry a single state in the election. However, revisionism was later to gain more adherents, especially in academic circles. These university-based revisionists returned in their studies to the events of 1944–47, examined the origins of the Cold War, and found America, not Russia, wanting. United States leaders, such as President Truman, Secretaries Byrnes and Acheson, Senators Vandenburg and Taft, perceived aggressive designs in what were really defensive moves on Moscow's part. While it was true that the USSR wanted "friendly" nations in Eastern Europe, revisionists claimed this did not indicate a general expansionist drive. Refusing to adjust to the realities of sphere-of-influence politics, Washington adopted a moralistic pose to hide its real intentions, which were motivated by economic necessity. American policies such as the Truman Doctrine, the Marshall Plan, and the establishment of NATO were intended to facilitate economic domination of Europe to protect American export markets. Concealing this behind the rhetoric of containment, President Truman "bombarded the American people with a 'hate the enemy' campaign,"[1] blaming it all on Soviet "aggression". This "campaign" also, according to the revisionists, contributed to the "militarization" of American foreign policy.

Revisionists, of course, represent a distinctive minority point of view, even in the universities. For although they labored most diligently to blame the Cold War on the West, certain facts would not go away. Among the most difficult of these was the Soviet annexation, between 1939 and 1945, of some 180,000 square miles of territory, including in Europe all of Estonia, Latvia, and Lithuania and parts of Finland, Poland, and Rumania. The USSR also annexed southern Sakhalin and the Kurile Islands in the Far East and acquired a satellite in North Korea. In contrast, only China among the other major victorious powers acquired new territory. First Britain and later France divested themselves of large colonial empires and the United States granted independence to the Philippines.

As the Soviet Union approached strategic nuclear parity with the United States a new school of thought emerged—the detentists. Basically, this group came to believe that the shared superpower position which arrived with parity—the total vulnerability of the United States and the Soviet Union vis-a-vis each other and virtual invulnerability of the two countries to all other actors in the system— could become the basis for an understanding which would usher in an era of peace. At the

Even a superpower has to tread a tightrope and often, at least in outward appearance, encounters terrible difficulties in securing long- or short-term advantages for itself or its friends. Lending six T-38 Talon supersonic trainers to Portugal (unloading from C-5A, far left) is a simple case of keeping difficult friends well-disposed; the T-38s are surplus to requirements anyway. A Presidential chat with the First Secretary of the Central Committee of the Polish United Workers' Party (left) is all part of the welcome process of détente. But what can the superpower do when its personnel are murdered by N Korean border guards (below)?

minimum, strategic parity coupled with the doctrine and policy of assured destruction, would provide sufficient stability so that nuclear war could be prevented and a less antagonistic superpower relationship could be established.[2]

Although the detente concepts were articulated as early as the Kennedy–Johnson era, it was not until Nixon and Kissinger assumed power that detente became official American policy. Superpower strategic parity, it was argued, had produced a situation in which neither the United States nor the Soviet Union could expect to win a war with each other in any meaningful sense. Thus the basis for a new and more stable relationship existed which would eliminate superpower strategic conflict so long as each possessed invulnerable second-strike forces.

At the same time, the danger of escalation of a local conflict existed, so that it had become imperative to improve Soviet–American relations. Specifically, detente would permit agreements to be made to limit the strategic arms race and other actions intended to "replace confrontation with negotiation". This less dangerous situation, according to President Nixon and Secretary Kissinger, had been realized in the SALT agreements of May 1972 and June 1973, ushering in a new era in American–Soviet relations.

Limitations of space do not permit here the detailed critique which the detente concept deserves. Suffice it to say that central to it is the notion of the "unwinnability" of nuclear war.[3] This, in turn, rests heavily on certain assumptions about future technological developments in weapons systems. Also, recent evidence that the USSR is continuing to expand its strategic forces far beyond imaginable defense requirements is beginning to raise doubts among those hitherto less alarmed about Soviet military power.

Finally, the containment school of thought is still with us in 1977. It has slipped from the majority position it enjoyed in 1947, however, and now represents a minority point of view. The proponents of containment have also acquired a new name: cold warriors (to their detractors) and realists (as they call themselves). The realists, unlike the revisionists and detentists, tend to accord more attention to Soviet capabilities and less to Soviet intentions. Unlike the detente group, the realist school believes that there is such a thing as politically usable military superiority.[4] While they also think a nuclear war is unlikely, they think that in such a war there will be an outcome which clearly distinguishes the victor from the vanquished, even if nuclear war would wreak such devastation that costs to the victor would be extremely high. They point out that the USSR has undertaken civil defense and other preparations which might, indeed, reduce Soviet casualties under certain circumstances to levels below those suffered by the Soviet Union in World War II. For these reasons, realists call for strengthening both US strategic forces and NATO defenses. Realists substantiate their calls for greater US–European defense efforts by citing such Soviet statements as the following: "There is profound erroneousness and harm in the disorienting claims of bourgeois ideologies that there will be no victor in a thermonuclear world war".[5]

When realists focus on Soviet intentions, they are no less concerned. Unlike revisionists and detentists, realists basically take Soviet statements about the victory of communism seriously. Some realists, in fact, think the evidence is substantial that the USSR is indeed now strongly embarked upon a "war-winning" strategy and that both Soviet statements and the Soviet military buildup are consistent with such a policy, however inconceivable it might appear both to American and West European political leaders.

By and large, there is broad consensus now (1977) on the Soviet military buildup—the disagreement lies in its meaning and the requirements for an appropriate NATO and American response.[6] The meaning attached to the Soviet military effort, in turn, to a significant degree turns on the weight accorded ideology as a factor in actual Soviet behavior. Soviet ideology is just one of the many facets ignored by revisionists; detentists, on the other hand, do not ignore Soviet pronouncements but explain them as fulfilling other needs of the Soviet system. In contrast, realists take Soviet ideology as not the only factor but a significant one pointing to deteriorating, not improving, Soviet–American and NATO–Warsaw Pact relationships in an "era of detente".

While, at present, detente advocates dominate American policy-making in the Carter Administration, the controversy over American–Soviet relations will not die away. Indeed, if the Soviet military buildup continues at anything like its present pace, the debate in national security circles will almost certainly intensify. The outcome will not only affect Soviet–American relations but American relationships with Europe and Japan as well. Accordingly, West Europeans, Japanese and others should not be reluctant to enter into the fray. On the contrary, they should join vigorously and uninhibitedly, the coming

detente–realist debate. The future of NATO—and indeed US security commitments around the world—rest on the outcome.

US Force Presence in Asia

While NATO–Europe has been and remains the principal focus of United States security concerns, Washington also maintains a substantial, although sharply declining, military presence in Asia. In fact, when the Nixon Administration took office in 1969, the United States had much larger military forces in Asia than in Europe. Of course, the Vietnam forces, which at their largest totalled some 550,000 troops, were a significant element in this situation. Additionally it was US policy at that time to maintain military forces sufficient to fight "two and a half wars". This was defined as including a possible conflict between NATO–Warsaw Pact forces, a war between the United States and the Peoples Republic of China, and a "half-war" contingency elsewhere. In fact, between 1969 and 1975 the United States withdrew from Asia some 702,000 military personnel. In contrast, not a single soldier was withdrawn from Europe. Empirically, if not in theory, the Nixon Administration not only terminated the Vietnam conflict but reverted to a "European-first" military posture. Military aid was to take the place of American soldiers. Europe was to get US troops, Asians were to get US dollars.[7]

Such a policy was both required and was justified by the downgrading of the "Chinese threat" to non-communist Asian nations and to US national security. This was accomplished through the secret Kissinger mission to Peking in 1971 followed by the Nixon trip in 1972, although full diplomatic relations with the PRC were not established. By the end of the Ford Administration, Nixon's statement that "Asian hands must shape the Asia future"[8] had been given concrete reality.

To say that international relations in Asia are in a state of flux is to understate vastly the dramatic changes of the 1970s. These include not only the developing rapprochement with China, first by the United States and then by Japan but also a sharpening of the already hostile Sino-Soviet conflict; the steady buildup of Soviet forces in the Asian area; a "cooling" in American–Japanese relations for a variety of reasons generally subsumed under the heading of "Nixon shocks"; increased tension between Moscow and Tokyo; the American withdrawal from Indochina and the subsequent collapse of the Saigon and Phnom Penh governments; and an acceleration of the decline of American military power in the Pacific. When President Carter took office, the only remaining American forces on the continent of Asia were some 42,000 personnel, including air and naval units and tactical nuclear weapons, stationed in and around South Korea, where they had been since the Korean War began in 1950. By mid-1977, in addition to US forces in Korea, there were only some 68,000 US military personnel, plus the US 7th Fleet, in East Asia.[9]

As regards Korean–American relations, these have been subjected to increasing stresses and strains. Although the two events may not be related, when the United States withdrew the Seventh Division from Korea in 1971–72, President Park declared (in December 1971) a state of emergency; martial law followed some months later (in October 1972) and in December a new

constitution—referred to as the Yushin constitution—conferred new powers on the chief executive. Subsequently, four emergency decrees were issued and a number of prominent opposition leaders were arrested, including a former ROK president, Yun Po-son.[10] Supporters of President Park cited the new security situation in Asia and Korea in justifying more stringent political controls; critics claimed that these were only excuses to maintain a dictator whose support in the populace had waned.

These charges were echoed in the United States. Sentiment for removing the remaining US ground forces, which had surfaced periodically in the past, began building again in Washington.[11] "Trial balloons" were floated, suggesting various "options" to the retention of American forces in South Korea, especially involving the Second Division which was positioned along the DMZ guarding the approaches to Seoul. Whether or not there was serious sentiment in the executive branch for removing or repositioning the Second Division, the collapse of South Vietnam in April 1975

effectively eliminated the possibility of such a move by the Ford Administration: in May, President Ford reaffirmed US treaty commitments to the Republic of Korea and in August Secretary of Defense Schlesinger journeyed to Seoul to emphasize the President's statement by pledging that American troops would remain in Korea and that the United States would continue to assist South Korea in its armed forces improvement program.

Reviving the arguments of the 1972–74 period, presidential candidate Jimmy Carter in May 1976 called for the withdrawal from Korea of the remaining American ground forces and the tactical nuclear weapons available to these forces. Subsequently, the new president had been in office only about a week when his Vice President, Walter Mondale, announced in Tokyo that US force withdrawals would begin but would be accompanied by "consultations" between Washington and Tokyo and Seoul. It was not mentioned precisely what these "consultations" would include since indeed the decision had not only been

Left: For the Soviet audience this unloading of a 40-ton superconducting magnet at Moscow Sheremetyevo is their first contact with the United States, the supposed last bastion of wicked capitalism, seen in a new cooperative light.

Right: One of the few visible responses of the United States to the killing of two of its Army officers by N Koreans (page 21) was to send a squadron of F-111F attack aircraft to S Korea, on TDY (temporary duty). Here Mk 82 bombs are off-loaded at a sodden Taegu AB.

made prior to talks with the Koreans and the Japanese, but even before the new Secretary of State and National Security Advisor had had an opportunity to assess the situation. Undaunted by these rather peculiar circumstances, President Carter reaffirmed in March 1977 his intention to withdraw American ground forces, but in phases, and accompanied by "consultations", from the Republic of Korea.

President Carter's decision quite naturally raises the question as to whether adequate consideration has been given to the reasons for retaining the status quo. Possibly the most important of these is the belief that the presence of US forces in Korea is a highly significant symbol of American determination to play an important (although clearly not a dominant) role in shaping the course of change in Asia. It can be argued that the Second Division, placed as it is on the DMZ in "harm's way", is a symbol of US will and resolve to uphold its treaty obligations and its commitments in an era when there is, regrettably, substantial reason to doubt that it intends to do so. President Carter in his press conference of May 26, 1977, replying to criticisms of his withdrawal policy, stated that the American "commitment to South Korea is undeviating and is staunch".[12] But will the Koreans and Japanese believe that this is true when the troops depart? Or will this action be perceived as yet another step in the waning of American power in Asia? Responding to these fears and to pleas by the South Korean government, in July 1977 Secretary of Defense Harold Brown announced in Seoul that two of the three brigades of the Second Division would remain in South Korea until 1982, the final year of the phased withdrawal. The US also announced that South Korea would be given additional military aid in "compensation" for the withdrawal of troops.[13]

It is difficult to determine whether the South Koreans or the Japanese are the most concerned about an American withdrawal from Korea.[14] Japan's policy—indeed its entire postwar posture—has been predicated on the alliance with the United States, the American nuclear shield, and on Washington's determination to prevent an overturn of the balance in Northeast Asia. Tokyo's concerns can be readily understood when it is recalled that Japan is indeed an anomaly in world history: a truly great power, with the third largest GNP in the world, but dependent upon a former enemy six thousand miles away for its security.

The argument that South Korea's and Japan's ally is thousands of miles away while the two communist giants are immediately at hand will not impress those who no longer believe strategic location is of consequence. Certainly, it cannot be denied that modern technology has reduced the importance of geopolitical factors in world politics. But if one assumes that future international conflicts are much more likely to take limited (and probably conventional) form, rather than that of intercontinental superpower war, then strategic location will remain critically important. Thus, although opponents of the US force presence tend to regard this as "old balance of power politics", somehow conceptually inferior to a "dynamic new approach to world affairs", the fact that Northeast Asia is the only world region where four (China, the Soviet Union, Japan, and the United States) of the five centers of world power (with only Western Europe absent) interact must be a vital consideration.

An essential ingredient of this four-power system in Asia is the United States. And of the four Pacific powers, only the United States is not physically present in Northeast Asia. American troops are a "surrogate presence"; they serve to remind the others, as President Nixon stated in his famous Nixon Doctrine in Guam in 1969, that the United States is and will remain a Pacific power. Failure to so remain might set in motion a train of events that might very quickly lead to destablilizing the four-power balance in East Asia. Indeed, it is possible that the current stable system might then undergo alliance partner shifts with the most serious implications for American security.

At present there seems to be broad agreement in policy-making circles that US national security interests require, above all else, close relations and cooperation with Japan. Opponents of the troop withdrawal argue that Japanese security would be gravely threatened and that the Japanese might take actions, such as extensively rearming, including possibly acquiring nuclear weapons, that would seriously undermine US security policy in East Asia. If Japan thought that the US was abandoning its security commitment to Korea, this could bring changes in Japanese policy, ranging from pacifism to belligerent nationalism. In any case, the US would be a certain loser.[15] Perhaps this dispute should be resolved by actually consulting Tokyo, as distinct from merely informing the Japanese of decisions already made in Washington. And in a world increasingly hostile to American interests, where the list of allies diminishes almost every year, President Carter might also give weight to the views of the South Koreans.

Irrespective of Tongsun-Park related scandals, and notwithstanding the distaste Americans feel for regimes violating human rights, the security of the Republic of Korea and America are closely bound together. To pretend otherwise is to place in jeopardy the future not only of Korea but the entire postwar posture of the United States in Northeast Asia. Thus, as in American–Soviet relations, a great new debate on what constitutes US national interests in Asia appears nearly certain to occur.

American Security Concerns in the Middle East

In addition to Western Europe and Northeast Asia, the United States has important interests in one other world region: the Middle East. In contrast to the sharp disagreements that exist over American policy to the USSR and the concomitant preservation of European security, and the arguments over the utility of Korea to Northeast Asian stability, there seems to be a broad consensus concerning US interests in the Middle East, even if there are questions as to how best secure those interests. American policy goals are: to assist Israel in maintaining its independence and security and to settle the Arab–Israel conflict on equitable terms; to secure access to Persian Gulf oil at "reasonable" prices, both for the United States and other oil-dependent nations, especially Western Europe and Japan; and finally, to deny "undue" influence over the Middle East to the Soviet Union.

Arab–Israel Policies

Policy choices with regard to the Arab–Israeli conflict must begin with the fundamental premise that the United States of necessity will have important relationships with both Israelis and Arabs for the foreseeable future. Polarization of the political forces in the Middle East, which would be a likely consequence of a US decision to abandon "even-handedness" and strongly favor one or the other side, would jeopardize important American interests. Accordingly, courses of action such as reversing alliances and "abandoning" Israel on the one hand or deliberately seeking confrontation with the Arab world through total and unquestioning support of Tel Aviv on the other, are not feasible.

While there are certain aspects of the Arab–

Left: A welcome handshake for Menachem Begin, Prime Minister of Israel, at the White House on 21 March 1978. But later Mr Begin went home after what he described as the "most difficult" talks of his career. It was clearly a matter of clashing attitudes and unyielding positions.

Right: Arrival at an Israeli airbase of one of 25 F-15 Eagles, for which Israel paid $600 million. A further 15 have been ordered, but American popularity in Israel has been badly hit by large arms sales to Arab countries, notably 45 F-15A fighters and 15 F-15B trainers for Saudi Arabia.

Above: One of the larger potential threats to stability is Libya, whose armed forces have grown with almost explosive rapidity. Here a US Navy F-4J has a close look at a Libyan Tu-22 supersonic reconnaissance bomber supplied by the Soviet Union

Israeli dispute which lend themselves to the formulation of alternative options, there are other aspects which have come to be imperatives in US policy. These are:

1. The existence of Israel is not negotiable. Most Arabs have now come to accept this and the United States must not adopt a policy position which leaves any room for doubt on this question. To do otherwise, aside from the moral implications, would do irretrievable damage to US credibility and lead an isolated and desperate Israel to adopt a declaratory nuclear retaliation policy with possibly dangerous consequences.

2. While the United States is committed to defend Israel's right to exist, it is not committed to particular boundaries. The United States supports UN Resolution 242 which calls for Israeli withdrawal from territories occupied in the 1967 war. That resolution envisions such withdrawal in the context of Arab recognition of Israel's rights to live in peace within secure and recognized borders, not mere armistice lines.

3. The United States supports "normalization" of the conflict. This means direct negotiations of issues by the immediate participants, with external powers assisting but not dictating outcomes. It also means the acceptance of negotiations as a bargaining process in which each side makes certain concessions in order to arrive at a solution not wholly satisfactory but at least minimally acceptable to all concerned.

4. Pending resolution of the dispute, the United States must attempt to maintain a balance of military power between the two parties. This does not necessarily mean matching in all particulars Soviet (and other) arms transfers to the Arab countries. A serious imbalance of forces must be avoided, however, as either an Arab attack or Israeli preemption may result. Arab military preponderance may also result in an Israeli decision to inform the

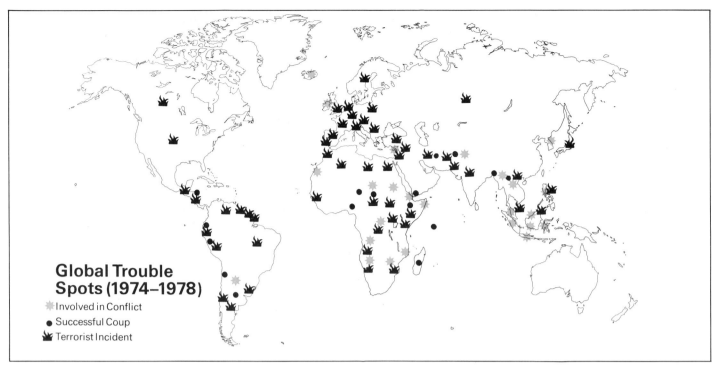

Global Trouble Spots (1974–1978)

✳ Involved in Conflict

● Successful Coup

🔥 Terrorist Incident

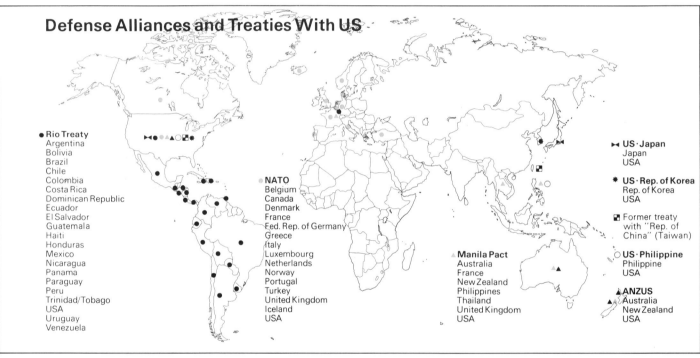

Defense Alliances and Treaties With US

● **Rio Treaty**
Argentina
Bolivia
Brazil
Chile
Colombia
Costa Rica
Dominican Republic
Ecuador
El Salvador
Guatemala
Haiti
Honduras
Mexico
Nicaragua
Panama
Paraguay
Peru
Trinidad/Tobago
USA
Uruguay
Venezuela

● **NATO**
Belgium
Canada
Denmark
France
Fed. Rep. of Germany
Greece
Italy
Luxembourg
Netherlands
Norway
Portugal
Turkey
United Kingdom
Iceland
USA

▲ **Manila Pact**
Australia
France
New Zealand
Philippines
Thailand
United Kingdom
USA

◄ **US·Japan**
Japan
USA

✳ **US·Rep. of Korea**
Rep. of Korea
USA

◨ Former treaty
with "Rep. of
China" (Taiwan)

○ **US·Philippine**
Philippine
USA

▲ **ANZUS**
Australia
New Zealand
USA

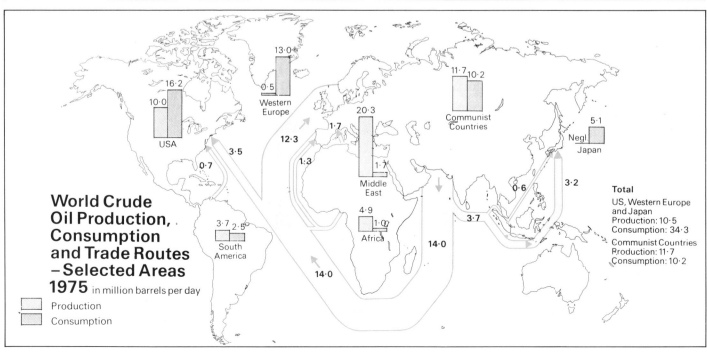

World Crude Oil Production, Consumption and Trade Routes – Selected Areas

1975 in million barrels per day

Production

Consumption

USA 10·0 / 16·2
Western Europe 0·5 / 13·0
Communist Countries 11·7 / 10·2
Japan Negl. / 5·1
Middle East 20·3 / 1·7
South America 3·7 / 2·5
Africa 4·9 / 1·0

3·5
0·7
12·3
1·7
1·3
14·0
14·0
0·6
3·2
3·7

Total
US, Western Europe and Japan
Production: 10·5
Consumption: 34·3

Communist Countries
Production: 11·7
Consumption: 10·2

Left: The facing page contains some of the fundamental features of today's unquiet world. In fact, many—perhaps most—of the terrorist incidents are due to either pure ideology, as in the case of the Baader-Meinhof group and the so-called Red Brigade, or to localized pressure groups such as the so-called South Moluccans in the Netherlands. In a few cases geopolitical and economic factors throw tremendous importance on a region which before 1939 was never an issue at all. An outstanding case is South Africa, whose strategic importance—even after the reopening of the Suez canal—has made it the focus of a global campaign ostensibly based on Apartheid but actually aimed at using any weapon to weaken the position of the government in Pretoria. Many other trouble-spots hinge on border disputes, old tribal antipathies and, increasingly, successful fanning of embers by the Soviet Union. Over the period covered, 1974-78, the United States has seen its influence dramatically decline and its previously valuable CIA discredited, while cost-escalation and dwindling defense budgets have thrown all kinds of important weapon, aid and other globally significant programmes into disarray. Even more fundamentally, where are the boundaries of national interest? The United States, like many other great trading nations, is vitally dependent on free sea traffic, collective security and the most cautious yet effective opposition to forces of aggression, coercion and unrest.

Below: USS Barnstable County, a high-speed tank landing ship, passing freely through the Suez canal. Such great waterways are natural foci of subversive or aggressive forces. In the long term President Carter made a wise decision to hand over the Panama canal by the year 2000.

world that it has adopted a nuclear stance and will respond to an Arab attack with nuclear weapons.

5. It is not sufficient to maintain a military balance between Israel and the Arab opponents. While it is possible that a no-war, no-peace situation could persist a long time, the inherent instabilities make it essential to move beyond this condition to some form of settlement and US policy should be geared to this goal.

Oil Policies

Choices with regard to oil policy must be formulated to cope with the many and varied facets of the problem. The most basic policy requirement, however difficult to implement, is simple and obvious: the United States can and it must bring energy production and energy consumption into a much closer balance than presently exists. The existing situation will worsen in the future unless present trends—an annual increase in consumption and level or declining production—are reversed.

Given these facts, it is clear that the United States needs to cooperate with Saudi Arabia. Saudi Arabia is the key to the oil problem. Saudi Arabia in 1976 was estimated to possess about one-third of the oil reserves in the entire world. Indeed, not only is an embargo impossible without Saudi cooperation, but the Saudis, with substantial spare capacity, have the power virtually to dictate lower oil prices through substantially increasing their oil production. Between October 1973 and December 1976, the Saudis agreed to regular OPEC price increases, although presumably counseling price moderation. At the OPEC meeting on December 17, 1976, however, the Saudis (and also the United Arab Emirates) refused to agree to a ten percent increase in posted prices decided upon by the other eleven members of OPEC. Instead, Saudi Arabia and the UAE raised prices by five percent. This signalled the first open break in the oil cartel. Other OPEC members, such as Iran, were particularly incensed at Riyadh's decision to increase oil production, which should have the effect not only of diverting some of their customers to

cheaper Saudi oil but also will lead to a further accumulation of oil surpluses and at least some price reductions. (Posted prices for Saudi and UAE oil as of January 1, 1977, reflecting a five percent increase, were $12.08 a barrel, as contrasted to $12.70, reflecting a ten percent increase for other OPEC members.) For the United States, unless prices are reduced, or consumption cut, the oil import bill is expected to total about $40 billion in 1977, with approximately forty percent of US needs supplied by imports.[16]

The Saudi Oil Minister, Sheik Zaki Yamani, made it clear that he expects the United States to be grateful to Saudi Arabia for its "restraint" in oil pricing; this "gratitude", in his view, should take the form of additional progress on the Arab–Israeli situation and on the North–South dialogue in Paris with regard to the "new international economic order".[17]

The Superpowers:
The Conflict of Interests

Soviet actions in the Middle East just prior to, during and immediately after the 1973 Arab–Israeli War were wholly inconsistent with either the spirit or letter of the detente agreements of 1972 and 1973.[18] More critical is the fact, however, that even if their conceptions of detente were identical, the interests of the two superpowers in the Middle East are sufficiently divergent as to make continued tension and possibly a renewal of outright conflict in the area likely. More important examples of asymmetries in goals and divergences of interests are:

1. The United States, and even much more so its European and Japanese allies, need the oil of the Middle East and do not want to disrupt the oil supplies. The Soviet government, while it finds the oil useful, can view with equanimity disruptions in the supply of oil, at least for the near term.

2. The Soviet Union and before it Czarist Russia has long regarded the Middle East and the Indian Ocean as areas of critical importance to its security. The United States, on the other hand, has not historically had a clear and consistent policy regarding the Middle East, and

has only since the crisis of the 1973 war taken an active and leading role in Middle East affairs.

3. The United States has been more closely associated in a diplomatic and military sense with the non-Arab regimes in the Middle East, Israel and Iran. The USSR has been a supporter of the Arabs, anti-Israeli and, to a lesser extent, anti-Iranian. Currently the United States is attempting to be "even-handed", whereas the Soviet Union is not.

4. The Soviets have associated themselves with the "radical" Arabs of the Gulf, in opposition to conservative regimes such as that in Saudi Arabia. The United States supports the existing governments and opposes their replacement by radical regimes.

5. The Soviet Union regards the Persian Gulf–Indian Ocean area as an arena essential to the general Soviet policy of containing China; the United States has no interest at present in containing Chinese activities in the region.

6. The United States would benefit from a "just" and peaceful resolution of the Arab–Israeli conflict while the Soviets wish to exploit its continuation.

7. Disruption in the Middle East and conflicts in the area, such as that between Greece and Turkey over Cyprus, will weaken the southern flank of NATO and hence adversely affect the US alliance system. This problem does not exist for the USSR.

American and Russian interests are in sharp conflict in the Middle East; to expect these differences to be eliminated through a Soviet–American detente is wholly unrealistic. Super-power rivalry will continue in the Middle East, Persian Gulf, and Indian Ocean areas, restrained primarily by the mutual interest both sides have in preventing this conflict of interest from escalating into a nuclear confrontation.

Egypt, Saudi Arabia, and Iran

Three countries—in addition to Israel—are keys to any successful US policy in the Middle East: Egypt, Saudi Arabia, and Iran. Egypt, the strongest of the Arab countries, is decisive in determining overall Arab–Israeli relations. It was Egypt which initiated the 1967 War and the

1970 War of Attrition; it was Egypt's Sadat who planned the October 1973 conflict; it is Egypt which controls the Suez Canal and which has long been a target for Soviet influence.

Egypt is the only Arab state which posseses all the recognized attributes of nationhood, including an ancient political tradition, historically accepted territorial dimensions, linguistic and cultural homogeneity and a centralized, bureaucratic administration in the Western mold. Furthermore, unlike the case with Syria, the geography of the conflict area favors an Israeli–Egyptian peace settlement.

Above: Cordial meeting of three of the world's great leaders, President Carter, King Hussein and the Shah of Iran. At the time all wielded great power, but the subsequent deposition of one of their number showed his power to be fragile.

Below: Sometimes violence erupts into full-scale war, and normal life becomes impossible. On 27 July 1976 about 300 Americans were evacuated from West Beirut by US Navy LSU-1643, seen easing into the dock of USS *Coronado*.

There are not only no insurmountable issues in Israeli–Egyptian relations; both sides have certain common interests. As part of the "Arab nation", however, and in the interests of maintaining a united front, Egypt has not at present agreed to a separate peace with Israel, even though this would result in the restoration of Egyptian territory under Israeli occupation.

Saudi Arabia's claim to leadership is based on oil and on its religious leadership of Islam. Saudi Arabia was the key to the Arab oil embargo; Saudi Arabia alone can determine whether there is an oversupply or shortage of world oil. It was Saudi Arabia's agreement to employ the oil weapon that played a significant role both in Egypt's and Syria's decision to go to war and in denying Israel any benefits from its fourth military victory.

It is now indisputedly true that the United States needs to cultivate the closest possible relations with Saudi Arabia. In practical terms, in addition to the Arab–Israeli and North–South questions, this means continued access for Saudi Arabia to US technology, expertise, and management assistance, as well as providing an outlet for the investment of surplus Saudi revenues. These are not really controversial issues; what is more likely to cause problems is the resistance by some in the United States, including influential Congressmen, to large-scale Saudi purchases of American weapons. President-elect Carter also criticized the quantity of arms sales to Saudi Arabia during the 1976 election campaign, on the grounds that

Right: In late 1977 President Sadat of Egypt displayed immense personal courage in openly seeking a rapprochement with the Arabs' arch-enemy, Israel. President Carter had by mid-1978 been unable to sustain the initial momentum of this work.

Below: The Iranian revolution in early 1979 left vast amounts of modern US weaponry in the hands of a new and unfriendly regime. This F-14A, seen on delivery to Iran in US markings, represents the pinnacle of Western technology.

the weapons might be used against Israel and on the moral implications of the US being "the world's leading arms salesman".

It is certainly true that US arms sales to the Persian Gulf have risen dramatically in the last four years. In fiscal year 1972, the combined arms sales totals for Saudi Arabia and Iran was $854 million; three years later, in fiscal year 1975, the dollar value of US arms sales worldwide totaled $9.5 billion, with $4.8 billion accounted for by Israel, Iran, and Saudi Arabia. In fiscal year 1976, worldwide US sales of arms was $8.4 billion, of which just under a billion went to Israel, £1.3 billion went to Iran, and $2.5 billion to Saudi Arabia. Estimates for new sales during fiscal year 1977 are $1 billion for Israel, $1.2 billion for Iran, and $1.5 billion for Saudi Arabia.[19]

Iran, with a population five or six times larger than that of Saudi Arabia, a developing economy, an emerging middle class and all the major ingredients to become a modern state, is in a very different situation from Saudi Arabia. Large scale arms for Iran are clearly more justified than for Saudi Arabia. Further, since Iran is not an Arab nation, there is no need to be concerned that American weapons will be used against Israel. Iran's commitment to maintaining stability in the oil-rich Gulf is also vital and consistent with American policy of substituting regional power centers for US direct military presence in the Third World.[20] Finally, Iran has for many years maintained a staunchly anti-Soviet posture, thus making Tehran a valuable ally in containing possible Soviet penetration of the Gulf area.[21]

At the same time, Americans naturally question whether the US should continue to contribute to the military buildup of a nation which has been in the forefront of the drive for higher oil prices. If the Iranians were in a position to influence significantly oil prices, then it would be valid to argue that the US should demand Iranian oil price moderations as a quid pro quo for US arms sales. But the reality is that Iranian oil price rhetoric should be ignored; Iran has little power to affect oil prices. Furthermore, it must be remembered that the prices Iran pays for American imports have

also risen, in some cases drastically. Finally, the United States has a decided interest in a strong and viable Iran, especially in an era when it is not regarded as permissible for the United States to maintain significant military forces of its own in the Persian Gulf area.

Note: Since the preceding two paragraphs were written the revolution in Iran has changed the picture. The Iranian Islamic republic poses problems to the West.

Emerging Issues
While United States security interests at present are most strongly engaged in Europe, Northeast Asia, and the Middle East, other regions appear to be increasing in importance. In Latin America, current concern is over the Panama Canal and the emergence of possible leftist political regimes which might cooperate

with Moscow or Peking, and future relations with Cuba. For the near future, Latin America is likely to remain less than critical to United States policy. Over the long run, Latin American oil, immigration from Latin America, especially from Mexico, to the United States, and hemispheric security seem destined to claim more attention from Washington than it has in the recent past.

Sub-Saharan Africa, like Latin America, has been on the policy back-burner. This un-

Below: Vast amounts of materiel change hands in the modern world. Here Zaïrian troops off-load "rations and non-lethal equipment" from a C-5A at Kinshasa. The items are said to have been ordered by Zaïre and paid for with "military sales credit". The US provided the airlift.

Table 1 : United States Security Assistance

The term "security assistance" includes:
1. Foreign Military Sales (FMS), by which defense articles and services are sold to foreign countries and international organizations.
2. The FMS Credit Program through which credits are provided or guaranteed.
3. The Military Assistance Program (MAP).
4. The International Military Education and Training Program (IMETP).
5. Security Supporting Assistance. MAP, IMETP and Security Supporting Assistance are carried out under the Foreign Assistance Act as grant aid for which the US receives no reimbursement from the recipient.

Security Assistance Programs (Requested FY 1978)

Military Assistance Program (MAP)	$284.6 million
International Military Education and Training Program (IMETP)	$36.3 million
Foreign Military Sales program	$7.7 billion (projected)

Foreign Military Sales ($ billions)*

	FY 1972	FY 1974	FY 1977	FY 1978 Projection of FMS orders
Total	3.3	10.6	8.7	7.7

* FMS orders only. In FY 1974 total of all US military export programs and orders, including FMS, grant aid and commercial exports, was $12.4 billion. This includes $784.9 million in Military Assistance Programs (MAP), $0.6 billion in FMS orders and slightly over $1 billion in estimated commercial orders for defense articles and services. Commercial deliveries in FY 1974 amounted to $502 million.

From 1950 to 1976, 60 percent of total FMS orders dealt with supporting equipment, spare parts and supporting services, while only 40 percent were for weapons and ammunition.
Over 63 percent of US FMS between FY 1974 and FY 1976 have been in the Middle East, primarily to Iran, Israel and Saudi Arabia.

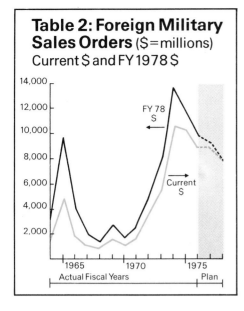

Table 2: Foreign Military Sales Orders ($=millions)
Current $ and FY 1978 $

FY 78 $

Current $

14,000

12,000

10,000

8,000

6,000

4,000

2,000

1965 1970 1975

Actual Fiscal Years Plan

doubtedly results from its geographical remoteness from the zone of superpower confrontation, its poverty, and the tendency of American policy-makers to follow the lead in Africa set by European powers. Increasing racial tensions in Africa, coupled with a growing awareness of their African heritage among black Americans, make it likely that Africa will receive more attention in US policy than it has in the past.

Finally, there loom on the horizon a number of problems not associated with particular regions which will be of increasing concern to American policy-makers. One is the consideration to be given to North–South issues as distinct from East–West problems. These involve the so-called "new economic order" and the alleged growing interdependence of nations throughout the world. A second problem rapidly nearing the critical stage concerns nuclear proliferation: how dangerous is it and what to do about it. Last, but not least, there is the extent to which the United States should allow the state of human rights in other countries, normally

regarded as falling within their domestic jurisdiction, to impinge upon or even govern international relationships.

While it is generally agreed that these emerging problems are becoming more critical, no greater error could be made than to assume that they are not adding to but replacing the more traditional national security concerns. In a world of sovereign states, power is still the principal arbiter of international affairs. Furthermore, in an increasingly populated planet, resource conflict will become the rule rather than the exception. Local hostilities will increase in frequency and intensity, not diminish.

Finally, the military confrontation between the superpowers and allied states, especially in Europe, Northeast Asia, and the Middle East, however regrettable, will remain the dominant national security problem for the foreseeable future.

Footnotes

1. Walter A. Williams, *The Tragedy of American Diplomacy* (New York: Dell Publishing Co., 1962), pp. 268–74. This is one of the better known revisionist works expounding an economic interpretation of US cold war behavior.
2. See Walter Slocombe, *The Political Implications of Strategic Parity* (London: ISS, Adelphi Paper No. 77, 1971), pp. 1–4. This theme is argued more extensively in Jerome Kahan, *Security in the Nuclear Age* (Washington: Brookings Institution, 1975), especially in chapters 4 and 6.
3. According to one observer, "The most extreme fear—the potential Soviet capacity to fight and survive a nuclear war—is clearly far-fetched." See Barry Blechman, *et al., The Soviet Military Buildup and US Defense Spending* (Washington: Brookings Institution, 1977), p. 22.
4. Johan Holst argues, for example, that the Soviet government is at least "verbally committed to a notion of superiority...." See his "Parity, Superiority or Sufficiency? Some remarks on the Nature and Future of the Soviet-American Strategic Relationship" in *Soviet-American Relations and World Order: Arms Limitations and Policy* (London: ISS, Adelphi Paper No. 65, 1970), p. 35.
5. As quoted by Richard Pipes, "Why the Soviet Union Thinks it Could Fight and Win a Nuclear War", *Commentary* (July 1977). See also Leon Goure, *et al., War Survival in Soviet Strategy* (Miami: University of Miami Press, 1976), *passim.*
6. Blechman, *op. cit.* Blechman states (p. 54) that "With each passing year it has become more difficult to

explain the continuing momentum in the Soviet defense buildup."
7. Stephen P. Gibert, "Implications of the Nixon Doctrine for Military Aid Policy", *Orbis* (Fall, 1972), pp. 671–678.
8. Richard Nixon, *US Foreign Policy for the 1970s: A New Strategy for Peace* (Washington: GPO, 1970), p. 60.
9. These were: Japan, 18,500; Okinawa, 23,400; Taiwan, 1,200; Guam, 8,800; and the Philippines, 16,200. Figures furnished the author by the Dept. of Defense.
10. Sungjo Han, "South Korea in 1974: the 'Korean Democracy' on Trial", *Asian Survey* (January 1975), pp. 35–36.
11. Criticisms of South Korea by some in the Congress were so vehement that "assault" is probably the best word to describe them. Especially vocal was Congressman Donald Fraser, the chairman of the Subcommittee on International Organizations and Movements, who, however, did not "want to suggest by this that North Korea is any better". US House of Representatives Subcommittee on Asian and Pacific Affairs, *Hearings: Our Commitments in Asia* (Washington: GPO, 1974), p. 61.
12. As quoted in *The Washington Post* (May 27, 1977).
13. *New York Times* (July 27, 1977).
14. See, for example, the statement by Japanese Prime Minister Sato in a joint 1969 Japanese–American communique that "the security of the Republic of Korea is essential to Japan's own security". Quoted in Kunio Muraoka, *Japanese Security and the United States* (London: ISS, Adelphi Paper No. 95, 1973), p. 7.
15. Leslie Brown, *American Security Policy in Asia* (London: ISS, Adelphi Paper No. 132, 1977), pp. 13–14.
16. US oil imports were 6 million b/d in 1975. Depending upon a number of factors, imports could range from 7.8 to 9.3 b/d in 1980. Projections are by the International Energy Agency, as reported in *The Economist* (April 10, 1976).
17. Interview on NBC-TV, December 19, 1976.
18. Foy Kohler, Leon Goure, and Mose Harvey, *The Soviet Union and the October 1973 Middle East War* (Miami: University of Miami Press, 1974), *passim.*
19. US Congress, Committee on International Relations, *International Security Assistance and Arms Export Control Act of 1976* (Washington: GPO, 1976), pp. 91–92.
20. Rouhollah K. Ramazani, "Iran and the United States: An Experiment in Enduring Friendship", *The Middle East Journal* (Summer 1976), pp. 333–334.
21. Lawrence Martin, "The Future Strategic Role of Iran" in A. Amirsedeghi, *Iran in the Twentieth Century* (London: Heinemann, 1977), pp. 227–228, 249–251.

Below: LHA-1, name-ship of the new Tarawa class of large amphibious-warfare vessels, heads through the Panama Canal soon after commissioning. This great seaway has never been closed, and US control has meant stability.

The US Defense Organization

Dr. Lawrence J. Korb, Professor of Management, US Naval War College; Adjunct Scholar of American Enterprise Institute for federal budgetary analysis and national security policy.

The heart of the US war machine is the Department of Defense (DOD), which is the largest bureaucracy within the American political system. It was created three decades ago by the National Security Act (NSA) of 1947. Prior to that time, the American military establishment was divided into two separate cabinet level departments: War and Navy. Over the past thirty years, the structure of DOD has been modified several times by legislation, executive order, and administrative fiat. The structure of the department as it now exists is outlined in Table 1.

The current organizational structure of DOD can be best understood if it is broken down into its five major levels. These are: the Office of the Secretary of Defense (OSD), the Joint Chiefs of Staff (JCS), the military departments, the defense agencies, and the field or operational commands.[1]

The Office of the Secretary of Defense (OSD)

The Department of Defense is under the control of the Secretary of Defense. He is the individual responsible for exercising the President's authority over DOD. The Secretary performs three main functions for the Chief Executive. First, he is the manager of DOD. In this capacity, the Secretary controls the Department's resources and directs all activities of the subunits of the Department. Second, he is the deputy commander-in-chief with authority and responsibility for controlling the actions of US military forces. Third, the Secretary is a principal advisor to the President on national security policy.

To assist him in carrying out his multiple responsibilities, the Secretary has a Deputy Secretary, eleven assistant secretaries of defense or equivalent level positions, and a General Counsel. Collectively, this group and their staffs are referred to as the Office of the Secretary of Defense (OSD). OSD is comprised of about 2,000 people, 1,500 of whom are civilians and 500 of whom are military personnel.

When the Department was first created, the Secretary of Defense was limited to three special assistants and his total staff was only 50 people. As his responsibilities grew, so too did the size of OSD. It reached its apex in 1969, at the height of the war in Vietnam, when it climbed to 3,500 people. The 40 percent reduction in OSD over the last decade has paralleled the cut in the size of the entire defense establishment.

A 1949 amendment to the NSA authorized the creation of a Deputy Secretary of Defense, and a 1972 amendment authorized the creation of a second Deputy. However, except for a brief period in 1976, the post of the second Deputy has not been filled. The intent of Congress in establishing the second Deputy was to allow the incumbent to focus on operational matters,[2] but the other Deputy and the Chairman of the Joint Chiefs of Staff both argued that this would encroach upon their areas of responsibility. When Robert Ellsworth served briefly as the second Deputy Secretary of Defense, he was given responsibility for intelligence activities instead of operational matters.

The Deputy Secretary of Defense is the alter ego of the Secretary. He is responsible for coordination and supervision of the Department as directed by the Secretary. Normally the Secretary delegates a great deal of his authority to the Deputy. The number two man can issue directives to all the subunits of governmental agencies, and to international bodies in the name of the Secretary. In recent years, the Deputy has also been given complete authority to deal with specific problem areas. David Packard, Deputy 1969–72, reformed DOD's weapons acquisition process, while William Clements, 1972–77, revised the Department's educational system.

The Assistant Secretary of Defense, Program Analysis, Planning and Evaluation, and his personnel serve as the Secretary's analytical staff. It is their job to evaluate all of the proposals submitted to the Secretary to ensure that they are in accord with the established objectives and are cost effective. As will be noted later, their main function is to analyse the programs submitted by the military departments and agencies during the budgetary process.

This group was established in 1961 as the Systems Analysis Division in the Comptroller's office. In 1965, Systems Analysis was raised to the Assistant Secretary level, in 1976 was placed in a staff capacity to the Secretary, and in 1977 it was restored to the Assistant Secretary level. Despite the changes in its status, the functions of systems analysis have remained the same.

Current legislation allows the Secretary of Defense to have nine assistant secretaries of defense plus a Director of Defense Research and Engineering, a Director of Telecommunications and Command and Control Systems, and a General Counsel. The law does not specify the functional responsibilities or titles of the nine assistant secretaries, but permits the Secretary to alter them as he sees fit. The current designations of each of these 12 individuals are self explanatory; descriptions of their responsibilities are listed in Table 1.

The job of the people at the assistant secretary level is to develop and control the implementation of policy in their areas of responsibility. They are in effect executive vice presidents of DOD. For example, the Director of Defense Research and Engineering supervises all research, development, testing and evaluation of weapons, weapons systems, and defense material. The Assistant Secretary of Defense for International Security Affairs develops and coordinates defense positions, policies, plans, and procedures in the field of international politico-military and foreign economic affairs.

Each of the assistant secretaries normally has several deputies and a staff of 150 to 200 people to enable him to carry out his responsibilities. Like the Secretary and Deputy Secretary of Defense, the Assistant Secretary level positions are subject to Senate confirmation.

The Joint Chiefs of Staff (JCS)

According to law, the Joint Chiefs of Staff are composed of four military officers: The Chief of Staff of the Army, the Chief of Naval Operations (CNO), the Chief of Staff of the Air Force, and a Chairman.[3] The latter is a member of one of the armed services but during his tenure on the JCS

Most things about the US defense establishment are on an astronomic scale. From his seat in the National Security Council (left) the President of the United States controls the world's largest employer, spender of the biggest budget (outside the Soviet Union) and, in theory if not in practice, provider of the world's most effective defense system. But even before SecDef McNamara shook it up in 1960 many Americans felt the DoD (Department of Defense) a wasteful bureaucratic juggernaut. From the Pentagon (below, with five 921-foot sides enclosing 44,200 telephones and almost as many people) the scene looks different.

has no service responsibilities. The Commandant of the Marine Corps is not a voting member of the JCS but is permitted to participate in JCS deliberations whenever matters in which the Marine Corps has an interest are under consideration. As a practical matter, this means that the Commandant is involved in nearly all JCS deliberations and is the de facto fifth member of the JCS.

All of the Joint Chiefs are appointed by the President subject to Senate confirmation. The service chiefs are appointed for a fixed nonrenewable term of four years. The chairman is appointed for a two-year term, and, except in wartime, can only be reappointed once. His term is not fixed and he serves at the pleasure of the President. Because of their tenure in office, the terms of the Chiefs carry over from one administration to the next.

The JCS perform four functions within DOD. First, they serve as the principal military advisors to the President and the Secretary of Defense. Their input to these two individuals is made primarily through the NSC system. Second, they prepare seven short, medium, and long range strategic and logistic plans which provide guidance for the development of the defense budgets, military aid programs, industrial mobilization plans, research and development programs, and the contingency plans of operational commanders. Third, they review and comment upon the plans, programs, and requirements of the separate services and the

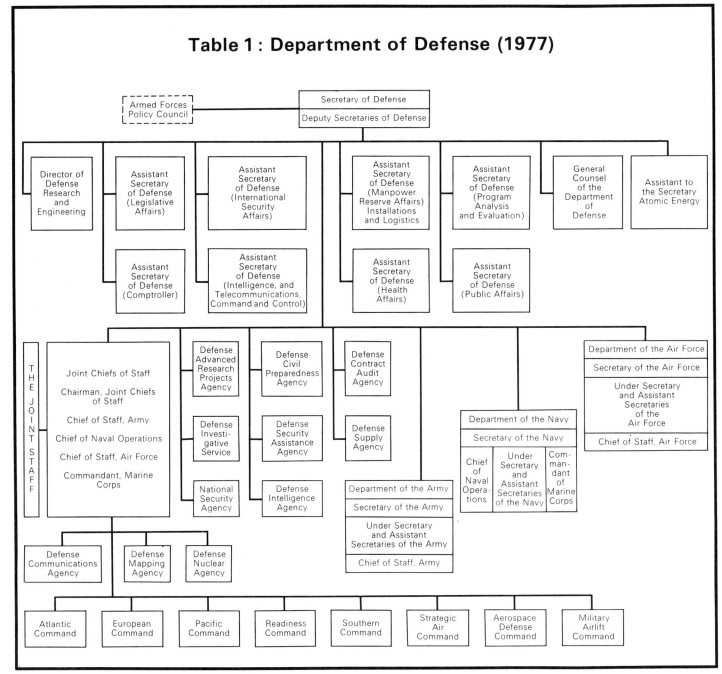

Table 1 : Department of Defense (1977)

field commands. Fourth, the Chiefs assist the President and the Secretary of Defense in carrying out their command responsibilities; that is, the JCS provide strategic direction over the operational commands for the Commander-in-Chief and the Deputy Commander-in-Chief.

The JCS are assisted in the exercise of their functions by a group known either as the Organization of the Joint Chiefs of Staff (OJCS) or the Office of the Joint Chiefs of Staff. OJCS is composed of 1,400 military personnel and 350 civilians and has two major components: the Joint Staff and the other groups which support the JCS but are not part of the Joint Staff.

The Joint Staff cannot by law exceed 400 military officers and is composed of equal numbers of officers from the three military departments, with the Marine Corps being allotted 20 percent of the Navy complement. The Joint Staff is headed by a director and divided along conventional military staff lines into three sections: operations, logistics, plans and policy. The intelligence function is performed for the JCS by the Defense Intelligence Agency. The director of the Joint Staff is a three-star general or admiral appointed for a two-year term by the chairman with the approval of the

Two recent photographs of the top US defense officials. Above left, on 10 March, 1978, Dr Harold Brown, Secretary of Defense (far left) introduces the Israeli Defense Minister, Mr Ezer Weizman, to (from left) John Stetson, Air Force Secretary, General David C. Jones, Air Force Chief of Staff, now Chairman Joint Chiefs of Staff, Adm James L. Holloway III until mid-1978 Chief of Naval Operations, and General Louis H. Wilson, Jr., Marine Commandant. Below, the President with (from left) Dr Harold Brown, Dr Zbigniew Brzezinski, National Security Adviser, and General Alexander M. Haig, Supreme Allied Commander Europe.

Secretary of Defense and the other members of the JCS. Although there is no legal requirement to do so, the positions of Director, Joint Staff, and the heads of the three directorates are normally rotated among the armed services. The primary function of the 400 member Joint Staff is to prepare staff studies on which the JCS base their decisions.

In order to fulfill its responsibilities while not violating the 400 man limit on the Joint Staff, the JCS have created a number of groups outside the Joint Staff but within OJCS. These groups include officers working on Strategic Arms Limitation, Mutual and Balanced Force Reduction, Law of the Sea, and Automatic Data Processing. Although this is technically illegal, Congress has given its tacit approval to the arrangement by funding these additional groups over the past two decades.

The Military Departments

Within the Department of Defense there are three military deparments separately organized and administered: Army, Navy, and Air Force. However, these organizations are departments in name only. The secretaries of these departments do not have cabinet level status nor are they responsible directly to the President or Congress. For all practical purposes, the Army, Navy, and Air Force are agencies or bureaus within the Department of Defense. They carry the designation of Department because up until the formation of DOD they had cabinet level status and were masters of their own affairs. Three decades after unification, the military departments are left with but few vestiges of their former prerogatives.

The primary function of the Departments of the Army, Navy, and Air Force is to recruit, train, and equip forces for the unified and specified commands. These departments have no control over military operations. The chain of command goes from the President through the Secretary of Defense and the JCS to the unified or specified commands. Moreover, in the areas "reserved" to the military departments—that is, recruiting, training, equipping—OSD can

and does intervene to establish guidelines and procedures; for example, the length of recruit training, development of weapon systems. Moreover, whenever there is a conflict between a departmental position and an OSD position, the Army, Navy, and Air Force must give way.

Each military department is headed by a secretary who is in effect president of a DOD subsidiary. These individuals are usually referred to as service secretaries. The departments are organized essentially along hierarchical staff lines which are a rough microcosm of the organization of the entire Department of Defense. Each service secretary has an under-secretary, a service secretariat and a military staff.

The secretariat is composed of approximately 10 civilian officials whose responsibilities roughly parallel those of the assistant secretaries of defense; e.g., research and developing, manpower and reserve affairs, general counsel. Each of these ten officials presides over a mixed staff of civilians and military personnel, the total size of which is now about 100.

The military staff of each department is headed by the uniformed Chief of Service. Each service chief has a vice chief who is in charge of conducting the day-to-day operations of the service staff so that the service chief has time to devote to his corporate duties as a member of the JCS. The military staffs are normally divided into approximately 15 sections which represent the different line and staff functions performed by the services; for example, personnel and medicine. Just as the responsibilities of the secretariat overlap with those of OSD, many of the functions of the military staff overlap with those of the defense agencies; for example, intelligence. Finally, there are the non-headquarters organizations or commands of each military department which actually carry out the work of recruiting, training, and equipping the force. When these forces become operational, i.e., assigned to a unified or specified command, the departments maintain only administrative control over them. The field commanders—for example, Commanding General,

US Seventh Army or Commander-in-Chief US Pacific Fleet—become component commanders in the unified or specified commands.

There are certain differences in the organizational arrangements of the military departments. Generally speaking the Departments of the Army and Air Force are much more hierarchical in nature than the Navy Department, in which certain bilineal elements of pre-World War II organizational arrangements have persisted. In the Army and Air Force, the military staffs support and report to the service secretary through both the appropriate assistant secretary, and the undersecretary. In the Navy, the CNO and the Commandant of the Marine Corps report directly to the Secretary of the Navy through a chain entirely separate from the civilian secretariat. Moreover, in the Navy department there are two distinct military staffs, one led by the CNO and the other managed by the Commandant of the Marine Corps.

Defense Agencies

At the present time there are 11 organizations or groups within DOD which have the status of defense agencies. These organizations perform functions which are common to or cut across departmental lines. There are no specific restrictions on the number or functions of these organizations. The McCormack-Curtis amendment to the 1958 Defense Reorganization Act empowers the Secretary to create such agencies whenever he determines that it would be advantageous in terms of effectiveness, economy, or efficiency to provide for the performance of a common function by a single organization. Implicit in the amendment is the Secretary of Defense's power to disestablish or disband such agencies.

Secretaries of Defense Gates, McNamara, and Laird have used the provisions of the McCormack-Curtis amendment to create 10 defense agencies. The eleventh agency, the National Security Agency, was established in November, 1952, by Presidential directive and

Table 2: Selected Characteristics of the Defense Agencies in 1977

Agency	Founded	Reports To	Personnel		
			Military	Civilian	Total
National Security Agency	1952	OSD	Classified	Classified	Classified
Defense Advanced Research Projects Agency	1972	OSD	43	107	150
Defense Nuclear Agency	1972	JCS	600	631	1,231
Defence Communications Agency	1960	JCS	1,600	1,610	3,210
Defense Intelligence Agency	1961	JCS/OSD	2,000	2,541	4,541
Defense Supply Agency	1961	OSD	1,446	47,083	48,529
Defense Contract Audit Agency	1965	OSD	—	3,520	3,520
Defense Security Assistance Agency	1971	OSD	100	116	216
Defense Mapping Agency	1972	JCS	819	7,371	8,190
Defense Civil Preparedness Agency	1972	OSD	—	604	604
Defense Investigative Service	1972	OSD	1,529	1,490	3,019
Total			8,137	65,073	73,210

placed under the control of the Secretary of Defense.

Seven of the agencies are under the direct management control of the Secretary of Defense; that is, their tasks are given by and they report directly to the Secretary. Three other agencies, Defense Communications, Defense Mapping, and Defense Nuclear, report directly to the JCS. The status of the Defense Intelligence Agency (DIA) is somewhat ambivalent. From its creation in 1961 through 1976, it was under the control of the JCS. In fact, as noted above, the Director of DIA serves as the J-2 for the Joint Staff. However,

in 1976 control over DIA was transferred to OSD, with the provision that the JCS could still assign tasks to it directly. Table 2 contains a list of the 11 agencies along with their dates of inception, controlling agent and personnel assigned.

Seven of the agencies are headed by three-star

Below: Not an agency of the defense establishment, the CIA, whose Washington HQ is pictured, serves political rather than military objectives. It has no direct links with the uniformed military.

generals or admirals, while the other four organizations, Defense Advanced Research Projects, Defense Civil Preparedness, Defense Contract Audit and Defense Investigative Service, are headed by a senior civilian. All of the agencies are staffed by a mixed civilian military complement. The civilians are generally in a permanent career status while the military personnel are assigned for a three-year tour.

The 11 defense agencies employ over 70,000 people. About 90 percent of the personnel are civilian while the remaining 10 percent are military on temporary assignment. The agencies vary widely in size. They range from the mammoth Defense Supply Agency, which employs nearly 50,000 people, to the miniscule Defense Advance Research Projects Agency, which has only 150 people on its payroll. Most of the agencies are comparatively small. Only the Defense Supply Agency and Defense Mapping Agency have more than 5,000 people in their group. The median size is just about 3,000 and three agencies actually have less than 1,000 people in their employ.

Although the defense agencies are the largest single organizational unit within DOD, their total budget is comparatively small. The total budget of these 11 agencies for FY 1978 was less than $4 billion or about 3 percent of the total defense budget.[6] There is one organizational reason for the fact that these groups consume such a relatively small amount of resources; that is, each of the military departments has groups within its military staff with responsibilities similar to that of the defense agencies. These service groups perform much of the basic work in the area, while the defense agencies function more or less as integrators.

The responsibilities of the agencies vary widely. This section will conclude with a brief description of the role of each of these eleven organizations.

The *National Security Agency* (NSA) is officially designated the National Security Agency/Central Security Service. It has a two-

fold responsibility. NSA safeguards the communications of the armed forces and monitors the communications of other nations for the purpose of gathering intelligence. The NSA was established in 1952 by President Truman as a replacement for the Armed Forces Security Agency. The Central Security Service was added to NSA in 1972 to emphasize the fact that NSA was being given responsibility for developing a unified cryptologic program within DOD. The three star director of NSA also heads the

Above: The White House is at once a home, office, center for diplomatic functions—and focal point for all who love or hate America. The highest defense decisions are taken here.

Central Security Service. Because of the classified nature of its operation, there are no figures available on the number of NSA employees. Nor does the NSA appear on many organizational charts of DOD.

US Mainland Military Districts

First US Army includes:
District of Columbia,
Commonwealth of Puerto Rico,
Virgin Islands of the
United States.

Naval Districts (HQ in blue)

Army Areas

Air Force Reserve Regions
(HQ in black)

The purpose of the *Defense Advanced Research Projects Agency* (DARPA) is to maintain technological superiority for the US in the field of military hardware. DARPA undertakes and carries through to feasibility demonstration those projects which meet one of the following criteria: those with high potential payoffs but with too high a risk for the individual services to obtain budget approval; projects which may involve major technological advances or breakthroughs; and projects which could have broad utilization within the entire department. After DARPA has explored a concept and determined it to be feasible, control of the project is turned over to the department or agency most directly concerned.

The *Defense Nuclear Agency* (DNA) is the present name of the group known initially as the Armed Forces Special Weapons Project and later as the Defense Atomic Support Agency. DNA manages the nuclear weapons stockpile, develops and monitors a National Nuclear Test Readiness Program, and maintains liaison for DOD with other governmental bodies concerned with nuclear matters.

The primary function of the *Defense Communications Agency* (DCA) is to manage the World-Wide Military Command and Control System. DCA also directs the National Communications System and the Defense Satellite Communications System. The operations of these systems will be discussed more fully in the section on command and control.

The *Defense Intelligence Agency* (DIA) manages all of the defense intelligence programs and provides intelligence support to the Secretary of Defense and the JCS. DIA relies upon the resources of the armed services for intelligence collection and supervises the development of intelligence by the services to meet their own particular needs.

The *Defense Supply Agency* (DSA) handles the procurement, storage and distribution of all common consumable items used within DOD.

Non-consumables and items peculiar to individual service weapon systems are managed by the military services. DSA presently handles 60 percent of all requisitions processed by DOD and administers military contracts with a value of more than $75 billion.

The role of the *Defense Contract Audit Agency* (DCAA) is to perform all the required contract auditing for DOD and to provide accounting and financial advisory service regarding defense contracts to DOD components which have responsibility for procurement and contract administration. The functions of DCAA include evaluating the acceptability of costs claimed as proposed by contractors and reviewing the efficiency and economy of contractor operations. Many other agencies of the Federal government also make use of DCAA services.

The *Defense Security Assistance Agency* (DSAA) was established to provide greater emphasis to the management and control of such aid programs as military assistance and foreign military sales. Besides controlling these programs the Director of DSAA also functions as a deputy assistant secretary of defense under the Assistant Secretary of Defense for International Security Affairs.

The *Defense Civil Preparedness Agency* (DCPA) is responsible for creating and maintaining an effective national civil defense program and for providing planning guidance and technical assistance to state and local governments in their achievement of disaster preparedness. DCAA was created in 1972 to replace the Army's Office of Civil Defense. It was given the status of a defense agency in order to emphasize the role of civil defense in the total US national security policy and to upgrade the entire civil defense program.

The *Defense Mapping Agency* (DMA) was established to consolidate and improve the efficiency of defense mapping, charting, and geodetic operations. DMA relies almost completely on the individual services for research

and development and data collection.

The primary function of the *Defence Investigative Service* (DIS) is to conduct personnel security investigations on DOD civilians, military personnel, and industrial and contractor personnel involved in defense business. DIS also conducts some criminal investigations and crime prevention surveys for DOD.

Field Commands

The operational forces of DOD are placed under the control of either a unified or specified commander. A unified command is one which has a broad continuing mission and is composed of forces of two or more services. A specified command also has a broad continuing mission but is normally composed of forces from only one service.

The operating forces of the Department of Defense are presently broken down into five unified and three specified commands. Four of the five unified are theater or area commands: Atlantic, Pacific, European, and Southern. The fifth unified command, the Readiness Command,

Right: Army Sec Clifford L. Alexander Jr with (left) Under-Sec Walter P. LaBerge and VCofS Gen Walter T. Kerwin Jr. The occasion was the somewhat controversial announcement that the German 120mm gun had been chosen for the XM1.

Right below: Gen Bernard W. Rogers, US Forces Commander in Hawaii, looks through the sight of an infantry TOW missile launcher on a visit to Schofield Barracks.

Below: Gen Louis H. Wilson Jr, Commandant of the Marine Corps, pauses to speak with a member of the Recruit Honor Guard during a visit to the Marine Corps Recruit Depot, San Diego.

is composed of forces from the Army and Air Force based in the continental United States. The Readiness Command is in effect a contingency command. Its primary mission is to make its forces available to reinforce the other unified or area commands.

The three specified commands are the Strategic Air Command, Aerospace Defense Command, and Military Airlift Command. Each of these commands is composed primarily of Air Force components.

The present command structure had its origins in World War II when the creation of theater joint and combined commands demonstrated the value of unified commands for broad military missions. The National Security Act of 1947 authorized the President to establish combatant commands for the performance of assigned military missions. However, it was not until the 1958 Reorganization Act became law that the unified and specified commands were placed directly under the control of the Secretary of Defense. Prior to that time, the unified commands were subject to the authority of the military departments and service chiefs.

Each unified command is headed by a four-star general officer. The Atlantic and Pacific Commands have always been headed by Navy admirals, while the European, Southern, and Readiness Commands are normally under the control of an Army officer. The three specified commands are headed by Air Force generals. The commanders of the unified and specified commands are responsible to the President and the Secretary of Defense for the accomplishment of their military missions. They have full operational control over the forces assigned to them and these forces cannot be reassigned or transferred except by the Secretary of Defense. The JCS provide strategic guidance and direction to these commands through the various

Above: General Haig, SACEUR, in the field —easing into a British Army Scorpion during Allied Command Europe (ACE) Exercise Avon Express on Salisbury Plain, England, in November 1977.

joint planning and intelligence documents, but do not exercise operational control over them. The JCS may issue orders to the unified commands only on the authority and direction of the Secretary of Defense. On their own, the Chiefs cannot move a ship or squadron.

The unified and specified commands are assisted by a joint staff and the commanders of the service forces or components assigned to them. In some of the commands, the unified commander also functions as a component commander. For example, the Commander-in-Chief of the Atlantic also serves as the Commander of the Atlantic fleet. Some of the unified commanders also are allied commanders. For example, the Commander-in-Chief of Europe is also the Supreme Allied Commander Europe.

As noted above, logistic and administrative support of the eight combat commands is the responsibility of the military departments. This permits the operational commander to focus on strategic and tactical matters and to take advantage of preexisting channels for logistic and administrative support.

Table 3 contains the organizational arrangements of the European Command. These arrangements are similar to those in each of the eight operational commands.

The Budgetary Process
The annual formulation of the budget within DOD involves all of the organisational elements within the Department and is probably the most important part of the policymaking process within DOD. Planning becomes irrelevant and

operations impossible if the proper mix of men and material are not purchased. To a great extent in DOD, dollars are policy.

As with other federal agencies the budgetary process in DOD has two clearly delineated phases: executive formulation and legislative authorization and appropriation. The executive phase lasts about 20 months, while the legislative portion takes another nine months.[7] Thus, the process begins about $2\frac{1}{2}$ years before the budget becomes operational.

Executive Phase
Since 1961 DOD has formulated its budget through the use of the Planning, Programming and Budgeting System (PPBS). This system divides the executive phase of the budgetary process into three clearly defined cycles: planning, programming, and budgeting, and has as its foundation the Five Year Defense Plan (FYDP). The FYDP is the master plan for the entire budget process. At any given moment, it contains the approved programs with their estimated costs projected out over a five year period. Each year the FYDP is updated to reflect decisions made in the budgetary process.

The planning cycle is the first and largest of the cycles. It begins in May and goes on for 10 months; that is, until the following February.

The planning cycle consists of four steps. The first step involves production of Volume I of the Joint Strategic Objectives Plan (JSOP) by the JCS for the Secretary of Defense. This volume is the Chiefs' assessment of the military threat facing the United States and of the national commitments projected over the next five years. In formulating JSOP I, the JCS are guided by the decisions made by the National Security Council (NSC) in this area. Generally speaking, in JSOP I, the JCS present a very foreboding view of the military capabilities of the adversaries of the United States.

During the summer the Secretary of Defense and his staff review JSOP I, and, in the fall, the Secretary completes the second step in the cycle by issuing his own draft or tentative policy, planning, and programming guidance to the defense community. The Secretary's guidance is based upon the inputs of the JCS, the NSC, and his own conception of what the national security policy should be. This document, referred to as the Draft or Tentative Planning and Programming Guidance (DPPG), is normally issued in September or October.

While the defense community is reviewing the DPPG, the JCS completes work on Volume II of the JSOP and sends it to the Secretary. This third step of the cycle is normally completed in December. JSOP II contains the JCS recommendations on the optimum force structure which the Chiefs feel is necessary to implement the guidance received from the Secretary of Defense in the DPPG. JSOP II is prepared without regard to fiscal limitations and usually recommends a total force structure about 50 percent larger than DOD can fund. In formulating JSOP II the Chiefs receive inputs from both the services and the unified and specified commanders.

The Secretary completes the planning cycle in February by issuing a Planning Programming Guidance Memorandum (PPGM). This document presents definitive fiscal constraints and policy assumptions under which the upcoming budget will be produced.

The fiscal constraints set forth a total for the entire Department as well as targets for each of the subunits of the organization. The DOD target comes from the Office of Management and Budget and is arrived at through a complex series of negotiations and bargaining between the President's advisors for national security and economic affairs. The ultimate decision on the defense total is highly susceptible to such influences as the state of the US economy, the chief executive's own monetary philosophy, and the demands of other agencies as well as the international situation.

Rather than funding a particular policy, the process is generally reversed. The administration decides on the size of the entire federal budget, adds up the essentially uncontrollable items in the budget, and then allocates some portion of the remainder to defense.

The shares of the defense total which are allocated to the individual components are based upon the missions or programs supported by each of these agencies. For example, the Navy supplies: the submarine launched ballistic missile portion of the Triad in DOD's strategic program; surface combatants and tactical air for the general purpose forces program, and transport ships for the sealift mission.

The planning assumptions in the PPG are influenced to some degree by guidance received from the National Security Council and to a lesser extent by inputs from the JCS in JSOP I and II. These assumptions are primarily a product of the Secretary of Defense's own interpretation of NSC and JCS inputs and his views on the likely scenarios which may lead to armed involvement by US military forces.

The programming cycle commences upon receipt of the PPG by the departments and agencies and lasts through the summer. This cycle contains three steps. First, the military departments and agencies complete their Program Objective Memoranda (POM) and the JCS

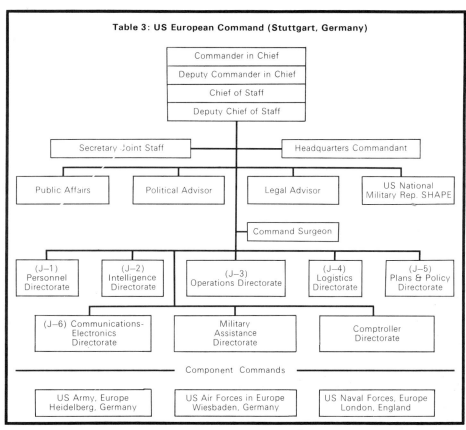

Table 3: US European Command (Stuttgart, Germany)

Below: What motivates (foreground, from left) US Ambassador to NATO Robert Strausz-Hupé, SecDef Harold Brown, ASecDef (ISA) Eugene McAuliffe and the then-JCS Gen George Brown, USA, as they discuss the billion-dollar AWACS at NATO HQ in 1977?

their Joint Force Memorandum (JFM). Both of these documents are submitted to OSD in May.

The POMs express total program requirements in terms of forces, manpower and costs for each mission area of the defense budget in which the organization plays a part. The POMs must provide a rationale for any deviations from the FYDP or PPG.

The Joint Force Memorandum (JFM), which is drawn up by the JCS, presents the corporate view of the uniformed leaders on the force levels that they feel ought to be provided within the fixed constraints of the PPG. The JFM also includes an assessment of the degree of risk that the Department is taking by not funding all of the forces recommended in the JSOP II. Finally, this document highlights the major force issues which the Chiefs feel should be resolved during the current budget process.

Theoretically, the JFM and POM should be different since the former is prepared from a collective viewpoint while the latter represents the views of a single department or agency. In actual practice, there is no appreciable difference between the two documents. The Chiefs simply add together the programs of their own services and label it a joint plan. This unified military position gives the military leaders important leverage in their subsequent dealings with their civilian superiors.

The POM and JFM are scrutinized during June by the systems analysts in OSD for conformity with the fiscal and policy guidance of the PPG. On the basis of this analysis, issue papers are prepared for the Secretary of Defense. These issues are the major questions that the analysts feel the Secretary should address in his review of the POM and JFM. They normally reflect those areas where OSD feels that the departments or agencies could meet their assigned objectives in a more cost effective manner. The analysts normally prepare a series of options for the Secretary on each issue.

During July and August the Secretary of Defense and his staff meet with the service chiefs and department secretaries to discuss and debate these issues. These "issue paper" meetings are considered the second "step" in the programming cycle. On the basis of these meetings, the Secretary makes a decision on each issue which he promulgates in the form of a Program Decision Memorandum (PDM). The PDMs are circulated throughout the Department for review and comment. If the JCS or the individual services disagree with any of the Secretary's judgments, they ask for a reconsideration or rehearing on the issue. The decisions which are not contested or reclaimed are allowed to stand. Normally about 10 percent of the issues are reclaimed and about half of these decisions are altered. The PDM-reclamation process is the third and final step in the cycle.

The budgetary cycle commences on October 1 when the departments and agencies submit their budget estimates for the fiscal year beginning twelve months hence. These estimates are reviewed jointly by personnel assigned to the Assistant Secretary of Defense (Comptroller) and the National Security Analysis Branch of the Office of Management and Budget (OMB). Theoretically this joint examination is technical in nature; that is, the reviewers are supposed to determine such things as whether a particular weapons system is costed out correctly. In practice, the comptroller and OMB often raise many issues with policy implications; for example, how many weapons are needed.

On the basis of this review, the Secretary of Defense makes certain changes in the budgets of his subunits which he issues in the form of Program Budget Decisions (PBD) throughout November and early December. These are circulated throughout the Department, and the military departments and agencies are given the opportunity to reclama those with which they disagree.

The PBD reclama process is finished in late December and the budget is then sent to the President. If the OMB examiners are not satisfied with certain decisions of the Secretary, the Director of OMB brings these to the attention of the Chief Executive. The President normally reviews the defense budget in early January and submits it to the Congress by the middle of the month. In his review, the President usually meets with the JCS as a group to ascertain their views on the final product. The Chief Executive generally makes only marginal changes to the proposed budget. However, there are some occasions when the President will make substantial modifications. These occasions arise if the Chief Executive needs to achieve specific monetary goals which necessitate a change in the size of the total federal budget. Since the defense budget represents two-thirds of all of the controllable expenditures in the entire federal budget, it is the easiest area to change in order to alter the size of the federal budget. Table 4 recaps the steps in the budgetary process.

Legislative Phase

The legislative phase of the defense budget process begins in mid-January upon receipt of the budget from the President and lasts until late September when the budget is sent to the White House for signature. This phase has three separate stages.

The first stage consists of setting a target for, or a ceiling on, the size of the defense budget. Under the provisions of the Congressional Budget Control and Impoundment Act of 1974, the Congress must pass a budget resolution by May 15. Among other things, this resolution must establish the overall size of the federal budget. This is made on the basis of recommendations of the House and Senate Budget Committees which conduct hearings on the subject. During the past three years, the Budget Committees have set a target for the defense budget about 4 percent below the amount requested by the administration. The budget resolution deals only with the size and not the distribution of the defense budget.

The second stage in the legislative phase of the budget process consists of authorizing or approving the major weapon systems and manpower levels of DOD. Before funds can be appropriated to DOD for men and material, the substance of the program must be approved. The authorization hearings are conducted by

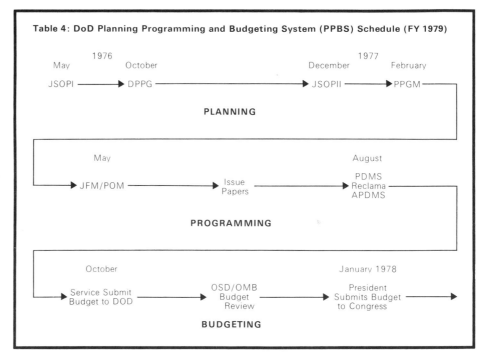

Table 4: DoD Planning Programming and Budgeting System (PPBS) Schedule (FY 1979)

World Military Command and Control Network

BMEWS	Ballistic Missile Early Warning System
WWMCCS	Worldwide Military Command and Control System
MEECN	Minimum Essential Emergency Communications Network
SIOP Forces	Strategic Integrated Operations Plan Forces
NMCC	National Military Command Centre (Pentagon)
ANMCC	Alternate National Military Command Centre (Washington)
NEACP	National Emergency Airborne Command Post

Above: In contrast with Communist countries' systems, on 21 January 1978 Fred P. Wacker, ASecDef (Comptroller) has to explain the DoD FY79 (Fiscal Year 1979) budget publicly to the media.

the Armed Services Committees of each chamber. These committees take about one thousand hours of testimony from the Secretary of Defense, the assistant secretaries, service secretaries and the JCS before making their recommendations. Many times issues which were decided within the executive branch are reopened again, and the services make their case once more to the Armed Services Committees which, for the most part, are composed of defense partisans. On many occasions these committees will authorize a program which the Secretary of Defense or the President does not want; e.g., a nuclear powered strike cruiser. The

Congress normally completes action on the authorization by the end of June.

The final stage of the legislative phase is the appropriations process. The Congress may appropriate funds for any authorized program but does not have to appropriate funds for all authorized programs. The appropriations process is conducted by a subcommittee of the House and Senate Appropriations Committees. These groups take another six hundred hours of

Diagram 2: The Changing Role of Communications, Command and Control (C³) in Escalation Control

Posture of forces		Levels of Activity		C³ Support Function	Required C³ Capability
Strategic Reserve Engaged Strategic Forces Engaged		Strategic Nuclear War		Reconstitution Termination Execution Info for Decision	Function under Attack Physical Survivability Jam Nuclear Effects Resistant
Selected Strategic Forces Engaged Tactical Nuclear Forces Engaged		Theater Nuclear War		Positive Control over Employment of Tactical Nuclear Weapons	Secure Communications Jam Nuclear Effects Resistant and Support for Planning
General Purpose Forces Engaged (Non-Nuclear)	Negotiate/Terminate	Theater Conventional War	Control of Escalation	Interoperate with Allies Joint Worldwide Operations	Systems Interoperability Secure Communications Survive Conventional Attack
Isolated Engagements Limited Deployment (Show of Force)		Crisis		Rapid Effective Response Two Way Info Flow	Mobility of C³ Assets Secure Communications Jam Resistant
Normal Readiness		Day-to-Day		Training and Exercises Situation Monitoring Access to Intel and Warning* Contingency Planning	Efficient Operations Quality Service Force Connectivity Secure Communications

Areas Indicate Transition Between Levels. Capabilities in these Areas are Key to Smooth Orderly Transition
*Warning Systems Covered Under Strategic Defense Programs

testimony on the defense budget from most of the same witnesses who appeared before the Armed Services Committees. In effect, each program in the DOD budget is subject to double jeopardy. It must be approved in both the authorization and appropriations process. Work on the defense appropriation bill is normally completed in late September.

While the defense appropriation bill is making its way through each chamber, the Congress adopts a second and binding resolution on the size of the defense budget. This figure, which must be established by September 15, is nearly identical to the May 15 target. If the defense appropriation bill falls within the binding target, the legislative phase is concluded. If not, the bill is sent back to the Appropriations Committee or the guideline is changed. Thus far, the size of the defense appropriations bill has not exceeded the binding target.

Command, Control, and Communications

The command, control, and communications (C³) systems of DOD are the means through which the National Command Authorities (The President and the Secretary of Defense) and, under their direction, the military commanders control and employ the military strength of the United States.[8] These C³ systems are composed of satellites for warning, surveillance, meteorology, and communications; ground and undersea systems; ground, shipborne, and airborne command facilities, worldwide voice, telephone, teletype, and automatic data networks; and information processing systems. A secure, well designed, and efficient C³ system is vital to the success of DOD in fulfilling its primary mission of employing military force in support of national policy. A poor C³ system can undo the best efforts of even an administratively sound organizational structure and a cost effective military force.

An overview of the present C³ structure is portrayed in Diagram 1. At the center are the National Command Authorities (NCA)—the President and the Secretary of Defense. The NCA exercise command and control over deployed forces through the Joint Chiefs of Staff. The JCS are supported directly by the National Military Command System (NMCS), which consists of the National Military Command Center (NMCC) in the Pentagon, the Alternate National Military Command Center

(ANMCC), based near Washington, and the National Emergency Airborne Command Post (NEACP), along with their interconnecting telecommunications and Automated Data Processing (ADP) support. These facilities provide the personnel and equipment which can receive, evaluate and display information as well as execute national decisions for direction and control of the forces. Alerting procedures and the redundancy of the facilities, coupled with the NEACP's airborne capability, provide for an important degree of survivability if the system should come under attack.

The NMCS is under the control of the JCS. The chairman of the JCS is responsible for the operation of the three elements in this system. He is assisted in this job by the Director and Deputy Director of Operations (J-3). The Director of the Defense Communications Agency is the NMCS systems engineer and technical supervisor for the entire NMCS.

The second diagrammatic ring around the NCA represents the Defense Communications System (DCS). The DCS is the "in-place" worldwide system which serves as the foundation for wartime communications while concurrently satisfying peacetime communication needs. It provides for common-user communication requirements and extends high volume command and control capability throughout the United States, Europe and the Pacific. Included are subsystems for voice communications by the Automatic Voice Network (AUTOVON), secure voice communications by the Automatic Secure Voice Network (AUTOSEVOCOM), and secure message and data transmission by the Automatic Digital Network (AUTODIN). For the most part, these systems consist of fixed equipment and facilities and interconnect with the primary and alternate fixed or mobile command posts of the key decision makers.

Overseas, the DCS is mostly government-owned; in the US, it is leased from commercial carriers. It serves the entire Defense community with over 1,500 AUTODIN terminals and 17,000 direct AUTOVON subscribers. The systems which comprise the DCS have a preempt capability so that essential command and control messages can be accorded precedence over routine traffic. The DCS system is operated and maintained by the Defense Communications Agency.

The last ring in the diagram represents the

mobile and transportable facilities and tactical networks organic to the military field forces. Also included here are the post, camp, station and base fixed, internal communications systems. The communications networks of the operating forces are the means by which the highly mobile forces are maneuvered by their commanders. DOD has the capability to link the various tactical systems through the DCS to the NMCS to allow the National Command Authorities to communicate with unified and specified commanders in crisis spots and then to the on-scene commanders represented on the outer ring.

Funding and Control

The pie-shaped segments in the diagram represent the Worldwide Military Command and Control System (WWMCCS). This system includes the communication systems of the Unified and Specified commands, and the special systems used for control of nuclear forces. This portion of the communications network has survivability characteristics which are too expensive for incorporation in all systems but which are necessary for execution of essential functions in the event of stress, degradation, or deliberate attack. Some of the survivability characteristics are physical hardening, mobility, redundancy, antijam protection and electromagnetic pulse protection. That portion of WWMCCS designated the Minimum Essential Emergency Communications Network (MEECN) encompasses the maximum survivability and reliability features needed for essential network performance in a stressed environment. The MEECN is dedicated to providing the highest possible assurance of command and control of US strategic nuclear forces during and after any nuclear attack on the United States, which includes an attack on the communications systems.

The perimeter of the second ring contains examples of the intermediaries through which directives would flow on their way to and from the field forces. For example, communications with most operating or deployed forces would be channeled through the unified and specified commands, while communications with a military advisory group in a particular country would be handled by the embassy.

The perimeter of the outer ring contains selected examples of different areas and types of forces. The strategic nuclear forces or SIOP (Strategic Integrated Operations Plan) forces use the MEECN while theater or tactical nuclear forces communicate through WWMCCS. Communications between the NCA and the Sixth Fleet in the Mediterranean or the US Seventh Army in Germany would use the Defense Communications System and would go via the European Command. Communications among units of the Sixth Fleet and the Seventh Army would take place via the tactical communications net.

The C³ systems and procedures must be adaptable to rapidly changing situations ranging from day-to-day activities, through crisis

In time of crisis the hub of US national strategic and economic command decision-taking would be eight miles above the ground, where a Boeing E-4B would have on board a team of about 60 including the President, selected DoD officials and the Commander of SAC. Flight refuelling (a KC-135 is the tanker at right) would maintain the airborne command post indefinitely, secure from any conceivable hostile attack. All decision-taking is on the main deck, where there are more command, control and communications (C³) items than in any other vehicle on Earth. Aft in the lower lobe is a technical control facility (left) whose task is to manage the domestic power supplies of the Advanced Airborne National Command Post (AABNCP) itself.

to conventional and nuclear war—including surprise attack on the United States—and programs have been structured to address this need. The interrelationship of force postures, levels of conflict and the command and control function required at each level is illustrated by Diagram 2.

Defense Organizational Issues

If any organizational theorist were designing an organization from scratch, it is not likely that he would design an organization in the form of the Department of Defense in 1978. However, it is important to keep in mind that DOD was not created from a *tabula rasa*. The three military departments, the four services, and the JCS all antedated the establishment of DOD, and their continued existence has never been seriously challenged.

Moreover, the efficiency of defense organization has always had to take a secondary role to the desire of Congress to maintain its ability to influence defense policy. The legislative branch operates on the premise that a truly centralized military establishment would decrease the impact of the Congress in the policy process. For example, the legislature has not allowed an increase in the number of assistant secretaries since 1953, nor in the size of the joint staff since 1958. Moreover, each branch has a legislative veto on the power of the Secretary to transfer roles and missions among the services.

Nonetheless, in spite of these limitations, there are still some things that can and should be changed to improve the effectiveness of defense organization. These changes can be grouped into three categories.

First, the Secretary of Defense needs to reduce his span of control. Under the present arrangement, it is simply too great. At the present time, the Secretary has twenty-three people who report directly to him. As indicated in Table 1, these include his deputy, the assistant secretaries, service secretaries, and heads of defense agencies. This situation could be remedied by creation of four or five super assistant secretaries or undersecretaries.

Second, the service secretariats ought to be eliminated or substantially reduced. There is simply no need for the large secretariats. These groups merely duplicate the work of OSD and have no real import on the policy process. The secretaries of the military departments could function more effectively by using the staff of their military chiefs.

Third, the operational command situation needs to be clarified. At present there is a great deal of potential confusion between the area or unified and the functional or specified commands. For example, it is not clear who would have control over strategic forces in the Pacific—CINCPAC or CINCSAC? The problem could be solved by dividing and placing the operational forces into strategic, tactical and logistic commands.

In addition there are also some changes which could be made in the budgetary process. As it presently exists the process is too long and cumbersome. The executive phase could easily be shortened to twelve months and many of the documents and steps combined. For example, the JCS and OSD need to issue only one planning document instead of JSOP I, II, the DPPG and DPGM. Similarly, the JFM could easily be eliminated from the programming cycle.

The command control and communications system has the opposite problem. It is simply too efficient. As it exists, the C³ system can easily lead to overcontrol of field operations by Washington. During the Mayaguez incident the Pentagon and the White House were actually issuing orders to individual aircraft. Moreover, information was being made available to Washington before the on-the-scene units. No structural changes can solve this problem. The National Command Authorities must have the capability to exert whatever degree of control they feel is appropriate. The ability to resist the tendency toward overcontrol requires the development of the proper respect for military professionalism.

Footnotes

1. Data on the present organizational structure of DOD can be gathered from *United States Government Manual*, 1976–77, pp. 160–75. See also Theodore Bauer and Eston White, *Defense Organization and Management*, Industrial College of the Armed Forces, 1975, and my *Thirty Years of Service Unification*, Naval Institute Proceedings, June 1978.
2. The post was established as a result of the unauthorized bombing of North Vietnam by the Seventh Air Force.
3. For an analysis of the organization and function of the JCS see my *The Joint Chiefs of Staff: The First Twenty-Five Years*, Bloomington: Indiana University Press, 1976.
4. Up until World War II, the Department of the Navy was composed of separate bureaux, each of which was subject to the control of the Secretary of the Navy.
5. Donald Rumsfeld, *Annual Defense Department Report, FY 1978*, January 17, 1977, p. 304.
6. *Ibid.*, p. A-1.
7. For a detailed analysis of the defense budgetary process, see my "The Budget Process in the Department of Defense, 1947–77," *Public Administration Review*, July–August, 1977, pp. 334–46.
8. This discussion is drawn from Donald Rumsfeld, *Annual Defense Department Report FY 1977*, January 27, 1976, pp. 172–85 and *FY 1978 Report*, pp. 254–62.

The US Intelligence Machine

Dr. Ray S. Cline, Executive Director, Georgetown University Center for Strategic and International Studies; former Deputy Director for Intelligence, Central Intelligence Agency.

Throughout the sweep of history military commanders have emphasized the difficulty of penetrating the "fog of war" that obscures the movement of forces as well as the intentions of opposing military leaders on the battlefield. Intelligence is the sum of reliable information available at a military headquarters; it is also the apparatus by which the commander extends the capacity of his own eyes and ears to collect the information he needs. Intelligence should encompass as much as possible of the pattern of maneuver and concentration of forces in the theater of combat. It has always been eagerly sought by great military leaders, and superior intelligence often provides the margin which wins the battle. The extraordinary achievements of British troops in North Africa and US naval forces in the Pacific in the early days of World War II, for example, were due less to superior generalship or brilliant seamanship than to the precision of data on enemy forces provided by code and cipher breaksthrough. When intelligence is good enough to give advance warning to the military high command of what the enemy is going to do as well as what he is now doing, the fortunes of war will nearly always swing to the side with the better information.

In the early days of the history of the United States, the importance of intelligence was fully appreciated by the founding fathers of the Republic. In what, after all, was a quasi-guerilla war against the generally superior British forces in North America, the supreme commander George Washington depended enormously on the superiority of the information which he could gather because of the sympathy of most of the citizens of the countryside. In this way time and again he was able to offset what was usually comparative weakness in the numbers, training, supply, and equipment of his troops.

Washington's first large expenditures, after he took command of the Continental armed forces, were made for the purpose of sending secret agents into the town of Boston, and he encouraged the procurement of spies as a central part of his plans for coping with the better organized and trained British forces in Boston. He also gave orders for the stationing of lookouts at all commanding heights. Washington urged that prisoners be captured in all skirmishes so that they could be interrogated. His view, he said, was: "do not stick at any expense" in organizing an espionage net to penetrate the enemy-controlled area.

Intelligence Requirements Today

The technology of war and the destructiveness of weapons have changed enormously in the past two centuries, but the imperative of basing military decisions on sound information about the capabilities of enemy forces and their potential movements is just as great as ever. In fact, the commanders of the armed forces of the United States today have an even more difficult job than George Washington did. He at least knew the terrain of the battles of the Revolutionary War, and he had friendly populations everywhere in British-occupied areas. Today's US armed forces have virtually a global battlefield to be concerned with in preparing for defense of their country, their soldiers, sailors, and airmen on duty overseas, their military bases, and the territory of their allies.

Moreover, in the broadest context, armies today are intended primarily to deter potential enemies from resorting to military force as an instrument of their international policy. Hence the battlefield not only has expanded, in a sense, to cover the whole world but also the requirements for knowledge of the strength and the intentions of every potential combatant has become overwhelming. In many ways it is more important than ever before to be prepared to respond instantly and appropriately to opening phases of hostilities since the name of the game is to avoid escalation. In order to deter an enemy from attacking in some locale where the interests of the United States may force it to become involved, or to counter a local attack in such a way as to prevent further escalation, it is absolutely essential for the US to be prepared in all respects with knowledge of the ground, air, and naval capabilities of potential enemies as well as the geographical, military, and economic conditions in adversary, friendly, and neutral territory. It is also imperative to be aware of the psychology and the political factors which go into military decision-making by all parties to the potential conflict. The peacetime requirements for intelligence are staggeringly voluminous and complex.

It is necessary, therefore, for modern military intelligence officers to think not merely of the circumstances on the battlefield where armies fire on one another, although in the last analysis that is where both capabilities and the intentions of planners are tested out; it is essential in addition to make the more subtle distinctions to enable not only military commanders but all of the government officials responsible for national security affairs to understand fully the dangers around them, the risks they should or should not take, and the probable outcome of interdependent political, military, and economic factors that condition the outcome of military conflicts in which the United States may become involved.

Today the American unit commander has at his fingertips details about the locale of his operations and the character of potential enemy forces which exceed anything ever available before. The danger today is less with the paucity of information than it is with the difficulty of comprehending all of the information. Here the automation of knowledge has helped in some ways but created additional difficulties in other ways. The armed forces of the United States have in the tactical military field achieved extraordinary breakthroughs in creating display systems which provide the commander with the routine elements of information about the forces which he might meet in battle, and which give him instant retrieval of data which in the past would have had to be processed through the minds of men in his intelligence section. However, the data on the automated display system can only be as good as the input into the computers which supply that data. The computer experts are absolutely right in enunciating the idea they abbreviate as "GIGO"—which means, "garbage in, garbage out".

Below: This vertical photograph of Washington D.C. was taken on 2402-type film from 50,500ft. Different kinds of film defeat most attempts at camouflage, and detail is much finer than anything reproducible on this page. The SR-71 (far left) is the chief American strategic reconnaissance aircraft, and like most modern reconnaissance platforms uses radar and infra-red as well as optical photography. Just as important as information-gathering is data processing and transmission. The DSCS II (Defense Satellite Communications System II, near left) will be a key network of 18 space platforms girdling the Earth and enabling all kinds of information to be relayed in split-seconds.

In a sense, the automation of information processing is only a special modern circumstance for intelligence operations, a tool of the trade, rather than a fundamental change in the character of intelligence operations. It is still crucial to get the information to go into the automated memory bank and appear on the display panels, whatever they may be, on board ship or in command posts in battle areas.

There are two types of intelligence needed by military commanders, tactical and strategic. There is no clean dividing line between the two but units in the field have a primary concern for tactical detail about immediately opposing forces. At higher headquarters the broader sweep of information about nations and potential conflicts of all kinds is what is needed. The key point for the tactical commander is to know how to sift out of the vast data banks at national levels of intelligence analysis exactly what is relevant to his problems. Thus the fighting soldier at any level of command will have a greater chance of getting what he needs for military success if he understand the structure and functioning of the great central intelligence system that is a component part of the American military machine.

Tactical military intelligence continues to be of prime importance to the combat forces, and in time of war the intelligence (G-2) sections of every command echelon extract all the information possible from reconnaissance sweeps, prisoner interrogations, and local espionage sources. Tactical intelligence in combat situations, just as in the time of George Washington, will depend to a remarkable extent on contact with the enemy, ability to capture prisoners and interrogate them efficiently, conduct aerial and patrol reconnaissance, communicate with agents behind the enemy lines, and intercept documentary evidence about opposing forces.

The Vietnam war, in this respect, was not very different from earlier wars. It was marked primarily by the sophistication of the gadgetry, not the difference in the essential elements of information which commanders needed to know. In fact, advanced technology in gadgetry imposed an additional burden of deploying manpower and a tremendous complication in the processing of information. Interrogation centers for the interviewing of military and civilian prisoners turned out reams of information which had to be evaluated, assimilated and related to secret agent reporting, search patrols, intercepted messages (a prime source of data particularly valuable because in some cases it revealed forward plans of the enemy), and the voluminous files of film from overflying airplanes—especially the old reliable workhorse, the U-2.

These elements of tactical military intelligence, however, are not the main resource of the American military machine. In peacetime, in view of the complexity of possible future conflicts and, in fact, uncertainties as to where the battlefields may be, the main data base for United States military forces comes from the national intelligence community, which deals primarily with strategic intelligence. It is the provision of this strategic intelligence to the armed forces in the field, along with nuggets and titbits of information that are of tactical import to individual units in the field (although part of the strategic intake), that gives the American military machine its margin of superiority in being alert and ready for hostilities, able to comprehend enemy force maneuvers and deceptions, and prepared to go into combat effectively in fighting any first-phase battles.

The main element of the intelligence component of the American military machine is not the standard G-2 unit which appears under one name or another in almost all military organizations, but the national intelligence system. Encompassing all of the elements of government agencies that collect or evaluate and analyze intelligence information, this central intelligence community provides most of the basic data on which they will operate in peacetime, and on the basis of which they will go into

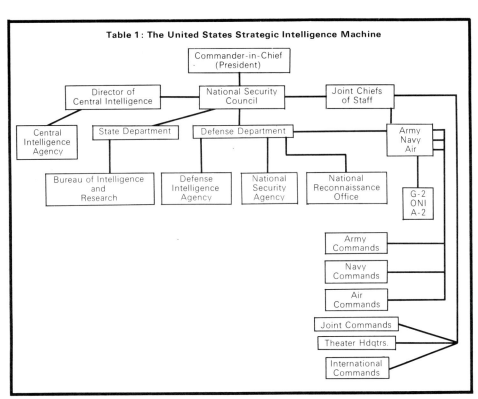

Table 1: The United States Strategic Intelligence Machine

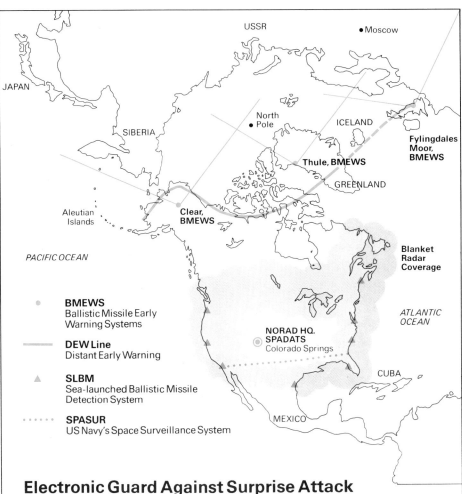

Electronic Guard Against Surprise Attack

These are the lacings of the electronic network covering air approaches to North America. All are tied to the North American Air Defense Command's underground Combat Operations Center within Cheyenne Mountain near Colorado Springs, Colo. At three sites near the top of the world, high-powered radar antennas of the Ballistic Missile Early Warning System (BMEWS) reach out 3,000 miles to give the alert of an intercontinental ballistic missile attack from the north. Eight radar sites of the Sea-Launched Ballistic Missile Detection and Warning System (SLBM) along the sea approaches to the US would detect a missile attack launched from submarines. Space satellites would also flash an alarm to NORAD's Combat Operations Center of a missile attack against North America. Against the manned bomber threat, NORAD employs the Distant Early Warning (DEW) Line, extending across the top of the continent, and a system of radars guarding all approaches to the US and the populated areas of Canada. Stretched across the southern US is the US Naval Space Surveillance System (SPASUR), one of the satellite detection and tracking nets reporting data on earth-orbiting space objects to NORAD's Space Defense Center inside Cheyenne Mountain.

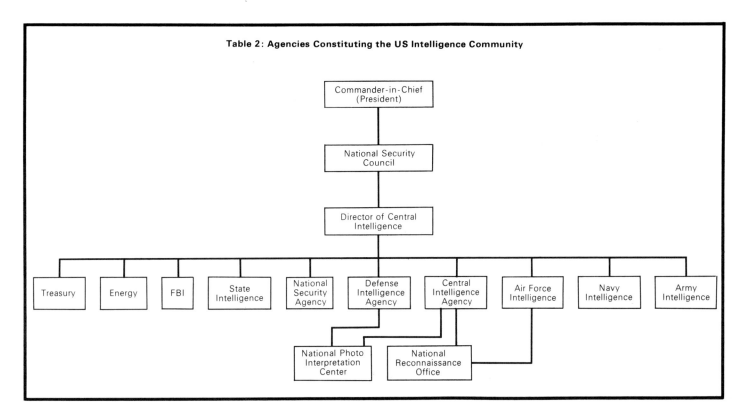

Table 2: Agencies Constituting the US Intelligence Community

Commander-in-Chief (President)
→ National Security Council
→ Director of Central Intelligence
→ Treasury | Energy | FBI | State Intelligence | National Security Agency | Defense Intelligence Agency | Central Intelligence Agency | Air Force Intelligence | Navy Intelligence | Army Intelligence
→ National Photo Interpretation Center | National Reconnaissance Office

battle, if deterrence fails and war comes. Viewed in this sense, the American military machine is almost entirely dependent on the cogs and wheels of the intelligence community in Washington.

At present the structure of the US intelligence community is being reviewed and reorganized by the Executive Branch of the government and by the Congress. Nevertheless, the essential elements are long established and clearly identified. The military agencies provide to their own forces in the field the informational output not only of the intelligence agencies under the command of the Secretary of Defense and the Joint Chiefs of Staff, but those that are directly or indirectly tasked by civilian agencies of

Right: Routes that space satellites take as they circle the earth can be displayed on screens in NORAD's Command Post. By relaying a command to a computer, battle staff members can look at the paths a satellite will follow for as many as 12 global revolutions and know what part of the earth it will soon be crossing.

Below: High technology bases, of top strategic importance, are dotted over many remote regions, giving the USAF Satellite Control Facility global coverage.

Air Force Satellite Communications System (AFSATCOM)

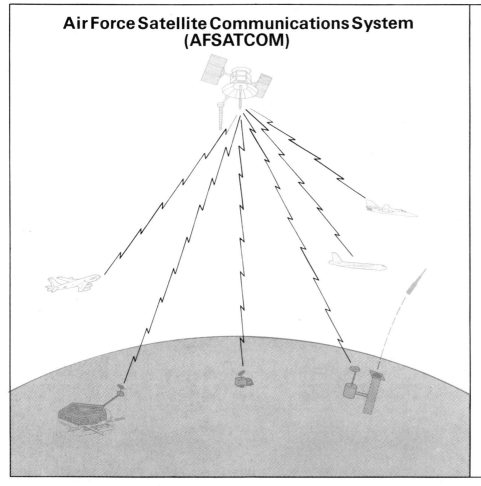

AFSATCOM (Air Force Satellite Communications System) is one of the major American systems providing "C³": command, control and communications. Providing ground and air teletype terminals and the satellites is only a minor part of the task. Every user has to have secure access to the system, to be alerted instantly of any change in the status of any satellite (caused by malfunction or possibly enemy action) and be able to "talk" to any other part of the Air Force. A fundamental part of the requirement is that it must "withstand massive physical as well as jamming attacks in the execution of its mission". Though reliability and resistance to nuclear explosions and other attacks must be high, the whole system incorporates a degree of redundancy so that loss of one or more satellites, or many ground terminals, does not degrade system capability. The links illustrated are two-way, most of them uhf (ultra high frequency), with instant-response transponders in the satellites to re-broadcast amplified and possibly clarified messages to the allotted destination(s). Of course, any major nuclear attack decision could be taken only by the President of the United States and Commander of SAC, and in any time of crisis both would be airborne in an E-4 AABNCP aircraft, as explained on pages 164–165. In 1978 various Air Force agencies were still engaged in research and testing prior to awarding AFSATCOM contracts.

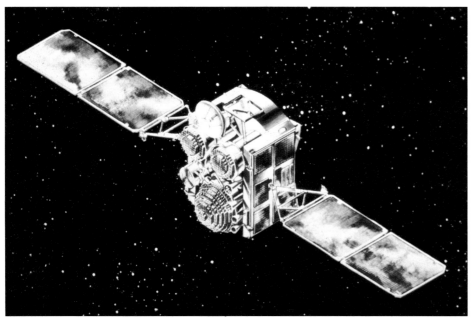

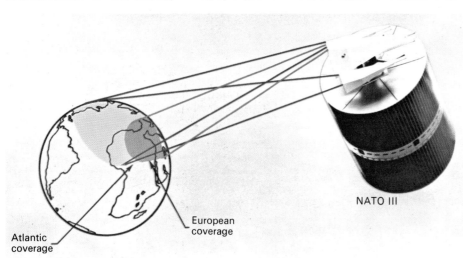

government like the State Department and the Central Intelligence Agency (CIA). The superiority of strategic intelligence holdings in Washington is mainly due to the 30-year effort to coordinate and share intelligence among all agencies at the national level as prescribed in the National Security Act of 1947, which set up the Central Intelligence Agency. To know what the danger of the outbreak of hostilities is and what the character of potential attacks might be, requires more than the individual unit commander can possibly have resources to discover. Hence, from the front line back through the echelons of command of each theater, the military intelligence units are holding data which come from the massive machine managed from Washington. It is the structure and functioning of this central intelligence machine which a US military commander must appreciate if he is to use it well and to get the best information out of the sources available to him.

The first thing to realize is that a great deal of information comes from what we think of as open sources. Newspaper accounts of foreign events, periodical literature on economic, political and scientific trends, foreign broadcasts of speeches and news, the proceedings of scholarly conferences in American or foreign "think tanks": all these must be mined and the valuable nuggets distributed to the right staffs. Beyond this, US Embassy diplomatic reporting brings in data openly procured from foreign sources but passed back to Washington in confidential channels of official communications. Military intelligence and related background information of military value derive in good part from these open sources.

Among them, reporting from military

Left: Though quite different in appearance, the American DSCS III (upper) and NATO III (left) both fulfil similar functions. Each satellite holds its station over the same point whilst processing and re-transmitting many voice, teletype, facsimile (picture) and data channels. There will be 18 DSCS III satellites but only one NATO III plus a single "back-up".

attachés stationed in embassies abroad—what could be called semi-open intelligence—is extremely useful in focusing on the weapons characteristics and the force levels of nations all over the world, including the forces of allies and friends of the US, as well as these allies' views of potential enemies' forces. The attachés, of course, mainly concentrate on the information more difficult to procure, information about the forces of the Soviet Union, the greatest military power opposing the United States, and other nations which are, by political and strategic force of circumstance, adversaries if not actual enemies of the United States; for example, the People's Republic of China (Peking) and the Warsaw Pact countries of East Europe. These attaché reports are often procured through the services of friendly military agencies abroad and their detailed accounts of the structure and training levels, the readiness for combat of all kinds of forces, and the technical specifications of weapons provide the US with the basic data on which the worldwide order of battle is built. A surprising amount of useful knowledge is available from close scanning of the open broadcasts of the governments and the governmental units in the totalitarian states. Because information is so tightly controlled, things that are said about the armed forces and their plans are sometimes very revealing. CIA is the principal agency responsible for procuring foreign broadcasts and documents, though all the other intelligence components assist.

For the major adversary nations, however, like the Soviet Union and China, which try to conceal from the United States the military data which the US military machine needs to know in order to do its job of deterrence and preparedness, the open sources and semi-open official reports are not full enough to permit full reliance on them. These countries can only be brought under surveillance by the sophisticated instrumentalities of the secret and clandestine agencies of the national intelligence community.

Another reason why central intelligence at the Washington level is crucial to all military units is the fluid and problematic nature of modern conflicts. If the crucial value of intelligence is one main characteristic of military affairs today, others are the mobility of military forces, the fuzziness of battle lines, and the melding or merging of tactical and strategic considerations as military dispositions in one region or another reveal clues to the intentions of military planners in Moscow or Peking and vice versa. The whereabouts of Soviet strategic air forces and, in particular, of missile-launching submarines, becomes a prime element in calculating the probabilities of conflict throughout the regions of the world where US forces are deployed. In a total war, strategic warning would be as likely to come from the first indicators of movement to sea of Soviet submarines in unusual force in the Atlantic and the Pacific as from troop mobilization or concentrations on any front.

An American combat unit in Korea, say, might get no inkling of attack until the actual jumping off of forces near the Demilitarized Zone and yet be enormously aided in being ready for an attack by a report from the Iceland area confirming the movement to sea of unprecedented numbers of submarines from Murmansk.

All of this is to say that the subject matter of military intelligence is basically what it has

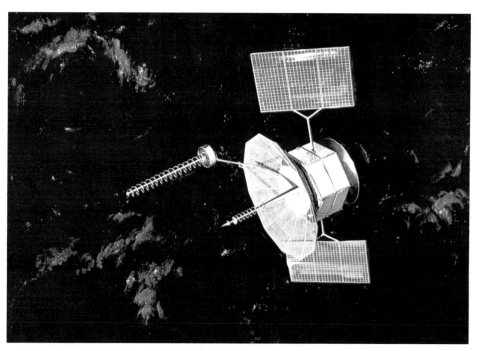

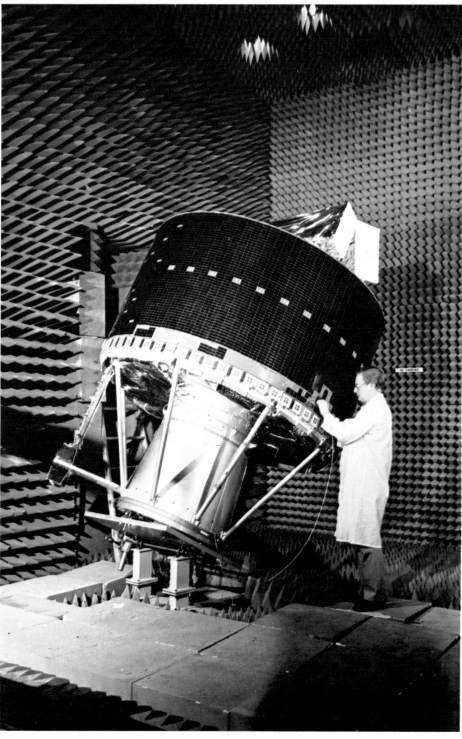

Top: FLTSATCOM (Fleet Satellite Communications) satellites began operating in 1977. Four, plus a spare, will link US Navy aircraft, ships, submarines, SAC and the Presidential command network.

Right: Second of the NATO III series, IIIB was placed in orbit hovering over a point on the Equator on January 27, 1977. It can simultaneously handle hundreds of different communications.

always been, but that the elaborate structure of the modern US intelligence community extends the range of observation—the eyes and ears of each unit commander—to a virtually unlimited global surveillance. At tactical unit or strategic force levels the intelligence sections of all commands try to keep up-to-date, reliable order of battle (strength and deployment of potential enemy forces), technical intelligence about weapons characteristics and the capabilities and vulnerabilities of all support facilities—especially transportation and communications equipment, and the main features of the terrain of potential battlefields.

All of this kind of data, when and if collected in the field, goes up the chain of command as well as directly back to Washington. In Washington all sources and all service interests are melded into one big evaluation process, from which emerges the general picture confronting the American military machine as a whole. From this national picture of the world around the US, the military agencies of the Defense Department, the Joint Chiefs of Staff, the Army, the Navy, the Air Force, the Marines, and the Coast Guard abstract the data relevant to their respective missions and construct an intelligence data base for their own reference in operational planning and also to send out to the joint theater commands and service headquarters all over the world. The theater command staffs sort out the intelligence applicable to the units under them and pass it along. Thus there is a flow of intelligence to the field for combat unit readiness purposes that is the finished product from all of the various kinds of intelligence that flows into Washington from the many agencies collecting military information and related strategic data for the entire intelligence community.

The President of the United States is under the Constitution the Commander-in-Chief of the US armed forces. Hence, at a high level of interdependence, he is nominally the recipient of all military intelligence that affects his extremely broad strategic responsibilities. A schematic rendition of the military command system in which the main cogs in the strategic intelligence machine operates is shown in Table 1.

At every command level there is an intense demand for reliable intelligence on the basis of which to prepare strategic plans, train and deploy forces, and maintain combat readiness. While reporting goes up in the various chains of command, strategic intelligence mainly goes down after it has been coordinated, evaluated, and amalgamated at the top level of each intelligence element in Washington. These tasks in peacetime simply must be done in an active interrelationship with all the other elements of the intelligence community, civilian as well as military.

After all, the best indication that hostilities may break out in some specific region where US armed forces are exposed may not be any kind of military action, but, for example, a piece of political intelligence to the effect that Soviet advisors are being withdrawn (as they were from Syria and Egypt a few days before the Yom Kippur war in October 1973), or a piece of economic intelligence (the importation or domestic production of commercial items—such as medicines—in such quantity as to exceed normal civilian requirements and reveal an urgent need for military end-use materiél).

Thus the American military machine runs primarily on the output of the strategic intelligence machine in Washington, that is, the agencies and elements of agencies operating under the interagency coordinating mechanisms headed by the Director of Intelligence. These agencies constituting the intelligence community shown in Table 2.

The ten agencies are very uneven in the contributions they make to the American military machine, but among them the work is done which creates the national intelligence data base on which all force planning, deployment, and combat readiness depend.

Principle of the Earth Orbiting Satellite

North Pole

Near-Polar Orbit

Earth Rotation

Above: A satellite travelling at about 17,500mph about 100 miles above the Earth's surface makes one orbit every 90 minutes. In a near-Polar orbit the Earth turns about 1,500 miles (at the Equator) between orbits, so the whole globe is eventually covered. Below 100 miles, atmospheric drag slows the satellite down quickly and it burns up. At a height of about 22,300 miles a satellite in eastwards equatorial orbit (wide band) appears to hover over one spot.

The Treasury Department's input is in the form of economic statistics and financial information derived from its intricate involvement with foreign and international financial organizations. It is represented by a Special Assistant to the Secretary of the Treasury and works very closely with the Economic Research Office of CIA.

The new Energy Department has a most specialized function to perform, mainly to contribute its specialized knowledge of energy in all its forms, but especially nuclear energy, to estimates made by the CIA and the military intelligence analysis staffs of foreign nuclear weapons inventories and characteristics. While it will also contribute to economic estimates on other forms of energy, the technical detail based on weapons development programs in the US is the best guide, or the only guide, to

Below: This black Lockheed U-2 ultra-high-flying aircraft is carrying special equipment behind the cockpit for use in upper-air and electronic surveillance experiments. They are the main intelligence research platforms.

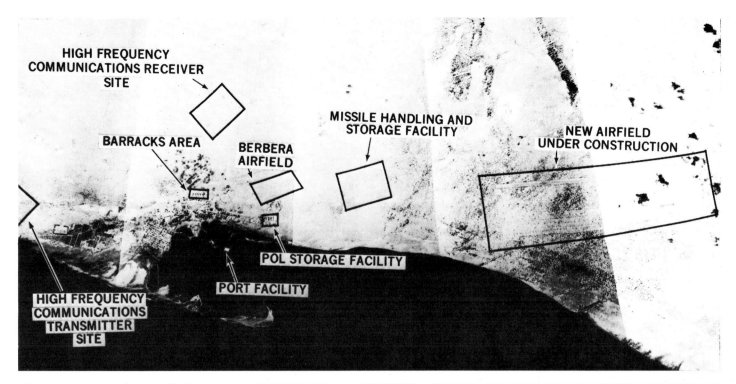

HIGH FREQUENCY COMMUNICATIONS RECEIVER SITE

BARRACKS AREA

BERBERA AIRFIELD

MISSILE HANDLING AND STORAGE FACILITY

NEW AIRFIELD UNDER CONSTRUCTION

POL STORAGE FACILITY

PORT FACILITY

HIGH FREQUENCY COMMUNICATIONS TRANSMITTER SITE

Above: An "orientation view" of the Somali port of Berbera, assembled from five USAF reconnaissance photographs taken during the Soviet arms build-up in 1975. Three enlargements (right) show Soviet ships unloading, a missile storage facility and the vast military airbase under construction. With modern methods of multi-spectral (many wavelengths) photography virtually no significant event can take place on the Earth's surface undetected, even by aircraft flying at great height. But with Britain's global presence gone, only the United States has the capability of watching the Soviet Union's widespread military operations.

VYN CLASS (BARRACKS SHIP)

AMUR AS

Submarine Tender

CARGO FREIGHTER

METERS
SCALE APRX

the meaning of evidence about Soviet or Chinese nuclear weapons production. Similar technical know-how for calculations of nuclear energy use for generation of power in civilian economies—a matter of prime importance for economic research by CIA—will become increasingly important in calculating the resources of nations; but the crucial military contribution will for a long time be in the nuclear weapons field.

The FBI has a limited but important function in the intelligence community—counterespionage in the United States. It is the agency responsible for discovering and countering hostile penetrations of US government organizations and facilities by foreign governments and intelligence agencies. In this capacity the FBI works closely with CIA, which is responsible for counterespionage abroad, and with the counterintelligence staffs of the armed services. FBI information on penetration efforts could be extremely valuable tip-off evidence in the event of planned attack or sabotage of military installations. It was a crucial failure when the combined efforts of the fragmentary US intelligence services at the time of the Pearl Harbor attack of 1941 did not put together the FBI reports of Japanese data collection efforts in Hawaii with intercepted communications indicating a breakdown of diplomatic talks and an impending attack somewhere.

The US State Department is one of the most important cogs in the intelligence community machine. In the first place, it operates the embassy installations in foreign countries where US military attaches and the CIA clandestine station officers do their work. Thus, open reporting on military subjects garnered from foreign sources and the secret data passed to attaches and CIA agent-handlers are dependent upon the official hospitality and

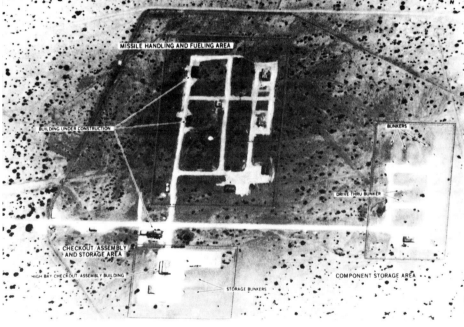

MISSILE HANDLING AND FUELING AREA

BUILDING UNDER CONSTRUCTION

BUNKERS

DRIVE THRU BUNKER

CHECKOUT ASSEMBLY AND STORAGE AREA

HIGH BAY CHECKOUT ASSEMBLY BUILDING

STORAGE BUNKERS

COMPONENT STORAGE AREA

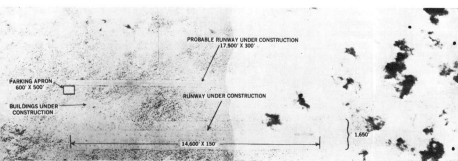

PROBABLE RUNWAY UNDER CONSTRUCTION
17,500' X 300'

PARKING APRON
600' X 500'

BUILDINGS UNDER CONSTRUCTION

RUNWAY UNDER CONSTRUCTION

14,600' X 150'

1,650'

Intelligence Asset Availability

This chart depicts the various intelligence assets and organizations which work to satisfy the operational requirements of US Army generals, colonels, and captains, and the echelons at which these assets are normally assigned, attached, or in direct support.

Information demands which cannot be fulfilled with organic resources must be satisfied by those of a higher commander. For example, national level collection supports corps requirements far beyond the scope of organic capabilities, and feeds both combat information and intelligence into the corps fusion center. Division and brigade centers similarly support their commanders' needs as well as those of subordinate commanders which exceed their organic capabilities.

	GENERALS		COLONELS		CAPTAINS
	CORPS	DIVISION	BRIGADE	BATTALION	COMPANIES
National Strategic System	●				
USAF/USN Systems	●	●			
Tactical Systems					
Electromagnetic					
SIGINT					
☐COMINT	●	●	●		
☐ELINT	●	●	●		
REMS		●	●	●	●
GSR		●	●	●	●
Weapon Locating Radar		●	●		
Imagery					
Photo	●	●			
IR	●	●			
SLAR	●	●			
Human Observation					
Reconnaissance Units	●	●		●	
Troops				●	●
IPW	●		●		

SIGINT	Signal intelligence	**GSR**	Ground surveillance radar
COMINT	Communications intelligence	**IR**	Infra-red
ELINT	Electronic intelligence	**SLAR**	Side-looking aircraft (or airborne) radar
REMS	Remote sensors	**IPW**	Interrogation of prisoners of war

Relative Intelligence/Combat Information to Various Echelons, US Army, Europe

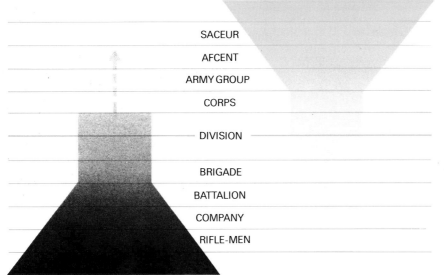

Strategic Intelligence

SACEUR
AFCENT
ARMY GROUP
CORPS
DIVISION
BRIGADE
BATTALION
COMPANY
RIFLE-MEN

Combat Information

SACEUR Supreme Allied Commander Europe
AFCENT Allied Forces Central Europe

Intelligence of varying detail is required by generals, colonels, and captains. The typical requirements at corps and division are normally general in nature. Commanders at this echelon need intelligence products which provide the basis for timely decisions—they need the answers to what, where, when and in what strength. Their intelligence must be primarily decision-oriented and directed toward telling them where to concentrate their forces.

Brigade commanders move forces and assign delivery of fires; hence, they need approximately equal ratios of intelligence and combat information. Battalion commanders need some intelligence and a great deal of combat information—*they need information on enemy movements, as they take place.* Commanders of companies are almost exclusively concerned with combat information—targets.

Combat information is used for rapid tactical execution of maneuvers and fire support which respond to the fast moving enemy situation in the battle area.

Just as the lower echelons need less intelligence and more combat information, so do they perform more reporting and less analysis. The higher echelons, primarily corps and to a lesser extent division, analyze and fuse. Normally, brigades and battalions and companies report combat information up and receive combat intelligence down.

administrative housekeeping of the embassies. In particular, the worldwide diplomatic communications net runs through embassy facilities where secure ciphers can be used to funnel intelligence data back to the intelligence agencies in the United States. The worldwide CRITICOM (Critical Communications) Net includes State Department and CIA communications facilities as well as US overseas military headquarters channels. Through CRITICOM, intelligence reports with evidence indicating the possibility of imminence of hostilities reach the desks of senior officials in Washington promptly, often in ten minutes, nearly always in less than an hour.

Embassy reporting is supplemented in ways often invaluable for assessing military information on foreign armed forces by political and economic officers who file official dispatches on the structure, evolutionary trend, and strengths or weaknesses of the political system and the economy of the host countries. If an army, navy, or air force is caught up in domestic political strife or if an economy is riddled with corruption of sheer inefficiency in its heavy industry and weapons production facilities, such facts may tell more about military capabilities than order of battle analyses or technical training levels of armed forces. Official reporting of this kind makes up, along with open information filed from foreign press, radio, TV, and periodical literature, about half of the information circulating at top levels of government in Washington. It provides the framework which secret military information fits into or modifies.

The National Security Agency (NSA) is the central code and cipher facility of the US Government, and its cryptanalytic reports have often supplied the small but indispensable bits of information which enable analysts to fit together a jigsaw puzzle of other fragmentary intelligence. While modern high-level ciphers are extremely hard to break into, mechanical and human errors sometimes reveal significant messages meant to be hidden from outsiders. More important, traffic analysis of the senders and receivers of enciphered messages, derived from sophisticated direction-finding equipment, reveals a great deal about the structure and activity of the armed forces units to which the signals organizations being overheard are attached. Even without reading the messages, skilled NSA analysts can reconstruct radio networks that parallel armed forces organization and deployment.

During peacetime industrial production and weapons testing data from signals intelligence is vital in providing clues to armaments levels, weapons characteristics, and readiness patterns of all combat forces. Mobilization and maneuver exercises reveal strategic warning indicators and alert military commands to the possibilities of hostilities. In actual military conflict situations, such as the recent Vietnam, Korean, and Arab-Israeli wars, forces in combat of necessity resort to lower security level codes and ciphers to meet the urgencies of field situations, and in these circumstances signals intercepts become one of the richest sources of detailed knowledge about the size and deployment of armies. The Army, Navy, and Air Force provide cryptanalytic field units for operation under central NSA task guidance. A commander without signals intelligence in a local war is like a man without hearing; he is handicapped in his movements and in his awareness of dangers. Some of this intelligence is produced and used directly in the field, but most of it to be fully productive is guided from Washington and is funneled back to Washington for correlation with other data and distribution to all elements of government and the armed forces.

In view of the electronic nature of command, guidance and radar-interrogation devices in almost all military units and weapons systems, the recorded blips and beeps of electronic gadgetry are crucial pieces of knowledge for opposing combat forces. This ELINT (electronic intelligence) is a vast field of technical informa-

tion about the ever-changing technical specifications of each weapons system and the overall pattern of electronic order of battle—the deployment of radars, electronic counter-measures (jamming) equipment and defensive electronic devices (counter-countermeasures). This is the true wizard war, with the most advanced gadgetry giving a sharp edge in battle provided it does not become known sufficiently to enemy electronic intelligence collectors to be offset, evaded, or countered by devices tailored for the purpose. While much of this kind of intelligence is tactical military intelligence, it requires constant sorting out and updating at NSA Headquarters to avoid obsolescence, and possible surprise.

Since the range of interception is vastly increased by putting receivers on satellites orbiting the earth, the wizard war in the strategic field has gone into space. The electronic gear essential for recording earth-generated signals from space and sifting out the meaningful military evidence from the noise is the most difficult—and costly—of modern intelligence collection techniques. In the field of strategic warning stationary satellites positioned in orbit at the right height and speed to stay in place where certain important signals can be sensed provide the best guarantee of noting missile firings, particularly in test modes.

The electronic monitoring and reporting equipment attached to missiles by their own test headquarters so that they can observe how the weapons are performing can be overheard by others if the listening devices are correctly positioned and tuned. This particular kind of data is called telemetry and is followed closely by NSA and CIA so as to get early warning about research and development breakthrough as well as warning of readiness for hostilities. Modern military intelligence holdings are saturated with information derived from signals and telemetry.

The CIA led the way to another development of an intelligence technique that changed the nature of modern warfare. Satellites orbiting the earth can be used for sensing light and heat

Above: Right down to the level of individual ships, squadrons and army brigades advanced electronic systems are necessary to display tactical information for quick and correct decisions.

waves as well as electronic pulses. About 1960 the CIA, working closely with the US Air Force, developed satellite vehicles with extraordinarily sensitive cameras and other sensing devices that enable US intelligence analysts to survey large portions of the earth's surface in relatively short periods of time so as to detect objects of a very small size (generally of about one foot in length in any dimensions). The photographic imagery, developed for the old U-2 high-flying aircraft, has become so complex and effective that it provides a truly indispensable first-phase data base for any research or reporting that depends on counting and measuring visible objects on the earth's surface.

Right and below: Two Soviet-made T-55 tanks knocked out in south Laos, and SA-2 SAMs travelling out of Haiphong in 1972. These are examples of low-level photographs, taken by manned aircraft or RPVs, needed for pre- and post-strike intelligence. With modern ground forces such pictures are required instantly.

It is not possible to collect imagery at night or under heavy cloud cover or inside buildings and shelters. It is also impossible to photograph ideas inside men's heads. But everything else is fair game for the photo interpreter's file. There are few analytical problems, especially in military intelligence, that do not start with the skilled interpreters and analysts using the facilities of the National Photographic Interpretation Center (NPIC), a joint facility administered by CIA but used extensively by the armed services. If CIA had accomplished nothing in its 30 years but to bring the United States into the world of modern overhead reconnaissance imagery—at least five years ahead, technically, of the Soviet Union, its only rival in this exotic field of intelligence—CIA would have well repaid the country for supporting its entire effort. The costs are so great that only the richest nations can support a modern overhead reconnaissance program.

The principle of the earth-orbiting satellite is simple. A certain velocity attained by a satellite projected into space by a missile will cause it to go into orbit around the earth—its outward thrust being equalized by the pull of the earth's gravity, like a man-made moon, at heights from around 100 to a few hundreds of miles above the surface of the globe. The speed of the camera carrying satellites is so great that they circle the earth approximately every 90 minutes. If the satellite is in a near-Polar orbit, the earth turns under it about 1,500 miles at each orbit so that the camera can cover successive broad swaths of the Eurasian Continent, for example, moving across the land surface at each orbit and filling in the interstices between swaths on successive days as the earth keeps turning. This particular mode of surveillance is especially good for covering the Soviet Union which, at 8.6 million square miles, is by far the largest territory under one government, and to a lesser extent China, which is, after Canada, the next largest, that is the third largest, at 3.7 million square miles. The United States itself is the fourth largest nation with 3.6 million square miles.

Mapping large parts of the territory of the Soviet Union in very short order (a number of days) is quite feasible when weather permits. The imagery thus captured can either be catapulted out of the satellite in a film capsule, with a parachute, to be hooked by a waiting aircraft, or transmitted to ground stations in coded signals when the satellite is orbiting the right part of the earth. It is all an expensive, technically complex process taking much time, manpower, skill, and money; nevertheless, it gives US intelligence agencies a capability without which its intelligence estimates would be much spongier and its own population and the populations of US allies would be infinitely less secure.

A final important point to remember is that it is the surveillance of potential enemy territory by photographic sensors, aided by electronic intercepts of all kinds, lumped together under the term "national technical means" of verification of levels of strategic arms that makes arms limitation agreements between the USSR and the United States feasible. The precision with which the United States is able to count missile launchers in the Soviet Union, and vice versa, reassured Soviet and US national leaders sufficiently to permit the signing of the ABM limitation treaty and the SALT I missile limitation agreement. In many ways the future of arms control and limitation depends on the virtuosity of the US intelligence services. Only with adequate verification of numbers of weapons and compliance with all limitation provisions can the United States afford to limit the numbers and capabilities of its own strategic weapons. Military commanders and military intelligence agencies therefore have a tremendous vested interest in the effectiveness of these verification techniques which include the use of all kinds of analytical skills and confirming types of evidence as well as the "technical" photographic and signals intelligence itself.

One of the vital "technical means" is the array of sound-sensing devices which can be planted on ocean floors or carried in ships and submarines to detect the movement of submarines under water in the same way that other sensors detect missile and aircraft movements. This "sound ranging"—i.e. SONAR—evidence supplements photography of the construction of missile-launching submarines, filling in what would otherwise be a missing gap in US knowledge of Soviet strategic weapons and US capability to verify compliance with SALT agreements limiting submarines as well as missiles and aircraft.

CIA and the US Air Force jointly manage the operational program which develops the specific missiles and sensors and fires the payloads of imagery collecting devices into orbit. The Navy has some satellite capabilities of its own aimed at peculiarly naval targets, and, of course, it is first and foremost in the field of underwater sensors of all kinds. The whole program of national reconnaissance and imagery interpretation is the embodiment of the intelligence community at work, sharing resources, skills and intelligence products. While the State Department does not get involved in the collection program as such, it has a lively interest in tasking or targetting the sensors, and it becomes immediately and directly involved when international crises occur involving disputes over the location and activity of military forces. For instance, the State Department took the intelligence lead during the Suez Canal Zone missile controversy of 1970, when the USSR built the anti-aircraft missile defenses in depth near the Canal that eventually provided one of the key ingredients of the Egyptian initial victory in the Yom Kippur cross-Canal attack in October 1973. Consequently no intelligence agency can afford to be ignorant of the findings of the national reconnaissance and imagery interpretation

Above: How can one detect intruders and avoid false alarms (caused, for example, by animals)? This US Army device is a seismic detector for the lightest human footfall; another detector is magnetic.

machinery. No military commander could do his job properly today without having his own planners, intelligence section, and targetting staffs fully informed of the national holdings of photography and other imagery covering his area of responsibility.

The CIA itself, much maligned as it has been for the fairly limited domestic security operations and covert political interventions abroad which it got into in the Nixon-Watergate era, is fundamentally and primarily an intelligence collection and analysis agency. Clandestine services operations are aimed at using secret agents to try to elicit, buy or steal useful information that other nations are trying to hide. While the military intelligence agencies collect some clandestine information, mainly in their own areas of expertise, CIA tries to collect all of the information of strategic value — political, economic, scientific, or military—that is needed by decision-makers and policy planners at the national level of government. It operates in almost every country of the world and in countries friendly to the United States; the clandestine information taken from its own agents is supplemented by secret intelligence given in exchanges with friendly intelligence services of the host governments. CIA information reports go directly to all agencies concerned with the subject matter, although the need to protect sources often limits distribution to higher levels of officialdom.

The CIA also provides secret information reports to other agencies based on its open collection of confidential data from willing American sources who travel and work abroad. This procedure is open, not clandestine, but the

data collected must be protected in order to protect the sources who give it to the US Government as a patriotic duty but naturally do not want their foreign interlocutors to think of them as intelligence agents—which they are not. Surprisingly often some tidbit of technical international trade data that has come to light in this way provides the central clue to interpretation of a military program that cannot be properly understood on the basis of other information available.

CIA sources, clandestine and open-confidential, are targetted to get at the kind of hidden information that cannot be overheard electronically or detected by imagery sensors. It deals mainly with people, their thoughts and plans, and the future direction of government policies of all kinds. Naturally some of the most valuable material is in the military intelligence field. For example, the penetration of the Soviet Union by the CIA agent, Colonel Oleg Penkovsky in the early 1960s, gave the American military agencies bales of secret documents on Soviet weapons, forces, and military thought; our basic understanding of the Soviet military threat would be greatly impoverished if this material had not become available. With less happy results, CIA distributed some sensitive clandestine reports on Syrian and Egyptian plans to attack Israel in 1973 that proved to be remarkably accurate. Unfortunately they were dismissed by most military intelligence analysts as contrary to their estimates of Arab intentions based on other factors, until after hostilities began.

This brings us then to the most difficult and most crucial task of the intelligence community—research, analysis, and estimating. Hard factual evidence must be weighed in the light of "softer" but crucial evidence of human purposes and perceptions to make an overall assessment of capabilities, intentions, and possible courses of action. Here CIA has the richest and largest talent pool, ranging over the spectrum of research in economic, scientific, political, and strategic-military intelligence. Its staffs do depth research and reporting; they provide the tidbits of new data that make up the staple of current intelligence reporting to the top-levels of government, and they work with State and Defense intelligence research analysts to arrive at coordinated views on the truly difficult estimative problems where evidence is insufficient to illuminate with certainty what is going or is likely to develop.

If the policymakers and strategic planners of the national security complex of agencies require answers on the probability of various situations existing or likely to develop in some foreseen set of circumstances, the CIA-State-Defense analytical teams must give the best answers possible on the basis of the evidence held by the whole intelligence community. Often these problems are military: Will Syria attack Israel? Will North Korea attack South Korea? How many large modern missiles does the USSR have? How large a stockpile of weapons-grade nuclear energy material does Communist China have? Will there be a Thai-Cambodian war? What African countries will Cuban troops be used in? What will be the shape of the Soviet Navy in 1985? How much superior in combat capability are Warsaw Pact troops in Central Europe compared with the capability of opposing NATO forces?

These are bread-and-butter intelligence analysis tasks. CIA analysts, the analysts of the Defense Intelligence Agency (DIA), and the analysts of the State Department's Intelligence Bureau (INR) must pull together the best guesses possible on these hard questions—not necessarily (because it would not be possible) always exactly right, but as objective and accurate a setting out of real probabilities as evidence allows. On good estimates good policy can be made, as well as good military force

Above: In South-East Asia the techniques of air-dropping acoustic, seismic and combined sensors for trucks and humans reached a high pitch in the Igloo White programme. These photographs show an even more sensitive sensor, which can be dropped with a braking parachute (by F-111, above) or with its own petal-type airbrakes (inset), normally into areas where they are concealed.

projections, theater deployment plans, weapons procurement, and troop training programs. Just as the local military field commander strains to hear and see everything in his sector of command that pierces the fog of war and lets him see into the minds of potential armed enemies so as either to deter them or to counter them in battle, the whole central strategic intelligence system strains to provide the eyes and ears of national strategic high command.

As weapons become lighter, more mobile, more accurate, and more destructive, the more imperative it is for military commanders to know their terrain (whether local, regional, or global), the strength and disposition of opposing forces, and, above all, the degree of probability of various military moves of a threatening or damaging character. While every military unit struggles to increase its own alertness to local intelligence on these matters, every unit and every echelon of command must also be familiar with and extract every possible element of essential information from the vast array of experts and data that constitute a vital part of the American military machine, that is, the central intelligence collection and analysis apparatus of the United States intelligence community. It is this advanced national intelligence machine that gives US forces a potential edge in every area of the world in deterring war or winning conflicts when they occur.

The US Strategic Triad

Dr. William R. Van Cleave, Professor of International Relations, and Director of Defense and Strategic Studies Program, University of Southern California; US Delegate to SALT 1 talks, 1969-1971.

The term "strategic forces" is an ambiguous one and trying to define it precisely can be a fruitless task. In any traditional strategic sense, confining the term to those intercontinental nuclear forces directed essentially toward the USSR, as is the tendency in the US, is an impoverishment of the term. This is not the place, however, to seek a more proper application, and since other sections of this book cover other forces, this section will deal with forces implied by the narrow sense of the term "strategic nuclear forces"—those intercontinental offensive and defensive systems designed principally to cope with similar Soviet forces. Following the categorization of the Annual Defense Department Report,* strategic nuclear forces encompass intercontinental ballistic missiles (ICBMs), modern submarine launched ballistic missiles (SLBMs) on nuclear powered launcher submarines (SSBNs), intercontinental bombers, possibly some future cruise missiles, and the defenses against such forces. Due to the paucity of American bomber defenses, the absence of a ballistic missile defense, the general-purpose force nature of antisubmarine defense, and the very small and unorganized civil defense effort in the US, this section must of necessity focus on the strategic offensive forces.

The existing mix of strategic offensive forces—the Minuteman and Titan II ICBMs, the Polaris and Poseidon SLBMs, and the B-52 heavy bomber—has become known as the Triad, a descriptive term that has come to connote prescriptively the complementarity or synergism of the three forces. The term and its rationale have become so entrenched that it is difficult to remember that the particular Triad forces were developed and their deployment begun before their complementarity was well appreciated. Nevertheless, as diagrams 1 to 4 show, the rationale for a force mix that presents an enemy with very different offensive and defensive problems and that dovetails individual strengths and weaknesses into a more capable whole is eminently persuasive. That does not imply necessarily that *three* is the correct number. There are proponents of a Diad, or two-force mix, and a Diad could result willy-nilly from a failure to preserve the viability of one of the forces. Current US policy, however, does not contemplate a Diad, but rather a somewhat different Triad, or even perhaps a Quadrad. For the near future, that means adding long range cruise missiles to the bomber force. In the longer term, it may mean supplanting the bomber penetration mission entirely with cruise missiles launched from stand-off aicraft, complemented by a mix of fixed and possibly mobile land-based ICBMs, SLBMs, and possibly (SALT allowing) submarine launched long range cruise missiles.

Before moving to present and future US strategic forces and policies, it will be helpful to outline the development of American strategic nuclear forces and the changes in American thinking about those forces.

Prologue to a Strategic Force

US demobilization after World War II was so thorough that, in 1946, Army Air Force testimony before Congress indicated that not one fully operational air wing existed. While the United States had pioneered the development of atomic weapons and held the sole capability to produce and stockpile these weapons, it did not in fact start to produce such a stockpile until the late 1940s. "Atomic diplomacy" certainly did not exist without the atomic military means. A foreign policy of containment, formulated by 1947-1948, lacked the military support and military strategy necessary to such a policy. A growing recognition within the United States Government that American military strength was seriously lacking was nurtured by the developing Cold War and Russia's acquisition of atomic weapons technology in 1949. Early in 1950, a National Security Council Report (NSC-68) summed up the situation, warned of broad-gauged Soviet military superiority and increasing threats to the West unless appropriate countermeasures were immediately taken, and recommended a crash program to build up America's nuclear and general-purpose forces. The attack on the Republic of Korea then served as the catalyst for a rearmament that would in all probability have otherwise not taken place at that time or with the rapidity which occurred.

In 1953, the new Eisenhower Administration inaugurated a broad economically oriented strategic program, the "New Look", which imposed severe budget constraints on the military, but at the same time selectively emphasized strategic air power, the development of a family of nuclear weapons, and North American air defense.

At the start of the Korean War, American strategic forces were centered on a small number of World War II B-29 or modified B-29 (B-50) bombers. The huge six-engine (propeller) B-36, a bomber initially contracted at the start of World War II, and the six-jet B-47 medium bomber, however, began service in 1951, and also began the rejuvenation of the Strategic Air Command. Due to the range-limitations of the B-47, bases for it were established overseas and an air refueling technique was developed. By the time production of the B-47 ended, some 2,000 of these aircraft, in different versions, had been produced.

The Korean War also gave impetus to the development and production of the B-52, an eight-jet-engine heavy bomber, which continues to be the bomber mainstay of the Triad today. The B-52 was first flown in 1952 and was first delivered to SAC in 1955. Between 1955 and 1962, when the last B-52 was delivered, a total of more than 700 B-52s of various classifications and capabilities were producted.

The speed and range, or radius (normally one-half the range), of a bomber are variable measurements. Not only does each influence the other, but each is also influenced by altitude of flight, flight profile, payload, and refueling. With optimum payload and cruising speed, and high altitude flight, the B-52 could hit a target in the USSR and return to the US without refueling, a total trip of 9,000 to 10,000 miles. At higher speeds (maximum speeds ranged from about 550 to 650mph, depending upon the model of B-52), more payload, and low-level penetration, the range would be reduced substantially, and refueling required for mission performance.

The Strategic Triad comprises the three forms of strategic attack: SLBM (far left), ICBM (left) and bomber (below). The examples are, respectively, Polaris A3, Minuteman III and B-52H. Once demonstrably the leader in each, the United States has progressively declined until it is today outnumbered by the Soviet Union in all three categories. Even more serious is the complete absence of any new bomber or ICBM except for various proposals. As it takes many years for a new strategic delivery system to get into service, the two superpowers will by 1982 be grossly unbalanced.

The 1950s also saw the development of a supersonic medium bomber, the B-58, which was first flown in 1956, but of which less than one hundred ever entered the force. A B-70 bomber, with speed near Mach-3, designed during the mid-late 1950s as successor to the B-52, was cancelled in 1961 by the Kennedy Administration.

The story of American strategic ballistic missiles is an interesting one, and clearly one where technology did not lead automatically to decisions on strategic forces; rather, technology encountered much resistance and was successfully turned into modern weapons systems only after the efforts of a few dedicated and determined people. One recent study of the American ICBM program summarizes it as "a long pattern of disbelief, neglect, and delay".[1]

Despite the technological headstart provided after World War II by the acquisition of German rocket experience and expertise, long-range missile weapons were subordinated in research and development priority to manned aircraft and air-breathing (cruise) missiles. In 1947, US Air Force research on long-range ballistic missiles was cancelled altogether and not resumed until after the start of the Korean War. By 1953, less than $2 million was spent on such research. During 1953–1955, however, technological developments, evidence of a concerted Soviet rocket program, and—most particularly —the efforts of a few civilians changed neglect into a high priority development program, prudently placed outside of normal Air Force channels (but under the direction and management of an Air Force General, Bernard Schriever).[2] With strong Congressional backing, General Schriever took his case for the ICBM to President Eisenhower and the National Security Council in the middle of 1955. The result was a Presidential directive assigning the highest national priority to the ICBM. Funding for strategic ballistic missile development (ICBM and IRBM) rose to $159 million in 1955, $1.4 billion in 1957, and $2 billion in 1958.

The initial US ICBM programs, the Atlas and Titan, involved large liquid-fueled missiles. In 1955, however, a breakthrough in solid fuel technology led to the Air Force Minuteman ICBM and the Navy Polaris SLBM programs— more compact, solid-fuel missiles for deployment, respectively, in underground silos and submarines, which resulted in a missile force with much greater survivability against a surprise attack.

The shock produced in America by the full range flight test of a Soviet ICBM in August, 1957, well before any US ICBM was ready, followed by the launches of the world's first man-made satellites, Sputnik in October and Sputnik II in November, caused further acceleration of the American missile programs. A full range ICBM flight test was accomplished with Atlas in November 1958. Despite progress being made in solid-fuel ballistic missiles, the decision was made to proceed with interim deployment of the liquid-fueled Atlas and Titan I ICBMs, and the Thor and Jupiter IRBMs. The latter, having ranges of only 1,500nm, were deployed in the United Kingdom, Turkey, and Italy between 1959 and 1962, when they were phased out. Approximately 200 Atlas and Titan I ICBMs and 100 IRBMs were deployed by 1962 when the Minuteman I ICBM became operational, at which time they were phased out.

Minuteman I, with a 5,500nm range and somewhat less than 2,000 pounds throw-weight or payload, was flight tested in February, 1961, and first became operational in December, 1962. The first fully operational Minuteman squadron was assigned to SAC in February, 1963. Titan II (a liquid-fueled ICBM, four to five times the size of the Minuteman) was developed along with Minuteman, and also first became operational

Right: Biggest USAF ICBM is the Titan II, but there are only 54 silos and the whole weapon system is old and needs continual updating. The two rocket stages burn storable liquid propellants.

Table 1 : Polaris/Poseidon Submarines

Name	Hull Number	Shipbuilding Program	Commissioned
1. George Washington	SSBN-598	1958	December 30, 1959
2. Patrick Henry	SSBN-599	1958	April 9, 1960
3. Theodore Roosevelt	SSBN-600	1958	February 13, 1961
4. Robert E. Lee	SSBN-601	1959	September 16, 1960
5. Abraham Lincoln	SSBN-602	1959	March 8, 1961
6. Ethan Allen	SSBN-608	1959	August 8, 1961
7. Sam Houston	SSBN-609	1959	March 6, 1962
8. Thomas A. Edison	SSBN-610	1959	March 10, 1962
9. John Marshall	SSBN-611	1959	May 21, 1962
10. Lafeyette	SSBN-616	1961	April 23, 1963
11. Alexander Hamilton	SSBN-617	1961	June 27, 1963
12. Thomas Jefferson	SSBN-618	1961	January 4, 1963
13. Andrew Jackson	SSBN-619	1961	July 3, 1963
14. John Adams	SSBN-620	1961	May 12, 1964
15. James Monroe	SSBN-622	1961	December 7, 1963
16. Nathan Hale	SSBN-623	1961	November 23, 1963
17. Woodrow Wilson	SSBN-624	1961	December 27, 1963
18. Henry Clay	SSBN-625	1961	February 20, 1964
19. Daniel Webster	SSBN-626	1961	April 9, 1964
20. James Madison	SSBN-627	1962	July 23, 1964
21. Tecumseh	SSBN-628	1962	May 29, 1964
22. Daniel Boone	SSBN-629	1962	April 23, 1964
23. John C. Calhoun	SSBN-630	1962	September 15, 1964
24. Ulysses S. Grant	SSBN-631	1962	July 17, 1964
25. Von Steuben	SSBN-632	1962	September 30, 1964
26. Casimir Pulaski	SSBN-633	1962	August 14, 1964
27. Stonewall Jackson	SSBN-634	1962	August 26, 1964
28. Sam Rayburn	SSBN-635	1962	December 2, 1964
29. Nathanael Greene	SSBN-636	1962	December 19, 1964
30. Benjamin Franklin	SSBN-640	1963	October 22, 1965
31. Simon Bolivar	SSBN-641	1963	October 29, 1965
32. Kamehameha	SSBN-642	1963	December 10, 1965
33. George Bancroft	SSBN-643	1963	January 22, 1966
34. Lewis and Clark	SSBN-644	1963	December 22, 1965
35. James K. Polk	SSBN-645	1963	April 15, 1966
36. George C. Marshall	SSBN-654	1964	April 23, 1966
37. Henry L. Stimson	SSBN-655	1964	August 22, 1966
38. George Washington Carver	SSBN-656	1964	June 15, 1966
39. Francis Scott Key	SSBN-657	1964	December 3, 1966
40. Mariano G. Vallejo	SSBN-658	1964	December 16, 1966
41. Will Rogers	SSBN-659	1964	April 1, 1967

Source: Naval Nuclear Propulsion Program. Joint Committee on Atomic Energy, Congress of the United States. 93rd Congress, 2nd session. Superintendent of Documents, United States Government Printing Office, Washington, DC, 1974, p. 49.

in 1963, but a total of only 54 of the missiles was deployed. By the mid-1960s, Minuteman II, a follow-on missile of somewhat longer range and slightly more payload, but with more accuracy, became operational.

The first SLBM nuclear-powered submarine, the USS *George Washington* successfully launched a Polaris from underwater in July, 1960, and became fully operational in 1961. (The table shows the schedule of Polaris submarines). Early boats were equipped with an interim 1,200nm missile (the A-1), until the 1,500nm A-2 and later the 2,500nm A-3, equipped with three warheads (not independently targetable) became standard.

Transition to a Modern Force and New Doctrine

The Eisenhower strategic doctrine, initially based upon maintaining superiority in strategic nuclear forces, was changed to one of "sufficiency" by 1956–1957. As Secretary of the Air Force Quarles expressed it, sufficiency depended, not necessarily upon being superior in forces or capabilities, but upon having the "forces required to accomplish the mission assigned". By the end of the 1950s a dual debate developed, centered, first, upon the nature of the mission and, second, upon whether US programs were "sufficient" to provide the forces necessary to mission success. The Eisenhower Administration left office with neither part of the debate being resolved.

In 1961, a new Administration and a new civilian team in the Department of Defense assumed office, persuaded that a change was in order away from Eisenhower's Sufficiency doctrine and the strategy of "Massive Retaliation". "Flexible Response", a phrase gleaned by President Kennedy from the writings of Army General Maxwell Taylor, and supported by RAND Corporation studies, whereby the flexibility of both general-purpose and strategic nuclear forces was to be increased, was adopted as policy. At the same time, however, the "systems analysts" who came to dominate the Pentagon sought a more systematic and mensurable approach to planning strategic forces, an analytical and quantifiable theory to determine as precisely as possible "How Much is Enough?".[3] The evolution of American strategic thinking during the 1960s was the story of a contest between true Flexible Response, which tended to drive strategic force requirements upwards, and the analytical techniques and arms control corollaries of calculable force limitations, which depressed requirements.

From this contest, the term "Flexible Response" was supplanted by the doctrine of "Assured Destruction" (AD) and the later concept of "Mutual Assured Destruction" (MAD). Originally only one of several analytical tests to aid judgment on the adequacy of forces, AD became the principal criterion, then the dominant strategic concept of the American defense community, and finally a philosophical base for theories of mutual deterrent strategic stability, and strategic arms limitation. It became the necessary "conceptual framework for measuring the need and adequacy of our strategic forces".

While these concepts were evolving, force level decisions had to be made. The Eisenhower Administration left office planning some 1,100 Minuteman, Titan, and Polaris missiles under the concept of Sufficiency. The new Administration, having been critical of the "passiveness" of the Eisenhower Administration and having campaigned on a warning of "missile gap" and a cry for US strategic superiority, moved initially to redeem campaign pledges. Superiority was reinstituted as American policy for strategic force relations with the USSR (in testimony before Congress in 1963, Administration spokesmen termed US strategic superiority the *"sine qua non"* of Western security), and planned levels of Minuteman and Polaris were increased: Polaris to 44 boats (with 16 missiles each) and Minuteman, by some accounts, to as many as 1,600–2,000.

As strategic ballistic missiles were becoming operational, decisions were made to reduce the bomber force of SAC. In 1961, that force consisted of over 2,000 B-47s and B-52s. Secretary of Defense McNamara accelerated the phase-out of B-47s and cancelled developmental work on the advanced B-70 strategic bomber. The last B-52s and B-58s were delivered to SAC in 1962, and by then no new strategic bomber was either in production or under development. By the time that Minuteman and Polaris were fully operational, US bomber strength had been reduced to less than 700 B-52s and B-58s. (The latter were phased out in 1969, and the former suffered attrition through fatigue and Vietnam, to reduce the force further.)

Cost-effectiveness considerations along with the progressive development of American Assured Destruction thinking led to reductions in planned levels of Minuteman and Polaris early in the 1960s. ICBM levels were lowered to 1,200 Minuteman and 120 Titan II, and then to 1,000 Minuteman and 54 Titan II. Polaris levels were set at 41 boats with 656 missiles. By the mid-1960s the decision had been made to level off American strategic offensive forces at the levels then existing.

Evolution of American Doctrine: The 1960s, Superiority to Parity

In his famous Ann Arbor, Michigan, address in 1962, Secretary McNamara set forth the tenets of a Flexible Response Doctrine based upon counterforce and damage limiting. Military strategy, he said, "should be approached in much the same way that more conventional military operations have been regarded in the past. That is to say, principal military objectives... should be the destruction of the enemy's military forces, not of its civilian population."[4] Deterrence of nuclear war would be based upon the ability to limit damage in the event of war, which would be accomplished by US possession of the means to destroy an enemy's military capability and by targeting restraint (*vis-a-vis* cities) on our own part, backed by the ability to escalate should the enemy do so. In 1963, McNamara said:

> "We should not think of ourselves as forced by limitations of resources to rely upon strategies of desperation and threats of vast mutual destruction. . . . The damage-limiting capability of our numerically superior force is, I believe, well worth its incremental cost."

Clearly, cost-effectiveness arguments against damage limiting had not yet impressed the Secretary, nor had the notion that MAD parity was synonymous with strategic stability.

Although biographers of McNamara generally agree that his thinking was moving away from this strategy by 1964–1965, the Defense Reports of those years repeated the same theme: In addition to an Assured Destruction capability, American forces "should have the power to

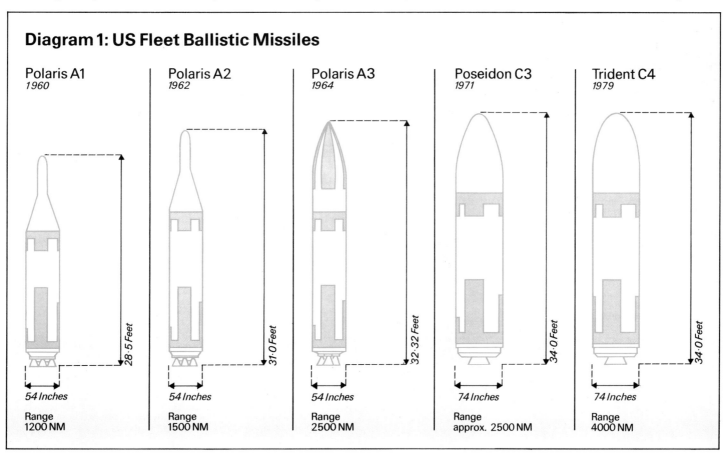

Diagram 1: US Fleet Ballistic Missiles

Polaris A1
1960

28·5 Feet

54 Inches

Range
1200 NM

Polaris A2
1962

31·0 Feet

54 Inches

Range
1500 NM

Polaris A3
1964

32·32 Feet

54 Inches

Range
2500 NM

Poseidon C3
1971

34·0 Feet

74 Inches

Range
approx. 2500 NM

Trident C4
1979

34·0 Feet

74 Inches

Range
4000 NM

limit the destruction of our own cities and population to the maximum extent practicable ...a damage-limiting strategy appears to be the most practical and effective course for us to follow." Moreover, contradicting later assertions that Pentagon studies did not support damage-limiting strategies, one Report stated directly: "In every pertinent case we found that forces in excess of those needed simply to destroy Soviet cities would significantly reduce damage to the US and Western Europe." Assured Destruction and Damage Limiting were thus this time the dual pillars of American strategic policy.

Change, however, came rapidly. More emphasis in public statements (and in target and force planning) came to be placed on Assured Destruction, now based upon the judgmental criterion of "unacceptable damage" measured in presumed population fatalities and gross industrial destruction. Concurrently, Secretary McNamara began to disparage both damage limiting and countermilitary targeting. Flexible Response options gave way in emphasis to countercity AD. In 1966 and 1967, he said: "Our forces must be sufficiently large to possess an 'Assured Destruction' capability." It is this capability "and not the ability partially to limit damage to ourselves" that must command our attention.

From Assured Destruction grew the mutual deterrence concept of Mutual Assured Destruction (MAD). *Both* sides were to have an AD capability against the other, and—ideally—essentially no other strategic force capabilities.

Neither should develop capabilities that would appear to call into question the other's AD capability; hence, offensive and defensive capabilities that might do so were to be avoided to the extent feasible.[5] It was not merely that such capabilities were not achievable at prices the decision makers were willing to pay; they were to be avoided as incompatible with stability based upon MAD. MAD was as much an arms limitation concept as a strategic one. Thus, it was not so much that forces to counter the enemy's AD capability would upset mutual deterrence as that they would "fuel an arms race". As McNamara's Assistant Secretary of Defense expressed it, "any attempt on our part to reduce damage to our society would put pressure on the Soviets to strive for an off-setting improvement in their assured-destruction forces, and vice versa . . . This 'action-reaction' phenomenon is central to all strategic force planning as well as to any theory of an arms race." The corollary to this presumed "action-reaction" determinism was inaction-inaction. If the US were to refrain from challenging a Soviet AD capability, the Soviets would be satisfied and would have no need to build up their forces further. Stability would result, and strategic arms limitation agreements codifying that stability could be reached. Hence, a policy of self-restraint was adopted, and strategic force parity (later termed Sufficiency by the Nixon Administration) was substituted for the goal of Superiority. American strategic nuclear force expenditures declined, from over $18 billion (in fiscal year 1974 dollars) at the start

Above: First launch of the Trident SLBM took place on January 18, 1977, from the US Air Force Station at Cape Canaveral, which is handling preliminary flight tests of this Navy missile. Trident deployment has been hit by ship delays.

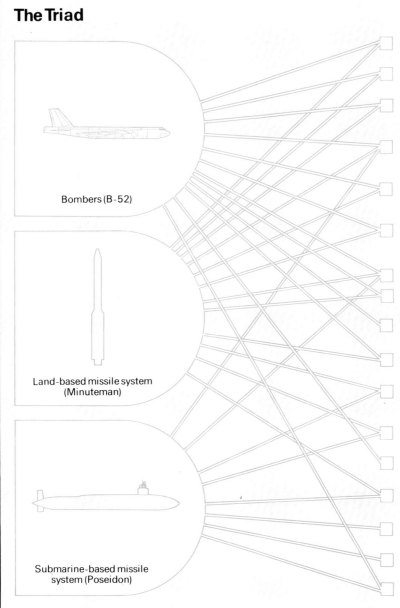

The Triad

Bombers (B-52)

Land-based missile system (Minuteman)

Submarine-based missile system (Poseidon)

Diagram 2: Capabilities of the Triad

RANGE – Up to 5500 nmi to allow full target coverage from any of several "safe" basing positions

PAYLOAD – Sufficient yield and quantities to allow conservative targeting and compensation for system errors

ACCURACY – Sufficient accuracy in conjunction with weapon yield to allow targeting of soft or hard targets with acceptable probability of destruction

PENETRATION – Capability to penetrate enemy strategic defense systems through inherent adaptability to advanced penetration techniques

FLEXIBILITY – Instantaneous capability to retarget or reallocate weapons with a choice of many engagement options and modes

COMMUNICATIONS – Constant, two-way, high-speed, reliable secure communications between command levels and weapon system

RELIABILITY – Extremely low failure rate

SECURITY – Ability to maintain constant surveillance over the physical security of the weapon

RECALL – Capability to recall, recover and reuse weapon at any point in conflict until it reaches the target area

AVAILABILITY – Capability to maintain a high state of operational alert status for the force

SURVIVABILITY – Provides characteristics such that the enemy cannot destroy the weapon system and thus nullify its deterrent capability

POST-ATTACK LIFE – Capability to operate in a post-attack mode for an extended time; i.e., many weeks to several months

ASSESSMENT – Capability to provide instantaneous assessment of weapon success or failure to accomplish its intended mission.

REACTION TIME – Capability to complete weapon mission within seconds of the time an engagement decision is made

COLLATERAL DAMAGE – Capability to limit damage to U.S. cities and population should an enemy first strike occur

ARMS CONTROL – Capability to adapt to any arms control agreement which might be desirable and negotiable

CRISIS MANAGEMENT – Capability to keep a low level of conflict or limited nuclear engagement from escalating into an all-out engagement

of the 1960s to less than one-half that by 1967–68.

Soviet strategic forces were growing during this period of time, but it seems clear that this growth was not the reason for the changes in American policy. The US intelligence community chronically underestimated the growth of that force and placed very modest AD objectives on the growth. In 1965, Secretary McNamara asserted that the "Soviets have decided that they have lost the quantitative race and they are not seeking to engage us in that contest . . . there is no indication that the Soviets are seeking to develop a strategic nuclear force as large as our own."

The changes came, instead, from the progressive development of the concepts and beliefs noted above, a presumed disutility of strategic forces for anything save AD, and the goal of strategic stability (MAD) through arms limitations agreements that would be possible only when the Soviets were satisfied with their own AD capability. The "slow pace" of Soviet strategic programs perceived by US officials was to be encouraged by US restraint. As an American arms control enthusiast later acknowledged, "the strategic parity which was a prerequisite for strategic arms limitation could not have come about except for conscious restraint on the part of the US government."[6]

Technological Developments

Technological development may be constrained by neglect or by policy, but it is very seldom by either. While these policies were evolving, technological progress was occurring in three notable areas that seemed incompatible with those policies: ballistic missile guidance, which promised very good accuracies for ICBMs; multiple warheads, or reentry vehicles, for single missiles, each of which could be independently targeted (MIRV); and antiballistic missile (ABM) systems.

The MIRV (Multiple Independently Re-Targeted Vehicle) was originally a cost-effectiveness concept whereby expanded target coverage could be provided without increasing the size of the missile force. As evidence began to accumulate in the middle 1960s of a Soviet ABM program and air defense expansion, and in the later 1960s of a Soviet counterforce capability against American ICBM silos, two supplementary reasons for MIRV were added: to counter a Soviet ABM and to reduce the ABM capability of Sam (Surface-to-Air Missile) air defenses; and to increase the capability of deterrent forces surviving any possible first strike. The quandary of MIRV and MAD was eased by deliberately avoiding effective hard target MIRVs (high yield, high accuracy), and designing them mostly to offset ABM and to increase soft target coverage.[7] (Hence, many reasoned, should ABM be banned in SALT, neither side should have any reason for MIRV, and MIRV could also be banned or stringently limited.) While the concept of MIRV was first proposed under an Air Force contract, the Navy Special Office, studying options to improve Polaris, adopted MIRV for future SLBMs. In 1965, development of Poseidon—a new SLBM eventually to be equipped with some ten small,

.04 MT warheads—was approved. The system seemed ideal for countering an ABM and targeting soft urban-industrial targets; it did not pose a threat to ICBM silos.

MIRV was also adapted to an Air Force follow-on to Minuteman. Minuteman III (with about 2,200 pounds of throw-weight or payload capability) was designed to be equipped with three MIRV warheads, each of .17 MT. This system, with MIRV, was first tested in 1968, but neither it nor Poseidon would be deployed prior to the beginning of SALT in 1969. Deployment of the first Minuteman III was scheduled for summer, 1970, and the first Poseidon-equipped SSBN was to be delivered in 1971. Hence, MIRV became a major SALT issue in the US. Major segments of the US Government wished to reach an agreement with the USSR banning MIRV before deployment began. In the second session of SALT, in the spring of 1970, the US proposed an agreement banning MIRV, which was rejected by the USSR, even though it

Below: Model of one of the proposed USAF CML (Cruise-Missile Launcher) aircraft, in this case based on the Boeing 747. It could carry 72 cruise missiles, but the vulnerability of such a weapon platform had not been tested in 1979. Foot of page: Test launch of a Boeing AGM-86A ALCM from an NB-52G trials aircraft. The cruise missile promises to carry megaton cruise missiles long distances from the launch aircraft; but can they penetrate modern defenses?

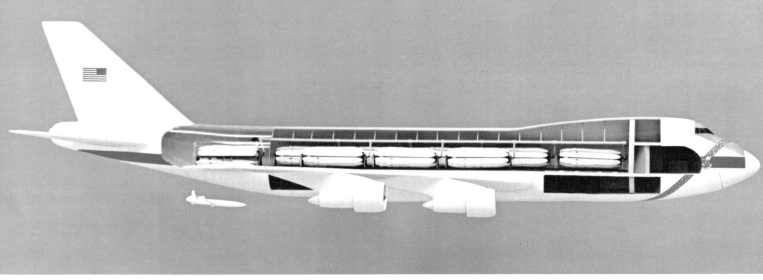

Right: Fitting a new Mk 12 re-entry vehicle to a Minuteman III in its silo in 1970. The Mk 12 houses three W-62 warheads each with a yield of 200 kT. Today the Mk 12A may be fitted instead.

would have also banned ABM. The Soviet Union did not link the two systems in the US arms control sense.

ABM, even more than MIRV, was widely deemed inconsistent with MAD concepts and US SALT aspirations. American policy through the 1960s had been to continue ABM development but to forgo deployment. Steady advances in the technology, however, combined with the same Soviet development that urged MIRV and other considerations, such as expected Peoples Republic of China (PRC) ICBM development, strained that policy. A reluctant decision to proceed with deployment was made in 1967, but the deployment was designed and rationalized to be consistent with a MAD relationship with the USSR. Initially, that meant casting the program in terms of a light area defense against such threats as the PRC might pose in the future, but not heavy enough to cause Soviet concern about its AD capability.

Early in 1969, the new Nixon Administration modified that plan. The new deployment plan, named Safeguard, was to emphasize first the defense of Minuteman ICBM silos, whose future vulnerability was projected by continuing Soviet ICBM developments. Eventual expansion of the deployment to twelve ABM sites would be decided on an annual basis, depending upon progress in SALT and developments in Soviet counterforce capabilities. SALT agreements could still be reached to limit, or possibly ban, ABM deployment. (It might be noted that ABM defense of retaliatory forces would be logically consistent with MAD. Such a defense would not reduce an enemy's AD capability, but would only preserve one's own. In SALT, that defense might be reduced or obviated altogether if agreements reduced the projected threats to US ICBM forces. In this vein, it is noteworthy that the major Soviet initiative to stop US ABM deployment in SALT came *after* the area defense component of Safeguard was abandoned by the US in 1970, and ABM plans became restricted to defense of Minuteman. Coupled with Soviet disinterest in banning MIRV, this should have clearly revealed the Soviet strategic emphasis on counterforce rather than MAD.)

By the end of the 1960s, the focus of US strategic force attention was on SALT. The Soviet Union had roughly drawn equal with the US, at least in the central strategic forces to be the subject of SALT, and "parity" was established. United States SALT expectations were high. While there were major studies of future US strategic force requirements and force modifications, they were SALT dominated and their recommendations were largely held in abeyance pending the outcome of SALT.

Early American expectations were not met. United States ABM deployment was limited by SALT to one ICBM site (since dismantled), but neither MIRV nor the continued growth and improvement of Soviet forces was constrained. The earlier US decisions to freeze numerical levels of the TRIAD and to improve the capabilities of the force qualitatively at only a modest, SALT-related pace failed to induce the Soviets to freeze their own strategic force levels or to show any similar restraint. In retrospect it must be concluded that US restraint and the concept of MAD merely contributed to the opportunity for the Soviet Union first to achieve parity, then to gain superiority in major quantitative comparisons of strategic forces, and finally to convert the latter to a counterforce and warfighting advantage.

A "New" American Strategic Doctrine

The Nixon Administration had formalized a set of criteria that defined "Sufficiency" for American strategic forces. In addition to the Assured Destruction criterion, Crisis Stability (i.e.,

Diagram 3: Triad force delivery vehicles on alert

Bombers 20%
LBMS 50%
SBMS 30%

% Total delivery vehicles

Bombers 9%
SBMS 23%
LBMS 68%

% Total delivery vehicles on alert

LBMS Land based ballistic missile systems
SBMS Submarine launched ballistic missile systems

avoiding major force vulnerabilities), equivalent destructive capability with the USSR, and defense against light attacks were to comprise Sufficiency. In practice, however, there was no major departure from the policies and concepts of the 1960s. In the early 1970s, after SALT had failed to dampen the Soviet build-up, a Government study spearheaded by the Office of Secretary of Defense produced what might be regarded as a new doctrine of Sufficiency (it is not yet clear that this doctrine is accepted by the Carter Administration).

On the basis of this study, Secretary of Defense James R. Schlesinger first announced in a press conference on January 10, 1974, that there had taken place "a change in the strategies of the United States with regard to the hypothetical employment of central strategic forces. A change in targeting strategy as it were." He went on: "To a large extent the American doctrinal position has been wrapped around something called 'assured destruction', which implies a tendency to target Soviet cities initially and massively and that this is the principal option that the President would have. It is our intention that this not be the only option and possibly not the principal option."

Because of the enormous growth of Soviet strategic force capabilities, he said, "the range of circumstances in which an all-out strike against an opponent's cities can be contemplated has narrowed considerably and one wishes to have alternatives for the employment of strategic forces."

Diagram 4: Strategic Triad Payload comparison

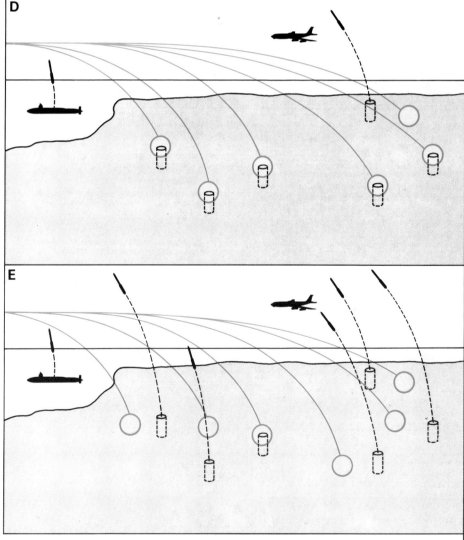

Assigned Strategic Payload

Available Strategic Payload
(on alert ready to go)

LBMS Land based ballistic missile systems
SBMS Submarine launched ballistic missile systems

The FY 1975 Department of Defense Report set forth what might be regarded as a new set of "sufficiency criteria", describing as the "principal features that we propose to maintain and improve in our strategic posture" the following:

". . . a capability sufficiently large, diversified, and survivable so that it will provide us at all times with high con-

fidence of riding out even a massive surprise attack and of penetrating enemy defenses, and with the ability to withhold an assured destruction reserve for an extended period of time.

". . . employment of the strategic forces in a controlled, selective, and restrained fashion.

Diagram 5: Counterforce Capability

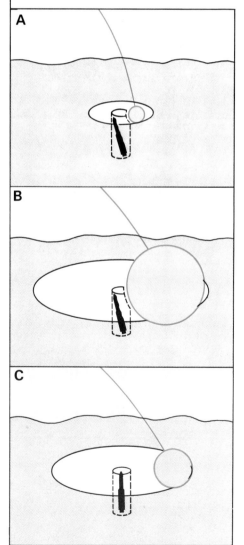

From "The SALT Negotiations" by Herbert Scoville, Jr. © 1977 by Scientific American Inc. All rights reserved.

Above: Counterforce capability depends on circular error probability (CEP) of the attacking missile (shown as a white disc representing the area within which there is a 50-50 chance of a hit) and the yield of its warhead (shown as a blue sphere of radius proportional to yield). A hardened ICBM can be knocked out by an accurate small-yield missile (A) or a less-accurate one with very large warhead (B), but a less-accurate small-yield missile will probably fail (C). An effective counterforce attack (D) leaves SLBMs and alert bombers; an ineffective one (E) leaves most of the ICBMs able to fire.

"... the forces to execute a wide range of options in response to potential actions by an enemy, including a capability for precise attacks on both soft and hard targets, while at the same time minimizing collateral damage.

"... an offensive capability of such size and composition that all will perceive it as in overall balance with the strategic forces of any potential opponent".[9]

To a large extent, American official strategic thinking seemed to have gone full circle back to the 1962 Ann Arbor statement of McNamara. Assured Destruction was not replaced; it was essential, but inadequate; furthermore, it was again to be perceived as a last ditch coercive reserve with the objective of dampening escalation even after deterrence initially failed and strategic weapons were used. As made clear later, AD was not to be measured arbitrarily in terms of population fatalities, but rather in terms of objectives of greater political-military relevance to a war and its aftermatch (hence, linking deterrence to political postwar objectives and relationships); principally, reduction of the enemy's post attack political-economic recovery capability and postwar political-military power.

Short of such major exchanges, however, the US goal was again to limit damage to the extent feasible, through targeting restraint and discriminate targeting, multiple options to fit the situation, and targeting of military forces, soft and hard.

It was ironic that counterforce and damage limiting were eschewed as major US objectives and strategic force planning criteria in order to exercise a self-restraint that was to induce Soviet reciprocity, but again had to be seriously reconsidered precisely because the lack of any reciprocity produced a Soviet strategic force capability rendering Assured Destruction thoroughly inadequate and highly questionable as a planned response to *any* threat save a massive Soviet attack on American cities as well as on US strategic forces. The steady growth of Soviet capabilities and steadfast rejection of MAD forced American rethinking of strategic doctrine.

Existing and Future Forces

How the 1974 strategic force criteria will influence future strategic forces, or even if they will be maintained as a matter of policy by the new Administration, remains to be seen. Neither President Carter nor Secretary of Defense Harold Brown seems closely in tune with such strategic doctrine, and may decide on a different reaction to Soviet capabilities, namely to restrict rather than to expand the role and capabilities of American strategic nuclear forces. There are, however, program requirements based upon other considerations: replacing aging systems, maintaining the minimum necessary force survivability and destructive capability in the face of continuing Soviet force improvements, and preventing too great a relative deterioration of the strategic balance. The current Administration is presently studying these matters.

The present American force consists of 41 SSBNs with 656 missiles; of these, 31 SSBNs have been retrofitted for the Poseidon C-3 missile, and 10 remain equipped with Polaris A-3. The 1,000 Minuteman force is divided between Minuteman II (450) and the MIRVed Minuteman III (550); the 54 Titan II missiles remain operational. There are now active only 316 B-52s (models D, G, H), plus 66 FB-111 medium bombers assigned to SAC.

Follow-on systems to each of these forces have been under research and development, and either proposed or programmed: Trident for the SSBN/SLBM force; M-X for the ICBM force; and the B-1 plus the long-range air-launched cruise missile (ALCM) for the strategic bomber force. Of these, the Carter Administration has cancelled the B-1 program after four aircraft were built (funding and possible production of

a fifth and sixth remain uncertain at the time of writing), and the future of the ALCM seems dependent upon further development of the technology, the question of a carrier aircraft, and SALT restrictions (such as range). The Trident is still programmed, but delayed, and the eventual force levels uncertain. The M-X remains mostly in the concept stage and is also highly dependent upon SALT. (The Carter Administration has reportedly offered to ban testing and deployment of such new missiles, at least for a period of time, and has proposed to ban mobile ICBMs.)

The Navy, not wishing to imply that the Polaris/Poseidon boats might be vulnerable ("... it is obvious that our current Polaris/Poseidon force is essentially invulnerable today," according to RADM A. L. Kelln, former Trident Program Manager), has supported Trident as "further enhancing the most survivable component" of the TRIAD, and extending that survivability into the 21st century. Advances in Soviet antisubmarine warfare (ASW) capabilities could mean that the SSBN technology of the 1950s would dangerously lag behind the ASW technology of the '70s and '80s. Trident also is needed to replace the existing force before aging affects its performance.

The Trident program involves both a larger new submarine and two new missiles, each new submarine to carry 24 missiles. The Trident I

Above: Artist's impression of the FB-111H, a proposed improved version of the very limited FB-111A. This project remains no more than a proposal.

(C-4) missile—3-stage, solid-fuel, with better guidance and a 4,000nm range—will be retrofitted into some of the present Poseidon submarines as well as carried by the Trident sub. Future Trident subs would carry the even more advanced, longer range, and more accurate Trident II D-5 missile. Construction of the first Trident sub was begun in the summer of 1974, and the second a year later. Originally, completion of the first boat was projected for August, 1978; that schedule slipped to September, 1979, and recently it was reported that further delay would push it well into 1980 or even 1981.

The M-X ICBM concept is based upon the need to increase US ICBM capability against hard targets, to narrow the widening gap between US and Soviet counterforce and warfighting capabilities, to enhance the capability of ICBMs surviving any first strike, and—in a

Below: It is too early to be dogmatic over whether cancellation of the B-1 will prove to be the disaster it seems on the surface. Without it the whole deterrent posture of the West appears to crumble.

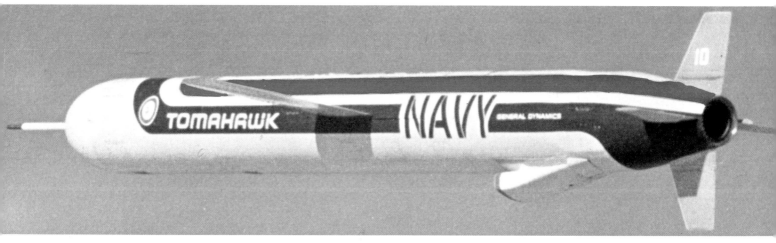

Top, above and right: How can a strategic missile system be made survivable? The ALCM Tomahawk (top) can be launched by aircraft or submarine, both of which offer pre-launch protection. One way of deploying the proposed MX is to hide it in the Buried Trench Concept (above). To fire, the missile tube is raised, pushing off the topsoil. The enemy never knows where the missiles are in the network of tunnels. Even the Minuteman ICBM, originally a fixed-base weapon, has been carried aloft in a C-5A and successfully launched on its mission in mid-air (right), though there is no present plan to deploy any of these missiles in this way.

mobile or mobile/concealed mode—to ensure future ICBM survivability. The missile, which would be nearly double the size and three to [four times the throw weight of the Minuteman III (or about the size of the Soviet SS-19), is designed for either present silos, reconfigured (which would not alleviate the vulnerability problem), or for deployment in some mobile or multiple aim point mode. Of several options studied, three have been considered by the USAF to show enough promise for further study and consideration: mobility within a buried trench, mobility among above-ground shelters, and containment in hardened capsules (perhaps to be covertly dispersed in fields of many more unhardened silos than there are missiles). At this time, no final choice has been made, nor has there been any final commitment to deployment of any version of the M-X.

The B-1 bomber was programmed by the previous Administration for a production of 244 aircraft, 210 of which would be operational bombers. The B-1 was designed to meet future problems both of prelaunch survivability against SLBM attack (by faster getaway time and hardening to nuclear effects) and penetration of Soviet air defenses (by very low level penetration at mach .85, high altitude penetration at supersonic speed, and use of SRAMs and ALCMs, the latter possibly in a "stand-off" mode outside air defenses). At about two-thirds to three-quarters the size and weight of the B-52, the B-1 could carry twice the payload over the same intercontinental range at much higher speeds. As noted, however, the Carter Ad-

ministration, incorrectly viewing the B-1 and the ALCM as alternatives, cancelled the program in favor of ALCM.

The ALCM, currently under development as is a possible alternative for both air and submarine launch (the Navy's *Tomahawk*), would be a long-range, subsonic air-breathing missile, small in size and in radar cross section, and hopefully cheap enough to produce in large numbers (consistent with any SALT limitations). The technology looks promising, but its effectiveness, as well as the vulnerability of the missile and whatever carrier aircraft is selected for the missile, remain to be demonstrated.

The future of these systems, the mix of American strategic forces, and the doctrine and objectives for those forces are yet to be decided definitively by the present Administration. An increasing number of American strategic specialists grow more and more concerned about the continuing viability and equivalence of American strategic forces against the still rapidly improving Soviet strategic force capability. Earlier 1977 projections by the Administration of "Essential Equivalence" with Soviet strategic forces in the mid-to-late 1980s were based upon full production of B-1, Trident, and some 550 M-X ICBMs. With B-1 cancelled and the other two uncertain and delayed, such projections may have to be revised, although there is no official notice of this as yet.

Politically, some Congressional concern over the state of affairs seems to be growing, as typified by an October, 1977, letter to President Carter from the Chairman of the House Armed Services Committee, Melvin Price (D., Ill.), which said, "I have attempted to comprehend the rationale behind the combination of decisions leading to cancellation of the B-1, cancellation of production of the SRAM, termination of production of the Minuteman III missile, and the reduction in funds for the development of the advanced MX system."

Footnotes

*The most recent DOD Report has separate sections covering Strategic Nuclear Forces, Theater Nuclear Forces, and Conventional Forces.
1. Edmund Beard, *Developing the ICBM* (New York: Columbia University Press, 1976). While the history of the development and deployment of US strategic ballistic missiles is most thoroughly contained in assorted Congressional Hearings and US Government histories, the reader is encouraged to refer to this excellent account for the ICBM story and to Harvey M. Sapolsky, *The Polaris System Development* (Cambridge, Mass: Harvard University Press, 1972) for the Polaris story.
2. The principal civilian mover was Trevor Gardner, Special Assistant for Research and Development to the Secretary of the Air Force. Under Gardner's sponsorship and guidance, a civilian Strategic Missile Evaluation Committee chaired by John von Neumann, validated the feasibility of an ICBM and urged a greater US effort.
3. This approach is best described in Alain C. Enthoven and K. Wayle Smith, *How Much is Enough?* (New York: Harper & Row, 1971), pp 176 and *passim*. Mr. Enthoven was Assistant Secretary of Defense for Systems Analysis during these years.
4. This address may be found in William W. Kaufmann, *The McNamara Strategy* (New York: Harper & Row, 1964). The other quotations that follow are taken from that book, annual Department of Defense reports, or Pentagon news releases.
5. This rationale and the following quote can be found in *How Much is Enough?*, op. cit.
6. Alton Frye, "US Decision Making for SALT", in Mason Willrich and John Rhinelander, *SALT: The Moscow Agreements and Beyond* (New York: The Free Press, 1974), p. 66.
7. The throw-weight and payload limits of the light Minuteman ICBM did not allow large MIRVs anyway; a new, larger ICBM would have had to be developed and produced. One designed and proposed by the USAF was rejected by the Administration precisely to avoid the deployment of larger MIRVs and a good hard-target counterforce capability.
8. For further analysis and documentation of the new policy, see William R. Van Cleave and R. W. Barnett, "Strategic Adaptability," ORBIS, XVIII, 3 (Fall 1974), pp. 655–676.
9. Report of Secretary of Defense Schlesinger to the Congress on the FY 1975 Defense Budget and FY 1975–1979 Defense Program, 93rd Congress, 2nd Session, March 4, 1974.

The United States Army

Lt. Col. Donald B. Vought, US Army (Ret.), former specialist instructor, US Army Command and General Staff College, Fort Leavenworth, Kansas, and
Lt. Col. J. R. Angolia, JCOS, DUCO, currently instructor at CGSC Fort Leavenworth.

The 790,000 men and women of the US Army constitute the main land fighting element of the American armed forces. This Army currently enjoys an advantage unique among the armies of the world powers—major combat experience. The Vietnamese War (circa 1965–1973) caused most of the current officer and senior non-commissioned officer corps to function professionally in an active combat environment. While the Vietnam struggle provided the US Army with two professional generations of leaders with combat exposure, the experience is not an unmixed advantage. In the intervening years since the withdrawal of US ground forces from Vietnam, the reorientation from a specific Southeast Asian war to a defensive posture on a global scale has been difficult.

Geopolitical factors pose some considerations which affect Army structure and doctrinal development. The most prominent of these is the problem of projecting military power abroad. A question which influences Army planners is how to structure forces for possible employment anywhere in the world when the various areas and different types of employment each call for a fundamentally different force. The current approach to a workable solution to the dilemma is the General Purpose Force.

The possible need to project power across vast expanses of ocean also influences the US Army in ways other than force structure. One of these is budgetary emphasis. The American defense budget for Fiscal Year 1977 called for the following service appropriations: Army, $26.9 billion; Navy, $36.4 billion; and Air Force, $32.2 billion. While not finalized at the time of writing, the FY 1978 budget calls for a similar proportionate distribution. Another area influenced by the problems of power projection is the inordinate need for interservice cooperation (that is, Army, Navy, and Air Force). The US military have developed unusually close working relationships between the armed services in which the Army, ever sensitive to the logistics of overseas operations, has been a leading voice.

The previously-referred-to concept of a General Purpose Force entails orienting the Army toward what is determined to be the principal threat to US interests while attempting to maintain sufficient flexibility so that major elements could be deployed elsewhere. Currently, the Army is oriented toward Europe. The European orientation drives both structure and doctrine, giving the Army of today an essentially defensive posture.

Integration of US Army elements into NATO forces poses no problems of doctrinal incompatibility, since the alliance is defensive in philosophy and form. With no offensive plans, NATO—and the US Army in Europe as an integral part of the alliance's ground forces—must be prepared to hold an enemy invasion force until either a negotiated peace or until NATO can reinforce itself to initiate large scale offensive action. Following is a brief description of how the US Army has organized itself and the tactics it would use to accomplish this.

The Division

The division is the basic combined arms formation that provides infantry and armor maneuver elements as well as artillery to support tactical operations. A total of sixteen divisions—four armored, five mechanized infantry, five infantry, one air assault and one airborne—make up the active army ground combat force. These forces comprise the combat force of the United States Army, and are those maneuver elements charged with the fighting mission. Within these divisions are found combat support elements consisting of artillery, air defense artillery, military intelligence, signal, chemical and engineers. Combat service support elements consisting of quartermaster, transportation, military police, medical services, and those other responsible for the care and maintenance of the Army are also organic to the division.

The division is the largest force that is trained and fought as a combined arms team. It is a balanced, self-sustaining force that normally conducts operations as part of a larger force, but is capable of conducting independent operations, especially when supplemented by additional combat support and combat service support elements. Normally, the division fights as part of a corps, with two to five divisions making up the corps force. The division is designed to fight conventional operations, or a mixture of conventional and nuclear operations in any part of the world as the force deployment requires. Nine of the sixteen divisions are armor and mechanized infantry, which are designed to fight most effectively in open terrain where their mobility, speed of movement, and long range firepower can be fully exploited. The current mechanized infantry and armored divisions are, in most respects, identical in their make-up except for the balance of maneuver battalions. The armored divisions deployed in or to Europe each consist of six tank battalions and five mechanized infantry battalions, while the mechanized infantry divisions each have the tank and infantry battalion ratio reversed.

While the division is the basic combined arms formation, it is the battalion (rather than the regiment, as is the case with the Soviet Ground Forces) that is the basic maneuver unit. The battalion fights as a part of a brigade, with normally three to five battalions comprising a brigade. Each division has three brigade headquarters to which battalions are assigned as the command sees fit.

Heavy maneuver battalions—armor and mechanized infantry—fight best in open country using terrain to its maximum advantage. The light maneuver forces—rifle infantry, air assault infantry, airborne infantry, and ranger infantry—are ideally suited for more restricted terrain where close-in fighting becomes the norm. Other maneuver elements of the division are the air or ground cavalry squadrons, and in some divisions, attack helicopter companies. The maneuver elements of the division are grouped together under brigade control in accordance with the terrain, the enemy they face, and the mission they must accomplish. Each tactical operation—offense, defense, or retrograde—requires that these elements be deployed differently.

In the offense, attacking forces concentrate and use maneuver against weak spots or gaps to gain a quick advantage over the enemy.

In the defense, maneuver is employed so that the

What is the US Army? Most observers would say it is primarily personnel, and in particular combat troops (below). But they can today do little without the backing of modern weaponry, exemplified by the launch of a Lance missile (left). The experience in South-East Asia did not help morale, and compared with the Soviet Union the re-equipment of the Army with new tanks and anti-aircraft missiles has been gravely harmed by delays and escalation in cost. Today the morale problems have been overcome, but the problems with modern weaponry are still serious.

Table 1: Organization of the Department of the Army

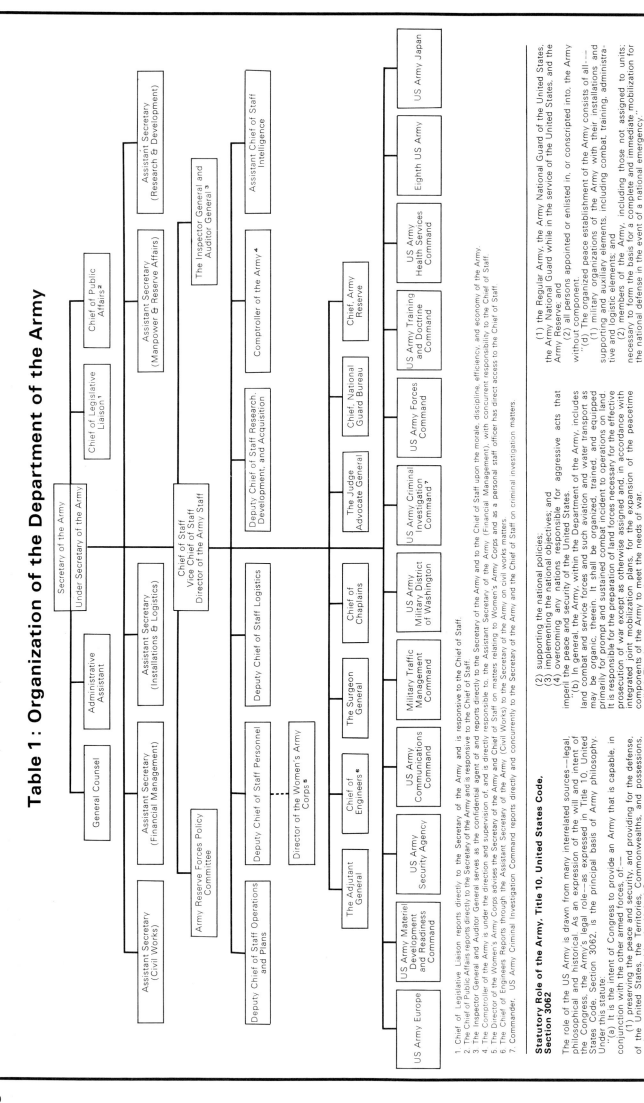

1. Chief of Legislative Liaison reports directly to the Secretary of the Army and is responsive to the Chief of Staff.
2. The Chief of Public Affairs reports directly to the Secretary of the Army and is responsive to the Chief of Staff.
3. The Inspector General and Auditor General serves as the confidential agent of and reports directly to the Secretary of the Army and to the Chief of Staff upon the morale, discipline, efficiency, and economy of the Army.
4. The Comptroller of the Army is under the direction and supervision of, and is directly responsible to, the Assistant Secretary of the Army (Financial Management), with concurrent responsibility to the Chief of Staff.
5. The Director of the Women's Army Corps advises the Secretary of the Army and Chief of Staff on matters relating to Women's Army Corps and as a personal staff officer has direct access to the Chief of Staff.
6. The Chief of Engineers Reports through the Assistant Secretary of the Army (Civil Works) to the Secretary of the Army on civil works matters.
7. Commander, US Army Criminal Investigation Command reports directly and concurrently to the Secretary of the Army and the Chief of Staff on criminal investigation matters.

Statutory Role of the Army, Title 10, United States Code, Section 3062

The role of the US Army is drawn from many interrelated sources—legal, philosophical and historical. As an expression of the will and intent of the Congress, the Army's legal role—as expressed in Title 10, United States Code, Section 3062. is the principal basis of Army philosophy. Under this statute:

"(a) It is the intent of Congress to provide an Army that is capable, in conjunction with the other armed forces, of:—

"(1) preserving the peace and security, and providing for the defense, of the United States, the Territories, Commonwealths, and possessions, and any areas occupied by the United States;

"(2) supporting the national policies;

"(3) implementing the national objectives; and

"(4) overcoming any nations responsible for aggressive acts that imperil the peace and security of the United States.

"(b) In general. the Army, within the Department of the Army, includes land combat and service forces and such aviation and water transport as may be organic. therein. It shall be organized. trained. and equipped primarily for prompt and sustained combat incident to operations on land. It is responsible for the preparation of land forces necessary for the effective prosecution of war except as otherwise assigned and, in accordance with integrated joint mobilization plans, for the expansion of the peacetime components of the Army to meet the needs of war.

"(c) The Army consists of:—

"(1) the Regular Army, the Army National Guard of the United States, the Army National Guard while in the service of the United States, and the Army Reserve; and

"(2) all persons appointed or enlisted in, or conscripted into, the Army without component.

"(d) The organized peace establishment of the Army consists of all—

"(1) military organizations of the Army with their installations and supporting and auxiliary elements, including combat, training, administrative and logistic elements; and

"(2) members of the Army, including those not assigned to units; necessary to form the basis for a complete and immediate mobilization for the national defense in the event of a national emergency.''

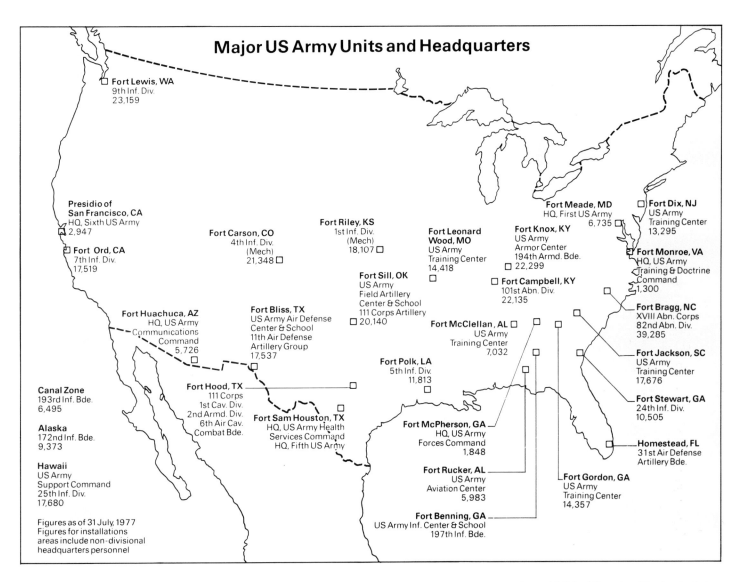

Major US Army Units and Headquarters

Fort Lewis, WA
9th Inf. Div.
23,159

Presidio of San Francisco, CA
HQ, Sixth US Army
2,947

Fort Ord, CA
7th Inf. Div.
17,519

Fort Carson, CO
4th Inf. Div.
(Mech)
21,348

Fort Riley, KS
1st Inf. Div.
(Mech)
18,107

Fort Leonard Wood, MO
US Army
Training Center
14,418

Fort Knox, KY
US Army
Armor Center
194th Armd. Bde.
22,299

Fort Meade, MD
HQ, First US Army
6,735

Fort Dix, NJ
US Army
Training Center
13,295

Fort Monroe, VA
HQ, US Army
Training & Doctrine
Command
1,300

Fort Huachuca, AZ
HQ, US Army
Communications
Command
5,726

Fort Bliss, TX
US Army Air Defense
Center & School
11th Air Defense
Artillery Group
17,537

Fort Sill, OK
US Army
Field Artillery
Center & School
111 Corps Artillery
20,140

Fort Campbell, KY
101st Abn. Div.
22,135

Fort McClellan, AL
US Army
Training Center
7,032

Fort Bragg, NC
XVIII Abn. Corps
82nd Abn. Div.
39,285

Fort Jackson, SC
US Army
Training Center
17,676

Canal Zone
193rd Inf. Bde.
6,495

Alaska
172nd Inf. Bde.
9,373

Hawaii
US Army
Support Command
25th Inf. Div.
17,680

Fort Hood, TX
111 Corps
1st Cav. Div.
2nd Armd. Div.
6th Air Cav.
Combat Bde.

Fort Sam Houston, TX
HQ, US Army Health
Services Command
HQ, Fifth US Army

Fort Polk, LA
5th Inf. Div.
11,813

Fort McPherson, GA
HQ, US Army
Forces Command
1,848

Fort Rucker, AL
US Army
Aviation Center
5,983

Fort Benning, GA
US Army Inf. Center & School
197th Inf. Bde.

Fort Gordon, GA
US Army
Training Center
14,357

Fort Stewart, GA
24th Inf. Div.
10,505

Homestead, FL
31st Air Defense
Artillery Bde.

Figures as of 31 July, 1977
Figures for installations
areas include non-divisional
headquarters personnel

---

enemy is constantly confronted by strong forces in depth, i.e., to deny the enemy weak spots to exploit.

In the retrograde, maneuver elements are positioned to delay and destroy enemy forces from pre-selected successive positions which give the advantage to the defender.

Tank and mechanized infantry battalions rarely fight as pure organic units, but are cross-attached or task-organized by the brigade commanders to perform specific mission tasks to utilize more fully their capabilities and offset each other's vulnerabilities. After the division commander has visualized how he wishes to fight the battle, he allocates maneuver units to the brigade commanders, who in turn cross-attach these forces to optimize the weapon systems of each unit. The resultant battalion task forces are a combination of tank and mechanized infantry companies under the command of a battalion commander. A tank heavy force would normally be structured to operate in open, rolling terrain, while the mechanized infantry heavy task force is better suited to operate in more restricted terrain and built-up areas. An even mix of tank and mechanized infantry results in a balanced task force that provides great flexibility to the commander. A balanced force would normally be structured when information about the enemy is vague or when the terrain is mixed and variable.

Armored Battalion Organization
The armored battalion has 550 officers and men, and is found in the armored, infantry, and mechanized divisions, and the separate armored, infantry, and mechanized brigades. The armored battalion is structured with a Headquarters and Headquarters Company, three Tank Companies and a Combat Support Company. The Combat Support Company has four 4.2in mortars, five Redeye anti-aircraft weapons, an armored-vehicle-launched bridge and a scout platoon.

Units in Europe also have four TOW and four Dragon anti-tank weapons. The two main weapon systems are the main battle tank and the wire-guided anti-tank guided missile TOW. The current main battle tank is the M60A1. There are 54 of these tanks organic to a battalion. It is armed with a 105mm main gun which is highly effective up to 2,187yds (2,000m). It has a cruising range of 310 miles (500km). Some battalions are equipped with the M60A2 tank which uses the M60 chassis, but is equipped with a 152mm main gun that can launch the Shillelagh missile in addition to firing conventional ammunition. There are currently more M60A1s in the weapons inventory than there are

M60A2s. Additionally, the M60A1 is being product-improved to the M60A3, which has a fully stabilized main gun system, improved suspension for increased cross-country mobility, a laser range finder with a solid state computer for greater accuracy and an improved engine and tracks. Because of the restricted range of

Below: Though the basic M60 is an out-dated tank, the M60A2 version has the unique gun/launcher for either conventional shells of 152mm calibre or the Shillelagh guided missile. Most of the 500 in use have infra-red night vision (looking like a TV screen).

Above: Trials at Pope Air Force Base with an M60 tank and 175mm SP gun being loaded aboard a Lockheed C-5A Galaxy. Virtually every field item in the Army can be airlifted in this monster aircraft, but some US Army items are badly sized and much can still be done to design-in an airlift capability to front-line equipment. The Soviet Union still leads in air-dropping capability.

the main gun and the thickness of frontal armor in modern tanks, the 105mm gun is most effective against other tanks at ranges less than 2,187yds (2,000m). To increase the killing range of the tank battalion against enemy armor, the armored battalion is equipped with four guided missile launchers (TOWs) with a range of 3,280yds (3,000m).

In the offense, tanks use their mobility and combat power to outflank the enemy or to penetrate the enemy defenses. Once armor has broken through to the enemy rear, it destroys or disrupts the defenses in depth. Tanks are also well suited for rapid and dynamic exploitation and pursuit operations.

In the defense, tanks can maneuver rapidly from one part of the battlefield to another to increase firepower in critical sectors as required. They can also be used to counterattack an exposed or weakened enemy to regain territory critical to the defense.

Mechanized Infantry Battalion
The structure of the Mechanized Infantry Battalion is the same as the armored battalion, but the manpower base is larger—891 officers and men. It is found in all the same organizations as the tank battalion except the infantry division, which does not have an organic mechanized infantry battalion. The mechanized infantry battalion has 69 organic M113A1 armored

personnel carriers that enable the infantrymen, to a degree, to maneuver with the tanks, and provide limited armor protection against small arms and shell fragments. The M113A1 is air transportable, air droppable, and has an amphibious capability. Its cruising range is 310

miles (500km). However, the M113A1 is scheduled to be replaced by a vastly improved infantry fighting vehicle that will provide greater protection, firepower and mobility. Dismounted infantry provide close-in protection for tanks when operating in restricted terrain or built-up areas. They are also an excellent source of combat information during tactical operations.

The most effective anti-armor weapons in the battalion are the antitank guided missiles. The mechanized infantry battalion has 18 guided missile TOW launchers, each mounted on a M113A1, and having a very high probability of hit out to 3,280yds (3,000m). To supplement these long range launchers there are 27 medium range 1,093yds (1,000m) Dragon guided missile launchers.

In the offense, the mechanized infantry usually attacks as part of a combined arms force. The infantrymen remain mounted in their carriers until they are required to assault or forced to dismount by the enemy. The carriers displace to protected positions to provide supporting fire with their .50 calibre machine guns. The new infantry fighting vehicle (IFV) with its 20mm cannon will greatly enhance the infantryman's ability to fight while mounted and protected.

In the defense, infantrymen dismount to occupy defensive positions, and the carriers are positioned in prepared defilade positions to deliver suppressive fire. The carriers also provide the commander with the flexibility to shift his forces rapidly to concentrate against an enemy breakthrough, or to strengthen thinned out sectors of the defense.

Infantry Battalion
The 749-man strong infantry battalion is identically structured (i.e., HQ, 3 Infantry Companies and Support Company), but is only organic to the infantry division and the separate infantry brigade. Infantry battalions are designated to fight as light infantry, air assault infantry, airborne infantry or ranger infantry. The basic infantry battalion is well suited for fighting in restricted terrain regardless of the obstacles or weather. Each battalion (airborne excepted) has an anti-tank capability identical to the guided missile capability of the mechanized infantry battalion. As a result of special training, air assault, airborne and ranger units have unique capabilities.

Table 2: US Armored and Mechanized Infantry Divisions Deployed to or in Europe	Armored Division	Mechanized Infantry Division
Tank battalions	6	5
Infantry battalion (mechanized)	5	6
Weapon system		
M60A1	216	270
M60A2	108	0
M551	27	27
M113	376	415
M113 TOW	154	168
Dragon	200	240
M109A1	54	54
M110	12	12
Chaparral	24	24
Vulcan	24	24
Redeye	72 teams	72 teams
CEV	8	8

Table 3: Major US Air Defense Artillery (ADA) Units in US mainland and overseas

United States
Fort Bliss, Texas—4th Battalion/1st ADA Group
    1st Battalion/55th ADA Group
    2nd Battalion/55th ADA Group
    5th Battalion/57th ADA Group
    4th Battalion/62nd ADA Group
Fort Campbell, Kentucky—1st Battalion/3rd ADA Group
Fort Bragg, North Carolina—3rd Battalion/4th ADA Group
Fort Hood, Texas—11th ADA Group
    2nd Battalion/5th ADA Group
    1st Battalion/68th ADA Group
Alaska—1st Battalion/43rd ADA Group
Fort Ord, California—1st Battalion/51st ADA Group
Fort Riley, Kansas—2nd Battalion/51st ADA Group

Homestead—2nd Battalion/52nd ADA Group
Florida: 3rd Battalion/68th ADA Group
Boca Chica—1st Battalion/65th ADA Group
Fort Carlson, Colorado—4th Battalion/61st ADA Group
Hawaii—1st Battalion/62nd ADA Group
Fort Lewis, Wichita—1st Battalion/67th ADA Group

Germany
32nd Army Air Defense Command
10th ADA Group
69th ADA Group
94th ADA Group
108th ADA Group

South Korea
38th ADA Group

The air assault infantry can be assigned the same missions as other infantry units, but they are afforded the capability of bypassing enemy forward defenses, and attacking positions in the enemy rear. This capability is provided by organic troop-lift helicopters that greatly increase the mobility and extend the range of the infantry.

Airborne infantry are normally considered to be the ground forces' strategic reserve. They can move great distances quickly to seize critical terrain deep in the enemy rear or to conduct a show of force. Once on the ground, airborne units are assigned tasks appropriate to their armament. The airborne infantry battalion is primarily equipped with 12 jeep-mounted TOW launchers and 30 Dragon missile launchers.

The ranger battalion is specially trained and organized to conduct decentralized and independent combat operations anywhere in the world. They may be required to:

Establish a credible American presence to demonstrate US resolve.

Conduct strategic and long-range tactical reconnaissance, raids, and other combat operations.

Infiltrate and exfiltrate by air, sea, or land, using parachute assault, small boats and navy vessels or on foot.

Armored Cavalry Squadron

The purpose of cavalry units is to perform reconnaissance, provide security, and engage in offensive, defensive, and delay operations as an economy of force unit for the division. Cavalry will normally be allocated to forces in the covering force area where they assist by fighting

a significant battle to force the enemy to deploy his first echelon regiments and conduct deliberate attacks, thereby revealing the main thrust of his attack before he reaches the main battle area. The armored cavalry squadron is structured with a Headquarters and Headquarters troop, three armored cavalry troops, and one air cavalry troop with an aggregate strength of 876 officers and men.

The M551 light armor vehicle (often referred to as a light tank) is the principal weapon system of the armored cavalry (ground) troop. The armored cavalry squadron has a total of 27 M551s, which mount a 152mm gun/missile launcher, and is air transportable and amphibious. The conventional round gives the M551 a high probability of hit out to 1,640yds (1,500m), while the missile's range is 3,280yds (3,000m). The cruising range for the light armor vehicle is 370 miles (596km). However, these are being replaced by the M60A1s to simplify maintenance and resupply problems.

The air cavalry troop consists of aeroscouts, aeroweapons, and aerorecon. The aeroscouts are the eyes and ears of the troop, while the aerorecon provides limited ground reconnaissance capability. The aeroweapons platoon consists of nine attack helicopters—5 AH-1Gs and 4 AH-1Ss (TOW COBRA)—which make up the air maneuver unit. They are highly mobile, with multiweapon systems capability. However, all helicopters will become AHs in the 1980s. The attack helicopters maneuver in a similar manner to ground units to engage the enemy from the front, flanks or rear, using terrain for cover and concealment. The AH-1 attack helicopters have a variety of configurations and ordnance loads, and have the capability

of attacking area targets or a point target. They can carry a mixture of ordnance to include 7.62mm machine guns, 40mm grenade launchers, 20mm and 30mm automatic cannon, 2.75in aerial rockets and TOW missiles. In addition to air cavalry troop, attack helicopters are found in the assault helicopter battalion, and as pure attack helicopter units. This weapon system is considered to be one of the most versatile and lethal on the modern battlefield.

Air Cavalry Squadron

The tasks assigned to the air cavalry squadron are much the same as those assigned to the armored cavalry squadron. The air cavalry squadron is organic to the infantry and airborne divisions, and is structured with one Headquarters and Headquarters troop, three air cavalry troops, and one armored cavalry troop with an aggregate of 963 officers and men (935 for airborne).

All available combat support and combat service support organic to the division or provided by Corps is directed in support of the maneuver units. Each division artillery, for example, has approximately 2,300 officers and men, and a variety of weapons. The armored division supports with 12 8-in self-propelled heavy howitzers, and 54 155mm medium self-propelled howitzers. The mechanized infantry division has a like number and types of artillery

Below: M60A1 battle tanks offloaded at the railhead at Illisheim, Germany, in August 1976 for Exercise Reforger. The unit is the famed 101st Airborne Division, since June 6, 1944, one of the top Army units.

Division Defensive Operations

The Active Defense

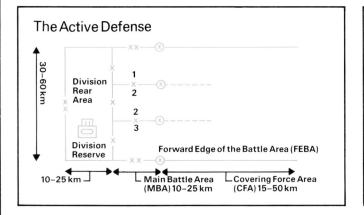

30–60 km

Division Rear Area

Division Reserve

1
2
2
3

Forward Edge of the Battle Area (FEBA)

10–25 km — Main Battle Area (MBA) 10–25 km — Covering Force Area (CFA) 15–50 km

Brigade Defense in Depth

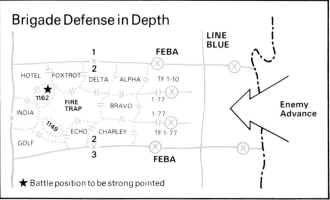

LINE BLUE

FEBA

HOTEL FOXTROT DELTA ALPHA TF 1-10
1162 FIRE TRAP BRAVO 1-77
INDIA
1149 ECHO CHARLEY TF 1-77
GOLF
FEBA

Enemy Advance

★ Battle position to be strong pointed

Weighted Defense

If intelligence on the enemy is accurate, and/or if terrain is so restrictive that no other feasible enemy avenue of approach constitutes a significant threat to the sector, the division commander may conclude that the enemy main effort will be directed against a specific place in the defensive sector. In such a situation, the defensive scheme is weighted against the anticipated avenue of approach. Risks are accepted in the remainder of the sector. The division, therefore, achieves favorable force ratios at the right place *before* the attack begins.

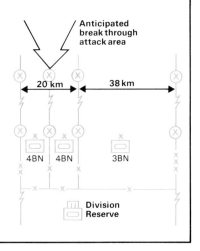

Anticipated break through attack area

20 km   38 km

4BN 4BN 3BN

Division Reserve

Balanced Defense

If the terrain throughout the defensive sector does not restrict vehicular movement and if the enemy situation is vague, initial allocation of combat power to the forward brigades may be relatively balanced to insure flexibility. In this option, "where" and "when" the division commander concentrates forces to achieve the required force ratios of 1:3 can only be determined *after* the attack begins and the enemy's major effort has been identified.

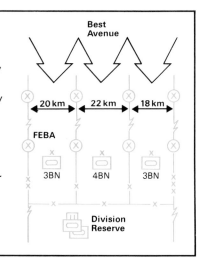

Best Avenue

20 km 22 km 18 km

FEBA

3BN 4BN 3BN

Division Reserve

Division Offensive Operations

Movement to Contact

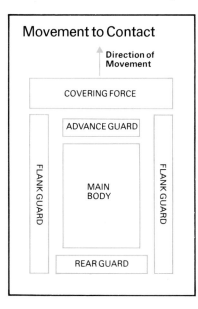

Direction of Movement

COVERING FORCE

ADVANCE GUARD

FLANK GUARD

MAIN BODY

FLANK GUARD

REAR GUARD

Concentrating Forces when Attacking from Positions on Line

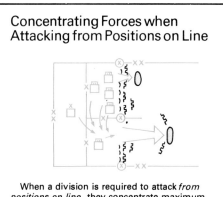

When a division is required to attack *from positions on line,* they concentrate maximum combat power on a narrow front against a selected weak spot. A limited objective operation or a deception operation is conducted to deceive the enemy and fix enemy forces in place. In this case a reinforced battalion task force conducts a feint.

Executing the Penetration

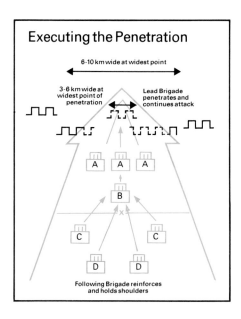

6-10 km wide at widest point

3-6 km wide at widest point of penetration

Lead Brigade penetrates and continues attack

A A A
B
C   C
D   D

Following Brigade reinforces and holds shoulders

Executing the Envelopment

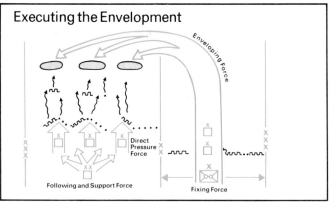

Enveloping Force

Direct Pressure Force

Following and Support Force

Fixing Force

XX ▭	Armored division
X ▭	Armored brigade
⊞	Reinforced tank battalion Task force
X ▢	Armored or Infantry brigade
⋈	Combat Support Services
X X X	Corps area of operations
X X	Division area of operations

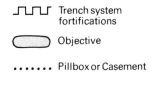

ⅬⅬⅬ Trench system fortifications

Objective

...... Pillbox or Casement

but the airborne division has only 54 105mm (towed) while the air assault division has 54 105mm (towed) and 18 155mm (towed) howitzers. The other supporting elements provide information concerning the enemy, weather, and terrain, the necessary communications for command and control, and the fuel, ammunition and food to maintain the maneuver units in combat.

US Army Tactical Doctrine

The principles of US Army doctrine, and therefore the shape and form of the ground forces, are heavily influenced by economics, existing attitudes of the American people, and the perceived potential threat. US and NATO strategists envision the greatest threat as coming from the Soviet Union or the Warsaw Pact, and being principally directed against the Western European landmass. Therefore, US ground forces are structured and doctrine is developed to cope with a potential war in Europe. Given an attack by the Warsaw Pact with little or no early warning, the Warsaw Pact enjoys a quantitative advantage in numbers of divisions, tanks, artillery and aircraft. To counter this numerical advantage, the United States has developed qualitatively superior equipment, and a tactical doctrine that is designed to neutralize or defeat an attacking numerically superior enemy. A tactical concept that combines maneuver forces with artillery and close air support in addition to the other elements of the combined arms formation has been emphasized in the development of today's tactical doctrine. Tanks and infantry are mutually supporting, long range and highly effective antitank guided missiles kill tanks and artillery and close air support are directed against infantry and soft targets.

Similarly, the Soviet force structure and doctrine are influenced by economics and the perceived threat, but additionally they are influenced by geography. The Soviet Union west of the Urals is primarily an open plain with low density population centers. Her historical enemies are the Germans in the west and the Chinese in the east, and she fears that an attack by one might stimulate an attack by the other, thus causing a two-front war. These factors—not to mention that they were the successful ingredients in World War II—are why the Soviet Union relies so heavily on masses of men and materiel. Offensive operations in Western Europe are, however, not afforded the wide geographic expanse for maneuver these massed formations require. Instead, ground forces would be restricted by urban sprawl, numerous water obstacles, and terrain-restricted directions of attack. Blitzkrieg-type offensive operations that would be very appropriate for the Soviet landmass may no longer be as feasible in Western Europe as was once the case. Concentrating masses of men and materiel would provide the defender with a lucrative nuclear target. If nuclear weapons were not used, the various obstacles and defenses would slow, halt, or fragment advancing forces. Even if the attacking force is able to concentrate a six-to-one or better favorable combat ratio (judged to be necessary in the offense), the attacker would still sustain staggering losses. His ability to sustain continuous operations in view of these losses and the disruption of successive echelons to the rear of the disintegrating forward elements is questionable.

Thus the Soviet war machine, offensive in nature, will be faced with critical limitations. Certainly not all Soviet forces can be or would be directed against operations in Western Europe. US strategists realize full well that, in the event of hostilities in Europe, NATO will initially be on the defensive, and the United States will be forced to fight with available European-based forces until such time as NATO

Right: A Dragon anti-tank team (one launcher flanked by a rifle/grenade launcher) covers Sicily drop zone at Fort Bragg as 82nd Airborne troops make a practice airborne assault.

Major US Army Units and Headquarters in Germany

NETHERLANDS

•Bremen

•Hannover

•Dortmund

Hamburg

Berlin

EAST GERMANY

•Cologne

•Bonn

**WEST GERMANY
193,324**
(Federal Republic
and West Berlin)

□ **Frankfurt**
V Corps
3rd Armored
Division

□ **Würzburg**
3rd Infantry
Division

Bad Kreuznach □
8th Infantry
Division

□ **Heidelberg**
HQ, US Army
Europe and
Seventh Army

□ **Ansbach**
1st Armored
Division

Moerhingen
VII Corps

FRANCE

🏭 Munich

SWITZERLAND

Figure as of 30 June 1977

can be heavily reinforced. As a result, there has recently been a major modification to US defensive doctrine.

The Active Defense

Inherent in the execution of the defense is the necessity to understand the fundamentals of the defense. First, it is necessary for the defender to understand the enemy—how he fights, the capabilities and limitations of his weapon systems, and the techniques for using them. Since it is anticipated that the Warsaw Pact would attack along a broad front with their forces massed in depth at preselected sectors, NATO forces would be hard pressed to concentrate against any single breakthrough effort. As a result, it is equally necessary to "see" the battlefield through extensive intelligence gathering means, and to assess the information to determine the plan of attack in sufficient time to employ countermeasures. Because limits on manpower and equipment preclude a defense along the entire NATO front, commanders would have to decide exactly when and where they must concentrate their defensive forces. Commanders would use every means at their disposal to prevent being outnumbered at any point by more than three to one in terms of equivalent combat power. The active defense is designed to capitalize on the mobility of the maneuver and fire support systems of the division in order to concentrate sufficient combat power at the decisive time and place. It is characterized by the initial deployment of strong combined arms forces as far forward as possible, and the subsequent repositioning of those forces during the course of the battle to achieve depth throughout the defensive sector. Realizing full well that he would be outnumbered, the defender would use terrain to its maximum advantage—obstacles would be positioned to enhance the capabilities of the defending weapon systems;

field artillery fire would be massed to disrupt the attacker; tactical air support would be concentrated against the massed main enemy effort; electronic warfare resources would be used to disrupt enemy command and control nets, as well as to intercept communications; ground and helicopter-mounted antitank guided missiles would be employed to destroy and disrupt the attacking force before the enemy could bring the full weight of his force to bear.

To perform the defensive mission the division allocates maneuver forces and necessary combat support and combat service support elements for operations in three defensive areas: *Covering Force Area; Main Battle Area;* and the *Division Rear Area*. The width, depth, organization, and mission of the forces in these areas vary, depending on the commander's analysis of the division mission, knowledge of the terrain, strength and tactics employed by the attacking enemy, and the capabilities of the division forces.

The covering force area extends forward of the forward edge of battle area, and may extend out as far as 60 to 70 kilometers. The force in this area may equal one-third or more of the entire combat force, and is structured to provide a combat shield behind which the bulk of the division's combat force deploys and prepares to fight the main defensive battle. It is in the covering force area that defending forces attempt to force the enemy to reveal his intended point of major effort, destroy leading security forces, destroy large segments of the first echelon attacking force, and to cause enemy supporting artillery to deploy thus making them cease fire to redeploy before they can support the attack on the main battle area. As the covering force fights back to the main battle area, the battle is handed off to the bulk of the forces deployed in the main battle area. The covering force then breaks contact with the enemy, and either thickens the main battle areas as a defensive force, reverts to a

Major US Army Units and Headquarters in Korea

Additionally, there are 3,167 US Army personnel serving in Japan

Below: An armored column on the march, led by an M557A1 command vehicle and M113 APC. This particular chassis has been built in greater numbers (over 65,000) than any other since 1945.

combat reserve role, or conducts a rear area security mission.

It is in the main battle area, that area from the forward edge of the battle area back to the brigade-designated rear boundaries, that the main defensive battle is fought. Previous US Army defensive doctrine for Europe implied giving up terrain in exchange for time to develop desired combat forces and to position them where required. Current doctrine calls for the defense to be conducted as far forward as possible, holding critical terrain for as long as possible, and counter-attacking to reoccupy lost terrain. The bulk of the defending force is deployed in the main battle area, and through the use of engineer support, they prepare their positions for the coming battle. Selection of key terrain, the placement of weapon systems to maximize their capabilities, and the establishment of selected strong points prepare them for the defense. While current doctrine envisions the lateral shifting of forces to block or destroy a massed attacking force, it is expected that this can only be accomplished at the local level once the battle has begun. Limitations in non-organic transport, battle losses to vehicles providing mobility, and constant interdiction efforts on the part of the enemy will make lateral movement over great distances difficult. The commander will have to make his decision early, but accurately, to blunt effectively the enemy thrust. Furthermore, current doctrine calls for tanks and antitank guided missiles to be sited so that they can effectively engage the enemy at maximum range, and begin the attrition of the attacking force as early as possible. Considering the nature of the terrain in Western Europe, with limitations in line-of-sight visibility likely to be worsened by battlefield obscuration, it is doubtful that existing antitank guided missiles can be employed at the limit of their 3,000 meter range capability. Instead, war games and studies indicate that the main battle will be fought at a range of less than 1,200 to 1,500 meters.

The division rear area is located behind the main battle area. The division commander insures that combat service support is projected forward from this area to sustain the defending forces. It is here that ammunition supply points, and petroleum, oil and lubricant distribution points are located, as well as the administrative and communications facilities. Because the rear area is vulnerable to air attack, as well as to airmobile, airborne, or air-landed attacks, it is necessary for the units located in the rear area to be trained and prepared for self-defense. Any maneuver reserve elements from the division or corps that might also be located in the rear area would add to the defense capability.

One of the main features of the active defense is the size of the reserve. The reserve is usually small—one or two battalions at division level. This allows the commander to bring maximum firepower to bear against the attacking enemy, and defeat him during the early stages of battle.

Determining how the battle will be fought is the responsibility of each tactical commander at each level of commande. In the defense, the commander has two basic alternatives—weight the defense or balance it. In the weighted defense, the commander is able to estimate the most feasible enemy avenue of approach, and concentrate forces in that area while accepting risks in the remainder of the sector. However, if the nature of the terrain does not restrict vehicular movement, and if the enemy situation is vague, the forward brigades of the division might be relatively balanced to provide flexibility. In the latter case, the commander can only concentrate his forces after the battle has begun and the major enemy thrust identified.

The Offense

Once the enemy attack has been halted, it will be necessary for the defender to seize the initiative and mount offensive operations to drive the enemy back and reestablish control over lost ground. The division commander will seek to concentrate overwhelming combat power in a ratio of at least six to one at the point where he wishes to conduct his penetration. Forces are concentrated on a very narrow front, with the commander again accepting the risk in the thinned-out areas. The attacking force will maneuver over covered and concealed routes, with movement supported by well timed and intense artillery and tactical air strikes designed to suppress the defending enemy. The attack is continuous, with enemy strongpoints bypassed to be engaged by follow-on forces. Mechanized and armored forces attempt to penetrate deep into the enemy rear, and disrupt his ability effectively to continue the defensive. Offensive operations would continue until such time as the enemy was destroyed or his willingness to continue hostile operations was visibly diminished.

Four major types of offensive operations are undertaken by US ground forces—movement to contact, attack (hasty and deliberate), exploitation, and the pursuit. In addition, there are limited operations such as reconnaissance in force, the raid, and the spoiling attack, or tactical deception operations such as the feint, demonstration, ruse or display.

A movement to contact is conducted to gain or reestablish contact with the enemy, and when the situation is vague. It is characterized by control at the lowest possible level of command, the ability to reinforce leading forces rapidly,

Below: Night attack by Shillelagh guided missiles fired by M60A2 battle tanks. Since 1960 the US Army has needed a completely new battle tank; delays and cost-escalation have become crucial.

and once contact is established, responsive field artillery and air support. The force conducting the movement to contact will normally be made up of a covering force, advance guard, flank guard, rear guard and the main body.

The covering force is designed to develop the situation, prevent delays of the main body, and provide early warning to the tactical commander. The commander allocates sufficient strength to the covering force, to include attack helicopters, field artillery, air defense artillery, and engineers, to allow it to operate well forward of the main body, and fight battles short of a decisive commitment.

The flank and rear guards are designed to protect the main body, and to provide early warning should a threat arise. If required to operate beyond the range of supporting artillery, the force is allocated sufficient supporting means to fight with relative independence from the main body similar to covering force. However, to do so requires the division commander to evaluate the resultant risk to the main body as a result of diminished firepower.

The advance guard assists the covering force, and insures the uninterrupted movement of the main body.

The main body consists of the bulk of the

Below: AH-1G HueyCobras at Norfolk, Virginia, awaiting shipment to Europe for Exercise Reforger in August 1976, give a hint of the Army's investment in rotary-wing hardware.

division combat power. At division level, movement to contact is usually conducted on multiple columns to take advantage of available road nets, and prevent the enemy from slowing movement by using small pockets of resistance. When the enemy is encountered, the commander will commit forces from the main body to maintain the momentum of the advance. Once the main body is committed, movement to contact ceases, and the assaulting division begins its attack.

If, during a movement to contact, the division encounters the main enemy defensive positions and locates a point where the enemy is weak, surprised or poorly organized, a hasty attack is conducted from the line of march without hesitation or major preparation. However, when the commander encounters a well-organized enemy defense in prepared positions, time is required to concentrate sufficient combat power—usually five or six to one—to overcome the defensive system by conducting a deliberate attack.

In determining how the attack is to be conducted, the commander has the option of weighting his attack by concentrating forces at a perceived weak point, or balancing his attack should the terrain or nature of the resistance so dictate. Reserves, which are small in number, will be committed to maintain the momentum of the attack to widen the point of the penetration, destroy bypassed forces, defeat a counterattack, or exploit where the situation permits.

An exploitation is initiated when the enemy

has recognizable difficulty in maintaining his defensive position. This will largely be determined by the division commander when he receives reports that enemy fire has diminished, the volume of captured prisoners has increased, large quantities of abandoned enemy materiel have been encountered, and artillery and command positions have been overrun. At this time, the division commander reinforces his success by shifting fire and maneuver units to the point of greatest opportunity. After notifying corps of his success, corps will normally provide another force to follow-and-support by clearing bypassed pockets of resistance and taking over some of the tasks of the exploiting force. Once the exploitation has begun, the commander deploys his attacking forces on multiple routes to increase the speed of the exploitation. Command at this time is relegated to the lowest possible level.

The pursuit is the culmination of a successful attack and exploitation, and is designed to cut off and annihilate the retreating enemy. It differs from the exploitation in that it focuses on the destruction of the enemy and emphasizes where possible enveloping or encircling them.

Direct pressure forces are employed to prevent the enemy from breaking contact or reconstituting his defense. The attack is continuous, day and night, and is oriented on the enemy rather than the seizure of terrain objectives.

The commander attempts to place an enveloping force behind the enemy to crush the enemy between the direct pressure force and the

enveloping force. The enveloping force is also a combined arms force capable of fighting sustained independent operations. If the enveloping force is unable to outdistance the enemy to get behind him, it will attack the flanks, and another enveloping force will be designated by the commander.

A successful attack requires continuous combat support and combat service support to sustain the weapon systems essential for maintaining the momentum of the attack. Field artillery, engineers, air defense, and other combat support and combat service support elements carefully plan movement to keep pace with the maneuver elements. Ammunition and fuel, critical to sustaining the battle, either on the offense or defense, are of prime importance. For this reason the support commander and combat commanders work together as a team to keep the combined arms team moving and shooting.

Deployment Considerations

While most ground forces are organized, equipped, and trained to fight in a European environment, building around the basic maneuver battalion or employing specially trained forces such as air assault, airborne or rangers, allows for ready deployment anywhere in the world should the need arise. It should be noted that certain modifications are currently being made to the basic organization of forces deployed to Europe. More tanks have been added for greater fire power and mobility, and a greater number of antitank guided missiles to combat enemy tank strength.

Theoretically, the conventional ground force is capable of fighting in a tactical nuclear environment without modification. No one has actually experienced a battle using tactical nuclear weapons; thus it is not clear precisely how thoroughly dual-capable existing organization, equipment and tactics are.

It should be apparent that a comparison between US and Soviet tactics indicates few substantive differences. What distinguishes the two forces is (a) that NATO forces have superior knowledge of the terrain over which at least the initial battles will be fought, technically superior equipment, a sustaining logistical support capability, and the flexibility and tactical latitude accorded the commanders at all levels, and (b) that the Soviets/WTO possess

Below: October 1975 and one of the first MABs (Mobile Assault Bridge) in Europe returns across the Donau near Ingolstadt, West Germany, for another load of vehicles of the 1st Armored Division.

Table 4: US Maneuver Forces mix and Locations

Armored Divisions
Ansbach, Germany
1st Armored Division
6 Armored   5 Mechanized

Fort Hood, Texas
2nd Armored Division
5 Armored   5 Mechanized
(3d Brigade in Germany)
(2 Armored   1 Mechanized)*

Frankfurt, Germany
3d Armored Division
6 Armored   5 Mechanized

Fort Hood, Texas
1st Cavalry Division
4 Armored   4 Mechanized
(2 Armored   1 Mechanized)*

Mechanized Divisions
Wurzburg, Germany
3d Infantry Division
6 Mechanized   4 Armored

Fort Carson, Colorado
4th Infantry Division
5 Mechanized   5 armored
(3d Brigade in Europe)
(1 Mechanized)

Fort Polk, Louisiana
5th Infantry Division
2 Armored   1 Mechanized (3 Infantry)*

Bad Kreuznach, Germany
8th Infantry Division
6 Mechanized   5 Armored

Fort Riley, Kansas
1st Infantry Division
5 Mechanized   5 Armored
(3d Brigade in Europe)
(1 Mechanized)*

Infantry Divisions
Korea
2nd Infantry Division
5 Infantry   2 Mechanized   1 Armored
(Still has HJ Battalion)

Fort Ord, California
7th Infantry Division
6 Infantry   (3 Infantry)*

Fort Lewis, Washington
9th Infantry Division
7 Infantry   1 Mechanized   1 Armored

Fort Stewart, Georgia
24th Infantry Division
6 Infantry   (1 Armored   3 Mechanized)*

Hawaii
25th Infantry Division
6 Infantry

Air Assault Divisions
Fort Campbell, Kentucky
101st AASLT Division
9 Infantry (Ambl)   1 Tank Dest   1 Attack Hel

Airborne Divisions
Fort Bragg, North Carolina
82nd Airborne Division
9 Infantry (Abn)   1 Armored (Lt)

6th ACCB
Fort Hood, Texas
2 Attack Battalions   1 Air Cavalry Battalion

172d Infantry Brigade (Sep)
Fort Richardson, Alabama
3 Infantry

197th Infantry Brigade
Fort Benning, Georgia
1 Infantry   1 Mechanized   1 Armored (1 Mech)*

194th Armored Brigade
Fort Knox, Kentucky
2 Armored   1 Mechanized

Berlin Brigade
3 Infantry   1 Armored Company

193d Infantry Brigade
Panama
2 Infantry   1 Mechanized

2d Armored Cavalry Regiment
Nürnburg, Germany
3 Cavalry Squadron

3d Armored Cavalry Regiment
Fort Bliss, Texas
3 Cavalry Squadron

11th Armored Cavalry Regiment
Fulda, Germany
3 Cavalry Squadron

Ranger Battalions
Fort Stewart, Georgia
1st Battalion (Ranger)   75th Infantry

Fort Lewis, Washington
2d Battalion (Ranger)   75th Infantry

Airborne Task Force (TF)
Italy
1 Airborne (+)

Totals (Active/Roundout)
Infantry 39/9   Armored 48/6
Airborne 10   Armored Cavalry 21
Ambulance 9   Air Cavalry 6
Mechanized 47/8   Attack 3
Ranger 2   Tank Des 1

*Reserve Component Roundout Battalions.

important numerical advantages in numbers of troops, tanks, artillery tubes, and the like. The Soviets regard the firm, centralized control at high levels of command to be one of their main strengths. Conversely, Western analysts view this to be one of their potentially most debilitating weaknesses.

Trends

The war in the Middle East in 1973 has provided some possible insights into the nature of warfare in the immediate future. Technical advances in equipment, more accurate firepower systems, and greater destructiveness of weapons will make the modern battlefield devastatingly lethal. A single tank battle can affect planned tank distribution for as much as two years. A single well-positioned attack helicopter may be expected to destroy tanks at a fifteen to one ratio in a single engagement. Tank strength remains the foundation of the combined arms team in the Western world. But tanks are expensive to build, expensive to deploy, and expensive to lose. US tanks and those of some NATO allies have undergone considerable systems improvement—improved armor, which may invalidate existing antitank concepts, more accurate range finders that will increase the first-round hit capability and more lethal tank ammunition that will increase the kill potential.

For the first time in modern warfare, the infantryman has the capability of killing his most feared opponent—the tank—at ranges greater than the tank itself can effectively shoot. Already the TOW antitank guided missile has a high probability of hit and kill. Every effort will be made to suppress the antitank guided missile (ATGM) gunner by use of high explosive and smoke rounds. The successor to the highly effective TOW is a missile that can be launched, and once fired, will guide in on a laser-designated

Right: As far as possible all combat troops are trained to fight efficiently in all extremes of climate. Here men of the 10th Special Forces Group ski through woods near Fort Drum, NY. First and third men are towing a supply sledge.

Below: The tailfins flick open as a TOW (Tube-launched, Optically tracked, Wire guided) anti-tank missile leaves its Jeep-mounted launcher. This missile has the great advantages of high flight speed, and such wide use by many armies that its price is very low.

target without the use of wire control. As for overcoming the obscuration problem, future launchers (to include tank gun systems) will detect their targets by the heat they emit through the use of thermal imagery sights.

Increased lethality in conventional munitions is signalling the end of the practical employment of massed, dismounted, and exposed infantrymen. As a result, more helicopters, and improved armored personnel carriers will provide the mobility and protection needed by the infantrymen. These vehicles will not simply move the force into battle, but will support it by fire throughout the attack and have a tank killing capability.

One of the greatest technological advances found on the modern battlefield is in the area of artillery munitions. US artillery has made revolutionary advances in lethality to the point where it is four times more lethal against personnel targets than its World War II forerunner. Precision guided projectiles fired from a standard cannon now have the capability of destroying single tanks with a high probability of first round success. Artillery is not only more lethal, and more accurate, but it is also more versatile. It can effectively deliver small scatterable antitank mines in the path of an advancing

tank assault, or it can deliver rounds that will rapidly clear wide areas of an enemy deployed minefield. Besides enhanced ability to kill, US artillery can be rapidly deployed with the advancing tanks and armored personnel carriers. All artillery currently found in the US armored and mechanized infantry divisions are entirely self-propelled. The US has also re-learned the importance of the multiple rocket launcher. This system is expected in the inventory in the not too distant future.

The high mobility and armor-killing capability of attack helicopters already makes these weapon platforms capable of defeating the entire spectrum of battlefield targets. Ongoing development of the advanced attack helicopter includes an advanced fire control system to provide extended range target acquisition and engagement, and a laser integrated Hellfire missile system that enables the gunner to "fire-and-forget" while enjoying a greater probability of a first round kill. In addition, product improvement of the existing 2.75-in aerial rocket and the introduction of the 30mm cannon will further improve the killing capability of the attack helicopter.

Night vision aids permit night maneuvers and engagement similar to those conducted during

daytime. Passive image intensifiers, impossible to be detected by the enemy, are currently in use on tanks, helicopters, and armored personnel carriers enabling defending or assaulting forces to engage the enemy at night in a like manner to daylight operations. Passive thermal sights, capable of penetrating smoke, atmospheric haze, light foliage, and camouflage, will also soon find their way into the inventory. These night vision aids will be of particular use during the first four or five days of battle since Soviet doctrine insists that pressure be maintained night and day. However, it is fully expected that the intensity of night combat will diminish with time since the combatants need to eat, rest, and resupply in order to sustain future operations.

The United States currently has nothing to equal the Soviet chemical warfare capability, although older systems remain stockpiled. Treaty restrictions on the production and use of chemical munitions have been closely adhered to by the United States. Even though the Soviet Union is a signatory of this treaty, chemical munitions are still produced and tested in the USSR, and military doctrine calls for the use of chemical warfare as a matter of course. Should the United States undertake to develop a viable chemical warfare capability, it is estimated

that it would take two or three years before sufficient chemical munitions would be available.

Progress is being made in the human engineering aspects of the modern Army. US divisions are being organizationally fine-tuned to reduce administrative distractions for small unit leaders, since these key individuals may be called upon to make increasingly crucial combat decisions and employ ever more complex technology on the battlefield.

Examples of current organizational changes which affect combat operations are the combat electronic warfare intelligence battalion (CEWI) and the tactical operations system (TOS). The CEWI integrates intelligence and electronic warfare planning and operations at the division level, thus centralizing control of radar, sensors, jamming equipment, etc., under the division commander's direction. TOS is designed to provide automated support to the command and control functions of the division and corps headquarters. Automated equipment will assist the commander in the critical decisions demanded by the high technology battlefield and the tactics this entails.

The US Army's response to a potential enemy enjoying numerical superiority has been shown to encompass both tactical techniques and

weapons technology. Another aspect of this response is the use of reserve component forces. The Army is currently authorized to maintain some 660,000 men and women in reserve component units. Some of these units are combat formations, some are combat support and some are combat service support. Reserve component units designated as "Round Out" habitually train with specific active Army organizations and in effect constitute organic elements of their designated divisions. In the event of hostilities, these units would deploy with their active organizations to facilitate training while still others become theater (of operations) assets when activated and deployed in accordance with existing mobilization plans. (See the chapter on reserve forces for details.)

Below: The Roland mobile SHORADS (short-range air-defense system) comprises two missiles ready to fire in tubes plus two four-round drum magazines, all carried with the radars on an M109R AFV. Despite massive engineering effort by the US licensees of this Franco-German system, Boeing and Hughes, the US Army version is very late and is costing considerably more than the estimates.

Tactical Nuclear Weapons and US Military Capabilities*

The changing strategic balance between the US and the USSR together with growing Soviet conventional military capabilities, especially in Europe, have in recent years revived interest in the role of tactical nuclear weapons in US defense planning. Some analysts have responded to the growing Soviet challenge by advocating greater reliance on tactical nuclear weapons for both deterrence and defense; others have argued that the increased Soviet threat, including deployment by the USSR of more numerous and sophisticated theater nuclear weapons in Europe, renders ever more doubtful claims that tactical nuclear weapons add to the credibility of the Western deterrent against war in Europe and provide useful military options in the event of war.

Tactical nuclear weapons, of course, have been a source of considerable controversy since the middle 1950s. There has never been any consensus among analysts, for example, on precisely what constitutes a tactical nuclear weapon. One approach stresses the explosive power of warheads as the key indicator. The yields of US weapons deployed in Europe range from the sub-kiloton level to more than a megaton. The latter weapons have an explosive power seventy times that of the bomb which devastated Hiroshima. Emphasis on the explosive power of bombs and warheads, moreover, tends to downgrade the significance of the ranges of delivery systems and the value of targets. An attack on Moscow which employed even the smallest nuclear weapons would certainly have to be judged a strategic attack. On the other hand, even very large strategic weapons can be employed in a tactical mode, and strategic delivery systems (such as the B-52) can be utilized tactically. For these and related reasons, most analysts now prefer to discuss tactical nuclear weapons in terms of modes of deployment and the types of targets against which they are to be utilized. Some attempt to avoid the term altogether, and talk instead about "theater nuclear weapons".

The origins of the existing United States tactical nuclear stockpile can be traced back to the late 1940s. As early as 1949 General Omar Bradley, the Chairman of the Joint Chiefs of Staff, proposed that the United States deploy tactical nuclear weapons in Europe to counter Soviet advantages in conventional military power. Testing of such weapons began in 1951, and by October 1953 the initial deployment of the 280mm "atomic cannon" in Europe was begun. "Regulus" and "Honest John" missiles followed in 1954.

The deployment of these systems, however, was not accompanied by the development of a carefully worked out doctrine for their use in war. Top Eisenhower Administration officials basically considered their deployment to represent the extension of the doctrine of massive retaliation to Europe and Northeast Asia. MC-14/2, for example, which laid down basic strategy for NATO during this period, called for a relatively light "shield" of conventional forces to serve as a tripwire to activate the US strategic "sword" in the event of a Soviet attack. Tactical nuclear weapons, as American planners saw it, further reduced the need for large conventional forces along the Iron Curtain. Such weapons were believed to afford distinct advantages to the side seeking to defend itself against an attack, and to compensate for Soviet advantages in conventional military power, especially manpower, at a bearable cost.

Insofar as attention was paid to the development of doctrine for the actual use of tactical nuclear weapons, analysts argued that allied conventional forces would "channel" first echelon elements of an invading force into massed formations which would constitute convenient targets for tactical nuclear systems.

*Editor's note: the following analysis was contributed by Dr James E. Dornan, Jr.

it was usually assumed as well that the use of tactical nuclear weapons against appropriate communist bloc targets behind the lines would seriously disrupt second and third echelon formations and help bring the attack quickly to a halt.

Almost immediately, however, doubts arose concerning the validity of such analyses. Some commentators challenged the assertion that tactical nuclear weapons would provide a cheaper means of defense against a communist bloc attack, and denied that a nuclear equipped NATO force would require fewer troops. It was only a matter of time, they suggested, before the USSR also would deploy tactical nuclear systems; since a war in Europe in which both sides utilized nuclear weapons would result in extremely high casualty rates, they argued, NATO would require far larger forces than would be necessary to fight a conventional war. Other analysts denied that tactical nuclear weapons necessarily favored the defense. While the deployment of nuclear systems with NATO forces might act as a deterrent against the massing of troops and armor, Pact deployment of similar weapons would also force defending NATO forces to spread out, rendering NATO defense lines vulnerable to penetration by small mechanized units. Finally, grave doubts were expressed concerning the adequacy of NATO's command, control and communications systems for controlling a nuclear war in the theater. Widespread fears arose in Europe, especially after the notorious *Carte Blanche* exercise in 1955, that any use of nuclear weapons in response to a Soviet attack would result in civilian casualties on a massive scale and the consequent destruction of all of Western Europe.

Above: The Pershing 1A is by far the most powerful battlefield missile system in the West. The heavy tracked vehicles of Pershing 1 have been replaced by a smaller number of wheeled vehicles, all of them airliftable in a C-130. A more accurate Mk II missile is in prospect.

Such doubts and fears led over time to new emphases in discussions by Western leaders of the role of nuclear weapons in the defense of Europe. Increasingly the role of theater nuclear weapons in *deterring* a Soviet attack was emphasized, and the *warfighting* role of such systems played down. American articulations of the doctrine of "flexible response" as developed under the Kennedy Administration, in fact, essentially argued that the role of such systems was to deter the use of tactical nuclear weapons by the Warsaw Pact; NATO, conversely, would employ such weapons only as a last resort—in the event of an "overwhelming enemy conventional breakthrough", in the words of a recent Department of Defense posture statement. Such statements, of course, have generated fears of their own, especially in Europe. Would NATO commanders receive permission to employ tactical nuclear weapons in sufficient time to influence the outcome of the conflict? Would the use of such weapons late in the game, presumably after the Warsaw Pact had achieved substantial breakthroughs along the FEBA (Forward Edge of the Battle Area), succeed in halting the attack? Given the size of many currently deployed nuclear bombs and warheads and the ranges of existing delivery systems, the utilization of such systems after Warsaw Pact breaksthrough would mean that most of the weapons would be detonated on

West German soil, with devastating impact on the industrial infrastructure and civilian population of the FRG. Reflections on these and related issues have led most European analysts to reject the American formulation of the doctrine of flexible response, and to stress instead the deterrent role of NATO-deployed nuclear systems.

By December of 1966, in any event, then-Secretary of Defense Robert S. McNamara announced that there were approximately 7,000 US nuclear warheads deployed in Western Europe. In 1968 Defense Secretary Clark Clifford stated that the total had reached 7,200. Some sources believe that by 1970 there were more than 10,000 nuclear warheads in Europe, although in that year obsolescent "Honest John" and "Sergeant" missiles began to be withdrawn and the level gradually receded once again to about 7,000. Some "Honest John" and "Sergeant" missiles remain, although these are gradually being replaced by the newer "Lance" tactical missile. The US also deploys nuclear warheads for "Pershing" missiles, "Nike-Hercules" anti-aircraft missiles (which also could be employed in a surface-to-surface mode), nuclear projectiles for some 500 8-inch and 155mm howitzers, and a number of atomic demolition munitions. The following chart lists the ground-launched tactical nuclear systems now deployed with US NATO-based forces in Europe. It should be noted, however, that there are also 72 "Pershings" and 20 "Sergeant" missiles plus a number of nuclear-capable 8-in and 155mm howitzers in the hands of the FRG, 44 "Lance" missiles deployed by the FRG, Great Britain and Italy, and 112 "Honest Johns" in the hands of the smaller NATO countries. France has also deployed 24 "Pluton" missiles with a range of 72 nautical miles and warheads with a yield estimated at approximately 20 KT.

In addition, the United States has deployed about 550 nuclear-capable tactical aircraft in the European theater. These consists primarily of F-4s and F-111s, plus A-6 and A-7 attack aircraft deployed aboard carriers in the Mediterranean. The new F-16 will be nuclear-capable. Nuclear bombs delivered by such aircraft have yields ranging from .1 KT to 1+ MT, although

Ground-launched Tactical Nuclear Weapons Deployed with US NATO-based Forces					
Name of System		Number Deployed	Max. Range (nm)	Yield of Warhead	IOC
MGR1B	Honest John	(being replaced)	22	20 KT	1953
MGM29A	Sergeant	(being replaced)	84	sub-to-low KT	1962
MGM52C	Lance	36	70	1 KT[1]	1973
MGM31A	Pershing[2]	108	395	60–400 KT[3]	1962
	Nike-Hercules	144	20	1 KT	1958
M110A1	8-in howitzer	c. 200	8.75[4]	sub-to-low KT	1964[5]
M109A1[6]	155mm howitzer	c. 300	9.47[7]	sub-to-low KT	1962[5]
Atomic Demolition Munitions (ADM)		n.a.	3	sub-to-low KT	1953

Source: International Institute of Strategic Studies, *The Military Balance*, 1977–1978; Jeffrey Record, *U.S. Nuclear Weapons in Europe* (Washington, DC: The Brookings Institution, 1974); Eric C. Ludvigsen, "Weapons Directory, 1977", *Army* (October, 1977).
1. Can be fitted with a variable-yield nuclear warhead in which the explosive energy is selected before launching.
2. The Pershing II, now under development, will utilize a radar area guidance system, and will be capable of CEPs measured in tens of feet.
3. Most published sources indicate that the bulk of the Pershings are armed with 400 KT warheads.
4. The M110A2, now being procured, will be capable of a range of 11.5nm (and of 15.6nm when firing the M650 rocket-assisted projectile now under development). A new nuclear round, the XM753, is also being developed for the M110A2.
5. IOC dates refer to early versions of the M109 and M110.
6. The M109A1 is the longer-cannoned version of the M109, and is now the standard general-support artillery weapon deployed with US Army units. Procurement is expected to be completed in 1979.
7. The M109A1 is also capable of ranges up to 15nm when firing the M549 rocket-assisted projectile.

most are said to be in the high KT range. Some —like the B-61 bomb—are variable-yield weapons. There are also well over 1,000 nuclear-capable aircraft in the air forces of the West European states. It is worth noting, however, that it is unlikely that more than a small fraction of these aircraft could be used to deliver nuclear ordnance in the event of war, given the demand for conventional battlefield support which would inevitably arise.

Finally, numbered among the 7,000 US nuclear warheads are a variety of sea-based ASW systems such as ASROC, SUBROC and ASTOR torpedoes and depth charges as well as "Talos" and "Terrier" surface-to-air missiles. None of these, however, would be useful against land targets, and many are being withdrawn from service due to obsolescence in any case.

Precise data concerning US nuclear systems deployed in Asia have never been made available. Published sources suggest, however, that there are approximately 300 nuclear weapons of all types deployed in Korea. These presumably include at present projectiles for 155mm and

8-in artillery pieces and a variety of air-deliverable nuclear bombs. All of the artillery projectiles and perhaps the Air Force weapons as well are scheduled to be withdrawn as US ground troops are pulled out of Korea over the next four years.

During the tenure of James A. Schlesinger as Secretary of Defense, United States planners began to give serious attention to the possibility of a failure of deterrence in Europe, and to reconsider ways in which nuclear weapons might be employed in the event of a Warsaw Pact attack. Although still emphasizing the deterrent role of US strategic and theater based nuclear systems, Schlesinger sought credible options for the actual utilization of

Below: If the development of a neutron warhead had not been terminated it would probably have been built into 203mm (8in) shells for the various US Army howitzers of this calibre, such as those fitted to the M110 SP armored vehicle shown here.

	Troops in open killed by heat/blast (red) or, several days later, radiation (blue)
	Crew killed inside
	Electronics destroyed by EMP; crew probably later succumb
	Tank knocked out but crew might survive (whereas with enhanced radiation bomb crew would die eventually)
	Radiation
	Reduced heat/blast effects
	Heat/blast effects
	Electromagnetic pulse (EMP)

such weapons in the event that deterrence failed, and he consequently became an advocate of the modernization of the US tactical nuclear force. Recent and impending advances in military technology have made possible the development and deployment of nuclear weapons which would both improve the military effectiveness of NATO's defense forces and avoid wholesale slaughter of civilians in the process. Technology either in hand or under development, for example, will greatly improve the accuracy with which ordnance can be delivered on targets. Electro-optical, laser-designated, infra-red seeking, beacon-guided and map-matching guidance systems are being developed and deployed both for conventional and nuclear weapons which will make possible higher "target" kill probabilities and at the same time permit the use of lower-yield nuclear weapons and the greater use of conventional ordnance against certain classes of targets. New methods are being developed for estimating desired target damage and for matching weapons and targets. Finally, so-called "tailored effects" weapons, i.e. weapons designed to

achieve specific military purposes, are being developed. So-called shallow-burst nuclear munitions, for example, detonated at sufficient depths in the ground, can minimize or eliminate fireball effects on the surface, thus reducing unwanted collateral damage to civilian population, buildings, and so on.

Of the various special effects weapons now under development, the so-called neutron bomb, more properly the enhanced radiation (ER) warhead, has received the most publicity. Contrary to many press reports, the ER warhead is not entirely new, nor is it a "people killer" weapon which is somehow less humane than existing nuclear weapons. Research and development on the ER warhead began in 1960. It is a nuclear weapon with special characteristics: it employs a relatively low-yield fission reaction to trigger a fusion reaction, and thus can release up to 80 per cent of its yield in very high-energy, deadly neutrons with a longer range than neutrons generated by standard fission weapons. It thus has a larger effective radius against personnel than normal fission weapons of the same yield, which kill primarily by blast and

heat. High velocity heavy neutrons easily penetrate the human body; moreover, while modern tanks are relatively impervious to blast and heat, such neutrons can easily penetrate armor, and react with it to produce deadly gamma radiation.

Such characteristics mean that lower yield weapons of the ER type, with reduced blast effects and lower levels of thermal radiation, and little or no fallout, can be used to perform certain military tasks. The use of such weapons would result in substantially less damage to nearby civilian and military structures. A 1-KT enhanced radiation weapon can deliver 5,000 to 8,000 rads (the standard measure of radiation) up to a distance of one-half mile, but would have little impact beyond a radius of a mile and a half. It would thus be highly useful against massing enemy troop and armor formations, even on the highly populated and heavily industrialized North German plain. ER weapons would also be especially valuable to defending forces, which can dig in and shield themselves against retaliatory nuclear attacks by the attacking force—even an attacking force equip-

1KT ENHANCED RADIATION (NEUTRON) BOMB

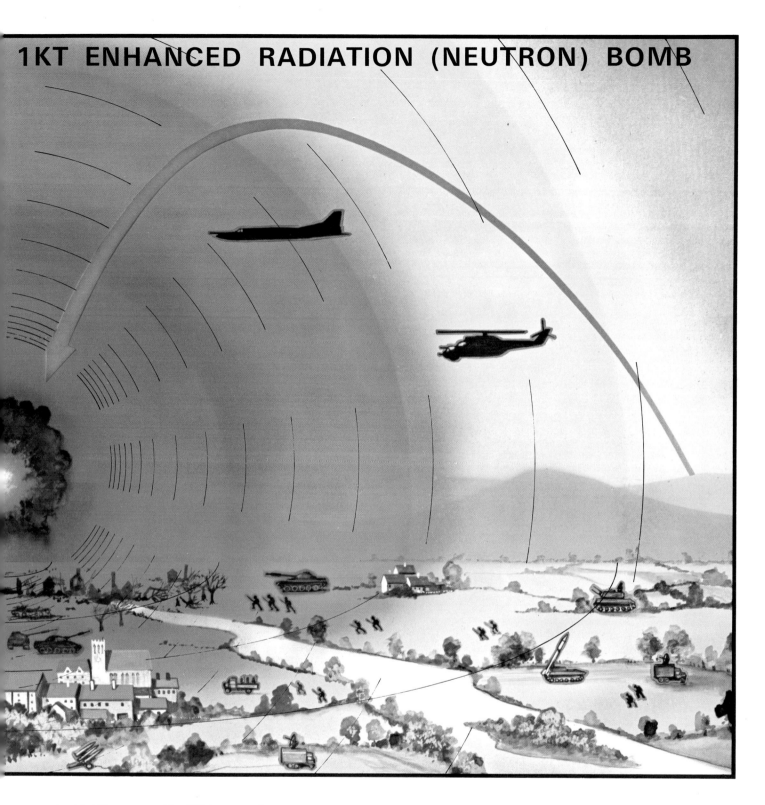

ped with ER weapons. The US is presently developing the W70-3 warhead for the "Lance" missile, and the W70-9 1-KT projectile for the 8-in howitzer; a projectile for the 155mm howitzer is also under discussion.

The deployment of ER weapons with US forces in Europe would by no means solve all of the military problems presently confronting the NATO alliance. An effective NATO deterrent, not to mention a viable alliance warfighting capability, depends upon the capabilities of the total military force at NATO's disposal. But ER weapons, particularly if utilized in connection with the new high-accuracy delivery systems now becoming available, could certainly enhance NATO's capacity to deal effectively with a Warsaw Pact mechanized assault, with substantially reduced destruction of civilian assets in the battle area. This would be particularly true if the weapons were utilized before massive Pact armored penetrations through the FEBA had occurred.

Whatever the decision on deployment of ER weapons, however, the debate over the role of tactical nuclear systems is certain to continue.

This diagram attempts the difficult task of illustrating some of the effects of a conventional nuclear weapon (left half of drawing) compared with a neutron bomb (right half). The nuclear weapon is of 10 kilotons yield and the neutron bomb of 1 kiloton, and both are air-burst at a height of 330ft (100m). (The blue trajectory shows a possible rocket delivery.) A, B, C and D respectively denote radii from ground zero of 250, 880, 1,320 and 2,220 yards (229, 805, 1,207 and 2,030m). The entire area hit by the conventional weapon is desolate, affected by blast and heat (red). Yet inside the tank (foreground) the crew could survive and carry on fighting. In contrast the red area on the right is localised. EMP (electromagnetic pulse) effects are augmented, and would destroy the electronics in the radar vehicle (foreground) and in the overflying aircraft. Most important of all, the radiation (yellow) is enormously intensified on the right, killing the crews in the tanks and in the aircraft. The popular media misled the public in the West in suggesting the neutron bomb was intended to "kill humans but protect property". This misses the point, and there would be no point in protecting property about to be occupied by the enemy. The entire purpose behind the neutron bomb was to kill immediately or disable the crews of tanks, aircraft and other strongly protected manned weapons, which could not be readily knocked out in any other way except by painstakingly picking off each one with an individual counter-weapon.

US Ground Forces Weapons

Christopher F. Foss, Author of Jane's *World Armoured Fighting Vehicles*; author of several military reference books, including Salamander's *The Illustrated Encyclopedia of Tanks and Fighting Vehicles.*

This section describes and illustrates all major Army weapons, including armored fighting vehicles, artillery and small arms. Army guided missiles are covered in the US rockets and missiles section.

M48 Medium Tank

M48, M48A, M48A1, M48A2, M48A2C, M48A3, M48A5, M67, M67A1, M67A2, M48A VLB

Crew: 4. **Armament:** One 90mm gun M41; one 0·3in M1919A-4E1 machine-gun co-axial with the main armament (some have a 7·62mm M73 MG); one 0·5in machine-gun in commander's cupola. **Armor:** 12·7mm– 120mm (0·50–4·80in). **Dimensions:** Length (including main armament) 24ft 5in (7·442m); length (hull) 22ft 7in (6·882m); width 11ft 11in (3·631m); height (including cupola) 10ft 3in (3·124m). **Weight:** Combat 104,000lbs (47,173kg). **Ground pressure:** 11·80lb/in² (0·83kg/cm²). **Engine:** Continental AVDS-1790-2A 12-cylinder air-cooled diesel developing 750hp at 2,400rpm. **Performance:** Road speed 30mph (48km/h); range 288 miles (463km); vertical obstacle 3ft (0·915m); trench 8ft 6in (2·59m); gradient 60 per cent. **History:** Entered service with the United States Army in 1953. Used by Germany, Greece, Israel, Jordan, Morocco, Norway, Pakistan, South Korea, Spain, Taiwan, Thailand, Turkey, United States and Vietnam.

Once the M47 was authorized for production, development started on a new medium tank as the M47 was only a stop-gap measure. So in October 1950 Detroit Arsenal started design work on a new medium tank armed with a 90mm gun. This design study was completed two months later and

Above: An M67A1 in action in Vietnam in 1966 (picture by 1st Marine Division). The M67A1 has the gun replaced by the M7A1-6 flamethrower.

in December 1950 Chrysler was given a contract to complete the design work and build six prototypes under the designation T48. The first of these prototypes had to be completed by December 1951. Production started in 1952 and first deliveries were made to the US Army the following year. The M48, as it was now called, was followed in production by the M60, essentially an M48A3 with a 105mm gun and other detailed changes, production of this model being undertaken at the Detroit Tank Plant.

The hull of the M48 is of cast armour construction, as is the turret. The driver is seated at the front of the hull with the other three crew members located in the turret, with the commander and gunner on the right and the loader on the left. The engine and transmission are at the rear of the hull, and are separated from the fighting compartment by a fireproof bulkhead. The suspension is of the torsion-bar type and consists of six road wheels, with the drive sprocket at the rear and the idler at the front. Depending on the model there are between three and five track-return rollers, and some models have a small track tensioning wheel between the sixth road wheel and the drive sprocket. The main armament consists of a 90mm gun with an elevation of +20° and a depression of −9°, traverse being 360°. A 0·3in M1919A4E1 machine-gun is mounted co-axially with the main armament, although most M48s in US (except on the M48A1 which has a simple mount). This cupola can be traversed through 360°, and the machine-gun can be elevated from −10° to +60°.

The M48 can be fitted with a dozer blade, if required, at the front of the hull. All M48s have infra-red driving lights and some an infra-red/white searchlight mounted over the main armament. The type can ford to a depth of 4ft (1·219m) without preparation or 8ft (2·438m) with the aid of a kit.

The first model to enter service was the M48, and this has a simple cupola for the commander, with the machine-gun mounted externally. The second model was the M48C, which was for training use only as it has a mild steel hull. The M48A1 was followed by the M48A2, which has many improvements including a fuel-injection system for the engine and larger capacity fuel tanks. The M48A2C was a slightly modified M48A2. The M48A3 was a significant improvement as this has a diesel engine, which increases the vehicle's operational range considerably, and a number of other modifications including a different fire-control system. Latest model is the M48A5, essentially an M48A1 or M48A2 with modifications including a new 105mm gun, new tracks, a 7·62mm M60D co-axial machine-gun and a similar weapon on the loader's hatch, plus many other detail modifications. Three flamethrower tanks were developed: the M67 (using an M48A1 chassis), the M67A1 (using an M48A2 chassis) and the M67A2 (using an M48A3 chassis). Also in service is an M48 Armoured Vehicle-Launched Bridge. This has a scissors bridge which can be laid over gaps up to 60ft (18·288m) in width.

Below: An M48A5, used only by National Guard units, fitted with an M60-type turret with 105mm gun and Xenon searchlight (above the main gun).

M60 Main Battle Tank

M60, M60A1, M60A2, M60A3, M60 AVLB, M728 CEV

Crew: 4. **Armament:** One 105mm gun; one 7·62mm machine-gun co-axial with main armament; one 0·5in anti-aircraft machine-gun in commander's cupola. **Armor:** 12·7mm–120mm (0·50–4·80in). **Dimensions:** Length (gun forward) 30ft 6in (9·309m); length (hull) 22ft 9½in (6·946m); width 11ft 11in (3·631m); height 10ft 8in (3·257m). **Weight:** Combat 108,000lbs (48,987kg). **Ground pressure:** 11·24lb/in² (0·79kg/cm²). **Engine:** Continental AVDS-1790-2A 12-cylinder diesel developing 750bhp at 2,400rpm. **Performance:** Road speed 30mph (48km/h); range 310 miles (500km); vertical obstacle 3ft (0·914m); trench 8ft 6in (2·59m); gradient 60 per cent. **History:** The M60 entered service with the United States Army in 1960 and is also used by Austria, Ethiopia, Iran, Israel, Italy, Jordan, Saudi Arabia, Somalia, South Korea, Turkey and the United States Marine Corps.

In the 1950s the standard tank of the United States Army was the M48. In 1957 an M48 series tank was fitted with a new engine for trials purposes and this was followed by another three prototypes in 1958. Late in 1958 it was decided to arm the new tank with the British 105mm L7 series gun, to be built in the United States under the designation M68. In 1959 the first production order for the new tank, now called the M60, was placed with Chrysler, and the type entered production at Detroit Tank Arsenal in late 1959, with the first production tanks being completed the following year.

From late in 1962, the M60 was replaced in production by the M60A1, which has a number of improvements, the most important being the redesigned turret. The M60A1 has a turret and hull of all-cast construction. The driver is seated at the front of the hull with the other three crew members in the turret, commander and gunner on the right and the loader on the left. The engine and transmission are at the rear, the latter having one reverse and two forward ranges. The M60 has torsion-bar suspension and six road wheels, with the idler at the front and the drive sprocket at the rear; there are four track-return rollers. The 105mm gun has an elevation of +20° and a depression of −10°, and traverse is 360°. Both elevation and traverse are powered. A 7·62mm M73 machine-gun is mounted co-axially with the main armament and there is a 0·5in M85 machine-gun in the commander's cupola. The latter can be aimed and fired from within the turret, and has an elevation of +60° and a depression of −15°. Some 63 rounds of 105mm, 900 rounds

of 0·5in and 5,950 rounds of 7·62mm ammunition are carried. Infra-red driving lights are fitted as standard and an infra-red/white light is mounted over the main armament. All M60s have an NBC system. The tank can also be fitted with a dozer blade on the front of the hull. The M60 can ford to a depth of 4ft (1·219m) without preparation or 8ft (2·438m) with the aid of a kit. For deep fording operations a schnorkel can be fitted, allowing the M60 to ford to a depth of 13ft 6in (4·114m). The M60A2 was developed in 1964–65 and consists of an M60 chassis with a new turret armed with the 152mm gun/launcher, which can fire a variety of ammunition with a combustible cartridge case or a Shillelagh missile. The M60A2 entered production in 1966, but it was not until 1974 that the first M60A2 unit was formed as many problems were encountered with the whole Shillelagh/M60A2/Sheridan programme. The M60A2 is used only by the United States Army and just over 500 were built. The M60A2 also has a 7·62mm co-axial machine-gun and a 0·5in M85 anti-aircraft machine-gun. Thirteen Shillelagh missiles, and 33 rounds of conventional 152mm, 5,950 rounds of 7·62mm and 900 rounds of 0·5in ammunition are carried. A major improvement program for the M60A1 is currently under way, and this is scheduled to be completed in a few years time. Tanks built with these modifications will be known as the M60A3. Not all of these modifications have been cleared for production yet, but the full list of improvements is as follows: a stabilization system for the main armament, a laser rangefinder which is being developed by Hughes, new night-vision equipment, an improved engine and air cleaners, new tracks, a modified cupola and a thermal sleeve for the main armament. There are two other variants of the M60 series, the M728 Combat Engineer Vehicle and the M60 Armoured Vehicle-Launched Bridge.

Altogether some 4,000 M60 series MBTs have been built at the Detroit Tank Plant. Initially production was running at only 30 tanks per month, but since 1973–74 production has been increasing and today about 100 tanks are being built each month and production should continue until the early 1980s, when the tank will be replaced in production by the XM1.

Below left: This M60A1, pictured on NATO exercises in Turkey in 1977, is fitted with the prominent IR night vision unit on the front of the turret. This model of M60 will later benefit by a computer for cross-wind and other factors.

Below: The M60A2 was taken out of production after a mere 526 had been built. Like the Sheridan, technical problems caused delays and crippling escalation in costs.

Left: The high silhouette of the M60 cannot be eliminated, but much has been done by various update programmes to keep the M60 effective. This is an M60A2.

U.S. ARMY 9B-9057

XM1 Abrams Main Battle Tank

Crew: 4. **Armament:** One 105mm M68 gun; one 7·62mm machine-gun co-axial with main armament; one 0·5in machine-gun on commander's cupola; one 7·62mm machine-gun on loader's hatch (see text). **Armor:** Classified. **Dimensions:** Length (hull) 25ft 7in (7·797m); width 11ft 8in (3·555m); height (to top of turret) 7ft 8½in (2·438m). **Weight:** Combat 116,000lbs (52,616kg). **Engine:** Avco Lycoming AGT-T 1500 HP-C turbine developing 1,500hp. **Performance:** Road speed 45mph (72·4km/h); range 300 miles (482km); vertical obstacle 3ft 6in (1·066m); trench 9ft (2·743m); gradient 60 per cent. **History:** Will enter production in 1979 for the United States Army. (Note: Above data relate to prototype tanks, and production tanks may differ.)

In June 1973 contracts were awarded to both the Chrysler Corporation (which builds the M60 series) and the Detroit Diesel Allison Division of the General Motors Corporation (which built the MBT-70) to build prototypes of a new tank designated XM1, and later named the Abrams tank. These tanks were handed over to the US Army for trials in February 1976. In November 1976 it was announced after a four-month delay that the Chrysler tank would be placed in production. Production will commence at the Lima Army Modification Centre at Lima in 1979 at the rate of 10 tanks per month, increasing to 30 tanks per month the following year. When production of the M60 is completed at Detroit Tank Arsenal early in the 1980s, this will also become available for production of the XM1. The

United States Army has a requirement for 3,312 XM1s and the total cost of the program will be $4,900,000,000.

The first 300 or so tanks will have the standard 105mm rifled gun as fitted to the current M60A1, but later production tanks will have the German 120mm smooth-bore gun, which was selected in preference to the British 120mm rifled gun. To complicate matters even further, the XM1 may well use parts of the German Leopard 2(AV), which was specially developed for the United States under a memorandum of understanding signed in December 1974.

The XM1 has a hull and turret of the new British Chobham Armour, which is claimed to make the tank immune to attack from both missiles and tank guns. Its crew consists of four, the driver at the front, the commander and gunner on the right of the turret, and the loader on the left. The main armament consists of a standard 105mm gun developed in Britain and produced under license in the United States and a 7·62mm machine-gun is mounted co-axially with the main armament. A 0·5in machine-gun is mounted at the commander's station and a 7·62mm machine-gun at the loader's station. No details of the exact quantities of ammunition carried have been released yet. The main armament can be aimed and fired on the move. The gunner first selects the target, and then uses the laser range-finder to get its range and then depresses the firing switch. The computer makes the calculations and adjustments required to ensure a hit.

The fuel tanks are separated from the crew compartment by armored bulkheads and sliding doors are provided for the ammunition stowage areas. The suspension is of the torsion-bar type with rotary shock absorbers. The tank can travel across country at a speed of 35mph (56km/h) and

Left: One of the original Chrysler-built Abrams prototypes. It is tragic for the American military posture that this tank was not started ten years earlier, because the time and money spent fruitlessly on the MBT-70 did little to hasten this all-American AFV which should by 1980 be in production. In the meantime, cost-inflation has forced a rate of production so low that the M60 will still be No 1 tank in 1985.

accelerate from 0 to 20mph (0 to 32km/h) in six seconds, and this will make the XM1 a difficult tank to engage on the battlefield. The XM1 is powered by a turbine developed by Avco Lycoming, running on a variety of fuels including petrol, diesel and jet fuel. All the driver has to do is adjust a dial in his compartment. According to the manufacturers, the engine will not require an overhaul until the tank has travelled between 12,000 to 18,000 miles (19,312 to 28,968km), a great advance over existing tank engines. This engine is coupled to an Allison X 1100 transmission with four forward and two reverse gears. Great emphasis has been placed on reliability and maintenance, and it is claimed that the complete engine can be removed for replacement in under 30 minutes.

The XM1 is provided with an NBC system and a full range of night-vision equipment for the commander, gunner and driver. When the XM1 enters service as the M1 in 1980, the US Army should at last have the tank it has been wanting for 20 years.

It is not often realized that there are hundreds of sub contractors to a major program such as a tank. On the Chrysler XM1 there are eight major subcontractors: the government for the armament, Avco Lycoming for the engine, Cadillac Gage for the turret drive and the stabilization system, the Control Data Corporation for the ballistic computer, the Detroit Diesel Allison Division of General Motors for the transmission and the final drive, the Hughes Aircraft Company for the laser rangefinder, the Kollmorgen Corporation for the gunner's auxiliary sight and the Singer Kearfott Division for the line-of-sight data link.

Above right: A prototype firing its 105mm gun. In early 1978 the German smooth-bore gun was selected over the well-proven British rifled gun, apparently for political reasons.

Right: The frontal aspect of the XM1 is a great advance over the earlier M48 and M60, which are fully 3ft higher. Oddly, the front turret panels are vertical—but very thick.

Below: The XM1 has an infinitely better shape than the M60, much higher performance and British "Chobham" laminated armor. But a new tank is now many years late. (In this drawing the main gun is shortened to fit the page.)

US ARMY JE0001

M551 Sheridan Light Tank

Crew: 4. **Armament:** One 152mm gun/missile launcher; one 7·62mm machine-gun co-axial with main armament; one 0·5in anti-aircraft machine-gun; four smoke dischargers on each side of turret. **Armor:** Classified. **Dimensions:** Length 20ft 8in (6·299m); width 9ft 3in (2·819m); height (overall) 9ft 8in (2·946m). **Weight:** Combat 34,898lbs (15,830kg). **Ground pressure:** 6·96lb/in² (0·49kg/cm²). **Engine:** Detroit Diesel 6V53T six-cylinder diesel developing 300bhp at 2,800rpm. **Performance:** Road speed 45mph (70km/h); water speed 3·6mph (5·8km/h); range 373 miles (600km); vertical obstacle 2ft 9in (0·838m); trench 8ft 4in (2·54m); gradient 60 per cent. **History:** Entered service with United States Army in 1966 and still in service.

In August 1959 the United States Army established a requirement for a "new armoured vehicle with increased capabilities over any other weapon in its own inventory and that of any adversary". The following year the Allison Division of General Motors was awarded a contract to design a vehicle called the Armored Reconnaissance Airborne Assault Vehicle (ARAAV) to meet the requirement. The first prototype, designated XM551, was completed in 1962, and this was followed by a further 11 prototypes. Late in 1965 a production contract was awarded to Allison, and the first production vehicles were completed in 1966, these being known as the M551 or Sheridan. Production was completed in 1970 after 1,700 vehicles had been built.

The hull of the Sheridan is of all-aluminium construction whilst the turret is of welded steel. The driver is seated at the front of the hull and the other three crew members are in the turret, with the loader on the left and the gunner and commander on the right. The engine and transmission are at the rear of the hull. The suspension is of the torsion-bar type and consists of five road wheels, with the drive sprocket at the rear and the idler at the front. There are no track-return rollers. The most interesting feature of the Sheridan is its armament system. This consists of a 152mm gun/launcher which has an elevation of +19° and a depression of −8°, traverse being 360°. A 7·62mm machine-gun is mounted co-axially with the main armament, and there is a 0·5in Browning machine-gun on the commander's cupola. The latter cannot be aimed and fired from within the turret, and as a result of combat experience in Vietnam many vehicles have now been fitted with a shield for this weapon. The 152mm gun/launcher, later fitted to the M60A2 and MBT-70 tanks, can fire either a Shillelagh missile or a variety of conventional ammunition including HEAT-T-MP, WP and canister, all of them having a combustible cartridge case. The Shillelagh missile was developed by the United States Army Missile Command and the Philco-Ford Corporation, and has a maximum range of about 3,281 yards (3,000m). The missile is controlled by the gunner, who simply has to keep the crosshairs of his sight on the target to ensure a hit. This missile itself weighs 59lbs (26·7kg) and has a single-stage solid-propellant motor which has a burn time of 1·18 seconds. Once the missile leaves the gun/missile-launcher, four fins at the rear of the missile unfold and it is guided to the target by a two-way infra-red command link which eliminates the need for the gunner to estimate the lead and range of the target. A Sheridan normally carries eight missiles and 20 rounds of ammunition, but this mix can be adjusted as required. In addition, 1,000 rounds of 0·5in and 3,000 rounds of 7·62mm ammunition are carried. The Sheridan is provided with a flotation screen, and when erected this enables the vehicle to propel itself across rivers and streams by its tracks. Night-vision equipment is provided as is an NBC system.

Above: Though now giving satisfactory service, the M551 suffered severe development problems which were far from resolved even during service in Vietnam. Production was halted after 1,700 had been built, and though effective the Sheridan today is regarded as a costly AFV calling for prolonged crew-training.

Below: The MGM-51A Shillelagh missile is a clever and complex weapon that kills tanks reliably over long ranges. At least as much trouble in the development of the M551 was caused by the use of the 152mm gun firing ordinary shells from combustible-case cartridges. The vehicle was overlight for this gun.

M113 Armored Personnel Carrier

M113, M113A1, M106, M132, M163 and variants
Crew: 2 plus 11. **Armament:** One Browning 0·5in (12·7mm) machine-gun. **Armor:** 12mm—38mm (0·47—1·58in). **Dimensions:** Length 15ft 11in (4·863m); width 8ft 10in (2·686m); height 8ft 2in (2·5m). **Weight:** Combat 24,600lbs (11,156kg). **Ground pressure:** 7·82lb/in² (0·55kg/cm²). **Engine:** General Motors Model 6V53 six-cylinder water-cooled diesel developing 215bhp at 2,800rpm. **Performance:** Road speed 42mph (67·6km/h); water speed 3·6mph (5·8km/h); range 300 miles (483km); vertical obstacle 2ft (0·61m); trench 5ft 6in (1·68m); gradient 60 per cent. **History:** Entered service with the United States Army in 1960. Also used by 40 other countries.

In the early 1950s the standard United States Army APC was the M75, followed in 1954 by the M59. Neither of these was satisfactory and in 1954 foundations were laid for a new series of vehicles. In 1958 prototypes of the T113 (aluminium hull) and T117 (steel hull) armoured personnel carriers were built. A modified version of the T113, the T113E1, was cleared for production in mid-1959 and production commenced at the FMC plant at San Jose, California, in 1960. The vehicle is still in production today and so far over 60,000 have been built. It is also built in Italy by Oto Melara, which has produced a further 4,000 for the Italian Army and for export. In 1964 the M113 was replaced in production by the M113A1, identical with the earlier model but for a diesel rather than a petrol engine.

The M113A1 has a larger radius of action than the earlier vehicle. The M113 has the distinction of being the first armoured fighting vehicle of aluminium construction to enter production. The driver is seated at the front of the hull on the left, with the engine to his right. The commander's hatch is in the center of the roof and the personnel compartment is at the rear of the hull. The infantry enter and leave via a large ramp in the hull rear, although there is also a roof hatch over the troop compartment. The basic vehicle is normally armed with a pintle-mounted Browning 0·5in machine-gun, which has 2,000 rounds of ammunition. The M113 is fully amphibious and is propelled in the water by its tracks. Infra-red driving lights are fitted as standard. FMC has developed a wide variety of kits for the basic vehicle including an ambulance kit, NBC kit, heater kit, dozer-blade kit, various shield for machine-guns and so on.

There are more variants of the M113 family than any other fighting vehicle in service today, and there is room here to mention only some of the more important models. The M577 is the command vehicle, with a much higher roof and no armament. There are two mortar carriers: the M125 with an 81mm mortar, and the M106 with a 107mm mortar. The flamethrower model is known as the M132A1, and is not used outside the United States Army. The M806A1 is the recovery model, and this is provided with a winch in the rear of the vehicle and spades at the rear. The anti-aircraft model is known as the Vulcan Air Defense System or M163; this is armed with a six-barrelled 20mm General Electric cannon. The M548 tracked cargo carrier is based on an M113 chassis, can carry 5 tons (5,080kg) of cargo and is fully amphibious. There are many models of the M548, including the M727, which carries three HAWK surface-to-air missiles, and the M730, which carries four Chaparral short-range surface-to-air missiles. Yet another version, the M752, carries the Lance tactical missile system, whilst the M688 carries two spare missiles.

Above: Though amphibious, M113 versions are slow in the water; corresponding Soviet vehicles are fitted with water-jet propulsion and have speeds from 60 to 100 percent higher.

Left: The high outline of the M113, with vertical sidewalls, increases its vulnerability on the battlefield. This was the price paid for a revolutionary hull of welded aluminium which makes the whole vehicle float with about one foot freeboard even when fully loaded. Production has never let up; the US Army alone is buying almost 1,000 in 1978.

Below: The squat shape of the M113 is distinctive even amidst the snows of Alaska, as a squad from Company A, 1st BG, 23rd Infantry, goes through a tactical demonstration at the Fort Richardson training aids area. Future APCs may have turbine engines, but the Army is pleased with the 113's diesel.

M107 Self-propelled Gun/M110 Self-propelled Howitzer

M107, M110, M110E2 Self-propelled gun

Crew: 5. **Armament:** One 175mm gun. **Armor:** 20mm (0·79in) maximum, estimated. **Dimensions:** Length (including gun and mount in travelling position) 36ft 11in (11·256m); length (hull) 18ft 9in (5·72m); width 10ft 4in (3·149m); height (to top of barrel in travelling position) 12ft 1in (3·679m). **Weight:** Combat 62,098lbs (28,168kg). **Ground pressure:** 11·52lb/in² (0·81kg/cm²). **Engine:** Detroit Diesel Model 8V71T eight-cylinder turbocharged diesel developing 405hp at 2,300rpm. **Performance:** Road speed 35mph (56km/h); range 450 miles (725km); vertical obstacle 3ft 4in (1·016m); trench 7ft 9in (2·362m); gradient 60 per cent. **History:** Entered service with the United States Army in 1963. Also used by Germany, Greece, Iran, Israel, Italy, the Netherlands, Spain, Turkey, and Vietnam (probably non-operational).

In 1956 the United States Army issued a requirement for a range of self-propelled artillery which would be air-transportable. The Pacific Car and Foundry Company of Washington were awarded the development contract and from 1958 built three different self-propelled weapons on the same chassis. These were the T235 (175mm gun), which became the M107, the T236 (203mm howitzer), which became the M110, and the T245 (155mm gun), which was subsequently dropped from the range. These prototypes were powered by a petrol engine, but it was soon decided to replace this by a diesel engine as this could give the vehicles a much greater range of action. When fitted with a diesel engine the T235 became the T235E1 and after further trials this was placed in production as the M107 in 1962, entering service with the army the following year. The M107 has in fact been built by three different companies at various times: FMC, Bowen-McLaughlin York and the Pacific Car and Foundry Company. It is not currently in production. The hull is of all-welded aluminium construction with the driver at the front on the left with the engine to his right. The gun is mounted towards the rear of the hull. The suspension is of the torsion-bar type and consists of five road wheels, with the fifth road wheel acting as the idler; the drive sprocket is at the front. Five crew are carried on the gun (driver, commander and three gun crew), the other eight crew members following in an M548 tracked vehicle (this is based on the M113 APC chassis), which also carries the ammunition, as only two ready rounds are carried on the M107 itself. The 175mm gun has an elevation of +65° and a depression of −2°, traverse being 30° left and 30° right. Elevation and traverse are both powered, although there are manual controls for use in an emergency. The M107 fires an HE round to a maximum range of 35,870 yards (32,800m). A large hydraulically-operated spade is mounted at the rear of the hull and is lowered into position before the gun opens fire, and the suspension can also be locked when the gun is fired to provide a more stable firing platform. The gun can officially fire one round per minute, but a well trained crew can fire at least two rounds a minute. As the projectile is

very heavy, an hydraulic hoist is provided to position the projectile on the ramming tray; the round is then pushed into the breech hydraulically before the charge is pushed home, the breechlock closed and the weapon is then fired. The M107 can ford streams to a maximum depth of 3ft 6in (1·066m) but has no amphibious capability. Infra-red driving lights are fitted as standard but the type does not have an NBC system.

The M110 8in (203mm) self-propelled howitzer has an identical hull and mount as the 175mm M107, and the 8in howitzer has the same elevation and traverse as the 175mm gun. The M110 is easily distinguishable from the M107 as the former has a much shorter and fatter barrel. The howitzer can fire both HE and tactical nuclear rounds to a maximum range of 18,372 yards (16,800m). Both the M110 and the M107 are now being replaced in service with the United States Army and Marines by the M110E2. This has a much longer barrel than the standard M110 and will be able to fire a variety of ammunition including HE, improved conventional munitions, chemical, dual-purpose, nuclear and rocket-assisted projectiles to a maximum range of 22,966 yards (21,000m), although the rocket-assisted projectiles will have a longer range than this. It has been estimated by the US Army that the total cost to convert all M107s and M110s to the new standard will be about $40,000,000, a great deal less than the cost of building a new vehicle. The M110E2 will be known as the M110A1 or as the M110A2 when fitted with a muzzle-brake. The installation of the muzzle-brake will enable it to fire an even better round. The M107/M110 is normally fielded in battalions of 12 guns. One of the problems with heavy artillery of this type is keeping the guns supplied with sufficient ammunition. As noted above the weapon is supported by an M548 tracked vehicle, and this in turn is kept supplied by 5- or 10-ton trucks. Another problem is that the M107 has a very high muzzle velocity which means that its barrel, like tank barrels, wears out after about 400 rounds have been fired. It takes about two hours to change the barrel on the M107 and spare barrels are held in reserve for just this purpose.

LVTP-7 Amphibious Assault Vehicle

LVTP-7, LVTC-7, LVTE-7, LVTH-7

Crew: 3 plus 25. **Armament:** One M85 0·5in (12·7mm) machine-gun. **Armor:** 7mm—30mm (0·28—1·18in). **Dimensions:** Length 26ft 1in (7·943m); width, 10ft 9in (3·27m); height, 10ft 9in (3·27m). **Weight:** Combat 52,150lbs (23,655kg). **Ground pressure:** 8lb/in² (0·57kg/cm²). **Engine:** Detroit Diesel Model 8V53T eight-cylinder turbocharged diesel developing 400bhp at 2,800rpm. **Performance:** Road speed 39·5mph (63·37km/h); water speed 8·5mph (13·7km/h); range (road) 300 miles (482km); vertical obstacle 3ft (0·914m); trench 8ft (2·438m); gradient, 70 per cent. **History:** Entered service with United States Marine Corps 1971. Also in service with Argentina, Italy, Spain and Thailand. No longer in production.

The standard amphibious assault carrier in service with the United States Marines in the 1950s was the LVTP-5 (Landing Vehicle Tracked Personnel-5). Although an improvement over earlier vehicles, the LVTP-5 proved very difficult to maintain in service. So, in 1964, the Marines issued a requirement for a new LVTP and the FMC Corporation was selected to build 17 prototypes. The first of these was completed in 1967 under the designation of LVTPX-12. Trials were carried out in Alaska, Panama and various other Marine installations, and in 1970 FMC was awarded a production contract for 942 vehicles. The first production LVTP-7 was completed in August 1971 and production continued until September 1974. It has now completely replaced the older LVTP-5. The role of the LVTP-7 is to transport Marines from ships off shore to the beach, and if required, to carry them inland to their objective. The hull of the LVTP-7 is of all-welded aluminium construction and varies in thickness from 20 to 45mm. The engine and transmission are at the front of the hull and can be removed as a complete unit if required. The driver is seated at the front, on the left, with the commander to his rear. The LVTP-7 is armed with a turret-mounted M85 0·5in machine-gun. This is mounted on the right side and has an elevation of +60° and a depression of −15°; traverse is a full 360° and a total of 1,000 rounds of ammunition is carried. The personnel compartment is at the rear of the hull, where the 25 Marines are provided with bench type seats which can be quickly stowed so that the vehicle can be used as an ambulance or cargo carrier. The usual

method of entry and exit is via a large ramp at the rear of the hull. Hatches are also provided over the troop compartment so that stores can be loaded when the vehicle is alongside a ship.

The LVTP-7 is propelled in the water by two water-jets, one in each side of the hull towards the rear. These are driven by propeller shafts from the transmission. Basically pumps draw water from above the track, and this is then discharged to the rear of the vehicle. Deflectors at the rear of each unit divert the water-jet stream for steering, stopping and reversing.

There are two special versions of the LVTP-7 in service. The first of these

Below: An LVTP-7 climbing up a beach from the sea, during Exercise Display Determination in Turkey in 1977. Future developments will retain a welded-aluminum hull but may have a better shape for deflecting projectiles and reducing wave drag.

Above: An M107 in action. This excellent gun was designed at Watervliet Arsenal, NY, which also makes production guns. Most chassis are made by Bowen, McLaughlin York.

Left: Firing lanyard on an M110 of the US Army about to be pulled. Pacific Car and Foundry designed the chassis used on this and the M107, from which the dozer blade is extended hydraulically prior to opening fire.

is the LVTR-7. This is used to repair disabled vehicles, for which a wide range of equipment is carried, including an hydraulic crane and winch. The second model is the LVTC-7, a special command model with additional radios and other equipment. Two other models, the LVTE-7 (Engineer) and LVTH-7 (Howitzer) were not placed in production.

It is now planned to bring all LVTP-7s up to a new standard as the LVTP-7A1. Modifications include a new engine, smoke generation capability, passive night vision equipment, and automatic fire suppression system. The LVTP-7A1 should enter service in 1983.

Below: This rear view of an LVTP-7 shows the large full-section tailgate, which when closed is sealed against water ingress. On each side are the large curved deflectors at the rear of the square-section water jets for sea propulsion.

M109 Self-propelled Howitzer

Crew: 6. **Armament:** One 155mm howitzer; one ·5in (12·7mm) Browning anti-aircraft machine-gun. **Armor:** 20mm (0·79in) maximum, estimated. **Dimensions:** Length (including armament) 21ft 8in (6·612m); length (hull) 20ft 6in (6·256m); width 10ft 10in (3·295m); height (including anti-aircraft machine-gun) 10ft 10in (3·295m). **Weight:** Combat 52,438lbs (23,786kg). **Ground pressure:** 10·95lb/in² (0·77kg/cm²). **Engine:** Detroit Diesel Model 8V71T eight-cylinder turbocharged diesel developing 405bhp at 2,300rpm. **Performance:** Road speed 35mph (56km/h); range 242 miles (390km); vertical obstacle 1ft 9in (0·533m); trench 6ft (1·828m); gradient 60 per cent. **History:** Entered service with the United States Army in 1963. Also used by Austria, Belgium, Canada, Denmark, Germany, Great Britain, Ethiopia, Iran, Israel, Italy, Libya, the Netherlands, Norway, Spain and Switzerland. Still in production.

The first production models of the M109 were completed in 1962, and some 3,000 examples have now been built, making the M109 the most widely used self-propelled howitzer in the world. It has a hull of all-welded aluminum construction, providing the crew with protection from small arms fire. The driver is seated at the front of the hull on the left, with the engine to his right. The other five crew members are the commander, gunner and three ammunition members, all located in the turret at the rear of the hull. There is a large door in the rear of the hull for ammunition resupply purposes. Hatches are also provided in the sides and rear of the turret. There are two hatches in the roof of the turret, the commander's hatch being on the right. A 0·5in (12·7mm) Browning machine-gun is mounted on this for anti-aircraft defense. The suspension is of the torsion-bar type and consists of seven road wheels, with the drive sprocket at the front and the idler at the rear, and there are no track-return rollers.

The 155mm howitzer has an elevation of +75° and a depression of −3°, and the turret can be traversed through 360°. Elevation and traverse are powered, with manual controls for emergency use. The weapon can fire a variety of ammunition, including HE, tactical nuclear, illuminating, smoke and chemical rounds. A total of 28 rounds of separate-loading ammunition is carried, as well as 500 rounds of machine-gun ammunition. The latest model to enter service is the M109A1, identical with the M109 apart from its much longer barrel, which is provided with a fume extractor as well as a muzzle-brake. The fume extractor removes propellant gases from the barrel after a round has been fired and thus prevents fumes from entering the fighting compartment. The M109 fires a round to a maximum range of 16,076 yards (14,700m), whilst the M109A1 fires to a maximum range of 19,685 yards (18,000m). The M109 can ford streams to a maximum depth of 5ft (1·524m). A special amphibious kit has been developed for the vehicle but this is not widely used. It consists of nine inflatable airbags, normally carried by a truck. Four of these are fitted to each side of the hull and the last to the front of the hull. The vehicle is then propelled in the water by its tracks at a maximum speed of 4mph (6·4km/h). The M109 is provided with infra-red driving lights and some vehicles also have an NBC system.

Below: Head-on view of an M109 of the 2nd Field Artillery in Exercise Reforger 76 in Germany. By mid-1978 output of the long-barrel M109A1 and new-production M109A2 exceeded 3,450.

XM723 Mechanized Infantry Combat Vehicle

Crew: 2 plus 9. **Armament:** One 20mm cannon; one 7·62mm machine-gun co-axial with main armament; twin launcher for TOW ATGW. **Armor:** Classified. **Dimensions:** Length 20ft 5in (6·223m); width 10ft 6in (3·2m); height 9ft 1in (2·768m). **Weight:** Combat 43,000lbs (19,504kg). **Ground pressure:** 6·82lb/in² (0·48kg/cm²). **Engine:** Cummins VTA-903 water-cooled turbo-charged diesel developing 450hp at 2,600rpm. **Performance:** Road speed 45mph (72km/h); water speed 5mph (8km/h); range 300 miles (483km); vertical obstacle 3ft (0·914m); trench 8ft 4in (2·54m); gradient 60 per cent. **History:** Should enter service with the United States Army in 1980.

The United States Army has had a requirement for an MICV for well over 10 years. The first American MICV was the XM701, developed in the early 1960s on the M107/M110 self-propelled gun chassis. This proved unsatisfactory during trials. The Americans then tried to modify the current M113 to meet the MICV role: a variety of different models was built and tested, but again these vehicles failed to meet the army requirement. As a result of a competition held in 1972, the FMC Corporation, which still builds the M113A1, was awarded a contract to design an MICV designated the XM723. Prototypes are now being tested, and the vehicle should enter low-scale production in 1978–79 and enter service with the US Army in 1980.

The XM723 will replace some, but not all, of the current M113 APCs, as the latter are more than adequate for many roles on the battlefield. The XM723 will have three major advances over the existing M113 APC. First, the MICV will have greater mobility and better cross-country speed, enabling it to keep up with the XM1 MBT when acting as part of the tank/infantry team. Second, it has much greater firepower. Third, it has superior armor protection. The tank provides long-range firepower whilst the MICV provides firepower against softer, close in targets. The XM723's infantry also assist the tank by locating and destroying enemy anti-tank weapons.

The hull of the XM723 is of all-welded aluminum construction with an applique layer of steel armour welded to the hull front, upper sides and rear for added protection. The hull sides also have a thin layer of steel armor, the space between the aluminium and steel being filled with foam to increase the buoyancy of the vehicle. The driver is seated at the front of the vehicle

on the left, with the engine to his right and the vehicle commander to his rear. The turret is in the centre of the hull and the personnel compartment is at the rear. Personnel entry is affected through a large power-operated ramp in the hull rear. First prototypes carried 12 men; driver, gunner and 10 men. During trials it was found that this left little space for additional equipment, however, so only nine infantrymen are now carried. Prototypes and early production vehicles will be armed with a turret-mounted dual-feed 20mm cannon and a co-axial 7·62mm machine-gun. These have an elevation of +60° and a depression of −9°, traverse being a full 360°. A stabilization system is provided, allowing the gunner to lay and fire the armament on the move across country. From 1980 it is expected that the 20mm cannon will be replaced by a new 25mm weapon now being developed by Philco-Ford. There are six firing-ports, two in each side of the hull and two in the rear. In addition to the infantry's rifles and M60 machine-gun, the vehicle carries four Light Anti-Tank Weapons and three Dragon ATGWs. The vehicle is fully amphibious and is propelled in the water by its tracks. An NBC system is installed, as is a full range of night-vision equipment. The XM723 should be in service in substantial numbers by the early 1980s, some 15 years after the Russians first fielded their BMP-1.

Above: A revealing view from above. Unlike most M113 versions the XM723 is completely enclosed and is expected not only to protect its occupants from enemy fire but also to afford complete NBC immunity. As with most US Army programs for major hardware, the chief problems with the MICV revolve around lateness and cost-escalation.

Left: Rear view of an MICV showing infantry doors. Though fully amphibious, this vehicle has no water jets and thus has a poor performance in the water-borne operating mode.

Below: Though good-looking, the XM723 is considerably larger than needed to carry 12 troops across country. It is more than 50 percent heavier than FMC's AIFV (armored infantry fighting vehicle) which carries ten and has a 25mm gun. Later the XM723 is to have a two-man TBAT (Tow/Bushmaster Armored Turret) with Tow missiles and 25mm Bushmaster cannon.

155mm M114 Howitzer

Calibre: 155mm. **Crew:** 11. **Weight:** 12,786lb (5800kg). **Length traveling:** 23·9ft (7·315m), **Width traveling:** 7·99ft (2·438m). **Height traveling:** 5·9ft (1·8m). **Elevation:** −2° to +63°. **Traverse:** 25° right and 24° left. **Range:** 15,966 yards (14,600m).

In 1939, Rock Island Arsenal started the development of a new 155mm towed howitzer to replace the 155mm M1918 howitzer which at that time was the standard 155mm howitzer of the US Army (this was basically a modified French 155mm weapon built in the United States). This new 155mm weapon was designated the M1 and first production weapons were completed in 1942. Production continued until after the end of the war by which time over 6,000 weapons had been built. After the war the M1 was redesignated the M114. The 4·5 inch gun M1 used the same carriage as the M114 but none of these remain in service today. A self-propelled model called the M41 was also built, but again, none of these remain in service with the US Army. There is also a model of the M114 with an auxiliary propulsion system, this being called the M123A1. This has a four-cylinder petrol engine mounted on its trails and this is connected to a hydraulic unit which in turn drives the main wheels of the gun. Maximum road speed is 4·3mph (7km/hr).

When the weapon is in the firing position, it is supported on its trails and a firing jack which is mounted under the carriage. When in the traveling position, the trails are locked together and attached to the prime mover, which is generally a 6×6 truck. The M114 can also be carried slung under a Boeing CH-47 Chinook helicopter.

Its recoil system is of the hydropneumatic variable type and its breech-block is of the stepped thread/interrupted screw type. The M114 can fire a variety of ammunition of the separate loading (eg, the projectile and a charge) including an HE round weighing 95lb (43kg), tactical nuclear, illuminating and chemical. Sustained rate of fire is one round per minute. It cannot however fire the new Rocket Assisted Round which has a longer range than the standard 155mm round.

Armored and mechanized divisions of the US Army use the 155mm M109/M109A1 self-propelled howitzers, but the infantry, airborne and airmobile divisions still use the M114, although it is to be replaced from 1978 by the new 155mm M198 howitzer. The armored and mechanized divisions do not use the M114 as these weapons are towed by trucks and therefore have limited cross-country mobility and would be unable to keep up with mechanized forces. Each M114 battalion normally has 18 M114 s in three batteries, each with six weapons. In addition to being used by the United States the weapon is also used by some thirty other countries and is likely to remain in service for some years to come.

Above: A typical M114 with trail legs splayed apart but the road wheels still on the ground. The whole gun is jacked up until the wheels are clear of the ground prior to firing.

155mm M198 Towed Howitzer

Crew: 10. **Weight:** 15,256lb (6920kg). **Length firing:** 37ft 1in (11·303m). **Length traveling:** 23ft 3in (7·087in). **Width firing:** 28ft (8·534m). **Width traveling:** 9ft 2in (2·79m). **Height firing (minimum):** 5ft 9in (1·749m). **Height traveling:** 9ft 4in (2·845m). **Ground clearance:** 13in (0·33m). **Elevation:** −5° to +72°. **Traverse:** 22½° left and right; 360° with speed traverse. **Range:** 32,808 yards (30,000m) with RAP; 24,864 yards (24,000m) with conventional round.

In the late 1960's, Rock Island Arsenal started work on a new 155mm howitzer to replace the M114, and this was given the development designation of the XM198. The first two prototypes were followed by eight further prototypes, and during extensive trials these weapons fired over 45,000 rounds of ammunition. The M198 is now in production at Rock Island, although at a later date it is expected that production will be transferred to a commercial company. For Fiscal Year 1978 the Army requested $45 million for 148 weapons, and for Fiscal Year 1979 a further $67 million for 240 weapons. The M198 will be used by airborne, airmobile and infantry divisions, other divisions will continue to use self-propelled artillery. The weapon will be deployed in battalions of 18 guns, each battery having 6 weapons. The M198 is normally towed by a 6×6 5-ton truck or a tracked M548 cargo carrier, the latter being a member of the M113 family of tracked vehicles. It can also be carried under a Boeing CH-47 Chinook or a CH-54 helicopter.

When in the traveling position, the barrel is swung through 180° so that it rests over the trails. This reduces the overall length of the weapon. When in the firing position the trails are opened out and the suspension system is raised so that the weapon rests on a non-anchored firing platform. A hydraulic ram cylinder and a 24in (0·609m) diameter float mounted in the bottom carriage at the on-carriage traverse centreline, provides for rapid shift of the carriage to ensure 360° traverse. This enables the weapon to be quickly laid onto a new target.

The weapon has a recoil system of the hydropneumatic type and the barrel is provided with a double baffle muzzle brake. The M198 uses separate loading ammunition (e.g. a projectile and a separate propelling charge) and can fire an HE round to a maximum range of 24,000m, or out to 30,000m with a Rocket Assisted Projectile. The latter is basically a conventional HE shell with a small rocket motor fitted at the rear to increase the range of the shell. The weapon will also fire the new Cannon Launched Guided Projectile (or Copperhead), nuclear and Improved Conventional Munitions as well as rounds at present used with the M114. It will also be able to fire the range of ammunition developed for the FH70. The latter is a joint development between Britain, Germany and Italy and is now in production. Maximum rate of fire is four rounds per minute and a thermal warning device is provided so that the gun crew know when the barrel is becoming too hot.

Below: A prototype XM198 seen at 40° elevation during tests at Rock Island Arsenal in November 1970. Heavier than the M114, it has much greater muzzle velocity and range.

105mm M101A1 Howitzer

Calibre: 105mm. **Crew:** 8. **Weight:** 4,977lb (2258kg). **Length traveling:** 19·6ft (5·991m). **Width traveling:** 7ft (2·159m). **Height traveling:** 5·163ft (1·574m). **Ground clearance:** 14in (0·356m). **Elevation:** −4·5° to +66°. **Traverse:** 23° left and right. **Range:** 12,029 yards (11,000m).

After the end of World War I, the United States Army formed a committee called the Westervelt Board to examine the performance of the field artillery in that war, and also to lay the foundations for a complete range of new artillery. One of the requirements was for a 105mm howitzer which, after many years of development owing to a shortage of funds, entered production at Rock Island Arsenal as the 105mm M2 in 1939. During World War II the M2 (later known as M101) was made by a number of companies and by the time production was completed in 1953, no less than 10,202 weapons had been built. Many self-propelled models were also developed and one of these, the M7 Priest (on a Sherman chassis), remains in service to this day, although not with the United States Army. Since the end of the war, there have been many attempts to reduce the weight and improve the mobility of the M101, but none of these have progressed past the trials stage. Today at least fifty armies around the world still use the M2 (M101). The main difference between the M101 and the M101A1 is that the M101 has the M2A1 carriage while the M101A1 has the M2A2 carriage.

The M101A1 has a carriage with split trails and is provided with a shield to protect the crew from small arms fire and shell splinters. Its breechblock is of the horizontal sliding wedge type and its recoil system is of the hydropneumatic type. The barrel, which is not provided with a muzzle brake, has a life of 20,000 rounds. The weapon can fire a wide variety of ammunition including an HE round weighing 33lb, High Explosive Anti-Tank — this round will penetrate 102mm of armor at 1,640 yards (1500m) — smoke, white phosphorous, chemical, illuminating, High Explosive Plastic – Tracer (an anti-tank round), leaflet, anti-personnel and the more recent Rocket Assisted Projectile. The latter has a range of 15,857 yards (14,500m). Its maximum rate of fire is 8 rounds per minute for 30 seconds, or 3rpm sustained. The M101 is normally towed by a 6×6 truck and can be airlifted by a Boeing Chinook helicopter.

Although obsolete by today's standards, the M101 is still in service in some numbers with the United States Army as each infantry division has three battalions each of which has 18 M101A1's (in three batteries of six guns). In Vietnam, it was found that the M101 was rather heavy in this type of terrain and as a result the 105mm M102 was developed at Rock Island Arsenal, this is however only used by Airborne and Airmobile Divisions. Both the M101 and the M102 were to have been replaced by the 105mm XM204, but development of this weapon has recently been stopped by Congress.

Above: The M101 is still standard light artillery of the US Army, despite obsolescence. Picture taken during annual operational readiness tests at Grafenwohr, Germany.

105mm M102 Light Howitzer

Calibre: 105mm. **Crew:** 8. **Weight:** 3,196lb (1450kg). **Length firing:** 22ft (6·718m). **Length traveling:** 17ft (5·182m). **Height firing:** 4·29ft (1·308m). **Height traveling:** 5·22ft (1·594m). **Width:** 6·44ft (1·964m). **Ground clearance:** 1·08ft (0·33m). **Elevation:** −5° to +75°. **Traverse:** 360°. **Range:** 12,576 yards (11,500m); standard ammunition: 16,513 yards (15,100m) with RAP.

The 105mm M102 was developed at Rock Island Arsenal to replace the standard 105mm M101 howitzer in both airborne and airmobile divisions. The first prototype was completed in 1962 and the weapon entered service in 1966. It was widely used in Vietnam. Improvements over the M101 include a reduction in weight, longer range, and it can be quickly traversed through 360°. Both the M101 and M102 were to have been replaced by a new 105mm howitzer called the XM204, but this was cancelled by Congress in 1977 owing to both tactical and technical problems.

The M102 is normally deployed in battalions of 18 guns (each of these having three batteries each with 6 guns), and both the 82nd Airborne and 101st Airmobile/Air Assault Divisions each have three battalions of M102s. It is normally towed by the M561 (6×6) Gama Goat vehicle or a 2½ ton 6×6 truck, and can be carried slung underneath a Boeing Chinook CH-47 helicopter.

When in the firing position the wheels are raised off the ground and the weapon rests on a turntable under the front of the carriage, a roller tyre is mounted at the rear of the trail and this enables the weapon to be quickly traversed through 360° to be laid onto a new target. The M102 has an unusual bow shape box type trail which is of aluminum construction to reduce weight. Its breechblock is of the vertical sliding wedge type and its recoil system is of the hydropneumatic type. The barrel is not provided with a muzzle brake, although this was fitted to the prototype weapons. A wide range of ammunition can be fitted including high explosive, high explosive anti-tank, anti-personnel, illuminating, smoke, chemical, HEP-T and leaflet. Ten rounds per minute can be fired for the first three minutes, and 3 rounds per minute in the sustained fire role.

Right: Layout of ammo at Normandy drop zone at Fort Bragg for fire mission support. The M102 is one of the lightest 105mm weapons and can be lifted by quite small helicopters.

Above: With the XM204 cancelled the M102 is the only modern light artillery in the US Army. It is far more stable than most other towed weapons.

M88 Medium Armored Recovery Vehicle

Crew: 4 (commander, driver, co-driver, mechanic). **Armament:** One 0·50 M2 HB machine gun. **Dimensions:** Length (without dozer blade): 27ft (8·254m); width 11·24ft (3·428m); height with anti-aircraft machine gun 10·58ft (3·225m). **Weight:** 111,993lb (50,800kg). **Ground pressure:** 1·63lb/cm² (0·74kg/cm²). **Engine:** Continental AVSI-1790-6A, twelve cylinder petrol engine developing 980bhp at 2,800rpm. **Performance:** Road speed: 30mph (48km/hr); range 223 miles (360km); vertical obstacle 3·49ft (1·066m); trench 8·58ft (2·616m); gradient 60 percent.

The standard medium armored recovery vehicle used by the US Army in the early 1950s was the M74. This was based on a Sherman tank chassis but could not handle the heavier tanks which were then entering service. In 1954, work on a new medium armored recovery vehicle commenced and three prototypes, designated the T88, were built by Bowen-McLaughlin-York. After trials, a batch of pre-production vehicles were built and then Bowen-McLaughlin-York were awarded a production contract for the vehicle which was standardized as the M88. Just over 1,000 M88s were built between 1961 and 1964, and some were also exported abroad. The M88 uses many automotive components of the M48 tank, and can recover AFV's up to and including the M60 MBT. Its role on the battlefield is to recover damaged and disabled tanks and other AFV's, and it can, if required, remove major components from tanks such as complete turrets. When the M88 first entered service it was armed with a 0·50 calibre machine gun mounted in a turret but this was subsequently replaced by a simple pintle mounted 0·50 machine gun.

The hull of the M88 is of cast armor construction and provides the crew with protection from small arms fire and shell splinters. The crew compartment is at the front of the hull and the engine and transmission is at the rear. A hydraulically operated dozer blade is mounted at the front of the hull and this is used to stabilize the vehicle when the winch or "A" frame is being used, and can also be used for normal dozing operations. The "A" type frame is pivoted at the front of the hull, and when not required this lays in

Above: Despite being 25 years old in concept, the M88 is still in production. Many kinds of gear are slung externally, but there are no combat electronics normally fitted.

the horizontal position on top of the hull. This frame can lift a maximum load of six tons (5443kg), or 25 tons (22,680kg) with the dozer blade in the lowered position.

The M88 is provided with two winches and both of these are mounted under the crew compartment. The main winch is provided with 200ft (61m) of 32mm cable and has a maximum pull of 40 tons, whilst the secondary winch, which is used for hoisting operations, has 400ft (122m) of 16mm cable. The vehicle is provided with a full range of tools and an auxiliary fuel pump. This enables the vehicle to transfer fuel to other armored vehicles.

Many M88s have been rebuilt with the AVDS-1790-2A diesel engine which is used in the M60 series of MBTs. These also have a diesel auxiliary power unit and personnel heaters, and are known as M88A1s. For Fiscal Years 1976, 1977 and 1978, the US Army requested a total of 198·7 million dollars for a further 370 M88A1s, and these will also be manufactured by Bowen-McLaughlin-York.

M578 Light Armored Recovery Vehicle

Crew: 3. **Armament:** One 0·50 M2 HB machine gun. **Dimensions:** Length overall 21ft (6·42m); width 10·331ft (3·149m); height with machine gun 10·87ft (3·314m). **Weight:** 53,946lb (24,470kg). **Ground pressure:** 1·56lb/cm² (0·71kg/cm²). **Engine:** General Motors Model 8V71T eight cylinder liquid diesel developing 425bhp at 1,700rpm. **Performance:** Road speed 37mph (59km/hr); range 450 miles (725km); vertical obstacle 3·3ft (1·016m); trench 7·76ft (2·362m); gradient 60 percent.

In the mid-1950s, the Pacific Car and Foundry Company of Renton, Washington, were awarded a contract by the US Army to build a new range of self-propelled artillery, all of which were to use the same common chassis. These three weapons were the T235 (which eventually entered service as the 175mm M107), the T236 (which entered service as the 8inch M110) and the T245 (this was a 155mm weapon but was not developed past the prototype stage). In 1957, it was decided to build a range of light armored recovery vehicles using the same chassis as the self-propelled guns. Three different prototypes were built. Further development resulted in the T120E1 which had a diesel engine, and this entered service as the M578.

The first production M578 was completed by the FMC Corporation in 1962, and since then the vehicle has been produced by the designers,

Pacific Car and Foundry, and more recently by Bowen-McLaughlin-York. Between FY 1976 and FY 1978, the US Army requested some 64 million dollars to purchase an additional 283 M578s.

The M578 is used by all arms including self-propelled artillery battalions, mechanized infantry battalions and armored cavalry regiments. Apart from recovering such vehicles as the M110 and M109, the vehicle is also used to change major components in the field, such as engines, transmissions and tank barrels.

The hull of the M578 is identical to that of the M107 and M110 self-propelled guns, with the driver being seated at the front of the hull on the left side and the engine to his right. The crane is mounted at the rear of the hull and this can be traversed through a full 360 degrees. The commander and mechanic are seated in the turret and a standard 0·50 Browning M2 HB machine gun is mounted on the roof for anti-aircraft protection. The crane can lift a maximum of 13 tons (11,793kg) and the main winch is provided with 229ft (70m) of 25mm cable. This has a maximum capacity of 27 tons (24,494kg). A large spade is mounted at the rear of the hull to stabilize the vehicle when the winch or crane is being used, in addition, the suspension can be locked out if required. Unlike most MBTs, the M578 is not provided with a NBC system and it has no amphibious capability, infra-red driving lights are normally fitted.

Below: The M578 standard light ARV of the US Army. There are no variants in service.

40mm M79 Grenade Launcher

Calibre: 40mm. **Weight of grenade:** 0·610lb (0·277kg). **Length of launcher:** 29in (73·7cm). **Length of barrel:** 14in (35·6cm). **Weight of launcher:** (empty) 5·99lb (2·72kg); loaded, 6·5lb (2·95kg). **Muzzle velocity:** 249ft/s (76m/s). **Range:** 437·4 yards (400m) maximum; 383 yards (350m) effective, area targets; 164 yards (150m) effective, point targets. **Effective casualty radius:** 5·46 yards (5m). **Rate of fire:** 5 rounds per minute.

The 40mm M79 Grenade Launcher was developed to give the infantryman the capability to deliver accurate firepower to a greater range than could be achieved with a conventional rifle grenade. The M79 is a single shot, break-open weapon and is fired from the shoulder. It is breech loaded and fires a variety of different types of ammunition including high explosive, high explosive air burst, CS gas and smoke. Its fore sight is of the blade type and its rear sight is of the folding leaf adjustable type. The latter is graduated from 82 yards (75m) to 410 yards (375m) in about 27 yards (25m) increments. When the rear sight is in the horizontal position, the fixed sight may be used to engage targets up to 109·3 yards (100m). The M79 is now being replaced by the M203 grenade launcher which is fitted to the standard M16A1 rifle.

Right: Standard infantry M79; there is also a version for use by US Army helicopters with automatic feed of grenades.

81mm M29 Mortar

Calibre: 81mm. **Weight of barrel:** 27·99lb (12·7kg). **Weight of base-plate:** 46lb (21kg). **Weight of bipod:** 40lb (18·15kg). **Total weight with sight:** 115lb (52·2kg). **Elevation:** +40° to +85°. **Traverse:** 4° left and 4° right. **Maximum range:** 5,025 yards (4595m) with M374A2 HE bomb. **Rate of fire:** 27rpm for 1 minute; 4rpm sustained.

In service with US Army and some Allied countries, the 81mm M29 mortar is the standard medium mortar of the US Army and is in service in two basic models, infantry and self-propelled. The standard infantry model can be disassembled into three components, each of which can be carried by one man—baseplate, barrel, mount and sight. The exterior of the barrel is helically grooved both to reduce weight and to dissipate heat when a high rate of fire is being achieved.

The mortar is also mounted in the rear of a modified member of the M113 APC family called the M125A1. In this vehicle the mortar is mounted on a turntable and this enables it to be traversed quickly through 360° to be laid onto a new target. A total of 114 81mm mortar bombs are carried in the vehicle.

The mortar can fire a variety of mortar bombs including HE (the M374 bomb has a maximum range of 5,025 yards (4595m)), white phosphorus (the M375 bomb has a maximum range of 5,180 yards (4737m)) and illuminating (the M301 bomb has a maximum range of 3,444 yards (3150m)). The 81mm M29 mortar is to be replaced in certain units by the new 60mm M224 lightweight mortar. The 107mm M30 mortar is to be phased out of service in the near future.

Right: Here seen in the infantry role, the M29 is the standard US Army medium mortar. It is also used by many NATO countries, some of which claim up to 32 bombs in one minute.

60mm M224 Lightweight Company Mortar

Below: The M224 60mm Lightweight Company Mortar can be used with a circular base plate and a bipod, or hand held.

During the Vietnam campaign, it was found that the standard 81mm M29 mortar was too heavy for the infantry to transport in rough terrain, even when disassembled into its three main components. In its place the old 60mm M19 mortar was used, but this had a short range. The M224 (development designation XM224) has been developed to replace the 81mm M29 mortar in non-mechanized infantry, airmobile and airborne units at company level, and will also be issued to the US Marine Corps. The weapon comprises a lightweight finned barrel, sight, baseplate and bipod, although if required it can also be used without the baseplate and bipod. The complete mortar weighs only 45lb (20·4kg) compared to the 81mm mortar which weighs 115lb (52kg). The M224 fires an HE bomb which provides a substantial portion of the lethality of the 81mm mortar with a waterproof "horseshoe" snap-off propellant increments, and a multi-option fuze. The latter allows proximity, near surface, point detonating and delay options, simply by the rotation of the fuze head.

The mortar will be used in conjunction with the AN/GVS-5 hand held laser rangefinder, this can range up to 10,936 yards (10,000m) to an accuracy of ±10·936 yards (±10m), this enables the mortar to engage a target without firing a ranging bomb first. The Fiscal Year 1978 request is for 190 mortars at a cost of 2·7 million dollars, and production will be undertaken at Watervliet Arsenal.

20mm Vulcan Air Defense System

Crew: 1 (on gun). **Weight (firing and traveling):** 3,500lb (1588kg). **Length traveling:** 15·4ft (4·7m). **Width traveling:** 6·49ft (1·98m). **Height traveling:** 6·66ft (2·032m). **Elevation:** −5° to +80°. **Traverse:** 360°. **Effective range:** 2,187 yards (2000m).
Note: the above data relate to the towed version.

The 20mm Vulcan is the standard light anti-aircraft gun of the US Army and has been in service since 1968, it is also used by Belgium, Israel and Jordan. There are two versions of the Vulcan system in service, one towed and the other self-propelled. The towed version is known as the M167 and this is mounted on a two wheeled carriage and is normally towed by an M715 or M37 truck. When in the firing position the weapon rests on three outriggers to provide a more stable firing platform. The self-propelled model is known as the M163 and this is mounted on a modified M113A1 APC chassis, the chassis itself being the M741.

The 20mm cannon used in the system is a modified version of the air-cooled six-barrel M61 Vulcan cannon developed by General Electric. It is also the standard air-to-air cannon of the US Air Force and is installed in many aircraft including the F-104, F-111, F-15 and F-16. The Vulcan cannon has two rates of fire, 1,000 or 3,000 rounds per minute, and the gunner can select either 10, 30, 60 or 100 round bursts. The M163 has 500 rounds of linked ready-use ammunition while the self-propelled model has 1,100 rounds of ready-use ammunition.

The fire control system consists of an M61 gyro lead-computing gun sight, a range-only radar mounted on the right side of the turret (developed by Lockheed Electronics), and a sight current generator. The gunner normally visually acquires and tracks the target while the radar supplies range and range rate data to the sight current generator. These imputs are converted to proper current for use in the sight. With this current the sight computes the correct lead angle and adds the required super elevation.

The turret has full power traverse and elevation, slewing rate being 60°/second, and elevation rate being 45°/second. Power is provided by an auxiliary generator.

The Vulcan air defense system is normally used in conjunction with the Chaparral SAM. Each Vulcan/Chaparral battalion has 24 Chaparral units and 24 self-propelled Vulcan systems. Airborne and Airmobile divisions have a total of 48 towed Vulcan systems. The Vulcan system is normally used in conjunction with the Saunders TPQ-32 or MPQ-49 Forward Area

Above: The M167 towed version. Vulcan guns in fighter aircraft fire at rates up to 6,000 shots/minute.

Alerting Radar, which provides the weapons with basic information such as from which direction the targets are approaching.

The 20mm cannon has a maximum effective range in the anti-aircraft role of 2,187 yards (2000m) but can also be used in the ground role, and was deployed to Vietnam for this purpose. A variety of different types of ammunition can be fired, including armor piercing, armor piercing incendiary, and high-explosive incendiary.

Currently undergoing trials is the Automatic Vulcan Air Defense System. Basically, this has the radar/optical tracking system replaced by a new system which relies primarily on an auto-tracking radar, and the standard range-only radar has been modified to give it an angle tracking capability.

In addition to being used by the Army and Air Force, a modified version of the 20mm Vulcan is being used by the US Navy for its Close-In Weapon System (or Vulcan Phalanx). This has been developed to protect warships against attack from cruise missiles.

66mm M72 Light Anti-tank Weapon

Calibre: 66mm. **Length of rocket:** 20in (50·8cm). **Weight of rocket:** 2·2lb (1kg). **Muzzle velocity:** 476ft/s (145m/s). **Maximum effective range:** 984ft (300m). **Length of launcher closed:** 25·7in (65·5cm). **Length of launcher extended:** 35in (89·3cm). **Weight complete:** 5·22lb (2·37kg).

The M72 is the standard Light Anti-Tank Weapon (LAW) of the US Army and is also used by many other armies around the world. Development of weapon started in 1958 with the first production LAWs being completed by the Hesse Eastern Company of Brockton, Massachusetts, in 1962. It is

also manufactured under licence in Norway by Raufoss. The LAW is a lightweight, shoulder-fired rocket launcher and its rocket has a HEAT warhead which will penetrate over 11·8in (300mm) of armor. It can also be used against bunkers, pillboxes and other battlefield fortifications.

When the M72 is required for action, the infantryman removes the safety pins, which open the end covers, and the inner tube is telescoped outwards, cocking the firing mechanism. The launcher tube is then held over the shoulder, aimed and the weapon fired. The launcher is then discarded. Improved models are known as the M72A1 and the more recent M72A2.

Below: Range practice with M72A2 LAW projectors. These have improved sights and fire a projectile having greater armor penetration than the original M72 (about 305mm, 12in).

90mm M67 Recoilless Rifle

Calibre: 90mm. **Crew:** 2. **Weight:** 34·98lb (15·876kg). **Length:** 53in (134·6cm). **Range:** 503 yards (460m) effective anti-tank; 2,296 yards (2100m) maximum.

The M67 was the standard Medium Anti-Tank Weapon (MAW) of the US Army for many years, but has now been replaced in many units by the M47 Dragon anti-tank guided missile. The M67 consists of a front-mounting bracket group, cable assembly, face shield group, breech and hinge mechanism group, rear mounting bracket group and the rifled tube itself. The telescopic sight has a magnification of ×3 and a 10° field of view. A normal team would consist of two men, one M67 MAW and five rounds of ammunition. It can be fired from the shoulder, or from the ground using the rear bipod mount and forward monopod for stability.

The M371 HEAT round is fin-stabilized and has a maximum effective range of 437 yards (400m), it weighs 9·2lb (4·19kg). The M590A1 anti-personnel round weighs 6·7lb (3·04kg) and has a maximum effective range of 328 yards (300m). A training round, weighing 9.23lb (4·19kg), is also available.

After firing five rounds in quick succession, a 15 minute cooling off period must elapse before fire is resumed as the barrel quickly overheats. The weapon also has a danger area, due to backblast, which extends 33 yards (30m) to the rear.

Below: The M67 is one of very few types of recoilless rifle of around 4in (100mm) calibre usable by a single infantryman.

0.50 Calibre Browning M2 Heavy Machine Gun

Calibre: 0·50in (12·7mm). **Length overall:** 65·07in (165·3cm). **Length of barrel:** 44·99in (114·3cm). **Weight (gun only):** 83·33lb (37·8kg); 127·8lb (57·98kg) with tripod. **Range:** 1,996 yards (1825m) effective in ground role; 7,470 yards (6830m) maximum; 820 yards (750m) anti-aircraft role. **Rate of fire:** 450/575rpm.

The 0·50 calibre M2 Heavy Barrel (HB) machine gun was developed for the US Army in the early 1930s, as the replacement for the 0·50 M1921A1 MG. The weapon was developed by John Browning (who designed many other famous weapons including the Browning Automatic Rifle and the Browning 0·30 machine gun), and the Colt Firearms company of Hartford, Connecticut.

The M2 is air-cooled and recoil operated, and is fed from a disintegrating metallic link belt. The weapon can fire either single shots or fully automatic, and various types of ammunition can be fired including ball, tracer, armor-piercing and armor-piercing incendiary. For ground targets the weapon is mounted on the M3 tripod while for the anti-aircraft role the M63 mount is used. It is also mounted on many armored fighting vehicles including the M113A1 series of APC (and variants), the M109/M108 SPH and the M578 and M88 ARV. The M55 anti-aircraft system (no longer in front line service with the US Army) has four M2s, and the M2 is also mounted in helicopters and in some commanders' turrets as the M85.

Above: The M55, still available, has a semi-armored mount for four M2s. It is fired resting on three jacks.

7.62mm M60 General Purpose Machine Gun

Calibre: 7·62mm. **Length:** 43·3in (110cm). **Length of barrel:** 22in (56cm). **Weight:** 23lb (10.48kg) with bipod; 39·6lb (18kg) with tripod. **Maximum effective range (bipod):** 984 yards (900m). **Maximum effective range (tripod):** 1,968 yards (1800m). **Rate of fire:** 550rpm (cyclic); 200rpm (automatic).

The M60 is the standard GPMG of the US Army and has now replaced the older 0·30 Browning machine gun. The weapon was developed by the Bridge Tool and Die Works and the Inland Division of General Motors Corporation, under the direction of Springfield Armory. Production of the M60 commenced in 1959 by the Maremont Corporation of Saco, Maine, and the weapon is still in production today.

The M60 is gas-operated, air-cooled and is normally used with a 100-round belt of ammunition. To avoid overheating the barrel is normally changed after 500 rounds have been fired. Its fore sight is of the fixed blade type and its rear sight is of the U-notch type and is graduated from about 656ft to 3,937ft (200 to 1200m) in about 328ft (100m) steps. The weapon is provided with a stock, carrying handle and a built in bipod. The M60 can also be used on an M122 tripod mount and other applications include helicopters and armored fighting vehicles.

Above: The M60 in standard infantry form, with stock, pistol-grip trigger and bipod. The helicopter model, illustrated on page 161, has twin grips at the rear and pintle mount.

5.56mm M16A1 Rifle

Calibre: 5·56mm. **Length overall (with flash suppressor):** 38·9in (99cm). **Length of barrel:** 19·9in (50·8cm). **Weight (including 30 round loaded magazine):** 8·42lb (3·82kg). **Range:** 503 yards (460m) (maximum effective). **Rate of fire:** 700–950rpm (cyclic); 150–200rpm (automatic); 45–65rpm (semi-automatic). **Muzzle velocity:** 3,280ft/s (1000m/s).

The M16 (previously the AR-15) was designed by Eugene Stoner and was a development of the earlier 7·62mm AR-10 assault rifle. It was first adopted by the US Air Force, and at a later date the US Army adopted the weapon for use in Vietnam. When first used in combat numerous faults became apparent and most of these were traced to a lack of training and poor maintenance. Since then the M16 has replaced the 7·62mm M14 as the standard rifle of the United States forces. To date over 4,000,000 have been manufactured, most by Colt Firearms and the weapon is also made under licence in Singapore, South Korea and the Philippines. Twenty-one armies use the M16. The weapon is gas-operated and the user can select either full automatic or semi-automatic. Both 20- and 30-round magazine can be fitted, as can a bipod, bayonet, telescope and night sight. The weapon can also be fitted with the M203 40mm grenade launcher, and this fires a variety of 40mm grenades to a maximum range of 382 yards (350m). The M203 is now replacing the M79 grenade launcher on a one-for-one basis. The Colt Commando is a special version of the M16 and this has a shorter barrel, flash supressor and a telescopic sight, reducing the overall length of the weapon to 27·9in (71cm).

Below: Training with an M16 fitted with a laser transmitter and receiver simulator system (clipped under the muzzle) with which accuracy can be checked without necessarily firing.

0.45 Calibre M1911A1 Pistol

Calibre: 0·45in (11·43mm). **Length:** 8·63in (21·93cm). **Length of barrel:** 5·03in (12·78cm). **Weight loaded:** 2·99lb (1·36kg). **Weight empty:** 2·49lb (1·13kg). **Effective range:** 65ft (20m). **Muzzle velocity:** 826ft/s (252m/s).

The 0·45 calibre M1911 pistol was the standard American sidearm of World War I. In 1923, work on an improved model commenced at Springfield Armory, and this was standardized as the M1911A1 in 1926, and since then the weapon has been the standard sidearm of the US Army. The Army does, however, use other pistols for special missions, as the M1911A1 is rather heavy and has quite a recoil. Between 1937 and 1945, over 19 million M1911A1 pistols were manufactured by Colt, Ithaca and Remington. The weapon is semi-automatic, and all the user has to do is to pull the trigger each time he wants to fire. The magazine, which is in the grip, holds a total of seven rounds. The fore sight is of the fixed blade type and the rear sight consists of a fixed groove. The weapon has three safety devices: the grip safety on the handle, the safety lock, and the half cock position on the hammer.

Right: Demonstrating the position used in competition shooting with sidearms; this body and arm posture provides the shooter with maximum stability. Without doubt, the next standard US Army sidearm will have much smaller calibre.

The United States Navy

Bruce F. Powers, Director of (Research) Planning and Director of a Study of Sea-Based Aircraft, Center for Naval Analyses, University of Rochester, Arlington, Virginia.

All nations that have navies do so to exert some control over portions of the oceans. The United States is no exception. The far-flung successes of the US Navy as World War II ended made it dominant in many parts of the world. Despite demobilization, this dominance continued into the 1960s. Today, the US Navy has half as many ships as it had 15 years ago. Even so, it deploys versatile, capable fleets overseas and operates additional effective forces closer to the United States during peacetime. Today's US Navy has 458 ships and 540,000 men and women on active duty. It is still the most capable navy in the world.

Forces That Have Shaped the Navy

The US Navy—the ships and aircraft in it and how they are used—has been shaped by many forces. The most important of the forces that have shaped the Navy are the broad objectives the United States has for it. These are discussed now, followed by descriptions of the conflicts the US Navy is most likely to fight in and the peacetime posture used to prepare for them. Those conflicts help set the objectives; they also point out the characteristics of opposing navies most needing US Navy attention. Improvements in technology create opportunities to shape a navy; limited budgets impose constraints. These, too, are discussed.

Objectives of the US Navy

The United States has a Navy in order to achieve several broad objectives. Among the peacetime objectives are insuring use of the seas by friendly merchant shipping, and influencing events far from US shores. In wartime, one of the primary missions of the Navy is to keep the conflict confined to areas of US choice. The US Congress requires that the Navy be prepared to fight quickly when called upon, and to keep fighting when necessary. In order to achieve these objectives, US Navy officers focus on more specific missions—establishing control of sea and air space and projecting air, missile, or amphibious forces ashore.

As the United States became increasingly dependent on foreign trade during the past century, its Navy grew to insure the uninterrupted flow of that trade. One reason US Navy ships are deployed far from US shores is to maintain that flow by deterring potential threats to it.

These deployed forces also affect events ashore by their ability to intervene. Earlier in this century, intervention ashore meant several miles—the range of a naval gun or an independent landing party. More recently, carrier-based aircraft have extended potential intervention ranges to hundreds of miles. Cruise missiles abord ships could, one day, extend the range still farther.

Naval forces can move freely in peacetime. This flexibility becomes very important in crises, when naval forces can help signal their governments' intent by the stations they assume. Some of this stationing can be threatening but, if done outside territorial waters, the option to stop short of combat and pull away is retained. If, on the other hand, land forces are to influence crises, they must generally be so placed that the act of placement is itself hostile.

Naval forces are therefore preferred for crisis management. US Naval forces bring a wide range of potential capabilities to a crisis—from a few interceptor sorties that can cover the ground forces of a small ally to large air strikes or amphibious assaults. This versatility gives added flexibility to US government policy in a crisis. If the crisis turns to combat, the versatility permits US participation without the full-scale commitment implied by the introduction of sizable ground forces. If a full-scale commitment is decided upon, Naval forces are often—because of their position and the range of their capabilities—the first committed. (The first American strikes against North Vietnam, for instance, were conducted by US Navy forces in 1964. The demand for air sorties to support friendly troops in South Vietnam rose quickly in 1965. Even though it may be less expensive to fly air sorties from land bases, they take months to build. While construction was going on in 1965, an extra carrier flew the sorties needed.)

When a crisis does turn into a conflict, one US objective is to control it. Employing necessary US Navy capabilities far from US shores enhances the likelihood of keeping conflict confined and away from North America or other areas of vital concern. Because the United States has major interests overseas, including the well-being of many allies there, local conflicts that spill over can be very damaging.

Prompt and Sustained Operations

In addition to operating at long distances, the US Navy is expected to respond promptly and continue to fight for months or even years. The requirements to go into action quickly means that naval forces must be ready. This is achieved by keeping them manned and equipped and exercising them regularly. The exercises stress likely combat employment and tend to be more sophisticated the closer the forces are to the scene of their likely employment. In particular, the forces regularly stationed in the Mediterranean Sea and in the western Pacific Ocean conduct multi-ship exercises that stress several types of naval warfare within the space of a few days.

The requirement to be able to sustain combat over a period also influences the design of the US Navy. Staying power is built into individual ships; it is also achieved by providing both relief warships and ships that can replenish warships engaged in combat with ammunition, fuel, spare parts, and food. The replenishment ships permit warships to keep fighting, and to do so several thousand miles from the United States rather than returning home for replenishment. A network of overseas bases increases the flexibility and decreases the distances over which these replenishment ships must sail. Typically, warships retire a hundred miles or more from the combat area to replenish and then return to it. When warships need repairs or crews rest, the relief warships fill their place. Relief warships operate near the coasts of the United States in peacetime.

Specific Missions

To achieve the objectives described above, US Navy officers tend to focus on specific missions. The most important is establishing and main-

After World War II the United States Navy was much larger than any three others combined, although since 1960 the meteoric rise of the Soviet Navy has presented major global problems. The most significant new development in naval warfare, the SSBN (nuclear missile-armed submarine) was pioneered by the USN, which in the Trident (left) has taken this weapon to its highest point (although actual deployment of Trident is hit by delays and cost-inflation). Another area in which the US Navy pioneered is nuclear propulsion, exemplified by the picture below of (from left) CGN-9 *Long Beach*, CVN-65 *Enterprise* and the frigates *Bainbridge* and *Truxtun*, all nuclear-powered.

taining control of sea and air space. Others are projecting military forces ashore and operating in peacetime to make allies and potential foes aware of a US Navy presence. Establishing sea control is generally viewed as a prerequisite to projecting naval forces ashore, as in a large-scale amphibious assault, for example. Moving a division or more of troops to assault a distant shore requires many transports. Such ships are lightly armed; their path must be kept safe from opposing forces. Even if the path is cleared beforehand, heavily armed escorts are needed to fend off opposing forces that may enter the cleared lane afterward. The clearing and escort tasks amount to establishment of control over sea and air space. Similar tasks are obviously required for a massive resupply by unarmed convoys, and even for the transit of task forces whose principal ships are aircraft carriers. Once an amphibious or carrier force has reached its operating area, control of the sea and air space there is necessary. If control of the operating area is subject to interruption, projection of air or landing forces ashore cannot be achieved reliably.

Shifts in Missions
Emphasis has been shifting among US Navy missions since World War II. Such broad objectives as ensuring free use of the seas and influencing distant events have remained fixed. But specific Navy missions, such as projecting

forces ashore, have shifted in relative importance as technology and the capabilities of potential opponents have evolved.

After World War II, the US Navy quickly demobilized from 3.4 million men and thousands of ships to 350,000 men and a few hundred ships. Because the fleets of the United States and its allies faced no important opponents at sea, the smaller US Navy was still able to dominate the oceans. During the Korean War of 1950–53, for instance, ships of the US Navy and the navies of some other UN members operated several thousand miles from the United States. Unchallenged at sea, this force devoted itself entirely to air attacks, shore bombardment with naval guns, and amphibious landings.

About that time, US Navy aircraft aboard carriers were assigned the mission of delivering nuclear weapons on targets in the Soviet Union. This mission influenced the design of carriers and their aircraft. Some aircraft became larger to carry the large nuclear devices of the time and to strike targets at ranges of a thousand or more miles. The carriers themselves grew larger to accommodate the large aircraft. Except for amphibious transports, the Navy subordinated its other large surface ships to escort or replenishment of the carriers. Beginning in 1960, the carriers gradually transferred the long-range delivery of nuclear weapons to submarines.

The US Navy has operated nuclear-powered

submarines since 1960 whose mission is firing ballistic missiles with nuclear warheads. These "Polaris" and "Poscidon" missiles can be launched from beneath the ocean's surface against targets in the Soviet Union or elsewhere. The submarine-launched missiles account for only part of the ability of the United States to shoot intercontinental nuclear weapons; it is described in more detail in the chapter on "strategic" forces.

When the carriers turned over the mission of delivery of nuclear weapons against the Soviet Union to submarines, they resumed their earlier attention to closer targets. This shift of attention was accelerated in 1964–72 by the requirements for air sorties during the Vietnam War. Here, as in Korea, the absence of a naval threat permitted the carriers to mount sorties with maximum bombloads from close to shore and free their escorts occasionally to bombard it.

Potential challenges at sea have also caused shifts in emphasis among Navy missions. The Soviet Navy began its first regular deployments outside home waters by deploying to the Mediterranean Sea in 1964. In 1967, such deployments became continuous. During that year, an Egyptian ship launched a cruise missile at the Israeli destroyer *Eilat* and sank it. Similar missiles were carried by some of the Soviet ships that had recently arrived in the Mediterranean. There—and, later, elsewhere as US Navy operations in Vietnam decreased—the Navy

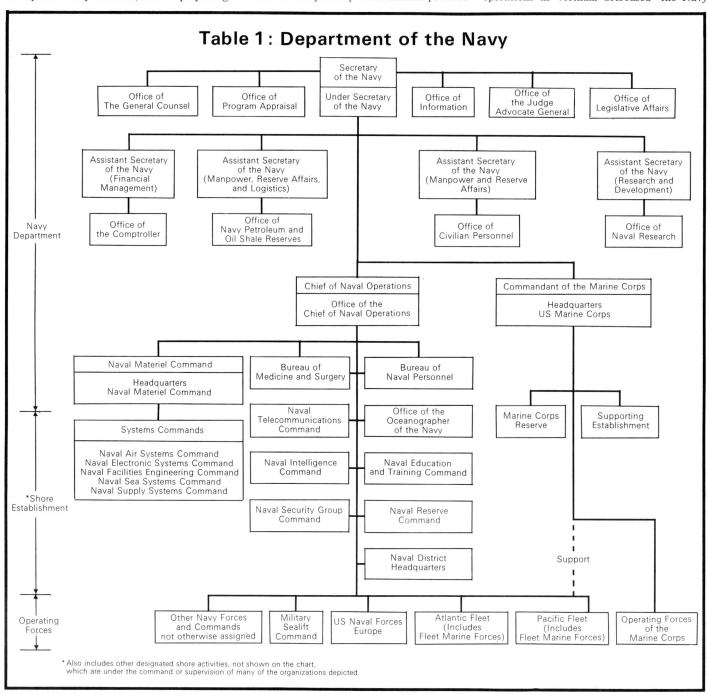

Table 1: Department of the Navy

* Also includes other designated shore activities, not shown on the chart, which are under the command or supervision of many of the organizations depicted.

developed and exercised procedures for dealing with opposing surface forces.

Submarines have been a major concern to the US Navy even longer, particularly in the Atlantic Ocean. German submarines nearly stopped the Atlantic flow of supplies to Europe in 1918 and again in 1942. After 1945, the Soviet Union acquired a large submarine force. Beginning in the mid-1950s, some older US aircraft carriers were assigned exclusively to anti-submarine duty. They were therefore allotted anti-submarine helicopters and fixed-wing anti-submarine aircraft. Beginning in the early 1970s, for budgetary reasons, the carrier-capable anti-submarine aircraft have been placed aboard all carriers; the older carriers devoted to anti-submarine work have been retired. At the same time, nuclear-powered submarines besides those fitted with ballistic missiles have entered the US Navy in large numbers, adding significantly to its anti-submarine strength. However, the ongoing modernization of the Soviet Navy's attack submarines with nuclear-powered ones, which are much more difficult to detect than diesel-powered submarines, has increased the US Navy's concern over the threat posed by Soviet submarines. So has the regular appearance in sizable numbers of Soviet submarines in the Mediterranean and, less so, in the Pacific and Indian Oceans.

Although nuclear weapons for delivery by carrier-based aircraft were at first designed for use against the Soviet homeland, later nuclear weapons were developed for both offensive and defensive war at sea. Such weapons are no longer limited to aircraft carriers.

Likely Wartime Employment

The US Secretary of Defense has directed the Navy to be ready for a NATO war with Warsaw Pact forces, for a lesser contingency elsewhere, and for managing crises. US forces are to be able to deal with the NATO war and a lesser contingency at the same time. This "one and one-half war" strategy has been US policy for almost a decade. (Earlier, national policy directed the armed services to be prepared for two large wars and a lesser contingency.)

A NATO war would place great stress on US Naval forces. In such a war, they might be called upon to provide NATO ground forces with air support from carriers or to assist by landing Marines. To do either would require control of sea and air space in the vicinity. If the war went on for weeks or months, extensive sea

control operations would be required of NATO navies so that NATO armies and air forces engaged in Europe could be supplied by merchant shipping from North America. Any of these missions, moreover, might involve use of tactical nuclear weapons (further discussion on these weapons occurs toward the end of the chapter on the US Army).

With or without nuclear weapons, the US Navy might be expected to participate extensively in such sea control while providing NATO land forces with more direct support. In such a conflict, the US fleet would have to help fend off Soviet attacks at sea and cope with Warsaw Pact air defenses ashore. NATO, with the combined capabilities of its navies including the US, would find its hands full in dealing with these threats. If the US Navy were called upon to fight a lesser war elsewhere at the same time, NATO would be especially taxed.

Lesser contingencies that might require US forces could include incidents in the Middle East, Persian Gulf, and Korea. The US Navy would probably play a large role in these contingencies. Besides its access to each area from the sea, the capabilities that the Navy has developed to be ready for a NATO war make it a tool the US government is apt to use in these smaller wars. Third World combat would probably be slower than NATO combat and the opponents might be weaker than the Soviet Union. It is because of the potential Soviet foe

Above: Since withdrawal from the Mediterranean of the Royal Navy the main NATO peacekeeping force in that theatre has been the US 6th Fleet. Of the units seen here on exercise the largest is a Fast Combat Support Ship (AOE).

that the US Navy has acquired highly sophisticated weapons systems, such as the F-14 interceptor. Without the demands of a NATO war, they might not be needed in the US fleet. But, because they are there, the US fleet would probably prevail in lesser conflicts.

Peacetime Deployment Posture

The peacetime deployment posture of the US Navy reflects where it is most likely to be employed in wartime and crises. The details of the peacetime disposition of the Navy will be described later, but the general character of the Navy's peacetime posture bears description now. It, too, has shaped the Navy.

The US Navy deploys forward one-seventh to one-third of its warships—depending on class—in peacetime. Current practice has almost a third of the aircraft carriers deployed forward.

Below: The Kaman SH-2F Seasprite is a neat helicopter serving as interim LAMPS (Light Airborne Multi-Purpose System). The larger SH-60 is now being bought.

Changes in US/USSR Naval Force Levels (1966–1976)

Attack Submarines

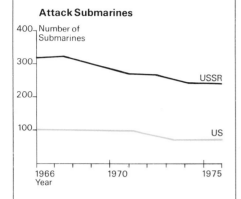

Main Surface Combatants

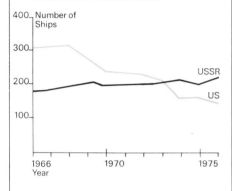

Standoff Weapon Ship Delivery Platform

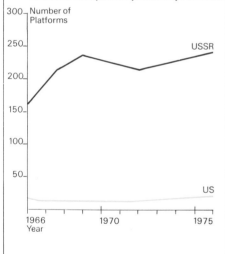

Amphibious Ships

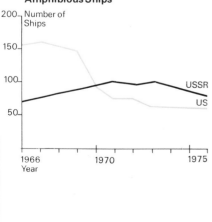

On a typical day, two US carriers are deployed to the Mediterranean Sea and two others to the western Pacific Ocean. (Carriers deploy overseas for approximately six months at a time.) these four carriers are backed up by nine others assigned to bases in the continental United States. The nine carriers based in the US are in various states of operational training and repair, including one or two in overhaul. A fourteenth carrier — one without ammunition storage—is used for training new pilots. It does not deploy.

A carrier, its embarked aircraft, their pilots, the escorting ships, and their crews customarily train together for a deployment. This period of preparation builds working relationships and mutual confidence. Training includes advanced exercises in, for example, the North Atlantic during preparation for deployment to the Mediterranean. When a group of ships and aircraft deploys, it generally operates as a task group.

This arrangement takes advantage of the smooth working relationship built during work-up training. Amphibious ships are similarly grouped; because the embarked Marines make up a single fighting unit once they have landed and their effectiveness ashore depends partly on how well their landing is coordinated, there are obvious advantages to grouping their transports.

The areas to which Navy task groups deploy forward are compromises between expected combat areas and points from which ships can be dispatched to more distant areas if the need arise. (Forward deployed ships move regularly for exercises and port visits.) The forces deployed forward are ready for combat, some of those to the rear are ready to augment those forward, and all have the ability common to all naval forces—the freedom to move in crises.

In case of potential conflict, the carriers in that part of the world, together with escorts and other ships such as transports, are usually moved closer to the trouble spot. An additional carrier with supporting ships is sometimes dispatched from the United States. At least one such carrier on each coast can be dispatched immediately, arriving in the Mediterranean in 4–5 days or in the western Pacific in 8–10. Another carrier on each coast can be dispatched 3–5 days later.

If a war lasted at least 6 months, and the forces in the Mediterranean or western Pacific could spare a temporary loan of forces, as many as 10–11 carriers could be sent to the combat theater. A much longer war would permit construction of additional carriers.

Below: Major elements in the Navy's shore-based power are the VP (fixed-wing patrol) squadrons flying the P-3 Orion. Here a crewman at NAS Patuxent River, Maryland, loads a sonobuoy into a P-3C Update II Orion of VP-24. These ASW sensors are usually used in multiple.

US/USSR Maritime Bases and Facilities

· United States Bases and Facilities · Soviet Bases and Facilities · Soviet Anchorages

Naval Bases

Naval bases in the United States provide the full range of services needed, including: overhaul, refueling, aircraft rework, ordnance storage, sensor calibration, and recreation. Recoring of nuclear power plants is also available. The many US Navy bases overseas tend to provide a narrower range of services. Overhauls, including recoring, are not done overseas. Nor are repairs that can be deferred until the end of a deployment. Overseas bases exist to provide the services a deployed fleet must have to stay ready. In wartime, large-scale operations are often conducted to seize such bases overseas.

One way to ease the burden of a peacetime policy that puts so much of the fleet's warships forward is to station some of them overseas indefinitely, saving transit times. But, because all overhauls are done in the United States, indefinite overseas stationing has not been adopted. Instead, a compromise has been arranged for submarine and destroyer tenders and cruisers that serve as flagships overseas. It is known as "homeporting", and assigns some ships overseas for the full 4 to 7 years between major overhauls. More recently, a squadron of destroyers was "homeported" in Greece for three years. An aircraft carrier and a squadron of destroyers are now "homeported" in Japan.

Past Technological Improvements

About a hundred years ago, the United States Navy converted its ships from sail to steam. Steam was faster but required coaling stations along the routes. Moreover, because steam made large-scale operations more reliable, fleets covered larger areas. Since conversion from coal to oil, which is more easily transferred at sea than coal, direct and frequent dependence on bases for refueling has decreased. (The bases now serve more as storage points for such consumables as ammunition, jet fuel, and oil for ships, and as transit points for the spare parts on which the fleet increasingly depends.) Eleven of the Navy's surface ships, being propelled by nuclear power plants, are virtually free of the usual refueling requirements; however, the three large aircraft carriers, *Enterprise*, *Nimitz*, and *Eisenhower*, need occasional replenishment of the aviation fuel. (A conventionally propelled carrier must, every few days, take on ship fuel as well as aviation fuel.) All US Navy submarines constructed since 1960 have nuclear propulsion, making them less vulnerable to radar and visual detection than the diesel-electric submarines that regularly have to break the surface of the water.

The outcome of sea battles has always depended, in large part, on the ranges at which ships could detect each other, on weapon ranges, and on the ability of ships to absorb hits. The introduction of ironclad ships over a hundred years ago was followed by the development of armour-piercing ammunition for naval guns. The range of these guns was slowly extended to the range of the visual horizon, about 20 miles, and then slightly beyond. Accuracy also improved. Aircraft first operated from ships to extend the range at which targets could be detected and identified—beyond ship horizons—so that naval gunfire could be concentrated against them. Later, the aircraft began to carry bombs and torpedoes. World War II proved surface ships to be vulnerable to attacks by aircraft; the carrier became the pre-eminent ship of the line. As with naval guns earlier, the range of aircraft operating from ships was increased. Their speed was improved by the introduction of jet engines in the late 1940s. This was followed by increases in the speed and altitude of aircraft designed to fight other aircraft and in the range and bombload of aircraft designed to strike surface targets, on sea and land.

Detection of targets had been largely visual, but World War II brought radar and sonar to ships, and radar to aircraft. Shipborne radar permitted detection of air targets far beyond the range of naval guns; guided anti-air missiles named "Tartar", "Terrier", and "Talos" began

US/USSR Ballistic Missile Submarines

Union of Soviet Socialist Republics

	Year Operational	Propulsion		Missile
Typhoon Class *(size unknown)*	1980	Nuclear	18–24	SS–NX–18 5,800 NM
Delta I Class *450 feet*	1973	Nuclear	12	SS-N-8 4,200 NM
Delta II Class *500 feet*	1976	Nuclear	16	SS-N-8 4,200 NM
Delta III Class *500 feet +*	1978	Nuclear	20	SS–NX–18 5,800 NM
Yankee Class *428 feet*	1968	Nuclear	16	SS-N-6 1,300/1,600 NM
Hotel II Class *380 feet*	1964	Nuclear	3	SS-N-6 700 NM
Golf Class *320 feet*	1960	Diesel	3	SS-N-5/4 350-700 NM

United States

	Year Operational	Propulsion		Missile
Polaris *383 and 410 feet*	1960	Nuclear	16	A-3 2,500 NM
Poseidon *425 feet*	1971	Nuclear	16	C-3 2,500 NM
Trident *560 feet*	1982?	Nuclear	24	C-4 4,000 NM

0 Feet   200   400   600

to replace guns aboard US Navy ships in the late 1950s, to take advantage of the larger detection range made possible by the radars and the greater accuracy of the missiles. In the late 1970s, "Harpoon" surface-to-surface missiles began to supplant still more naval guns.

Similarly, high-powered shipborne sonars, such as the SQS-26, which arrived in the 1960s, extended the range at which submerged submarines could be detected. Airborne radar used for anti-submarine work and detection of surface ships at first was later extended to anti-air warfare. Radar allowed interceptors to detect other aircraft beyond visual range; air-to-air missiles of greater range than air-to-air guns soon followed. The heat-seeking (passive infra-red homing) "Sidewinder" of 2 to 3 miles range came first. It had to attack from the rear of

Above: USS *Los Angeles* (SSN 688) is lead-ship of the new class of attack submarines intended to counter the latest Soviet nuclear submarine forces. By 1990 a force of 40 is planned.

Top: When the US Navy authorized the 41-vessel FBMS (Fleet Ballistic-Missile Submarine) force it looked uncatchable. But the Soviet Yankee and Delta classes outnumber the American, and Trident lags.

the target. The "Sparrow" missile, permitting attack at 10 to 15 miles and from any heading because of its radar guidance, followed. Only one "Sparrow" at a time could be controlled by the F-4 interceptor that had fired it. This limitation was recently overcome by introduction of the F-14 interceptor with "Phoenix" missiles which have a range of over 90 miles; the F-14 can control six at a time.

Force Coordination

The arrival of long-range weapons and sensors in quantity in the US fleet has made coordination of forces especially useful. When several ships and aircraft operate together in a task group, as is customary, the capabilities of their sensors and weapons overlap, often beyond the range at which any one of the ships or aircraft could, alone, destroy the target. Coordination of the sensors or weapons on several ships or aircraft is needed to take advantage of the overlap.

Coordination occurs by visual signals, as well as by radio, which was added in the past 70 years, and by high-speed computers, which arrived in the past 20. All US Navy aircraft carriers, most cruisers, and several other surface ships have the Navy Tactical Data System (NTDS), providing computer-assisted target tracking and quick radio exchange of tracking data among ships.

The carrier-based E-2 aircraft, whose capabilities include a look-down radar for detecting and tracking targets that ships may not be able to detect, has a comparable Air Tactical Data System. It permits linking with the ships' NTDS, so that tracking data can be shared among all units. The most recent version of the land-based P-3 anti-submarine aircraft has the computer and communications capability to participate in this linking; carrier-based interceptors do, too. Though ships without NTDS have significant radio capacity and other means of control, the margin provided by NTDS often leads to an NTDS ship to be chosen by a task group commander as his flagship.

The coordination capability of the US Navy was displayed in 1972. Five aircraft carriers with attendant escorts, air control ships and replenishment ships operated together in the Gulf of Tonkin. At times, this force operated more than a hundred aircraft in combat, tracking both them and potentially hostile aircraft, providing airborne refueling aircraft as needed, recovering pilots whose planes had been shot down over North Vietnam, tracking surface targets, and refueling and rearming ships while in motion.

Because ships now carry computers, large radars, large sonars, and missile systems, they are larger than ever before. The equipment itself, the need for larger crews that must operate it, and the objective of providing greater comfort for those crews have all contributed to this growth; so have greater magazine and fuel capacities, to lengthen the time between replenishments. Most classes of US Navy ships have at least doubled in size since World War II. The newest aircraft carriers displace 93,000 tons

when fully loaded; in World War II, the largest ships were 59,000 ton battleships.

Constraints

The US Navy faces a number of obstacles in achieving the objectives determined for it by national policy and in taking advantage of the technological opportunities it creates and that are presented to it. Opposing navies have already been mentioned. Another obstacle is limited funds. Although almost $40,000 million will be spent in 1978 on the US Navy and Marine Corps (whose budgets are closely coordinated), many programs compete for these funds. In anti-air warfare, for example, shipborne surface-to-air missiles compete with interceptors. Should new missiles be funded or existing interceptors be provided with more spare parts? Once such issues are resolved within the Navy Department, a proposed budget is sent forward. That budget competes with others for the limited funds available to the Defense Department, and so forth. The net result is that most programs do not receive the funds their Navy sponsors ask for. The reductions take on meaning when the capabilities of potential opponents are considered.

The principal potential opponent of the US Navy is the Soviet Navy. It has more ships than the US Navy, though less tonnage. The quality and sophistication of its operations have increased substantially in the past 20 years. The posture of the Soviet Navy, at least until recently, has been principally defensive, emphasizing protection of the Soviet homeland by denying portions of the sea to Western navies. In the past decade or so, deployments far from the Soviet Union have become common.

Today the Soviet Navy has about as many ships in the Mediterranean as the US Navy. Occasionally, they deploy a ship—such as the *Moskva, Leningrad,* or *Kiev*—that is capable of operating aircraft. More important, several of the ships and submarines on the scene carry anti-ship cruise missiles. Both the number of missile-equipped ships and the total number can be doubled within a month, as was done in October 1973. Although the Soviet ships tend to stay in the eastern Mediterranean and the US ships in the western Mediterranean in routine peacetime operations, ships of both nations roam throughout the seas. During crises, they tend to intermingle. At such close quarters, the potency of the Soviet shipboard missiles, combined with the proximity to Soviet bases for missile-equipped aircraft, make a massed attack particularly threatening. If US forces were to take the initiative in such circumstances, they would pose a serious threat to the Soviet Navy. The advantage to the force that strikes first inhibits the action both governments take with their fleets.

Some obstacles to orderly development of a

navy cannot be foreseen. In the case of the US Navy, the Vietnam War was such an interruption. Its emphasis on projection ashore demanded funds for carriers and their aircraft, for amphibious ships, for ships with naval guns, and for the unexpectedly large amounts of ammunition used. At the same time, the Navy's share of the Defence budget shrank because the combat loss rates of Army and Air Force equipment ashore had been unforeseen. The net result for Navy forces designed for sea control was accelerated obsolescence and relative inattention to replacement forces. That is still being corrected, as will be seen later.

Below: Notable features of the 30 DD-963/ DDG-47 *Spruance* class destroyers include (1) SQS-53 sonar. (2) WQS-2 sonar communications. (3) Mk 45 guns. (4) ASROC launcher (eight missiles). (5) Central Control Station. (6) Bridge. (7) SPQ-9A surface track radar. (8) SPG-60 pulse doppler air track radar. (9) Possible space for Harpoon missile launchers. (10) Upper deck spaces for SAMs, Phalanx guns and chaff launchers. (11) SPS-40B air surveillance radar. (12) Tacan dome and EW aerial mounts (not fitted). (13) Helicopter hangar. (14) Helicopter platform. (15) Left/right triple Mk 32 tubes for Mk 46 torpedoes. (16) Provision for Sea Sparrow SAM launcher. (17) Allison 501 gas-turbine/electric generator group.

Table 2: Composition of the US Navy, 1978		
Active Ships		
Aircraft carriers		13
Conventionally powered	10	
Nuclear-powered	3	
Cruisers (7,800–17,500 tons)		28
Conventionally-powered	20	
Nuclear-powered	8	
Destroyers (4,000–7,300 tons)		70
Frigates (2,600–3,500 tons)		65
Attack submarines		78
Diesel-electric	7	
Nuclear-powered	71	
Amphibious transports		63
Mine warfare ships		3
Patrol boats		3
Underway replenishment ships		39
Auxiliaries		55
Ballistic missile submarines		41
With Polaris missiles	10	
With Poseidon missiles	31	
Total		458
Reserve Ships		
Destroyers		28
Amphibious transports		3
Mine warfare ships		22
Auxiliaries		4
Total		57

Above: Launch of Harpoon cruise missile from DE 1064 (USS *Lockwood*), one of the 46-strong DE escort class. Harpoon has been fired from submarines, hydrofoils and various types of aircraft.

Table 3: Fleets of the US Navy

Fleet	Operating Area	Home Port of Flagship
Second	Atlantic Ocean	Norfolk, Virginia
Third	Eastern Pacific Ocean	Pearl Harbor, Hawaii (headquarters ashore)
Sixth	Mediterranean Sea	Gaeta, Italy
Seventh	Western Pacific Ocean	Yokosuka, Japan

Table 4: Peacetime Composition of Deployed US Fleets, 1978

Sixth Fleet

Task Force 60
2 carriers
14 surface combatants

Task Force 61
5 amphibious ships

Task Force 62
1 reinforced USMC battalion

Task Force 63
6–7 underway replenishment ships
4 auxiliaries

Task Force 67
1½ maritime patrol squadrons
1 reconnaissance squadron

Task Force 69
4–5 attack submarines

Seventh Fleet

Task Force 72
3½ maritime patrol squadrons
1 reconnaissance squadron

Task Force 73
7–9 underway replenishment ships —
7–8 auxiliaries

Task Force 74
6 attack submarines

Task Force 76
8 amphibious ships

Task Force 77
2 carriers
19 surface combatants

Task Force 79
2 reinforced USMC battalions

Table 5: Fleet Organization, US Navy, 1978

Commander-in-Chief Pacific Fleet	Commander-in-Chief Atlantic Fleet	Commander-in-Chief Naval Forces, Europe
Pearl Harbor, Hawaii	Norfolk, Virginia	London, England

Seventh Fleet	Third Fleet	Second Fleet	Sixth Fleet	MidEast Force

The US Navy Today

Having traced the forces that have shaped the Navy, the discussion now turns to what today's Navy is like—its composition, disposition, organization, leadership (Tables 1 to 5), manning, and capabilities.

Table 2 shows the current composition of the US Navy, as of mid-1978. (The designation of cruisers, destroyers, and frigates has changed recently.) Groups of US Navy surface ships tend to be built around a carrier, amphibious ships or replenishment ships. Each such task group will need surface combatants with it in wartime. The total number of cruisers, destroyers and frigates is about 13 times as large as the number of carriers. Twenty or thirty surface combatants will provide defense as the lightly armed amphibious ships transit to the landing area and shore bombardments once there. A like number would escort the 8 to 10 groups of underway replenishment ships that would be needed to keep fighting ships on station. Yet others would be needed for convoy duty. All these wartime demands, when combined with the other demands likely in the Indian Ocean (where a MidEast Force of three Navy ships is maintained continuously in peacetime), in South American waters and elsewhere, would quickly top the 163 surface combatants.

Besides the 458 ships assigned to the Navy, there are 4,663 aircraft assigned to the Navy and Marine Corps. Approximately 1,000 are aboard large aircraft carriers. Another few hundred, mostly helicopters, are aboard smaller ships, including amphibious assault ships. Land-based aircraft include 24 squadrons of nine P-3s each.

Some attack submarines would be assigned to anti-submarine work in wartime, including 1 to 3 submarines to each of the task groups built around a carrier. These groups also would each include 4 to 7 surface combatants and be supported by P-3s and their own carrier-based aircraft.

Each ship and aircraft in the US Navy is assigned to one of four fleets for operational control. Table 3 shows the four fleets and their customary operating areas. The fleet to which any one ship or aircraft is assigned changes with time. Deployments overseas mean assignment to the Sixth or Seventh Fleet for several months. The approximate peacetime composition of those fleets is in Table 4. After a deployment is concluded, the ship or aircraft squadron returns to the Second or Third Fleet, respectively. Then, the ship or squadron begins a new training cycle.

The overall management of this rotation is conducted by theater commanders-in-chief. The organization for operational control is shown in Table 5, where the locations of the headquarters of the commander-in-chief are also shown.

The US Navy organization for management of force rotation is not symmetrical. In the Pacific Fleet, forces in the Third Fleet preparing for deployment are still controlled by the same commander-in-chief when assigned to the Seventh Fleet. When forces are deployed to Sixth Fleet from Second Fleet, their operations are controlled by separate commanders-in-chief. This asymmetry stems from the unified command structure for worldwide US forces. That structure stresses three theaters, the Pacific, Atlantic, and Europe. Unlike US Navy and US Marine Corps forces, which are integrated within fleets as shown in Table 4, the forces of the US Army, the US Navy, and the US Air Force report to their unified theater commanders-in-chief through commanders-in-chief of each service such as those shown in Table 5. In Europe, the unified US commander-in-chief has an Army component commander-in-chief, an Air Force component commander-in-chief, and a Navy component commander-in-chief (the C-in-C, US Naval Forces, Europe).

The Commanders-in-Chief of the Pacific and Atlantic Fleets each have several subordinate commanders charged with administrative control of various types of forces. Each of these subordinate commanders tends to be concerned with one type of ship only—such as submarines—and is responsible for development of tactics and doctrine and for provision of manpower, spare parts, safety standards, and so on to the ships. The ships and aircraft assigned to the Sixth Fleet are under the administrative control of the Commander-in-Chief, Atlantic Fleet.

The Navy commanders-in-chief are autonomous. Operating doctrine and procedures for their forces can vary. Because the forces and personnel under their control rotate, these variations are not great. The ultimate unifying influence in the US Navy is provided by the Chief of Naval Operations (CNO). Despite his title, the CNO commands no forces. He does, however, select the forces that will make up the Navy. He does so by considering the operational problems faced by fleet commanders, the postulated threat, guidance on US strategy from the Secretary of Defense, emerging technologies, available manpower, and budget constraints. In selecting the forces that will make up the Navy, the CNO's effect on it comes five to 35 years after his decisions. The CNO is also responsible for more immediate concerns—the provision of manpower and other resources to the fleet commanders-in-chief and for overall Navy policies. Admiral J. Holloway III, completed his four-year term as CNO in summer 1978, being replaced by Adm. Thomas B. Hayward. The CNO also serves as the Navy member of the Joint Chiefs of Staff, who direct worldwide US forces through the unified commanders-in-chief.

The US Navy has about 540,000 men and women on active duty; all are volunteers. About 62,000 are officers, and 4,350 are cadets. Before 1973, when the United States ended conscription, the Navy was composed almost entirely of volunteers, but some of them might otherwise have been drafted into the Army. The end of conscription has been accompanied by substantial increases in pay, now about $5,000, for recruits. In the post-conscription period, Navy manpower managers have stressed proper selection of recruits. Such indicators as graduation from secondary school are scrutinized to increase the chances of successful completion of enlistment and of the Navy's many schools that prepare recruits to operate and maintain increasingly sophisticated equipment.

Capabilities

The operational strengths and weaknesses of the US Navy are best viewed by recalling that it is structured to assert control over the oceans and, when necessary, over adjacent territory. Its principal potential opponent, the Soviet Navy, is, on the other hand, structured to deny that control.

In anti-submarine warfare, the US Navy enjoys significant technological advantages that are buttressed by geographical advantages. US anti-submarine sensors permit detections that allow attacks to be made at long range. Off-ship sensors and information-processing capabilities permit tracking of submarines, thus increasing the likelihood that attacks will be successful. Widespread and well-placed US air bases for operation of P-3 anti-submarine planes give them an advantage. Because the large Soviet submarine force must move out of home waters to be useful in wartime and since the exit from those waters to the North Atlantic, in particular, is narrow, US defenses could be concentrated. Attack submarines could be stationed in barriers to take advantage of this. Despite these US advantages, the size of the Soviet force and the slow pace of any anti-submarine campaign is apt to present vexing problems. If the Soviets deployed their submarines significantly before combat, high initial US losses would be possible.

Table 6: Platform Type Capabilities for Warfare Tasks

● Major Capability   Planned Capability ( )

Warfare Tasks	Carrier	Combatant	Surface SSN	Surface SSBN	Amphibious	Maritime Patrol Aircraft (MPA)	Support
Fundamental Tasks							
Anti-Air Warfare							
Air Superiority	●						
Air Defense	●	●					
Anti-Submarine Warfare							
Distant Operations	●		●			●	
Close Operations	●	●	●			●	
Anti-Surface Ship Warfare							
Distant Operations	●	(1)	●			(2)	
Close Operations	●	●	●			(2)	
Strike Warfare							
Nuclear	●	(3)	(3)	●			
Conventional	●	(4)	(4)				
Amphibious Warfare							
Vertical Assault					●		
Over the Beach					●		
Close Support	●	●			●		
Mine Warfare							
Offensive	●		●			●	
Countermeasures		●			●		
Special Warfare			●		●		
Supporting Tasks							
Intelligence							
Imagery	●						
Reconnaissance	●		●			●	
Surveillance	●	●	●			●	●
Command, Control and Communications	●	●	●	●	●	●	●
Logistics							
Long Haul Resupply							●
Local Resupply							●
Repair	●						●

Notes:
(1) Sea-launched cruise missile (SLCM) with extended range, over-the-horizon targeting.
(2) Harpoon capability enables maritime patrol aircraft to attack surface ships.
(3) SLCM with terrain contour matching (TERCOM) will provide nuclear strike capability.
(4) SLCM (second generation) with guidance accuracies to permit conventional warheads.

Table reproduced from report to Congress by CNO Adm. James L. Holloway III, US Navy, "Posture of the US Navy", February 1978.

The Soviets learned well the lesson taught by Japanese kamikaze attacks on American and British surface ships toward the end of World War II. Cruise missiles (low-flying homing weapons) have been fitted on some Soviet submarines and are now widely deployed on Soviet cruisers and destroyers. These pilotless missiles are directed against surface ships; they can be redirected in flight. They have proved their potency, as in the *Eilat* sinking and in the 1971 Indo-Pakistani War. As described earlier, the intermingling of forces that sometimes occurs in crises tends to offer great advantage to the side that shoots first if it is willing to incur the risks of a war. The potential harm to US surface ships from Soviet cruise missiles fired from intermingled positions is made more severe by the added possibility of prompt follow-up attacks with torpedoes fired by submarines. This combination, if effectively delivered, could disable large numbers of US ships.

With reasonable prospects for eventual, if not immediate, establishment of sea control, US capabilities to project naval power ashore can be assessed. It is here that most of the combat experience gained in Vietnam resides. Each US aircraft carrier is a potent force. Its 24 A-7s, 13 A-6s, 24 F-4s or F-14s, and 20 to 25 other aircraft can mount a devastating strike of about 40 aircraft on several hours' notice. In a strike of this kind, half the aircraft may carry bombs or air-to-surface missiles. The loads possible on today's carrier-based aircraft mean that such a strike could deliver 75 tons of bombs on targets as far as 300–400 miles from the carrier. When, instead of major strikes, more routine production of sorties is required, as often happened in Vietnam, a large carrier is capable of 110 to 120 sorties a day when operating aircraft for 12 hours and then resting for 12. This performance is possible at night as well as in daylight, and is readily sustained for a month or more.

Such output can be interrupted, however. The example of the North Vietnamese Air Force shows how. This force of no more than 100 fighter aircraft prevented carriers in the Gulf of Tonkin and larger numbers of US Air Force bases ashore from achieving maximum output. The usual way to measure fighter performance is the exchange ratio: in the case of the Vietnam War, MiGs lost versus US fighters lost. The MiGs initially held their own at that, but were later overwhelmed. However, detections of MiGs near strike groups over North Vietnam sometimes caused heavily-laden attack aircraft to jettison their bombloads before reaching the target so as to decrease vulnerability to the MiGs. This, too, is a useful measure of the effect of the North Vietnamese Air Force. The most subtle measure captures the most pervasive effect the MiGs had. Ten to fifteen percent of the sorties flown from carriers in the Gulf of Tonkin were launched with air-to-air missiles instead of air-to-ground bombs in case MiGs should appear; they almost never did. Thousands of sorties that might have carried bombs did not.

Despite the possibilities for interruption of carrier strikes or diversion of some of their aircraft to other missions, a carrier near a friendly country's shoreline poses a considerable problem for a potential invader. Similarly, the amphibious assault capabilities of US Marines embarked in Navy ships permit rapid landing of an effective force. Most amphibious transports can move at 20 knots and thereby create uncertainty regarding the choice of a

Top: USS *Mississinewa* (AO-144) is an oiler of 40,000 tons full-load displacement, but she is dwarfed by the *"JFK"*, CVA-67, one of the monster super-carriers with a flight deck over 1,000ft by 250ft.

Right: With her sister, *Eisenhower*, the *Nimitz*—CVA-68—named for the great US Navy commander of World War II—is the largest warship in the world. With full-load 92,000 tons, few drydocks fit her.

landing site. The large replenishment force of the US Navy can keep up with the amphibious force. It can also replenish the faster carrier task forces while they are underway, day or night.

Despite many strengths, the US Navy is noticeably weak in some areas. The problems of dealing with massed missile attacks have already been described. Task groups without carriers are limited in their ability to detect, identify, and track ships beyond visual range. As a result, effective use of the surface-to-surface "Harpoon" missiles that are being installed in large numbers of surface combatants will be limited to visual or radar ranges unless friendly aircraft can help. The threat of large-scale use of mines by the Soviet Navy is not matched by large-scale mine countermeasure forces or exercises in the US Navy—the present active mine inventory includes only three mine warfare ships. The substantial ability of the US Navy to manage massed forces at sea has depended on high-frequency (HF) radio communications. These signals, readily detectable at ranges beyond the horizon and susceptible to interference by jamming, are another weakness of the US fleet.

The US Navy Tomorrow

The composition of any navy changes only slowly because ships normally have useful lifetimes of 20 to 40 years. (Aircraft last about half as long.) In 1963, the US Navy was composed of 916 ships, twice as many as it has now. Many of these 916 were ships built toward the end of World War II and were retired by the mid-1970s; many others were constructed during the 1950s, as Korea and the Cold War pushed up the size of the Navy. In 1963, the US Navy had 24 aircraft carriers; nine were smaller ones configured for anti-submarine work. There were 280 surface combatants, mainly World War II destroyers. The conversion to a nuclear-powered submarine force had just begun. There were 12 nuclear-powered ballistic missile submarines and 16 such attack submarines. By 1977 there were 41 and 71, respectively. Seventy-nine of the 86 diesel-powered submarines that were

in the 1963 inventory had been retired by mid-1977. Most of the reduction in inventory since 1963 has come in mine warfare ships (from 87 ships to 3), underway replenishment ships (from 75 to 39), and auxiliaries (from 189 to 55).

Continued reduction in the number of US Navy ships is not expected. In fact, moderate growth may occur in the next few years. Since the US Congress authorizes shipbuilding only one year at a time, the fleet's future composition cannot be specified. However, the CNO and Secretary of Defense have based planning for a 1982 fleet on more than 500 ships. A few ships of each type (except carriers) might be added, but the most substantial growth would be in the numbers of frigates and attack submarines.

One of the new ship types that will begin entering the inventory by 1982 is *Trident*. These large (18,700-ton) submarines will carry 24 ballistic missiles each. The missiles will have a 4,000-mile range, permitting operation of the new submarines over a much wider area than the *Polaris* and *Poseidon* submarines they will slowly replace. The increase in operating area, the increased number of missiles per submarine, the quieter operation, and the expected reduction in frequency of overhauls should all make the *Trident* force a less vulnerable and more potent ballistic missile force.

Before proceeding with a description of other weapons systems that will soon be entering the US fleet, it is worth noting that eventual performance in the fleet seldom matches the claims made for a system before it is deployed. Those claims are generally made with implicit assumptions of near-perfect maintenance, a cooperative atmosphere or ocean, and perfect information available to commanders. Though such assumptions are unjustified, they color nearly all descriptions of future weapon systems.

Anti-submarine helicopters called LAMPS (Light Airborne Multi-Purpose System) are already aboard approximately 75 surface combatants. They are there to permit weapon delivery more quickly after detection and at longer range than possible while waiting for the surface combatant to move toward the contact. A replacement, LAMPS Mark III, will begin

Table 7: Five Year Shipbuilding Program						
Vessel	**'78**	**'79**	**'80**	**'81**	**'82**	**Total**
Trident	2	1	2	1	2	8
SSN 688	1	2	2	2	2	9
CV (SLEP)	—	—	(1)	—	(1)	(2)
CVV	—	1	—	1	—	2
DDG-47	1	—	3	3	3	10
DDG-2 (conversion)	—	—	(6)	(6)	(6)	(18)
FFG-7	9	11	12	12	12	56
FFGX	—	—	—	1	1	2
LX (LSD-41)	—	1	—	2	3	6
MCM	—	1	6	6	6	19
AO	4	4	2	2	2	14
AOE	—	—	1	—	—	1
AD	—	1	1	—	—	2
AR	—	1	—	—	1	2
T-AGOS	—	3	5	4	—	12
T-ATF	5	2	—	—	—	7
T-ARC	—	1	1	—	—	2
T-ASR	—	—	2	2	—	4
Total						
New Ships	22	29	37	36	32	156
( ) Conversion/ SLEP	(—)	(—)	(7)	(6)	(7)	(20)

Trident: Ballistic missile submarine. **SSN 688:** *Los Angeles* class nuclear attack submarine. **CV (SLEP):** Carrier service life extension programme (eight *Forrestal* and *Kittyhawk* class). **CVV:** Medium-size aircraft carrier. **DDG-47:** 'Aegis'-equipped gas turbine guided missile destroyer. **DDG-2:** Guided missile destroyer conversion. **FFG-2:** Guided missile destroyer conversion. **FFG-7:** Guided missile frigate (lead ship *Oliver Hazard Perry*). **FFGX:** Guided missile frigate (new class). **LX (LSD-41):** Landing ship dock (new class). **MCM:** Mine countermeasures ship. **AO:** Fleet oiler. **AOE:** Fast combat support ship. **AD:** Destroyer tender. **AR:** Repair ship. **T-AGOS:** Ocean surveillance ship. **T-ATF:** Fleet tug. **T-ARC:** Cable repair ship. **T-ASR:** Submarine rescue ship.

Below: The vessel in the background looks like a carrier, but in fact is one of the *Iwo Jima* class of LPH amphibious assault ships, designed for the job from a clean sheet of paper. Nearer the camera is one of the much newer LPD amphibious transport docks, LPD-11 *Coronado*.

entering the fleet in the early 1980s. Its longer range, sonobuoy capacity, and information-processing capability will permit it to take advantage of the longer range detections expected from high-powered sonars and towed passive sonar arrays on surface combatants. These arrays consist of hydrophones imbedded in a cable several hundred feet in length that is towed behind a surface combatant or submarine. Engine or other characteristic noise emitted by an opposing submarine can be heard through the hydrophones. The wide separation between hydrophones permits accurate determination of the opposing submarine's bearing, and the separation of the array from the noise made by the towing ship as it moves through the water permits clear interpretation of the submarine's emitted noise. These capabilities, combined with improved data processing aboard the ship, should make possible more effective attacks with LAMPS III or other anti-submarine weapons aboard surface combatants.

Another anti-submarine weapon, but one that does not require a ship's presence to be effective, is entering the inventory now. It is CAPTOR, for enCAPsulated TORpedo. After drop by aircraft or ship, it moors itself to the bottom, and waits. Mine-like, it senses the passage of a submarine and then releases its torpedo at the submarine. The potential cost savings over maintaining barriers continually with ships or planes are obvious.

It has been 20 years since nuclear-powered attack submarines began joining the US fleet in quantity. These early boats were of 3,000 to 4,000 tons submerged displacement. Their replacements, the SSN-688 class of 6,900 tons submerged displacement, have begun to join the fleet and will continue to do so through the 1980s. The 688-class boats can exceed 30 knots underwater, are much quieter than their predecessors, and are fitted with the long-range BQQ-5 hull-mounted sonar. By 1990, there will be almost 40 of them in the US fleet.

Anti-air warfare capabilities in the US Navy should also be upgraded by the arrival of new systems. Prominent among these is the "Aegis" surface-to-air missile system. It will depend on the SPY-1 phased array radar, permitting automatic detection and tracking, and on the 13-mile "Standard" missile. Beginning in the early 1980s, "Aegis" is to be deployed on variants of the *Spruance* (DD-963) hulls propelled by gas turbines that were introduced in the mid-1970s. (These *Spruance* destroyers were the first US ships constructed in large blocs by modular assembly techniques in a single shipyard. The Iranian Navy has ordered four of them.) Anti-air capabilities are also to be upgraded by installation of the Phalanx gun system, a 6-barreled 20mm rapid-fire system designed to shoot down cruise missiles that pass through such outer defenses as "Aegis".

The sophisticated swing-wing F-14s began replacing F-4 interceptors in the mid-1970s. The F-14s are very expensive, and a less costly complement to them has therefore been sought for carrier service. The F-18 will begin appearing in the Navy and Marine Corps in the early 1980s. The saving it brings will be increased by using the same airframe for an attack airplane, the A-18. It will replace the A-7s that are now aboard the carriers. The effectiveness of carrier-based interceptors will be increased by deployment of an improved version of the first air-to-air missile, "Sidewinder". Because of greatly increased sensitivity to the heat emitted by opposing aircraft, the new "Sidewinder"

Top: Practice with the radar-directed 3-in (76mm) guns of the frigate *Richmond K Turner*, DLG-20 of the Leahy class. The prospects are that such guns will be replaced by missiles by 1982.

Right: The AV-8A Harrier, bought by the Marine Corps in 1969, gradually won over those who did not believe in jet V/STOL. But in 1979 the Carter administration refused funds for the new AV-8B.

will not be limited to attacks from the rear of its target aircraft, but can be used from any bearing.

In the mid-1980s, the longer range "Tomahawk" will augment the 60-mile "Harpoons" that will, by then, be on many ships, unless their deployment is restricted or banned in SALT. (These surface-to-surface missiles are intended to restore offensive punch to surface ships after a long eclipse. The eclipse began when surface combatants were assigned primarily to defend aircraft carriers and thus some of their guns were therefore removed to make way for surface-to-air missile systems.) When LAMPS is aboard the firing ship, identification of targets at ranges beyond the horizon is possible. LAMPS III will extend that range further. So should satellite systems for the detection and identification of surface targets. In fact, systems that stress management and processing of information rather than direct destruction of targets will claim an increasing share of US Navy resources as it moves into the 21st century. Another current example is a set of communications satellites that use ultra-high-frequency (UHF) radio signals. Unlike the widely used high-frequency (HF) signals that bounce off the ionosphere, UHF radio cannot be detected beyond the 20-mile line-of-sight horizon of the transmitting ship. Since the satellite is above the ship, it can receive the signal and relay it to distant points without betraying the position of the transmitting ship.

The US Navy's amphibious force is being upgraded by delivery of five large ships called LHAs. As with the *Spruance* destroyers, they were constructed by modular shipbuilding techniques. They offer large flight decks for helicopter lift of troops and cargo to the beach, well decks for ship-to-shore landing craft carrying tanks and other heavy equipment, and enough internal capacity to carry a reinforced battalion of troops and equipment. Until now, USMC battalions deployed at sea were spread among four or five ships.

Unanswered Questions

Certain characteristics of the future US Navy cannot be seen clearly at this point. The major question marks include:
1. Which should be stressed more in structuring the Navy, NATO or the Third World?
2. What is the role and future distribution of aircraft at sea?
3. How vulnerable are surface ships?
4. Can distant targets be located and identified accurately enough to use Navy surface-to-surface missiles at their maximum ranges?
5. How many surface ships should have nuclear propulsion?
6. How should attacks that employ nuclear weapons be countered?

Should the Navy be structured for NATO wars or for intervention in the Third World? Put another way, should sea control or projection ashore be stressed more? These questions underlie much of the current debate, both inside and outside the US Defense Department, over the future of the US Navy. The choice will affect the entire Navy, but its effect is seen most clearly in carrier and amphibious forces. If the US Navy and Marine Corps are to participate in a NATO conflict with the Warsaw Pact, enough carriers must be built to make sure that enough will be near Europe when their air sorties are needed. (They are expected to be necessary in the Mediterranean, may be necessary in northern Europe, and could even be required in central Europe.) Similarly, a plan to employ USMC ground forces in central Europe would require them to have more tanks and other heavy equipment than they do now. If they were to move to Europe in amphibious ships, those ships would need more capacity, and other ships of the US Navy would have to see to it that the amphibious ships could get to their objective area despite opposition. If, on the other hand, land bases can be depended upon to provide all the needed air sorties in Europe, and NATO land armies can hold the line without help from amphibious troops, the carriers and

Marines can concentrate on preparations for Third World operations. This might mean that fewer carriers will be needed in the US inventory, and also that carrier aircraft might not face opponents as sophisticated or as concentrated as those in Europe. For the Marines, it would probably mean lighter forces designed to intervene quickly and withdraw quickly. In either case, significant forces to keep the supply line to Europe open would be necessary in a long war.

Whether the Navy is oriented toward Europe or toward the Third World, the future of sea-based aircraft will be the subject of major debate over the next few years. There is general agreement that aircraft based on ships will be a continuing feature of the US Navy, but how many aircraft, their design, and the nature of the ships that will operate them is not clear. As noted earlier, the number of carriers has been going

Above: Lead-ship of the very important FFG-7 class of guided-missile frigates, USS *Oliver Hazard Perry* is one of the new era of American gas-turbine vessels —compared with Soviet counterparts, strangely devoid of weapons.

Facing page top: Display console operators working in the air detection and tracking section of the Amphibious Control Center of the Blue Ridge class amphibious command ship *Mount Whitney*, LCC-20.

Below: An overcast day in Virginia as trucks work their way ashore along a pontoon causeway from Tank Landing Ship *Wahkiakum County*, LST-1162. Like the Soviet Union, the United States does not yet lack military training areas.

down as the size of their aircraft has been going up. Meanwhile, the Soviets have deployed cruise missiles in quantities that might be able to put some carriers out of action early in a war. If the Soviets can attack several carriers successfully, a significant portion of the US Navy's offensive punch would be blunted.

Admiral Holloway sees a possible answer in aircraft that can take off and land vertically or over a runway a few hundred feet in length. This technology, known as V/STOL, may produce aircraft that can perform in flight as well as conventional aircraft. If such aircraft can be developed, then smaller, more numerous ships could operate the aircraft. What size ships and how many? How many aircraft per ship? To begin to find out, a squadron of V/STOL Harriers was deployed to the Sixth Fleet along with conventional aircraft aboard the carrier

USS *F. D. Roosevelt* at the end of 1976. The Harriers provided some answers and also re-emphasized some questions. How reliable must aircraft be that are dispatched to smaller ships so that they will continue operating from them—rather than filling their limited deck space with aircraft awaiting the arrival of spare parts? How should aircraft maintenance be managed? If many ships with aircraft operate far apart, will they need additional communications to coordinate all the aircraft? Which is more easily defeated—a force of many smaller ships or a force of a few large ships?

How vulnerable are surface ships in an era of widespread cruise missiles? Proponents of submarines and of land-based aircraft say the era of navies built around surface ships is passing. Surface ships, however, cannot be matched for a combination of easy communica-

tions and on-station times running to weeks or months. Because of this, efforts to fashion effective defenses against anti-ship cruise missiles continue. These include direct defenses, such as "Aegis", "Phalanx", and F-14s, and indirect ones, such as dispersion of aircraft and shifting radio communications to UHF.

Another element of the decentralization of

Below: The 3,000-ton SES (Surface-Effect Ship, the US Navy name for an oceangoing air-cushion vehicle) has been a long time maturing, and even now can be illustrated only in artwork. Bell, Aerojet, Litton and Lockheed received design contracts in 1972, and the first two companies have delivered SES craft.

Above: An artist's impression of a Sparrow medium-range AAM being fired from an F-18 Hornet of the Navy. This multi-role combat aircraft is intended to replace the F-4 as a fighter and A-7 as an attack bomber.

Right: Fast shooting by the cat crews of CVA-59 *Forrestal*, with three F-4Js slammed off her two bow catapults in about two minutes and another about to go (followed on the right cat by an E-2C and F-4)

US Navy offensive power is the widespread deployment of "Harpoon" aboard surface combatants. As described earlier, taking advantage of the range of "Harpoon" and, later, the much longer range of "Tomahawk" requires a capability to detect, identify, hit and assess the damage to targets well beyond the horizon. This means integrating and passing information among ships and aircraft in such timely and reliable fashion that doing it presents major problems to the US Navy—a navy that has already made important advances in the management of information.

How many surface ships should be propelled by nuclear power? The advantages of nuclear power can be substantial. For an aircraft carrier, though, the investment in such propulsion can be up to twice as much as that for conventional propulsion. Over the ship's lifetime, however, the costs for aircraft are dominant and they do not depend on the means of propulsion. Freedom from the constraints of ship refueling, especially under sustained high-speed operating conditions, has to be balanced against the cost differences. Building programs in the remainder of the century can produce somewhat different numbers of ships, depending on which propulsions plants are selected for them.

Attacks conducted with nuclear weapons present acute problems in defending a fleet. Soviet naval writers tend not to distinguish between the use of nuclear and conventional weapons as US writers do. Soviet writers also stress "decisive strikes" and intimate that naval conflict will be brief. If strikes with nuclear weapons are to be the means to achieve these goals, defeating them may require more than defeating conventional strikes. Because nuclear weapons are more powerful and therefore need not be as accurate, stopping more of them is necessary to protect a fleet. Depending on the size of the warheads on the attacking weapons, it may be necessary to stop all of them —a much more demanding task than stopping most. If systems such as "Aegis" and "Phalanx" cannot achieve it, then dispersal of defending ships may be necessary to prevent more than one from being disabled by a nuclear detonation. As the separation distance between ships increases, the communications that permits coordination of ships and aircraft becomes more difficult to maintain. If attacks with nuclear weapons are thus disruptive to a fleet, then their use offers more advantage to the side whose mission is sea denial than to the assertive side.

The world's naval officers and other students of naval warfare have not yet reached agreement on which factors are most important in winning war at sea. Although it is possible to get general agreement on which factors—the ranges of weapons, quality of fighting personnel, staying power of ships, ability to mass and co-ordinate forces, and the many other considerations discussed in this chapter—are important, it is much more difficult to rank the factors in order of importance. It is presently impossible to relate changes in one factor to changes in another in any systematic way. Because of that, debate over how to build and operate more effective navies and how to predict which one of them will prevail in combat continues. Such debate is ordinarily illuminated by combat experience, but there has been no major conflict between navies for more than 30 years. Navies are already quite different from what they were then; they will continue to change. The debate will go on.

Right: Many expensive ($25 to 28 million) F-14A Tomcats have been lost. This one rolled off *JFK* off northern Scotland in November 1976. The Soviets would have liked to have salvaged it, but the US Navy fished it up after prolonged search.

Below: Frame from a film taken by a ship, probably USS *Bigelow*, armed with CIWS, Close-In Weapon System. This uses the 20mm Vulcan gun to pour out 3,000 shells per minute, tracking them with radar to bring them on-target—in this case a Walleye missile, whose warhead has been detonated.

US Warships

Hugh Lyon, founder member of "Warships Society", London; author of technical reference books, including Salamander's *The Encyclopedia of the World's Warships.*

The following technical descriptions cover the more important warships, auxiliary classes and torpedoes in the US Navy inventory. The warships are presented by ship type, with combat vessels arranged approximately by size.

Nimitz Class Aircraft Carriers

Displacement: 81,600 tons (91,400 full load).
Dimensions: Length overall 1,090ft 3in (332·9m); deck width overall 251ft 6in (76·8m); beam 133ft 9in (40·8m); draught 42ft 6in (13m).
Aircraft: Over 90 aircraft and helicopters.
Armament: Surface-to-air missiles, three BPDMS Sea Sparrow 8-tube launchers on sponsons one to starboard forward and one each side aft.
Propulsion: Two A4W reactors, four sets GE steam turbines. Total approx 280,000shp on four shafts, maximum speed approx 33kts.

It was decided in October 1963 that *John F Kennedy* (CV-67) should be conventionally powered because of the massive expense of nuclear powered carriers, and in February 1965 Secretary of Defense McNamara announced in Congress that the attack carrier force was to be reduced by two ships to 13 because of growing doubts about their utility and vulnerability, especially in view of their immense cost. However, the effectiveness of the carrier operations off Vietnam brought a change of heart, and in February 1966 McNamara told Congress that he had reassessed the need and was planning to ask for 15 attack carriers again. *Enterprise* (CVN-65) had demonstrated how valuable the extra freedom of action allowed by using nuclear power could be, and four nuclear powered aircraft carriers were included in McNamara's new total. On 1 July 1966 funds were provided for *Nimitz* (CVN-68), and she was then due for completion in 1971 with her sisters CVN-69 and CVN-70 due in 1973 and 1975. The facts of the future were to be very different. Only one American shipyard,

Above: Almost half of *Nimitz's* aircraft complement are on the flight deck. Note the cluttered box-like island and the BPDMS mount on a sponson aft.

the Newport News Shipbuilding and Dry Dock Co. which built *Enterprise* (CVN-65), was able to build them. *Nimitz* (CVN-68) was laid down in 1968, but problems beset her construction at all points. Though she required only two reactors as opposed to eight in *Enterprise* (CVN-65), delays in delivering and testing the components of the new A4W/A1G reactors caused slippage which was exacerbated by shortages of labor. As a result *Nimitz* (CVN-68) was not commissioned in 1971 but on 3 May 1975; her next sister, *Dwight D Eisenhower* (CVN-69), in 1977 instead of 1973; and *Carl Vinson* (CVN-70) was not laid down until October 1975 with a tentative delivery date in 1981 instead of 1975. As a result, costs have shot up, and while the price of *Nimitz* (CVN-68) was $1·881 billion, the next pair will be over $2 billion each.

These three ships are slightly larger than *Enterprise* (CVN-65), but their machinery is smaller, advantage having been taken of improvements in reactor design to reduce their number from eight to two with only a slight reduction in power and speed. This enables them to carry a fifth again as much aviation fuel as the earlier nuclear carrier, and they can also carry more ammunition and stores, thus further reducing their dependence on external supply. They also have a greater complement, more aircraft, and a different radar (SPS 48 in place of SPS 32/33). Planning for a fourth ship was temporarily in abeyance as a result of continuing doubts over these ship's utility and cost effectiveness. However, although it appeared almost certain in 1975–76 that the nuclear aircraft carrier would be abandoned in favor of a spartan, conventionally powered *Essex* sized ship, the proponents of the nuclear powered carrier again appeared to be coming to the fore in 1977, and preliminary funding has been provided for a fourth *Nimitz* class aircraft carrier.

Above: The three catapults, the lowered starboard deck edge lifts and the starboard rear BPDMS mount are clearly visible as *Nimitz* replenishes at sea.

Below: *Nimitz.* Note the deck edge lifts, the BPDMS mounts, the deck parks, and the SPS-43A 2-D radar on the lattice mast aft of the island.

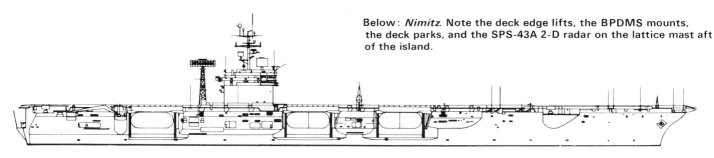

Kitty Hawk Class Aircraft Carriers

Displacement: 61,000 tons (80,000 full load).
Dimensions: Length overall 1,062ft 6in (323·9m); deck width overall 252ft (76·8m); beam 129ft 6in (38·5m); draught 35ft 10in (11m).
Aircraft: Over 80 aircraft and helicopters.
Armament: Surface-to-air missiles, two twin Terrier launchers on sponsons one each side aft.
Propulsion: Four sets Westinghouse steam turbines. Total 280,000shp on four shafts, maximum speed 35kts.

Although the hull of the *Kitty Hawk* class is very similar to that of the *Forrestals*, so many improvements were incorporated in these ships that they are counted as a different class. They followed on directly from the *Forrestals*, *Kitty Hawk* (CV-63) being built between 1956–61, *Constellation* (CV-64) between 1957–61 and *America* (CV-66) between 1961–65. Each has slightly different dimensions (the data applies to *Kitty Hawk* (CV-63)), and *America* (CV-66), which was laid down later than the other two, has a bow sonar. The weakest point in the layout of the *Forrestals* is in the arrangement of their lifts, particularly in the positioning of the port lift at the forward end of the angled deck, where it cannot be used if flying operations are in progress. Also, the arrangement of the starboard lifts, with one forward and two behind the island is inconvenient when planes are being marshalled for the forecastle catapults. On the *Kitty Hawks* and subsequent US aircraft carriers the port lift has been moved aft to a point where it no longer encroaches on the angled deck. In addition the island has been moved aft so that there are two lifts forward and one aft on the starboard side. The *Kitty Hawks* can launch and recover large numbers of aircraft continuously without difficulty, whereas the decks of the *Midways* and *Forrestals* soon become clogged with aircraft. *Kitty Hawk* (CV-63) was the first American warship to be armed totally with missiles. In place of the *Forrestals'* eight single 5in 54-cal guns arranged on sponsons each side of the hull at bow and stern, the *Kitty Hawks* were completed with two twin

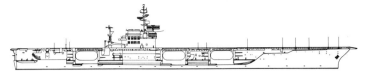

Above: *Kitty Hawk*. Note crane abaft island.

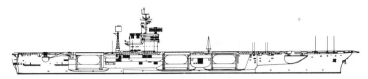

Above: *John F Kennedy*. Note BPDMS mounts.

Terrier SAMs aft. This medium range SAM system is unnecessarily large and expensive for a ship that is already protected against hostile aircraft by its own aircraft and by accompanying escorts, so later carriers and the refitted *Forrestals* have only mounted the much lighter and cheaper short range Sea Sparrow SAM system as a 'last ditch' weapon.

In 1963 it was decided that the carrier to be laid down in FY 1964 would be nuclear powered, but the immense cost caused second thoughts, and she was eventually laid down as the conventionally powered *John F Kennedy* (CV-67). She closely resembles the last *Kitty Hawk*, *America* (CV-66), and she also has a bow sonar, but she can be distinguished externally by having two BPDMS Sea Sparrow SAM launchers in place of Terriers and by having her funnel canted to starboard to direct the hot funnel gases away from the radars and the flight path.

Below: A Phantom has just been launched from *Kitty Hawk's* starboard bow catapult, and a Crusader is about to be catapulted from the angled deck.

Enterprise Aircraft Carrier

Displacement: 75,700 tons (89,600 full load).
Dimensions: Length overall 1,102ft (335·9m); deck width overall 252ft (76·8m); beam 133ft (40·5m); draught 35·8ft (10·8m).
Aircraft: Over 90 aircraft and helicopters.
Armament: Surface-to-air missiles, two BPDMS Sea Sparrow 8-tube launchers on sponsons one each side aft.
Propulsion: Eight A2W reactors, four sets Westinghouse steam turbines. Total approx 280,000shp on four shafts, maximum speed approx 35kts.

USS *Enterprise* (CVN-65) was designed at a time when fierce argument was taking place in the USA over the future value of aircraft carriers, and she was commissioned in the first year of the Kennedy administration whose Secretary of Defense, Robert McNamara, was by no means convinced of the cost-effectiveness of a ship which had cost $451,300,000. Her hull design was a modification of that of the *Forrestal* class conventionally powered aircraft carriers but the inclusion of nuclear propulsion and other differences resulted in her being the largest warship built up to that time. With the cruiser *Long Beach* (CGN-9) completing shortly before her, *Enterprise* (CVN-65) was the second nuclear powered warship and probably the most distinctive. Having no requirement for funnel uptakes the bridge is box-shaped with a cone top. At the lower level "bill-board" fixed array radar antennae for the SPS 32 and 33 "3-D" sets are fitted to the sides and the cone is fitted with aerials for electronic counter-measures. The design of the nuclear plant was initiated in 1950, deferred from 1953–54 to obtain full value from developments in submarine nuclear propulsion, and then continued to the production stage by the Bettis Atomic Power

Laboratory. On 2 December 1960, just two months after launching, *Enterprise's* first reactor went critical, and in the next 11 months all eight, feeding 32 heat exchangers and with two reactors for each shaft, reached criticality. From her commissioning in November 1961 until her first refit and nuclear refuelling which started in November 1964 she steamed nearly 210,000 miles. With a range such as this, to be steadily and notably increased as future refuellings provide improved cores, with a higher speed than previous carriers and with 50 percent more aviation fuel than the *Forrestals*, stored in space taken up by the ship's own fuel in conventionally powered units, she proved many of the points advanced by the supporters of nuclear propulsion. But with over 90 aircraft and helicopters to operate and 5,500 men to be fed there is still the continual need for underway replenishment groups to provide fuel, munitions and food. Although the frequency of such replenishments is much less than the conventional weekly rendezvous with a tanker, under intensive operating it will still cause problems for planners. The requirement for ammunition and missiles for ship-board systems is, however, minimal as *Enterprise* (CVN-65) has no guns and, although allowance was originally made for a Terrier SAM system, her sole armament is a pair of BPDMS Sea Sparrow SAM launchers. Like all US carriers, she relies mainly on aircraft for long range defense and on escorts for close range protection. With the embarkation of AS aircraft, she was reclassified from CVAN to CVN on 30 June 1975.

Below: *Enterprise* **with a Corsair on deck and a Hawkeye on the lowered starboard lift. Note the "bill-board" radar arrays on the small island.**

Forrestal Class
Aircraft Carriers

Displacement: 60,000 tons (78,700 full load).
Dimensions: Length overall 1,039ft (316·8m); deck width overall 252ft (76·8m); beam 129ft 6in (39·5m); draught 37ft (11·3m).
Aircraft: Over 80 aircraft and helicopters.
Armament: Surface-to-air missiles, three BPDMS Sea Sparrow 8-tube launchers on sponsons one to starboard forward and one each side aft.
Propulsion: Four sets Westinghouse steam turbines. Total 280,000shp on four shafts, maximum speed 34kts.

United States (CVA-58), the first postwar American aircraft carrier to be laid down, had a designed displacement of 65,000 tons. She was to have had funnels flush with the flight deck and a retractable bridge to provide the maximum possible deck space for operating the large postwar carrier aircraft. However, she was cancelled almost immediately after being laid down in April 1949 because of doubts about her design and function, and because of pressure from the USAF Strategic Air Command. The subsequent "Admirals' revolt" and a reassessment of the value of aircraft carriers in the light of the Korean War resulted in the US Navy being allowed to build a

Below: *Forrestal* **with full deck parks. Note the lift at the forward end of the angled deck and the midships position of the cramped island.**

Above: A small launch can be seen just ahead of *Enterprise*, whose unique island makes her unmistakeable. Note the BPDMS mount. The large Tomcat fighters are mostly parked aft, and the other aircraft on the flight-deck are Corsairs, Hawkeyes, Vigilantes, Intruders and Prowlers, with Sea King A/S and SAR helicopters.

Below: *Independence.* Note the BPDMS mount forward and the search radar cantilevered from the funnel.

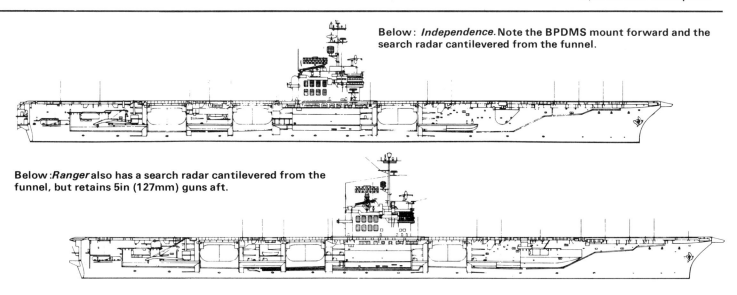

Below: *Ranger* also has a search radar cantilevered from the funnel, but retains 5in (127mm) guns aft.

fleet based on large aircraft carriers. A *Forrestal* was authorized each year from 1952–55, and *Forrestal* (CV-59), *Saratoga* (CV-60), *Ranger* (CV-61) and *Independence* (CV-62) were built between 1952–59. They were the largest aircraft carriers to be built since the Japanese *Shinano* of 1944. Their design was based on that of the *United States* (CVA-58), but it was modified to take advantage of the new British angled deck. This underwent very successful trials on the *Essex* class aircraft carrier *Antietam* (CV-36) in 1952, and gave the necessary deck space whilst still retaining a fixed island and funnel. *Forrestal* (CV-59) is the first American aircraft carrier to be built with an angled deck. This is angled at 8° and the flight deck and island are sponsoned out to twice the width of the hull. The four lifts, each 52ft 3in by 62ft (15·9m by 18·9m) are external to the hull, eliminating a source of weakness in previous carriers' flight decks. *Forrestal* (CV-59) is also the first American carrier to be built with steam catapults (another British invention), having two forward and two on the angled deck enabling four aircraft to be launched in very rapid succession. To improve seaworthiness

the *Forrestals* have a fully enclosed hurricane bow, the first fitted to an American carrier since the pre-war *Lexingtons*. However, when first completed they were unable to maintain high speed in rough weather because the forward 5in gun sponsons were liable to structural damage because of their size and position. They were therefore removed, and most eight single 5in 54-cal have since been replaced by three BPDMS Sea Sparrow SAM launchers. Another weak point in the design is the positioning of the port lift at the forward end of the angled deck where it interferes with flying operations. *Saratoga* (CV-60), *Ranger* (CV-61) and *Independence* (CV-62) are slightly larger than *Forrestal*, and have more powerful engines giving a knot more speed. *Ranger* (CV-61) has a wider flight deck and *Independence* (CV-62) is slightly longer. The data applies to *Saratoga* (CV-60). Since the phasing out of the *Essex* class carriers, they all now operate a mix of fighter, attack, airborne radar, reconnaissance and AS aircraft and helicopters, and were reclassified from (CVA) to (CV) on 30 June 1975.

Midway Class
Aircraft Carriers

Displacement: 51,000 tons (64,000 full load).
Dimensions: Length overall 979ft (298·4m); deck width overall 237ft 3in (72·5m); beam 121ft (36·9m); draught 35ft 3in (10·8m).
Aircraft: 60–75 aircraft and helicopters.
Armament: Guns, three single 5in 54-cal on sponsons one to starboard forward and one each side aft.
Propulsion: Four sets Westinghouse or GE steam turbines. Total 212,000 shp on four shafts, maximum speed 33kts.

Above: *Midway.* **Note search radar on funnel.**

Above: *Coral Sea.* **Note search radar on mast.**

The three *Midway* class aircraft carriers (CV) are the smallest ships of that type currently in service in the USN, but when they were built in 1943–47 they were by far the largest. Six were originally ordered in the first years of the Pacific war, but three were cancelled and only *Midway* (CV-41), *Franklin D Roosevelt* (CV-42) and *Coral Sea* (CV-43) were built. They were intended to combine the best features of the US *Essex* class carriers currently in large scale production with the armored flight deck fitted to the British *Illustrious* class carriers. Although they only had the same aircraft capacity and maximum speed of the 30,800 ton *Essex*s, the *Midway*s displaced about 45,000 tons when first completed, which was the penalty to be paid for the extra protection and the other additional features worked into these ships. Unlike the *Essex*s, the *Midways'* completion was not rushed, and none was ready before the end of World War II. Their original armament consisted of eighteen single 5in 54-cal guns distributed round the hull, and they also carried large numbers of 40mm and 20mm AA guns. They carried about 130 aircraft in an open hangar, with three lifts, two on the centre line and one at the deck edge to port. They had an open bow. They were the first US warships to be built too wide for the Panama canal. After serving in the Atlantic and Mediterranean during the Korean War, they were all modernized between 1953–60. All three ships had angled decks, steam catapults and enclosed bows fitted, and their elec-

Below: The advantages of an angled deck can clearly be seen in this bow view of *Midway.* **Note large overhang, and Intruders on flight deck.**

Above: Although *Midway* **still retains some 5in (127mm) guns, she has been extensively modernized. Note the large deck-edge lifts, and new radar.**

tronics were updated. *Midway* (CV-41) and *Franklin D Roosevelt* (CV-42) were fitted with a deck edge lift at the forward end of the angled deck and another behind the island to starboard, whilst retaining their centerline lift forward. *Coral Sea* (CV-43), which was the last to be converted, was fitted with a deck edge lift fore and aft of the island to starboard and a lift at the forward end of the angled deck to port. *Midway* was again modernized between 1967–70 when she was given a starboard deck edge lift forward of the island in place of the one on the centerline, and all the lifts were enlarged. Her angled deck was extended, her steam catapults replaced by more powerful ones and her arrester gear renewed. She can now operate F-14 Tomcats, but the other two were not modernized. They are very old, and are worn out. *Franklin D Roosevelt* (CV-42) grounded badly in the mid-1960s, and since then has been used purely as a training carrier. The two unmodernized ships will soon be scrapped, and *Midway* (CV-41) will also have to be taken out of service in the next few years.

Virginia Class Cruisers

Displacement: 10,000 tons full load.
Dimensions: Length overall 580ft (177·3m); beam 60ft 6in (18·5m); draught 29ft 5in (9m).
Aircraft: Facilities for AS helicopters right aft.
Armament: Surface-to-air and AS missiles, two ASTOR twin launchers one forward and one aft; guns, two single 5in 54-cal one in front of bridge and one aft of superstructure; torpedo tubes, two triple Mk 32 12·7in (324mm) mounts one each side of the superstructure aft.
Propulsion: Two D2G reactors, two sets steam turbines. Total 100,000shp on two shafts, maximum speed over 30kts.

Above: *Virginia* **class. Note large bow sonar.**

The four *Virginia*s, two of which have been completed and two of which are under construction, are the first US warships to be fitted with the new Aegis weapons control system. This integrated system gives much better and faster control for the ship's weapons, and is also highly resistant to ECM. The *Virginia* class Nuclear-powered Guided Missile Cruisers (CGN) are based on the preceding *California* class, but have a combined SAM/ASM/SSM Mk 26 twin launcher. This fires either Standard 2 MR or ER SAMs, ASROC ASMs or Harpoon SSMs, and in addition to adding Harpoon SSMs to the ship's weapons it also enables the separate ASROC launcher to be dispensed with, thereby saving 16ft in hull length. It also provides all round defense with all three types of missile in the *Virginia*s' arrangement of one

launcher forward and another aft. The Mk 26 launcher is fed from specially developed magazines which can feed any type of missile in any order to the launcher. Besides having no separate ASROC launcher or reload house, and having a slightly shorter hull, the *Virginia*s can be distinguished from the *California*s by having the aft 5in 54-cal gun mounted one deck lower. The USN has been pressing for several years for a somewhat larger nuclear powered guided missile cruiser (CSGN) optimized for the sea control rather than the escort role, but such is the cost of these ships that it is unlikely that any CGNs other than those necessary to escort the CVNs will be built, at least in the near future. Meanwhile the *Virginia*s could be fitted with tactical cruise missiles to uprate their surface capability. As yet, no other ships have been fitted with Aegis, though the DDG-47 enhanced *Spruance*s, which have not yet been authorized, are intended to have it.

California Class Cruisers

Displacement: 10,150 tons full load.
Dimensions: Length overall 596ft (181·7m); beam 61ft (18·6m); draught 31·5ft (9·6m).
Aircraft: Facilities for A/S helicopter right aft.
Armament: Surface-to-air missiles, two Tartar single launchers one right forward and one aft; guns, two single 5in 54-cal one forward and one superimposed aft; AS weapons, one ASROC 8-tube launcher in front of bridge; torpedo tubes, four Mk 32 12·7in (324mm) two each side at stern.
Propulsion: Two D2G reactors, two sets steam turbines. Total 100,000shp on two shafts, maximum speed over 30kts.

Because the full advantages of a nuclear powered aircraft carrier cannot be obtained unless they also have nuclear powered escorts, the building of the three *Nimitz* class CVNs meant a new program of nuclear powered guided missile cruisers. The first to be built were the two *California* class Guided Missile Cruisers (CGN), *California* (CGN-36) and *South Carolina* (CGN-37), built between 1970–75. They are developed versions of *Bainbridge* (CGN-25) and *Truxtun* (CGN-35), but are considerably larger and more sophisticated ships. They can easily be distinguished by their enclosed masts and their flush decks. They are armed primarily for AA and AS duties, though they have a limited surface capability. This reflects their function as escorts for the nuclear aircraft carriers, whose aircraft are intended to provide protection against major surface ships. However, they may soon be fitted with Harpoon SSMs which will enable them to operate independently. A third *California* was authorized in FY 1968, but its construction was deferred and later cancelled in favour of the improved *Virginia* class CGNs in 1970. Each of these ships cost about $200 million, but they are highly sophisticated vessels, and are essential for a nuclear powered carrier force. Since completion, the two *Californias* have served as escorts to *Nimitz* (CVN-68).

Above: The *Californias* can be distinguished from the *Virginias* by having a separate ASROC launcher and a superimposed 5in (127mm) gun aft.

Below: *California* at speed. Note the absence of funnels and the helicopter platform aft.

Above: *California* class. Note ASROC launcher.

Long Beach Cruiser

Displacement: 14,200 tons (17,100 full load).
Dimensions: Length overall 721ft 2in (220m); beam 73ft 2in (22·3m); draught 31ft (9·5m).
Aircraft: One Kaman SH-2F Seasprite on pad right aft.
Armament: Surface-to-air missiles, two superimposed Standard ER launchers forward, one Talos twin launcher aft; AS weapons, one ASROC 8-tube launcher immediately behind the bridge amidships; guns, two single 5in 38-cal one each side amidships; torpedo tubes, two triple Mk 32 12·7in (324mm) mounts one each side of the superstructure just forward of the bridge.
Propulsion: Two Westinghouse C1W reactors, two sets GE steam turbines. Approx 40,000shp each, maximum speed over 30kts.

Long Beach (CGN-9, ex CGN-160, ex CLGN-160) was the first surface warship to have nuclear propulsion, and was also the first to be armed entirely with guided missiles. She was originally intended to be a 7,800 ton standard displacement guided missile frigate with a single Terrier SAM launcher. Before the design was finalized in 1956 the size had almost doubled and the armament considerably increased. She was completed with two Terrier SAM twin launchers superfiring forward and a Talos launcher aft. She was originally designed to carry Regulus II SSMs. This was a nuclear armed strategic cruise missile with a range of about 1,000 miles at a speed of Mach 2. When this was cancelled in favor of Polaris ICBMs, it was planned to fit eight of these in tubes amidships. However, Polaris has only been fitted in submarines and *Long Beach* was finally completed without any SSMs or ICBMs. Instead, she mounts an ASROC launcher amidships. Laid down in 1957, she was completed in 1961 at a cost of nearly $333 million. The forward superstructure is similar to that fitted to the nuclear aircraft carrier *Enterprise* (CVN-65). It is a large square structure with fixed "Billboard" antennae for the SPS-32 surface search and target

designation and SPS-33 height finding radars. The aft superstructure is much smaller, and since the 1962–63 refit it has been flanked by two 5in guns, which were fitted to counter the threat from low-flying aircraft and fast patrol boats, neither of which could be dealt with by missiles. *Long Beach* was completed as an escort for nuclear aircraft carriers, and is intended to deal with air and sub-surface threats. At present she relies mainly on carrier-borne aircraft for defense against surface attack, though her present missiles have a limited surface-to-surface capability. In company with *Enterprise* (CVN-65) and *Bainbridge* (CGN-25), *Long Beach* showed the advantages of an all nuclear task force during Operation Sea Orbit in 1964, when these three nuclear powered ships sailed round the world in 65 days without needing to replenish. *Long Beach* underwent her first major refit and refuelling in 1966–67, after steaming over 160,000 miles on her first reactor cores, much of it at sustained high speed. Her radars were updated in 1970, and she will shortly be undergoing her "mid-life" refit. She will probably be refitted with the Aegis system at a cost of over $400 million, which will eliminate some of the shortcomings in her surface-to-surface and close range weapons and update her electronics.

Below: *Long Beach* has a similar "bill-board" radar array to the nuclear carrier *Enterprise*.

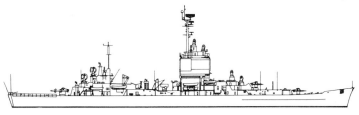

Above: *Long Beach* showing unique silhouette.

Albany Class Cruisers

Displacement: 13,700 tons (17,500 full load).
Dimensions: Length overall 673ft 6in (205·3m); beam 70ft 10in (21·6m); draught 30ft (9·1m).
Aircraft: Facilities for two AS helicopters aft.
Armament: Surface-to-air missiles, two twin Talos launchers one forward and one aft and two twin Tartar launchers one each side of the superstructure forward; guns, two single 5in 38-cal one each side of the second Mack; AS weapons, one ASROC 8-tube launcher between the Macks; torpedo tubes, two triple Mk 32 12·7in (324mm) mounts one each side of the forward superstructure.
Propulsion: Four sets GE steam turbines. Total 120,000shp on four shafts, maximum speed 33kts.

The three *Albany* class Guided Missile Cruisers (CG) were built between 1943–46 as members of the two funnelled *Baltimore* class and improved, one funneled *Oregon City* class heavy cruisers. The *Baltimores* were the largest class of heavy cruiser ever built. They were originally armed with three triple 8in (203mm) turrets, two forward and one aft, six twin 5in 38-cal and 48 40mm and 22 20mm AA guns. After the Terrier SAM had undergone successful trials on the trials ship *Mississippi* (ex BB-41), two *Baltimores*, *Boston* (CA-69 later CAG-1) and *Canberra* (ex *Pittsburgh*, CA-70 later CAG-2) were converted into single ended guided missile cruisers between 1951–56. The twin funnels were replaced with a single funnel, and the aft turret was removed and replaced by two twin Terrier SAM launchers. The superstructure was also modified. It had been intended to convert all the *Baltimores* to this standard, but the conversion was so expensive and complicated for the results achieved that the plan was dropped. However, *Chicago* (CA-136, later CG-11) and *Columbus* (CA-74, later CG-12), together with *Albany* (CA-123 later CG-10) of the *Oregon City* class were completely reconstructed as double-ended guided missile cruisers. They were converted between 1959–64. The superstructure was completely removed and replaced with a new aluminum structure and two tall macks. A twin Talos SAM launcher was fitted fore and aft, and a twin Terrier SAM launcher was fitted either side of the bridge. Space was left amidships to fit Polaris ICBMs, but these were never carried, and an ASROC 8-tube ASM launcher was fitted amidships instead. Originally no

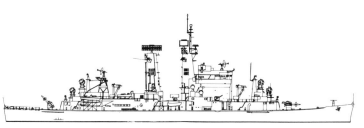

Above: *Chicago*. Note enormous macks.

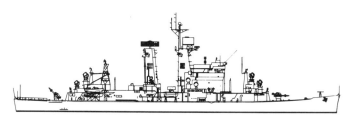

Above: *Albany*, with modernised radar.

guns were mounted, but the SAMs could not cope with fast low flying aircraft or with the even more difficult target posed by small high speed surface vessels, and like all the early US missile armed escorts, guns have been added to deal with these threats. All the conventionally armed *Baltimores* and *Oregon Citys* had been discarded by 1974, and *Boston* (CAG-1) and *Canberra* (CAG-2) have also been deleted. Both *Chicago* (CG-11) and *Columbus* (CG-12) have been taken out of service, but *Albany* (CG-10), which was modernized between 1967–68, still remains in service. Although these ships were very capable, it is doubtful that the money expended on converting them to missile cruisers was well spent. They cost so much and spent so long in dock that it would have been wiser to build new ships, especially after the experience with the two *Boston* single ended conversions. That this was belatedly recognized by the USN is shown by the fact that the planned total conversion of two more *Baltimores* was not proceeded with, and no more World War II cruisers were rebuilt afterwards.

Belknap Class Cruisers

Displacement: 6,570 tons (7,930 full load).
Dimensions: Length overall 547ft (166·7m); beam 54ft 10in (16·7m); draught 28ft 10in (8·8m).
Aircraft: One Kaman SH-2F Seasprite with hangar and pad at aft end of superstructure.
Armament: Surface-to-air and AS missiles, one ASTOR (Standard and ASROC) twin launcher forward; guns, one single 5in 54-cal right aft, two single 3in one each side amidships; torpedo tubes, two triple Mk 32 12·7in (324mm) mounts one each side of the superstructure abreast the forward mack.
Propulsion: Two sets GE or De Laval steam turbines. Total 85,000shp on two shafts, maximum speed 34kts.

Above: *Belknap* has her missile launcher forward, where there is most room for a large magazine.

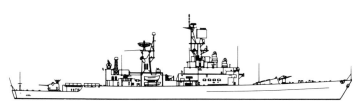

Above: *Belknap* class cruiser *Fox*. Note macks.

Below: The nuclear powered *Truxtun* can be distinguished from her conventionally powered half-sisters by her lattice masts and by having the gun forward and the missile launcher aft.

The *Belknaps* are the last conventionally powered US cruisers to be built up to the present. They are anti-aircraft and anti-submarine escorts for the US carriers and they have been developed from the smaller conventionally powered *Leahys*. Like them, the *Belknaps* are long-ranged, seaworthy ships with sophisticated electronics, but these features have been attained at the expense of weapons systems. The most serious lack is the absence of an adequate SSM, though this is being remedied by the addition of Harpoon. By the time the *Belknaps* were designed, the USN had realized the advantages of carrying a helicopter on board, and they had also appreciated the continued advantages of guns. As a result, the *Leahys'* aft Terrier SAM launcher was replaced by a 5in 54-cal gun and a pad and hangar for a helicopter. Space was also saved forward by firing ASROC ASMs from the same launcher as the SAMs. As in the Leahys, the two uptakes are incorporated into macks. Ten *Belknap* class Guided Missile Cruisers (CG) were to have been built, but as with the earlier class Congress insisted that one should be nuclear powered, so only nine conventionally powered *Belknaps* were built between 1962–67. Their nuclear powered half-sister, *Truxtun* (CGN-35), was built between 1963–67, and like *Bainbridge* (CGN-25) has two D2G reactors in a slightly larger hull. She differs from her conventionally powered half-sisters not only because she is nuclear powered and has lattice masts instead of macks, but also because she has the 5in 54-cal gun on the forecastle and the SAM/ASM launcher on the quarterdeck. One problem with ships fitted with the joint SAM/ASM launcher is that if the launcher were damaged or broke down, the ship would be deprived of a large part pf its AA and AS capability. *Belknap* (CG-26) was severely damaged in collision with the US carrier *John F Kennedy* (CV-67) in the Mediterranean on 22 November 1975. Her entire upperworks were removed by the carrier's overhang, and a serious fire followed. There was a possibility that she might be scrapped, but she is now being refitted with improved weapons systems.

Leahy Class Cruisers

Displacement: 5,670 tons (7,800 full load).
Dimensions: Length overall 534ft 6in (163·1m); beam 54ft 6in (16·2m); draught 24ft 6in (7·4m).
Aircraft: Pad but no facilities for AS helicopter aft.
Armament: Surface-to-air missiles, two twin Terrier launchers one forward and one aft; guns, two twin 3in one each side of the superstructure aft; AS weapons, one ASROC 8-tube launcher in front of bridge; torpedo tubes, two triple Mk 32 12·7in (324mm) mounts one each side amidships.
Propulsion: Two sets GE, De Laval or Allis Chalmers steam turbines. Total 85,000shp on two shafts, maximum speed 34kts.

The nine ships of the *Leahy* class were originally classed as Frigates (DLG) but they are now rated as Guided Missile Cruisers (CG). They were built between 1959–64 and belong to the period when the USN believed that the gun had been completely superceded by the missile. As a result, they are "double-ended" ships, with twin Terrier SAM launchers fore and aft. The main AS weapon is the ASROC 8-tube ASM launcher. There is a helicopter pad aft, but no hangar, so one cannot be permanently embarked.

Above: *Leahy* class firing a Terrier SAM from the aft launcher. Note SPG-55 missile control radars.

Above: *Leahy* showing twin SAM launchers and ASROC launcher.

They have a very weak gun armament of two twin 3in (76mm) amidships. The hull is based on that of the *Coontz* class, but above water the silhouette is completely different. There is a long forecastle extending over three-quarters the length of the ship, and they have a large, bulky superstructure. The *Leahy*s are the first new-built US ships to be fitted with macks, with all their attendent saving of space. From 1968 onwards the entire class has been refitted with the more modern electronics carried in the *Belknap*s, and can now operate the extended-range Standard SAM. As with all US escorts of this period, they lack a credible SSM, though ER Standard does have a limited SSM capability. However, since they are intended to operate as carrier escorts, emphasis has quite rightly been given to AA and to a certain extent AS capability, leaving the carrier aircraft to cope with the surface threat. If they receive Harpoon SSMs, they will then be able to operate independently. Like the later *Belknap*s, the *Leahy*s were intended to be a ten ship class. However, Congress insisted that one ship should be nuclear powered. This was *Bainbridge* (CGN-25). She is based closely on the *Leahy*s, but has a slightly larger hull to allow two D2G reactors to be fitted. Like the *Leahy*s she has a twin Terrier SAM launcher fore and aft, and she has the ASROC 8-tube ASM launcher in front of the bridge. She can be distinguished from her conventionally powered half sisters by having open lattice masts in place of macks. She was built between 1959–62, and was the first small surface ship to receive a nuclear reactor. From 1974 she was modernized in the same way as the *Leahy*s, receiving SPS 40 radar and ER Standard SAMs.

Ohio Class
Missile Submarines

Displacement: 16,000 surface (18,700 submerged).
Dimensions: Length overall 560ft (170·7m); beam 42ft (12·8m); draught 35ft 6in (10·8m).
Armament: Submarine launched ballistic missiles, twenty-four vertical tubes for Trident 1 in two rows of twelve in hull behind fin; torpedo tubes, four 21in (533mm) in bow.
Propulsion: One GE S8G reactor, one set GE steam turbines. Total shp on one shaft, and submerged speed not known.

While the program of upgrading the later Polaris SLBM submarines to carry the Poseidon SLBM was underway in the early 1970s, a new SLBM program was under development. This was to provide a much longer range missile, the Trident 1 SLBM with a range of 4,000 miles, and a huge 18,700 ton submarine to carry 24 of them. In due course, probably in the early 1980s, it was intended to introduce the improved Trident II SLBM with a 6,000 mile range to be retrofitted in place of the earlier missile. While Congress baulked at the immense cost of this new system, the Soviet Navy introduced their own long range SLBM, the 4,200 mile range SSN-8, in the *Delta* class SSBN in 1972. In 1976 the first increased range SSN-8s (6,450 miles) were fired. The US reaction was to speed up development of the Trident programme, and the first *Ohio* class Nuclear Ballistic Missile Submarine (SSBN) *Ohio* (SSBN-726) was laid down on 10 April 1976. *Michigan* (SSBN-727) has also been laid down, and a further eight are on order. They were due to enter service from 1979 but have slipped three years. The eventual number of Trident SLBM-carrying submarines depends on two main factors. The first is the result of the SALT (Strategic Arms Limitation Talks) agreement currently being negotiated between America and Russia, and any subsequent agreements. These will once again determine the maximum number of SLBMs that each side will tolerate the other having. The other factor is the development of the new types of long range cruise missiles, some of which can be used in a strategic role when launched from an ordinary 21in (533mm) submarine torpedo tube. Further developments in this field may restrict the need for a large number of SLBMs. However, the great advantage of the current generation of extremely long range SLBMs is that they can be launched from America's and Russia's home waters, thus making it extremely difficult to destroy the missiles before they have been fired. This makes the immense size of the *Ohio*s less significant, because although they are an immense target they are unlikely to be exposed to serious attack.

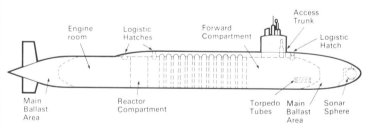

Above: Simplified drawing of *Ohio* class.

Below: Artist's impression of *Ohio* class showing long casing over the Trident SLBM tubes.

Lafayette Class
Missile Submarines

Displacement: 7,320 tons surface (8,250 submerged).
Dimensions: Length overall 425ft (129·5m); beam 33ft (10·1m); draught 31ft 6in (9·6m).
Armament: Submarine launched ballistic missiles, sixteen vertical tubes for Poseidon in two rows of eight in hull behind fin; torpedo tubes, four 21in (533mm) in bow.
Propulsion: One S5W reactor, two sets steam turbines. Total approx 15,000shp on one shaft, submerged speed approx 30kts.

The thirty-one *Lafayette* class Nuclear Ballistic Missile Submarines (SSBN), built between 1961–67, are the definitive US SSBNs of the 1960s and 1970s. The first eight ships were originally fitted with Polaris A-2 SLBMs, whilst the remaining twenty-three were fitted with the improved Polaris A-3 SLBMs, which have a range of 2,880 miles and can carry three 200 kiloton warheads. The first five ships in the class launched their missiles by compressed air, but the later 25 vessels used a rocket motor to produce a gas-steam mixture to eject the missiles from their tubes. Most of the *Lafayette*s have now been refitted with Poseidon C-3 CLBMs, and the remaining vessels were to reenter service in 1978. The Poseidon C-3 SLBM has a range of about 2,500 miles, and can carry ten 40 kiloton MIRVs. Problems were discovered in the first of these missiles to be fitted in the *Lafayette*s, and these have since been replaced by modified versions. The *Lafayette*s are slightly enlarged and improved versions of the *Ethan Allen*

Above: *Lafayette* **class. Note casing over SLBMs.**

design, and are almost indistinguishable from them except by the number on the fin. The last twelve *Lafayette*s differ considerably from the earlier ships in the class, and are sometimes referred to as the *Benjamin Franklin* class. They have improved and quieter machinery and 28 more crew members. Ten will be refitted with the larger three-stage Trident 1 (C-4) SLBM between 1981–85. This missile has a range of about 4,000 miles, and carries 100 kiloton MIRVs. Although these SSBNs do not have the underwater performance of the SSNs, they still have a considerable offensive capability against ships or other submarines, and they can be armed with conventional and wire-guided torpedoes and Subroc. Normally, however, they keep well out of the way of other ships and submarines, in order to make it as difficult as possible to locate them. In addition, their immense size would put them at a considerable disadvantage once they had been discovered. *Daniel Webster* (SSBN-626) has been experimentally fitted with diving planes on a raised bow sonar instead of on the fin, as in other US nuclear submarines; but although this was successful (it is the method used by other countries' nuclear submarines), it has not led to any change in the position of diving planes in other US submarines.

Lafayette **class** *John Adams* **cruising on the surface of the Pacific off Guam.**

Ethan Allen Class
Missile Submarines

Displacement: 6,900 tons surface (7,900 submerged).
Dimensions: Length overall 410ft 6in (125·1m); beam 33ft (10·1m); draught 30ft (9·1m).
Armament: Submarine launched ballistic missiles, sixteen vertical tubes for Polaris A-3 in two rows of eight in hull behind fin; torpedo tubes, four 21in (533mm) in bow.
Propulsion: One S5W reactor, one set geared turbines. Total approx 15,000shp on one shaft, submerged speed approx 30kts.

Whereas the *George Washington* class were built to a modified attack submarine design in order to get the Polaris SLBM into service in the shortest possible time, the five *Ethan Allen* class Nuclear Ballistic Missile Submarines (SSBN) were the first to be specially designed for the purpose. They are very similar to the *George Washington*s but are nearly 30ft (9·1m) longer and were armed when built with the Polaris A-2 SLBM, which has a range of 1,725 miles. They have greatly improved crew quarters, an important consideration when these vessels remain submerged on patrol for over 60 days at a time. They can be distinguished externally from the *George Washington*s by the blended-in casing over the missile tubes. On the earlier class this starts abruptly at the forward end of the fin, and it is much more noticeable. *Ethan Allen* (SSBN-608) was the first SSBN to fire a live missile, on 6 May 1962. This detonated successfully on the Christmas Island test range. Like all nuclear submarines in the USN, these ships have two crews, Blue and Gold, who take the submarine out on patrol alternately. In this way the nuclear boats are at sea for most of the time between refits, whilst their crews get an adequate rest from the stressful living conditions submerged. In practice, the endurance of these ships is not limited by the vessel itself, but by the length of time the crew can operate efficiently in them. Like all US SSBNs, the *Ethan Allen*s have an adequate underwater performance, but for most of the time they cruise at under 5 knots in their operational areas, and the missiles are usually launched at a speed of about only 3 knots. These ships have been refitted with Polaris A-3 SLBMs, but like the *George Washington*s they will not be fitted with Poseidon C-3 SLBM. Both of these classes have now been in service for fifteen years or more, and they will soon be replaced by the *Ohio* class Trident SLBM submarines.

Below: *Ethan Allen's* **elongated teardrop hull produces an enormous wake on the surface.**

George Washington Class Missile Submarines

Displacement: 6,019 tons surface (6,888 submerged).
Dimensions: Length overall 381ft 8in (116·3m); beam 33ft (10·1m); draught 29ft (8·8m).
Armament: Submarine launched ballistic missiles, sixteen vertical tubes for Polaris A-3 in two rows of eight in hull behind fin; torpedo tubes, six 21in (533m) in bow.
Propulsion: One Westinghouse S5W reactor, one set GE steam turbines. Total 15,000shp on one shaft, submerged speed approximately 30kts.

In 1955 the Soviet Union began the conversion of six *Zulu* class conventionally powered submarines to fire ballistic missiles. The modification involved the fitting of two launch tubes in the fin for the surface-discharged 300 mile range SSN-4 Snark SLBMs. A year earlier the USN had laid down the first of two *Grayback* class conventionally powered submarines, firing the Regulus I surface-launched cruise missile, and in 1957 laid down a nuclear powered Regulus I submarine, *Halibut*, which entered service in 1960. However, at that time cruise missiles were considerably more vulnerable than ballistic missiles, and in the early 1950s the US Navy, in collaboration with the US Army, started development of the Jupiter ICBM. This was to be fueled by liquid oxygen and kerosene, and three of these monster 60ft (18·3m) surface-launched missiles were intended to be carried in a 10,000 ton nuclear submarine. At the same time as the Russian developments made a US ballistic missile submarine more urgently required, developments in solid fuel and miniaturization had produced the Polaris A-1 SLBM. Not only did this have solid fuel, with all its attendent advantages, it could be launched submerged and had a range of 1,380 miles and it was so small that sixteen could be carried in the hull of a submarine

Above: *George Washington* at speed on the surface. This class can easily be distinguished by the short casing over the SLBMs.

only half the size of the projected Jupiter armed SSBN. The submerged launch capability and the for that period long range of the Polaris A-1 SLBM meant that the Polaris armed submarines were virtually undetectable before they had launched their missiles, whereas their Russian contemporaries had to close virtually to American coastal waters and were forced to surface to fire their missiles. In order to put Polaris into service as soon as possible, the five *George Washington* class Nuclear Ballistic Missile Submarines (SSBN) were basically lengthened versions of the *Skipjack* class SSNs, *George Washington* (SSBN-598) herself was laid down as the nuclear attack submarine *Scorpion*, and was lengthened 130ft (40m) on the stocks. This additional section, which contained the launch tubes, was inserted immediately aft of the fin. The original powerplant and much of the attack submarine's equipment were retained in the SSBN. The five *George Washington*s, built between 1957–61, were in service for seven years before the first Russian equivalents, the *Yankee* class SSBNs, became operational. By the mid-1960s the relatively short range of the Polaris A-1 SLBMs, which restricted the waters that the SSBNs could operate in whilst still allowing their missiles to reach targets inside Russia, was making the *George Washington*s more vulnerable to Russian countermeasures. Therefore during their first recoring between 1964–67 the class were fitted with the 2,880 mile Polaris A-3 SLBM. Their electronics has also been upgraded.

Above: *George Washington* class. Note casing.

Left: The doors over the Polaris SLBM tubes can clearly be seen in this view of *George Washington*.

Los Angeles Class Submarines

Displacement: 6,900 tons submerged.
Dimensions: Length overall 358ft 10in (109·7m); beam 32ft 11in (10·1m); draught 31ft 11in (9·8m).
Armament: Torpedo tubes, four 21in (533mm) amidships.
Propulsion: One D2G reactor, two sets steam turbines. Total approx 30,000shp on one shaft, submerged speed approx 35kts.

The first *Los Angeles* class Nuclear Attack Submarine (SSN) entered service in 1976, and a total of twenty-three are on order at present. These follow the experimental *Glenard P Lipscomb* (SSN-685), built between 1971–74 and are much larger than previous SSNs. They have a much higher submerged speed, and the increase in displacement is necessary to allow this and to enable them to carry all the electronics and weapons systems that are fitted. They have the BQQ 5 sonar system, and can operate Subroc, Sub-Harpoon and submarine launched cruise missiles as well as conventional and wire-guided torpedoes. Thus, like all the later US SSNs, although they are basically intended to hunt other submarines and to protect the SSBNs, they can also be used without modification to sink ships at long range with Sub-Harpoon, and when they enter service they can use the new cruise missiles to fire nuclear warheads at targets well inland. It is possible that with the new US emphasis on strategic cruise missiles, this role may be increased, and the new cruise missiles will in any case be used to attack surface targets at ten times the range of the existing 70 miles range Sub-Harpoon in a tactical role.

Above: *Los Angeles.* Her hull form is optimised for high speed submerged rather than on the surface. **Below:** The *Los Angeles* class submarine *Philadelphia* being launched. The flag covers the bow sonar.

Above: *Los Angeles* class. Note length of hull.

Sturgeon Class Submarines

Displacement: 3,640 tons surface (4,640 submerged).
Dimensions: Length overall 292ft 3in (89m); beam 31ft 8in (9·7m); draught 28ft 6in (8·8m).
Armament: Torpedo tubes, four 21in (533mm) amidships.
Propulsion: One S5W2 reactor, two sets GE or De Laval steam turbines. Total approx 20,000shp on one shaft, submerged speed approx 30kts.

The thirty-seven *Sturgeon* class Nuclear Attack Submarines (SSN) are slightly enlarged and improved versions of the preceding *Permit* class. Like them, the *Sturgeon*s have an elongated teardrop hull with the torpedo tubes set amidships and with the bow taken up by the various components of the BQQ-2 sonar system. They can be distinguished visually from the *Permit*s by the taller fin with the diving planes set further down. They can also fire Subroc, Sub-Harpoon and cruise missiles. There have been several problems between the USN and the builders of this class, *Pogy* (SSN-647) was reallocated to another yard for completion and *Guitarro* (SSN-665) was delayed for over two years. In an attempt to reduce noise, they are fitted with two contra-rotating propellers on the same shaft. Noise is the normal method of locating submarines, and though the American vessels are significantly quieter than the Russian submarines, any developments which can reduce noise and therefore the distance at which a submarine can be detected still further are speedily introduced in US submarines. These boats are primarily intended to hunt other submarines, and the ability to detect hostile submarines at long ranges is even more important

Above: This view of *Sturgeon* clearly shows the elongated teardrop hull form.

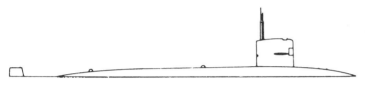

Above: *Sturgeon* class. Note forward position of fin.

than reducing the chances of the boat being herself detected. The *Sturgeon*s, like the *Permit*s, will therefore be fitted as soon as possible with the BQQ-5 sonar system introduced in the *Los Angeles* class SSNs. An experimental SSN based on the *Permit/Sturgeon* design, *Narwhal* (SSN-671), was built between 1967–69 to test the S5G free-circulation reactor, which has no pumps and is therefore quieter than previous US reactors.

Permit Class Submarines

Displacement: 3,750–3,800 tons surface (4,300–4,470 submerged).
Dimensions: Length overall 278ft 6in–297ft 4in (84·9–90·6m); beam 31ft 8in (9·6m); draught 28ft 4in (8·7m).
Armament: Torpedo tubes, four 21in (533mm) tubes amidships.

Propulsion: One Westinghouse S5W reactor, one set GE or De Laval steam turbines. Total 15,000shp on one shaft, submerged speed approx 30kts.

This class was originally known as the *Thresher* class, but after the loss of the name-ship (SSN-593) in the Atlantic in April 1963 the class was renamed the *Permit* class. They were preceded by the smaller *Tullibee* (SSN-597). Displacing only 2,640 tons submerged, this was an attempt to build the ideal hunter-killer submarine. The small size increased the manoeuvrability and meant that she was more likely to detect the hostile submarine before she herself had been detected, and the torpedoes were fitted amidships in an elongated teardrop hull. The entire bow was therefore freed for use to contain the new BQQ-2 sonar. She was also fitted with turbo-electric drive to eliminate the noise made by the reduction gears in earlier boats. However, the small size meant that she had a low submerged speed, and she lacked the room to carry all the necessary equipment and electronics, so no more SSNs of this size have been built. However, all the best features are incorporated in the thirteen surviving members of the *Permit* class, built between 1960–68. Four of these ships were originally designed to carry the Regulus II cruise missile, but they were reordered as SSNs when the Regulus II program was cancelled in favor of the Polaris SLBM in 1958. The first ten have a smaller hull than the last three, and *Jack* (SSN-605) has a modified hull to accommodate the machinery for contra-rotating propellors in an attempt to reduce noise. Their principal hunter-killer weapon is Subroc, which is controlled by the BQQ-2 sonar system, and they can also fire the anti-ship Sub-Harpoon. They are also capable of firing the new submarine launched cruise missiles. They will be refitted with the BQQ-5 sonar system.

Left: *Tullibee* is an experimental submarine. The larger *Permit*s do not have the casing abaft the fin. The three small domes on the hull are part of the BQG-4 PUFFS passive fire control system.

Skate Class Submarines

Displacement: 2,570 tons surface (2,860 submerged).
Dimensions: Length overall 267ft 8in (81·4m); beam 25ft (7·6m); draught 20ft 6in (6·1m).
Armament: Torpedo tubes, six 21in (533mm) four in bow and two in stern.
Propulsion: One S3W or S4W reactor, two sets steam turbines. Total 13,200shp on two shafts, submerged speed approx 25kts.

The *Skate* class Nuclear Attack Submarines (SSN) were the first non-experimental nuclear submarines to enter service. The four ships in this class were built between 1955–59, and are smaller versions of *Nautilus* (SSN-571), with the same type of hull, optimized for underwater performance. *Skate* (SSN-578) and *Swordfish* (SSN-579) have an S3W

reactor, whilst *Sargo* (SSN-583) and *Seadragon* (SSN-584) have an S4W. The S3W and S4W are both pressurized water cooled reactors, but they differ in design although they both develop the same power. Together with the two prototype nuclear submarines these vessels were used to explore the advantages conferred by the nuclear submarine's ability to remain submerged virtually indefinitely. The only real limit is imposed by the ability of the crew to continue functioning after a long spell cooped up inside the hull. Two more nuclear submarines were built virtually simultaneously with the *Skate*s, the Regulus I cruise missile armed *Halibut* (SSN-587) and the radar picket *Triton* (SSN-586). Both these ships were optimized for performance on the surface. *Halibut* needed to surface to fire her missiles. This and the greater vulnerability of the Regulus missiles than the Polaris SLBM meant that future construction was devoted to SSBNs rather than cruise missile submarines, and the Regulus launcher and associated equipment was removed in 1965. Since then she has served as

Skipjack class Submarine

Displacement: 3,075 tons surface (3,500 submerged).
Dimensions: Length overall 251ft 9in (76·8m); beam 31ft 8in (9·8m); draught 28ft (8·5m).
Armament: Torpedo tubes, six 21in (533mm) in bow.
Propulsion: One S5W reactor, one set Westinghouse or GE steam turbines. Total approx 15,000shp, submerged speed approx 30kts.

The *Skipjack* class Nuclear Attack Submarines (SSN) are the first nuclear submarines to incorporate the teardrop hull developed on the conventionally powered *Albacore* (AGSS-569). Instead of having a twenty plus knot submerged speed, the new hull form gave a thirty plus knot speed submerged, though their surface performance is poor in comparison. As well as the improved speed, the underwater manoeuvrability is also increased though the use of only one screw brings its own problems, and means that stern torpedo tubes can no longer be fitted. One of this class, *Scorpion*, was modified on the slip to become the first of the *George Washington* class SSBNs, and the materials for another were appropriated for the second. Ultimately six *Skipjacks* were built between 1956–61, including a replacement *Scorpion* (SSN-589), which was lost in the Atlantic in May 1968. All the engine fittings are duplicated (except for the reactor and propeller) to minimize the danger of a breakdown. They have had their original sonar equipment updated, but these old ships will not be fitted with the new BQQ-5 sonar because part of the bows are taken up by the torpedo tubes. They were the first class to use the S5W reactor. They will soon be taken out of service.

Above: *Skipjack* class, with teardrop hull-form.

Above: *Skipjack* was the first nuclear submarine to have a teardrop hull, a single screw, and the diving planes mounted on the fin.

Nautilus Submarine

Displacement: 3,764 tons surface (4,040 submerged).
Dimensions: Length overall 319ft 4in (97·4m); beam 27ft 7in (8·4m); draught 22ft (6·7m).
Armament: Torpedo tubes, six 21in (533mm) in bow.
Propulsion: One S2W reactor, two sets Westinghouse steam turbines. Total 15,000shp on two shafts, submerged speed 28kts.

The first funds for the construction of a nuclear submarine were authorized by Congress in the FY 1952 Budget and were the follow-on to research and development on a submarine reactor which had been started by the Argonne National Laboratory at the beginning of 1948 and continued by Westinghouse at the Bettis Atomic Power Laboratory. The Submarine Thermal Reactor Mark II which resulted from this work became known as the S2W and was installed in the hull of the *Nautilus* during her two and a quarter years of construction. It was a pressurized water cooled reactor and formed the basis of US submarine reactor design for the next decade. *Nautilus* has a conventional hull design, based on that of the German World War II *Type XXI*, with two screws and a streamlined fin. It is optimized for high performance submerged, but does not give as good manoeuvrability or as high a submerged speed as the teardrop hull pioneered on the conventionally powered experimental submarine *Albacore* (AGSS-569), which

was under construction at the same time. *Nautilus* (SSN-571) was the first nuclear-powered ship, and she got under way for the first time on 17 January 1955. She performed very well, and proved quite capable of undertaking long voyages submerged. By August 1958 she had established sufficient confidence in her reliability to be sent on the first submarine Polar transit, leaving from Hawaii and finishing in Portland, England. She is now no longer used operationally, and has been refitted for research. Almost simultaneously with *Nautilus* (SSN-571) another nuclear submarine, *Seawolf* (SSN-575), was built to test the rival liquid sodium cooled reactor, the S2G. This did not prove successful and it was replaced by a pressurized water cooled one similar to that fitted in *Nautilus* during her first refit in 1958–60.

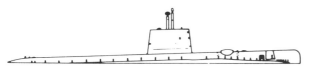

Above: *Nautilus.* Note conventional hull-form.

Right: *Nautilus,* seen here on trials, was the first nuclear submarine, and had an active career of over twenty years.

an attack submarine. She went into reserve in 1976. *Triton* was intended to act as a radar warning picket for surface task forces, and was for some time the largest nuclear submarine, and the only one with two reactors. She could easily be recognized by the long, flat topped hull and the enormous fin, intended to accommodate the radar. Her function was taken over by aircraft before she was even built, and she was a white elephant. She was too big to be used as an attack submarine, and in any case was not very manoeuvrable submerged. She was finally decommissioned in 1969. The *Skate* class are also now in reserve.

Left: *Halibut,* seen here after reconstruction, was the first purpose-built cruise missile submarine. The bulge forward was on the site of the launcher, aft of the Regulus II SSM hangar.

Barbel Class Submarines

Displacement: 2,150 tons surface (2,895 submerged).
Dimensions: Length overall 219ft 6in (66·8m); beam 29ft (8·8m); draught 28ft (8·5m).
Armament: Torpedo tubes, six 21in (533mm) in bow.
Propulsion: Three Fairbanks Morse diesels, one Westinghouse electric motor, diesel-electric drive. Total 4,800shp, submerged speed 25kts.

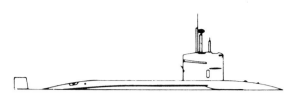

Above: *Barbel* class. Note teardrop hull-form.

The three *Barbel* class are the last conventionally powered submarines (SS) to be built for the USN, and are the only ones to remain in service. The *Albacore* (AGSS), built between 1952–53, had demonstrated the advantages of the short beamy "tear-drop" hull in reducing underwater drag by lessening the surface area for a given displacement. This opened the way to higher underwater speeds, whereas the *Tang* class submarines built between 1949–52 and based on the German World War II Type XXI design could make about 18 knots submerged, the *Barbel* class, built between 1956–59, can better this by about 7 knots, though at some expense to performance on the surface. When first built, the forward diving planes were positioned on the bows, but they have since been relocated on the fin. This class forms the basis of the Japanese *Uzushio* class submarine design. When the *Barbel*s were authorized in 1956, it was considered that the nuclear attack submarines (SSN) would be too expensive to be built in sufficient numbers, so the *Barbel*s were to be built to provide a sufficient number of attack submarines for the USN's needs. However, the nuclear attack submarine proved to be so superior in performance and the nuclear ship lobby under Admiral Rickover has been so powerful that all subsequent operational submarines have been nuclear powered. The *Barbel*s still perform a useful function as training ships, demonstrating the problems and abilities of conventional submarines in training exercises with nuclear attack and ballistic missile submarines and surface ships and AS aircraft and helicopters. The *Barbel* class can be distinguished from the nuclear attack submarines by their small size and the flat top to the hull, which has a clearly defined edge on each side.

Above: *Barbel* at speed. Note the flat top to the hull which distinguishes this class from the later and larger nuclear attack submarines.

Coontz Class Destroyers

Displacement: 4,700 tons (5,800 full load).
Dimensions: Length overall 512ft 6in (156·2m); beam 52ft 6in (15·9m); draught 25ft (7·6m).
Armament: Surface-to-air missiles, one Terrier twin launcher right aft; guns, one single 5in 54-cal forward; AS weapons, one ASROC 8-tube launcher superimposed forward; torpedo tubes, two triple Mk 32 12·7in (324mm) mounts one each side between the funnels amidships.
Propulsion: Two sets De Laval or Allis Chalmers steam turbines. Total 85,000shp on two shafts, maximum speed 34kts.

but this was replaced by the ASROC launcher before they were laid down. As built, they had two twin 3in (76mm) mounts abaft the aft funnel, but these were removed when the class was modernized between 1968 and 1975. This was intended to improve their AA capabilities, and they have been fitted with Standard in place of Terrier SAMs, NTDS and improved radar. *King* (DLG-10, later DDG-41) and *Mahan* (DLG-11 later DDG-42) were used with the *Essex* class carrier *Oriskany* (CVA-34 later CV-34) as trials ships for NTDS in 1961–62. *King* was later used between 1973–74 for sea trials of the Vulcan–Phalanx 20mm CIWS (Close In Weapon System) gun. This class can be distinguished by the large superstructure and absence of a gun aft. Ten ships were built though it had originally been intended to construct twenty. However improvements in weapon design and the introduction of macks meant that the class were curtailed, and the money allocated for the remaining ten went towards the completely redesigned *Leahy*s. As refitted the *Coontz* class are powerful AA and AS escorts, but they have only a limited surface capability and the lack of room for a hangar means that they cannot permanently embark a helicopter though one can be operated from the pad aft.

Above: *Coontz* class *Farragut* with ASROC reload house.

Above: *Coontz* was built as a frigate but the class were re-rated as destroyers on 30 June 1975. Note the separate lattice masts and funnels.

The *Coontz* class were originally rated as Frigates (DLG), but they are now classified as Guided Missile Destroyers (DDG). They were the first American escorts to be designed to carry guided missiles, and are based on the earlier *Mitscher* class, which were armed with guns and AS weapons. The *Coontz* class were the only US Frigates to have separate masts and funnels, and are single-ended ships, with a 5in 54-cal gun and a superfiring ASROC ASM launcher forward and a twin Terrier SAM launcher aft. They were originally designed to have a second single 5in 54-cal gun in B position,

Right: *Coontz* class *Prebble* refuelling in heavy seas from a *Neosho* class fleet oiler.

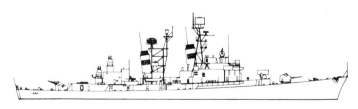

Above: *Coontz* class *Mahan.* Note guns abaft funnels.

Mitscher Class Destroyers

Displacement: 3,680 tons (5,155 full load).
Dimensions: Length overall 493ft (150·3m); beam 50ft (15·2m); draught 21ft (6·4m).
Armament: Surface-to-air missiles, one single Tartar launcher superimposed aft; guns, two single 5in 54-cal one forward and one aft; AS weapons, one ASROC 8-tube launcher superimposed forward; torpedo tubes, two triple Mk 32 12·7in (324mm) one each side of the superstructure.
Propulsion: Two sets GE steam turbines. Total 75,000shp on two shafts, maximum speed 35kts.

The four *Mitscher* class Destroyer Leaders (DL) were built between 1949–54 as large fast AA and AS escorts, with a long range and accommodation and facilities for an escort commander and his staff. Unlike the contemporary 5,600 ton *Norfolk* (DL-1), which was based on a cruiser hull, the *Mitscher*s had an enlarged destroyer hull and were armed with a single 5 in 54-cal and a superfiring twin 3in (76mm) fore and aft, with a Weapon Able AS rocket launcher superfiring over each 3in mount. The aft 3in and Weapon Able were replaced in the early 1960s by a helicopter pad, and in 1966–69 two of the *Mitscher*s were converted into Guided Missile Destroyers (DDG). The superstructure has been enlarged and a lattice main mast fitted, and the Mk 13 Tartar single SAM launcher has been installed in X position aft. An ASROC 8-tube ASM launcher is fitted in place of the forward 3in (76mm) mount. Modern electronics have also been fitted. The two unconverted ships have been discarded.

Right: *Mitscher* in Suda Bay, Crete, with the aircraft
carrier *America* and other ships of the US 6th
Fleet in the background.

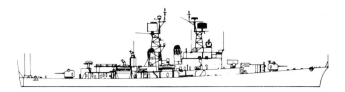

Above: *Mitscher*. Note funnels set very close together.

Spruance Class Destroyers

Displacement: 7,300 tons full load.
Dimensions: Length overall 563ft 4in (171·1m); beam 55ft (17·6m); draught 29ft (8·8m).
Aircraft: Two Kaman SH-2F Seasprite or one Sikorsky SH-3D Sea King with hangar and pad at aft end of superstructure.
Armament: Surface-to-air missiles, one BPDMS Sea Sparrow 8-tube launcher to be fitted on break of quarterdeck aft; guns, two single 5in 54-cal Mk 45 one forward and one right aft; AS weapons, one ASROC 8-tube launcher in front of bridge; torpedo tubes, six Mk 32 12·7in (324mm) tubes three each side at stern.
Propulsion: Four sets GE gas turbines. Total 80,000shp on two shafts, maximum speed over 30kts.

Above: *Spruance* class *Elliot* showing how the funnels
are offset over the gas turbines. Note the bulky
box-shaped superstructure.

Above: *Spruance* on trials. The large lattice masts carry
the radar and ECM arrays.

Whilst the US built up a considerable force of carrier-escort guided missile destroyers in the years after World War II, she relied on the ageing wartime destroyers to provide the bulk of her general purpose escorts. Although many of the *Fletcher*, *Allen M Sumner* and *Gearing* class destroyers were modernized in the early 1960s, no new hulls were built, and by the late 1960s they were worn out and well overdue for replacement. Although some still remain in reserve, most have been transferred to other navies or scrapped. The *Spruance* class were designed to replace them. They are the first large American warships to be powered totally by gas turbines, and are intended primarily for AS work. Because the weapons systems and crew cost more than the ship herself, the *Spruance*s are large and extremely seaworthy ships with a relatively small number of weapons, so that a large number could be built with the available money. This policy has excited a great deal of criticism, not least amongst officers in the USN, and their lack of armament has been widely deplored. However, sheer numbers of ships were necessary in a hurry to replace the enormous quantity of World War II vessels, and the large size of the ships, combined with the rectangular shape

of the superstructure, means that new weapons can easily be installed, and new electronics modules added to the ones already there. The only problem is the cost. In keeping with the desire to keep the ships as simple and cheap as possible, the funnels are arranged directly over the engines, so they are staggered on different sides of the hull. In an attempt to reduce costs still further, the entire class is being built by one firm on one specially constructed production line. Unfortunately, this Total Ship Procurement Package, so far from reducing costs, has itself caused many problems and expenses. Thirty *Spruance*s were authorized. The first was delivered in 1976, four years after it was begun and they are still under construction. They will be retrofitted with Harpoon as soon as it becomes available. Perhaps the most successful aspect of these ships is the very small number of crew. It is possible that the basic hull design may be used for a new anti-aircraft escort. A version fitted with the new Mk 26 combined SAM/ASM/SSM launcher and Aegis, the DDG-47, has been designed to replace the *Charles F Adams* class DDGs, but it has not been authorized as yet by Congress.

Above: *Spruance* class. Note pad and hangar aft.

Charles F Adams
Class Destroyers

Displacement: 3,370 tons (4,500 full load).
Dimensions: Length overall 435ft 6in (133·2m); beam 47ft (14·3m); draught 20ft (6·1m).
Armament: Surface-to-air missiles, one single or twin Tartar launcher at the end of the superstructure aft; guns, two single 5in 54-cal mounts one forward and one on superstructure aft; AS weapons, one ASROC 8-tube launcher between the funnels; torpedo tubes, two triple Mk 32 12·7in (324mm) mounts one each side of the bridge.
Propulsion: Two sets GE steam turbines. Total 70,000shp on two shafts, maximum speed 35kts.

The twenty-three *Charles F Adams* class Guided Missile Destroyers (DDG) built between 1958–64 are improved versions of the *Forrest Sherman* class

Above:*Charles F Adams* class *Sampson* firing Tartar SAM. Note single 5in (127mm) gun in foreground.

Above: *Charles F Adams* class *Barney* with twin launcher.

Above:*Charles F Adams* class *Waddell* with single launcher.

destroyer design. They have a slightly enlarged hull and mount a twin or single Tartar launcher in place of the earlier ships' Y position 5in 54-cal, and an ASROC 8-tube ASM launcher between the funnels. No 3in (76mm) guns were fitted. The later ships in the class differ somewhat from the earlier ones. The first thirteen ships have a Mk 11 twin launcher for the Tartar SAM whereas the later ships have a Mk 13 single launcher, and the last five ships have the bow mounted SQS-26 sonar in place of the hull mounted SQS-23 fitted in the others. Three ships of this class have been built for Australia and three more for West Germany. These differ slightly from the American vessels. In 1964 *Biddle* (DDG-5) was renamed *Claude V Ricketts* and for the next year operated with a mixed crew composed of officers and men from a number of different NATO navies to test the concept of NATO mixed manned surface ballistic missile ships. Although the experiment was reasonably successful, the concept was abandoned, partly because the surface ships would have been much more vulnerable than ballistic missile submarines. *Claude V Ricketts* therefore reverted to being manned by the USN. When built, these ships were excellent AA and AS escorts, but they lack an adequate surface capability, cannot operate a helicopter and their electronics are no longer adequate.

Forrest Sherman
Class Destroyers

Displacement: 2,780–2,850 tons (4,200 full load).
Dimensions: Length overall 418ft 5in (127·4m); beam 45ft 2in (13·7m); draught 20ft (6·1m).
Armament: (ASW version) Guns, two single 5in 54-cal one forward and one aft; AS weapons, one ASROC 8-tube launcher behind rear funnel; torpedo tubes, two triple Mk 32 12·7in (324mm) mounts one each side of the bridge (DLG version). Surface-to-air missiles, one single Tartar launcher aft; guns, one single 5in 54-cal forward; AS weapons and torpedo tubes as in ASW version.
Propulsion: Two sets GE or Westinghouse steam turbines. Total 70,000shp on two shafts, maximum speed 33kts.

The eighteen *Forrest Sherman* class Destroyers (DD) were the first US postwar destroyer design. They were slightly larger versions of the wartime *Gearing* class, some of which, converted for ASW, still remain in reserve. However, in place of the *Gearings'* three twin 5in 38-cal, arranged with two superfiring turrets forward and one aft, the *Forrest Shermans* had one single 5in 54-cal forward and two aft. They also had two twin 3in (76mm) mounts, and four fixed 21in (533mm) as torpedo tubes amidships. Four *Forrest Shermans* were rebuilt between 1965–68 as Guided Missile Destroyers (DDG), and they were redesigned as the *Decatur* class. These ships are armed with a Tartar Mk 13 SAM launcher aft, and retain a 5in 54-cal gun forward. They have an ASROC ASM 8-tube launcher amidships

Above: *Decatur* class *Somers* (converted *Forrest Sherman*).

and two triple Mk 32 12·7in (324mm) torpedo tubes, one each side just ahead of the bridge. These positions were originally occupied by two Hedgehog AS weapon launchers. They can easily be distinguished by the missile launcher and extra superstructure aft and by the greatly enlarged main lattice mast. Their electronics have also been completely modernized. It was originally intended to convert more than four *Forrest Shermans* to this standard, but it proved to be too expensive. It was also intended to fit the *Decaturs* with DASH Drone AS Helicopters, but after the failure of this system ASROC was substituted instead. The remaining fourteen *Forrest Shermans* were next intended to be modernized with improved AS weapons and electronics, but in the event it only proved to be worth modifying eight of these old ships between 1967–71. The remainder are being discarded, and even the modernized ships will not be in service for much longer. One of the unmodernized ships, *Hull* (DD-945), has been used for trials with the new lightweight Mk 71 8in (203mm) gun. This may be fitted to new ships to provide them with a powerful anti-ship and shore bombardment weapon.

Knox Class Frigates

Displacement: 3,011 tons (3,877 full load).
Dimensions: Length overall 438ft (133·5m); beam 46ft 9in (14·25m); draught 24ft 9in (7·6m).
Aircraft: Kaman SH-2F Seasprite helicopter with hangar and pad aft.
Armament: Surface-to-air missiles, one BPDMS Sea Sparrow 8-tube launcher right aft; guns, one single 5in 54-cal forward; AS weapons, one

Right: *Bronstein* was the first of the US second generation post-war escorts. Note 3in (76mm) twin mount, mack set well forward, and low quarterdeck.

ASROC 8-tube launcher in front of bridge; torpedo tubes, four Mk 32 12·7in (324mm) tubes at stern.
Propulsion: One Westinghouse steam turbine. Total 35,000shp, maximum speed over 27kts.

The *Knox* class frigates are second generation US postwar escorts, and are the largest class of surface warships built in America since the war. The first generation postwar escorts were the *Dealey*, *Courtney* and *Claud Jones* classes, built between 1952–60. These are conventional turbine or diesel powered single-screw ships developed from World War II designs, but whereas the *Dealey*s and *Courtney*s were successful ships, too much was attempted on too small a displacement with the *Claud Jones* class, and a new type of ship was necessary. The first of the second-generation escorts are the *Bronstein* class, built between 1961–63. These are much larger ships with a new hull form, capable of carrying ASROC, DASH, a twin 3in (76mm) mount and modern electronics, including a bow sonar. To save deck space they have a mack. Two were built, and the ten *Garcia*s, an enlarged version built between 1962–68, have a similar layout but have a flush deck and two single 5in (127mm) guns. They introduced the very high pressure boilers, which save space and weight. Six *Brooke*s, a version with an improved anti-aircraft armament, were also built. A Tartar SAM single launcher replaced the aft 5in (127mm) gun, but this proved too expensive. The *Knox* class, forty-six of which have been built between 1965–74, are very similar but slightly larger than the *Garcia*s. Originally intended to mount the cancelled "Sea Mauler" short range SAM, some now have a BPDMS Sea Sparrow SAM launcher instead. In some ships the ASROC AS launcher can fire RIM-24B Tartar SSMs, conferring a surface offensive capability. Harpoon SSMs are now being retrofitted. The last 20 ships, built under a Total Procurement Contract by the Avondale Shipyards, Westwego, were at first known as the *Joseph Hewes* class, although they are virtually identical to the other *Knox*s. Like all US escorts with the new hull form, the *Knox*s are extremely seaworthy, but the single engine and shaft makes them vulnerable to damage or breakdown. However, this reflects the US wartime experience that it is engine rather than ship production that causes bottlenecks in the supply of escorts, and it also makes the ships cheaper.

Above: *Knox* has a large mack amidships. Note 5in (127mm) 54 cal gun and ASROC launcher forward. She has been retrofitted with a telescopic hangar and a BPDMS launcher at the extreme stern.

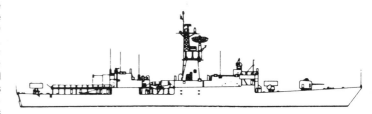

Above: *Knox* class with hangar and BPDMS launcher.

Above: Early *Knox* class with BPDMS launcher.

Left: *Garcia* is the leadship of the class from which the *Knox* class was developed. Note the two single 5in (127mm) 38 cal guns and the relatively small superstructure and mack.

Oliver H Perry Class Frigates

Displacement: 3,500 tons full load.
Dimensions: Length overall 412ft (126m); beam 43ft 2in (13·2m); draught 24ft (7·4m).
Aircraft: Kaman SH-2D Sea Sprite helicopter with hangar and pad aft.
Armament: Surface-to-air and AS missiles, one combined (Standard and ASROC twin launcher forward; guns, one single 3in (76mm) Compact on superstructure amidships, one Vulcan-Phalanx 20mm mount on hangar aft; torpedo tubes, two Mk 32 triple 12·7in (324mm) mounts one each side amidships.
Propulsion: Two sets GE gas turbines. Total 40,000shp on one shaft, maximum speed 28·5kts.

Although the *Oliver H Perry* class Patrol Frigates (FFG) have a similar basic layout and single screw hull as the preceding *Knox* class (FF), they differ very considerably. They have a completely different weapons fit and are powered by gas turbines. The use of two gas turbines, though they are coupled to a single shaft, reduces the possibility that the ship would be completely immobilized by the breakdown of the main engine, and they also give almost instantaneous power and very rapid acceleration. Their main drawback is that they use slightly more fuel. The use of a combined SAM/SSM launcher gives them a greatly improved anti-aircraft and surface capability, and the two LAMPS helicopters provide the long range AS weapon. The position of the single 3in (76mm) Compact is by no means ideal, but the blind spot astern is covered by the Vulcan-Phalanx gun. The light weight of these two weapons has enabled them to be carried very high up on the ship without greatly affecting the stability. The Vulcan-Phalanx was not fitted initially to the first ships, but it will be mounted later. These ships have a comprehensive electronics fit, and the large and bulky superstructure is well suited to carrying a large number of easily changeable modules. This will make updating the ship's capabilities during a refit a much easier task than on earlier vessels. Great efforts have been made, as

Above: Artist's impression of *Oliver H Perry* class frigate, with Interim LAMPS Seasprite helicopter.

on all modern warships, to reduce the number of the crew, and this class needs 35 fewer officers and men than the *Knox*s. Twenty-five *Oliver H Perry*s have been ordered, but only the first ships have so far been completed.

Agile Class Ocean Minesweeper

Displacement: 637–720 tons (735–780 full load).
Dimensions: Length overall 171–173ft (52·3–52·7m); beam 36ft (10·7m); draught 13ft 8in (4·1m).
Armament: Guns, one single 40mm forward, two single 20mm on bridge wings.
Propulsion: Two GE or Packard diesels. Total 1,520 or 2,280bhp on two shafts, maximum speed 13·75–15·5kts.

Ninety-three *Agile* class Ocean Minesweepers (MSO) were built between 1952–56. Based on World War II designs, they have wooden hulls and non-magnetic machinery and equipment. A number were built for foreign navies, and a number of those built for the USN have been transferred abroad. Others have been scrapped and only about thirty remain in reserve. Some have the more powerful Packard diesels, and although these do not raise the maximum speed by very much, the extra power enables sweeps to be towed faster. All the survivors are fitted for mechanical, magnetic and acoustic sweeping, and can detect mines by sonar. Four that have been fitted with more powerful Packard diesels, an SQS-14 sonar mine detector

Above: *Agile* class minesweeper *Dash*. The drums abaft the funnel are for towed sweeps.

Above: Modified *Agile* class minesweeper *Acme*. She has more powerful engines, better equipment and extra office space. Note short hull with wide beam.

and extra offices for use as squadron leaders have been designated the *Acme* class. Three larger MSOs of the *Alacrity* class were built between 1956–58. Two remain in service and they are used for ASW experiments. They have been reclassified as AGs. No more minesweepers have been built because the USN now mainly relies on helicopters to sweep mines. Not only do they do it faster, they are also less vulnerable. Those mines which cannot be swept by helicopter are dealt with by divers, guided by the minesweeper's sonar.

Asheville Class Patrol Gunboats

Displacement: 225 tons (245 full load).
Dimensions: Length overall 164ft 6in (50·1m); beam 24ft (7·3m); draught 9ft 6in (2·9m).
Armament: Guns, one single 3in (76mm) forward, one single 40mm aft, two twin 0·5in (12·7mm) one each side amidships.
Propulsion: One GE gas turbine and two Cummins diesels (CODAG drive). Total 15,250shp on two shafts, maximum speed over 40kts.

When the United States became involved in the war in Vietnam in a major scale in the mid-1960s, it was realized that the USN had no small fast patrol vessels that could be used for coastal work. Instead they had to rely on small craft and expensive frigates and destroyers. As a result sixteen *Asheville* class Patrol Gunboats (PG) were built between 1965–69. They are uncomplicated and relatively cheap vessels, and were well suited to their job. However, since the United States disengaged from Vietnam the USN's need for these vessels has diminished, and several have been

Above: *Asheville* class patrol gunboat *Antelope* fires a Standard MR SSM. Modified versions of this class are now under construction in both Taiwan and South Korea.

transferred to Greece, South Korea and Turkey. Their CODAG propulsion gives them a relatively long range on their diesels, whilst the gas turbine can accelerate them from rest to 40 knots in about one minute. *Chehalis* was disarmed in 1975 and is used for research, and several others have been fitted with two Tartar SSMs aft to give them some capability against major warships. They have a distinctive appearance with a large chunky superstructure amidships, with prominent intakes and a small funnel. The 3in (76mm) gun has an automatic fire control radar.

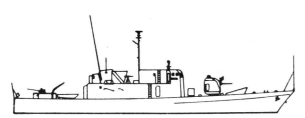

Above: *Asheville* class. Note large superstructure.

Pegasus Class Patrol Hydrofoils

Displacement: 190 tons (221 full load).
Dimensions: foilborne; length overall 131ft 2in (40m); beam 28ft 2in (8·6m); draught 7ft 6in (2·3m).
Armament: Surface-to-surface missiles, eight Harpoon aft; guns, one single 3in 62-cal forward.
Propulsion: Foilborne; one GE gas turbine. Total 18,000shp, maximum speed over 48kts. Hullborne; two MTU diesels. Total 1,600bhp, maximum speed 12kts.

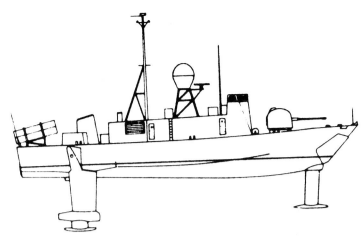

Above: *Pegasus* class with foils extended.

The *Pegasus* class Missile armed Patrol Hydrofoil (PHM) was developed by Boeing from several earlier civil and military craft, including the USS *Tucumcari* (PGH-2) which was built between 1966–68. They are all submerged foil hydrofoils, and they differ in having one hydrofoil at the bows and two (one each side) aft, whereas other hydrofoils have two foils forward and one aft. The Boeing system, combined with a computer, gives quicker reactions and a smoother ride in rough water. *Pegasus* (PHM-1) was originally intended to be the prototype for a number of hydrofoils with the same hull and machinery but with differing armaments for the United States, Italy and Germany. The German boats were to have been equipped with Exocet SSMs. However, by the time *Pegasus* (PHM-1) was built in 1973–6, all three countries had had second thoughts. Although the PHM offers a heavy armament on a small, very fast and highly manouvrable hull, it is also extremely expensive, and it was considered that cheaper and less sophisticated vessels might be better for the short range tasks that *Pegasus* was designed to perform. However, the project seems to have been revived by Congress, who have given the go-ahead for PHM 3–6. In addition to the PHMs, the USN has an interest in several other unconventional types of ship. This includes the SWATH (Small Waterplane Twin Hull) research ship *Kaimalino*, and the Hovercraft or SES (Surface Effect Ships). A number of British and American SES have been tested, including the 100 ton Bell SES-100B, and so impressed has the USN been by the potential of these vessels for ASW and Minesweeping that they have gone ahead with the design of a 3,000 ton LSES. This will be optimized for AS warfare and carry two helicopters or a V/STOL aircraft, and will be powered, if it is built, by six large gas turbines.

Above: *Pegasus* on the surface with its foils retracted, in the company of an *Asheville* class patrol gunboat. Note 3in (76mm) gun and Harpoon SSM tubes aft.

Above: *SES-100B* hovercraft on missile firing trials.

Below: *SES-100B* hovercraft setting a speed record of 103·038mph off Florida in 1976.

Blue Ridge Class Command Ships

Displacement: 19,290 tons full load.
Dimensions: Length overall 698ft 6in (213·6m); beam 82ft 8in (25·3m); draught 26ft 10in (8·2m).
Aircraft: Two Kaman UH-2C Seasprite and one Boeing Vertol CH-46A Sea Knight helicopters with pad at stern.
Armament: Surface-to-air missiles, two BPDMS Sea Sparrow 8-tube launchers one each side abaft the superstructure: guns, two twin 3in (76mm) one each side forward of the superstructure.
Propulsion: One GE steam turbine. Total 22,000shp on one shaft, maximum speed 21·5kts.

Command Ships were introduced during World War II, when the increasing size and complexity of the staff and communications network of the amphibious task force commanders made the provision of a special ship fully equipped with offices and extensive communications facilities a necessity. By the end of World War II the Americans standardized on the 15 *Mount Mckinley* class converted merchant ships, the last of which have only

Above: *Blue Ridge.* Note flat deck, sponsons, BPDMS launcher amidships, and flat topped tower aft.

Above: *Blue Ridge* at anchor during an amphibious exercise in the Philippines in 1976.

Above: *Blue Ridge.* Note the number of ariels.

recently been taken out of service. These 7,500 ton ships had a top speed of only 16 knots, but this was adequate for the existing fleet of amphibious assault ships. Five were later modernized and given improved communication facilities and a helicopter pad aft. It was essential that their successors should be both larger and faster, and the solution adopted was to use a lengthened version of the *Iwo Jima* class LPH's hull. This has proved ideal for the purpose. The large space occupied by the hangar on the LPHs has been turned into offices and accommodation for the enormous staff of nearly 700 officers and men who are carried in addition to the ship's crew. The large flat upper deck carries all the radio and radar aeriels necessitated by their role as command ships, and the area of the upper deck has been further increased by carrying it out over sponsons extending over half the length of the ship. These contain small landing craft and the ship's boats. There is a large helicopter pad aft which provides necessary mobility for the staff. The ships have an unmistakeable appearance, with a tall lattice mast forward, a box like superstructure amidships to which the funnel is blended and a flat-topped tower aft. This was intended to be surmounted by a large dome containing a search radar but this was never fitted to keep costs down. Apart from this they have a full radar and ECM fit, and are equipped with TACAN, NTDS (Naval Tactical Data System), ACIS (Amphibious, Command Information System) and NIPS (Naval Intelligence Processing System). Two command ships that have recently been taken out of service are *Northampton* (CC-1), built as an *Oregon City* class heavy cruiser and converted before completion, and *Wright* (CC-2), a converted light fleet carrier. Both these ships were capable of over 30 knots and were therefore suitable for use as fleet Command Ships as well as for amphibious operations. A third *Blue Ridge* class ship was originally projected which would have been fitted for use as a fleet command ship as well as a Command Ship for amphibious operations, but it was not built. Both the *Blue Ridge* class can, of course, be used in this role, but they are not specially equipped for it.

Tarawa Class Amphibious Assault Ships

Displacement: 39,300 tons full load.
Dimensions: Length overall 820ft (237·8m); beam 106ft (32·3m); draught 27ft 6in (8·4m).
Aircraft: Typically 30 Boeing Vertol UH-46 Sea Knight and Sikorsky CH-53 Sea Stallion helicopters.
Armament: Surface-to-air missiles, two BPDMS Sea Sparrow 8-tube launchers one just forward of the island and one on the port quarter; guns, three single 5in 54-cal one each side of the bow and one on the starboard quarter.
Propulsion: Two sets Westinghouse steam turbines. Total 70,000shp on two shafts, maximum speed 24kts.

The *Tarawa* class Amphibious Assault Ships (LHA) are designed to fulfil the functions of both the LPHs and the LPDs, by being able to carry a battalion group of about 1,800 Marines and land them and their equipment by both helicopters and landing craft. Although this means that the loss of one ship would be more damaging than before, it saves the cost of a large and complex vessel and its crew. They have a full length continuous flight

Below: Note *Tarawa's* bulky hull and superstructure.

Above: *Tarawa* in dock just prior to the launching ceremony in 1973.

deck, with a large rectangular island to starboard. The helicopter hangar is in the aft part of the ship, and it is connected to the flight deck by a portside elevator and another at the stern on the centerline. The forward part of the hull at hangar deck level is used for stores and equipment, which, as in the *Iwo Jimas*, is bought up to the flight deck by two small elevators. Beneath the hangar aft there is a dock large enough to contain four *1610* class LCUs. Side thrusters are fitted to make docking and undocking easier. Nine of these ships were ordered under a Total Package Procurement Contract from Litton Industries, but as in the case of the *Spruances* this has proved a failure. Cost overruns have been considerable and completion of the class has been delayed by between two to four years whilst the problems are resolved. Four *Tarawas* have been cancelled, and although the first was laid down in 1971, by mid 1977 only two were in service.

Iwo Jima Class
Amphibious Assault Ships

Displacement: 17,000 tons (18,300 full load).
Dimensions: Length overall 602ft (182·9m); deck width overall 105ft (31·9m); beam 84ft (25·6m); draught 26ft (7·9m).
Aircraft: Typically 20 Boeing Vertol CH-46 Sea Knight, 4 Sikorsky CH-53 Sea Stallion and 4 Bell UH-1 Iroquois helicopters.
Armament: Surface-to-air missiles, three BPDMS Sea Sparrow 8-tube launchers, one forward of island and one each side of stern.
Propulsion: One set steam turbines. Total 23,000shp on one shaft, maximum speed 20kts.

The seven *Iwo Jima* class Amphibious Assault Ships (LPH) were built between 1959–70. The LPH is complementary to the LPD, but whereas the LPD transports troops and equipment and lands them by landing craft, the LPH transports lightly equipped troops and lands them by helicopter. The LPH was evolved after the Suez operation of 1956 and the Lebanon crisis of 1958 had demonstrated the value of helicopters for landing troops. They operate twenty-eight helicopters from a continuous full length flight deck, on which seven can be loaded at any one time. There are no catapults or arrester wires, nor is the flight deck strengthened to operate conventional carrier aircraft, but V/STOL aircraft can be operated. There are two deck edge lifts, one amidships to port, and one behind the island to starboard. These can be hinged down to cover the opening in the hull. Below the flight deck is a hangar and accommodation for 2,090 fully equipped marines. They have extensive medical facilities with 300 beds, and casualties can be evacuated direct from the shore to the LPH by helicopter. These ships were originally armed with four twin 3in (76mm) guns, two at the stern and two superimposed in front of the island, but these have since been replaced

Above: *Iwo Jima* class *Okinawa.* **Note Sea Knight and Sea Stallion helicopters and BPDMS launcher.**

by BPDMS Sea Sparrow SAM launchers. It was originally proposed to build more of these ships, but it was decided to combine the functions of the LPH and LPD in one ship, the *Tarawa* class LHA, so only seven LPHs were built. In 1971–72 *Guam* (LPH-9) was converted into an Interim Sea Control Ship. One of the proposals for producing a cheaper alternative to keeping a 15 strong carrier force in commission was to build an updated version of the escort carrier. These 15,000 ton Sea Control Ships (SCS) were to have been fitted with AV-8 Harrier V/STOL aircraft and AS helicopters, and *Guam* (LPH-9) was modified to see if the idea was practical. She was fitted with a new tactical command center and Carrier Control Approach radar, and embarked Harriers and AS helicopters. Although these were operated successfully, no SCS have been built, and *Guam* reverted to her original role. LPHs have also been used to sweep mines, operating Sikorsky CH-53 Sea Stallion helicopters equipped for the purpose.

Austin Class Assault
Transports

Displacement: 11,050 tons (17,150 full load).
Dimensions: Length overall 576ft 10in (176·4m); beam 84ft (25·6m); draught 23ft (7m).
Aircraft: Six Boeing Vertol CH-46 Sea Knight helicopters with landing deck and telescopic hangar aft.
Armament: Guns, four twin 3in (76mm) one each side forward of the bridge and one each side on aft end of superstructure.
Propulsion: Two sets steam turbines. Total 24,000shp, maximum speed 20kts.

Above: *Austin* class *Cleveland* with minesweeping Sea Stallion helicopters on the flight deck.

The first Amphibious Transports Dock (LPD) were the three *Raleigh* class built between 1960–64. They were developed from the LSD design but were intended not only to carry landing craft but also to transport all their associated troops and accompanying equipment on one ship. Although LSDs are still necessary to transport and maintain additional landing craft, the use of LPDs means that a large number of accompanying troop and equipment transports can be dispensed with. In addition, the LPDs have ramps running from their vehicle decks to the dock so that the landing craft can be reloaded inside the LPD rather than alongside another vessel. This is a much faster, safer and more convenient method. The *Raleigh*s have a 168ft long docking well at the stern that can accommodate nine LCM 6, four LCM 8 or 20 LCVP. The dock is covered by an integral helicopter flight deck, and *Raleigh* (LPD 1) and *Vancouver* (LPD 2) have been fitted with telescopic hangars. *La Salle* has been reclassified as AGF-3 and serves as flagship in the Persian Gulf. It was originally intended to build more *Raleigh*s, but it was soon realized that by lengthening the hull the transport

capacity could be greatly increased, so the twelve *Austin* class LPDs have a 50ft extension to their hull forward of the dock. Otherwise they are very similar to the *Raleigh*s. They can carry 900 troops and their equipment, and also have the integral helicopter flight deck aft and a telescopic hangar. Some have been used to operate minesweeping helicopters. After the development of the *Tarawa* class LHA, which incorporates the features of the LPDs with those of the *Iwo Jima* class LPH, one *Austin* was cancelled and no more will be built.

Above: *Austin* class *Trenton.* **Note bulky superstructure and 3in (76mm) mounts forward.**

Right: *Raleigh* is a smaller version of the *Austin* class. She has an LCM alongside. There is a dock for landing craft beneath the flight deck aft.

Anchorage Class
Assault Transports

Displacement: 13,650 tons full load.
Dimensions: Length overall 553ft 4in (169·1m); beam 84ft (25·6m); draught 18ft 7in (5·7m).
Armament: Guns, four twin 3in (76mm) one each side at forward and aft ends of superstructure.
Propulsion: Two sets steam turbines. Total 24,000shp, maximum speed 20kts.

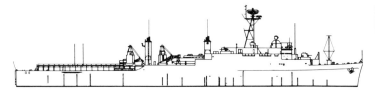

Above: *Anchorage.* **Note enclosed gun mounts forward.**

The five *Anchorage* class Landing Ships Dock (LSD) are intended to replace a larger number of the surviving wartime LSDs, which as well as being worn out were too slow to keep up with the rest of the amphibious assault force. They were built between 1967–72, and are considerably larger than the preceding *Thomastons.* Though they carry the same number of landing craft, the *Anchorages'* dock is 30ft longer, and they can carry 337 troops. Because their main function is to transport and maintain landing craft rather than to transport troops and their associated equipment, they, like the *Thomastons,* do not have any connections between the dock and the troop vehicle decks. Instead, there are two large cranes, one each side, at the forward end of the dock. At the rear end, there is a helicopter pad. As with the *Thomastons,* this is removable, though it is normally left in situ. The armament is smaller than on earlier ships because the emphasis is now on area defence by accompanying escorts. They have a fairly comprehensive electronics fit. They can be distinguished from earlier LSDs by their lattice mast and longer and higher hull.

Above: *Anchorage,* **showing staggered funnels, LCM in davits amidships, and dock aft.**

Thomaston Class
Assault Transports

Displacement: 6,880 tons (11,270 full load).
Dimensions: Length overall 510ft (155·5m); beam 84ft (25·6m); draught 19ft (5·8m).
Armament: Guns, six twin 3in (76mm) one each side at forward, middle and aft ends of superstructure.
Propulsion: Two sets steam turbines. Total 23,000shp, maximum speed 23kts.

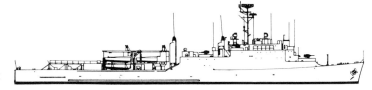

Above: *Thomaston* class *Hermitage.* **Note open gun mounts.**

The eight *Thomaston* class Landing Ships Dock (LSD) are improved versions of the later World War II LSD designs, some of which are still held in reserve. The *Thomastons* are larger and more powerful to enable them to keep up with the modern 20 knot amphibious assault force. They are intended to transport landing craft loaded with men, weapons, vehicles and supplies and have a 400ft long floodable dock aft. This can accommodate either three 1610 class LCUs or up to 21 LCM 8s, although normally only 18 would be carried. In the *Thomastons* the landing craft have to be pre-loaded with vehicles or supplies because there is no provision for transfering them in the dock. The aft end of the dock is covered by a large helicopter pad which is used to operate the larger transport helicopters to rapidly transfer men and supplies from the LSD to the shore. They originally had eight twin 3in (76mm), but two twin mounts were removed in 1962. They have a normal capacity of 109 troops, but more can be accommodated in an emergency. Like all LSDs and LPDs, the machinery is arranged so that the funnels are staggered.

Below: *Thomaston,* **with launch in landing craft davits amidships. Note small flight deck.**

511-1152 Series
Tank Landing Ships

Displacement: 1,653 tons (4,080 full load).
Dimensions: Length overall 328ft (100m); beam 50ft (15·2m); draught 14ft (4·2m).
Armament: Guns, none to eight 40mm in single or twin mounts at the bow and stern.

Above: *511-1152 Series* Tank Landing Craft at anchor, with *LCVP* in davits alongside bridge. She has bow doors, and the tank decks occupy the front three-quarters of the ship, with the engines aft.

Propulsion: Two diesels. Total 1,700bhp, maximum speed 11kts.

The *511-1152* series were the standard late World War II LST. Some still remain in reserve.

Newport Class
Tank Landing Ships

Displacement: 8,342 tons full load.
Dimensions: Length overall 523ft 3in (160m); beam 67ft 9in (20·7m); draught 15ft (4·5m).
Armament: Guns, two twin 3in (76mm) one each side of the superstructure amidships.
Propulsion: Six Alco diesels. Total 16,500hp on two shafts, maximum speed 20kts.

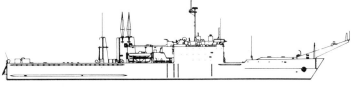

Above: *Newport* class. Note large gallows forward.

The twenty *Newport* class Tank Landing Ships (LST) are replacements for the World War II and 1950s LSTs, which are no longer fast enough to keep up with the 20 knot amphibious assault force. The *Newport*s are large seagoing ships, and in order to give them fine lines for high speed and sufficient draught for stability, whilst at the same time retaining the ability to land troops and equipment direct on to a beach, they have been fitted with a large gallows at the bows, which enables a ramp to be extended

Below: *Newport*, showing ramp stowed on foc'stle and bulky superstructure amidships, topped by a pole mast and twin 3in (76mm) gun mounts.

Above: *Newport* class LST beached and disembarking vehicles, with vehicle ramp extended.

over a hundred feet forward of the ship. They also carry pontoons slung vertically against the side of the hull aft, each of which can carry a main battle tank. Vehicles can be loaded and unloaded onto these or from a dock from the stern gate. The *Newport*s are fitted with a vertical propeller aft to improve manoeuvrability whilst beaching. Helicopters can be operated from the pad aft. These ships can carry about 500 tons of equipment in addition to 430 troops.

Suffolk County Class
Tank Landing Ships

Displacement: 3,860 tons (7,100 full load).
Dimensions: Length overall 440ft 5in (134·7m); beam 62ft (18·9m); draught 16ft 6in (5m).
Armament: Guns, three twin 3in (76mm) one each side at bows one at stern.
Propulsion: Six Nordberg diesels. Total 13,700bhp on two shafts, maximum speed 16kts.

The *Suffolk County* class are the ultimate development of the wartime LST, built 1956–58. They can carry 700 troops, an LCU and four LCVPs, and have a helicopter pad amidships. Seven were built, the survivors are in reserve.

Right: *Suffolk County* with deck cargo of vehicles. Note large superstructure and prominent funnel.

Charleston Class
Amphibious Cargo Ships

Displacement: 20,700 tons full load.
Dimensions: Length overall 575ft 6in (175·4m); beam 82ft (25m); draught 25ft 6in (7·7m).
Armament: Guns, four twin 3in (76mm) one each side on the forecastle and one each side of the funnel on the superstructure.
Propulsion: One set steam turbines. Total 22,000shp on one shaft, maximum speed 21kts.

The five *Charleston* class Amphibious Cargo Ships (AKA), built between 1966–69, carry four LCM 8, and transport the Marines' heavy equipment. They have a helicopter pad aft.

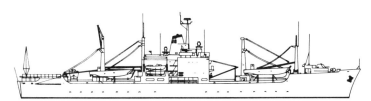

Above: *Charleston* class amphibious cargo ship. Note LCM in davits fore and aft, prominent masts, and helicopter pad at stern.

Above: *Charleston* and her four sisters replace a number of World War II vessels, and are used to carry the heavy equipment that cannot fit into amphibious assault ships.

Wichita Class
Replenishment Oilers

Displacement: 38,100 tons full load.
Dimensions: Length overall 659ft (206·9m); beam 96ft (29·3m); draught 33ft 4in (10·2m).
Aircraft: Two Boeing Vertol UH-46 Sea Knight helicopters with pad and hangar aft.
Armament: Guns, two twin 3in (76mm) one each side of the funnel.
Propulsion: Two sets steam turbines. Total 32,000shp on two shafts, maximum speed 20kts.

Six *Wichita* class Replenishment Oilers (AOR) were built between 1966–73. Seven more are building or authorized. These are armed with one BPDMS Sea Sparrow SAM launcher. The *Wichita*s are designed to replenish the fleet at sea.

Right: *Wichita* class *Roanoke* being launched in 1974. These ships form a vital part of the fleet train which replenishes US warships at sea.

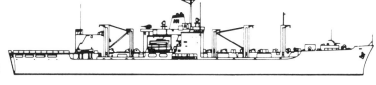

Mars Class Combat
Stores Ships

Displacement: 16,240 tons full load.
Dimensions: Length overall 581ft (177·1m); beam 79ft (24·1m); draught 24ft (7·3m).
Aircraft: Two Boeing Vertol UH-46 Sea Knight helicopters with pad and hangar at stern.
Armament: Guns, four twin 3in (76mm) one each side on forecastle and one each side on superstructure aft of bridge.

Above: *Mars* class. Note hangar and pad aft.

Propulsion: One set steam turbines. Total 22,000shp on one shaft, maximum speed 20kts.

The seven *Mars* class Combat Stores Ships (AFS) replenish stores at sea. They were built between 1962–70. Like the AOR, AOE and AE, they use their helicopters for vertical replenishment.

Above: A Sea Knight helicopter conducts a vertical replenishment from *Mars* helicopter pad. Note the equipment for horizontal replenishment.

Kilauea Class
Ammunition Ships

Displacement: 20,500 tons full load.
Dimensions: Length overall 564ft (171·9m); beam 81ft (24·7m); draught 25ft 8in (7·8m).
Aircraft: Two Boeing Vertol UH-46 Sea Knight helicopters with pad and hangar aft.
Armament: Guns, four twin 3in (76mm) one each side at break of forecastle forward and one each side on superstructure behind the funnel.
Propulsion: One set steam turbines. Total 22,000shp on one shaft, maximum speed 20kts.

Eight *Kilauea* class Ammunition Ships (AE), built between 1966–72, and two *Suribachi* and three *Nitro* class built between 1955–59 replenish the fleet with ammunition and explosive stores at sea.

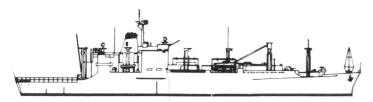

Above: *Kilauea* class *Santa Barbara*. Note pad aft.

Above: *Kilauea* at speed. The superstructure in this class is set well back, with the holds for the ammunition and explosives amidships.

Samuel Gompers Class
Destroyer Tenders

Displacement: 20,500 tons (21,600 full load).
Dimensions: Length overall 643ft (196·3m); beam 84ft 8in (25·9m); draught 23ft 7in (7·2m).
Aircraft: One helicopter with pad and hangar aft.
Armament: Guns, one single 5in 38-cal forward, six 0·5in (12·7mm) in superstructure.
Propulsion: Two sets steam turbines. Total 20,000shp on two shafts, maximum speed 18kts.

Samuel Gompers and *Puget Sound*, built between 1964–68, are designed to maintain up to six Guided Missile Destroyers and Cruisers simultaneously. They are America's only postwar Destroyer Tenders. Two more are projected, to be armed with one BPDMS Sea Sparrow launcher.

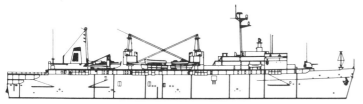

Above: *Samuel Gompers* class. Note large cranes.

Right: *Samuel Gompers* at sea off Hawaii. This class can maintain nuclear powerplants. The hull is similar to that of the *Simon Lake* and *L Y Spear* class submarine tenders.

Dixie Class
Destroyer Tenders

Displacement: 10,400 tons (17,175 full load).
Dimensions: Length overall 530ft 6in (161·7m); beam 73ft 4in (22·3m); draught 25ft 6in (7·8m).
Aircraft: One helicopter with pad and hangar aft.
Armament: Guns, two single 5in 38-cal superimposed forward.
Propulsion: Two sets steam turbines. Total 11,000shp on two shafts, maximum speed 18kts.

The five *Dixie* class Tenders were built between 1939–44 and were modernized in 1959–63 to support Guided Missile Destroyers. Several wartime *Arcadia* class Tenders are also still in service.

Above: *Dixie* class *Piedmont.* Note the 5in (127mm) guns forward, the large cranes abaft the second funnel, and the small hangar and helicopter pad aft. They have a large number of workshops and storerooms.

Left: *Dixie* and her four sisters were modernized under the FRAM II programme to maintain missile-armed destroyers. Although *Dixie* is seen here at sea they spend most of their career in harbour as base ships.

Simon Lake Class
Submarine Tenders

Displacement: 21,000 tons (32,650 full load).
Dimensions: Length overall 640ft 10in (196m); beam 86ft 7in (26·5m); draught 30ft (9·2m).
Armament: Guns, two twin 3in (76mm) one each side of the funnel.
Propulsion: One steam turbine. Total 20,000shp on one shaft, maximum speed 18kts.

Simon Lake and *Canopus*, built between 1963–65, are designed to serve nine Nuclear Ballistic Missile Submarines (SSBN) apiece. They are fully equipped to service reactors and ballistic missiles. There is a helicopter pad aft.

Right: *Simon Lake* at sea off Hawaii. Note the SLBM cranes amidships and the funnel aft. The hull is similar to that of the other modern submarine and destroyer tenders.

Spear Class
Submarine Tenders

Displacement: 12,770 tons (22,640 full load).
Dimensions: Length overall 640ft 10in (196m); beam 84ft 7in (25·9m); draught 23ft 2in (7·1m).
Armament: Guns, two 5in 38-cal one forward and one aft.
Propulsion: One steam turbine. Total 20,000shp on one shaft, maximum speed 20kts.

L Y Spear and *Dixon* are tenders for Nuclear Attack Submarines (SSN). They were built between 1966–71 and can each deal with 12 boats. Two more *Spear* class are projected. They will be armed with one BPDMS Sea Sparrow SAM launcher and four 20mm. There is a helicopter pad aft.

Above: *L Y Spear* class *Dixon.* This class was developed from the *Simon Lake* class, but maintains SSNs instead of SSBNs. Note the single 5in (127mm) gun forward.

Left: *L Y Spear.* Three modified versions of this class are being built to service and maintain the new *Los Angeles* class SSNs.

Hunley Class
Submarine Tenders

Displacement: 10,500 tons (18,300 full load).
Dimensions: Length overall 597ft 1in (182·6m); beam 82ft 8in (25·3m); draught 24ft (7·4m).
Armament: Guns, two twin 3in (76mm) one each side just behind the funnel.
Propulsion: Ten Fairbanks Morse diesels (diesel-electric drive). Total 15,000shp on one shaft, maximum speed 18kts.

Hunley and *Holland*, like the larger and better equipped *Simon Lake* class, serve SSBNs. They were built between 1960–63, and have a helicopter pad aft.

Above: *Hunley* as built with a single hammerhead crane aft for SLBMs. This class were the first purpose-built SSBN tenders in the world.

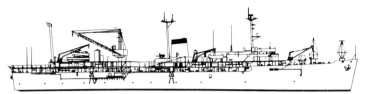

Above: *Hunley* as refitted with two cranes.

Fulton Class
Submarine Tenders

Displacement: 9,750 tons (18,000 full load).
Dimensions: Length overall 530ft 6in (161·4m); beam 73ft 4in (22·4m); draught 26ft 9in (8·2m).
Armament: Guns, two single 5in 38-cal superimposed forward.
Propulsion: General Motors diesels (diesel-electric drive). 11,500bhp on two shafts, maximum speed 15·5kts.

Seven *Fulton* class Tenders were built during World War II. In 1959–60 *Proteus* was lengthened and refitted to support SSBNs, and four others were modernized (see data) in 1960–62 to act as tenders for SSNs. In addition, other wartime ships have been modernized to provide logistic support for Submarine Tenders based overseas.

Above: *Fulton* at sea. Note the two single 5in (127mm) guns forward and the cranes aft. This class has a similar hull to the *Dixie* class destroyer tenders.

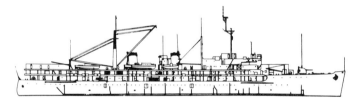

Above: *Fulton* class *Howard W Gilmore* (ex *Neptune*).

Pigeon Class
Submarine Rescue Ships

Displacement: 4,200 tons full load.
Dimensions: Length overall 250ft 2in (76·5m); beam 85ft 8in (26·2m); draught 19ft (5·8m).
Armament: Guns, two single 3in (76mm) one on each side in front of the bridge.
Propulsion: Four diesels. Total 6,000shp on two shafts, maximum speed 15kts.

The catamaran-hulled Submarine Rescue Ships (ASR) *Pigeon* and *Ortolan* were designed specially for this job. They have a helicopter pad aft.

Above: *Pigeon* underway. 10 ships of this class were planned but only two were ordered. They have heavy lift equipment, salvage gear, and multiple anchors.

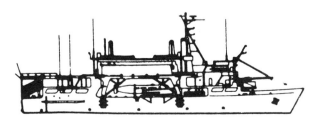

Above: *Pigeon* class. These ships can be used for rescue and salvage work. There is a 34ft (10·4m) well between the two hulls. Note travelling crane.

Edenton Class Salvage And Rescue Ships

Displacement: 2,650 tons (3,125 full load).
Dimensions: Length overall 287ft 9in (88m); beam 49ft 10in (15·25m); draught 15ft (4·6m).
Propulsion: Four Paxman diesels. Total 6,000shp on two shafts, maximum speed 16kts.

The three *Edenton* class Salvage and Rescue Ships (ATS) were built in Britain between 1967–72.

Above: *Edenton*, showing heavy lift gear in bows. Note *Asheville* PG behind bow and *Thomaston* LSD at stern.

Above: *Edenton* at sea. Note large cranes and fire-fighting mast at forward end of bridge.

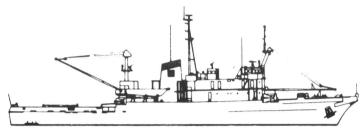

Above: *Edenton* can also be used for ocean towing.

Neosho Class Fleet Oilers

Displacement: 11,600 tons (38,000–40,000 full load).
Dimensions: Length overall 655ft (199·6m); beam 86ft (26·2m); draught 35ft (10·7m).
Armament: Guns, four or six twin 3in (76mm) one each side on the forecastle and one or two each side on the superstructure aft.
Propulsion: Two sets steam turbines. Total 28,000shp, maximum speed 20kts.

The five *Neosho* class Fleet Oilers (AO), built between 1952–55, are, like the other American AOs, fitted for underway replenishment.

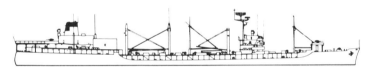

Above: *Neosho* class. Note helicopter pad aft.

Right: *Neosho* underway. This class are the largest US fleet replenishment oilers.

Compass Island Class Experimental Ships

Displacement: 9,200 tons (17,600 full load).
Dimensions: Length overall 552ft 8in (169m); beam 74ft 10in (22·9m); draught 24ft 2in (7·4m).
Propulsion: One set steam turbines. Total 15,000shp on one shaft, maximum speed 20kts.

Built in the early 1950s as Fast Cargo Ships, the Experimental Ships (AG) *Compass Island* and *Observation Island* are used to test launch SSBN missiles and are part of a small fleet of US Experimental Ships. They have a helicopter pad aft.

Above: *Compass Island* is used as an SSBN navigation systems trials and evaluation ship.

Left: *Observation Island* has SLBM tubes between the centre superstructure and the helicopter pad aft.

Sanctuary Hospital Ship

Displacement: 11,333 tons (15,226 full load).
Dimensions: Length overall 520ft (158·6m); beam 71ft 6in (21·8m); draught 24ft (7·3m).
Propulsion: Two sets GE steam turbines. Total 9,000shp on two shafts, maximum speed 18kts.

The Hospital Ship (AH) *Sanctuary* was built during World War II and has 750 hospital beds. There is a helicopter pad aft.

Right: *Haven* was one of *Sanctuary's* five World War II sister-ships, but is no longer in service.

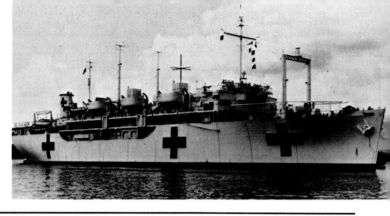

Major US Torpedoes

Type: Mk 16 Mod 8 ship and submarine torpedo.
Weight: 4,796lb (2,180kg).
Dimensions: Length 20ft 6in (6.25m): diameter 21in (533mm).
Manufacturer: Various.
Role: Anti-Ship.
Guidance: None.
Propulsion: Hydrogen peroxide.
Conventional unguided torpedo. Warhead 880lb (400kg).

Type: Mk 30 Mod 1 Training torpedo.
Weight: Not known.
Dimensions: Not known.
Manufacturer: Northrop.
Role: Acoustic or Magnetic Anomaly target for all AS detectors and weapons.
Guidance: Pre-programmed and acoustic.
Propulsion: Electric
Fired from 21in (533mm) tube or air-dropped.

Type: Mk 37 Mod 0 submarine torpedo.
Weight: 1,430lb (650kg).
Dimensions: Length 11ft 4in (3.45m): diameter 19in (485mm).
Manufacturer: Westinghouse.
Role: Anti-Submarine.
Guidance: Active-passive acoustic homing.
Propulsion: Electric.
Fired from 21in (533mm) tube. Originally also intended for use against ships, but guidance system only proved suitable for AS work. Maximum speed 25kts. Mod 3 is an improved version.

Type: Mk 37 Mod 1 submarine torpedo.
Weight: 1,694lb (770kg).
Dimensions: Length 13ft 5in (4.1m): diameter 19in (485mm).
Manufacturer: Westinghouse.
Role: Anti-Submarine.
Guidance: Wire-guided.
Propulsion: Electric.
Fired from 21in (533mm) tube. Developed from Mk 37 O. Mod 2 is an improved version.

Above and below: Deck launching trials of the Mk 37C torpedo in 1976 to enable it to be used in surface vessels as well as in submarines.

Type: Mk 37C submarine torpedo.
Weight:
Dimensions: Length 11ft 4in or 13ft 5in (3.45 or 4.1m): diameter 19in (485mm).
Manufacturer: Northrop.
Role: Anti-Submarine and Anti-Ship.
Guidance: Passive homing or none.
Propulsion: Otto fuel engine.
Fired from 21in (533mm) tube. Updated Mk 37 Mod 2 or 3 with dual-role. Maximum speed 35kts.

Type: Mk 43 Mod 1 Aircraft and Ship torpedo.
Weight: 264lb (120kg).
Dimensions: Length 7ft 8in (2.3m): diameter 12.7in (324mm)
Manufacturer: Various.
Role: Anti-Submarine.
Guidance: Active homing.
Propulsion: Electric.
Only useful against slow submarines.

Type: Mk 44 Mod 0 Aircraft and Ship torpedo.
Weight: 422lb (192kg).
Dimensions: Length: 8ft 4in (2.54m): diameter 12.7in (324mm).
Manufacturer: Various.
Role: Anti-Submarine.
Guidance: Active homing.
Propulsion: Electric
Mod 1 differs slightly. Being replaced by Mk 46.

Type: Mk 46 Mod 0 General purpose torpedo.
Weight: 568lb (258kg).
Dimensions: Length: 8ft 5in (2.57m): diameter 12.7in (324mm).
Manufacturer: Various.
Role: Anti-Submarine.
Guidance: Active Homing.
Propulsion: Solid Fuel (Monergol).
Standard lightweight AS torpedo, used in aircraft, ships and ASROC. Mod 1 has an Otto fuel engine. Mk 46 torpedoes are also used in CAPTOR AS mines.

Type: Mk 48 Mod 1 Ship and Submarine torpedo.
Weight: 2,750lb (1,250kg).
Dimensions: Length 19ft (5.8m): diameter 21in (533mm).
Manufacturer: Gould.
Role: Anti-Ship and Anti-Submarine.
Guidance: Active-passive acoustic homing or Wire-guided.
Propulsion:
Designed to replace other large ship- or submarine-launched torpedoes. Maximum speed about 40kts. Very long range and deep diving capability.

Below: A Mk 48 Mod 1 torpedo being loaded into the *Sturgeon* class SSN *Pargo.*

The United States Air Force

Maj. Gen. Robert N. Ginsburgh, USAF(Ret.), former Deputy Director, Joint Staff, Organization of the Joint Chiefs of Staff, Washington, former Director of Air Force Information, former Armed Forces Aide to the President.

Although the United States has been the world's preeminent air power for some 35 years, the US Air Force itself is relatively young. Born in mid-1947, the USAF is slightly more than half the age of Britain's Royal Air Force, which served as its inspiration and model.

Ironically, by the time of its birth the US Air Force was significantly smaller than during its period of gestation. Produced by the experience of World War II, the military strength of the Air Force in 1947 was only about 300,000—one-eighth of the Army Air Force's peak strength of 2,400,000 in the closing months of World War II.

Its lineage, of course, can be traced back many years. Some historical buffs trace the beginnings of the American Air Force to the use of balloons by the Union Forces during the Civil War. (Conceptually, the use of balloons by American military forces can be traced back much further, to proposals made during the Mexican War, the war with the Seminole Indians or even to Benjamin Franklin.)

In terms of continuous existence, however, America's air arm began on August 1, 1907, with the establishment of the Aeronautical Division of the Signal Corps—with a total strength of three people. The following year the Aeronautical Division acquired its first airship—a dirigible balloon—and the year after that its first heavier-than-air craft, built by the Wright brothers.

Although the Wright brothers were credited with making the world's first powered flight in December of 1903, the US was slow to exploit the new capability for military purposes. Thus in early 1917, on the eve of America's entry into World War I, the United States ranked fourteenth in the world in terms of military aviation, with a strength of a little over one thousand people and without a single aircraft capable of performing in combat.

The declaration of war by the United States in April 1917 triggered an explosive expansion of the infant American air arm. By the time of the Armistice eighteen months later, total strength had expanded to 190,000; pilot strength from 100 to 11,000; and training fields from 5 to 40. Although only one American-built plane, the DH-4, saw combat during the war, by the end of the war the US had produced more than 5,000 trainers (Curtiss Jennies, J-1s and JN-4s) in addition to the 1,200 de Havillands (DH-4s) which had been delivered to the American Expeditionary Forces. American industry had produced 30,000 aircraft engines and developed the capacity to produce nearly 50,000 engines and 20,000 airplanes a year.

Meanwhile, more than 1,200 American pilots, observers and gunners (45 American squadrons) saw action at the Front—observing, bursting balloons, directing artillery fire, conducting ground strafing, achieving several hundred aerial victories in dogfights with enemy aircraft, and even dropping 137 tons of explosives. These aerial exploits, many of which brought into the dreary trench warfare of World War I a sense of gallantry—a sense of hand-to-hand combat and a return to the days of knighthood and chivalry —captured the imagination of the American public.

Evaluating facts rather than potential, tra-ditional Army leaders were less impressed, and in the postwar evaluation of the air arm were inclined to look on aircraft as "merely an added means of communication, observation and reconnaissance". Thus the United States failed to follow Britain's example in establishing the independent Royal Air Force in 1918. Nevertheless, American airpower had achieved sufficient stature to be divorced from the Signal Corps and in May of 1918 became the Division of Military Aeronautics, US Army.

In the rapid demobilization of the World War I fighting machine, within two years American air strength was reduced by 95 percent to about 9,000 military personnel. The Army Reorganization Act of 1920 which recreated the Army Air Service provided the impetus for expansion to almost 12,000 by the following year. But a combination of limited budgets, control by "ground-minded" senior officers plus the general euphoria of the Disarmament talks led to a reduction of the Air Services to its postwar low of 9,500 by the end of 1923. Not until 1937 was the Army Air Corps actually to achieve the strength of 17,500 authorized by the Act of 1920.

The history of the Army Air Corps (in 1926 the name was changed from the Air Services) during the interwar years was marked by controversy: airpower versus seapower, continuing arguments over appropriations and personnel strengths, the struggle for an autonomous air arm, Congressional Commissions, a series of airship disasters, dispute over carrying the air mail, and the court martial of General Billy Mitchell, the enthusiastic, if untactful, proponent of airpower. Much of the controversy centered around the struggle of airpower proponents to create autonomous air forces based on the capability of independent strategic striking power. (Strategic airpower is dealt with in another chapter of this book).

Early Records in Private Aviation

Simultaneously, the Air Corps was improving its capability, successively establishing new records for distance, altitude, speed and endurance: coast to coast non-stop in 1923, thirty-seven hours in the air using aerial refueling in 1923, across America in a dawn to dusk flight in 1924, around the world in 175 days the same year, speed records by 1925 of 245 miles an hour, the 22,000 Pan American good will flight 1926–7, the first flight from California to Hawaii in 1927, almost a full week in the air in 1929, a non-stop en masse flight from Alaska to the state of Washington in 1934, a balloon altitude record of 72,000 feet by 1935.

Such exploits by Air Corps personnel, extensively barnstorming throughout the country by ex-army pilots from World War I, and Lindbergh's dramatic trans-Atlantic solo flight had created an air-minded American public which enthusiastically supported the development of private civil aviation.

America's preeminence in commercial aviation was not matched in military aviation. By the late 1930's France, Russia, Britain and Italy all led the US in aircraft production, with Germany and Japan rapidly catching up.

On the outbreak of World War II in 1939, the US Army Air Corps strength was less than

Though the youngest US armed force (1947) the Air Force has a reputation for unequalled political power, although this may be an impression voiced by less-successful rivals for declining funds. These rivals might suggest the F-15 Eagle (below) was an astronomically priced toy in which pilots can zoom through "the wild blue yonder". Such an assertion, which does not withstand critical examination, could not be levelled at the A-10A close-support tank killer (left) which, even without its heavy weapon load, is slower than World War II fighters. Fixed-wing close support is a role the Army wanted.

Table 1: Office of the Secretary of the Air Force*

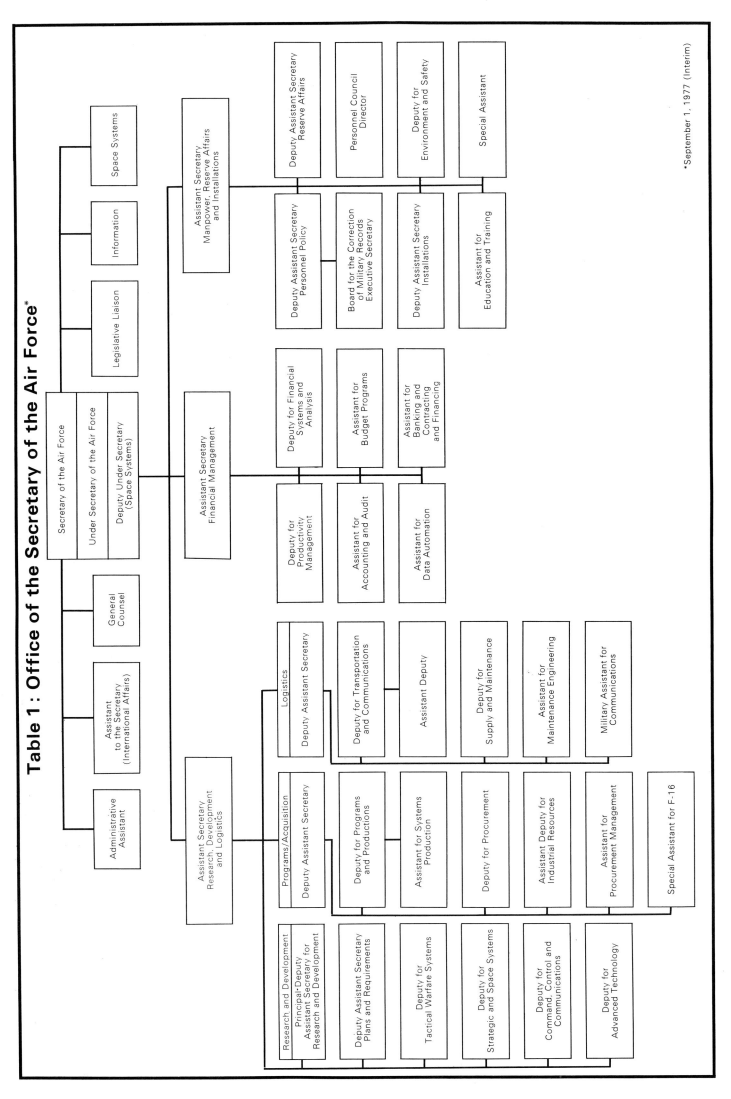

*September 1, 1977 (Interim)

148

24,000 men. Though this strength was dramatically increased in each of the following two years, at the time of the Pearl Harbor attack the Army Air Forces numbered only 150,000 men. However, its aircraft strength had been expanded from 800 in 1937 to 12,000, and in addition the US as the arsenal of democracy had supplied several thousand badly-needed planes to the Allied powers.

Before the end of the war three and a half years later, the Army Air Forces had expanded to a total of 2.4 million men and women, and American industry had produced more than 230,000 planes for the Allied war effort. Compared to the 137 tons of ordnance dropped by the Air Services during World War I, the Army Air Forces dropped 177,000 tons on Japan alone, and more than three times that much in the European theater—plus two atomic bombs on Hiroshima and Nagasaki.

In the process, the AAF lost 65,000 aircraft and suffered 120,000 overseas casualties, including 40,000 deaths. Within the US there were an additional 150,000 wartime air fatalities.

The decisive nature of the strategic air campaigns, the dramatic attacks on German and Japanese industry, the spectacle of 1,000-plane raids over Germany, the fire bombing of Tokyo-Yokohama, and finally the two atomic bomb attacks have tended to focus attention on the strategic air effort. Throughout the war, however, a significant part of the air effort had been devoted to tactical (now more commonly called theater) air operations.

Even while emphasizing the potential decisiveness of independent strategic airpower, Army Air Corps leaders had not neglected doctrine for joint air–ground operations. Essentially the employment doctrine envisaged three phases or tasks. First was the job of achieving air superiority, primarily by destruction of enemy air forces on the ground, but also in aerial combat. Next came the job of isolating the ground battlefield by interdiction tasks. Finally,

close air operations in support of ground troops were stressed, directed both by ground and aerial observers.

Not long after the initial employment of American forces in North Africa, Army leaders learned a tactical lesson on the battlefield which air leaders had long urged in the classrooms—the necessity of centralized control of airpower for maximum effectiveness. They quickly realized that the Allied defeat at the Battle of Kaserine Pass in the fall of 1942 resulted primarily from the greater effectiveness of the numerically inferior German air forces operating under centralized control. Ever since that time American ground forces have always fought under an umbrella of air superiority—and usually under conditions of air supremacy.

In the two wars the United States has waged since then, the US Air Force has followed essentially the same threefold pattern for employment of tactical air forces in joint air–ground operations, though the execution has been improved by significant technological advances in command, control, and communications.

Emphasis of Close Air Support

More recently there appears to be some shift in emphasis among the three tasks. The earlier conception of executing the three tasks sequentially—first the battle for air superiority, then the interdiction phase, and finally close air support—has been modified to include the allocation of air effort to pursue all three tasks simultaneously. Furthermore, many American tacticians argue that because of the overwhelming numerical superiority of Warsaw Pact ground forces on the Central Front in Europe first, rather than last, priority should be given to air support of the ground battle in the event of war in that theater. At the same time, Warsaw Pact practices of dispersion, concealment and protection of aircraft have led to increased emphasis on air-to-air operations to achieve

Above: Backbone of the Air Force's tactical strength is still provided by the old but versatile Phantom. Here a pair of F-4Es of the 35th Tac Ftr Wing recover at George AFB, California.

air superiority. It is an open question whether these modifications in the traditional air doctrine would prove to be more or less effective in the event of war.

Immediately upon the conclusion of World War II, expecting big power cooperation in the new United Nations, and judging that the "absolute weapon" of atomic power would deter war, the US rapidly demobilized its military machine. Though not quite as drastic as the post World War I pattern, by the end of 1947 the American air arm was down to about 300,000—significant in terms of pre-war strength but only one-eighth the peak wartime strength.

In the meantime, however, in the autumn of 1947 the United States Air Force achieved its long-sought independence as a separate force co-equal to the Army and Navy. Under the impetus of the Cold War, the Soviet explosion of an atomic bomb, the development of hydrogen weapons, and the Finletter Commission on airpower, the size of the Air Force had been increased 30 percent by the outbreak of the Korean War.

The requirement for waging a war in the Pacific while building up NATO to deter the Soviets in Europe led to a rapid air buildup, which eventually reached a strength of almost one million. The change from the Truman to the Eisenhower Administration brought a "New Look" in military affairs. Though the new strategy emphasized air-atomic power, this was to be "a bigger bang for a buck", which theoretically, would require fewer forces in being. Thus for each of the next eight years the Air Force's strength declined. Along with the Kennedy Administration in 1961, however, came another doctrinal change, to "flexible response" and its

Major Active Air Force Installations in the US

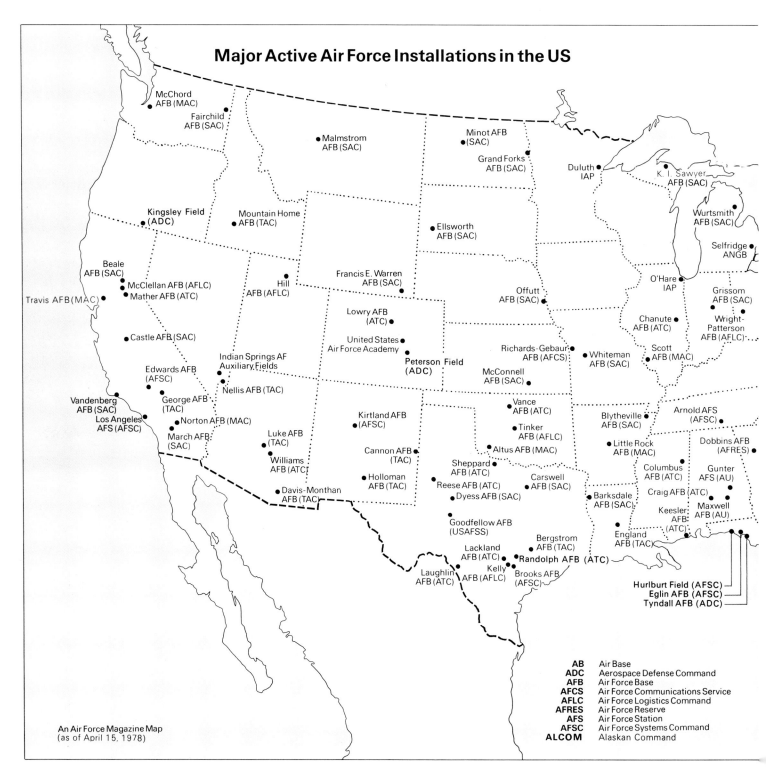

McChord AFB (MAC)
Fairchild AFB (SAC)
Malmstrom AFB (SAC)
Minot AFB (SAC)
Grand Forks AFB (SAC)
Duluth IAP
K. I. Sawyer AFB (SAC)
Wurtsmith AFB (SAC)
Selfridge ANGB
Kingsley Field (ADC)
Mountain Home AFB (TAC)
Ellsworth AFB (SAC)
O'Hare IAP
Grissom AFB (SAC)
Beale AFB (SAC)
McClellan AFB (AFLC)
Mather AFB (ATC)
Hill AFB (AFLC)
Francis E. Warren AFB (SAC)
Offutt AFB (SAC)
Chanute AFB (ATC)
Wright-Patterson AFB (AFLC)
Travis AFB (MAC)
Lowry AFB (ATC)
Richards-Gebaur AFB (AFCS)
Scott AFB (MAC)
Castle AFB (SAC)
United States Air Force Academy
Peterson Field (ADC)
Whiteman AFB (SAC)
Indian Springs AF Auxiliary Fields
McConnell AFB (SAC)
Edwards AFB (AFSC)
Nellis AFB (TAC)
Vance AFB (ATC)
Blytheville AFB (SAC)
Arnold AFS (AFSC)
Vandenberg AFB (SAC)
George AFB (TAC)
Kirtland AFB (AFSC)
Tinker AFB (AFLC)
Little Rock AFB (MAC)
Dobbins AFB (AFRES)
Los Angeles AFS (AFSC)
Norton AFB (MAC)
Luke AFB (TAC)
Cannon AFB (TAC)
Altus AFB (MAC)
Columbus AFB (ATC)
Gunter AFS (AU)
March AFB (SAC)
Williams AFB (ATC)
Holloman AFB (TAC)
Sheppard AFB (ATC)
Carswell AFB (SAC)
Craig AFB (ATC)
Maxwell AFB (AU)
Davis-Monthan AFB (TAC)
Reese AFB (ATC)
Dyess AFB (SAC)
Barksdale AFB (SAC)
Keesler AFB (ATC)
Goodfellow AFB (USAFSS)
Bergstrom AFB (TAC)
England AFB (TAC)
Lackland AFB (ATC)
Randolph AFB (ATC)
Laughlin AFB (ATC)
Kelly AFB (AFLC)
Brooks AFB (AFSC)
Hurlburt Field (AFSC)
Eglin AFB (AFSC)
Tyndall AFB (ADC)

An Air Force Magazine Map
(as of April 15, 1978)

AB	Air Base
ADC	Aerospace Defense Command
AFB	Air Force Base
AFCS	Air Force Communications Service
AFLC	Air Force Logistics Command
AFRES	Air Force Reserve
AFS	Air Force Station
AFSC	Air Force Systems Command
ALCOM	Alaskan Command

emphasis on general purpose as opposed to strategic forces. This generated a new expansion of the Air Force, which was further stimulated by the Vietnam War. This latest expansion peaked in 1968 at over 900,000 when another decline set in.

Ten years later, at the end of 1977, the Air Force stood at slightly over 570,000 military personnel, the lowest strength since the early days of the Korean War.

Against the ups and downs of the Air Force's personnel strengths a number of long range trends are evident. In thirty years the Air Force has made the transition from the propeller-driven World War II aircraft to an all-jet combat Air Force. Aircraft fly farther, higher, and faster but they are fewer in number. Instead of 20,000 aircraft, the Air Force today has fewer than 10,000—with the Reserve Forces comprising a significantly greater percentage than earlier. Fewer aircraft, longer ranges, aerial refueling and changes in national policy have significantly reduced the supporting base structure—especially overseas. Bases, budgets, and people for offensive and defensive strategic forces claim a much smaller percentage of the

total. Within the strategic forces increasing reliance is placed on missile forces as the number of manned bombers continues to decline; the Carter Administration's decision not to proceed with production of the new B-1 strategic bomber will accelerate that decline. Fifteen percent of the airmen are black. Seven percent of the airmen are women—and this number is increasing. Almost all of the airmen are high school graduates; most of the officers are college graduates.

Although there have been many changes in emphasis, the overall structure of the Air Force remains essentially the same as when it was first organized. It consists of thirteen major air commands with three quarters of a million military personnel and 13 separate operating agencies with 35,000. Civilian personnel and reserve forces of a quarter million each bring the grand total to over one million people.

Of the thirteen major air commands six of them, with 340,000 people, can be classified as combat commands. By far the biggest single command is still the Strategic Air Command numbering 127,000—more than four times larger than the air defense forces. These stra-

Table 2: Installations of the United States Air Force

Major Installations	FY '68	FY '77
US and Possessions	138	110
Foreign	60	27
Totals	**198**	**137**
Other Installations		
US and Possessions	2,723	2,371
Foreign	1,060	653
Totals	**3,783**	**3,024**
"Other Installations" includes:[1]		
Auxiliary	1,892	—
Ballistic Missile	1,158	1,157
Industrial	43	—
Radar	183	—
Air National Guard	106	127
Tenant, Non-Air Force	357	—
War Only	44	—
Electronics Station or Site		579
General Support Annex	—	1,140
Auxiliary Air Field	—	21

"Other installations" was redefined in 1972.

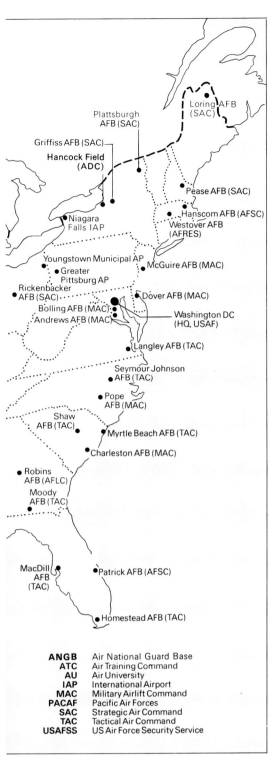

Loring AFB (SAC)

Plattsburgh AFB (SAC)

Griffiss AFB (SAC)
Hancock Field (ADC)

Pease AFB (SAC)

Hanscom AFB (AFSC)

Niagara Falls IAP

Westover AFB (AFRES)

McGuire AFB (MAC)

Youngstown Municipal AP
Greater Pittsburg AP

Rickenbacker AFB (SAC)

Dover AFB (MAC)

Bolling AFB (MAC)
Andrews AFB (MAC)

Washington DC (HQ, USAF)

Langley AFB (TAC)

Seymour Johnson AFB (TAC)

Pope AFB (MAC)

Shaw AFB (TAC)

Myrtle Beach AFB (TAC)

Charleston AFB (MAC)

Robins AFB (AFLC)

Moody AFB (TAC)

MacDill AFB (TAC)

Patrick AFB (AFSC)

Homestead AFB (TAC)

ANGB	Air National Guard Base
ATC	Air Training Command
AU	Air University
IAP	International Airport
MAC	Military Airlift Command
PACAF	Pacific Air Forces
SAC	Strategic Air Command
TAC	Tactical Air Command
USAFSS	US Air Force Security Service

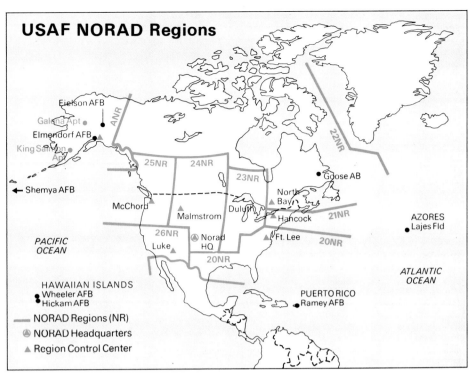

USAF NORAD Regions

Eielson AFB
Galena Apt
Elmendorf AFB
King Salmon Apt
Shemya AFB

ANR
25NR
24NR
23NR
22NR

Goose AB

McChord
Malmstrom
Duluth
North Bay
Hancock
21NR
20NR

AZORES
Lajes Fld

26NR
Luke
Norad HQ
Ft. Lee
20NR

PACIFIC OCEAN

ATLANTIC OCEAN

HAWAIIAN ISLANDS
Wheeler AFB
Hickam AFB

PUERTO RICO
Ramey AFB

— NORAD Regions (NR)
⬣ NORAD Headquarters
▲ Region Control Center

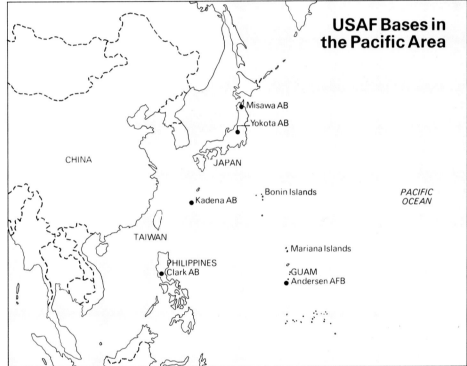

USAF Bases in the Pacific Area

Misawa AB
Yokota AB

CHINA

JAPAN

Kadena AB

Bonin Islands

PACIFIC OCEAN

TAIWAN

Mariana Islands

PHILIPPINES
Clark AB

GUAM
Andersen AFB

tegic forces, together with the contributions of strategic forces from the other services, are the subject of a separate chapter.

Although SAC is the largest single air command, the total of tactical forces is greater than the strategic forces, offensive and defensive. The tactical forces, however, are organized into four separate commands. These are the tactical Air Command (95,000) based in the United States, and the three overseas commands: United States Air Forces in Europe (50,000), Pacific Air Forces (31,000) and the Alaskan Air Command (10,000).

For operational purposes the tactical air forces are subordinated to the unified and specified command system. Thus the Pacific Air Forces form the air component of the Pacific Command under the control of the Commander-in-Chief, Pacific (CINCPAC). Similarly, the United States Air Forces in Europe are part of the

Right: Most effective tactical delivery system in any NATO air force is the F-111F. This powerful attack aircraft equips the 48th Tac Ftr Wing, based at RAF Lakenheath, England, administratively in USAFE.

US European Command under the Commander-in-Chief, US European Command (USCINCEUR). Historically, USCINCEUR has also worn the second hat of SACEUR (Supreme Allied Command Europe), thus simplifying the task of merging American operations into NATO operations. Formerly, the Alaskan Air Command was also subordinated to the unified Alaskan Command; however, with the elimination of the Alaskan Command, the Commander of the Alaskan Air Command, as the senior military officer in Alaska, has assumed responsibility for coordinating joint military matters. The Tactical Air Command actually serves as the USAF air component for two unified commands—the US Atlantic Command, Norfolk, Virginia, and the US Readiness Command, MacDill AFB, Florida.

Major subordinate commands of the Tactical Air Command (Langley AFB, Virginia) are the Ninth Air Force (Shaw AFB, South Carolina) with 9 tactical fighter wings, a special operations wing, 'a tactical reconnaissance wing, and a tactical air control wing; and the Twelfth Air Force (Bergstrom AFB, Texas) with 6 tactical fighter wings, a tactical reconnaissance wing, a tactical air control wing, and two tactical training wings. Other Tactical Air Command units include the Tactical Air Warfare Center, the Tactical Fighter Weapons Center, an early warning and control wing, and the Southern Air Division stationed in the Panama Canal Zone.

From Ramstein Air Base, Germany, the US Air Forces Europe commands the Third Air Force in England, the Sixteenth Air Force in Germany, and the Seventeenth Air Force in Germany—with a total of eight tactical fighter wings, two tactical reconnaissance wings, and one tactical control wing.

Pacific Air Forces in Hawaii command two numbered Air Forces in Japan and the Philippines plus three air divisions in Hawaii, Okinawa, and Korea, Alaskan Air Command, Elmendorf AFB, Alaska, commands a composite wing, a combat support group and 13 Aircraft

Table 3: Number of Aircraft Per Active-Duty USAF Squadron

Aircraft Type	Number
A-7	24
B-52	14
C-5	17
C-9	11
C-130	15
AC-130	10
KC-135	15
C-141	18
F-4	24
RF-4	18
F-5	18
F-15	24
F-106	18
F-111	24
FB-111	15

Projected Unit Equipment (UE) Assignments for New Weapon Systems

A-10	24
B-1	15
E-3A	10
F-16	24

NOTE: In addition, four USAF aircraft types are counted as total Unit Equipment, not by squadrons. These include the HC-130 (24 total), the WC-130 (13 total), and the T-39 (104 total), all of the Military Airlift Command; and the T-38 trainer (946 total, plus those assigned to the Thunderbirds demonstration team). Source: *Air Force Magazine*

warning squadrons.

Another measure of the current importance of tactical air forces is the fiscal year 1978 budget of $9.4 billion for the Air Force general purpose forces compared to $5.8 billion for Air Force strategic forces. Fifteen years ago the general purpose budget was less than half the strategic budget. Total tactical capability must also take into account the contribution of the Reserve Forces with a $2 billion budget and 250,000 people. Though the Reserve Forces serve as a back-up for the total Air Force, their greatest

contribution is to the tactical air forces. Finally, the total US tactical air capability would have to include the forces of the Navy, Marines, and Army—whose aircraft strength, in fact, exceeds that of the Air Force.

Since 1971 the total US tactical air strength has fallen below that of the USSR but now appears to have stabilized at a level about three-quarters of the total of Soviet tactical operating aircraft.

The Air Force element of these tactical air forces consists of eight major types. Most numerous are the more than 600 F-4 Phantoms. First developed as a naval fighter in the mid-1950's, the F-4 will continue to be a mainstay of tactical forces—though in declining numbers—into the 1980's. The total F-4 force, which includes several different models, has a wide range of missions and capabilities. The former include air superiority, attack, close-support, electronic counter measures, and defense suppression. Air-to-air capabilities include 20 millimeter multi-barrel guns, Sparrow and Sidewinder missiles. Air-to-ground capability now includes Shrike

Right: The A-10A's philosophy is one of survivability and first-pass lethality. Its pilots fly manually just above the ground, unlike this one turning high over the desert with eight of a possible 11 pylons loaded. The white pod under the nose is Pave Penny.

Below right: There are few US military loads that will not fit inside a C-5A. Here various configurations of ground vehicles and helicopters are being taken on board during exercise SADIP.

Below: Attack run by a Vought A-7D, an economical and effective close-support and tactical attack bomber first designed for the Navy. This one comes from the 354th Tac Ftr Wing at Myrtle Beach, S Carolina, which is now converting to the Fairchild A-10A.

Major Force Squadrons	FY '68	FY '74	FY '76	FY '77	FY '78
Bomber	40	28	26	24	24
ECM/Reconnaissance	3	1	1	1	1
IRBM/ICBM	26	26	26	26	26
Tanker	41	38	35	32	30
Interceptor	34	7	6	6	6
Bomarc	6	—	—	—	—
Command, Control and Surveillance	13	8	6	6	6
Tactical Bomber	1	—	—	—	—
Mace/Matador	2	—	—	—	—
Fighter	92	74	74	77	78
Reconnaissance	21	13	9	9	9
Tactical Air Control System	9	11	9	11	11
Special Operations Force	22	5	5	5	5
Tactical Airborne Command Control System	—	—	2	4	4
Tactical Airlift	31	17	15	15	15
Strategic Airlift	32	17	17	17	17
Aeromed Evacuation	6	3	3	3	3
Special Mission	2	2	2	2	2
Mapping	2	1	—	—	—
Weather	6	3	2	2	2
Air Rescue and Recovery	14	12	5	5	5
Intelligence	15	9	7	6	6
Other	9	2	2	2	2
Total, USAF	**427**	**277**	**252**	**253**	**252**
Air National Guard	78	91	91	91	91
Air Force Reserve (incl. Associate Squadrons)	37	53	53	53	53
Total, Major Force Squadrons	**542**	**421**	**396**	**397**	**396**

NOTE: Data in FY '68–76 columns are actual; FY '77 and FY '78 data are programmed.
Source: *Air Force Magazine*

(AGM-45), Standard ARM (AGM-78), HARM (AGM-88), Maverick missile (AGM-65) and the CBU Rockeye area weapon. "Smart-bomb" capability includes laser, infra-red, and electro-optical guidance. With a typical tactical load the F-4 has a maximum speed of Mach 2.2, a 40,000 feet altitude, and a range of 1,300 miles.

The RF-4C, a reconnaissance version of the F-4, is assigned to the nine tactical reconnaissance squadrons of the active and reserve forces. Though the number of tactical reconnaissance squadrons is far below the 21 squadrons of 1968, it is one greater than the 1964 strength.

A newer fighter-bomber, on which production was not completed until 1976, is the General Dynamics F-111. Originally conceived as a joint Air Force–Navy project, 437 were produced by the Air Force in four versions which are deployed with four Air Force tactical fighter wings. (Two additional models were produced for the Strategic Air Command and for the Royal Australian Air Force.) Compared to the F-4, the F-111 can fly higher, at two-and-a-half times the range, with a 50 percent greater bomb load.

Another current tactical aircraft scheduled to serve into the 1980s is Vought Corporation's attack fighter, the A-7D. Less expensive—though less versatile and less capable than the F-4 and F-111—the A-7 has proven to be an effective all-weather strike aircraft, and is becoming an increasingly important element of the reserve forces as newer aircraft replace it with active squadrons. Three other types of tactical aircraft currently assigned to the reserve forces are scheduled to be phased out of the inventory by mid-1981. Oldest of these is North American's F-100 Super Sabre, successor to the F-86 Sabre interceptor of Korean War fame. Of a total of 2,300 produced, 400 are still operational. The first operations fighter capable of supersonic speed in level flight, the original prototype of the F-100 was first flown in 1953. In addition to the original intercepter version, subsequent models were developed for the fighter-bomber role. Also being phased out is the F-105 Thunderchief. The F-105 was first flown in 1959, and eventually some 600 of these all-weather fighter-bombers were produced for use in both high and low level strike missions at night and in all weather. Several squadrons of the F-105 are in service with the reserve forces, and two squadrons of the F-105 "Wild Weasel" are assigned to the active forces for the suppression of surface-to-air missiles using electronic countermeasures. The newest and smallest of the aircraft being phased out is the A37B currently assigned to the reserve forces. Originally designed as a jet trainer, it was converted to use as a counter-insurgency aircraft.

As the F-100s, F-105s and A-37s are being phased out, three new aircraft types are being phased in.

Foremost of these is the McDonnell Douglas F-15 Eagle, which will become the Air Force's primary air superiority fighter. First flown in 1972, the presently planned production of more than 700 will be completed by 1981. Rated as the best air-to-air fighter operational in the world today, it is expected to remain superior to any potential enemy aircraft projected for the 1980s (including the Soviet Foxbat, MiG-25). Although designed primarily for the air superiority role, the F-15 also has an inherent air-to-surface capability and could carry an external bomb load of 15,000 pounds. Even without external fuel, the F-15 has a ferry range of 2,900 miles.

Of the same generation as the F-15 is Fairchild's A-10. The first aircraft designed specifically for the close air support of ground troops, the A-10 is a rugged, relatively low cost, subsonic jet featuring large payload, long loiter time, and survivability. The A-10 was selected for production after a competitive flyoff with the Northrop A-9 and a comparative evaluation with the A-7D. A total of over 700 aircraft is planned, with direct delivery into the reserve forces beginning in February 1979. The US, and hence NATO, will rely heavily on the A-10 to counter the Warsaw Pact's 5-to-1 armored advantage and overall 2-to-1 strength advantage in ground forces.

The third of the new generation of tactical aircraft is the General Dynamics F-16. Conceived of originally as a lower cost aircraft for sale to foreign air forces, almost 1,400 F-16s are now programmed for the US active and reserve forces, with introduction into the reserve forces beginning in February 1980. An additional 400 F-16s are programmed for Belgium, Denmark, the Netherlands, and Norway. As a complement to the F-15, the F-16 will help redress the quantitative deficiency of tactical aircraft at lower cost. Although it lacks the all-weather radar missile capability of the F-15, its air-to-air effectiveness is expected to parallel that of the F-15 in close visual combat. Although its design was optimized for clear air mass air-to-air operations, the F-16 will also have an air-to-ground capability which will allow the theater commander to use the F-16s as a "swing" force.

In addition to these current and projected major combat type aircraft of the tactical air forces, three additional types deserve mention: the O-2A, the OV-10A, and the E3A. The O-2A and the newer OV-10A were procured for the forward air control mission and are currently in service in reserve and active units within the United States and overseas. The OV-10A also

Left: A PQM-102 RPV target flying in the unmanned mode from Holloman AFB, New Mexico, in 1975. The PQM-102 is a rebuilt F-102A Delta Dagger all-weather interceptor.

Facing page upper: Two of the eight F-16A and F-16B development (pre-production) fighters flying together from Fort Worth. The one on the left has the Westinghouse pulse-doppler radar. All eight of these F-16s were flying by July 1978.

Right: A unique photograph secured by a TAC photographer at Nellis on the occasion of the 1977 William Tell weapons meet. Aircraft taking part included the F-4, F-15, A-7, F-111, F-100 and F-105.

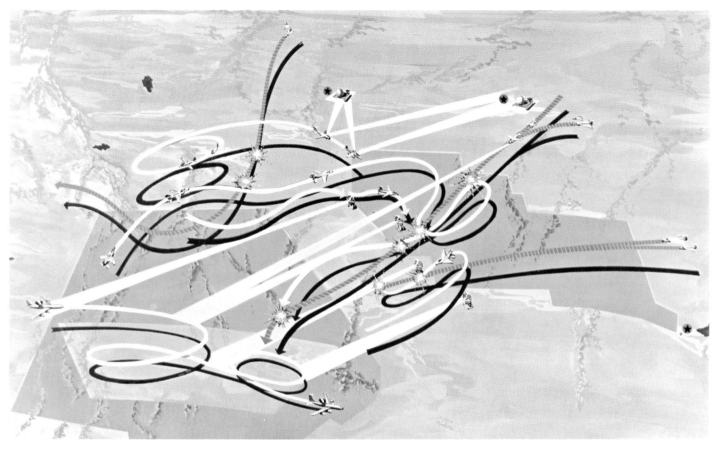

has a limited quick-response role in support of ground forces before the arrival of tactical fighters.

The E-3A, or AWACS (Airborne Warning and Control System) is the Air Force's top priority program for general purpose forces. AWACS is a jamming-resistant, surveillance, command, control, and communications system carried in a modified Boeing 707. It combines a sophisticated radar with advanced data processing and communications relay equipment. It is capable of all weather, long range, high or low level surveillance of all air vehicles over all kinds of terrain. In addition, the AWACS can detect and display maritime surface targets and the status of friendly ground positions (based on coded beacon returns).

It would be difficult to overstate the potential military significance of this system. In the World War II Battle of Britain, for example, radar control greatly magnified the effectiveness of RAF fighter units and made it possible for these relatively small forces to withstand the German aerial blitz. Similarly, a relatively crude airborne command and control system in Southeast Asia multiplied the aircraft kill ratio over North Vietnam by a factor of six.

The AWACS not only significantly improves the capability of airborne command and control for more efficient weapon allocation and control of the air battle; more importantly, it also provides a counter to the ability of sophisticated modern aircraft to underfly existing ground-based radar envelopes. Finally, it provides military commanders and political authorities up to the highest levels unprecedented access to a comprehensive near-real-time image of the conflict situation, whether crisis or major conflict. In addition to its role of controlling American tactical air forces, the AWACS is also designed to provide surveillance and control for the air defense of the United States—and NATO and Iran have taken steps toward procuring its own AWACS force.

Any broad assessment of American tactical air force capability must consider three additional elements: air defense, strategic forces, and airlift.

One of the traditional missions of tactical air forces has always been air defense in overseas theaters. In both the Korean War and the Vietnam War assets of the Air Defense Command were deployed to supplement tactical forces for theater air defense. Now, however, the shoe is on the other foot. With the aging and drastic shrinkage of the air defense forces, F-4s of the Tactical Air Command have had to assume 4 of the 26 alert locations for the air defense of the United States. (The current intercepter force of F-106s is 20 years old, and the 49 intercepter and 8 BOMARC squadrons of a generation ago are down to only 6). Additional TAC assets would be required in case of an actual attack on the United States.

Strategic forces, on the other hand, offer the potential for a significant reinforcement of tactical air forces capability. In the Korean War, Strategic Air Command B-50s significantly added to the bombing campaign, while in the Vietnam War conventionally-armed B-52s were used exclusively for close air support and interdiction as well as for attacks on the Hanoi-Haiphong areas. For the future, both the B-52s and FB-111s could provide a significant rein-

Above: Schematic representation of a test intended to demonstrate survivability of the E-3A (AWACS). A single E-3A was confined within a box about 50 by 80 nautical miles within the Edwards AFB Range area. Defending it were two F-15s, four F-4Es, two aircraft able to jam the two "hostile" GCI stations and an F-105G to attack the four hostile ground-based jammers. The E-3A initiated tracks on the hostile aircraft at distant ranges close to their initial points. On the basis of these tracks the defending fighters were successful in scoring multiple "kills" on all the hostiles, which simulated six MiG-23 Flogger and two Brewer E escorting jammers. Once it had detected the attackers, the E-3A descended to deny the enemy positive GCI control, but—it is claimed—maintained active radar surveillance at all times.

Table 5: Number of Active Aircraft and Flying Hours

Type of Aircraft	FY '68	FY '77	FY '78
Bomber, Strategic	714	491	489
Bomber, Other	65	—	—
Tanker	667	556	525
Fighter/Interceptor/Attack	3,985	2,588	2,667
Reconnaissance/Electronic Warfare	1,009	423	422
Cargo/Transport	2,358	863	853
Search and Rescue (Fixed Wing)	91	37	38
Helicopter (includes Rescue)	465	253	255
Special Research	5		
Trainer	2,584	1,772	1,786
Utility/Observation	663	216	213
Total, USAF	**12,606**	**7,199**	**7,248**
Air National Guard total	1,438	1,567	1,532
Air Force Reserve total	426	480	473
Free World Military Forces total	692	—	—
Aircraft earmarked (MAP, USN, and Other Non-USAF)	165	—	—
Total Active Aircraft: USAF, AFRES, ANG	**15,327**	**9,246**	**9,253**
Flying Hours (x1,000)			
USAF	7,068	2,713	2,676
ANG	465	405	406
AFRES	164	140	144
Total Flying Hours	**7,697**	**3,258**	**3,226**

Source: *Air Force Magazine*

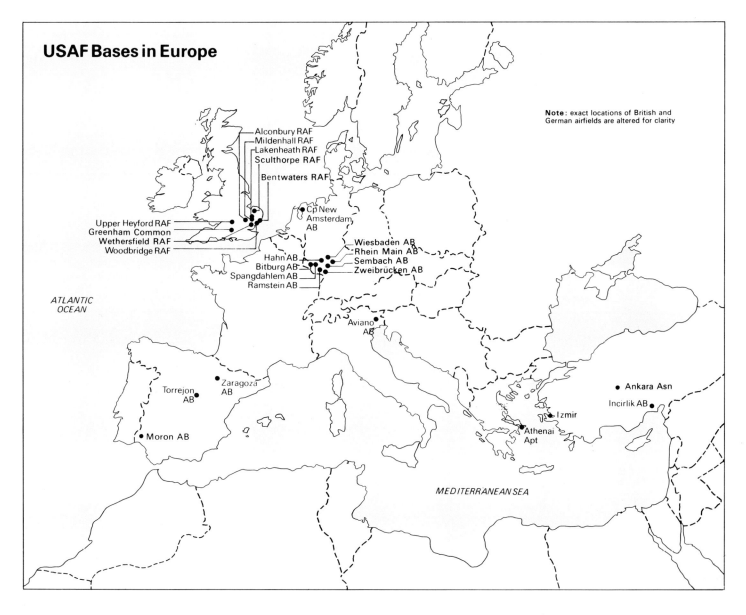

USAF Bases in Europe

Note: exact locations of British and German airfields are altered for clarity

Alconbury RAF
Mildenhall RAF
Lakenheath RAF
Sculthorpe RAF
Bentwaters RAF

Upper Heyford RAF
Greenham Common
Wethersfield RAF
Woodbridge RAF

Cp New Amsterdam AB

Wiesbaden AB
Rhein Main AB
Sembach AB
Zweibrücken AB

Hahn AB
Bitburg AB
Spangdahlem AB
Ramstein AB

ATLANTIC OCEAN

Aviano AB

Torrejon AB
Zaragoza AB
Moron AB

Ankara Asn
Incirlik AB
Izmir
Athenai Apt

MEDITERRANEAN SEA

forcement to tactical air capabilities using either conventional or nuclear weapons. These potential strategic assets might not always be available, however, since there might be circumstances when it would be essential to maintain them in a high state of readiness for their primary strategic role.

Normally, about half of the US Air Force's tactical forces are stationed in the United States. Most scenarios, however, would envision their combat employment in overseas theaters rather than within the continental limits of the United States. While most TAC aircraft can be redeployed overseas under their own power, using SACs KC 135s for aerial refueling where necessary, tactical air forces are heavily dependent upon strategic airlift to provide the combat and logistic support for early commitment to combat operations. In addition, both theatre air forces and ground forces count on tactical airlift to enhance their combat capabilities.

Traditionally, tactical airlift had been assigned as part of tactical air forces whether in the US or overseas. In early 1977, however, all US strategic and tactical airlift was consolidated under the Military Airlift Command, which has the responsibility for airlift support of all the military services.

The Military Airlift Command's strategic airlift capability is centered upon the 70 C-5s and 270 C-141s. In time of emergency this airlift capacity could potentially be doubled through the use of 100 widebody and 200 other jet transport aircraft of the Civil Reserve Air Fleet (CRAF). A number of programs are planned to enhance materially this strategic capability: procuring increased spare parts to improve wartime utilization rates for the C-5 and C-141, providing an aerial refueling capability for the

C-141 and stretching its fuselage to expand its cargo capacity 30 percent, strengthening the C-5 wing to quadruple its useful life, and modifying aircraft of the Civil Reserve Air Fleet. Capabilities will be further enhanced by procurement of the advanced tanker/cargo aircraft (ATCA) which is to be an off-the-shelf derivative of the McDonnell Douglas DC-10.

Below: Now given the Department of Defense designation of KC-10A, the McDonnell Douglas DC-10-30F is to be the basis of the ATCA (Advanced Tanker/Cargo Aircraft) now being developed to augment and replace the hard-pressed KC-135 force. There may be 20 ATCAs, costing the USAF a total of $800 million.

The tactical airlift capability is centered on the 234 C-130s. In addition, reserve forces have an additional 360 tactical airlift aircraft of varying cargo capacities. An Advanced Medium Short Take Off and Land Transport (the AMST, two versions of which are still being tested at the end of 1977) is proposed to modernize this aging and limited tactical airlift capability.

All of the major mission elements of the Air Force offensive and defensive strategic forces, tactical forces, and airlift forces are dependent on the Air Force's supporting elements. In fact these supporting elements comprise about 45 percent of the US Air Force's active strength. These elements are organized into six major air commands (Air Training Command, Air Force Logistics Command, Air Force Systems Command, Air Force Communication Service, Air Force Security Service, Air University) and 13 separate operating agencies (totalling 35,000 people).

Largest of these commands is the Air Training Command (92,000) which is responsible for personnel recruitment, basic training, flying training, technical training and combat crew training. In-service professional military education is the function of the Air University, which also directs the Air Force ROTC programs in colleges and high schools. The nucleus of the career officer corps, however, comes from the Air Force Academy.

Roughly the same size as the Air Training Command is the Air Force Logistics Command, which is responsible for the procurement, supply, transportation, and maintenance support for both the US Air Force and the air forces of Allied nations. The Logistics Command is unique in that its civilians outnumber its military 9 to 1.

Currently about one fourth of the Air Force's total budget goes to the Air Force Systems Command, which constantly wages the battle for technological superiority for the Air Force of the future. In addition to research and develop-

Above: Boeing's B-52 was designed in 1949-51, and nobody then dreamed it would have to remain as America's manned strategic delivery system until 1988 at the earliest and probably later. This is a SRAM-toting B-52G, No 1957-6518.

Below: The proverb about big fleas having lesser fleas applies to this DC-130H, operating from Hill AFB, in RPV research. Its two XQM-103 RPVs are each carrying a pair of free-fall stores (probably drop tanks).

ment, the Systems Command is also responsible for test, evaluation and production of Air Force missiles, aircraft and related hardware.

Rapid communications has always been an essential element of effective air operations. The need for fast, accurate, secure, survivable communications continue to increase in importance. Meeting these needs is the primary mission of the 50,000 men in Air Force Communication Service, maintaining 500 units at 400 different locations.

Last of the major air commands is the 16,000 man Air Force Security Service, responsible for

Above: The sharp ends of TAC Phantoms, that nearest the camera being F-4D-28 No 65-765A. Today the back-seater (as he is called) is styled WSO (Weapon-System Operator), and he is seldom a rated pilot. But the duplication of controls is fairly complete, and most backseaters could get the aircraft back in one piece if the pilot were incapacitated.

signals intelligence, communications security, and electronic warfare analysis service for all Air Force commands. The Security Service also serves as the Air Force element of the National Security Agency.

The contribution of the various US Air Force supporting elements to the combat capabilities of the tactical air forces is significant but difficult to quantify.

Easily discernible is the 25 percent Soviet numerical superiority over the US in operational tactical aircraft. Equally visible is the Warsaw Pact's 2-to-1 superiority in ground forces and 5-to-1 superiority over the armored forces of NATO.

To cope with the Soviets' quantitative advantages US tactical air forces are relying on a number of qualitative factors:

a continuing, though diminishing lead in technology;

modernization of tactical forces after a long relative lull in production;

superior aircraft such as the F-15 which is expected to outperform any opposition throughout the 1980s;

superior capabilities for surveillance, command, control, and communication;

improved defense suppression techniques, especially in the currently marginal electronics counter measures capability;

balancing of costs, quantity and quality through the concept of the high-low mix;

superior capabilities of American precision guided munitions;

more highly trained and combat-experienced personnel;

superior strategic and tactical air mobility to help compensate for potential Soviet geographical advantages;

superior logistics support of combat forces;

superior tactical nuclear capability;

potential reinforcement of tactical forces, under some scenarios, by the conventional or nuclear capability of strategic forces.

Undoubtably, these factors are impressive to the Soviets. Many analysts believe that they would be sufficient to cope with numerically

superior Soviet tactical air forces in the event of war. Less certain is their ability to compensate for Warsaw Pact superiority on the ground. Hopefully, tactical air forces, under the strategic nuclear umbrella, will not have to prove the point in combat.

Below: Approximating to a MiG-21, these Northrop F-5E Tiger II fighters serve with the DACT (Dissimilar Aircraft Combat Training) squadron at RAF Alconbury, England. They act the part of hostile "Aggressors" for other fighter pilots.

US Combat Aircraft

Bill Gunston, contributor to Jane's *All the World's Aircraft*: author of many technical books and papers on military affairs.

This catalogue does not attempt to include every USAF aircraft, and in addition to obsolescent or minor types omits aircraft not at present funded or whose programme has been terminated (except for the Rockwell B-1 which, despite its termination as a production programme, is still being funded as a research project).

Bell 209 HueyCobra

AH-1G to -1T HueyCobra (data for -1G)

Origin: Bell Helicopter Textron, USA.
Type: Two-seat combat helicopter.
Engine: 1,100shp Lycoming T53-L-13 turboshaft.
Dimensions: Main-rotor diameter 44ft (13·4m); overall length (rotors turning) 52ft 11½in (16·14m); length of fuselage 44ft 5in (13·54m); height 13ft 5½in (4·1m).
Weights: Empty 6,073lb (2754kg); maximum 9,500lb (4309kg).
Performance: Maximum speed 219mph (352km/h); maximum rate of climb (not vertical) 1,230ft (375m)/min; service ceiling 11,400ft (3475m); hovering ceiling in ground effect 9,900ft (3015m); range at sea level with 8% reserve 357 miles (574km).
Armament: Typically one 7·62mm multi-barrel Minigun, one 40mm grenade launcher, both in remote-control turrets, or 20mm six-barrel or 30mm three-barrel cannon, plus four stores pylons for 76 rockets of 2·75in calibre or Minigun pods or 20mm gun pod, or (TOWCobra) eight TOW missiles in tandem tube launchers on two outer pylons, inners being available for other stores.
History: First flight 7 September 1965; combat service June 1967 (TOW-Cobra January 1973).

Development: First flown in 1965 after only six months of development, the HueyCobra is a combat development of the UH-1 Iroquois family. It combines the dynamic parts – engine, transmission and rotor system – of the original Huey with a new streamlined fuselage providing for a gunner in the

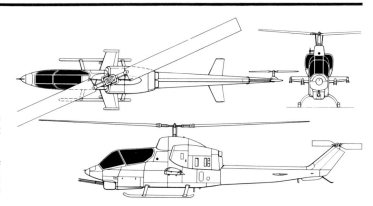

Three-view of Bell AH-1J (other Twin Pac models similar).

front and pilot above and behind him and for a wide range of fixed and power-aimed armament systems. The first version was the US Army AH-1G, with 1,100hp T53 engine, of which 1,124 were delivered, including eight to the Spanish Navy for anti-ship strike and 38 as trainers to the US Marine Corps. The AH-1Q is an anti-armour version often called TOWCobra because it carries eight TOW missile pods as well as the appropriate sighting system. The AH-1J SeaCobra of the Marine Corps and Iranian Army has twin engines, the 1,800hp UAC Twin Pac having two T400 power sections driving one shaft. Latest versions are the -1Q, -1R, -1S and -1T, with more power and new equipment. All Cobras can have a great variety of armament.

Left: The original AH-1G Cobra, which served in Vietnam in very large numbers from September 1967.

Below: In future the chief weapon of most Cobra versions will be the TOW missile. In most configurations two four-round boxes will be carried.

160

Bell "Huey" family

XH-40, UH-1 Iroquois series (Models 204, 205, 212 and 214), CH-118 and -135, and Isfahan

Origin: Bell Helicopter Textron, Fort Worth, USA; built under licence by Agusta, Italy; Fuji, Japan; and AIDC, Taiwan.

Type: Multi-role utility and transport helicopter.

Engine: Originally, one Lycoming T53 free-turbine turboshaft rated at 600–640shp, later rising in stages to 825, 930, 1,100 and 1,400shp; (some Agusta-built AB 204) Rolls-Royce Gnome, 1,250shp; (212) 1,800shp P&WC PT6T-3 (T400) coupled turboshafts, flat-rated at 1,250shp and with 900shp immediately available from either following failure of the other; (214) 2,930shp Lycoming LTC4B (T55) flat-rated at 2,050shp.

Dimensions: Diameter of twin-blade main rotor (204, UH-1B, C) 44ft 0in (13·41m), (205, 212) 48ft 0in (14·63m) (tracking tips, 48ft 2¼in, 14·69m); (214) 50ft 0in (15·24m); overall length (rotors turning) (early) 53ft 0in (16·15m) (virtually all modern versions) 57ft 3¼in (17·46m); height overall (modern, typical) 14ft 4¾in (4·39m).

Weights: Empty (XH-40) about 4,000lb (1814kg), (typical 205) 4,667lb (2116kg), (typical 212) 5,549lb (2517kg), (214/214B) about 6,000lb (2722kg); maximum loaded (XH-40) 5,800lb (2631kg), (typical 205) 9,500lb (4309kg), (212/UH-1N) 10,500lb (4762kg), (214B) 16,000lb (7257kg).

Performance: Maximum speed (all) typically 127mph (204km/h); econ cruise speed, usually same; max range with useful payload, typically 248 miles (400km).

Armament: See text.

History: First flight (XH-40) 22 October 1956, (production UH-1) 1958, (205) August 1961, (212) 1969, (214) 1974.

Development: Used by more air forces, and built in greater numbers, than any other military aircraft since World War II, the "Huey" family of helicopters grew from a single prototype, the XH-40, for the US Army. Over 20 years the gross weight has been almost multiplied by three, though the size has changed only slightly. Early versions seat eight to ten, carried the occasional machine-gun, and included the TH-1L Seawolf trainer for the US Navy and the Italian-developed Agusta-Bell 204AS with radar and ASW sensors and torpedoes. The Model 205 (UH-1D, -1H &c) have more power and carry up to 15 passengers. Dornier built 352 for the W German Army, and similar versions are still in production at Agusta, Fuji and AIDC. Canada sponsored the twin-engined 212 (UH-1N, Canada CH-135),

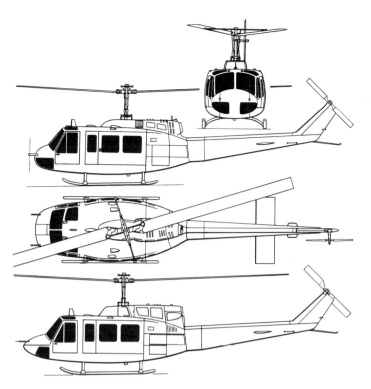

Above: Three-view of the Bell UH-1H Iroquois with additional side view (bottom) of the twin-engined UH-1N.

which again is made in Italy in an ASW version, with a new radar, AQS-13B variable-depth sonar and two torpedoes. Most powerful Huey is the 214 and 214B, first ordered by Iran, in whose service the 214A Isfahan has set several climb and altitude records. The 214 series have a new high-rated transmission system. "Noda-Matic" vibration-damping suspension and broad rotor blades allowing speed to rise to 150mph (241km/h). Many Hueys (called thus from the original "HU" designation, later changed to UH) carry guns, anti-tank missiles and special night-fighting gear, but most are simple casevac and assault transports. Official US military name is Iroquois. The HueyCobra "gunship" models are described on the previous page.

Left: First "stretched" version was the Army UH-1D of 1961.

Below: Several thousand Hueys of various kinds served in Vietnam. This air gunner is providing covering fire with an M60 from an almost new UH-1H troop transport and casevac ambulance. Altitude is about 100 feet.

Bell Kiowa and JetRanger

Variants, see text.

Origin: Bell Helicopter Textron, Fort Worth, USA; licence-built by Agusta, Italy (and some by Commonwealth Aircraft, Australia).
Type: Light multi-role helicopter.
Engine: One 317shp Allison T63-700 or 250-C18 turboshaft; (206B models) 420shp Allison 250-C20B or 400shp C20.
Dimensions: Diameter of two-blade main rotor 35ft 4in (10·77m), (206B) 33ft 4in (10·16m), (206L) 37ft 0in (11·28m); length overall (rotors turning) 40ft 11¾in (12·49m), (206B) 38ft 9½in (11·82m); height 9ft 6½in (2·91m).
Weights: Empty 1,464lb (664kg), (206B slightly less), (206L) 1,962lb (890kg); maximum loaded 3,000lb (1361kg), (206B) 3,200lb (1451kg), (206L) 4,000lb (1814kg).
Performance: Economical cruise (Kiowa S/L) 117mph (188km/h), (206B 5,000ft, 1525m) 138mph (222km/h); max range S/L no reserve with max useful load, 305 miles (490km), (206B and L) 345 miles (555km).
Armament: usually none (see text).
History: First flight (OH-4A) 8 December 1962, (206A) 10 January 1966, (206B) 1970.

Development: First flown as the OH-4A, loser in the US Army Light Observation Helicopter contest of 1962, the 206 was marketed as the civil JetRanger, this family growing to encompass the more powerful 206B and more capacious 206L LongRanger. In 1968 the US Army re-opened the LOH competition, naming Bell now winner and buying 2,200 OH-58A Kiowas similar to the 206A but with larger main rotor. US Navy trainers are TH-57A Sea Rangers, Candian designation is CH-136, and Australian-assembled models for Army use are 206B standard. Agusta builds AB

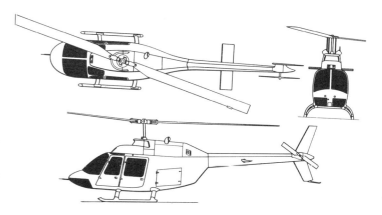

Above: Three-view of basic OH-58A without sensors or weapons.

206B JetRanger IIs, many for military use (Sweden uses the HKP 6 with torpedoes) and the big-rotor AB206A-1 and B-1. Sales of all versions exceed 5,500, most being five-seaters (206L, seven) and US Army Kiowas having the XM27 kit with Minigun and various other weapons (probably to be modified to OH-58C standard).

Right: One of the US Army's 2,200 OH-58A and improved OH-58C Kiowas, fitted with the XM27 armament option with two rapid-fire 7·62mm Miniguns on side sponsons, fed from internal ammunition boxes. The OH-58C is a rebuild with 420hp engine, IR suppressor over jetpipes and flat glass to reduce glint.

Boeing B-52 Stratofortress

B-52 to B-52H

Origin: The Boeing Company, USA.
Type: Strategic bomber and ECM platform with crew of six.
Engines: (B-52F, G) eight 13,750lb (6238kg) thrust (water-injection rating) Pratt & Whitney J57-43W two-shaft turbojets; (B-52H) eight 17,000lb (7711kg) thrust Pratt & Whitney TF33-3 two-shaft turbofans.
Dimensions: Span 185ft (56·4m); length 157ft 7in (48m); height 48ft 3in (14·75m); (B-52G, H) 40ft 8in (12·4m).
Weights: Empty 171,000–193,000lb (77,200–87,100kg); loaded 450,000lb (204,120kg) (B-52G, 488,000lb, 221,500kg; B-52H, 505,000lb, 229,000kg).
Performance: Maximum speed about 630mph (1014km/h) at over 24,000ft (7315m); service ceiling 45,000–55,000ft (13,720–16,765m); range on internal fuel with maximum weapon load (C, D, E, F) 6,200 miles (9978km); (G) 8,500 miles (13,680km); (H) 12,500 miles (20,150km).

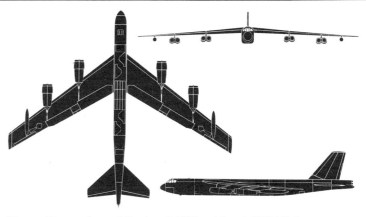

Above: Three-view of Boeing B-52H, without EVS blisters.

Armament: Remotely directed tail mounting for four 0·50in (B-52H, 20mm six-barrel ASG-21 cannon). Normal internal bomb capacity 27,000lb (12,247kg) including all SAC special weapons; (B-52D) internal and external provision for up to 70,000lb (31,750kg) conventional bombs; (B-52G and H) external pylons for two AGM-28B Hound Dog missiles or 12 AGM-69A SRAM missiles, with optional rotary dispenser for eight SRAM internally.
History: First flight (YB-52) 15 April 1952; (B-52A) 5 August 1954; combat service with 93rd BW, 29 June 1955; final delivery (H) June 1962.

Development: Still the heaviest and most powerful bomber ever to be built, the mighty B-52 was planned in 1946 as a straight-winged turboprop. At that time no jet engine existed capable of propelling an intercontinental bomber, because fuel consumption was too high. It was Pratt & Whitney's development of a more efficient turbojet, the two-shaft J57, that tipped the scales and led to the new bomber being urgently redesigned in October 1948 as a swept-wing jet. In some ways it resembled a scaled-up B-47, but in fact the wing was made quite different in section and in construction and it housed most of the fuel, which in the B-47 had been in the fuselage. Although the J57, with an expected rating of 10,000lb (4536kg), was the most powerful engine available, an unprecedented four double pods were needed. The two prototypes had pilots in tandem, as in the B-47, but the production B-52A had side-by-side pilots with an airline-type flight deck. The crew of six included a rear gunner in the extreme tail to look after his four radar-directed 0·5in guns. The B-52B had provision for 833 Imp gal (3800 litre) underwing tanks and could carry a two-crew camera or countermeasures capsule in the bomb bay. As the first true service version it encountered many problems, especially with the accessory power systems driven by high-speed air turbines using hot air bled from the engines. The four two-wheel landing gear trucks swivelled for cross-wind landings, the lofty fin could fold to enter hangars, and normal bomb load was 10,000lb (4536kg) carried for 8,000 miles (12,875km). The B-52C had much more fuel, the D was similar but used for bombing only (not reconnaissance) and the E and F introduced completely new nav/bombing systems. The G had an integral tank "wet wing" housing far more fuel, more powerful engines driving the accessories directly, as on the F, and many other changes including shorter fin, Quail countermeasures vehicles and a pair of Hound Dog stand-off missiles. Final model was the B-52H, the 102 of which brought

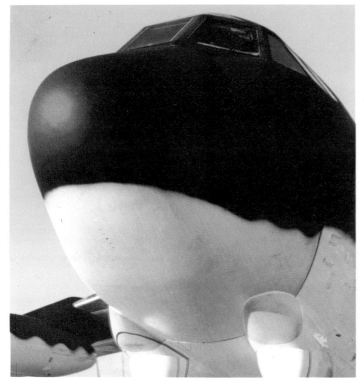

Above: Virtually all remaining B-52G and H bombers now have the ASQ-151 EVS (electro-optical viewing system). Under the nose are this system's twin steerable chin turrets, as described in the text. They serve added bright displays in front of the aircraft commander and co-pilot. At the other end of the aircraft ALQ-154(V) tail-warning radar may be added.

Above: In the war in South-East Asia the B-52D and B-52F were rebuilt to carry very heavy loads of conventional high-explosive bombs and painted black underneath. Called Buffs, from Big Ugly Fat Fella, by the natives of Guam where this picture was taken, they were naturally loathed by the Viet-Cong.

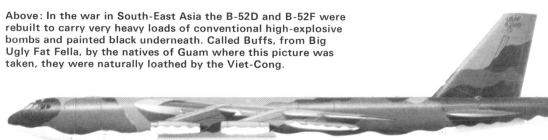

Left: A B-52G in the current SAC paint scheme and with EVS installation. Primary armament of the G and H today is the SRAM, with ALCM in view.

the total to 744. Powered by TF33 fan engines the H got rid of engine water injection, greatly extended range and performance, had a new tail stinger (a 20mm "Gatling" with operator up front as in the G) and many other improvements. In Vietnam D to F models carried up to 70,000lb (31,750kg) of "iron bombs", most of which were rained down without precision aiming (because targets were seldom seen), while the G and H remained in SAC service as multi-role low-level strategic systems pending the introduction of the Rockwell B-1.

Since 1961 new equipment installations and structural reinforcement and reconstruction of the airframes have cost several times the original price. In 1977 the main striking force of SAC comprised 13 Wings equipped with about 165 G and 90 H models. These have been completely rebuilt and later refurbished with SRAM capability, ALE-25 diversionary rocket pods under the wings, and the ASQ-151 electro-optical viewing system (which includes two steerable chin turrets under the nose, the left housing a Westinghouse low-light TV and the right a Hughes forward-looking infra-red). Another new device is the GBU-15 glide bomb, of the Pave Strike family, first tested from a B-52 in July 1976. Later, in 1979, the Boeing AGM-86A ALCM (air-launched cruise missile) may be available; a B-52G or H carry 12 externally and eight on the internal SRAM dispenser. The remaining long-range SAC force comprises 80 structurally rebuilt Ds devoid of the ASQ-151 and equipped only for free-fall bombs, but with updated defensive avionics. A Strategic Air Command training wing, detached to Okinawa, is equipped with 22 Fs.

Boeing C-135 family and military 707

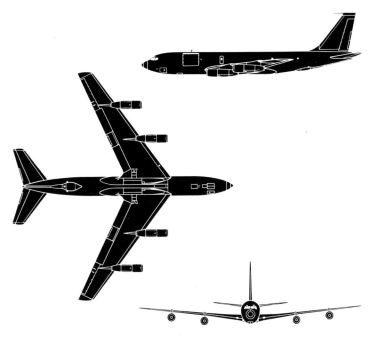

C-135 Stratolifter family, KC-135 Stratotanker family (data KC-135A)

Origin: The Boeing Company, USA.
Type: Originally, tanker/transport; now many other roles.
Engines: Four 13,750lb (6238kg) thrust (water injection rating) Pratt & Whitney J57-59W two-shaft turbojets.
Dimensions: Span 130ft 10in (39·7m); length 136ft 3in (41·0m); height 38ft 4in (11·6m).
Weights: Empty 109,000lb (49,442kg); loaded 297,000lb (134,715kg).
Performance: Maximum speed 600mph (966km/h); cruising speed 552mph (890km/h); service ceiling 40,000ft (12,192m); typical range 4,000 miles (6437km).
Armament: None.
History: First flight (civil 367–80) 15 July 1954; (KC-135) 31 August 1956; final delivery (RC-135S) mid-1966.

Development: Boeing jet transports all stemmed from a company-funded prototype, the 367-80, flown in July 1954. After evaluation of this aircraft the US Air Force decided in October 1954 to buy 29 developed versions to serve in the dual roles of tanker for Strategic Air Command and logistic transport for MATS (later Military Airlift Command). In fact, though all KC-135 Stratotankers can serve as transports, they have seldom had to

Above: Three-view of Boeing KC-135B with TF33-9 turbofans.

Boeing E-4A and 747

E-4 (AABNCP)

Origin: The Boeing Company, USA.
Type: Airborne command post, with crew/staff of 28–60.
Engines: (E-4A) four 45,500lb (20,639kg) thrust Pratt & Whitney F105-100 (JT9D) turbofans; (E-4B) four 52,500lb (23,815kg) thrust General Electric F103-100 turbofans.
Dimensions: Span 195ft 8in (59·64m); length 231ft 4in (70·5m); height 63ft 5in (19·33m).
Weights: Empty, probably 380,000lb (172,370kg); loaded 803,000lb (364,230kg).
Performance: Maximum speed 608mph (978km/h) at 30,000ft (9144m); maximum Mach number 0·92; normal operational ceiling 45,000ft (13,715m); normal unrefuelled range about 6,500 miles (10,460km).
Armament: None.
History: First flight (747) 9 February 1969; (E-4) January 1973.

Development: Since the late 1950s the United States has created a growing fleet of various kinds of EC-135 aircraft as airborne command posts.

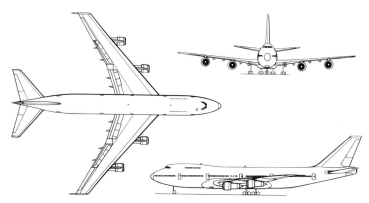

Above: Three-view of original Boeing E-4A as first delivered.

Operated by the National Military Command System and SAC, these are the platforms carrying the national strategic and economic command and decision-taking machinery, with perfect unjammable communications to all

Boeing-Vertol CH-47 Chinook

CH-47A, B and C Chinook (data for C)

Origin: Boeing Vertol Company, USA; built under licence by Elicotteri Meridionali and SIAI-Marchetti, Italy.
Type: Medium transport helicopter with normal crew of two/three.
Engines: Two 3,750shp Lycoming T55-L-11A free-turbine turboshafts.
Dimensions: Diameter of main rotors 60ft (18·29m); length, rotors turning, 99ft (30·2m); length of fuselage 51ft (15·54m); height 18ft 7in (5·67m).
Weights: Empty 20,616lb (9351kg); loaded (condition 1) 33,000lb (14,969kg); (overload condition II) 46,000lb (20,865kg).
Performance: Maximum speed (condition I) 189mph (304km/h); (II) 142mph (229km/h); initial climb (I) 2,880ft (878m)/min; (II) 1,320ft (402m)/min; service ceiling (I) 15,000ft (4570m); (II) 8,000ft (2440m); mission radius, cruising speed and payload (I) 115 miles (185km) at 158mph (254km/h) with 7,262lb (3294kg); (II) 23 miles (37km) at 131mph (211km/h) with 23,212lb (10,528kg).
Armament: Normally, none.
History: First flight (YCH-47A) 21 September 1961; (CH-47C) 14 October 1967.

Development: Development of the Vertol 114 began in 1956 to meet the need of the US Army for a turbine-engined all-weather cargo helicopter able to operate effectively in the most adverse conditions of altitude and temperature. Retaining the tandem-rotor configuration, the first YCH-47A flew on the power of two 2,200shp Lycoming T55 turboshaft engines and led directly to the production CH-47A. With an unobstructed cabin 7½ft (2·29m) wide, 6½ft (1·98m) high and over 30ft (9·2m) long, the Chinook proved a valuable vehicle, soon standardised as US Army medium helicopter and deployed all over the world. By 1972 more then 550 had served in Vietnam, mainly in the battlefield airlift of troops and weapons but also rescuing civilians (on one occasion 147 refugees and their belongings were

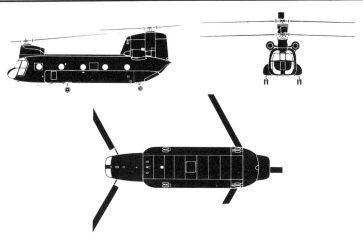

Above: Three-view of Boeing-Vertol CH-47C (blades cropped).

carried to safety in one Chinook) and lifting back for salvage or repair 11,500 disabled aircraft valued at more than $3,000 million. The A model gave way to the CH-47B, with 2,850hp engines and numerous improvements and, finally, to the much more powerful CH-47C. Over 800 Chinooks were built, all at Boeing Vertol at Philadelphia (successor to Piasecki). Small numbers of C models continue in production in Italy.

Right: These two Boeing-Vertol Chinooks were advanced CH-47C versions fitted with special night observation systems for research into use of attack transport helicopters for assault by night. A current Chinook customer of the USA is Britain, which ordered three times over ten years and cancelled twice.

do so, because production of C-135 Stratolifters has been considerable. The Boeing 717 tanker introduced a new high-speed Boeing Flying Boom refuelling system, mounted under the rear fuselage. This is aimed by aerodynamic controls at the receptacle on the receiver aircraft; then the boom operator "fires" the telescopic boom to make a fuel-tight joint. Total fuel capacity on the KC-135A is about 26,000 Imp gal (118,000 litres), leaving the upper fuselage free for cargo. Between June 1957 and January 1965 no fewer than 732 were delivered to SAC. Another 88 Model 739 aircraft have been supplied as various models of C-135, most having 18,000lb (8165kg) thrust TF33 fan engines. At least 28 species of modifications are in USAF service, including VC-135 VIP aircraft, command posts, and more than 21 types of 135 used for electronic intelligence, countermeasures and special research. Twelve KC-135F tankers were supplied to refuel the nuclear Mirage IVA *force de frappe* of the Armée de l'Air, these having booms modified for probe/drogue refuelling. Though not armed with guns or bombs, the huge and varied fleets of 135s are very much "combat" aircraft in the context of an electronically based form of warfare and will continue to pry, probe and spoof — and feed fuel to thirsty fighters "below bingo" — for many years.

In comparison with C-135 models the 707-320 has a considerably longer and fatter fuselage, bigger wing, greater fuel capacity and much greater weight. All 707-320 versions in military service have the TF33 turbofan engine. The USAF flies various VC-137s, including the two VC-137Cs flown by the 89th Military Airlift Wing and bearing the legend "United States of America" as the personal long-range transports of the President. The Canadian Armed Forces CC-137 fleet includes two aircraft with Beech flight-refuelling hosereel pods on the wingtips, while the Imperial Iranian AF fleet of 12 707-3J9Cs have optional pods on the wingtips and a Flying Boom installation on the rear fuselage.

Above: All current combat aircraft of Tactical Air Command, like those of Strategic Air Command, have receptacles for the KC-135 refuelling boom. These are F-4Es in Vietnam.

government and military organizations and the capacity to survive even a nuclear war. Since 1965 the EC-135 has become restrictive, and to meet future needs and provide for a larger staff in greater comfort, with the capability of more flexible action and response, the 747B airframe was adopted to carry the Advanced Airborne National Command Post (AABNCP). The first two were fitted with Pratt & Whitney JT9D engines, but the standard was later adopted as that of the fourth aircraft, bought for $39 million in December 1973 with GE engines and later equipment. Much of the special equipment has been taken from the EC-135A, H, J, K, L and P force. There are three decks, the main deck being a mixture of executive offices and luxurious living quarters and the rest being packed with advanced electronics. The first three (E-4A) aircraft are based at Andrews AFB near Washington; eventually, without cost to the Air Force, they will be retrofitted with F103 engines and they will also be provided with E-4B equipment. It is planned to base the E-4B and two further E-4B aircraft at Offutt AFB, headquarters of SAC in Nebraska. Since 1976 the E-4 has been carefully studied as a possible carrier of the SRAM and ALCM missiles; up to 96 of either could be launched.

Left: This E-4A is depicted as it was originally delivered, with Pratt & Whitney F105 engines. Subsequently, like other A-models, it was re-engined by General Electric with the F103. Pratt & Whitney now has engines as powerful as any F103.

Boeing E-3A Sentry (AWACS)

E-3A Sentry (AWACS)

Origin: The Boeing Company, USA.
Type: Airborne warning and control system platform, with crew of 17.
Engines: Four 21,000lb (9525kg) thrust Pratt & Whitney TF33-100A turbofans.
Dimensions: Span 145ft 9in (44·42m); length 152ft 11in (46·61m); height 42ft 5in (12·93m).
Weights: Empty 172,000lb (78,020kg); maximum, 325,000lb (147,420kg).
Performance: Maximum speed, about 600mph (966km/h) at high altitude (about 300mph, 483km/h at low levels); normal operating height, over 40,000ft (12,190m); endurance, at least 12hr on station without refuelling.
Armament: None.
History: First flight (EC-137D test aircraft) 9 February 1972; (E-3A) 31 October 1975.

Development: Developments in radars and airborne data processing led first to the basic early-warning aircraft, exemplified by the Douglas EA-1 series and Grumman E-1B, and then, around 1965, to the concept of the Airborne Warning And Control System (AWACS). This is a flying surveillance and management station from which the entire air situation of a small nation, or part of a large one, can be controlled. Carrying an extremely powerful surveillance radar, a mass of sensing and data-processing systems and advanced displays both for the crew and for transmission to the ground, an AWACS can maintain perfect watch on every kind of aerial vehicle, hostile and friendly, over a radius exceeding 200 miles (322km). This facilitates the most efficient handling of every situation, right down to air traffic control at a beach-head or the best route for helicopters to rescue a friendly pilot. The first AWACS is the Boeing E-3A. Derived from the 707-320B airliner, it was to have had eight TF34 engines but owing to their fantastic overall cost these aircraft now retain the TF33 and have emerged somewhat less complex than once planned. Trials with rival Hughes and Westinghouse radars were held with EC-137D test aircraft; the Westinghouse was chosen, with aerial rotating at six times a minute in a 30ft (9·14m) dome high above the rear fuselage. Except for the E-4A the E-3A is almost certainly the most expensive aircraft ever to enter military service. Initial operational service in 1977-78 is to be followed by a total of 34 planned aircraft for efficient protection of US airspace. The tenth E-3A was scheduled for delivery in July 1978. By the time this book appears the European NATO nations may also have decided to buy the E-3A. In late 1976 discussion had centred around 27 European-based aircraft costing $2,273 million.

The cutaway drawing shows how completely the 707-320C airframe of the E-3A is merely the platform for lifting the electronics to its surveillance vantage point. Until the 1960s the technology of "overland downlook radar" was not fully developed, and the small echoes from distant targets were blotted out by the giant reflections from the ground. Today the Westinghouse APY-1 radar of E-3A is proven, with high-PRF pulse-doppler signals processed by high-speed computer, with the aerial rotating every 10 seconds in a 30ft "rotodome"

Below: E-3As are painted grey; emitting parts of the rotodome are black.

U.S. AIR FORCE

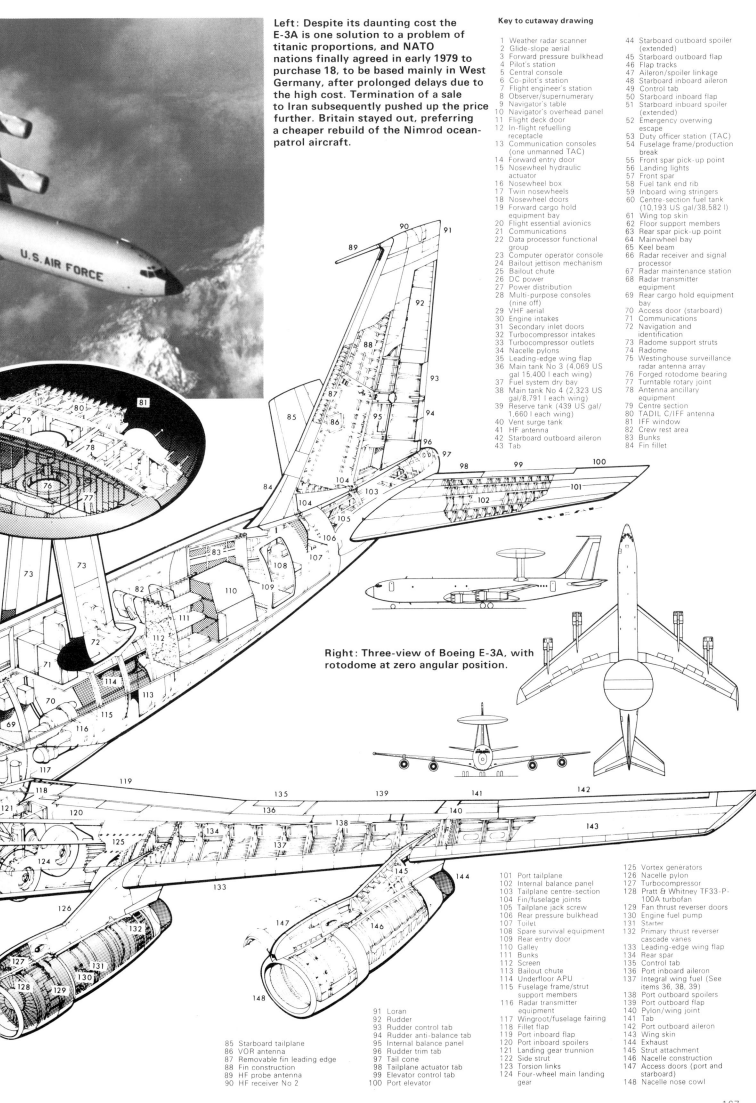

Left: Despite its daunting cost the E-3A is one solution to a problem of titanic proportions, and NATO nations finally agreed in early 1979 to purchase 18, to be based mainly in West Germany, after prolonged delays due to the high cost. Termination of a sale to Iran subsequently pushed up the price further. Britain stayed out, preferring a cheaper rebuild of the Nimrod ocean-patrol aircraft.

Right: Three-view of Boeing E-3A, with rotodome at zero angular position.

Key to cutaway drawing

1 Weather radar scanner
2 Glide-slope aerial
3 Forward pressure bulkhead
4 Pilot's station
5 Central console
6 Co-pilot's station
7 Flight engineer's station
8 Observer/supernumerary
9 Navigator's table
10 Navigator's overhead panel
11 Flight deck door
12 In-flight refuelling receptacle
13 Communication consoles (one unmanned TAC)
14 Forward entry door
15 Nosewheel hydraulic actuator
16 Nosewheel box
17 Twin nosewheels
18 Nosewheel doors
19 Forward cargo hold equipment bay
20 Flight essential avionics
21 Communications
22 Data processor functional group
23 Computer operator console
24 Bailout jettison mechanism
25 Bailout chute
26 DC power
27 Power distribution
28 Multi-purpose consoles (nine off)
29 VHF aerial
30 Engine intakes
31 Secondary inlet doors
32 Turbocompressor intakes
33 Turbocompressor outlets
34 Nacelle pylons
35 Leading-edge wing flap
36 Main tank No 3 (4,069 US gal 15,400 l each wing)
37 Fuel system dry bay
38 Main tank No 4 (2,323 US gal/8,791 l each wing)
39 Reserve tank (439 US gal/ 1,660 l each wing)
40 Vent surge tank
41 HF antenna
42 Starboard outboard aileron
43 Tab

44 Starboard outboard spoiler (extended)
45 Starboard outboard flap
46 Flap tracks
47 Aileron/spoiler linkage
48 Starboard inboard aileron
49 Control tab
50 Starboard inboard flap
51 Starboard inboard spoiler (extended)
52 Emergency overwing escape
53 Duty officer station (TAC)
54 Fuselage frame/production break
55 Front spar pick-up point
56 Landing lights
57 Front spar
58 Fuel tank end rib
59 Inboard wing stringers
60 Centre-section fuel tank (10,193 US gal/38,582 l)
61 Wing top skin
62 Floor support members
63 Rear spar pick-up point
64 Mainwheel bay
65 Keel beam
66 Radar receiver and signal processor
67 Radar maintenance station
68 Radar transmitter equipment
69 Rear cargo hold equipment bay
70 Access door (starboard)
71 Communications
72 Navigation and identification
73 Radome support struts
74 Radome
75 Westinghouse surveillance radar antenna array
76 Forged rotodome bearing
77 Turntable rotary joint
78 Antenna ancillary equipment
79 Centre section
80 TADIL C/IFF antenna
81 IFF window
82 Crew rest area
83 Bunks
84 Fin fillet

85 Starboard tailplane
86 VOR antenna
87 Removable fin leading edge
88 Fin construction
89 HF probe antenna
90 HF receiver No 2

91 Loran
92 Rudder
93 Rudder control tab
94 Rudder anti-balance tab
95 Internal balance panel
96 Rudder trim tab
97 Tail cone
98 Tailplane actuator tab
99 Elevator control tab
100 Port elevator

101 Port tailplane
102 Internal balance panel
103 Tailplane centre-section
104 Fin/fuselage joints
105 Tailplane jack screw
106 Rear pressure bulkhead
107 Toilet
108 Spare survival equipment
109 Rear entry door
110 Galley
111 Bunks
112 Screen
113 Bailout chute
114 Underfloor APU
115 Fuselage frame/strut support members
116 Radar transmitter equipment
117 Wingroot/fuselage fairing
118 Fillet flap
119 Port inboard flap
120 Port inboard spoilers
121 Landing gear trunnion
122 Side strut
123 Torsion links
124 Four-wheel main landing gear

125 Vortex generators
126 Nacelle pylon
127 Turbocompressor
128 Pratt & Whitney TF33-P-100A turbofan
129 Fan thrust reverser doors
130 Engine fuel pump
131 Starter
132 Primary thrust reverser cascade vanes
133 Leading-edge wing flap
134 Rear spar
135 Control tab
136 Port inboard aileron
137 Integral wing fuel (See items 36, 38, 39)
138 Port outboard spoilers
139 Port outboard flap
140 Pylon/wing joint
141 Tab
142 Port outboard aileron
143 Wing skin
144 Exhaust
145 Strut attachment
146 Nacelle construction
147 Access doors (port and starboard)
148 Nacelle nose cowl

Boeing-Vertol H-46 family

CH-46 Sea Knight, UH-46, CH-113, KV-107

Origin: Boeing Vertol, Philadelphia, USA; licence-built by Kawasaki, Japan.
Type: Transport, search/rescue, minesweeping.
Engines: Two 1,250–1,870shp General Electric T58 or Rolls-Royce Gnome turboshafts.
Dimensions: Diameter of each three-blade main rotor 50ft 0in (15·24m); fuselage length 44ft 10in (13·66m); height 16ft 8½in (5·09m).
Weights: Empty (KV-107/II-2) 10,732lb (4868kg), (CH-46E) 11,585lb (5240kg); maximum loaded (KV) 19,000lb (8618kg), (E) 21,400lb (9706kg).
Performance: Typical cruise 120mph (193km/h); range with 30min reserve (6,600lb, 3000kg payload) 109 miles (175km), (2,400lb, 1088kg payload) 633 miles (1020km).
History: First flight (107) April 1958, (prototype CH-46A) 27 August 1959.

Development: The CH-46A Sea Knight was an assault transport carrying up to 25 equipped troops or 4,000lb (1814kg) cargo. Over 600 of these were followed by more powerful CH-46D and F versions, the Navy UH-46A for ship replenishment and the CH-46E and UH-46D with 1,870hp T58-10 engines. Canada uses CH-113 Labradors and 113A Voyageurs, Sweden uses the HKP-7 with Gnome engines, and in Japan Kawasaki has built nearly 100 of various KV-107 versions.

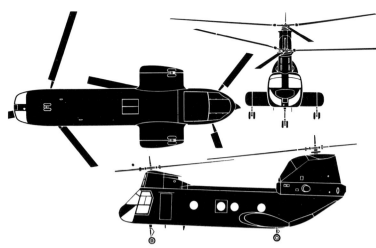

Above: Three-view of CH-46D (other versions generally similar).

Below left: CH-46F Sea Knight of the Marine Corps engaged in a para-dropping exercise. It can carry 25 troops.

Below: Another Marine Corps CH-46 at Landing Zone Falcon, near Camp LeJeune, N Carolina, during exercises in 1973. It was conveying Marines of the 2nd Marine Division, 8th Regiment.

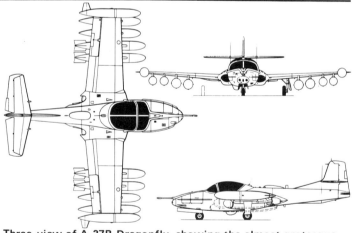

Cessna A-37 Dragonfly

A-37, -37A and -37B (Model 318E)
(data for -37B)

Origin: Cessna Aircraft Co, USA.
Type: Two-seat light strike aircraft.
Engines: Two 2,850lb (1293kg) thrust General Electric J85-17A single-shaft turbojets.
Dimensions: Span (over tip tanks) 35ft 10½in (10·93m); length (not including refuelling probe) 29ft 3in (8·92m); height 8ft 10½in (2·7m).
Weights: Empty 6,211lb (2817kg); loaded 14,000lb (6350kg).
Performance: Maximum speed 507mph (816km/h) at 16,000ft (4875m); initial climb at gross weight 6,990ft (2130m)/min; service ceiling 41,765ft (12,730m); range (maximum weapons) 460 miles (740km), (maximum fuel) 1,012 miles (1628km).
Armament: One 7·62mm GAU-2B/A six-barrel Minigun in nose; eight wing pylon stations, two inners for up to 870lb (394kg), intermediate for 600lb (272kg) and outers for 500lb (227kg); maximum ordnance load 5,680lb (2576kg).
History: First flight (XT-37) 12 October 1954; (YAT-37D) 22 October 1963; (A-37B) September 1967.

Development: The Cessna Model 318 was the first American jet trainer. It entered production for the US Air Force as the T-37A, powered by two 920lb (417kg) thrust Continental J69 (licence-built Turboméca Marboré) engines and with side-by-side ejection seats. All A models were subsequently converted to the standard of the main production type, the T-37B, with J69-25 engines of 1,025lb (465kg) thrust. Export versions were designated T-37C, with provision for underwing armament. Production of the T-37 was completed in 1975 with more than 1,300 delivered to the USAF and 14 other air forces. It was logical to fit the much more powerful J85 engine and restress the airframe to carry greater loads in arduous combat duties. The work began in 1960 at the time of the upsurge of interest in Co-In (counter-insurgency) aircraft to fight "brushfire wars". Deliveries of A-37A aircraft converted from T-37 trainers began in May 1967 and a squadron of 25 had flown 10,000 combat missions in Vietnam in an extensive evaluation by early 1968. The slightly more powerful A-37B is the definitive production version and by 1977 deliveries had exceeded 600.

Three-view of A-37B Dragonfly, showing the almost grotesque array of possible stores.

The A-37B is not pressurised, nor does it have ejection seats, but the dual pilots are protected by layered nylon flak curtains. The wealth of nav/com avionics and possible underwing stores is impressive and nearly all B models have a fixed nose refuelling probe.

Below: Camouflaged A-37s of various sub-types have been widely used as hacks, trials platforms and in research programmes. This example was engaged in limited-warfare mission research.

General Dynamics
F-106 Delta Dart

F-106A and F-106B

Origin: General Dynamics/Convair, USA.

Type: (F-106A) single-seat all-weather interceptor; (F-106B) operational trainer.

Engine: One 24,500lb (11,130kg) thrust Pratt & Whitney J75-17 two-shaft afterburning turbojet.

Dimensions: Span 38ft 3½in (11·67m); length (both) 70ft 8¾in (21·55m); height 20ft 3¼in (6·15m).

Weights: (A) empty 23,646lb (10,725kg); maximum loaded 38,250lb (17,350kg).

Performance: (Both) maximum speed 1,525mph (2455km/h, Mach 2·31); initial climb about 30,000ft (9144m)/min; service ceiling 57,000ft (17,375m); range with drop tanks (A) 1,700 miles (2735km); combat radius, about 600 miles (966km).

Armament: One internal 20mm M-61 multi-barrel cannon; internal weapon bay for air-to-air guided missiles, with typical load comprising one AIR-2A and one AIR-2G Genie rockets and two each of AIM-4E, -4F or 4G Falcons.

History: First flight (aerodynamic prototype) 26 December 1956; (F-106B) 9 April 1958, production delivery July 1959 to July 1960.

Development: Originally designated F-102B, the 106 was a natural development of the F-102A with new engine and avionics. By redesigning from scratch to the supersonic Area Rule the fuselage was made much neater and more efficient than that of the earlier aircraft and the more powerful engine resulted in a peak speed approximately twice as fast. The Hughes MA-1 fire control, though no bulkier or heavier than that of the 102, was far more capable and integrated with the SAGE (Semi-Automatic Ground Environment) defence system covering the continental United States in an automatic manner, the pilot acting as a supervisory manager. Though

bought in modest numbers, the 106 has had an exceptionally long life-span in the USAF Aerospace Defense Command front-line inventory. At several times the Improved Manned Interceptor program (IMI) has pointed the need for a replacement with longer-range look-down radar and long-range missiles, and much research has been done with the Lockheed YF-12 (described later). At present no replacement, other than the multi-role F-15, is in sight and the F-106 and tandem-seat F-106B force (respectively numbering originally 277 and 63) will continue until at least 1980. They have been repeatedly updated, with improved avionics, infra-red sensors, drop tanks, flight refuelling and a Gatling gun.

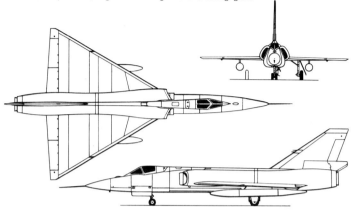

Above: Three-view of F-106A with drop tanks.

Left: An F-106A single-seater shown in the markings of an Aerospace Defense Command Squadron (which no longer uses Delta Darts).

Fairchild Republic A-10A Thunderbolt II

A-10A Thunderbolt II

Origin: Fairchild Republic Co, USA.

Type: Single-seat close-air-support aircraft.

Engines: Two 9,275lb (4207kg) thrust General Electric TF34-100 two-shaft turbofans.

Dimensions: Span 57ft 6in (17·53m); length 53ft 4in (16·26m); height 14ft 5½in (4·4m).

Weights: Empty 21,813lb (9894kg); maximum loaded 47,200lb (21,410 kg).

Performance: Maximum speed (clean) 460mph (740km/h), 380mph (612km/h) at maximum weight; initial climb 1,000ft (328m)/min at maximum weight; take-off distance (at maximum weight) 3,850ft (1173m), (at forward-airstrip weight with six Mk 82 bombs), 1,130ft (344m); steady speed in 45° dive with full airbrake 299mph (481km/h); close-air-support radius with reserves 288 miles (463km); ferry range 2,723 miles (4382km).

Armament: 30mm high-velocity GAU-8/A cannon in forward fuselage; 11 pylons for total external ordnance load of 16,000lb (7257kg) (exceptionally, 18,500lb, 8392kg).

History: First flight 10 May 1972; service delivery for inventory December 1974.

continued on page 170 ▶

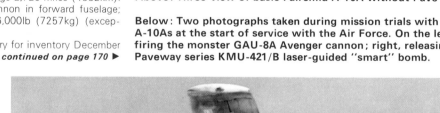

Above: Three-view of basic Fairchild A-10A without Pave Penny.

Below: Two photographs taken during mission trials with A-10As at the start of service with the Air Force. On the left, firing the monster GAU-8A Avenger cannon; right, releasing a Paveway series KMU-421/B laser-guided "smart" bomb.

▶Development: Despite the more overt attractions of Mach 2 aircraft the US Air Force was forced to consider the CAS (close air support) mission because of the total unsuitability of its existing equipment. In both the wars it had had to fight since World War II – Korea and Vietnam – its aircraft had been worldbeaters but planned for a totally different kind of war. What was needed, it appeared, was something like an up-to-date Skyraider that could carry a heavy load of ordnance, had good endurance and could survive severe damage from ground fire. Between 1963-69 extensive studies gradually refined the AX specification, which had begun by pre-supposing a twin turbo prop and ended with a larger aircraft powered by two turbofans. After an industrywide competition the Northrop A-9A and Fairchild A-10A were chosen for prototype fly-off evaluation, which took place with two of each type at Edwards in October-December 1972. The A-10A was announced winner and GE the winner of the contest to produce the 30mm tank-busting gun, the most powerful ever fitted to any aircraft, with very high muzzle velocity and rate of fire, and muzzle horsepower 20 times that of the 75mm gun fitted to some B-25s in World War II. Named Avenger, this gun is driven hydraulically at either 2,100 or 4,200rds/min, and is fed by a drum containing 1,350 milk-bottle-size rounds. Empty cases are fed back into the rear of the drum. By 1978 ground-reloading will probably be done by a special powered system. Underwing load can be made up of any stores in the Tactical Air Command inventory, the landing gears (which protrude when retracted for damage-free emergency landing) and all tail surfaces are interchangeable, the cockpit is encased in a "bath" of thick titanium armour, and the engines are hung above the rear fuselage where their infra-red signature is a minimum. Originally Tactical Air Command intended to buy 600 of these grey-painted brutes, but despite unavoidable escalation in cost and degradation in performance the planned number has grown to 735, to be operational by 1982. By mid-1976 orders had been placed for 95, all of which had flown or were on the line, and the 1977 budget included a further 100. In the course of 1979 the 81st Tac Ftr Wing is to re-equip with the A-10A at Bentwaters and Woodbridge, England. In May 1978, following TAC's acceptance of its 100th A-10, the aircraft was officially named Thunderbolt II, after the World War II P-47 Thunderbolt.

Above: USAF technicians and civilian engineers open boxes of GAU-8/A ammunition to reload the monster drum magazine of an A-10A.

Right: Airbrakes open, an A-10A lets go a Maverick AGM-65A, the most numerous air-to-ground missile in TAC's inventory. With the Pave Penny pod the laser-guided Maverick can be used.

Below: Cutaway of an A-10A, showing the size of the tank-killing gun and its vast ammunition drum containing up to 1,350 rounds each as big as a milk bottle. A Pave Penny laser pod is shown under the forward fuselage, but no ECM is depicted. Planned as a simple, "austere" aircraft, the A-10 has to get complex to survive.

Key to cutaway drawing

1 Flight refuelling probe (removable)
2 Universal aerial refuelling receptacle slipway (UARRSI) for drogue or boom
3 Nosewheel (retracted) position
4 Forward electrical compartment
5 Battery
6 Gun muzzle
7 Nosewheel door
8 Nosewheel leg (offset to starboard)
9 Twin landing/taxiing lamps
10 Forward retracting nosewheel
11 Nosewheel linkage
12 General Electric GAU-8A 30mm Gatling-type gun
13 Forward gun support pallet
14 Gun recoil pack
15 Linkless feed chutes
16 Hydraulic pump
17 Pave Penny laser target-seeker pod (offset to starboard)
18 Integral titanium armour (lower cockpit area and vital controls)
19 Rubber pedals
20 Control column
21 Head-up display
22 Bullet-resistant glass windscreen
23 Upward-hinged canopy
24 Headrest
25 Pilot's zero-zero ejection seat
26 Electrical and avionics equipment bays
27 Forward fuselage structure
28 Ammunition drum (1,350 rounds)
29 Ammunition chute interchange
30 Heavy skin panelling area (HE shell triggering)
31 LB warning aerial
32 Fuselage fuel cells forward wall (fire retardant foam filling)
33 Fuselage forward fuel cell
34 Fuselage 'notch' (wing centre-section carry-through)
35 Centre bulkhead
36 Fuselage aft fuel cell
37 Control runs/plumbing/wiring service trough
38 Port wing fuel cell (wing break to fuselage centreline)
39 Front spar
40 Leading edge structure
41 Fuselage port bomb pylon
42 Triple bomb-rack shoe
43 Fuselage starboard triple bomb cluster
44 Fuselage port triple bomb cluster
45 Wing centre-section bomb pylon

46 Mk 82 bomb (nominal 500 lb/227 kg)
47 Mainwheel gear door
48 Landing gear fairing
49 Wing strengthening
50 Wing centre/outer section break
51 Main landing gear (port and starboard identical)
52 Wing outer-section bomb pylons
53 Single Mk 82 bombs
54 Port mainwheel
55 Outboard pylon (extended forward)
56 Front spar (outer section)
57 Centre spar
58 Rear spar
59 Wing structure
60 Drooped wingtip
61 Port navigation light
62 Port aileron
63 Flaps
64 Port engine nacelle
65 X-band beacon
66 Hydraulic reservoirs (2)
67 Auxiliary power unit
68 Environmental control system
69 Aerials
70 APU exhaust
71 VHF Tacan
72 Port nacelle forward attachment
73 Port nacelle aft attachment
74 Control runs
75 Tailplane centre-section
76 IFF aerial (beneath fuselage)
77 Tailplane structure
78 Tailplane/fin bolt attachments
79 Rudder lower hinge
80 Port rudder (same as 91)
81 Port fin (same as 92)
82 Rudder upper hinge
83 Port elevator (same as 88)
84 Elevator hinge fairing
85 Rear navigation light
86 Tail cone
87 Elevator actuation system
88 Starboard elevator
89 Tailplane stringers
90 Starboard tailplane (same as 77)

91 Starboard rudder
92 Starboard fin
93 Upward canted exhaust pipe
94 Nacelle module installation fairing
95 Steel engine bearers
96 General Electric TF34-100 turbofan (9,065 lb/4,112 kg thrust, identical port and starboard)
97 Centrebody
98 Engine intake
99 VHF/AM aerial
100 VHF/FM aerial
101 Starboard wing centre-section
102 VHF Tacan aerial
103 Starboard bomb pylons
104 Single Mk 82 bombs
105 Outboard pylon (extended forward)
106 Flaps
107 Wing skinning
108 Starboard aileron
109 Drooped wingtip
110 Starboard navigation light

General Dynamics F-16

Model 401, YF-16, F-16A, F-16B

Origin: General Dynamics/Fort Worth, USA, with widespread sub-contract manufacture in Europe and European assembly of aircraft for European customers (see text).

Type: Single-seat fighter bomber; (B) operational trainer.

Engine: One 24,000lb (10,885kg) thrust Pratt & Whitney F100-PW-100 two-shaft afterburning turbofan.

Dimensions: Span (no Sidewinders) 31ft 0in (9·45m), (with Sidewinders) 32ft 10in (10·01m); length (excl probe) (YF-16) 46ft 6in, (F-16A) 47ft 7·7in (14·52m); height (F-16) 16ft 5·2in (5·01m).

Weights: Empty (YF) about 12,000lb (5443kg); (F) about 14,800lb (6733kg); maximum gross (YF) 27,000lb (12,245kg); (F) 33,000lb (14,969kg).

Performance: Maximum speed, Mach 1·95, equivalent to about 1,300mph (2090km/h); initial climb (YF) 40,000ft (12,200m)/min; service ceiling about 60,000ft (18,300m); range on internal fuel in interception mission, about 1,300 miles (2100km); attack radius at low level with maximum weapon load, 120 miles (193km); attack radius with six Mk 82 bombs, 339 miles (546km).

Armament: One 20mm M61 multi-barrel cannon on left side of fuselage; nine pylons for total external load of up to 15,200lb (6895kg) (YF, seven pylons for total of 11,500lb, 5217kg).

History: First flight (YF) 20 January 1974; service delivery, scheduled for mid-1978.

Above: The F-16 is markedly smaller than the F-4 Phantom but is likewise a "fighter" that has become a multi-role aircraft.

Development: One of the most important combat aircraft of the rest of the century was started merely as a technology demonstrator to see to what degree it would be possible to build a useful fighter that was significantly smaller and cheaper than the F-15. The US Air Force Lightweight Fighter (LWF) programme was not intended to lead to a production aircraft but merely to establish what was possible, at what cost. Contracts for two prototypes of each of the two best submissions were awarded in April 1972, the aircraft being the General Dynamics 401 and a simplified Northrop P.530. As the YF-16 and YF-17 these aircraft completed a programme of competitive evaluation, as planned, in 1974. By this time the wish of four European members of NATO — Belgium, Holland, Denmark and Norway — to replace their F-104Gs with an aircraft in this class had spurred a total revision of the LWF programme. In April 1974 it was changed into the Air Combat Fighter (ACF) programme and the Defense Secretary, James Schlesinger, announced that 650 of the winning design would be bought for the USAF, with a vast support depot in Europe. In December 1974 the YF-16 was chosen as the future ACF (announced the following month) and in June 1975, after protracted and tortuous discussions, it was chosen by the four European countries. As an aircraft the F-16 is exciting. It has a flashing performance on the power of the single fully developed engine (the same as the F-15) fed by a simple fixed-geometry inlet. Structure and systems are modern, with control-configured vehicle (CCV) flight dynamics, quad-redundant electrically signalled controls (fly-by-wire), graphite-epoxy structures and a flared wing/body shape. Pilot view is outstanding and he lies back in a reclining Escapac seat and flies the aircraft through a sidestick controller. In the nose is an advanced pulse-doppler radar suitable for attack or interception missions and armament can be carried for both roles, though the basic design was biased strongly in favour of air-to-air missions in good weather at close range. It remains to be seen to what degree the F-16 can be modified to make it a better ground attack, reconnaissance or all-weather interceptor aircraft. Main contractors include Westinghouse (radar), Marconi-Elliott (HUD-sight and portions of flight-control system), Westinghouse and Delco (computers), Kaiser (radar and

Key to cutaway drawing

1 Air data probe (Rosemount Engineering)
2 SSR-1 radar ranging system (General Electric) (Westinghouse multi-mode radar in F-16)
3 Angle-of-attack transducers (port and starboard)
4 Battery and avionics compartment
5 Central air-data computer (Sperry Flight Systems)
6 Air-data converter
7 Forward pressure bulkhead
8 Rudder pedals
9 Control wiring (fly-by-wire) junction
10 Raised heel-rest line
11 Instrument panel shroud
12 Head-up display unit (Marconi-Elliott Avionic Systems HUDWAS)
13 Side-stick controller
14 Starboard instrument console
15 Lightweight ejection seat (30-deg tilt-back Douglas Escapac IH-8)
16 Arm rest
17 Port instrument console (power lever mounting)
18 Fuselage forebody strakes
19 Cooling louvres
20 Gun gas-suppression nozzle
21 Gun-fairing frames
22 Boundary-layer splitter plate
23 Fixed-geometry air intake
24 Inlet duct
25 Aerial
26 Nosewheel leg (Menasco Manufacturing)
27 Aft-retracting nose gear (Goodyear Tire & Rubber)
28 Shock-absorber scissors
29 Retraction strut
30 Nosewheel door
31 Door hinge
32 Nosewheel well (below duct)
33 General Electric M61 20mm gun
34 Cannon barrels
35 Emergency power-unit pack (Sundstrand Avionics)
36 Canopy hinge
37 Headrest
38 Canopy lock
39 Frameless bubble canopy (Sierracin Corp)
40 Aft glazing
41 Forward fuselage fuel tank
42 Accelerometers (General Electric)
43 Ammunition drum
44 Ammunition feed and link return chutes (General Electric)
45 Forward/centre fuselage joint bulkhead
46 Inlet duct
47 Hydraulic equipment bay
48 Main (forward) fuselage fuel tank
49 Flight-refuelling receptacle
50 Multi-spar wing structure
51 Leading-edge flap hinge-line
52 Leading-edge manoeuvre flap
53 Wing-tip missile adaptor shoe
54 AIM-9 Sidewinder missile
55 Static dischargers
56 Fixed trailing-edge section
57 Starboard flaperon
58 Aerial
59 Forward support link
60 Glass-fibre root fairing
61 Fin/fuselage attachments
62 Aluminium multi-spar fin structure
63 Aluminium-honeycomb leading-edge
64 Steel leading-edge strip
65 Graphite-epoxy skin
66 Identification/navigation light
67 Static dischargers
68 Graphite-epoxy rudder skin
69 Aluminium-honeycomb rudder
70 Empennage flight controls
71 Fully variable articulated nozzle
72 Split trailing-edge airbrake (upper and lower surfaces)
73 Static dischargers
74 Aluminium-honeycomb tailplane
75 Graphite-epoxy skin

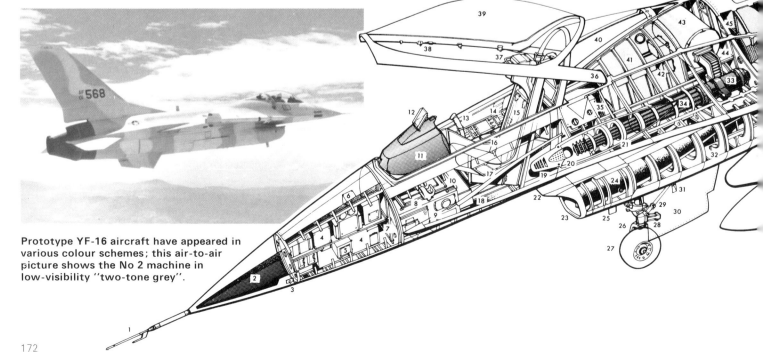

Prototype YF-16 aircraft have appeared in various colour schemes; this air-to-air picture shows the No 2 machine in low-visibility "two-tone grey".

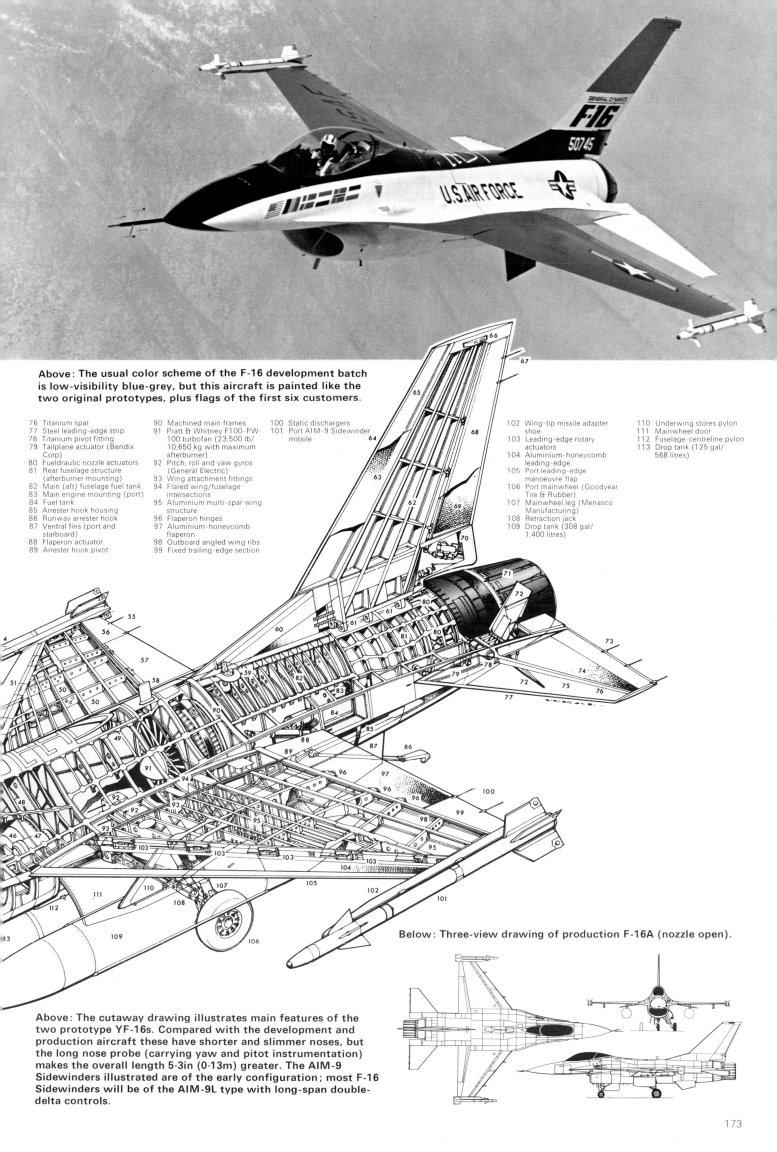

Above: The usual color scheme of the F-16 development batch is low-visibility blue-grey, but this aircraft is painted like the two original prototypes, plus flags of the first six customers.

76 Titanium spar
77 Steel leading-edge strip
78 Titanium pivot fitting
79 Tailplane actuator (Bendix Corp)
80 Fueldraulic nozzle actuators
81 Rear fuselage structure (afterburner mounting)
82 Main (aft) fuselage fuel tank
83 Main engine mounting (port)
84 Fuel tank
85 Arrester hook housing
86 Runway arrester hook
87 Ventral fins (port and starboard)
88 Flaperon actuator
89 Arrester hook pivot

90 Machined main frames
91 Pratt & Whitney F100-PW-100 turbofan (23,500 lb/10,650 kg with maximum afterburner)
92 Pitch, roll and yaw gyros (General Electric)
93 Wing attachment fittings
94 Flared wing/fuselage intersections
95 Aluminium multi-spar wing structure
96 Flaperon hinges
97 Aluminium-honeycomb flaperon
98 Outboard angled wing ribs
99 Fixed trailing-edge section

100 Static dischargers
101 Port AIM-9 Sidewinder missile

102 Wing-tip missile adapter shoe
103 Leading-edge rotary actuators
104 Aluminium-honeycomb leading-edge
105 Port leading-edge manoeuvre flap
106 Port mainwheel (Goodyear Tire & Rubber)
107 Mainwheel leg (Menasco Manufacturing)
108 Retraction jack
109 Drop tank (308 gal/1,400 litres)

110 Underwing stores pylon
111 Mainwheel door
112 Fuselage-centreline pylon
113 Drop tank (125 gal/568 litres)

Above: The cutaway drawing illustrates main features of the two prototype YF-16s. Compared with the development and production aircraft these have shorter and slimmer noses, but the long nose probe (carrying yaw and pitot instrumentation) makes the overall length 5·3in (0·13m) greater. The AIM-9 Sidewinders illustrated are of the early configuration; most F-16 Sidewinders will be of the AIM-9L type with long-span double-delta controls.

Below: Three-view drawing of production F-16A (nozzle open).

electro-optical display) and Singer-Kearfott (inertial system). In 1977 the USAF still intends to purchase 650 aircraft, mainly for use in Europe; in 1976 it set up a European System Programme Office to manage the project, and began work on the support depot. Orders are still subject to change, but the planned totals are: Belgium, 90 F-16A and 12 F-16B, with 14 aircraft on option; Denmark 48 (probably 40+8), and 10 on option; the Netherlands, 84, plus 18 on option; Norway, 72 (no options). In July 1976 General Dynamics finally signed co-production contracts with major companies in Belgium and Holland, specifying schedules and output rates of parts for 564 aircraft, a total that would increase with further F-16 sales. Aircraft will be assembled by General Dynamics (USAF), Fairey/SABCA (Belgium and Denmark) and Fokker-VFW (Netherlands and Norway); Kongsberg in Norway has a $163m co-production deal with Pratt & Whitney on more than 400 engines (all engines will be assembled by P & WA). Since early 1976 Turkey has been negotiating to join the European consortium (which has no formal title) and to buy up to 100 aircraft. In September 1976 Congress announced the sale to Iran of 160, costing $3·8 billion; it is doubtful that Iran can participate in manufacture. In December 1976 the first of eight development aircraft flew at Fort Worth, and delivery to the USAF is to begin in August 1978. Up to October 1976 $286 million had paid for basic development and flight test; Fiscal Year 1977 voted $620 million for the first 16 production aircraft, and FY78 is expected to provide $1,128 million. USAF buy in the next four years (1978-81) is planned to be 89, 145, 175 and 180, a total to that date of 605. First flight in Europe is planned to be at Schiphol (Fokker-VFW, Amsterdam) in July 1979.

Above: The second YF-16 prototype, pictured whilst undergoing weapon trials. It has just released 12 bombs each of a nominal 1,000lb. Maximum load, with reduced fuel, is 15,200lb.

Below: YF-16 No 2 in 1976 development configuration (nozzle closed).

Far right: Grey smoke spews from the Gatling exhaust port of a YF-16 on a low-level firing pass during weapon trials. Fighters are no longer built without guns.

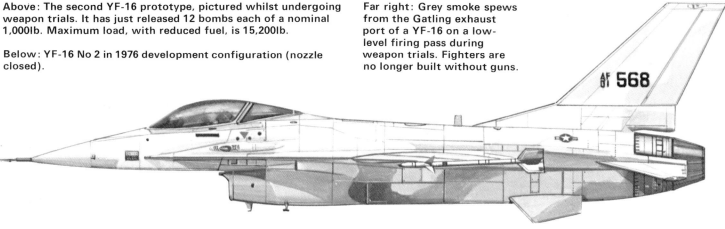

General Dynamics F-111

"TFX", F-111A to F-111F, EF-111A and FB-111A

Origin: General Dynamics/Fort Worth (EF-111A, Grumman Aerospace), USA.
Type: Two-seat all-weather attack bomber; (EF) two-seat electronic warfare; (FB) two-seat strategic bomber.
Engines: Two Pratt & Whitney TF30 two-shaft afterburning turbofans, at following ratings: (F-111A, C) TF30-3 at 18,500lb (8390kg); (D, E) TF30-9 at 19,600lb (8891kg); (F) RF30-100 at 25,100lb (11,385kg); (FB) TF30-7 at 20,350lb (9230kg).
Dimensions: Span, 72·5° sweep (A, D, E, F) 31ft 11½in (9·74m); (C, FB) 33ft 11in (10·34m); span, 16° sweep (A, D, E, F) 63ft (19·2m); (C, FB) 70ft (21·34m); length 73ft 6in (22·4m); height 17ft 1½in (5·22m).
Weights: Empty (A, C) 46,172lb (20,943kg); (D, E, F) about 49,000lb (22,226kg); (FB) about 50,000lb (22,680kg); maximum loaded (A, D, E) 92,500lb (41,954kg); (F) 100,000lb (45,400kg); (FB) 114,300lb (51,846kg); (EF) 87,800lb (40,270kg).

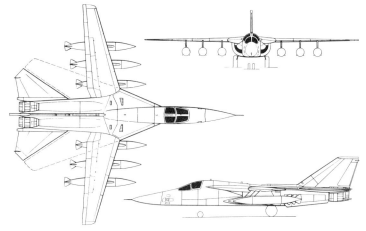

Above: Three-view of FB-111A bomber with six external tanks.

Performance: Maximum speed (clean), Mach 2·2 at 35,000ft or above, or about 1,450mph (2335km/h); maximum speed at low level (clean) Mach 1·2 or 800mph (1287km/h); maximum speed at maximum weight, subsonic at low level; service ceiling (clean) (A) 51,000ft (15,500m); (F) 60,000ft (18,290m); range on internal fuel (A, C) 3,165 miles (5093km).
Armament: Internal bay for two 750lb (341kg) bombs or 20mm M-61 multi-barrel gun; eight underwing pylons for total of 31,500lb (14,290kg) of stores, inner pylons swivelling with wing sweep and outer four being fixed and loaded only with wing at 16°.
History: First flight 21 December 1964; service delivery June 1967; first F-111F with -100 engine, May 1973; EF-111A (Grumman ECM conversion) 1976-7. *continued on page 176* ▶

Left: A powerful and effective F-111F, the final production model, seen in the TFR (terrain-following radar) mode among the Rockies. The F-111F wing is now based in Britain.

Right: One of the early development prototypes lets go a cluster of 24 Mk 82 (nominal 500lb, actual mass about 580lb) iron bombs from the two inboard pylons on each swing wing. Curiously, no pylons were provided for on the body.

▶Development: Developed to meet a bold Department of Defense edict that a common type of "fighter" called TFX should be developed to meet all future tactical needs of all US services, the F-111A proved both a world-beater and a great disappointment. Thrown into the public eye by acrimonious disagreement over which bidder should get the production contract, it then stayed in the news through being grossly overweight, up in drag and suffering from severe problems with propulsion, structure and systems. Eventually almost superhuman efforts cleared the F-111A for service, overcoming part of the range deficiency by a considerable increase in internal fuel. The RAAF bought 24 F-111C with long-span wings and stronger landing gear and took delivery after they had been nine years in storage. The RAF ordered 50 similar to the C but with updated avionics, but this deal was cancelled. Only 141 low-powered A-models were built, the US Navy F-111B fighter was cancelled, and the next batch was 94 of the E type with improved intakes and engines (20th Tac Ftr Wing at Upper Heyford, England). Then came the 96 F-111D with improved avionics (27th TFW in New Mexico) and finally the superb F-111F with redesigned P-100 engine of greatly increased thrust and cheaper avionics (366 TFW, in Idaho). The heavier FB-111A, with the ability to carry six AGM-69A SRAM missiles externally, was bought to replace the B-58 and early B-52 models in Strategic Air Command. Cost-inflation cut the FB order from 210 back to 76. With several RF and ECM conversions the total programme amounted to 539 plus 23 development prototypes. To keep the line open a further 12 were authorised in 1974 to be built at a low rate until 1976. In 1977 the only work on F-111s was structural improvement of aircraft in service and the Grumman programme to convert two A models to EF-111A configuration carrying comprehensive electronic-warfare equipment including ALQ-99 jammers of the type fitted to the Navy's EA-6B. If the EF-111A performs well Grumman may convert a further 40 to equip two USAF squadrons. The EF will not carry weapons, and will direct other aircraft. No aircraft has ever had worse luck or a worse press, and in combat in South East Asia the sudden loss of three of the first six aircraft was eventually found to be due to a faulty weld in the tailplane power unit. In fact all models of the F-111 are valuable machines with great range and endurance, excellent reliability and great ability to hit a point target in a first-pass strike, even in blind conditions. These aircraft are bombers, with much greater power and weight than four-engined bombers of World War II. It was unfortunate they were loosely launched as "fighters".

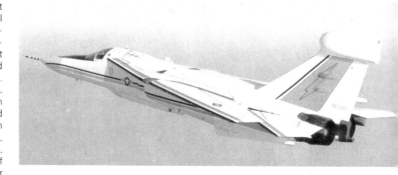

Above: The EF-111A electronic-warfare aircraft carries the ALQ-99 system with canoe (belly) and fin-top aerials.

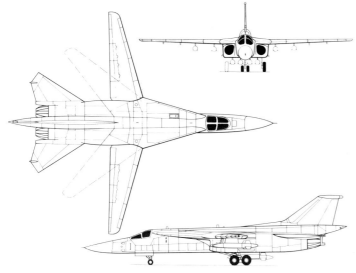

Above: Three-view of FB-111H strategic bomber proposal, from details supplied by General Dynamics.

Right: This cutaway shows the basic features of all tactical F-111 models, including the crew-escape module and six swivelling pylons (outers seldom used). In 1977 details were published of the proposed FB-111H, a lengthened strategic bomber powered by two F101 engines of the type developed for the B-1. New tandem-wheel main gears would allow six pylons to be added to the fuselage, and the longer internal bay could carry five B61 or four SRAMs. Intended to replace the B-1, this proposal was effectively killed by the 1979 defense budget.

Key to cutaway drawing

1 Hinged radome
2 General Electric APQ-113 attack radar
3 Texas Instruments APQ-110 terrain-following radar
4 Radome hinges (2)
5 Radar mounting
6 Nose lock
7 Angle-of-sideslip probe
8 Homing aerial (high)
9 Forward warning aerial
10 Homing aerial (low and mid)
11 ALR-41 aerial
12 Flight control computers
13 Feel and trim assembly
14 Forward avionics bay
14 Forward avionics bay Mk II digital computer)
15 Angle-of-attack probe
16 UHF Comm/TACAN No 2
17 Module forward bulkhead and stabilization flaps (2)
18 Twin nosewheels
19 Shock strut
20 Underfloor impact attenuation bag stowage (4)
21 Nosewheel well
22 Lox converter
23 Rudder pedals
24 Control column
25 Lox heat exchanger
26 Auxiliary flotation bag pressure bottle
27 Weapons sight
28 Forward parachute bridle line
29 De-fog nozzle
30 Windscreen
31 Starboard console

32 Emergency oxygen bottles
33 Crew seats
34 Bulkhead console
35 Wing sweep control handle
36 Recovery chute catapult
37 Provision/survival pack
38 Attenuation bags pressure bottle
39 Recovery chute
40 Aft parachute bridle line
41 UHF data link/AG IFF No 1 (see 123)

42 Stabilization-brake chute
43 Self-righting bag
44 UHF recovery
45 ECM aerials (port and starboard)

46 Forward fuselage fuel bay
47 Ground refuelling receptacle
48 Weapons bay
49 Module pitch flaps (port and starboard)
50 Aft flotation bag stowage
51 Flight refuelling receptacle
52 Primary heat-exchanger (air-to-water)

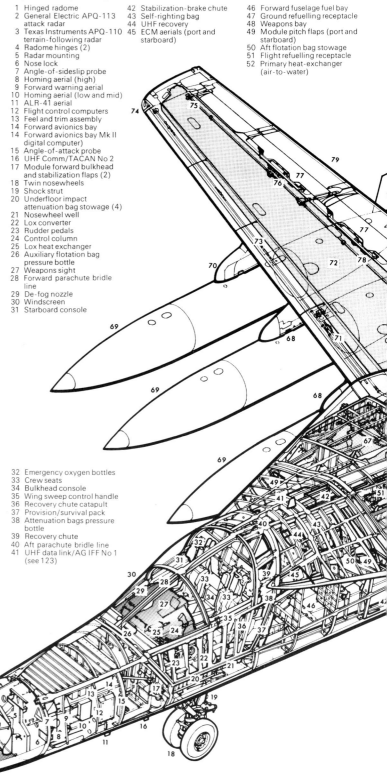

Above: An F-111E cruising with wings at 26° for subsonic efficiency. Like an A except for improved inlet ducts, the E equips the 20th TFW based at RAF Upper Heyford, England.

Above: Boomer's view of a SAC FB-111A with SRAM missiles. Only 76 of a planned 210 FB-111As were produced, supporting a mere two wings of only 30 aircraft each.

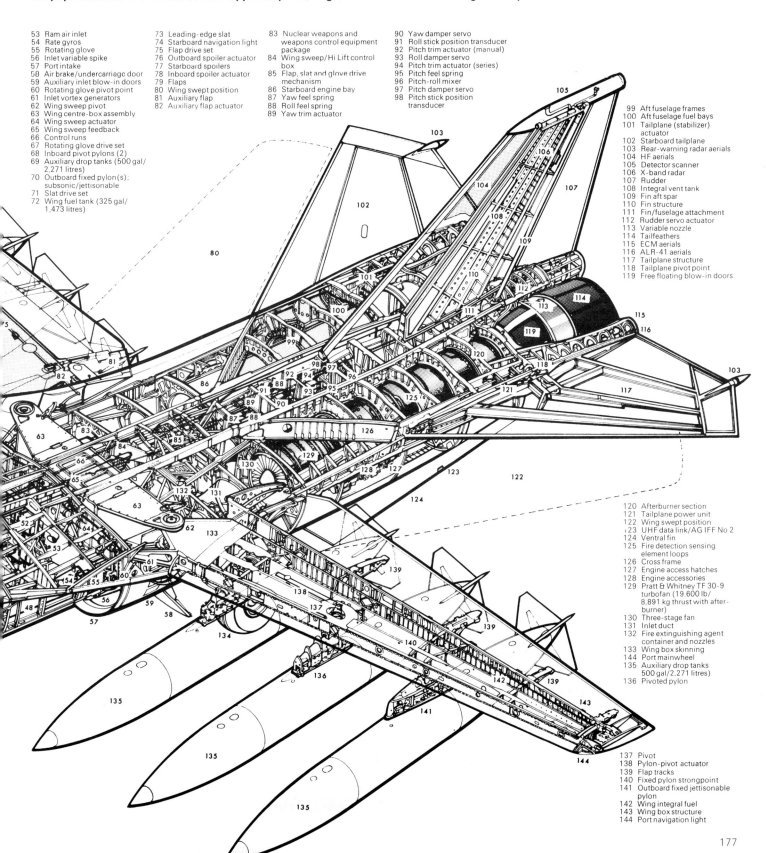

53 Ram air inlet
54 Rate gyros
55 Rotating glove
56 Inlet variable spike
57 Port intake
58 Air brake/undercarriage door
59 Auxiliary inlet blow-in doors
60 Rotating glove pivot point
61 Inlet vortex generators
62 Wing sweep pivot
63 Wing centre-box assembly
64 Wing sweep actuator
65 Wing sweep feedback
66 Control runs
67 Rotating glove drive set
68 Inboard pivot pylons (2)
69 Auxiliary drop tanks (500 gal/2,271 litres)
70 Outboard fixed pylon(s); subsonic/jettisonable
71 Slat drive set
72 Wing fuel tank (325 gal/1,473 litres)

73 Leading-edge slat
74 Starboard navigation light
75 Flap drive set
76 Outboard spoiler actuator
77 Starboard spoilers
78 Inboard spoiler actuator
79 Flaps
80 Wing swept position
81 Auxiliary flap
82 Auxiliary flap actuator

83 Nuclear weapons and weapons control equipment package
84 Wing sweep/Hi Lift control box
85 Flap, slat and glove drive mechanism
86 Starboard engine bay
87 Yaw feel spring
88 Roll feel spring
89 Yaw trim actuator

90 Yaw damper servo
91 Roll stick position transducer
92 Pitch trim actuator (manual)
93 Roll damper servo
94 Pitch trim actuator (series)
95 Pitch feel spring
96 Pitch-roll mixer
97 Pitch damper servo
98 Pitch stick position transducer

99 Aft fuselage frames
100 Aft fuselage fuel bays
101 Tailplane (stabilizer) actuator
102 Starboard tailplane
103 Rear-warning radar aerials
104 HF aerials
105 Detector scanner
106 X-band radar
107 Rudder
108 Integral vent tank
109 Fin aft spar
110 Fin structure
111 Fin/fuselage attachment
112 Rudder servo actuator
113 Variable nozzle
114 Tailfeathers
115 ECM aerials
116 ALR-41 aerials
117 Tailplane structure
118 Tailplane pivot point
119 Free floating blow-in doors

120 Afterburner section
121 Tailplane power unit
122 Wing swept position
123 UHF data link/AG IFF No 2
124 Ventral fin
125 Fire detection sensing element loops
126 Cross frame
127 Engine access hatches
128 Engine accessories
129 Pratt & Whitney TF 30-9 turbofan (19.600 lb/8,891 kg thrust with afterburner)
130 Three-stage fan
131 Inlet duct
132 Fire extinguishing agent container and nozzles
133 Wing box skinning
144 Port mainwheel
135 Auxiliary drop tanks 500 gal/2,271 litres)
136 Pivoted pylon

137 Pivot
138 Pylon-pivot actuator
139 Flap tracks
140 Fixed pylon strongpoint
141 Outboard fixed jettisonable pylon
142 Wing integral fuel
143 Wing box structure
144 Port navigation light

Grumman A-6 Intruder and Prowler

Grumman A-6A, B, C, E, EA-6A and B and KA-6D

Origin: Grumman Aerospace, USA.

Type: (A-6A, B, C, E) two-seat carrier-based all-weather attack; (EA-6A) two-seat ECM/attack; (EA-6B) four-seat ECM; (KA-6D) two-seat air-refuelling tanker.

Engines: (Except EA-6B) two 9,300lb (4218kg) thrust Pratt & Whitney J52-8A two-shaft turbojets; (EA-6B) two 11,200lb (5080kg) J52-408.

Dimensions: Span 53ft (16·15m); length (except EA-6B) 54ft 7in (16·64m); (EA-6B) 59ft 5in (18·11m); height (A-6A, A-6C, KA-6D) 15ft 7in (4·75m); (A-6E, EA-6A and B) 16ft 3in (4·95m).

Weights: Empty (A-6A) 25,684lb (11,650kg); (EA-6A) 27,769lb (12,596kg); (EA-6B) 34,581lb (15,686kg); (A-6E) 25,630lb (11,625kg); maximum loaded (A-6A and E) 60,626lb (27,500kg); (EA-6A) 56,500lb (25,628kg); (EA-6B) 58,500lb (26,535kg).

Performance: Maximum speed (clean A-6A) 685mph (1102km/h) at sea level or 625mph (1006km/h, Mach 0·94) at height; (EA-6A) over 630mph; (EA-6B) 599mph at sea level; (A-6E) 648mph (1043km/h) at sea level; initial climb (A-6E, clean) 8,600ft (2621m)/min; service ceiling (A-6A) 41,660ft (12,700m); (A-6E) 44,600ft (13,595m); (EA-6B) 39,000ft (11,582m); range with full combat load (A-6E) 1,077 miles (1733km); ferry range with external fuel (all) about 3,100 miles (4890km).

Armament: All attack versions, including EA-6A, five stores locations each rated at 3,600lb (1633kg) with maximum total load of 15,000lb (6804kg);

typical load thirty 500lb (227kg) bombs; (EA-6B, KA-6D) none.

History: First flight (YA2F-1) 19 April 1960; service acceptance of A-6A 1 February 1963; first flight (EA-6A) 1963; (KA-6D) 23 May 1966; (EA-6B) 25 May 1968; (A-6E) 27 February 1970; final delivery 1975.

Development: Selected from 11 competing designs in December 1957, the Intruder was specifically planned for first-pass blind attack on point surface targets at night or in any weather. Though area ruled, the aircraft

Key to cutaway drawing

1. Radome
2. APQ-92 radar antenna
3. Bulkhead
4. Rain removal nozzle
5. ALQ-126 receiver antenna fairing
6. Refuelling boom (detachable)
7. In-flight refuelling receptacle
8. Two-piece windscreens
9. Senior EWO's panoramic/video display consoles
10. Pilot's instrument panel shroud
11. Control column
12. Rudder pedals
13. Pitot static tubes (port and starboard)
14. Power brake
15. APQ-92 transmitter
16. Anti-collision beacon
17. "L"-band antenna
18. ALQ-92 (IFF) antenna
19. Taxi/landing light
20. Nosewheel leg fairing
21. Nosewheel leg
22. Tow link (landing position)
23. Tow link (launch position)
24. Dual nosewheel assembly
25. Nosewheel retraction jack
26. Nosewheel well door
27. Approach lights
28. Shock-absorber link
29. APQ-92 high and low voltage
30. APQ-92 modulator
31. Cockpit floor level
32. Anti-skid control
33. Fuselage forward frames
34. Pilot's ejection seat
35. Senior Electronic Warfare Officer's (ALQ-99 tactical jamming) ejection seat
36. Upward-hinged forward cockpit canopy
37. Canopy mechanism
38. Aft cockpit port EWO's console
39. Handgrips
40. Security equipment
41. Splitter plate
42. Port engine intake
43. Intake frames
44. Aft cockpit entry ladder
45. Electric hydraulic pump
46. Manual selector valves
47. Cockpit aft bulkhead
48. Third Electronic Warfare Officer's (ALQ-92 comms jamming) ejection seat
49. Second Electronic Warfare Officer's (ALQ-99 tactical jamming) ejection seat
50. Canopy mechanism
51. Upward-hinged aft cockpit canopy
52. Starboard outer ECM pod
53. Intake
54. Pod turbine power-source
55. ALQ-41/ALQ-100 starboard spear antenna
56. Leading-edge slats (deployed)
57. Starboard inner integral wing fuel cell
58. Starboard inner wing fence
59. Wing-fold cylinders
60. Hinge assembly
61. Wing-fold line
62. Starboard outer integral wing fuel cell
63. Fuel probe
64. Wing structure
65. Starboard outer wing fence
66. Starboard navigation light
67. Starboard formation light
68. Wingtip speed-brakes (open)
69. Speed-brake actuating cylinder fairing
70. Fence
71. Wingtip fuel dump outlet
72. Starboard single-slotted flap (outer section)
73. Starboard flaperons
74. Flaperon mechanism
75. Starboard single-slotted flap (inner section)
76. UHF/TACAN antenna
77. Directional control
78. Dorsal fairing frame
79. Computer power trim
80. Fuel lines
81. Control runs
82. Dorsal anti-collision beacon
83. Relay assembly group
84. Control linkage (bulkhead rear face)
85. Fuselage forward fuel cell
86. ALQ-126 receiver/transmitter
87. Hydraulic reservoir
88. Wingroot section front spar
89. Wingroot leading-edge spoiler
90. Engine bay frames
91. Port J52-P-408 turbojet
92. Mainwheel door mechanism
93. Engine accessories
94. Mainwheel well door
95. Port mainwheel well
96. Transducer/accelerometer
97. Power distribution/transfer panels
98. Fuselage mid fuel cell
99. Roll trim actuator
100. Lateral actuator control
101. ARA-48 antenna
102. Vent lines
103. Fuselage aft fuel cell
104. Longitudinal control
105. Air-conditioning scoop
106. Fuel vent scoop
107. TACAN receiver
108. ALQ-92 air scoop
109. LOX (3)
110. Heat exchanger
111. Gyroscope assembly
112. Fuel control relay box
113. Adaptor-compensator compass
114. Arresting hook lift
115. Analogue to digital converter
116. Relay box/blanking unit
117. Control runs
118. Frequency and direction encoder
119. Fuel vent
120. Dorsal fillet
121. Starboard horizontal stabilizer (tailplane)
122. Multi-spar vertical stabilizer (fin) structure
123. Horizontal stabilizer actuator
124. Transmitter remote compass
125. Power divider
126. System Integration Receiver (SIR) antennae/receiver fairing
127. SIR antennae (Bands 4 and 7/8)
128. SIR receivers (Bands 4-9)
129. SIR antennae (Bands 4 and 5/6)
130. ALQ-41 transmit antennae
131. Attenuator
132. RF divider
133. Rudder upper hinge
134. Rudder (honeycomb structure)
135. Antenna (Band 1)
136. Antenna (Band 2)
137. Rudder lower hinge
138. Rear navigation light
139. ALQ-126 transmit antenna
140. Fuel vent
141. Receiver antenna
142. Rudder actuator
143. Port horizontal stabilizer structure
144. Horizontal stabilizer pivot
145. Aft power supply
146. ALQ-41 transmitter
147. ALQ-41 receiver/transmitter
148. ALQ-100 receiver/transmitter
149. Chaff dispensers
150. UHF "L"-band antenna
151. Arresting hook
152. Extensible equipment platform (lowered)
153. APN-153 antenna
154. ALQ-41 power supply
155. ARC-105 radio receiver-transmitter

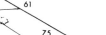

heavier than most of the heavy World War II four-engine bombers — the Intruder has excellent slow-flying qualities with full span slats and flaps. The crew sit side-by-side under a broad sliding canopy giving a marvellous view in all directions, the navigator having control of the extremely comprehensive navigation, radar and attack systems which are integrated into DIANE (Digital Integrated Attack Navigation Equipment). In Vietnam the A-6A worked round the clock making pinpoint attacks on targets which could not be accurately bombed by any other aircraft until the arrival of the F-111. The A-6E introduced a new multi-mode radar and computer and supplanted earlier versions in Navy and Marine Corps squadrons. The EA-6A introduced a valuable group of ECM (electronic countermeasures), while retaining partial attack capability, but the extraordinary EA-6B is a totally redesigned four-seat aircraft where the entire payload comprises the most advanced and comprehensive ECM equipment ever fitted to a tactical aircraft, part of it being carried in four external pods with windmill generators to supply electric power. The latest addition to attack versions was TRAM (Target Recognition Attack Multisensor), a turreted electro-optical/infra-red system matched with laser-guided weapons. In 1977 Grumman was building new Prowlers and the last A-6Es, and converting A-6A models to the latest E standard. In the course of 1977 the first Intruders were to be modified to fire the Harpoon active-seeker missile.

Above: A four-seat EA-6B Prowler parked with staircase extended. The outer jamming pods have windmill generators.

(originally designated A2F) was designed to be subsonic and is powered by two straight turbojets which in the original design were arranged with tilting jetpipes to help give lift for STOL (short takeoff and landing). Despite its considerable gross weight — much more than twice the empty weight and

156 Power supply boxes
157 Port engine exhaust outlet
158 Wing/fuselage fairing
159 Ram air turbine (stowed)
160 Flaperon gearing actuator
161 Wing centre-section fuel cell
162 Port inner integral wing fuel cell
163 Port inner wing fence
164 Leading-edge slat structure
165 Wing-fold cylinder bays
166 Hinge assembly
167 Port flaperons
168 Flap actuator bays
169 Port single-slotted flap (outer section)
170 Wingtip fuel dump outlet
171 Fence
172 Speed-brake actuating cylinder fairing
173 Wingtip speed-brakes (open)
174 Port formation light
175 Port navigation light
176 Port outer wing fence

177 Leading-edge slats
178 Port outer integral wing fuel cell
179 Fuel probe
180 Port outer ALQ-99 high-power (tactical) noise-jamming systems pod
181 Port outer wing pylon
182 Port mainwheel
183 Mainwheel leg
184 Port inner wing pylon
185 Mainwheel retraction strut
186 ALQ-41/ALQ-100 (radar deception) port spear antenna
187 Port inner ALQ-99 systems pod
188 Garrett-AiResearch four-bladed axial flow ram-air turbines
189 Ventral ALQ-99 high-power (tactical) noise-jamming systems pod

Left: Cutaway of an EA-6B Prowler, showing self-powered jammer pods and with the rear equipment pod extended. The ALQ-99 TJS (tactical jammer system) has now been fitted into the EF-111A with only two crew.

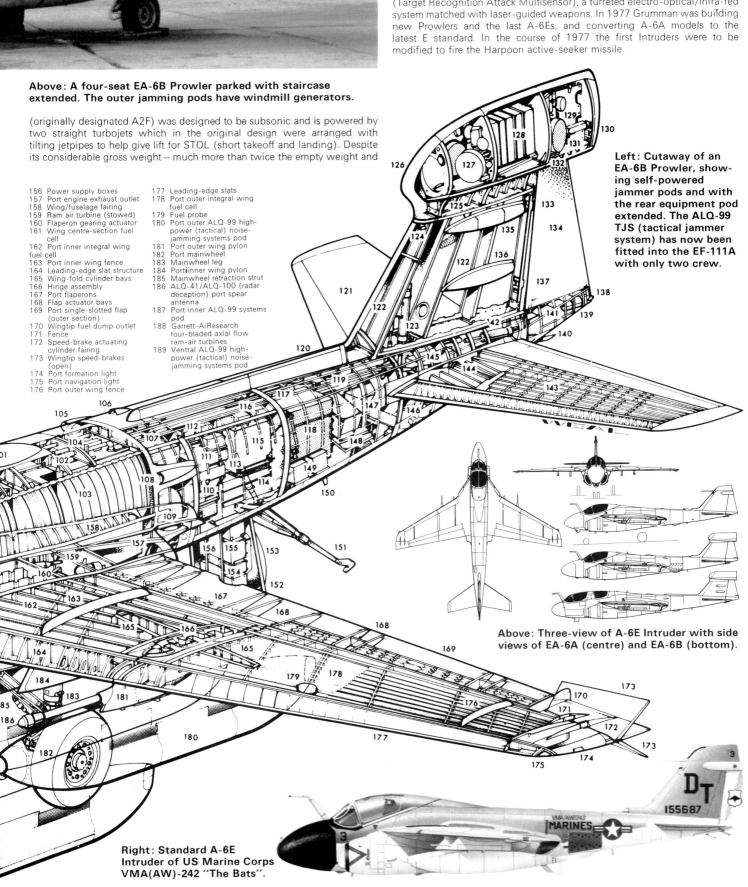

Above: Three-view of A-6E Intruder with side views of EA-6A (centre) and EA-6B (bottom).

Right: Standard A-6E Intruder of US Marine Corps VMA(AW)-242 "The Bats".

Grumman F-14 Tomcat

F-14A, B and C

Origin: Grumman Aerospace, USA.
Type: Two-seat carrier-based multi-role fighter.
Engines: (F-14A) two 20,900lb (9480kg) thrust Pratt & Whitney TF30-412A two-shaft afterburning turbofans; (B and C) two 28,090lb (12,741kg) thrust Pratt & Whitney F401-400 two-shaft afterburning turbofans.
Dimensions: Span (68° sweep) 38ft 2in (11·63m), (20° sweep) 64ft 1½in (19·54m); length 61ft 2in (18·89m); height 16ft (4·88m).
Weights: Empty 37,500lb (17,010kg); loaded (fighter mission) 55,000lb (24,948kg), (maximum) 72,000lb (32,658kg).
Performance: Maximum speed, 1,564mph (2517km/h, Mach 2·34) at height, 910mph (1470km/h, Mach 1·2) at sea level; initial climb at normal gross weight, over 30,000ft (9144m)/min; service ceiling over 56,000ft (17,070m); range (fighter with external fuel) about 2,000 miles (3200km).
Armament: One 20mm M61-A1 multi-barrel cannon in fuselage; four AIM-7 Sparrow and four or eight AIM-9 Sidewinder air-to-air missiles, or up to six AIM-54 Phoenix and two AIM-9; maximum external weapon load in surface attack role 14,500lb (6577kg).
History: First flight 21 December 1970; initial deployment with US Navy carriers October 1972; first flight of F-14B 12 September 1973.

Development: When Congress finally halted development of the compromised F-111B version of the TFX in mid-1968 Grumman was already well advanced with the project design of a replacement. After a competition for the VFX requirement Grumman was awarded a contract for the F-14 in January 1969. The company had to produce a detailed mock-up by May and build 12 development aircraft. Despite sudden loss of the first aircraft on its second flight, due to total hydraulic failure, the programme has been a complete technical success and produced one of the world's outstanding combat aircraft. Basic features include use of a variable-sweep wing, to match the aircraft to the conflicting needs of carrier compatability, dogfighting and attack on surface targets at low level; pilot and naval flight officer

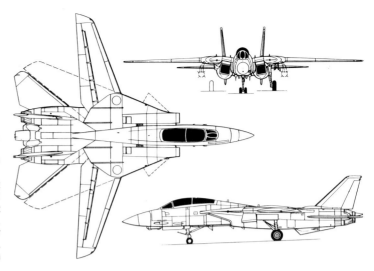

Above: **Three-view of an F-14A showing (broken lines) range of wing and glove movement.**

(observer) in tandem; an extremely advanced airframe, with tailplane skins of boron-epoxy composite and similar novel construction methods, and one canted vertical tail above each engine; and the extremely powerful Hughes AWG-9 radar which, used in conjunction with the Phoenix missile (carried by no other combat aircraft), can pick out and destroy a chosen aircraft from a formation at a distance of 100 miles. For close-in fighting the gun is used in conjunction with snap-shoot missiles, with the tremendous advantage that, as a launch platform, the Tomcat is unsurpassed (Grumman claim it to be unrivalled, and to be able — by automatic variation of wing sweep — to out-manoeuvre all previous combat aircraft). Introduction to the US Navy has been smooth and enthusiastic, with VF-1 and -2 serving aboard *Enterprise*

Opposite page, top: Head-on view of an F-14 Tomcat of US Navy VF-211. Armed here with an internal gun, two AIM-7F Sparrows and two AIM-9G Sidewinders, the Tomcat can also carry the Phoenix with over 100 miles' range.

Key to cutaway drawing

1 Anti-collision beacons
2 Countermeasures aerial
3 Honeycomb rudders
4 Honeycomb-sandwich fin skin
5 Rear navigation light
6 Fuel dump line
7 Variable nozzles
8 Engine rear mount/tailplane mounting spectacle beam
9 Tailplane actuator
10 Tailplane pivot mounting
11 Boron-epoxy tailplane
12 Honeycomb trailing edge
13 APR-25 receiving aerial
14 Wing position (fully swept)
15 Ventral fin
16 Engine oil-cooler air intake
17 UHF-band blade aerial
18 Aft fuselage structure
19 Multi-bolt fin attachments
20 Arrester-hook damper
21 Tailplane control linkage
22 Airbrake (upper surface)
23 Revised (reduced) aft fuselage planform (aircraft No 87 onwards)
24 Fin spigot mounting
25 Vent tank
26 Aft fuselage integral tanks
27 Fin root fairing
28 Port tailplane
29 Wing position (fully swept)
30 Inflatable seal (wing fully forward)

31 Port Pratt & Whitney TF30-P-412 turbofan (20,600 lb/9,344 kg thrust with afterburner)
32 Control runs
33 Aft fuselage attachment link
34 Carapace stiffeners (4)
35 VHF aerials
36 Wing spar box pivot support structure (titanium)
37 Wing-fold screw-jack
38 Flap drive shaft
39 Flaps
40 Wingtip formation lights (low intensity)
41 Port navigation light
42 Leading-edge slats
43 Wing integral tank
44 Slat drive shaft
45 Wing pivot
46 Mainwheel wells
47 Inlet bleed air doors

48 ECS (environmental control system) heat exchanger outlets
49 Navigation light (above and below glove vane)

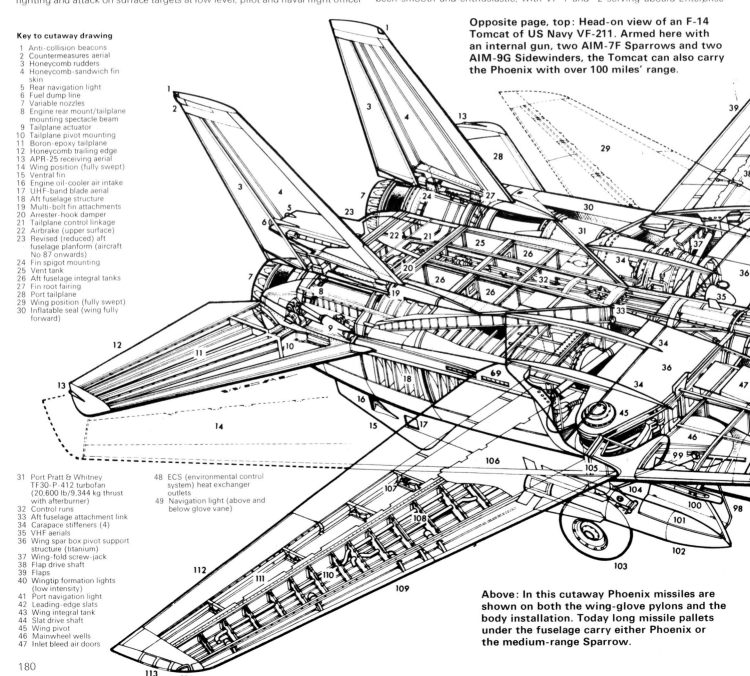

Above: **In this cutaway Phoenix missiles are shown on both the wing-glove pylons and the body installation. Today long missile pallets under the fuselage carry either Phoenix or the medium-range Sparrow.**

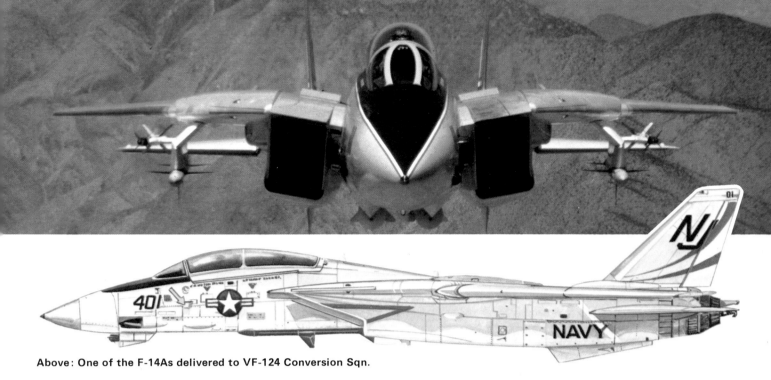

Above: One of the F-14As delivered to VF-124 Conversion Sqn.

in 1974. The export appeal of the F-14 is obvious and Iran is introducing 80 from 1976. But costs have run well beyond prediction, Grumman refusing at one time to continue the programme and claiming its existing contracts would result in a loss of $105 million. For the same reason the re-engined F-14B has been confined to two re-engined A-models, and the F-14C with new avionics and weapons remains a paper project. In 1975 production agreements were worked out and by 1977 total deliveries amounted to 243 aircraft, including about 12 for Iran. The US Navy (which includes the aircraft for the Marines) has funds for 306 F-14As and plans to buy 403 by 1981, but the requirement for an eventual total of over 500 is likely to be cut back as the F-18 comes into production. In 1976 severe trouble hit the F-14, affecting engines, fuselage structure, computer/weapon system and accidents attributed to pilot error. Efforts are being made to improve the operational-readiness rate and, if possible, increase installed engine thrust.

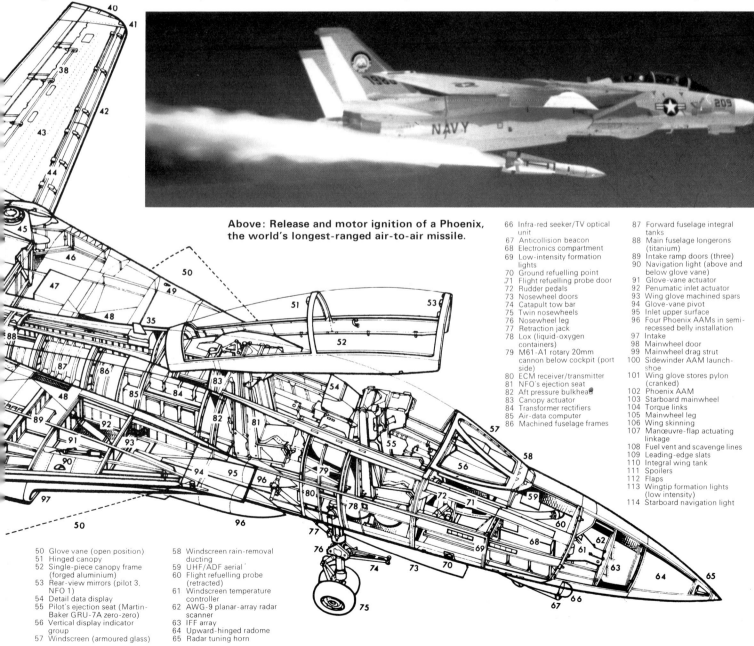

Above: Release and motor ignition of a Phoenix, the world's longest-ranged air-to-air missile.

50 Glove vane (open position)
51 Hinged canopy
52 Single-piece canopy frame (forged aluminium)
53 Rear-view mirrors (pilot 3, NFO 1)
54 Detail data display
55 Pilot's ejection seat (Martin-Baker GRU-7A zero-zero)
56 Vertical display indicator group
57 Windscreen (armoured glass)
58 Windscreen rain-removal ducting
59 UHF/ADF aerial
60 Flight refuelling probe (retracted)
61 Windscreen temperature controller
62 AWG-9 planar-array radar scanner
63 IFF array
64 Upward-hinged radome
65 Radar tuning horn
66 Infra-red seeker/TV optical unit
67 Anticollision beacon
68 Electronics compartment
69 Low-intensity formation lights
70 Ground refuelling point
71 Flight refuelling probe door
72 Rudder pedals
73 Nosewheel doors
74 Catapult tow bar
75 Twin nosewheels
76 Nosewheel leg
77 Retraction jack
78 Lox (liquid-oxygen containers)
79 M61-A1 rotary 20mm cannon below cockpit (port side)
80 ECM receiver/transmitter
81 NFO's ejection seat
82 Aft pressure bulkhead
83 Canopy actuator
84 Transformer rectifiers
85 Air-data computer
86 Machined fuselage frames
87 Forward fuselage integral tanks
88 Main fuselage longerons (titanium)
89 Intake ramp doors (three)
90 Navigation light (above and below glove vane)
91 Glove-vane actuator
92 Penumatic inlet actuator
93 Wing glove machined spars
94 Glove-vane pivot
95 Inlet upper surface
96 Four Phoenix AAMs in semi-recessed belly installation
97 Intake
98 Mainwheel door
99 Mainwheel drag strut
100 Sidewinder AAM launch-shoe
101 Wing glove stores pylon (cranked)
102 Phoenix AAM
103 Starboard mainwheel
104 Torque links
105 Mainwheel leg
106 Wing skinning
107 Manœuvre-flap actuating linkage
108 Fuel vent and scavenge lines
109 Leading-edge slats
110 Integral wing tank
111 Spoilers
112 Flaps
113 Wingtip formation lights (low intensity)
114 Starboard navigation light

Grumman E-2 Hawkeye

E-2A, B and C Hawkeye and C-2A Greyhound

Origin: Grumman Aerospace, USA.
Type: E-2 series, AEW aircraft; C-2, COD transport.
Engines: Two 4,050ehp Allison T56-8/8A single-shaft turboprops.
Dimensions: Span 80ft 7in (24·56m); length 57ft 7in (17·55m); (C-2A) 56ft 8in; height (E-2) 18ft 4in (5·59m); (C-2) 15ft 11in (4·85m).
Weights: Empty (E-2C) 37,616lb (17,062kg); (C-2A) 31,154lb (14,131 kg); loaded (E-2C) 51,569lb (23,391kg); (C-2A) 54,830lb (24,870kg).
Performance: Maximum speed (E-2C) 374mph (602km/h); (C-2A) 352mph (567km/h); initial climb (C-2A) 2,330ft (710m)/min; service ceiling (both) about 28,500ft (8650m); range (both) about 1,700 miles (2736km).
Armament: None.
History: First flight (W2F-1) 21 October 1960; (production E-2A) 19 April 1961; (E-2B) 20 February 1969; (E-2C) 20 January 1971; (C-2A) 18 November 1964; growth E-2C, possibly late 1977.

Development: Originally designated W2F-1, the E-2A Hawkeye was the first aircraft designed from scratch as an airborne early-warning surveillance platform (all previous AEW machines being modifications of existing types). Equipped with an APS-96 long-range radar with scanner rotating six times per minute inside a 24ft diameter radome, the E-2A has a flight crew of two and three controllers seated aft in the Airborne Tactical Data System (ATDS) compartment, which is constantly linked with the Naval Tactical Data System (NTDS) in Fleet HQ or the appropriate land base. The E-2A can handle an entire air situation and direct all friendly air operations in attacking or defensive missions. From the E-2A were derived the E-2B, with microelectronic computer, and the C-2A Greyhound COD (carrier on-board delivery) transport, able to make catapult takeoffs and arrested landings with 39 passengers or bulky freight. The final version was the dramatically new E-2C, with APS-120 radar and APA-171 aerial system, with OL-93 radar data processor serving a Combat Information Center (CIC) staff with complete knowledge of all airborne targets even in a land-clutter environment. Though it has an advanced and costly airframe, more than three-quarters of the price of an E-2C is accounted for by electronics. This version entered service with squadron VAW-123 at NAS Norfolk, Virginia, in November 1973. In 1977 Grumman is nearing the completion of E-2C manufacture, and with US government help is making a strong sales effort within NATO and in Middle East countries, emphasising the low price (about $13 million in 1975 US dollars). Four aircraft were

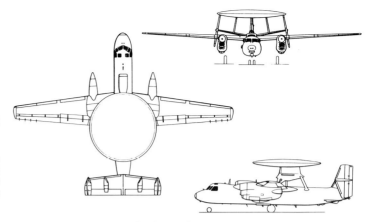

Above: Three-view of E-2C Hawkeye.

Above: A Grumman E-2C of VAW-125, embarked aboard the carrier USS *Constellation*. These early E-2Cs are being updated.

bought by Israel, but the NATO nations appear to prefer the Boeing E-3A. Grumman hope to sell the Growth E-2C with up to 50 per cent greater radar range, increased computer capacity and fuel in the outer wings.

Below: This VAW-125 Hawkeye serves aboard *John F. Kennedy*. The Advanced Radar Processing System (ARPS) is now being installed in all E-2C Hawkeyes.

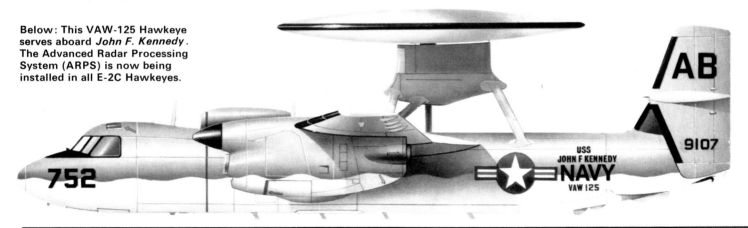

Grumman OV-1 Mohawk

OV-1A to -1D, EV-1, JOV, RV

Origin: Grumman Aerospace, USA.
Type: (OV) multi-sensor tactical observation and reconnaissance; (EV) electronic warfare; (JOV) armed reconnaissance; (RV) electronic reconnaissance;.
Engines: Two 1,005shp Lycoming T53-7 or -15 free-turbine turboprops; (OV-1D) two 1,160shp T53-701.
Dimensions: Span (-1A, -C) 42ft (12·8m); (-1B, -D) 48ft (14·63m); length 41ft (12·5m); (-1D with SLAR, 44ft 11in); height 12ft 8in (3·86m).
Weights: Empty (-1A) 9,937lb (4507kg); (-1B) 11,067lb (5020kg); (-1C) 10,400lb (4717kg); (-1D) 12,054lb (5467kg); maximum loaded (-1A) 15,031lb (6818kg); (-1B, C) 19,230lb (8722kg); (-1D) 18,109lb (8214kg).
Performance: Maximum speed (all) 297–310mph (480–500km/h); initial climb (-1A) 2,950ft (900m)/min; (-1B) 2,250ft (716m)/min; (-1C) 2,670ft (814m)/min; (-1D) 3,618ft (1103m)/min; service ceiling (all) 28,800–31,000ft (8534–9449m); range with external fuel (-1A) 1,410 miles (2270km); (-1B) 1,230 miles (1980km); (-1C) 1,330 miles (2140km); (-1D) 1,011 miles (1627km).
History: First flight (YOV-1A) 14 April 1959; service delivery, February 1961; final delivery December 1970.

Above: Three-view of OV-1D as originally built.

Armament: Not normally fitted, but in South East Asia the 1A, -1B and -1C all operated with a wide variety of air-to-ground weapons including grenade launchers, Minigun pods and small guided missiles.

Development: Representing a unique class of military aircraft, the OV-1 Mohawk is a specially designed battlefield surveillance machine with

Hughes AH-64

Model 77, AH-64 (to be named)

Origin: Hughes Helicopters, Culver City, USA.
Type: Armed tactical helicopter.
Engines: Two 1,536shp General Electric T700 turboshafts.
Dimensions: Diameter of four-blade main rotor 48ft 0in (14·63m); length overall (rotors turning) 55ft 8½in (16·96m); height overall 12ft 1¼in (3·69m).
Weights: Empty 9,500lb (4309kg); maximum loaded 17,400lb (7892kg).
Performance: Maximum speed at 13,200lb (5987kg) 191mph (307 km/h); cruise 180mph (289km/h); max vertical climb 3,200ft (975m)/min; range on internal fuel 359 miles (578km).
Armament: Hughes XM-230 30mm "chain gun" in turret on underside, 76 FFAR rockets, 16 TOW missiles and sight system, forward-looking infra-red and other sensors and range of other options.
History: First flight 30 September 1975; Phase 2 go-ahead November 1976.

Development: First helicopter in history to be adopted after having been planned from the start as a "gunship", the AH-64 was selected over the Bell YAH-63 at the end of 1976 after a tough but instructive competitive fly-off. Unlike the YAH-63 it seats the pilot behind the gunner/co-pilot, and it also has a small four-blade main rotor and tailwheel. Hughes developed the Chain Gun as a radically simpler and cheaper 30mm cannon with chain drive and rotary bolt action. Its turret is designed to fold under the armoured cockpit in a crash landing and the whole helicopter is designed to survive strikes at any point with shells up to 23mm calibre.

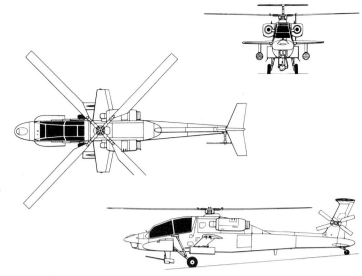

Above: Three-view of YAH-64 (note 60°/120° tail-rotor setting).

Below: Winner of the potentially enormous AAH competition, the first prototype YAH-64 blasts a ground target with folding-fin 2·75in rockets, 76 of which can be carried.

characteristics roughly midway between lightplanes and jet fighters. One of its requirements was to operate from rough forward airstrips and it has exceptional STOL (short takeoff and landing) qualities and good low-speed control with full-span slats and triple fins and rudders. Pilot and observer sit in side-by-side Martin Baker J5 seats and all versions have extremely good all-round view and very comprehensive navigation and communications equipment. All versions carry cameras and upward-firing flares for night photography. Most variants carry UAS-4 infra-red surveillance equipment and the -1B carries APS-94 SLAR (side-looking airborne radar) in a long pod under the right side of the fuselage, with automatic film processing giving, within seconds of exposure, a permanent film record of radar image on either side of the flight path. The -1D combined the functions of the two previous versions in being quickly convertible to either IR or SLAR missions. Underwing pylons can carry 150 US gal drop tanks, ECM (electronic countermeasures) pods, flare/chaff dispensers, or, in the JOV-1A such weapons as FFAR pods, 0·50in gun pods or 500lb (227kg) bombs — though a 1965 Department of Defense rule forbids the US Army to arm its fixed-wing aircraft! The EV-1 is the OV-1B converted to electronic surveillance with an ALQ-133 target locator system in centreline and tip pods. The RV-1C and -1D are conversions of the OV-1C and -1D for permanent use in the electronic reconnaissance role. Total production of the Mohawk was 375.

Right: A US Army OV-1D Mohawk, with the bulky APS-94 side-looking radar in a long pod offset under the right side.

Hughes OH-6 Cayuse and 500M

OH-6 Cayuse, 500M and NH-500M, 369HM, Defender and RACA-500

Origin: Hughes Helicopters, Culver City, USA; (NH) BredaNardi, Ascoli, Italy; (369HM) Kawasaki, Japan; (RACA) RACA, Buenos Aires, Argentina.
Type: Light multi-role helicopter.
Engine: One Allison turboshaft, (OH-6A) T63 5A flat rated at 252·5shp, (500M) 250-C18A flat-rated at 278shp.
Dimensions: Diameter of four-blade main rotor 26ft 4in (8·03m); length overall (rotors turning) 30ft 3¾in (9·24m); height overall 8ft 1½in (2·48m).
Weights: Empty (OH) 1,229lb (557kg), (500M) 1,130lb (512kg); maximum loaded (OH) 2,700lb (1225kg), (500M) 3,000lb (1361kg).
Performance: Max cruise at S/L 150mph (241km/h); typical range on normal fuel 380 miles (611km).
Armament: See text.
History: First flight (OH-6A) 27 February 1963, (500M) early 1968.

Development: Original winner of the controversial LOH (Light Observation Helicopter) competition of the US Army in 1961, the OH-6A Cayuse is one of the most compact flying machines in history, relative to its capability. The standard machine carries two crew and four equipped troops, or up to 1,000lb (454kg) of electronics and weapons including the XM-27 gun or XM-75 grenade launcher plus a wide range of other infantry weapons. The US Army bought 1,434, and several hundred other military or para-military examples have been built by Hughes or its licensees. BredaNardi is helping Pakistan get into production. The Spanish Navy 500Ms carry MAD and two Mk 44 torpedoes. The 500D-M is a more powerful seven-seater. In 1977 an armed model was named Defender, carrying four TOW missiles and sight system; it is to go into production in South Korea.

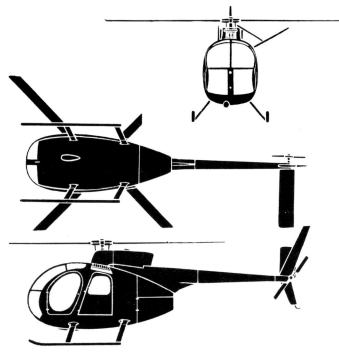

Above: Three-view of OH-6A Cayuse without mission equipment.

Below: Popularly called "The Loach" (from LOH, the original designation), the OH-6A is one of the most nimble helicopters and also exists in special gunship and ultra-quiet versions. Numerous sensors and weapons can be carried.

Kaman SH-2 Seasprite

UH-2, HH-2 and SH-2 in many versions (data for SH-2D)

Origin: Kaman Aerospace Corp, USA.
Type: Ship-based multi-role helicopter (ASW, anti-missile defence, observation, search/rescue and utility).
Engine(s): Original versions, one 1,050 or 1,250hp General Electric T58 free-turbine turboshaft; all current versions, two 1,350hp T58-8F.
Dimensions: Main rotor diameter 44ft (13·41m); overall length (blades turning) 52ft 7in (16m); fuselage length 40ft 6in (12·3m); height 13ft 7in (4·14m).
Weights: Empty 6,953lb (3153kg); maximum loaded 13,300lb (6033kg).
Performance: Maximum speed 168mph (270km/h); maximum rate of climb (not vertical) 2,440ft (744m)/min; service ceiling 22,500ft (6858m); range 422 miles (679m).
Armament: See text.
History: First flight (XHU2K-1) 2 July 1959; service delivery (HU2K-1, later called UH-2A) 18 December 1962; final delivery (new) 1972, (conversion) 1975.

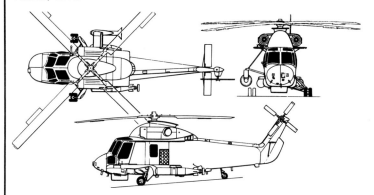

Above: Three-view of Kaman SH-2F Seasprite (gear extended).

Lockheed C-5A Galaxy

C-5A

Origin: Lockheed-Georgia Co, USA.
Type: Strategic transport.
Engines: Four 41,000lb (18,642kg) thrust General Electric TF39-1 two-shaft turbofans.
Dimensions: Span 222ft 8½in (67·88m); length 247ft 10in (75·54m); height 65ft 1½in (19·85m).
Weights: Empty 325,244lb (147,528kg); loaded 769,000lb (348,810kg).
Performance: Maximum speed 571mph (919km/h); initial climb 1,800ft (549m)/min; service ceiling at 615,000lb, 34,000ft (10,360m); range with maximum (220,967lb, 100,228kg) payload 3,749 miles (6033km); ferry range 7,991 miles (12,860km).
Armament: None.
History: First flight 30 June 1968; service delivery 17 December 1969; final delivery May 1973.

Development: On some counts the C-5A is the world's largest aircraft, though it is surpassed in power and weight by late models of B.747. Compared with the civil 747 it has less sweep and is considerably slower, because part of the Military Airlift Command requirement was that it should lift very heavy loads out of rough short airstrips. To this end it has a "high flotation" landing gear with 28 wheels capable of operating at maximum weight from unpaved surfaces. During development extremely difficult aerodynamic and structural problems had to be solved and there were

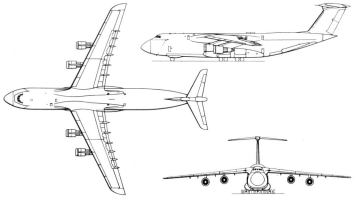

Above: Three-view of C-5A Galaxy as delivered to MAC.

Development: Originally designated HU2K-1 and named Seasprite, this exceptionally neat helicopter was at first powered by a single turbine engine mounted close under the rotor hub and was able to carry a wide range of loads, including nine passengers, in its unobstructed central cabin, with two crew in the nose. The main units of the tailwheel-type landing gear retracted fully. About 190 were delivered and all were later converted to have two T58 engines in nacelles on each side. Some are HH-2C rescue/utility with armour and various armament including chin Minigun turret and waist-mounted machine guns or cannon; others are unarmed HH-2D. One has been used in missile-firing (Sparrow III and Sidewinder) trials in the missile-defence role. All Seasprites have since 1970 been drastically converted to serve in the LAMPS (light airborne multi-purpose system) for anti-submarine and anti-missile defence. The SH-2D has more

Above: One of the world's neatest helicopter platforms, the SH-2F is the only helicopter to meet the US Navy interim LAMPS need for ASW and anti-ship missile defense. Clearly visible are radar, sonobuoys, MAD "bird", homing torpedo and extensive avionics aerials.

than two tons of special equipment including powerful chin radar, sonobuoys, MAD gear, ECM, new navigation and communications systems and Mk 44 and/or Mk 46 torpedoes. All will eventually be brought up to SH-2F standard with improved rotor, higher gross weight and improved sensors and weapons. The same basic design is one of the contenders for the future competition for a purpose-designed LAMPS helicopter of greater size and power.

severe difficulties concerned with fatigue and structure weight. As a result of these problems, combined with inflation, the price escalated and eventually the production had to be cut to a total of 81, equipping four squadrons. The original requirement of carrying 125,000lb for 8,000 miles was not met, but in most respects the final production C-5A is substantially above prediction and an outstanding logistic vehicle which has set an impressive record of capability and reliability. The unobstructed interior has a section 19ft wide and 13ft 6in high, not including the upper deck. Freight is normally carried in containers or, on 36 standard Type 463L pallets; two M-60 battle tanks can be driven on board and there is room for three packaged CH-47 Chinook heavy helicopters. Equipment includes a refuelling boom receptacle in the roof and a Norden multi-mode radar in the nose. In 1977 the trouble with wing fatigue was finally to be solved by a complete rebuild of the wing centre and inner sections. It will cost about $1,000 million to rebuild the 70 aircraft in the active inventory (seven others will not be rebuilt) in the years 1980-84.

Right: Few pictures better emphasize the gigantic size of the C-5A than this air-refuelling from a KC-135, itself no mean aircraft. A C-5A has a normal usable fuel capacity of 49,000 US gallons (41,000 Imp gal), weighing some 320,000lb.

Below: Take-off by a C-5A at Paris Le Bourget makes a normal ambulance and fire tender look inadequate. With a by-pass ratio of 8:1 the Lockheed monster is relatively quiet.

Lockheed C-130 Hercules

C-130 variants, see text (data for C-130H)

Origin: Lockheed-Georgia Co, USA.
Type: Basic aircraft, multi-role transport; for variants see text.
Engines: Four Allison T56 single-shaft turboprops; (C-130A) 3,750ehp T56-1A; (B and E families) 4,050ehp T56-7; (F and H families) 4,910ehp T56-15 or -16 flat-rated at 4,508ehp.
Dimensions: Span 132ft 7in (40·41m); length 97ft 9in (29·78m); (HC-130H and AC-130H and certain others are longer, owing to projecting devices); height 38ft 3in (11·66m).
Weights: Empty 65,621lb (34,300kg); maximum loaded 175,000lb (79,380kg) (YC-130, 108,000lb).
Performance: Maximum speed 384mph (618km/h); initial climb 1,900ft (579m)/min; service ceiling 33,000ft (10,060m); range (maximum payload) 2,487 miles (4,002km); (maximum fuel) 5,135 miles (8,264km).
Armament: Normally none; (AC-130H) one 105mm howitzer, one 40mm cannon, two 20mm cannon or T-171 "Gatlings", two 7·62mm "Gatling" Miniguns; optional grenade dispenser, rockets, missiles, bombs and various night or day sensors and target designators.
History: First flight (YC-130) 23 August 1954; (production C-130A) 7 April 1955; service delivery December 1956.
Development: Though actually conventional and logical and a synthesis of known techniques, the YC-130 appeared radical and bold in 1954. Among its features were a pressurized fuselage with full-section rear doors which could be opened in flight, very neat turboprop engines and rough-field landing gear retracting into bulges outside the pressure hull. Lockheed-Georgia delivered 461 A and more powerful B models, following in 1962 with 503 heavier E series with more internal fuel. The H introduced more powerful engines and gave rise to numerous other sub-types. Special role versions related to the E or H include DC RPV-directors, EC electronics, communications and countermeasures, HC search/rescue, helicopter fueller and spacecraft retrieval, KC assault transport and probe/drogue tanker (the US Marine Corps uses the KC-130R to refuel helicopters), LC wheel/ski and WC weather. One colour profile shows the AC-130H gunship, with formidable armament for night interdiction and equipped with forward-looking infra-red (FLIR), low-light-level TV (LLLTV), laser target designator and other fire control devices. Known and respected all over the world as the "Herky bird", the C-130 has remained in production for more than 23 years and no end to new orders can yet be seen. Constant

Above: A DC-130E RPV director carrying on its left outer pylon a Teledyne Ryan BQM-34B (supersonic Firebee RPV) which in turn is carrying an AGM-65A Maverick TV-guided missile (white).

product-improvement has steadily improved payload, range, fatigue life and reliability and in the mid-1970s the C-130 remained the standard transport and special-equipment platform for a growing list of users. Though the later fan-engined C-141 and C-5A were completed programmes, demand for the C-130 has actually increased as more and more military and civil customers find it meets their needs. Total sales by 1977 were close to 1,600 (including civil L 100 models) and the list of customer air forces speaks for itself. The C-130, in a vast range of sub-types, will have no difficulty meeting tactical airlift needs of most nations (except the United States) until the winner of the AMST competition becomes available — if it survives cutbacks and inflation — in the 1979-80 period.

Right: AC-130H night gunship of interdiction squadrons in South-East Asia, 1970-75.

Lockheed C-141 StarLifter

C-141A and B

Origin: Lockheed-Georgia Co. USA.
Type: Strategic transport.
Engines: Four 21,000lb (9525kg) thrust Pratt & Whitney TF33-7 two-shaft turbofans.
Dimensions: Span 159ft 11in (48·74m); length 145ft (44·2m); (B) 168ft 4in (51·3m); height 39ft 3in (11·96m).
Weights: Empty 133,773lb (60,678kg); loaded 316,600lb (143,600kg).
Performance: Maximum speed 571mph (919km/h); initial climb 3,100ft (945m)/min; service ceiling 41,600ft (12,680m); range with maximum (70,847lb, 32,136kg) payload 4,080 miles (6565km).
Armament: None.
History: First flight 17 December 1963; service delivery October 1964; final delivery July 1968.

Development: Designed to meet a requirement of USAF Military Airlift Command, the StarLifter has since been the most common of MAC's transports and has a very useful combination of range and payload. Compared with civil jet transports in the same weight category it has a less-swept wing and thus lower cruising speed (typically 495mph, 797km/h), but can lift heavier loads out of shorter airstrips. The body cross-section is the same 10ft by 9ft as the C-130, and this has proved the only real shortcoming in prohibiting carriage of many bulky items (though it is said the C-141 can carry "90 per cent of all air-portable items in the Army or Air

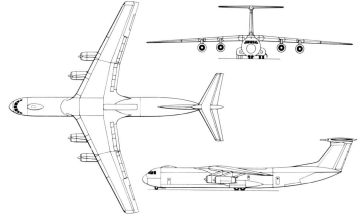

Above: Three-view of YC-141B showing 23ft 4in greater length.

Force"). The largest item normally carried is the packaged Minuteman ICBM, for which purpose several StarLifters have had the cargo floor slightly reinforced to bear the box skids of this 86,207lb load. Alternative loads are 154 troops, 123 paratroops or 80 stretchers (litters) and 16 attendants. A C-141 holds the world record for air-dropping, with a load of 70,195lb. Total production was 285 and these aircraft equip 14 MAC squadrons. During the Vietnam war they bore the main burden of airlifting supplies westwards and casualties eastwards. All are fitted with an all-weather landing system. The user has bitterly regretted not specifying a fatter fuselage, but is funding a major rebuild programme which is adding two "plugs" to extend the fuselage 23ft 4in (7·1m) whilst adding a flight refuelling receptacle and a new wing/body fairing to reduce drag. The first rebuild was flown in March 1977; the FY78 budget includes 70 rebuilds, and eventually 274 aircraft (all in the combat inventory) may be rebuilt as C-141Bs.

Left: Though restricted in cross-section of the cargo hold — which the stretched C-141B rebuild does not alter — vehicles such as the M113 family can easily be accommodated.

Right: Lockheed California Company is the producer of both America's fixed-wing ASW aircraft, the S-3A Viking (foreground) and P-3C Orion. Unlike the Viking, the Orion is still in new-build production, and has also succeeded in selling to nearly all America's allies who need such aircraft and do not produce their own. The equipment under the Orion may be an FLIR pod.

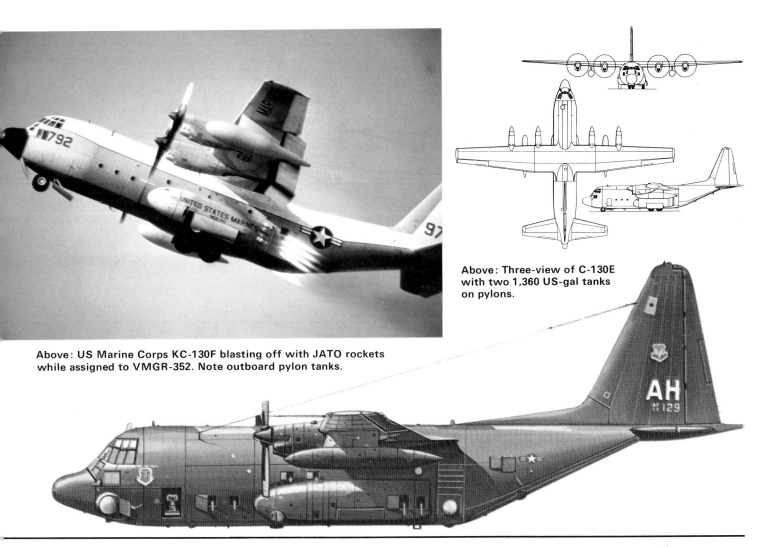

Above: Three-view of C-130E with two 1,360 US-gal tanks on pylons.

Above: US Marine Corps KC-130F blasting off with JATO rockets while assigned to VMGR-352. Note outboard pylon tanks.

Lockheed P-3 Orion

P-3A, -3B and -3C with derivatives

Origin: Lockheed-California Co. USA.
Type: Maritime reconnaissance and anti-submarine, normally with flight crew of five and tactical crew of five; variants, see text.
Engines: Four Allison T56 single-shaft turboprops; (P-3A) T56-10W, 4,500ehp with water injection; (remainder) T56-14, 4,910ehp.
Dimensions: Span 99ft 8in (30·37m); length 116ft 10in (35·61m); height 33ft 8½in (10·29m).
Weights: Empty (typical B, C) 61,491lb (27,890kg); maximum loaded 142,000lb (64,410kg).
Performance: Maximum speed 473mph (761km/h); initial climb 1,950ft (594m)/min; service ceiling 28,300ft (8625m); range 4,800 miles (7725km).
Armament: Very varied load in bulged unpressurized weapon bay ahead of wing and on ten wing pylons; maximum internal load 7,252lb (3290kg) can include two depth bombs, four Mk 44 torpedoes, 87 sonobuoys and many other sensing and marking devices; underwing load can include six 2,000lb (907kg) mines or various mixes of torpedoes, bombs, rockets or missiles. Maximum expendable load 20,000lb (9071kg).
History: First flight (aerodynamic prototype) 19 August 1958; (YP-3A) 25 November 1959; (production P-3A) 15 April 1961; (P-3C) 18 September 1968.

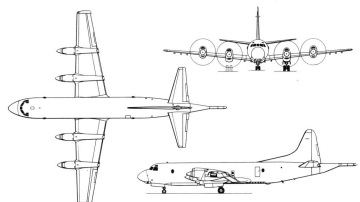

Above: Three-view of Lockheed P-3C Orion.

Development: In August 1957 the US Navy issued a requirement for an "off the shelf" anti-submarine patrol aircraft derived from an established type, and this was met in April 1958 by Lockheed's proposal for a conversion of the Electra turboprop airliner. The third Electra was quickly modified as an aerodynamic prototype and deliveries of production P-3As began in August 1962. From the 110th aircraft the Deltic system was fitted with more sensitive sensors and improved displays. Four early A models were converted as WP-3A weather reconnaissance aircraft, while others became EP-3A flying special electronic missions. Three As were supplied ex-USN to Spain. The B model introduced more powerful engines without water/alcohol injection and many were sold to Australia, New Zealand and Norway or modified, as EP-3B electronic reconnaissance and countermeasures, with huge "canoe radars" above and below and a radome under the forward fuselage. The completely different P-3C packages into the same airframe a new and more modern tactical system with sensors and weapons controlled by a digital computer. Derivatives include the P-3F for Iran and a variant for Australia. Other versions include the RP-3D for mapping the Earth's magnetic field and special reconnaissance and transport conversions. Production in 1977 was centred upon the P-3C Update, with computer memory increased from 65,000 to 458,000 words, a new computer language, receiver for the global Omega navigation system, increased acoustic-sensor capability, tactical displays for two of the sensor stations, and other improvements. Canada is buying yet another new version, the CP-140 Aurora, with the ASW systems of the S-3A Viking. Deliveries exceed 450, and output is being increased to deliver to the US Navy 12 in 1977, rising to 16 in 1980 and 24 in 1981.

Lockheed S-3A Viking

S-3A Viking, US-3A

Origin: Lockheed-California Co, USA.
Type: (S-3A) four-seat carrier-based anti-submarine aircraft; (US-3A) carrier on-board delivery transport.
Engines: Two 9,275lb (4207kg) General Electric TF34-2 or TF34–400 two-shaft turbofans.
Dimensions: Span 68ft 8in (20·93m); length 53ft 4in (16·26m); height 22ft 9in (6·93m).
Weights: Empty 26,600lb (12,065kg); normal loaded for carrier operation 42,500lb (19,277kg); maximum loaded 47,000lb (21,319kg).
Performance: Maximum speed 506mph (814km/h); initial climb, over 4,200ft (1280m)/min; service ceiling, above 35,000ft (10,670m); combat range, more than 2,303 miles (3705km); ferry range, more than 3,454 miles (5558km).
Armament: Split internal weapon bays can house four Mk 46 torpedoes, four Mk 82 bombs, four various depth bombs or four mines; two wing pylons can carry single or triple ejectors for bombs, rocket pods, missiles, tanks or other stores.
History: First flight 21 January 1972; service delivery October 1973; operational use (VS-41) 20 February 1974; final delivery after 1980.

Development: Designed to replace the evergreen Grumman S-2, the S-3 is perhaps the most remarkable exercise in packaging in the history of aviation. It is also an example of an aircraft in which the operational equipment costs considerably more than the aircraft itself. Lockheed-California won the Navy competition in partnership with LTV (Vought) which makes the wing, engine pods, tail and F-8 type landing gear. To increase transit speed the refuelling probe, MAD tail boom, FLIR (forward-looking infra-red) and certain other sensors all retract, while the extremely modern specially designed APS-116 radar is within the nose. Equipment includes CAINS (carrier aircraft inertial navigation system), comprehensive sonobuoy dispensing and control systems, doppler, very extensive radio navaid and altitude systems, radar warning and ECM systems, extensive communications, and a Univac

digital processor to manage all tactical and navigation information. By the end of 1975 more than 100 of the first buy of 186 Vikings were in service and foreign orders (beginning with Federal Germany) were being discussed. Procurement of the Navy force of 184 (plus two prototypes) was completed in FY77, but additional production is still a receding possibility in 1978. The first US-3A COD transport flew in July 1976. It carries a crew of two and six passengers plus 4,600lb (2087kg) cargo, of which 2,000lb can be accommodated in large underwing pods; the all-cargo payload is 7,500lb (3402kg), but production is unlikely.

Key to cutaway drawing

1. Radome
2. Texas Instruments AN/APS-116 radar scanner
3. Radome hinge line
4. Forward pressure bulkhead
5. Nosewheel well
6. Landing and taxi light
7. Launch bar
8. Nosewheel shock absorber
9. Twin nosewheels
10. Approach lights
11. Nosewheel doors
12. Nosewheel retraction mechanism
13. Forward (port) avionics bay
14. Rudder pedals
15. Control column
16. Instrument panel shroud
17. Windscreen wipers
18. Central console
19. Curved windscreen panels
20. Eyebrow instrument panel
21. Anti-glare roof panels
22. Centre section control housing
23. Co-pilot's side console
24. Co-pilot's seat (Douglas Escapac IE-1 all four seats)
25. Pilot's seat
26. Ryan Doppler ground velocity system
27. Texas Instruments forward-looking infra-red (FLIR) scanner stowage
28. Infra-red scanner (extended)
29. Hot-air exhaust panel (Williams Research APU)
30. Electronics compartment
31. Hartman Systems integrated control system (INCOS) tray sensor
32. Observation window
33. Sensor operator's seat
34. Tactical co-ordinator (TACCO) seat
35. In-flight refuelling probe (stowed)
36. UHF L-Band communications, IFF antenna
37. Preamp VHF antenna
38. Starboard engine pylon
39. Starboard stores pylon
40. Wing hinge line
41. Leading-edge flap actuator
42. Leading-edge flap
43. Electronic support measures (ESM) antennas
44. Wingtip ESM pod (IBM AN/ALR-47 system)
45. Wing skinning
46. Starboard aileron
47. Trailing edge flaps outer section
48. Aileron control system
49. Spoilers/speed brakes
50. Wing fold hydraulic actuator
51. Wing integral fuel system (shaded area)
52. In-flight refuelling point
53. LF-ADF antenna
54. Spoiler servos
55. Roll trim actuator
56. Aileron servo
57. Aft pressure bulkhead
58. Univac 1832 general-purpose digital computer
59. Mission avionics starboard console
60. Centre aisle
61. Starboard keelson
62. Attack stores port bay
63. Bomb bay door
64. Engine intake
65. Engine pylon
66. General Electric TF34-GE-400A turbofan
67. Mainwheel leg
68. Port mainwheel
69. Port external stores pylon
70. Aero 1D auxiliary fuel tank, 300-US gal (1136 l)
71. Leading-edge flaps
72. Wing spar
73. Spoiler actuators
74. Aileron actuator
75. Electronic support measures (ESM) system antennas
76. Port navigation light
77. Wingtip ESM pod
78. Port aileron
79. Aileron tab
80. Flap tracks
81. Trailing-edge flaps (extended)
82. Spoilers/speed brakes
83. Arresting hook
84. Wing hinge point
85. Mainwheel well
86. Sonobuoy chutes
87. Avionics cooling plant
88. UHF L-Band (Collins), TACAN (Hoffman) antenna
89. AiResearch environmental control system (ECS)
90. HF (Collins) antenna coupler
91. ECS intake
92. ECS intake trunking
93. Fuselage/empennage joint
94. Aft (port) avionics bay
95. MAD (Texas Instruments AN/ASQ-81) boom (stowed)
96. Elevator servo
97. Tailplane carry-through
98. ECS outlet
99. Fuel dump line
100. Fuel vent line
101. Heated leading-edge
102. Tailplane construction
103. Elevator mass balance
104. Static discharger
105. Port elevator
106. Elevator tab
107. MAD boom (extended)
108. Fin (hinged for stowage)
109. Rear navigation light
110. Pitch trim actuator
111. Rudder trim actuator
112. Fin hinge line
113. Starboard elevator
114. Fin-fold hydraulic actuator
115. Rudder servo
116. Rudder structure
117. Rudder tab
118. Rudder hinge
119. Sonobuoy ref and RCVR antenna
120. Rudder upper hinge
121. Static dischargers
122. Anti-collision beacon

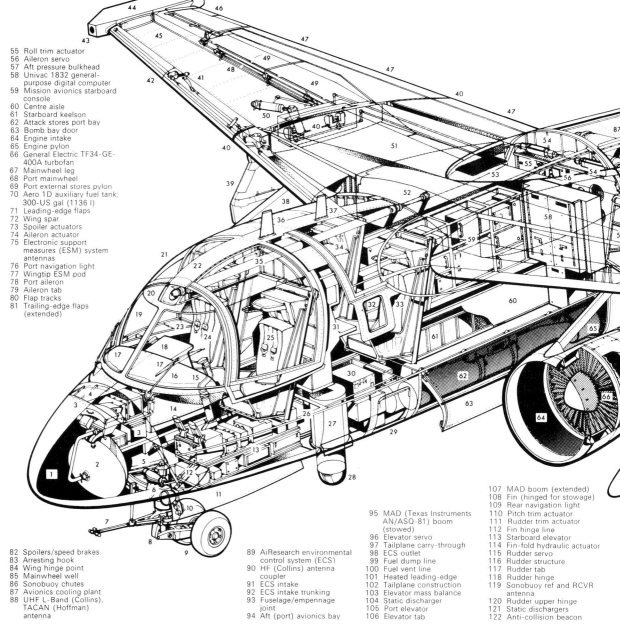

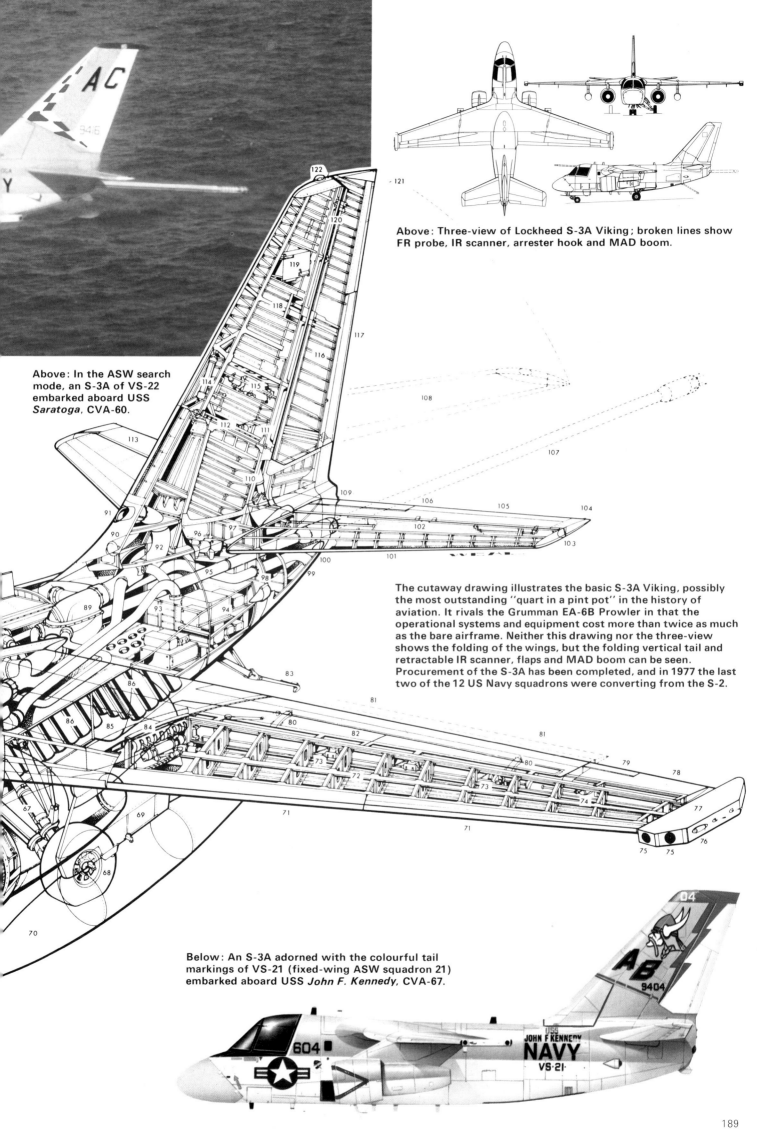

Above: Three-view of Lockheed S-3A Viking; broken lines show FR probe, IR scanner, arrester hook and MAD boom.

Above: In the ASW search mode, an S-3A of VS-22 embarked aboard USS *Saratoga*, CVA-60.

The cutaway drawing illustrates the basic S-3A Viking, possibly the most outstanding ''quart in a pint pot'' in the history of aviation. It rivals the Grumman EA-6B Prowler in that the operational systems and equipment cost more than twice as much as the bare airframe. Neither this drawing nor the three-view shows the folding of the wings, but the folding vertical tail and retractable IR scanner, flaps and MAD boom can be seen. Procurement of the S-3A has been completed, and in 1977 the last two of the 12 US Navy squadrons were converting from the S-2.

Below: An S-3A adorned with the colourful tail markings of VS-21 (fixed-wing ASW squadron 21) embarked aboard USS *John F. Kennedy*, CVA-67.

Lockheed SR-71

A-11, YF-12A and C, SR-71A, B and C
(data for SR-71A)

Origin: Lockheed-California Co, USA.
Type: YF-12, research interceptor; SR-71, strategic reconnaissance.
Engines: Two 32,500lb (14,740kg) thrust Pratt & Whitney J58 (JT11D-20B) single-shaft by-pass turbojets with afterburner.
Dimensions: Span 55ft 7in (16·95m); length 107ft 5in (32·74m); height 18ft 6in (5·64m).
Weights: Empty (typical) 60,000lb (27,215kg); loaded 170,000lb (77,110kg).
Performance: Maximum speed, in excess of 2,000mph (3220km/h, Mach 3); service ceiling, higher than 80,000ft (24,400m); range at Mach 3 at 78,740ft (24,000m), 2,982 miles (4800km). Performance limit, about 2,200mph and altitude of 86,000ft sustained.
Armament: SR-71 series, none; YF-12, see text.
History: First flight 26 April 1962; (production SR-71A) 22 December 1964; final delivery, about 1968.

Development: Despite their great size and intense noise these amazing aircraft were designed, built, test flown and put into use without a word leaking out into public until disclosed by President Johnson in February 1964. The A-11 was originally designed as a follow-on to the U-2, capable of flying even higher and many times faster in penetrating hostile airspace on clandestine overflights. Early in their career the three A-11s, with serial numbers 60-6934 to 6936, did overfly Communist territories in several parts of the world. Later they were completed as YF-12A research aircraft in the Improved Manned Interceptor programme, carrying Hughes ASG-18 pulse-doppler radar, infra-red sensors and eight Hughes AIM-47A large long-range air-to-air missiles in an internal bay. Made largely of a specially developed alloy of titanium, the YF-12A was the most advanced aircraft of its day and the only one to sustain a speed of Mach 3. One set a world speed record at 2,070mph on 1 May 1965, and another beat this at 2,189mph (3522km/h) in July 1976, in which month a 1,000km circuit was flown at 2,086mph (3356km/h) and an altitude of 86,000ft (26,212m) sustained. Surviving YF-12A variants have been stripped of weapon systems and used in supersonic transport research, flown by NASA. The SR-71 strategic

Above: Head-on view of SR-71A showing the unique broad chined body, whose lift and response to yaw are vital to safe flight.
Below: Standard SR-71A serving with the 9th SRW.

reconnaissance aircraft is longer and heavier, with a fuel capacity of over 80,000lb. Known as "Blackbirds" (though officially their external areas are painted indigo blue), they equip the 9th Strategic Reconnaissance Wing, from which detachments have operated over Vietnam, the Middle East and many other trouble-spots. Total production is at least 30, including SR-71B and C dual trainer versions. In September 1974 a standard A model set a transatlantic record at almost Mach 3 with a time from passing New York to passing London of 1hr 55min. Most SR-71s in the active inventory (some are stored) use special JP-7 high-temperature fuel, air-refuelled by specially equipped KC-135Q tankers.

Lockheed U-2

U-2A, C, D, R and CT, TR-1, WU-2
and HASP U-2

Origin: Lockheed-California Co, USA.
Type: High-altitude photo reconnaissance, multi-sensor reconnaissance and special reconnaissance; (CT) dual trainer; (TR) multi-sensor reconnaissance; (WU) weather research; (HASP) high-altitude sampling programme.
Engine: (U-2A) one 11,200lb (5080kg) Pratt & Whitney J57-13A or -37A two-shaft turbojet; (all other models) one 17,000lb (7711kg) Pratt & Whitney J75-13 two-shaft turbojet.
Dimensions: Span (except R) 80ft (24·38m), (U-2R) 103ft (31·39m); length (except R) 49ft 7in (15·1m), (U-2R) 63ft (19·2m); height (except R) 13ft (3·96m), (U-2R) 16ft (4·88m).

Above: Basic U-2B in non-reflective black but with USAF insignia, photographed in 1968 over Edwards AFB.

Below: Tandem-seat U-2D engaged in research projects at the Air Force Flight Test Center (6512th Test Squadron).

Weights: Empty (A) 9,920lb (4500kg), (others, except R) typically 11,700lb (5305kg), (U-2R) 14,990lb (6800kg); loaded (A) 14,800lb (6713kg), (others, except R, clean) 15,850lb (7190kg), (with two 89-gal wing tanks) 17,270lb (7833kg); maximum over 21,000lb (9526kg), (R) 29,000lb (13,154kg).
Performance: Maximum speed (A) 494mph (795km/h); (others) 528mph (850km/h); service ceiling (A) 70,000ft (21,340m); (others) 85,000ft (25,910m); maximum range (A) 2,600 miles (4185km); (others) 4,000 miles (6437km).
Armament: None.
History: First flight 1 August 1955; service delivery, early 1956; final delivery of new aircraft, July 1958.

Development: No aircraft in history has a record resembling the U-2. It was in operational use from Lakenheath (England) and Wiesbaden (Germany) in 1956, attracting the attention of spotters and amateur photographers who commented on its graceful glider-like appearance and on the odd fact that at take-off it jettisoned the small outrigger wheels under the outer wings, returning to land on small centreline wheels and the down-turned wingtips. When interest had reached fever-pitch the government blandly announced that the U-2, as it was called (a Utility designation) was used by the NACA (the National Advisory Committee for Aeronautics) for atmospheric research at heights up to 55,000ft. When one force-landed in Japan the public were frantically kept away at gun-point and it was clear the incident was regarded as serious. In fact the U-2 had been designed for clandestine reconnaissance over the territory of any nation. Aircraft were delivered to Watertown Strip, a remote airfield in Nevada, where CIA pilots converted and prepared for operational missions over Communist territory. Their aircraft bore no markings and operated — immune to interception, and often undetected — at far above the announced 55,000ft. Other U-2s were assigned to the 4080th Strategic Wing and carried USAF markings. Most were of the more powerful U-2B type with much greater height and range. On 1 May 1960 a U-2B flown by a CIA pilot took off from Peshawar (Pakistan) to fly across the Soviet Union to Bodø (Norway), but was shot down over Sverdlovsk, presenting the Russians with unprecedented material for a diplomatic incident. Later U-2s were shot down over China and Cuba, and the survivors were assigned to lawful missions involving many kinds of surveillance and sampling. The C and two-seat D make up the bulk of the fleet used today, numbering about 40 out of the 55 built. All have been extensively rebuilt, none more so than the enlarged U-2R special-reconnaissance platform which carries four times the 3,000lb (1361kg) payload of other models. The D was the original tandem-seat version, needing a second crew-member; the U-2CT dual trainer is a complete rebuild with instructor pilot seated high up behind the pupil (the U-2 needs extreme pilot skill near and on the ground); the C has a long dorsal "doghouse" housing avionics and equipment. The production line is to be reopened to deliver 25 TR-1 reconnaissance versions, with SLAR radar, by 1984 at a cost of $551·5 million.

McDonnell Douglas A-4 Skyhawk

A-4A to A-4S and TA-4 series

Origin: Douglas Aircraft Co, El Segundo (now division of McDonnell Douglas, Long Beach), USA.

Type: Single-seat attack bomber; TA, dual-control trainer.

Engine: (B, C, L, P, Q, S) one 7,700lb (3493kg) thrust Wright J65-16A single-shaft turbojet (US Sapphire); (E, J) 8,500lb (3856kg) Pratt & Whitney J52-6 two-shaft turbojet; (F, G, H, K) 9,300lb (4218kg) J52-8A; (M, N) 11,200lb (5080kg) J52-408A.

Dimensions: Span 27ft 6in (8·38m); length (A) 39ft 1in; (B) 39ft 6in (42ft 10¾in over FR probe); (E, F, G, H, K, L, P, Q, S) 40ft 1½in (12·22m); (M, N) 40ft 3¼in (12·27m); (TA series, excluding probe) 42ft 7¼in (12·98m); height 15ft (4·57m); (early single-seaters 15ft 2in, TA series 15ft 3in).

Weights: Empty (A) 7,700lb; (E) 9,284lb; (typical modern single-seat, eg M) 10,465lb (4747kg); (TA-4F) 10,602 (4809kg); maximum loaded (A) 17,000lb; (B) 22,000lb; (all others, shipboard) 24,500lb (11,113kg); (land-based) 27,420lb (12,437kg).

Performance: Maximum speed (clean) (B) 676mph; (E) 685mph; (M) 670mph (1078km/h); (TA-4F) 675mph; maximum speed (4,000lb, 1814kg bomb load) (F) 593mph; (M) 645mph; initial climb (F) 5,620ft (1713m)/min; (M) 8,440ft (2572m)/min; service ceiling (all, clean) about 49,000ft (14,935m); range (clean, or with 4,000lb weapons and max fuel, all late versions) about 920 miles (1480km); maximum range (M) 2,055 miles (3307km).

Armament: Standard on most versions, two 20mm Mk 12 cannon, each with 200 rounds; (H, N, and optional on other export versions) two 30mm DEFA 553, each with 150 rounds. Pylons under fuselage and wings for total ordnance load of (A, B, C) 5,000lb (2268kg); (E, F, G, H, K, L, P, Q, S) 8,200lb (3720kg); (M, N) 9,155lb (4153kg).

History: First flight (XA4D-1) 22 June 1954; (A-4A) 14 August 1954; squadron delivery October 1956; (A-4C) August 1959; (A-4E) July 1961; (A-4F) August 1966; (A-4M) April 1970; (A-4N) June 1972; first of TA series (TA-4E) June 1965.

Development: Most expert opinion in the US Navy refused to believe the claim of Ed Heinemann, chief engineer of what was then Douglas El Segundo, that he could build a jet attack bomber weighing half the 30,000lb

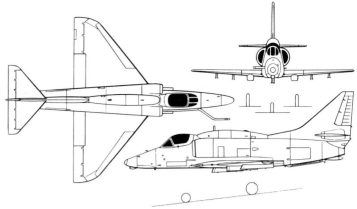

Above: Three-view of McDonnell Douglas A-4M Skyhawk II.

specified by the Navy. The first Skyhawk, nicknamed "Heinemann's Hot Rod", not only flew but gained a world record by flying a 500km circuit at over 695mph. Today, more than 23 years later, greatly developed versions are still in production, setting an unrivalled record for sustained manufacture. These late versions do weigh close to 30,000lb, but only because the basic design has been improved with more powerful engines, increased fuel capacity and much heavier weapon load. The wing was made in a single unit, forming an integral fuel tank and so small it did not need to fold. Hundreds of Skyhawks have served aboard carriers, but in the US involvement in SE Asia "The Scooter" (as it was affectionately known) flew many kinds of mission from land bases. In early versions the emphasis was on improving range and load and the addition of all-weather avionics. The F model introduced the dorsal hump containing additional avionics, and the M, the so-called Skyhawk II, marked a major increase in mission effectiveness. Most of the TA-4 trainers closely resembled the corresponding single-seater, but the TA-4J and certain other models have simplified avionics and the TA-4S (Singapore) is a rebuild by Lockheed Aircraft Service with two separate humped cockpits and an integral-tank fuselage. Production of the M for the US Marine Corps may continue until the AV-8B becomes available in 1983-84, 30 years after first flight. Deliveries in 1977 neared 3,000.

Below: A "Camel" (hump-backed A-4) of Navy attack squadron VA-55, firing a Shrike anti-radar missile. Despite its miniature proportions the A-4 can launch any Navy air weapon.

British Aerospace AV-8A Harrier and McDonnell Douglas AV-8B

AV-8A and TAV-8A

Origin: British Aerospace, Kingston, UK.
Type: Single-seat tactical attack; (TAV) dual trainer or special missions.
Engine: Same as AV-8B.
Dimensions: Span 25ft 3in (7·7m); length 45ft 6in (13·87m), (TAV) 55ft 9½in (17m); height 11ft 3in (3·4m), (TAV) 13ft 8in (4·2m).
Armament: Two 30mm Aden cannon in belly pods; four pylons with combined load up to 5,300lb (2400kg), plus two Sidewinder AAM.

Development: Adopted in 1969 by the US Marine Corps for use in beach assault and air-defense roles, the AV-8A is a simplified and Americanized version of the RAF Harrier GR.3. The vectored-thrust engine confers V/STOL capability for use from ship pads and small clearings ashore. The 112 delivered were supplemented by eight TAV-8A trainers, the main bases being Beaufort and Cherry Point.

AV-8B and proposed variants

Origin: McDonnell Douglas Corporation (MCAIR, St Louis), USA; principal associate, British Aerospace (Hawker Aircraft, Kingston), UK.
Type: V/STOL light attack; proposed versions include sea-based air defence, reconnaissance and dual trainer/multi-role.
Engine: One Rolls-Royce Pegasus 103 (Pratt & Whitney F402) vectored-thrust turbofan rated at 21,500lb (9752kg).
Dimensions: Span 30ft 3½in (9·20m); length 42ft 11in (13·1m); height 11ft 3½in (3·4m).
Weights: Empty 12,400lb (5625kg); design, 22,750lb (10,320kg); loaded (close-support seven Mk 82 bombs) 25,994lb (11,790kg); maximum over 29,000lb (13,150kg).
Performance: Maximum speed, clean, over Mach 1; operational radius (VTO, 7,800lb/3538kg weapons) 115 miles (185km), (STO, 12 Mk 82 Snakeye, internal fuel) 172 miles (278km), (STO, seven Mk 82, external fuel) 748 miles (1204km); ferry range over 3,000 miles (4830km).
Armament: Two 20mm Mk 12 cannon in single belly pods, six underwing pylons and centreline hardpoint for weapon/ECM/fuel load of 8,000lb (3630kg) for VTO or 9,000lb (4080kg) for STO.

Right: The first full-scale engineering model of the AV-8B is seen here in the 40ft×80ft wind tunnel at the NASA Ames Research Center. Though started at the same time as the F-18 Hornet, the latter has threatened to take money and manpower away from the AV-8B program, and in the FY79 and FY80 budgets the DoD has tried to kill the "foreign" import.

Below: An AV-8A flying with VMA-513 at Beaufort, SC.

McDonnell Douglas KC-10A

KC-10A (ATCA)

Origin: Douglas Aircraft Company, division of McDonnell Douglas Corporation, Long Beach, USA.
Type: Advanced tanker/cargo aircraft.
Engines: Two General Electric F103 (CF6-50C1) turbofans each rated at 52,500lb (23,815kg).
Dimensions: Span 165ft 4in (50·42m); length overall 182ft 3in (55·55m); height 58ft 1in (17·7m).
Weights: Empty, equipped (tanker) 239,747lb (108,749kg), (cargo) 243,973lb (110,666kg); maximum loaded 590,000lb (267,624kg).
Performance: Maximum permissible speed over 600mph (965km/h); critical field length 11,000ft (3353m); maximum still-air range (no reserves) with maximum payload of 170,027lb (77,124kg) 4,373 miles (7037km).
Armament: None.
History: First flight of commercial DC-10 29 August 1970; start of engineering work on ATCA 1971; selection of KC-10A December 1977; first flight of KC-10A and delivery programme not disclosed.

Development: The reason for this potentially large and costly programme is two-fold: to back up the ageing and in some ways unsatisfactory KC-135 force, and to augment the US global airlift posture dramatically despite the small number of new aircraft involved. Shortcomings in the KC-135 force had been obvious even during the early 1960s, and today these include limited aircraft range and payload, dependence on fuel supplies in overseas theatres, inability to "flush" (start engines and takeoff) in the brief time between warning and a nuclear attack on USAF airfields, and technical problems (mainly structural) with the KC-135 airframe. Throughout the early 1970s the Air Force studied and eventually defined a requirement for an ATCA (Advanced Tanker/Cargo Aircraft), with the following missions: refuelling combat aircraft on overseas deployment and simultaneously carrying their support equipment and personnel; refuelling strategic airlifters during overseas deployment and resupply missions; and augmenting the national defence cargo-carrying capability. Four aircraft were submitted, based on the 747, C-5A, TriStar and DC-10, and in December 1977 the Douglas submission based on the DC-10-30 was selected. Though commonality with the DC-10-30 is about 88 per cent there are many changes. The KC-10A has seven unpressurized fuel cells under the floor, four of them aft of the wing. At the tail is a completely new ARB (Aerial Refueling Boom) being developed by Douglas under separate contract, with digital fly-by-wire controls and a multitude of advanced features. Ahead of the ARB is a hose reel for refuelling Navy and other probe-equipped aircraft. Above the forward fuselage the KC-10A has a boom receptacle so that it can itself be flight-refuelled. The commercial airliner's passenger windows and lower-deck cargo doors are eliminated, but the upper deck has a large cargo door, improved cargo handling system and, ahead of the cargo area, seats for up to 80 crew and support personnel (normal flight crew is five). Gross weight is higher than for the DC-10, and another feature is military avionics including provision for near-blind landings. The initial 1978 contract for $28 million covers production engineering and tooling; numbers of KC-10As depends on funding in future years but the Air Force plans to buy about 20.

Right: A McDonnell Douglas drawing showing salient features of the KC-10A. Though based on the commercial DC-10-30 this aircraft will involve extensive additional engineering effort.

History: First flight (YAV-8B) late 1978; preliminary evaluation mid-1979; initial operational capability fourth quarter 1982.

Development: Following proposals in 1973 by Hawker Siddeley and McDonnell Douglas for an advanced development of the Harrier the then UK Defence Minister, Roy Mason, said there was "not enough common ground" for a joint programme. This caused a delay of many months, but the US government eventually studied an improved aircraft designated AV-16A with a new wing and the uprated Pegasus 15 engine, before deciding to try to achieve as much as possible of the same advantages in payload/range and weapon load with the existing engine. Rolls-Royce and Pratt & Whitney have studied the Pegasus 11D (800lb extra thrust) and 11+ (1,000lb more) but these remained mere proposals as this book went to press, despite the fact Rolls-Royce ran a Pegasus at over 25,000lb thrust in May 1972. Under the present programme all changes are confined to the airframe, the main improvement being a completely new wing, with greater span and area, less sweep, a supercritical section and graphite-epoxy construction throughout the main wing box and large single-slotted flaps and drooping ailerons. Strakes and a large hinged belly flap will increase air pressure under the fuselage in VTO, while other changes include inlets matched to the engine (they are too small on previous production Harriers) and front nozzles cut off square with the efflux.

Overall improvement in payload/range, compared with an AV-8A, is about 100 per cent. There is still a chance that further gains may result from improvement to the F402 engine, and production AV-8Bs may have the raised cockpit of the British Sea Harrier. The US Marine Corps requirement is for 336, and a variant might possibly be purchased by the US Navy for its own use. Present plans envisage the AV-8B having the Angle-Rate Bombing System, with dual-mode TV and laser spot coupled via IBM computer to the Marconi-Elliott HUD. Fixed or retractable probe refuelling is likely, but radar will not be fitted. McDonnell Douglas at St Louis has rebuilt two AV-8As as YAV-8Bs, the first beginning a very successful flight-test programme on 9 November 1978. But for political reasons the AV-8B has had an uphill fight for survival, and it was erased from the 1980 Defense Budget.

Above: This YAV-8B is an AV-8A rebuilt by McDonnell Douglas at St Louis and photographed during outdoor testing at Ames Research Center. New features include the wing, belly flap and strakes, and modified engine nozzles.

Below: A pair of AV-8As from VMA-231 at Cherry Point, NC. This aircraft lacks the inertial system and laser ranger of the RAF Harrier.

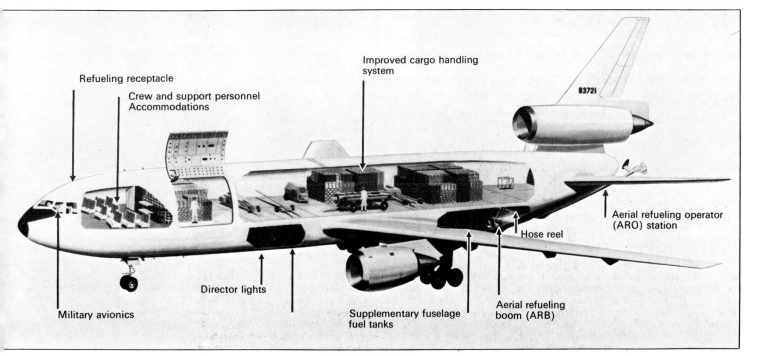

Refueling receptacle

Crew and support personnel Accommodations

Improved cargo handling system

83721

Aerial refueling operator (ARO) station

Hose reel

Aerial refueling boom (ARB)

Military avionics

Director lights

Supplementary fuselage fuel tanks

McDonnell Douglas F-4
Phantom II

F-4A to F-4S, RF-4, QF-4, EF-4

Origin: McDonnell Aircraft, division of McDonnell Douglas Corp, St Louis, USA; licence production by Mitsubishi, Japan (F-4EJ) and substantial subcontracting by W German industry.

Type: Originally carrier-based all-weather interceptor; now all-weather multi-role fighter for ship or land operation; (RF) all-weather multisensor reconnaissance; (QF) RPV; (EF) defence-suppression aircraft.

Engines: (B, G) two 17,000lb (7711kg) thrust General Electric J79-8 single-shaft turbojets with afterburner; (C, D) 17,000lb J79-15; (E, EJ, F) 17,900lb (8120kg) J79-17; (J, N, S) 17,900lb J79-10; (K, M) 20,515lb (9305kg) Rolls-Royce Spey 202/203 two-shaft augmented turbofans.

Dimensions: Span 38ft 5in (11·7m); length (B, C, D, G, J, N, S) 58ft 3in (17·76m); (E, EJ, F and all RF versions) 62ft 11in or 63ft (19·2m); (K, M) 57ft 7in (17·55m); height (all) 16ft 3in (4·96m).

Weights: Empty (B, C, D, G, J, N) 28,000lb (12,700kg); (E, EJ, F and RF) 29,000lb (13,150kg); (K, M) 31,000lb (14,060kg); maximum loaded (B) 54,600lb; (C, D, G, J, K, M, N, RF) 58,000lb (26,308kg); (E, EJ, F) 60,630lb (27,502kg).

Performance: Maximum speed with Sparrow missiles only (low) 910mph (1464km/h, Mach 1·19) with J79 engines, 920mph with Spey, (high) 1,500mph (2414km/h, Mach 2·27) with J79 engines, 1,386mph with Spey; initial climb, typically 28,000ft (8534m)/min with J79 engines, 32,000ft/min with Spey; service ceiling, over 60,000ft (19,685m) with J79 engines, 60,000ft with Spey; range on internal fuel (no weapons) about 1,750 miles (2817km); ferry range with external fuel, typically 2,300 miles (3700km) (E and variants, 2,600 miles (4184km).

Armament: (All versions except EF, RF, QF which have no armament) four AIM-7 Sparrow air-to-air missiles recessed under fuselage; inner wing pylons can carry two more AIM-7 or four AIM-9 Sidewinder missiles; in addition all E versions except RF have internal 20mm M-61 multi-barrel gun, and virtually all versions can carry the same gun in external centreline

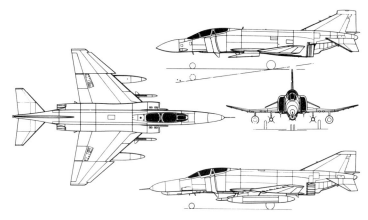

Above: Three view of standard F-4E with tanks and six Sparrows, with side view (top) of ECM-equipped FGR.2 of RAF.

pod; all except RF, QF have centreline and four wing pylons for tanks, bombs or other stores to total weight of 16,000lb (7257kg).

History: First flight (XF4H-1) 27 May 1958; service delivery (F-4A) February 1960 (carrier trials), February 1961 (inventory); first flight (Air Force F-4C) 27 May 1963; (YF-4K) 27 June 1966; (F-4E) 30 June 1967; (EF-4E) 1976.

Development: McDonnell designed the greatest fighter of the postwar era as a company venture to meet anticipated future needs. Planned as an attack aircraft with four 20mm guns, it was changed into a very advanced gunless all-weather interceptor with advanced radar and missile armament. In this form it entered service as the F-4A, soon followed by the F-4B used in large numbers (635) by the US Navy and Marine Corps, with Westinghouse APQ-72 radar, IR detector in a small fairing under the nose, and many weapon options. Pilot and radar intercept officer sit in tandem and the aircraft has blown flaps and extremely comprehensive combat equipment. A level Mach number of 2·6 was achieved and many world records were set

McDonnell Douglas
F-101 Voodoo

F-101A, B and C and RF-101A to H

Origin: McDonnell Aircraft Co (division of McDonnell Douglas Corp), USA.

Type: (A, C) day fighter-bomber; (B) all-weather interceptor; (RF) all-weather reconnaissance.

Engines: Two Pratt & Whitney J57 two-shaft turbojets with afterburner; (F-101B) 14,990lb (6800kg) J57-53 or -55 (others) 14,880lb (6750kg) J57-13.

Dimensions: Span 39ft 8in (12·09m); length 67ft 4¾in (20·55m); (RF) 69ft 3in; height 18ft (5·49m).

Weights: Empty (typical of all) 28,000lb (12,700kg); maximum loaded (B) 46,700lb (21,180kg); (all versions, overload 51,000lb, 23,133kg).

Performance: Maximum speed (B) 1,220mph (1963km/h, Mach 1·85); (others, typical) 1,100mph; initial climb (B) 17,000ft (5180m)/min; service ceiling 52,000ft (15,850m); range on internal fuel (B) 1,550 miles (2500km); (others) 1,700 miles (2736km).

Armament: (B) three Falcon (usually AIM-4D) air-to-air missiles semi-submerged in underside, sometimes supplemented by two AIR-2A Genie

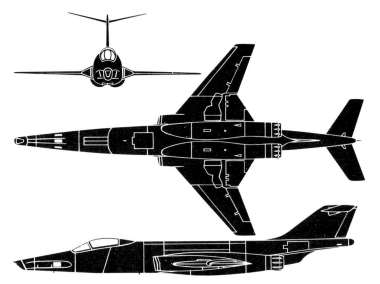

Above: Three-view of RF-101C Voodoo, unarmed reconnaissance.

Above: A trio of Phantoms being serviced by a KC-135A tanker. Taken in 1976, this picture shows two F-4Es and a D. Many F-4Ds lack the AAA-4 infra-red detector which occupies a prominent fairing under the nose in these, and in most F-4B and C versions except those for unarmed reconnaissance.

Left: Test launch of an early TV-guided AGM-65A Maverick from an F-4E Phantom. This aircraft is fitted with an experimental rudder assembled from panels of boron-fibre composite to gain service experience of this form of construction; under the right wing is a second missile. Mavericks are now issued to Tactical Air Command in large numbers.

for speed, altitude and rate of climb. Not replaced by the abandoned F-111B, the carrier-based Phantom continued in production for 19 years through the F-4G with digital communications, F-4J with AWG-10 pulse-doppler radar, drooping ailerons, slatted tail and increased power, and the N (rebuilt B). In 1961 the F-4B was formally compared with all US Air Force fighters and found to outperform all by a wide margin, especially in weapon load and radar performance. As a result it was ordered in modified form as the F-110, soon redesignated F-4C, for 16 of the 23 Tactical Air Command Wings. The camera/radar/IR linescan RF-4C followed in 1965. In 1964 the Royal Navy adopted the Anglicised F-4K, with wider fuselage housing Spey fan engines

and, of 48 delivered to Britain as Phantom FG.1, 28 served with the Royal Navy. The other 20 went to RAF Strike Command, which has also received 120 F-4M (UK designation Phantom FGR.2) which combine the British features with those of the F-4C plus the option of a multi-sensor centreline reconnaissance pod whilst retaining full weapons capability. In the US Air Force the C was followed by the much-improved D with APQ-100 radar replaced by APQ-109, inertial navigation added and many added or improved equipment items. This in turn was followed by the dramatically improved F-4E with slatted wing, internal gun and increased power, the EJ being the version built in Japan and the F being a Luftwaffe version. The Luftwaffe also operate the multi-sensor RF-4E. Australia leased F-4Es from the US government pending delivery of the F-111C. In 1977 deliveries of new aircraft, all assembled at St Louis except for the EJ, amounted to just on 5,000, and several batches remained to be built. Most were for export, but a few were outstanding for US services, and very large rebuild programmes were in hand including rebuilding 300 F-4J into F-4S with long-life slatted airframes, rebuilding Marine Corps RF-4Bs with new structure and sensors, rebuilding or refitting over 600 Air Force machines (for example with Pave Tack FLIR/laser pods or Pave Spike TV/laser pods) and complete rebuild of 116 F-4D or E Phantoms into the EF-4E Wild Weasel defence-suppression platform with weapons replaced by special electronics (especially the APR-38 system, with large pod on the fin) to detect, locate and classify hostile electromagnetic emissions, and assist other aircraft to destroy them. Some EF aircraft may do their own killing, with Standard ARM, Shrike and Harm missiles.

---

nuclear rockets on fuselage pylons; (C) three 20mm M-39 cannon (provision for four, with Tacan removed) in fuselage; (RF) none. As built, all A and C and derivatives fitted with centreline crutch for 1 MT tactical nuclear store and wing pylons for two 2,000lb (907kg) bombs, four 680lb (310kg) mines or other ordnance.

History: First flight 29 September 1954; service delivery (A) May 1957; final delivery (B) March 1961.

Development: By far the most powerful fighter of its day, the Voodoo was based on the XF-88 Voodoo prototype flown on 20 October 1948. Originally a long-range escort for Strategic Air Command, the F-101A became a tactical attack machine; 50 were followed by 47 improved C models, all of which set records for accident-free operation and were con-

verted to unarmed RF-101G and H for the Air National Guard, augmenting 35 RF-101A and 166 RF-101C built earlier and used intensively at all levels in Vietnam. The B interceptor sacrificed fuel for a radar operator to work the MG-13 radar fire-control; 478 were built and converted to F-101F or dual-control TF-101F for Air Defense Command (now Air National Guard). In 1961 66 ex-ADC aircraft were transferred to the RCAF as CF-101s; in 1970 the CAF exchanged the 58 survivors for 66 improved F and TF and there still serve as the only CAF all-weather fighters.

Below: One of the later rebuilds, a McDonnell Douglas RF-101H reconnaissance platform serving with the Air National Guard.

McDonnell Douglas
F-15 Eagle

F-15A, TF-15A

Origin: McDonnell Aircraft, division of McDonnell Douglas Corp, St Louis, USA.

Type: Single-seat all-weather air-superiority fighter; (TF) dual-control trainer.

Engines: Two Pratt & Whitney F100-100 two-shaft augmented turbofans, each rated at 14,871lb (6744kg) thrust dry and 23,810lb (10,800kg) with maximum augmentation.

Dimensions: Span 42ft 9¾in (13.05m); length 63ft 9¾in (19.45m); height 18ft 7½in (5.68m).

Weights: Empty, about 28,000lb (12,700kg); loaded (F or TF, clean) 39,500lb; (F with four Sparrows) about 40,500lb, (three 600gal drop tanks) 54,000lb, (three tanks and two FAST packs) 66,000lb (29,937kg).

Performance: Maximum speed (low) over 921mph (1482km/h, Mach 1.22), (high) over 1,650mph (2660km/h, Mach 2.5); initial climb, over 50,000ft (15,240m)/min; service ceiling, over 70,000ft (21,000m); range on internal fuel, about 1,200 miles (1930km); ferry range with maximum fuel, over 3,700 miles (5955km).

Armament: One 20mm M-61 multi-barrel gun with 960 rounds; four AIM-7 Sparrow air-to-air missiles on corners of fuselage and four AIM-9 Sidewinder air-to-air missiles on lateral rails at upper level of wing pylons; centreline pylon stressed for 4,500lb (2041kg) for 600 gal tank, reconnaissance pod or any tactical weapon; inner wing pylons stressed for 5,100lb (2313kg) for any tanks or weapon; outer wing pylons stressed for 1,000lb (454kg) for ECM pods or equivalent ordnance load. Normal external load limit, with or without FAST packs, 12,000lb (5443kg).

History: First flight 27 July 1972; (TF) 7 July 1973; service delivery March 1974 (Cat. II test), November 1974 (inventory).

Development: Emergence of the MiG-23 and -25 in 1967 accentuated the belief of the US Air Force that it was falling behind in true fighter aircraft. Studies for an FX (a new air-superiority fighter) were hastened and, after a major competition, McDonnell's team at St Louis was selected to build the new aircraft. The Air Force funded a new engine, won by Pratt & Whitney, and a new 25mm gun using caseless ammunition (abandoned after difficult

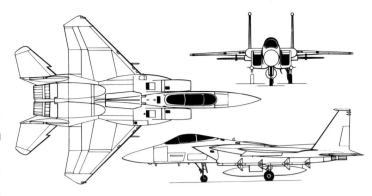

Above: Three-view of F-15A Eagle with drop tank but no FASTs.

development). The Eagle has emerged as probably the best fighter in the world, with thrust at low levels considerably greater than clean gross weight, a fixed wing of no less than 530 sq ft area, a single seat and an advanced Hughes X-band pulse-doppler radar. Though planned as an uncompromised machine for interception and air combat the Eagle also has formidable attack capability over intercontinental ranges. Undoubtedly its chief attributes are its combat manoeuvrability (it can outfly almost any other US machine without using afterburner) and the advanced automaticity of its radar, head-up display, weapon selectors and quick-fire capability. Internal fuel capacity of 11,200lb can be almost trebled by adding a FAST (fuel and sensor, tactical) pack on each side, a "conformal pallet" housing 10,000lb

Key to cutaway drawing

1 Nose radome
2 Planar-array radar scanner
3 Hughes APG-63 multi-mode radar
4 Forward bulkhead
5 Instrument panel shroud
6 Head-up display sight
7 Curved windscreen (polycarbonate with cast acrylic surfaces)
8 Polycarbonate one-piece canopy
9 Pilot's headrest
10 Ejection seat (Douglas Escapac)
11 Port control console
12 Nosewheel door
13 Retraction strut
14 Landing/taxi lights
15 Forward-retracting nosewheel
16 Nosewheel fairing door
17 Port intake
18 Variable inlet ramps
19 Inlet pivot line
20 Port missile station (Sidewinder, Sparrow or advanced missile)
21 Avionics stowage
22 Wing-intake fairing
23 Flight refuelling receptacle
24 Auxiliary intake (and grille)
25 Canopy hinges
26 Provision for second crew member (TF-15)
27 Starboard inlet
28 General Electric M61 20mm gun
29 Ammunition drum, 1,000 rounds
30 Ammunition feed
31 Dorsal speed-brake (shaded, shown retracted)
32 Centre-section fuel tanks (4)
33 Starboard wing tank
34 Vent tank

Above: Checking the flat (planar-array) scanner of the Hughes APG-63 computerized radar system.

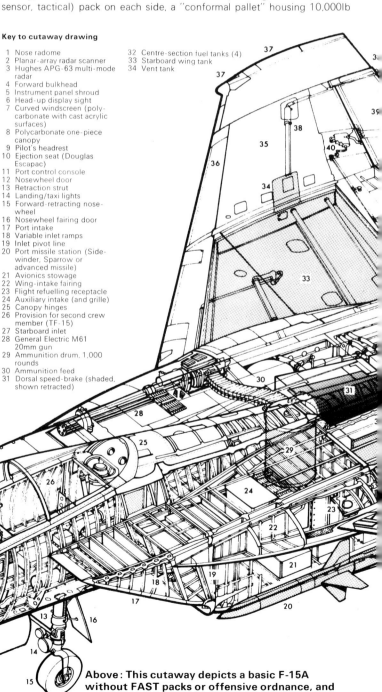

Above: This cutaway depicts a basic F-15A without FAST packs or offensive ordnance, and with the original shape of squared-off wingtip. Though originally planned as an uncompromised dogfighter and all-weather interceptor, the Eagle has been proved to have outstanding capability in certain attack situations demanding very heavy bomb loads delivered at moderate speeds and heights.

of fuel and target designators or weapons. Very extensive electronic systems for attack and defence, far beyond any standard previously seen in a fighter, are carried. A total USAF buy of 729 aircraft is planned, and though this has not changed since early in the programme the benefits of the "learning curve" (which reduces costs as production continues) are being much more than nullified by cost-inflation. The unit price of $7·5 million of 1975 had been more than doubled by late 1976 to over $16·7 million, with a figure in excess of $18 million predicted by Congress. Thus the 729 aircraft will now cost at least $12·2 billion, a figure rising by $500–600m each quarter. Nevertheless the outstanding qualities of this superbly capable fighter commend it to many governments; Israel has bought 21 new Eagles plus four reworked development aircraft, costing with support $600 million, and in mid-1976 the F-15 was chosen by Japan as the FX for the Air Self-Defence Force (with 78 of 100 bought scheduled to be made in Japan under licence). McDonnell Douglas are selling hard to Australia, Canada, France, W Germany and Saudi Arabia.

In 1980 the F-15A and two-seat F-15B (previously TF-15) will be replaced in production by the F-15C and two-seat F-15D. Both will have 2000lb (907kg) extra internal fuel and FAST packs, but the main improvement will be a programmable radar processor. It quadruples computer capacity, enables targets to be searched for whilst tracking others, and ability to transfer lock instantly to new targets. It also adds a new raid-assessment mode and opens the way to further improvements.

Above: F-15A Eagles peel off to recover at Langley AFB after a training sortie by the 1st Tac Fighter Wing. In 1977 the 36th TFW became operational with the Eagle at Bitburg AB, in West Germany, the first to be based outside the United States.

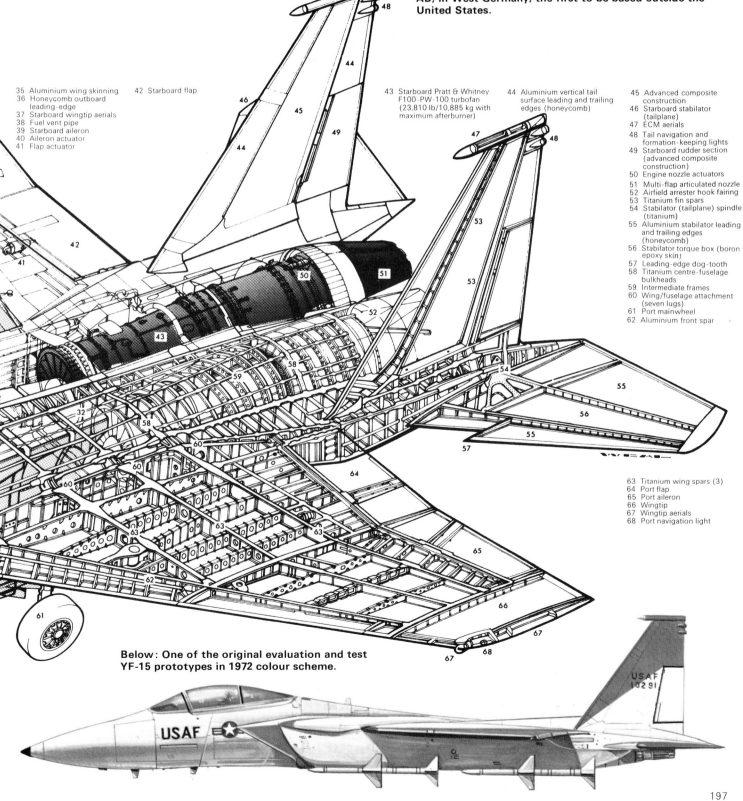

35 Aluminium wing skinning
36 Honeycomb outboard leading-edge
37 Starboard wingtip aerials
38 Fuel vent pipe
39 Starboard aileron
40 Aileron actuator
41 Flap actuator
42 Starboard flap
43 Starboard Pratt & Whitney F100-PW-100 turbofan (23,810 lb/10,885 kg with maximum afterburner)
44 Aluminium vertical tail surface leading and trailing edges (honeycomb)
45 Advanced composite construction
46 Starboard stabilator (tailplane)
47 ECM aerials
48 Tail navigation and formation-keeping lights
49 Starboard rudder section (advanced composite construction)
50 Engine nozzle actuators
51 Multi-flap articulated nozzle
52 Airfield arrester hook fairing
53 Titanium fin spars
54 Stabilator (tailplane) spindle (titanium)
55 Aluminium stabilator leading and trailing edges (honeycomb)
56 Stabilator torque box (boron epoxy skin)
57 Leading-edge dog-tooth
58 Titanium centre-fuselage bulkheads
59 Intermediate frames
60 Wing/fuselage attachment (seven lugs)
61 Port mainwheel
62 Aluminium front spar
63 Titanium wing spars (3)
64 Port flap
65 Port aileron
66 Wingtip
67 Wingtip aerials
68 Port navigation light

Below: One of the original evaluation and test YF-15 prototypes in 1972 colour scheme.

McDonnell Douglas/Northrop F-18 Hornet and Cobra

F-18, TF-18 and A-18

Origin: Original basic design, Northrop Corp; prime contractor, McDonnell Douglas Corp, USA, with Northrop building centre and aft fuselage.
Type: (F) single-seat carrier-based multi-role fighter, (TF) dual trainer, (A) single-seat land-based attack fighter.
Engines: Two 16,000lb (7257kg) thrust General Electric F404-400 two-shaft augmented turbofans.
Dimensions: Span (with missiles) 40ft 8½in (12·41m), (without missiles) 37ft 6in (11·42m); length 56ft (17·07m); height 14ft 9½in (4·50m).
Weights: (Provisional) empty 20,583lb (9336kg); loaded (clean) 33,642lb (15,260kg); maximum loaded (catapult limit) 50,064lb (22,710kg).
Performance: Maximum speed (clean, at altitude) 1,190mph (1915km/h, Mach 1·8), (maximum weight, sea level) subsonic; sustained combat manoeuvre ceiling, over 49,000ft (14,935m); absolute ceiling, over 60,000ft (18,290m); combat radius (air-to-air mission, high, no external fuel) 461 miles (741km); ferry range, not less than 2,300 miles (3700km).
Armament: One 20mm M61 Gatling in upper part of forward fuselage; nine external weapon stations for maximum load (catapult launch) of 13,400lb (6080kg), including bombs, sensor pods, ECM, missiles (including Sparrow) and other stores, with tip-mounted Sidewinders.
History: First flight (YF-17) 9 June 1974; (first of 11 test F-18) July 1978; (production F-18) 1980.

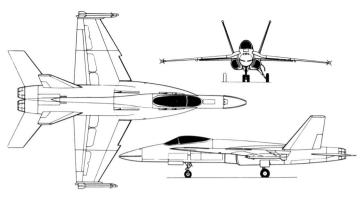

Above: Three-view of single-seater (F-18A and A-18).

Above: Takeoff of one of the two Northrop YF-17 prototypes. Originally built to compete in the USAF lightweight fighter programme, they are now supporting the re-launch of a Cobra.

Above: The two YF-17 prototypes in flight. Though their test flying has greatly underpinned the McDonnell Douglas-led Hornet, the latter will be a larger and very different aircraft.

North American (Rockwell) F-100 Super Sabre

F-100A to F-100F and DF-100F

Origin: North American Aviation Inc, Inglewood, USA.
Type: Single-seat fighter-bomber; (F-100F) two-seat operational trainer; (DF) missile or RPV director aircraft.
Engine: One Pratt & Whitney J57 two-shaft turbojet with afterburner, (most blocks of A) 14,500lb (6576kg) J57-7; (late A, all C) 16,000lb (7257kg) J57-29; (D, F) 16,950lb (7690kg) J57-21A (all ratings with afterburner).
Dimensions: Span (original A) 36ft 7in; (remainder) 38ft 9½in (11·81m); length (except F, excluding pitot boom) 49ft 6in (15·09m), (fuselage, 47ft exactly); (F) 52ft 6in (16·0m), (boom adds about 6ft to all models); height (original A) 13ft 4in; (remainder) 16ft 2¾in (4·96m).
Weights: Empty (original A) 19,700lb; (C) 20,450lb; (D) 21,000lb (9525kg); (F) 22,300lb (10,115kg); maximum loaded (original A) 28,935lb; (C, D) 34,832lb (15,800kg); (F, two tanks but no weapons) 30,700lb (13,925kg).
Performance: Maximum speed (typical of all) 864mph at height (1390 km/h, Mach 1·31); initial climb (clean) 16,000ft (4900m)/min; service ceiling (typical) 45,000ft (13,720m); range (high, two 375gal tanks) 1,500 miles (2415km).
Armament: Usually four (F, only two) 20mm M-39E cannon each with 200 rounds; (A) pylons for two 375gal supersonic tanks and four additional hardpoints (seldom used) for 4,000lb ordnance; (C, D) two tanks and six pylons for 7,500lb (3402kg) ordnance; (F) two tanks and maximum of 6,000lb (2722kg) ordnance.
History: First flight (YF-100) 25 May 1953; production (A) 29 October 1953; final delivery October 1959.

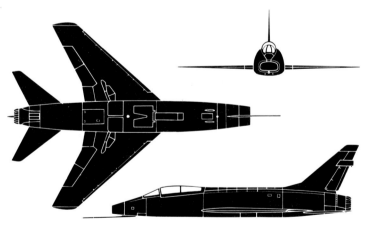

Three-view of tandem-seat F-100F in clean configuration.

Development: The success of the Sabre made it natural to attempt a successor, and in February 1949 this was planned as a larger and much more powerful machine able to exceed the speed of sound in level flight (had it been started two years later it might have been smaller, in view of the Korean pressure for simple fighters with the highest possible climb and performance at extreme altitudes). Unusual features were the 6 per cent wing with 45° sweep, no flaps, inboard ailerons, full-span slats and a slab tailplane mounted as low as possible. Level supersonic speed was achieved, for the first time with a combat aircraft, but after very rapid development, with the first (479th) wing fully equipped, the F-100A was grounded in November 1954. Trouble due to inertia coupling between the roll and yaw axes necessitated urgent modification, the wings and fin being lengthened. Subsequently the career of the "Hun" was wholly successful, the 203 A

Development: In 1971 the US Navy became concerned at the cost of the F-14 and the resulting reduced rate of procurement and total number that could be afforded. In 1973 it studied low-cost versions and compared them with navalised F-15 versions and improved F-4s. In 1974 the VFX specification emerged for a wholly new and smaller fighter somewhat along the lines of the Air Force Air Combat Fighter. In May 1975 the Navy and Marine Corps announced their choice of the F-18, developed from the existing land-based Northrop F-17 by McDonnell Douglas and Northrop. In fact the F-18 will be almost twice as heavy as the original F-17 proposal but, with more powerful engines, is expected to have adequate dogfight performance through the 1980s. Features include an unswept wing with large dogteeth and forebody strakes at the roots, twin canted vertical tails, simple fixed engine inlets and extensive graphite/epoxy structure. Search radar will be used in the interception and surface-attack roles, and a very wide range of weapons will be carried. In the Navy air-superiority mission the gun will be backed up by two Sparrows and two Sidewinders, and the F-18 is expected to show dramatic improvements over the F-4J in manoeuvrability, reliability and low cost. In Marine attack missions the maximum load can be

Above: Artist's impression of two Navy F-18 Hornets. The A-18, most of which will go to the Marines, will look similar. The first F-18 prototype flew on 18 November 1978.

14,000lb for airfield operation, and the inertial guidance and weapon-aiming are expected to offer a significant advance over the accuracy of any A-7. The Navy/Marines plan to buy 11 development aircraft plus 800 production machines by the end of 1990 at a unit cost of only $5·924 million in 1975 dollars, without spares. About every ninth aircraft will be a TF mission trainer, with 500lb (272kg) less fuel, rear cockpit (without HUD) and larger canopy.

In late 1976 Northrop — original designer of the YF-17 but a mere subcontractor on the F-18 — was trying to relaunch the land-based Cobra, but now as a modified F-18. Despite severe competition from the F-16 and other aircraft, Northrop aims to find worldwide sales for the Cobra replacing the F-4, F-104, A-7 and Mirage. It would have less internal fuel than the F-18, and thus even higher performance. Planned export delivery date is 1982, at $8 million in 1975 dollars.

fighters being followed by the stronger C fighter-bomber, the D with flaps and autopilot and the tandem-seat F. Total production was lower than expected at 2,294, many being built by NAA's newly occupied factory at Columbus, Ohio. In their early years the later versions pioneered global deployment of tactical aircraft by means of probe/drogue refuelling, and in Vietnam they proved outstandingly good at both low attack and top cover, flying more missions than over 15,000 Mustangs flew in World War II. In

1977 the survivors of what two decades earlier had been among the world's élite warplanes were in their final months of combat duty after countless inspection, repair and modification programmes.

Below: The F-100 is still an important item in the inventory of some of America's allies. Here an F-100C single-seater pops its braking parachute at an airbase of the Turkish air force.

Northrop F-5 Freedom Fighter and Tiger II

F-5A, B, E and F, CF-5A and D, NF-5A and B RF-5A, E and G, and SF-5A and B

Origin: Northrop Aircraft Division, Hawthorne, USA; made or assembled under licence by partnership Canada/Netherlands and by Spain.

Type: (With suffix A, E, and G) single-seat fighter-reconnaissance; (with suffix B, D and F) two-seat dual fighter/trainer.

Engines: (A, B, D, G) two 4,080lb (1850kg) thrust General Electric J85-13 single-shaft afterburning turbojets; (E, F) two 5,000lb (2268kg) J85-21.

Dimensions: Span (A, B, D, G) 25ft 3in (7·7m); (E, F) 26ft 8in (8·13m); length (A, G) 47ft 2in (14·38m); (B, D) 46ft 4in (14·12m); (E) 48ft 3¾in (14·73m); (F) 51ft 9¾in (15·80m); height (A, G) 13ft 2in (4·01m); (B, D) 13ft 1in (3·99m); (E, F) 13ft 4½in (4·08m).

Weights: Empty (A, G) 8,085lb (3667kg); (B, D) 8,361lb (3792kg); (E) 9,588lb (4349kg); (F) 9,700lb (4400kg); maximum loaded (A, G) 20,677lb (9379kg); (B, D) 20,500lb (9298kg); (E, F) 24,080lb (10,922kg).

Performance: Maximum speed at altitude (A, G) 925mph (1489km/h, Mach 1·40); (B, D) 885mph (1424km/h, Mach 1·34); (E) 1,060mph (1705km/h, Mach 1·60); initial climb (A, G) 28,700ft (8760m)/min; (B, D) 30,400ft (9265m)/min; (E) 31,600ft (9630m)/min; service ceiling (A, G) 50,500ft (15,390m); (B, D) 52,000ft (15,850m); (E) 54,000ft (16,460m); range with max fuel, with reserves, tanks retained, (A, G) 1,387 miles (2232km); (B, D) 1,393 miles (2241km); (E) 1,974 miles (3175km).

Armament: Two 20mm M-39A2 cannon each with 280 rounds in nose (can be retained in RF versions); five pylons for total external load of about 4,400lb (2000kg) in A, G (total military load for these models, including guns and ammunition, is 5,200lb) or 7,000lb (3175kg) in E; rails on wing-tips for AIM-9 Sidewinder missiles.

History: First flight (XT-38) 10 April 1959, (N-156F) 30 July 1959, (F-5A) 19 May 1964, (F-5E) 11 August 1972, (F-5F) 25 September 1974.

Development: In 1955 Northrop began the project design of a lightweight fighter, known as Tally-Ho, powered by two J85 missile engines slung in pods under a very small unswept wing. It was yet another of the many projects born in the Korean era when pilots were calling for lighter, simpler fighters with higher performance. Gradually Welko Gasich and his team refined the design, putting the engines in the fuselage and increasing the size, partly to meet the needs of the Navy. In June 1956 the Navy had pulled out, while the Air Force ordered the trainer version as the T-38 Talon. Over the next 15 years Northrop delivered 1,200 Talons, all to the USAF or NASA, as the standard supersonic trainer of those services! With this assured programme the company took the unique decision to go ahead and build a demonstration fighter in the absence of any orders – the only time this has ever been done with a supersonic aircraft. By the time it was ready for flight in 1959 the N-156F, dubbed Freedom Fighter had received some US Defense funding, and the prototype carried US serial and stencil markings but no national markings. It was a simple little fighter, carrying about 485 gallons of fuel, two cannon and an old F-86 style sight, and having racks for two little Sidewinder missiles. Today such a prototype would have remained unsold, but in October 1962 the Department of Defense decided to buy the so-called Freedom Fighter in large numbers to give, or sell on advantageous terms, to anti-Communist nations. More than 1,040 of the Freedom Fighter (suffixes A, B, D, G) have been built, all but 178 being exports from Northrop. The Netherlands built the NF-5A and B equipment, heavier mission load, 500lb (227kg) more fuel in the longer fuselage, new inlet ducts, revised body and wing, root extensions and manoeuvring flaps and an X-band radar. Deliveries began in 1972, followed

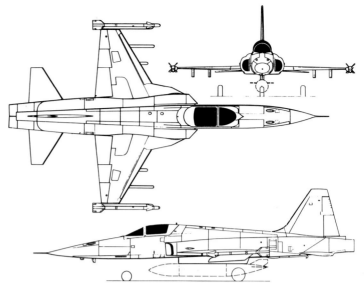

Three-view of F-5E Tiger II; the tandem-seat F-5F is 42in longer.

Below: Dive-bombing attack by an F-5A Freedom Fighter involved using the optical gunsight with manually depressed reticle.

by the two-seat F in 1975. The US Air Force uses the Tiger II to equip its Tac Ftr Training Aggressor units, simulating hostile aircraft; the US Navy uses it as an Air Combat Trainer for future F-4 or F-14 pilots. Basic price of an E is considerably higher than that of the more powerful Jaguar (a recent sale was 12 for Kenya, priced at $70·6 million), but over 1,000 of the Tiger II type are likely to be supplied on attractive terms to many countries.

Below: The later Tiger II seen in tandem-seat F-5F form, with AIM-9J Advanced Sidewinder AAMs for air-to-air interception.

Republic (Fairchild) F-105 Thunderchief

F-105B, D, F and G

Origin: Republic Aviation Corp (now Fairchild Republic Co), USA.
Type: Single-seat all-weather fighter-bomber; (F-105F) two-seat operational trainer; (G) two-seat ECM.
Engine: One Pratt & Whitney J75 two-shaft afterburning turbojet; (B) 23,500lb (10,660kg) J75-5; (D, F, G) 24,500lb (11,113kg) J75-19W.
Dimensions: Span 34ft 11¼in (10·65m); length (B, D) 64ft 3in (19·58m); (F, G) 69ft 7½in (21·21m); height (B, D) 19ft 8in (5·99m); (F, G) 20ft 2in (6·15m).
Weights: Empty (D) 27,500lb (12,474kg); (F, G) 28,393lb (12,879kg); maximum loaded (B) 40,000lb (18,144kg); (D) 52,546lb (23,834kg); (F, G) 54,000lb (24,495kg).
Performance: Maximum speed (B) 1,254mph; (D, F, G) 1,480mph (2382km/h, Mach 2·25); initial climb (B, D, typical) 34,500ft (10,500m)/min; (F, G) 32,000ft (9750m)/min; service ceiling (typical) 52,000ft (15,850m); tactical radius with 16 750lb bombs (D) 230 miles (370km); ferry range with maximum fuel (typical) 2,390 miles (3846km).
Armament: One 20mm M-61 gun with 1,029 rounds in left side of fuselage; internal bay for ordnance load of up to 8,000lb (3629kg), and five external pylons for additional load of 6,000lb (2722kg).
History: First flight (YF-105A) 22 October 1955; (production B) 26 May 1956; (D) 9 June 1959; (F) 11 June 1963; final delivery 1965.

Development: The AP-63 project was a private venture by Republic Aviation to follow the F-84. Its primary mission was delivery of nuclear or conventional weapons in all-weathers, with very high speed and long range. Though it had only the stop-gap J57 engine the first Thunderchief exceeded the speed of sound on its first flight, and the B model was soon in production for Tactical Air Command of the USAF. Apart from being the biggest single-seat, single-engine combat aircraft in history, the 105 was notable for its large bomb bay and unique swept-forward engine inlets in the wing roots. Only 75 B were delivered but 600 of the advanced D were built, with Nasarr monopulse radar and doppler navigation. Production was completed with 143 tandem-seat F with full operational equipment and dual controls. Known as "the Thud" the greatest of single-engined combat jets bore a huge burden throughout the Vietnam war. About 350 D were rebuilt during that conflict with the Thunderstick (T-stick) all-weather blind attack system — a few also being updated to T-stick II — with a large saddleback

Right: Pending the availability of numbers of EF-4E (F-4G) electronic-warfare aircraft, and the still later EF-111A, the Wild Weasel F-105G remains a vital multi-role EW platform in Tactical Air Command. A tandem-seater, it retains weapons capability, and this example from the 561st Tac Ftr Sqn, 35th Tac Ftr Wing, at George AFB, California, has a Standard ARM (anti-radar missile) under each wing. The main D/F and noise jammer pods are recessed on each side of the mid-fuselage.

Above: Three-view of a typical F-105D single-seater before being rebuilt with "saddleback" Thunderstick II avionics.

fairing from cockpit to fin. About 30 F were converted to ECM (electronic countermeasures) attackers, with pilot and observer and Wild Weasel and other radar homing, warning and jamming systems. Westinghouse jammers and Goodyear chaff pods were carried externally.

Rockwell International XFV-12

XFV-12A prototype, constructor's designation NR-356

Origin: Rockwell International, Columbus, USA.
Type: Fighter/attack technology prototype.
Engine: One modified Pratt & Whitney F401-400 two-shaft afterburning turbofan rated at 16,400lb (7438kg) dry and 28,090lb (12,741kg) with maximum afterburner.
Dimensions: Span (wing) 28ft 6¼in (8·69m), (canard) 12ft 1¼in (3·69m); length 43ft 11in (13·39m); height 10ft 4in (3·15m).
Weights: (Empty, fully equipped) 13,800lb (6259kg), (max VTOL) 19,500lb (8845kg), (max STOL) 24,250lb (11,000kg).
Performance: Maximum speed at maximum STOL weight, supersonic at low level, and in excess of Mach 2 (1,320mph, 2125km/h) at optimum height; take-off run at maximum STOL weight 300ft (91m).
Armament: Space for internal M61 gun in lower fuselage; provision for carrying air-to-surface or air-to-air weapons, with fuselage recesses for two Sparrow missiles.
History: Contract award November 1972; roll-out December 1976; first flight planned for 1977 but unlikely before 1981.

Development: In 1965–74 the US Navy studied the Sea Control Ship, an attractive form of small aircraft carrier with neither catapults nor arrester gear but equipped on a highly automated basis for use as a base for V/STOL aircraft. Though the Soviet Union is producing ships of this type, much bigger than the projected SCS, the US Navy had to abandon the proposal through lack of money. Work continued, however, on this extremely interesting technology-demonstrator aircraft, which to save money has

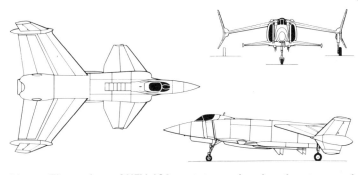

Above: Three-view of XFV-12A prototype, showing the staggered and semi-recessed Sparrow medium-range AAMs.

been designed by Rockwell's Columbus Aircraft Division in Ohio to incorporate the main wing box and parts of the inlet ducts of an F-4 Phantom, and the nose, cockpit and forward fuselage, and nose and main landing gears, of an A-4 Skyhawk. Pratt & Witney developed the large electro-hydraulic diverter valve which, for V/STOL, shuts off the engine nozzle and diverts the entire efflux through large high-temperature ducts. One duct feeds the canard's augmentor (ejector) flaps, while the larger duct feeds the similar flaps along the wings. Each surface has front and rear flaps across the full span, with endplates, and the ejector slits not only give direct lift and thrust but entrain an airflow 7½ times as great to give enough lift for VTOL or higher-weight STOL. All flap sections are of titanium honeycomb, fully powered to serve as control surfaces in forward flight, when the wing and canard are closed for forward speeds up to Mach 2. The fins carry small rudders above the wing but there are no leading-edge movable surfaces. There is no suggestion of producing an FV-12A in quantity, but the technology is expected to be valuable in refining the requirements for supersonic V/STOL fighter and attack aircraft for shipboard use in the late 1980s.

Rockwell International B-1

B-1

Origin: Rockwell International Corp, USA.
Type: Four-seat strategic bomber and missile platform.
Engines: Four 30,000lb (13,610kg) class General Electric F101-100 two-shaft augmented turbofans.
Dimensions: Span (15°) 136ft 8½in (41·7m); (67½°) 78ft 2½in (23·8m); length 150ft 2½in (45·8m); height 33ft 7in (10·24m).
Weights: Empty, about 140,000lb (63,500kg); maximum loaded 395,000lb (179,170kg), (gross weight likely to settle at about 400,000lb).
Performance: Maximum speed at sea level (std day) about 646mph (1040km/h, Mach 0·85); maximum speed at high altitude (prototypes) 1,320mph (2135km/h, Mach 2·0); service ceiling over 60,000ft (18,300m); range with maximum weapon load, 6,100 miles (9820km).
Armament: 24 Improved SRAM (AGM-69B thermonuclear missiles) internally, with provision for eight more externally; alternatively the same number of AGM-86A ALCM (air-launched cruise missiles) carried on the same mounts; 75,000lb (34,020kg) of free-fall bombs internally with provision for 40,000lb (18,144kg) externally.
History: First flight 23 December 1974; cancelled 30 June 1977.

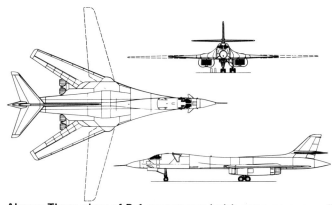

Above: Three-view of B-1 prototypes (with crew-escape pod) showing range of wing sweep.

Below: The first of the four B-1 prototypes, drawn as it was at the roll-out in mid-1974. Differences since then have been mainly internal.

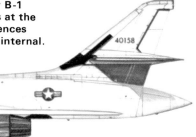

Development: By far the most expensive combat aircraft in history, the B-1 has also had by far the longest, most minutely studied and most costly gestation period. When the B-52 was bought for Strategic Air Command in 1951 it was just another aircraft – albeit a large and costly one, with a unit price of around $6 million – but in the late-1970s cost-inflation was the largest nail in the B-1's coffin. There are many, including Congressmen who vote on defence procurement, who cannot understand how a large manned vehicle can penetrate hostile airspace without getting shot down. This book is not the place to spell out the several compelling reasons for retaining a manned bomber in SAC's inventory, but the fact must be emphasised that the B-1 has been planned with unbelievable care and had to be professionally developed with inadequate funds in an environment of extreme parsimony. Only a single prototype was carrying the entire flight test programme for considerably more than a year, posing a frightening risk of severe delay should that aircraft have been lost. The technology of the B-1 is of immense breadth and depth, extending to every branch of aerodynamics, structures, propulsion and weapons. Much smaller than the B-52, it uses extremely advanced and efficient engines and a high-lift variable-sweep wing to carry twice the weapon load for a much greater distance at much higher speed and with many times greater penetrative capability. Almost all B-1 missions would be flown at about tree-top height; Mach 2·0 at high altitude would be used extremely rarely. Seen from the front a B-1's radar signature is approximately one-thirtieth as great as that of a B-52, and its defensive avionics (managed by associate contractor Boeing) are the most powerful and comprehensive ever fitted into a combat aircraft. These systems guard the B-1 against defensive radars by jamming, confusing and spoofing, in ways at present highly classified. Another design feature is the

ability to scramble quickly from an airfield under nuclear attack and to survive the effects of enemy thermonuclear explosions in fairly close proximity. All systems can be automatically checked and held at immediate readiness for long periods, so that on an alert being sounded the first man to reach the aircraft has only to hit a button behind the nose landing gear to energise all engines and systems for immediate take-off even before the crew are completely strapped in. Yet another design feature is low-altitude ride control (LARC) effected by gust sensors and operated by small canard surfaces on each side of the nose and the lowest section of rudder, to guide the speeding monster through turbulent air without the crew compartment suffering significant undulation. So vital is the need for the B-1 that even an economy-minded Congress, in the midst of a Presidential election, voted to commit funds for production in November 1976 but President Carter terminated production plans in 1977. The USAF had hoped to buy at least a small B-1 force, to form the third leg of the strategic deterrent Triad. The SAC requirement is for 241 aircraft, at an estimated unit price of $77 million (allowing for R&D and inflation), amounting to a total investment of $18,600,000,000.

Below: Three fine pictures of the B-1 in its current series of flight operations from Palmdale and Edwards in California. This program with three aircraft, is continuing despite President Carter's cancellation of the manufacturing program in the summer of 1977, stating that he hoped more could be done to update the B-52 and use cruise missiles. The fourth B-1 is expected to join the flight program in 1979.

Rockwell RA-5C Vigilante

A-5A, A-5B and RA-5C

Origin: North American Aviation, now Rockwell International, USA.
Type: (A, B) carrier-based attack; (C) carrier-based reconnaissance, with crew of two.
Engines: Two General Electric J79 single-shaft afterburning turbojets; (A, B) as originally built, 16,150lb J79-2 or -4; (RA-5C, pre-1969), 17,000lb (7710kg) J79-8, (post-1969) 17,860lb (8118kg) J79-10.
Dimensions: Span 53ft (16·15m); length 75ft 10in (23·11m), (folds to 68ft); height 19ft 5in (5·92m).
Weights: Empty (C) about 38,000lb (17,240kg); maximum loaded, 80,000lb (36,285kg).
Performance: Maximum speed at height 1,385mph (2230km/h, Mach 2·1); service ceiling (C) 67,000ft (20,400m); range with external fuel, about 3,200 miles (5150km).
Armament: None (A, see text).
History: First flight (YA3J-1) 31 August 1958; (A-5A) January 1960; (A-5B) 29 April 1962; (RA-5C) 30 June 1962; final delivery of new aircraft 1971.

Development: No aircraft in history introduced more new technology than the first Vigilante, planned in 1956 as a carrier-based attack aircraft. Among its features were automatically ‡scheduled engine inlets and nozzles, single-surface vertical tail, differential slab tailplanes, linear bomb bay between the engines (with two emptied fuel tanks and a nuclear weapon ejected rearwards in the form of a long tube) and a comprehensive radar-inertial navigation system. Another feature was flap-blowing, and in the A-5B full-span leading-edge droop blowing was added to allow a 15,000lb

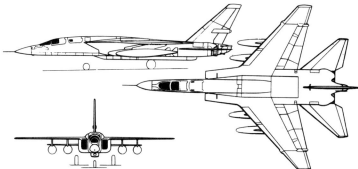

Above: Three-view of RA-5C with four external tanks but no ECM.

weight increase from saddle tanks in the new hump-backed fuselage. When carriers gave up a strategic nuclear role, the 57 A-5A were followed by the RA-5C, the airborne element of an integrated intelligence system serving the whole fleet and other forces. The RA-5C is extremely comprehensively equipped with multiple sensors including a side-looking radar under the fuselage. These valuable aircraft have been hard-worked in many theatres; 63 were built in 1962–66, 53 A-5A and the 6 A-5B were converted to RA-5C standard, and in 1969–71 the production line at Columbus was reopened for 46 Phase II with GE-10 engines and improved intakes and wing/body fillets.

Below: Unusual view of an RA-5C Vigilante as it leaves the catapult of the nuclear powered super-carrier USS *Enterprise*. It belongs to squadron RVAH-3.

Sikorsky S-64

S-64, CH-54A and B Tarhe

Origin: Sikorsky Aircraft, Division of United Technologies, Stratford, USA.
Type: Crane helicopter.
Engines: (CH-54A) two 4,500shp Pratt & Whitney T73-1 turboshafts, (CH-54B) two 4,800shp T73-700.
Dimensions: Diameter of six-blade main rotor 72ft 0in (21·95m); length overall (rotors turning) 88ft 6in (26·97m); height overall 18ft 7in (5·67m).
Weights: Empty (A) 19,234lb (8724kg); maximum loaded (A) 42,000lb (19,050kg), (B) 47,000lb (21,318kg).
Performance: Maximum cruise 105mph (169km/h); hovering ceiling out of ground effect 6,900ft (2100m); range with max fuel and 10 per cent reserve (typical) 230 miles (370km).
History: First flight (S-64) 9 May 1962; service delivery (CH-54A) late 1964, (B) late 1969.

Development: Developed from the first large US Army helicopter, the S-56, via the piston-engined S-60, the S-64 is an efficient weight-lifter which in Vietnam carried loads weighing up to 20,000lb (9072kg). The CH-54A Tarhes used in that campaign retrieved more than 380 shot-down aircraft, saving an estimated $210 million, and carried special vans housing up to 87 combat-equipped troops. The improved CH-54B, distinguished externally by twin main wheels, has lifted loads up to 40,780lb (18,497kg) and reached a height of 36,122ft (11,010m). There is no fuselage, just a structural beam joining the tail rotor to the cockpit in which seats are provided for three pilots, one facing to the rear for manoeuvring with loads. The dynamic components (rotor, gearboxes, shafting) were used as the basis for those of the S-65. With cancellation of the HLH (Heavy-Lift Helicopter) the S-64 remains the only large crane helicopter in the West.

Above: Three-view of the CH-54A Tarhe. The slightly more powerful CH-54B has twin-wheel main gears.

Sikorsky S-61

SH-3A and -3D Sea King, HH-3A, RH-3A and many other variants

Origin: Sikorsky Aircraft, Division of United Technologies, USA; built under licence by Agusta (Italy), Mitsubishi (Japan) and Westland (UK).
Type: See text.
Engines: Two General Electric T58 free-turbine turboshaft; (SH-3A and derivatives) 1,250shp T58-8B; (SH-3D and derivatives) 1,400shp T58-10; (S-61R versions) 1,500hp T58-5.
Dimensions: Diameter of main rotor 62ft (18·9m); length overall 72ft 8in (22·15m); (61R) 73ft; height overall 16ft 10in (5·13m).
Weights: Empty (simple transport versions, typical) 9,763lb (4428kg); (ASW, typical) 11,865lb (5382kg); (armed CH-3E) 13,255lb (6010kg); maximum loaded (ASW) about 18,626lb (8449kg); (transport) usually 21,500lb (9750kg); (CH-3E) 22,050lb (10,000kg).
Performance: Maximum speed (typical, maximum weight) 166mph (267km/h); initial climb (not vertical but maximum) varies from 2,200 to 1,310ft (670—400m)/min, depending on weight; service ceiling, typically 14,700ft (4480m); range with maximum fuel, typically 625 miles (1005km).
Armament: Very variable.
History: First flight 11 March 1959.

Development: Representing a quantum jump in helicopter capability, the S-61 family soon became a staple product of Sikorsky Aircraft, founded in March 1923 by Igor Sikorsky who left Russia after the Revolution and settled in the United States. He flew the first wholly practical helicopter in 1940, and his R-4 was the first helicopter in the world put into mass

Above. Three view of SH-3H showing radar, sonobuoys and MAD.

production (in 1942). A development, the S-51, was in 1947 licensed to the British firm Westland Aircraft, starting collloboration reviewed on later pages. The S-55 and S-58 were made in great numbers in the 1950s for many civil and military purposes, both now flying with various turbine engines. The S-61 featured an amphibious hull, twin turbine engines located above the hull close to the drive gearbox and an advanced flight-control system. First versions carried anti-submarine warfare (ASW) sensors and weapons, but later variants were equipped for various transport duties, minesweeping, drone or spacecraft recovery (eg lifting Astronauts from the sea), electronic surveillance and (S-61R series) transport/gunship and other combat duties.

Right: An SH-3D anti-submarine helicopter of US Navy squadron HS-2. The yellow disc is the drogue on the towed MAD "bird".

Sikorsky S-65

CH-53A Sea Stallion, HH-53, RH-53 and many other variants

Origin: Sikorsky Aircraft, Division of United Technologies, USA; licence-built by VFW-Fokker, Germany.
Type: See text.
Engines: (Early versions) two 2,850shp General Electric T64-6 free-turbine turboshaft; (CH-53D and G) 3,925shp T64 versions; (RH-53D) 4,380shp T64 versions; (CH-53E) three 4,380shp T64-415.
Dimensions: Diameter of main rotor (most) 72ft 3in (22·02m); (CH-53E) seven-blades, 79ft (24·08m); length overall (typical) 88ft 3in (26·9m); height overall 24ft 11in (7·6m).
Weights: Empty (CH-53D) 23,485lb (10,653kg); maximum loaded (most) 42,000lb (19,050kg); (RH-53D) 50,000lb; (CH-53E) over 60,000lb.
Performance: Maximum speed (most) 196mph (315km/h); (CH-53E) over 200mph; initial climb (maximum) typically 2,180ft (664m)/min; service ceiling, typically 20,400ft (6220m); range, typically 540 miles 869km).
Armament: most, none.
History: First flight 14 October 1964; service delivery (CH-53A) May 1966.

Development: Obviously developed from the S-61, the S-65 family includes the largest and most powerful helicopters in production outside the Soviet Union. The dynamic parts (rotors, gearboxes and control system) were originally similar to those of the S-64 Skycrane family, but using titanium and with folding main-rotor blades. Most versions served in Vietnam from

Above: CH-53D (other twin-engined versions similar).

January 1967, performing countless tasks including recovery of downed aircraft. In 1968 a standard CH-53A completed a prolonged series of loops and rolls, while others set records for speed and payload. Most of the 153 CH-53D for the German army were built in Germany, together with the engines. Latest versions are the RH-53D for mine countermeasures (MCM) with comprehensive tow/sweep systems and 0·5in guns for exploding surfaced mines, and the three-engined CH-53E for carrying slung loads up to 18 tons.

Below: The Marines use the CH-53A and much more powerful CH-53D; in high-density seating the D can carry 55 equipped troops.

Sikorsky UH-60A Black Hawk

S-70, UH-60A and SH-60B

Origin: Sikorsky Aircraft, Division of United Technologies, Stratford, USA.
Type: (A) Multi-role tactical transport; (B) US Navy LAMPS III.
Engines: Two 1,536shp General-Electric T-700-700 or -401 turboshafts.
Dimensions: Diameter of four-blade main rotor 53ft 8in (16·36m); length overall (rotors turning) 64ft 10in (19·76m); height overall 16ft 5in (5m).
Weights: Empty (A) 10,900lb (4,944kg), (B) 13,591lb (6,165kg); maximum loaded 21,400lb (9,/0/kg).
Performance: Maximum speed at 16,750lb (7,597kg) mission weight 198mph (318km/h); (B, 175mph, 282km/h).

Development: Sikorsky have won both the potentially largest helicopter programs for the US forces, since the "Huey": the UTTAS (Utility Tactical Transport Aircraft System) for the US Army and the Mk III LAMPS (Light Airborne Multi-Purpose System) for the US Navy. The S-70 was planned to fulfil the requirements of both, though the first three prototypes evaluated since 1974 were built for and flown chiefly by the Army for the UTTAS mission. This mission is primarily transport of an assault squad of 11 men plus crew of three, though other loads include four stretcher casualties or a slung load of 7,000lb (3175kg) (12,000lb, 5443kg, in the civil S-78 version). There is provision for a side-firing machine gun, and the whole machine is made squat so that when folded it fits a C-130; six can be carried

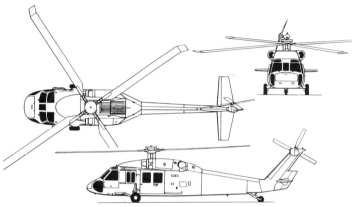

Above: Three-view of UH-60A Black Hawk.

in a C-5A.

The SH-60B has a basically similar airframe but is packed with ASW and other equipment, including radar, MAD, sonobuoys and two Mk 46 torpedoes. Engines are T-700-401s equipped for shipboard operation.

Below: One of the YUH-60A prototypes shows off its excellent manoeuvrability, which partially reads across to the SH-60B.

Vought A-7 Corsair II

Vought A-7A to E and TA-7C

Origin: Vought Systems Division of LTV, Dallas, USA.
Type: Single-seat attack bomber (carrier- or land-based); (TA) dual trainer.
Engine: (A) one 11,350lb (5150kg) thrust Pratt & Whitney TF30-6 two-shaft turbofan; (B, C) 12,200lb (5534kg) TF30-8; (D) 14,250lb (6465kg) Allison TF41-1 (Rolls-Royce Spey derivative) of same layout; (E) 15,000lb (6804kg) TF41-2.
Dimensions: Span 38ft 9in (11·80m); length 46ft 1½in (14·06m); (TA) 48ft 2in (14·68m); height 16ft 0¾in (4·90m); (TA) 16ft 5in (5m).
Weights: Empty (A) 15,904lb (7214kg); (D) 19,781lb (8972kg); maximum loaded (A) 32,500lb (14,750kg); (D) 42,000lb (19,050kg).
Performance: Maximum speed (all single-seat versions, clean) 698mph (1123km/h) at low level; climb and ceiling, not reported (seldom relevant); tactical radius with weapon load, typically 715 miles (1150km); ferry range with four external tanks, typically 4,100 miles (6600km).
Armament: (A, B) two 20mm Colt Mk 12 in nose; six wing and two fuselage pylons for weapon load of 15,000lb (6804kg). (D, E) one 20mm M61 Vulcan cannon on left side of fuselage with 1,000-round drum; external load up to theoretical 20,000lb (9072kg).
History: First flight 27 September 1965; service delivery October 1966; first flight of D, 26 September 1968.

Development: Though derived from the Crusader, the Corsair II is a totally different aircraft. By restricting performance to high subsonic speed, structure weight was reduced, range dramatically increased and weapon load multiplied by about 4. Development was outstandingly quick, as was production. Vought built 199 A-7A, used in action in the Gulf of Tonkin on 3 December 1967, followed by 196 B models. The C designation was used for the first 67 E models which retained the TF30 engine. In 1966 the Corsair II was adopted by the US Air Force, the A-7D having the superior

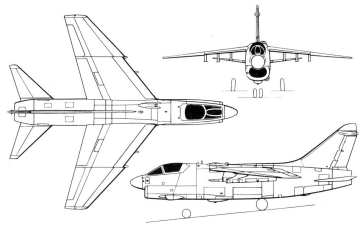

Above: Three-view of the Vought A-7D (A-7E generally similar).

TF41 engine, Gatling gun and more complete avionics for blind or automatic weapon delivery under all conditions, with head-up display and inertial/doppler navigation. By late 1976 over 480 had been delivered, with reduced production continuing. The Navy adopted the same model, with an even more powerful TF41, and by late 1976 about 540 E models had been built, bringing output to well over 1,400 within a decade. Vought funded development of a tandem-seat YA-7H, and is converting 81 B and C into the dual TA-7C. Greece is receiving 60 A-7H, similar to the D but without the on-board starter or flight-refuelling receptacle, at a price of $259·2 million. Pakistan accepted sale of 110, on condition (it was reported) it did not buy a nuclear reactor offered by France!

Below: A Vought A-7A Corsair II, the original production version. This example is (or rather was) serving with VA-195 aboard USS Kitty Hawk. It has been largely replaced by the much more advanced A-7E, which remains in low-rate production.

Right: A colorful formation of A-7E Corsairs from two Navy carriers, CVA-43 *Coral Sea* and the nuclear-powered CVAN-65 *Enterprise*. Ship names are near the jet nozzles. Though compact and smaller than most fighters the A-7 carries more bombs than World War II heavy bombers, and delivers them more accurately. The A-7E is still being built.

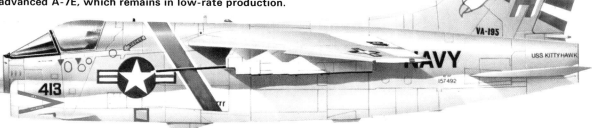

Vought F-8 Crusader

Vought F-8A to F-8J, RF-8, DF-8 and QF-8

Origin: Vought Systems Division of LTV, Dallas, USA.
Type: Originally single-seat carrier-based day fighter (see text).
Engine: One Pratt & Whitney J57 two-shaft turbojet with afterburner; (A, B, F, L) 16,200lb (7327kg) J57-12; (C, K) 16,900lb (7665kg) J57-16; others, 18,000lb (8165kg) J57-20A. About 100 F-8J re-engined with P&W TF30-420 afterburning turbofan, rated at 19,600lb (8891kg).
Dimensions: Span 35ft 8in (10·87m); (E, J) 35ft 2in; length 54ft 3in (16·54m); (E, J) 54ft 6in; height 15ft 9in (4·80m).
Weights: Empty (C) about 17,000lb (7710kg); (J) 19,700lb (8935kg); maximum loaded (C) 27,550lb (12,500kg); (J) 34,000lb (15,420kg).
Performance: Maximum speed, clean, at altitude (A, B, L, H) 1,013mph, (RF-8A) 982mph; (RF-8G) 1,002mph; (C, K, J) 1,105mph (1780km/h, Mach 1·68); (E) 1,135mph; (D) 1,230mph; initial climb (typical) 21,000ft (6400m)/min; service ceiling, from 38,400ft for J to 42,900ft (13,100m) for D; combat radius, from 368 miles for C, K to 440 miles (708km) for J and 455 miles (732km) for D.
Armament: (A, B, C) four 20mm Colt Mk 12 cannon each with 84 rounds; one Sidewinder on each side and 32 folding-fin rockets in belly pack; (D) four 20mm plus four Sidewinder; (E, H, J) four 20mm plus four Sidewinder plus 12 Mk 81 bombs, or two Bullpups or eight Zuni rockets; (K, L) as J but 144 rounds per gun; RF versions, none.
History: First flight (XF8U-1) 25 March 1955; (production F-8A) November 1956; service delivery 25 March 1957; final delivery 1965.

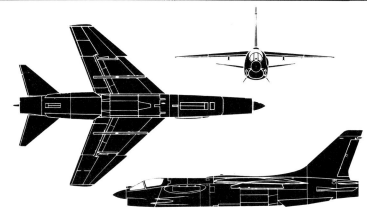

Above: Three-view of F-8J, a remanufactured F-8E now in use with the US Naval Reserve.

Left: A Vought F-8L of US Marine Corps squadron VMF-321. It is shown carrying the AIM-9H Sidewinder AAM; the Marines have a great interest in the air-to-surface mission for which all the rebuilt Crusaders are equipped.

Development: This outstanding carrier-based fighter, notable for its variable-incidence wing, outperformed the F-100 on the same engine, besides having 1,165gal internal fuel! Exceeding Mach 1 on the level on the first flight the F8U (as it then was) was rapidly developed for carrier service, and for 12 years was a popular combat aircraft of the US Navy and Marines. Altogether 1,259 were built, plus two prototypes, and in 1966–71 446 were rebuilt to a later standard (B to L, C to K, E to J and D to H). The continual process of improvement added all-weather radar, improved autopilot and weapon-delivery systems, air/ground weapons and, in the 42 F-8E(FN) for the French Navy, slower approach for small carriers. Variants include RF reconnaissance, DF drone RPV and QF RPV-control aircraft; a single dual trainer was also built. Many rebuilt versions remain in combat service, with long life ahead; total Crusader flight time exceeds 3,000,000hr.

Below: An F-8 (a remanufactured aircraft, probably a J) of Navy fighter squadron VF-201. To keep formation with the photographic aircraft it has set the wing at higher incidence.

The United States Marine Corps

Dr. Alan Ned Sabrosky, Ph.D., Assistant Professor of Politics, Catholic University of America, Washington D.C.; Research Associate, Foreign Policy Research Institute, Philadelphia.

Every nation has a *corps d'elite* whose military reputation stands above that of its other armed forces as a whole. Great Britain has its Brigade of Guards; France had its Foreign Legion, and then its paratroopers; and the United States has its Marine Corps. For over two hundred years, Marines have participated in every major war fought by the United States, as well as in innumerable police actions and armed interventions in virtually every part of the world. The list of battle honors earned by the Marine Corps from its inceptions in 1775 through the final days of the recent war in Indo-China bears testimony to its impressive record. Certainly, the performances of the Marine Corps at places such as Belleau Wood, Guadalcanal, Iwo Jima, and the Chosin Reservoir has earned it a prominent place in the lexicon of military history.

As with any military establishment, the US Marine Corps has its own set of traditions, reflecting an institutional interpretation of the Corps' past performance. In part, of course, such traditions are self-serving, highlighting only that which is worthy of emulation and ignoring or discarding anything that is not. Yet traditions cannot be dismissed lightly, especially in the case of a military institution. For such traditions not only influence the way in which the Corps sees itself, and how others view the Corps. They also shape the missions assigned to the Corps, and the way in which it organizes itself for battle.

Over the years, the Marine Corps has traditionally viewed itself as an elite force of infantry, highly disciplined and reliable (its motto is *Semper Fidelis*, or "Always Faithful"), which constituted the "cutting edge" of American diplomacy and power. The dictum that "every Marine was first and foremost a rifleman", while often only nominally accurate, reflected this perception. Even today, the fact that Marine ground combat formations are relatively large units with a high proportion of infantry is evidence of its continued significance. Further, the fact that Marines were stationed aboard major naval vessels, and traditionally operated in conjunction with the fleet, made them the logical choice for expeditionary forces abroad (sometimes in conjunction with members of the army and navy as well). This was particularly true in the years before strategic airlift capabilities became part of the American arsenal. But even then, Marines were still used as the initial ground combat forces in recent interventions (e.g., Lebanon in 1958, the Dominican Republic and South Vietnam in 1965), and as a "fire brigade" to relieve pressure on hard-pressed American forces (e.g., Korea in 1950) or evacuate American citizens in the face of enemy attack (e.g., Phnom Penh and Saigon in 1975). For the Marine Corps, in other words, being "first to fight" has had more than lyrical significance.

More recently, however, a new set of institutional traditions has been superimposed on those that originally existed. Since World War I, the Marine Corps has come to see itself as an elite assault force, in addition to whatever other qualifications it may have. The skill and ferocity of the Fourth Marine Brigade at Belleau Wood (subsequently renamed the "Wood of the Marine Brigade") earned them the accolade of Georges Clemenceau for "saving Paris", and the name of *Teufelhunde* ("devil dogs") from the Germans whom they defeated. Yet in that battle, and others like it, Marines had fought as line infantry. A unique mission was missing. That mission began to take shape in the years between the two world wars, at the same time as the Marine Corps was receiving a foretaste of Vietnam in the counterguerrilla operations in several Central American republics. During those interwar years, the Marines began experimenting with amphibious operations. When World War II began, and the Marines began to direct their activity to the problems confronting them in the Pacific Basin, these traditions merged to produce an amphibious assault force whose maintenance has since been the principal *raison d'être* for the US Marine Corps. Finally, the evolution of Marine aviation units not only provided the Corps with its own "air force", something which has been a bone of contention within the American armed services for years. After the reorganization of the US defense establishment in 1947, this capability allowed the Marine Corps to lay claim to being a unique, combined-arms, ground–air team with a special competence in amphibious warfare. This was the basic configuration of the Corps when it fought in the Korean and Vietnam wars, and which it retains today. The "Modern Marine Corps" had arrived.

The Modern Marine Corps

The position of the US Marine Corps in the American defense establishment today reflects a legislative legitimization of the status of the Corps at the end of World War II. That position was delineated by the National Security Act of 1947, as amended in 1952 and afterwards. It entailed a specification of: (1) the relationship of the Marine Corps to the other services in general, and to the Navy in particular; (2) the missions to be performed by the Corps; and (3) the basic force structure of the Corps.

The anomalous position of the Marine Corps within the US defense establishment is highlighted by its relationship to the other services. It is the only branch of the armed services not to be in a separate department. Instead, it has co-equal status with the Navy within the Department of the Navy, the Commandant Marine Corps (CMC) and the Chief of Naval Operations both reporting to the Secretary of the Navy. The Commandant Marine Corps, like the three other service chiefs, acts as a military advisor to the Commander in Chief. Yet unlike his Army, Navy, and Air Force counterparts, this "four services in three departments" organization precludes the Commandant from having a regular seat on the Joint Chiefs of Staff (JCS). However, when matters pertaining directly to the Marine Corps are being considered by the JCS, the Commandant participates in the discussions as a member co-equal in status with the other service chiefs.

The missions assigned to the Marine Corps fall into three broad categories. The principal mission of the Corps is to maintain an

Traditionally called Leathernecks or Grunts, the Marine has always been a tough fighting soldier who additionally has to be familiar with the sky and sea. The common combat image of the Corps is beach assault (below), but increasingly sophisticated and costly equipment has to be bought such as the Sea Stallion seen landing on LPH-10 *Tripoli* (left). Such equipment used to be bought by the Navy, but in 1969 the Marines boldly bought the Harrier V/STOL jet on their own account. By dogged persistence the Corps has added the jet to the rotor in vertical amphibious warfare, and V/STOL is now a key acronym for the Navy also.

US Marine Corps Posts and Stations

○ Aviation
● Marine Barracks
□ Detachments
△ Districts
▲ Installations
☆ State Departments

Marine Corps Personnel Strength by Country and Region (March 31, 1977).

Total Personnel	***188,845**	**Total: Foreign Countries**	**29,457**
Ashore	183,495	Ashore	25,842
Afloat	3,615	Afloat	3,165
US Territory and Special Locations	**159,388**	**Western and Southern Europe**	**2,914**
Continental US	138,693	European NATO	849
Transients	7,891	Afloat	1,800
Afloat	1,735		
		Western Hemisphere	**691**

Eastern Europe	**56**
Bulgaria	2
Czechoslovakia	6
Germany (Democratic Republic)	5
Hungary	5
Poland	6
Romania	6
USSR	18
Yugoslavia	8

amphibious capability to be used in conjunction with fleet operations, including the seizure and defense of advanced naval bases and the conduct of land operations essential to the successful conduct of a maritime campaign. In addition, the Corps was required to provide security detachments for naval bases and facilities, as well as the Navy's principal warships. Finally, the Corps would carry out additional duties at the discretion of the President, so long as they did not detract from the Corps' ability to conduct effective amphibious operations and to augment its operations forces upon wartime mobilization.

The third feature of the Marine Corps' position within the Department of Defense is also unique: the Corps is the only service to have its basic force structure defined by statutory law. According to the amended National Security Act of 1947, the Marine Corps will maintain a regular Fleet Marine Force of no less than three divisions and three aircraft wings, with the additional combat, combat support, and service units (force troops) necessary to maintain those divisions and air wings. Active-duty Marine Corps force levels could not exceed 400,000 personnel, although no minimum force levels were specified. Provision was also made for

reserve components to permit the expansion of the regular Marine Corps whenever mobilization occurred.

Current Strength and Deployment

The current active-duty strength of the Marine Corps is approximately 192,000 personnel, including 3,900 women. This represents a decline of 4,000 from the previously specified manpower levels brought about by recruiting difficulties during the initial years of the all-volunteer force in the US defense establishment as a whole. If recruiting conditions improve, however, the Corps plans to increase force levels to slightly over 194,000. The active-duty force is supplemented by a civilian workforce of approximately 20,000 personnel. Organized Marine Corps Reserves consist of approximately 33,500 personnel.

For nominal operational purposes, regular and reserve Marine Corps personnel are organized in four divisions (three regular and one reserve), four aircraft wings (three regular and one reserve), and supporting Force Troops. Traditionally, the Corps pairs a division (reinforced with Force Troops) and an aircraft wing into a so-called *division-wing team*, and divides

those teams among its two principal Fleet Marine Forces (FMF) which have responsibility for Marine Corps operations in the Atlantic / Mediterranean / Carribean and Pacific / Indian Ocean regions, respectively. Currently, one division-wing team, made up of the 2nd Marine Division (Reinforced) and the 2nd Marine Aircraft Wing are assigned to the Fleet Marine Force, Atlantic. Its principal units are based on the East Coast of the US. Two additional division-wing teams are assigned to the Fleet Marine Force, Pacific. One such team, composed of the 3rd Marine Division (Reinforced) and the 1st Marine Aircraft Wing, is based in the Western Pacific and Hawaii. Two-thirds of this division-wing team, with approximately 23,000 Marines, are deployed in the Western Pacific, principally on Okinawa. The remaining one-third of this division-wing team, organized into the 1st Marine Brigade (reinforced), is based in Hawaii. The second division-wing team with the Fleet Marine Force, Pacific, is based on the West Coast of the United States. This team, which is structured around the 1st Marine Division (Reinforced) and the 3rd Marine Aircraft Wing, provides rotation units for Marine formations based in the Western

East Asia and Pacific	25,165
Afloat	1,610
Africa, Near East and South Asia	629
Afloat	205
Undistributed	2
Total adjusted July 31, 1977	*190,855

Right upper: Two camouflaged Marines get their 81mm mortar zeroed-in on a possible "enemy" location during Exercise Bead Chevron. Marines are by definition amphibious and today are at home in the air as well.

Right: An amphibious assault team marches out to a waiting Sea Knight helicopter on board an amphibious warfare ship. This is effective against limited defenses.

Pacific, and is principally orientated toward operations in the Pacific Basin. However, it also provides back-up forces for Fleet Marine Force Atlantic, as in the Cuban crisis of 1962 and the intervention in the Dominican Republic in 1965.

In addition to its regular deployments, the Fleet Marine Forces provide contingents for the 6th Fleet (Mediterranean) and the 7th Fleet (Western Pacific). Each contingent, or Marine Amphibious Unit (MAU), provides an on-hand amphibious assault force capable of being placed ashore on its respective area on short notice. Similar units are sometimes deployed in the Caribbean (principally in support of the

US naval base at Guantanamo Bay, Cuba) and the Atlantic. Finally, the reserve division-wing team, made up of the 4th Marine Division and the 4th Marine Aircraft Wing, with supporting units, is located entirely within the US itself. Divided among localities within the six Marine Corps Districts, the units and personnel of this division-wing team are intended to augment and reinforce the regular division-wing teams.

Organization and Principal Weapons

Perhaps the dominant characteristic of both the divisional and aircraft wing organization within the Marine Corps is their size. Each is larger than its counterparts in the Army and the Air Force, respectively, and each reflects the basic doctrine emphasizing multi-purpose, combined-arms amphibious assault forces.

This is particularly apparent in the case of the Marine divisional structure. Even more than its advocacy of the combined-arms ground-air team organizing concept, the Marine Corps retains its basic faith in the central role of infantry in combat. Thus, the 18,000-man Marine Division (counting attached Navy personnel but excluding Force Troops personnel who would normally deploy with divisional units) includes a high proportion of infantry. The Marine divisions are the largest in the US defense establishment, exceeding by 20 per cent the size of their closest analogue in the US Army. Yet this advantage in size does not result in greater firepower or mobility for the Marine Division. In fact, with few exceptions, Marine ground combat formations are larger, less mobile, and possess less organic firepower than their principal Army counterparts.

The basic structure of the Marine Division, as it is presented in Chart 1, is essentially the old "triangular" model of World War II vintage. It is organized around three infantry regiments, each of which has three infantry battalions and a headquarters element. Each battalion, in its turn, has a headquarters company (including an assault/anti-tank/mortar capability) and four rifle companies, each of which is approximately two-thirds larger than its Army counterpart. Rifle company weapons include 60mm mortars, 3.5-in rocket launchers, 7.62mm M-60 machine guns, and individual weapons. Battalion-level weapons include eight 81mm mortars and eight 106mm recoilless rifles, with the latter scheduled to be replaced by the DRAGON weapons system now coming on line in the Corps. No organic heavy weapons exist at regimental level. In addition to the infantry regiments, each Marine division has an artillery regiment equipped with towed 105mm and 155mm howitzers, something of an anomaly in modern divisional structures. The division also includes a reconnaissance battalion, an engineer battalion, and other supporting units. However, the Marine division does not include any organic armored fighting vehicles or any heavy artillery. Those capabilities would be provided to the division by the Force Troops. Tank battalions include M60A1 tanks, plus an antitank company, and amphibious tractor (Amtrac) battalions equipped with LVTP-7 armored personnel carriers provide limited mobility for the division. Finally, Force artillery batteries are equipped with self-propelled 155mm and 8-in howitzers and 175mm guns.

For their part, the Marine aircraft wings, whose basic structure is presented in Chart 2, are both large and multipurpose. Unlike their Air Force counterparts, which usually include aircraft of only a single combat type, Marine Air Wings run the gamut from air-superiority (or air-air warfare) squadrons (F-4 N/S), to offensive air support squadrons (with A-4E/F/Ms, A-6/A/Es, and the controversial AV-8A V/STOL Harriers and AH-1J armed helicopters), and assault support squadrons (with light, medium, and heavy helicopter squadrons). Reconnaissance, electronic warfare, observation, and assault transport squadrons are also included in the inventory. Of all of its varied inventory, none has been more controversial than the British-built Hawker-Siddeley *Harrier*, a versatile yet complex aircraft which has a number of impressive characteristics. The Corps has had much difficulty with them, losing nearly a quarter of its original inventory of 110 aircraft in operational crashes.

Task Organization and Tactics

The size of both the Marine division and the Marine aircraft wing, the built-in reliance of the division on reinforcing elements from Force Troops, and the diversity and multipurpose flexibility of the aircraft wing reflect a basic element in Marine Corps organization, planning, and doctrine. This is the importance of "tailoring" combined-arms forces with a mix of ground and air components to perform a specific mission. Plans to the contrary notwithstanding, these task forces all too often tend to be *ad hoc* rather than programmed, relying on forces that are available rather than those that might provide an optimal force mix. The basic "building block" in this approach is the Marine Amphibious Unit (MAU). This comprises 1/9th of a division-wing team, including a battalion landing team (BLT)—an infantry battalion with attached divisional and force troops—and a composite helicopter squadron. Multiples of the MAU, which is intended to be a quick-reaction force, are the Marine Amphibious Brigade, or MAB (with from 2 to 5 MAUs), and the Marine Amphibious Force, or MAF (which can comprise up to two full division-wing teams). At present the MAB is considered in many circles to be the formation most capable of being de-

Right: Like the Navy the US Marine Corps uses the probe/drogue system of in-flight refuelling. Here at least six of the Corps' KC-130F Hercules tankers are topping up a Marine Corps fighter squadron, VMFA-232, with Phantom F-4Js.

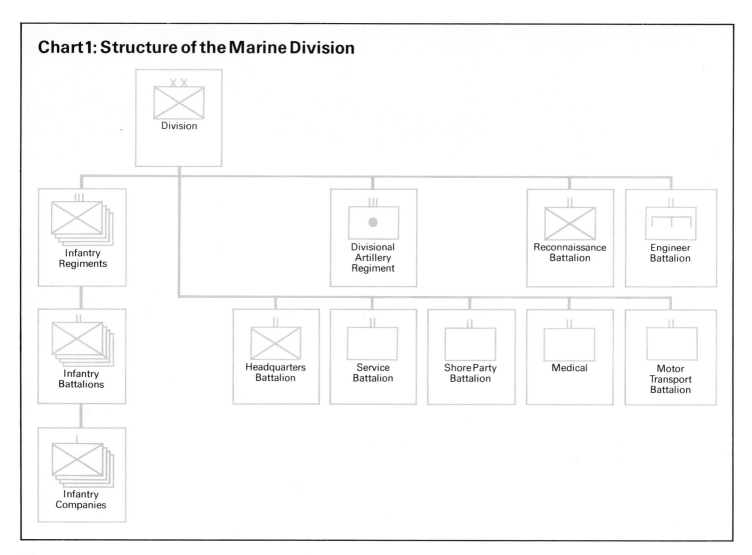

Chart 1: Structure of the Marine Division

Chart 2: Structure of the Marine Aircraft Wing

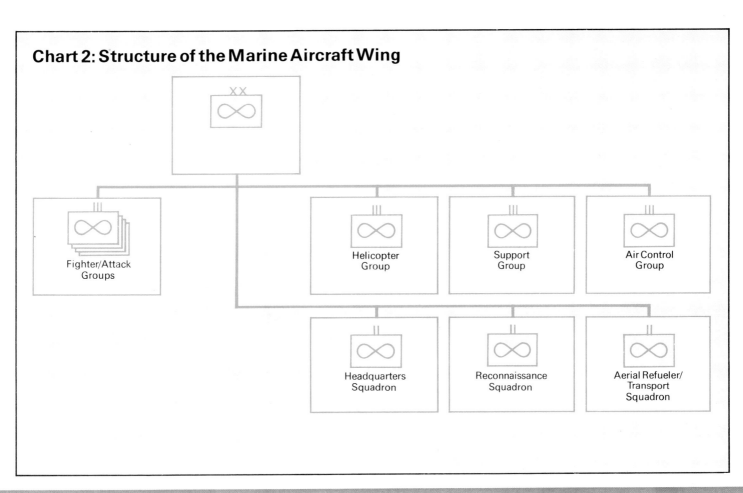

Fighter/Attack Groups

Helicopter Group

Support Group

Air Control Group

Headquarters Squadron

Reconnaissance Squadron

Aerial Refueler/ Transport Squadron

ployed in likely combat operations that are not amenable to being handled by a simple quick-reaction MAU. The MAF is more of an administrative than an operational entity, although operational plans for a MAF certainly exist.

Perhaps the single dominant characteristic of Marine tactical doctrine is the emphasis on the principle of the offensive. This applies not only to combined-arms amphibious operations, with their projected mix of seaborne and helicopter-borne assault groups attacking with naval gunfire and tactical air support, but to all other operations as well. In theory, the tactical repertoire of the Marine Corps is as varied as that of any other modern military organization. Certainly, it includes major emphasis on the closely coordinated employment of close air support and (where available and feasible) naval gunfire support as well. Yet, in practice, it often seems that the institutional precedence given to the ability to provide assault forces, coupled with the relatively limited tactical flexibility permitted to amphibious assault forces in the initial stage of an operation, continues to predominate.

Anti-Aircraft and Anti-Armor Capabilities
Control of the air has always been an important element in planning amphibious operations. It is equally essential for amphibious forces ashore to have an independent capability to defend themselves against attacking aircraft. Similarly, the relative dearth of armored fighting vehicles available to the MAU and its larger multiples argues for enhancing their anti-armor capabilities as well. Both anti-aircraft and anti-armor capabilities become of even greater importance to the Corps if one contemplates employing Marine units in either European or Middle Eastern theaters of operations.

Two basic weapons systems are available to the Marine Corps for anti-aircraft defense. First, each of the Fleet Marine Forces has a light anti-aircraft missile (LAAM) battalion equipped with HAWK surface-to-air missiles with its Force Troops. Second, for close-in defense, the Marine Air Control Group (MACG) of each Marine aircraft wing has a Forward Area Air Defense (FAAD) battery equipped with 75 "Redeye" shoulder-fired surface-to-air missile launchers. One section of this battery, with five "Redeye" launchers, would normally be deployed with each MAU. In addition, each Hawk LAAM battalion has four "Redeye" teams for close-in defense.

At present, Marine Corps anti-armor capabilities are principally based on its medium tanks (M60A1s), the 106mm recoilless rifles in the anti-tank platoons of each infantry battalion, the 3.5in rocket launchers in each rifle company, and the light assault weapons (LAW) distributed

Above: US Marines have often had to demonstrate their ability to move quickly off the beaches, under fire. Here, during training in Turkey, some hurry to take up position after having landed with M60A1 battle tanks.

among the infantry. This capability, however, is rapidly being augmented with the introduction of both heavy (TOW) and medium (DRAGON) missile systems. The first TOW missiles have been deployed, and it is anticipated that all regular and reserve Marine formations will be equipped with both the TOW and the DRAGON systems by 1980. It is now projected for each tank battalion to have (in addition to its complement of 70 tanks) an anti-tank company with 72 TOW launchers mounted on M151A1 jeeps. In addition, each infantry battalion will have an assault/anti-tank platoon which will include 16 DRAGON launchers. It is now planned to phase out both the 106mm recoilless rifles and the 3.5in rocket launchers when the TOW and DRAGON systems are deployed throughout the Corps.

On balance, it is clear that the Marine Corps, as it is presently configured, has a number of distinct assets. *First*, it is clearly a highly cost-effective force, providing a considerable degree of combat power at relatively low cost. In FY 1977, for example, only 4 percent of the entire defense budget was allocated to the Marine Corps. For that expenditure, the Corps provided 9 percent of the military personnel, 12 percent of the general-purpose forces, 12 percent of the tactical air forces, and 15 percent of the ground combat forces in the entire US defense establishment.

Second, within its basic ground combat

formations, the Marine Corps maintains a very high "teeth-to-tail" (combat : support) ratio of 60:40. This is the highest in the American defense establishment, and comes the closest of any American formation to the combat : support ratio of the very "toothy" Soviet formations. Combined with its previously mentioned cost-effectiveness, the ability of the Corps to provide "the most [combat power] for the least [outlay or personnel and resources]" seems demonstrated.

Third, the combined-arms ground-air team concept which is at the foundation of Marine Corps operational doctrine provides a framework for the integrated use of all combat arms to a degree greater than that which exists elsewhere in the US defense establishment. In this highly flexible and well-coordinated framework, the Marines employ a very high ratio of tactical air:infantry capabilities as a surrogate for the armor and artillery in which the Corps is lacking (at least by Army standards). This enhances the combat power of Marine formations beyond what might be expected from an inspection of the tables of organization and equipment of the ground combat elements.

Fourth, while there is some doubt about the utility of a large amphibious capability, there is little doubt about the need to have *some* ability to project combat power ashore via an amphibious assault, as that is currently conceived in US doctrine. Here, the Corps' forte stands out. It has the greatest experience with amphibious operations, and possesses the greatest number of personnel trained to manage such operations, of any force in the world. Airborne formations certainly can deploy more rapidly than seaborne Marines. But in some instances (e.g., Lebanon, 1958, Dominican Republic, 1965, and the Mayagüez incident, 1975) an amphibious force on station in a trouble spot may still be preferable to a more mobile force which would have to be deployed overseas from the US itself. Certainly, the new amphibious assault ships (LHA)—two of which are now operational, with three others to be available by 1980—which can carry 2,000 Marines with their artillery and armor, plus helicopters, will enhance the Corps' amphibious capability.

On the other hand, the Corps has a number of liabilities as well. *First,* the fact that approximately 71 percent of the funds authorized for the Marine Corps last year went for manpower-related costs underscores the "lightness" of the Marine ground combat formations. As Table 1 indicates, even a reinforced Marine infantry battalion comes out a distant third in comparison with equivalent Soviet ("threat force") and US Army motorized or mechanized rifle/infantry battalions. "Lightness" is, of course, a relative term. Against most Asian, African, or Latin American units, a Marine battalion (reinforced) would be considered a very *heavy* unit. Yet unless Marine operations in the future can be limited to the Third World, the ability of the Corps to operate effectively

Table 1 : Comparison of US/Soviet "Type" Battalion Major Weapons			
	Reinforced "Threat Force" (Soviet Union) Motorized Rifle Battalion	Cross-Attached US Army Mechanized Inf. Battalion	Reinforced US Marine Infantry Battalion
APCs	30 (BMP)	24 (APC)	10 (LVTP-7)
Tanks	13 (T-62)	17 (M60A1)	5 (M60A1)
HAWS*	33 (SAGGER) 30 (73mm auto. cannon)	22 (TOW) 9 (20mm auto. cannon)	8 (TOW) —
MAWS**	2 (SPG9RR)	22 (DRAGON)	32 (DRAGON)
LAWS***	29 (RPG7)	****(M72)	****(M72)
Mortars	6 (120mm)	4 (4.2 inch) 6 (81mm)	8 (81mm)

*Heavy Anti-tank Weapons.
**Medium Anti-tank Weapons.
***Light Anti-tank Weapons.
****Treated as a disposable round of ammunition; issued as needed.

Above: Two Marines firing Redeye man-portable surface-to-air missiles. Though used by the Corps in large numbers, Redeye suffers from severe deficiencies and is probably to be replaced by Stinger.

Right: Amphibious training in the Canal Zone (Panama), and two LVTP-7 tracked personnel carriers drive into USS *Tarawa* (General-Purpose Assault Ship LHA-1) in Balboa Harbor.

against much heavier Soviet formations must be considered questionable.

Second, it is very clear that the close-air support (CAS) on which the Corps has placed great reliance in the past may no longer retain the same usefulness. The family of Soviet-designed surface-to-air missiles and radar-directed multiple automatic AA cannon have, as the 1973 Arab-Israeli war demonstrated, made close-air support a very chancy thing. Yet this development, unless reversed, has a more profound implication for the Corps. That is, undermining the reliability of CAS also calls into question the utility of the air-ground team concept basic to USMC force structure and doctrine. Questions of interservice competition aside, it may become increasingly difficult to justify the "heavy" Marine aircraft wings in a combat environment ever more hostile to CAS. If those wings are attenuated, then the Corps would either have to acquire more armor and firepower to allow it to act without CAS, or forgo such augmentations and preclude engaging in operations outside of the Third World. Neither operation would justify a continuation of the Corps, as it is now constituted, at its present force levels.

Third, the Corps' ability to conduct amphibious operations with the support necessary for good prospects of success is decreasing, although not because of deficiencies on its part. The current fleet of amphibious warfare ships is relatively new, having an average age of less than 9 years. But trends in amphibious shipping over more than a decade (1964 to 1976) show that

there now exists: (1) fewer ships (–53 percent), with (2) less lift (–36 percent) than in the past. The fact that there is barely half the amphibious lift capability deemed necessary by US planners cannot be considered desirable. Moreover, naval gunfire (NGF) capability has decreased sharply in recent years to the point where the ability of a Marine landing force to receive essential support in the absence of tactical air superiority is doubtful. Unless these deficiencies can be remedied, the long-term ability of the US Marine Corps to retain a viable amphibious assault capability against established opposition will become highly questionable.

Three Basic Questions

In the aftermath of the Vietnam war and the general reassessment of American defense policy that has taken place, a number of questions have been raised about the place the US Marine Corps should have in the emerging defense establishment. Perhaps the most important point to be faced by the Corps is what it should become in order to be an effective instrument of US policy in the emerging world order. Three major issues have been raised which bear on this question. *First,* there is the issue of whether or not the US *needs* a Marine Corps, at least as it is presently constituted. Many question the need for a major amphibious capability; others wonder what the Marine Corps does that the Army cannot do; and still others argue simply that the Marine Corps has become both a second Army and a third Air

Force, and as such is an organizational redundancy.

Second, even if it is conceded that the US should retain a Marine Corps, there is considerable uncertainty about the size and the mission such a Corps should have. If it is reoriented toward NATO, then a major rearming effort would seem to be required to put Marine formations on an equal footing with both allied and threat forces in that theater. If it is not reoriented toward NATO, then it could well remain a "light" force oriented toward limited interventions and the Pacific Basin. Yet, in this case, many argue that its size could well be reduced significantly.

Third, there is the problem of manpower. The very foundation of the Corps is well-trained, well-disciplined personnel. Yet, for a period of time after the shift to the all-volunteer force, the Marine Corps was experiencing considerable difficulty in finding the "few good men" it needed. Turbulence and disciplinary problems within the Corps were widespread. This situation appears to have stabilized now, and is even improving in a number of respects. But there are serious reservations about the long-term ability of the Corps to recruit the numbers of high-quality personnel necessary to maintain current force levels. Equally pointed reservations have been placed regarding the long-term effect the modifications in the traditionally intense basic training may have on the overall quality of the Marine Corps.

The Future of the Marine Corps

It is readily apparent that the Marine Corps' history and record are sufficiently meritorious to commend it as a model for other military institutions to emulate. Recent criticism directed at the Corps as an institution is far from unusual. After World War II and the Korean War, the need for a Marine Corps was called into question, and the post-Vietnam experience simply fits the pattern. Yet it was, and is, clearly in the national interest of the US to have at its disposal an elite combat force, even—and, perhaps, especially—in an era of technologically sophisticated weaponry.

On the other hand, it must be recognized that the Corps' response to the most recent round of criticism has been less than persuasive. It can certainly be argued that there remains a need to retain an amphibious assault capability in the modern world. But it is a very different matter to argue that there is a need for a major, multi-division amphibious capability, and that the Marine Corps should be able to participate in operations in Europe, if the need arises. Memories of the past notwithstanding, it is all too likely that any adversary large enough to merit (e.g.) a MAF-level amphibious assault would also have the capability to concentrate massive firepower on a most inviting target: an amphibious force, lying (even at some distance) off a shoreline, preparing to send in the landing force via helicopter and assault landing craft or armored amphibians. What may have been perfectly feasible in the years before the advent of nuclear weapons and precision-guided munitions, or even in the era of US nuclear superiority, does not necessarily apply today. Furthermore, it should be clear that the only way that the Marine Corps could realistically hope to be able to conduct operations in a European war is for it to acquire a substantial mechanized capability. Yet this would make it functionally equivalent to the Army, thereby undermining the presumption of uniqueness on which its existence as a separate entity was, and remains, based.

One thing must be admitted fairly. The Marine Corps, despite extensive rationales to the contrary, has evolved to the point where its size and force structure bear only a tangential relationship to the purpose, scope, and realistic missions of an elite *force d'interventions.* Nor would augmenting the mechanized warfare capability of the Corps ease the problem. In fact, the Corps is caught on the horns of a dilemma, and one which is of its own making. If

it remains as it is presently configured, the Corps risks becoming a functional anachronism, as outmoded as horse cavalry in an era of machine guns, organizing itself around the doctrine of major amphibious operations in a world where the feasibility of such operations had become doubtful. Yet if it moves closer to the Army in terms of its organization, equipment, weapons, and tactical doctrine (e.g., regarding the conduct of mechanized operations), it risks losing both its institutional uniqueness *and* the mobility necessary for it to be able to carry out the rapid deployments essential for an intervention force, amphibious or not.

What, then, should the Marine Corps do? It is clear that there is no rational basis for the Corps to become a second Army, replete with mechanized formations; nor to compete with the other services for the possession of a major tactical air capability; nor even to remain a "light" force in a world of "heavy" conflicts. On the other hand, it is equally clear that what really gave the Marine Corps its presumptions of uniqueness and elite status in the past reflected its institutional values more than its operational characteristics. What made the Marine Corps different was not the missions it was intended to perform. It was the overall caliber of the forces available for *whatever* missions they were called upon to carry out. And it is there that the Corps should base its future position, and not simply retreat to periodic restatements of missions

Above: The main task of the Marines is amphibious warfare, and this needs special ships. Here an LCU landing craft is reversing out of the interior of an LSD dock landing ship.

that hark back to the days of Tarawa and Iwo Jima.

The United States needs a force capable of carrying out interventions in parts of the world that do not carry with them the spectre of nuclear war or an armored battle on the plains of Europe. The Marine Corps can become such a force with a mission and a structure appropriate to that role. To accomplish this would require a willingness on the part of the Corps itself to accept markedly lower force levels, and to divest itself of most of its aviation components. It would entail the Corps' adoption of an airmobile capability as well, making it the sole US intervention force, having both amphibious and airborne/airmobile capabilities, and allowing the Army to concentrate its attention on general war requirements. Ideally, the Marine Corps should separate itself from the Department of the Navy and form a separate service department, thus facilitating the shift in mission indicated above and underscoring the new mission of the Corps. Finally, a major unit of the restructured Corps should be stationed in Europe—not to participate in any conflict that might arise there, but to provide a forward-

Above: Largest helicopter of the Marine Corps, the Sikorsky CH-53D Sea Stallion can airlift 37 equipped "Grunts" or an eight-ton load of stores. This CH-53 is seen during exercises in mid-winter.

Right: The Marine Corps, like the Navy, is moving strongly towards new vehicles such as the ACV (air-cushion vehicle) and VTOL aircraft. This is the Bell Aerosystems amphibious assault ACV.

based intervention capability in Africa/Middle East analogous to the one that is maintained in the Western Pacific.

To effect this transformation would require radical changes, indeed, and the political obstacles to such a step would certainly be formidable. The Corps itself would oppose force reductions and the loss of its tactical aviation. The Army would resist losing the "airborne/airmobile" capability which has become a measure of status in that service. The Department of the Navy would object to losing control over the Marine Corps. Yet if these changes could be implemented, they could well produce the type of Marine Corps which would serve both its country and itself to the fullest measure possible in the coming years. Perhaps that would be a good lesson in the true meaning of "Semper Fidelis".

US Rockets and Missiles

Bill Gunston, contributor to Jane's *All the World's Aircraft*; author of many technical books and papers on military affairs.

The following inventory of weapons includes the major rockets and missiles in service with US armed forces, and important systems under development. They are arranged in system types.

STRATEGIC MISSILES

Boeing AGM-86A ALCM

Origin: Boeing Aerospace Company, Seattle.
Type: Air-launched cruise missile.
Dimensions: Length 14ft (4·27m); wing span 9ft 5in (289cm); fuselage diameter 25in (64cm).
Launch weight: 1,900lb (862kg) (with belly fuel tank, 2,400lb, 1089kg).
Propulsion: Williams Research F107-WR-100 two-shaft turbofan, rated in the 600lb (272kg) thrust class.
Guidance: McDonnell Douglas Tercom (terrain-comparison) backed up by inertial system.
Range: Maximum, hi, without belly tank, 760 miles (1200km).
Flight speed: Cruise, about Mach 0·65; terminal phase, possibly Mach 0·8.
Warhead: Thermonuclear, possibly 200kT.

This neat miniature aircraft is carried with its wings and tail folded and engine air inlet retracted. It then closely resembles a SRAM in bulk, and a B-52 can carry the same number: eight on the same rotary launcher and 12 (in two tandem triplets) on the external inner-wing pylons. The FB-111A can carry four externally and two internally. Derived partly from the cancelled AGM-86 SCAD (Subsonic Cruise Armed Decoy) missile, the ALCM can be used to hit hard point targets, and also for non-nuclear, reconnaissance and decoy missions. However used, it dilutes defenses, gives many fresh options and improves penetrability of the parent bomber. Flight development began with jettison tests in 1975 and continued with powered rounds from 5 March 1976. Despite several early failures the programme has moved satisfactorily, and operational deployment on the B-52G and H and FB-111A has been brought forward to 1980. With a belly fuel tank the range is extended about 30 percent. The proposed ALCM-B would be 60in (1·5m) longer and have double the range, but would be incompatible with the rotary launcher or B-52 internal bay. Despite this, AGM-86A will not go into the inventory, and if the Boeing ALCM is selected in preference to AGM-109 Tomahawk (p. 220) it will be the long B-version. A competitive fly-off took place in 1979.

Below and left: Sixth development AGM-86A at Boeing Aerospace. Its successor, AGM-86B, is seen on p. 253.

Bottom: An exploded drawing of the AGM-86A, which is the only version compatible with the internal eight-round rotary SRAM launcher of the B-52G and H, seen with ALCM below.

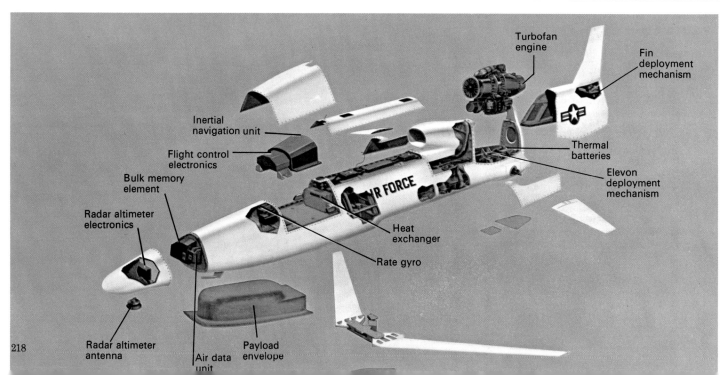

Boeing LGM-30 Minuteman

Origin: Boeing Aerospace Company, Seattle (missiles were assembled at a plant near Ogden, Utah).
Type: ICBM deployed in hardened silo.
Dimensions: Overall length 59ft 10in (18·2m); body diameter (first stage) 72in (183cm).
Launch weight: Minuteman II, 70,116lb (31,800kg); Minuteman III, 76,015lb (34,475kg).
Propulsion: First stage, Thiokol TU-120 (M55E) solid rocket, 200,000lb (91,000kg) thrust for 60 sec; second stage, Aerojet SR19 solid rocket, with liquid-injection thrust-vector control, 60,000lb (27,200kg) thrust; third stage (II) Hercules solid rocket, 35,000lb (16,000kg) thrust, (III) Aerojet/Thiokol solid rocket, 34,876lb (16,000kg) thrust, plus post-boost control system (see text).
Guidance: Rockwell Autonetics inertial.
Range: (II) over 7,000 miles (11,250km); (III) over 8,000 miles (12,875km).
Flight speed: At burnout, over 15,000mph (24,000km/h).
Warhead: (II) Avco Mk 11C with single thermonuclear device (about 2MT) with Tracor Mk 1A penaids; (III) three (sometimes two) General Electric Mk 12 MIRVs (see text).

Minuteman was designed in 1958–60 as a smaller and simpler second-generation ICBM using solid propellant. Originally envisaged as a mobile weapon launched from trains, it was actually deployed (probably mistakenly) in fixed hardened silos. Minuteman I (LGM-30B) became operational in 1963 but is no longer in use. Minuteman II (LGM-30F) became operational from December 1966 and today 450 are still in use, though replacement because of expired component-lifetimes cannot be long delayed. By 1978 all the re-entry vehicles should be of the Mk 11C type hardened against EMP; consideration has been given to prolonging missile life, and improving accuracy, by retrofitting the NS-20 guidance used on Minuteman III (LGM-30G). The latter, operational since 1970, has a new third stage and completely new re-entry vehicles forming a fourth stage with its own propulsion, guidance package and pitch-roll motors; as well as several warheads, individually targetable, it houses chaff, decoys and possibly other penaids. A new Mk 12A re-entry vehicle has been developed and will arm a proportion of the force of 550 missiles. It houses three 350kT W-78 warheads and has higher accuracy. Production of LGM-30G Minuteman III ended in late 1977, but the force is continually being updated, with improved silos, better guidance software, and the Command Data Buffer System which, with other add-ons, reduces re-targetting time per missile from around 24 hours to about half an hour, and allows it to be done remotely from the Wing's Launch Control Centre or from an ALCS (Airborne Launch Control System) aircraft.

Above right: Test launch of an early Minuteman III from Cape Kennedy Air Force Station, Cape Canaveral, in April 1969. This was one of about 34 test flights on the Atlantic Range in 1968–70.

Right: Minuteman II emplaced in a SAC SMW (Strategic Missile Wing) silo in the midwest. This example has the Avco Mk 11A re-entry vehicle with original Mk 1 penetration aids.

Boeing AGM-69A SRAM

Origin: Boeing Aerospace Company, Seattle.
Type: Fully manoeuvrable self-guided wingless rocket.
Dimensions: Length 14ft (4·27m) (with streamlined tailcone, 15ft 10¼in, 4·83m); body diameter 17·5in (44·5cm); fin span 35in (89cm).
Launch weight: 2,230lb (1010kg).
Propulsion: LPC-415 (former Lockheed Propulsion Co) re-startable two-pulse solid motor.
Guidance: Inertial, plus radar terrain-avoidance.
Range: Hi, up to 105 miles (170km); lo, up to 35 miles (56km).
Flight speed: Typically Mach 3.
Warhead: W-69 thermonuclear, 200kT.

A weapon of outstanding power, compactness and flexibility, SRAM (Short-Range Attack Missile) stemmed from the US Air Force Specific Operational Requirement 212 of 1964. In 1966 Boeing was selected as prime contractor, dropping a dummy from a B-52 in 1967 and completing all flight development in 1971. Production was authorized in January 1971 and production deliveries began in March 1972. By the end of 1975 the 1,500 missiles in the original orders had been delivered. SRAM is almost perfectly streamlined, and though it has three tail fins at 120° it has no wings, relying on body lift for trajectory control. SRAM can be launched at any altitude, in any direction, to hit a target in any direction from the bomber. Profile can be infinitely varied, including low terrain-following, ballistic, inertial plus sudden pull-up or any desired avoidance manoeuvres. The B-52G and H force of SAC (Strategic Air Command) each carry up to 20 SRAMS, each of which can be separately targeted. Eight are carried on a rotary launcher in the aft bomb bay, leaving space in the forward bay for four Mk 28 thermonuclear weapons. The other 12 are carried in tandem triple clusters on the external underwing pylons, these missiles having jettisonable tailcones to reduce drag before launch. The FB-111A carries two SRAMs in its bomb bay and four (with tailcones) on the swivelling underwing pylons. In 1977 a new motor was being developed (by Thiokol, LPC no longer being in business) because the LPC-415 has reached its five-year shelf life. The new motor will be retrofitted, at substantial cost. It was also to have powered an improved SRAM for the B-1.

Below: Fully loaded SRAM launcher inside the forward bomb bay of a B-52. Plans for an improved AGM-69B died with the B-1, but studies continue for a large SRAM carrier such as the 747 on p. 63. This could carry nine of these eight-missile dispensers.

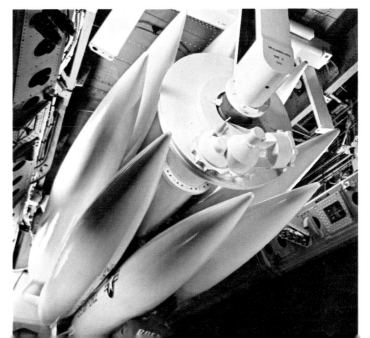

BGM-109 Tomahawk

Origin: General Dynamics/Convair, San Diego.
Type: Air-breathing cruise missile for submarine, surface ship, land-mobile or air launch.
Dimensions: Length 219in (556cm) (with tandem boost motor, about 21ft, 640cm); body diameter 21in (53cm); span 100in (254cm).
Launch weight: (strategic, sub-launched) about 4,000lb (1814kg), (strategic, land launched) about 3,000lb (1360kg), (strategic, air launched) about 2,500lb (1135kg), (tactical, air launched) about 2,200lb (1000kg).
Propulsion: (strategic) Williams Research F107 turbofan, about 600lb (272kg) thrust; (tactical) Teledyne CAE J402 turbojet, same rating.
Guidance: (strategic) McDonnell Douglas' Tercom and inertial, in complementary modes; (tactical) same guidance systems as AGM-84A Harpoon.
Range: (strategic, sub- or land) about 1,727 miles (2780km), (strategic, air) about 2,240 miles (3600km), (tactical) about 350 miles (560km).
Flight speed: Mach 0·72 (550mph, 885km/h).
Warhead: (strategic) thermonuclear, 1,000lb (454kg), (tactical) conventional, about same weight, with multiple fuze systems.

Development of Tomahawk began in December 1972 when the Navy ordered studies of an SLCM (Sea-Launched Cruise Missile). General Dynamics won the definitive prime contract in March 1976, by which time the program had greatly broadened to include tactical and strategic versions for launch from a wide range of platforms. All use similar airframes, though the tactical version has less fuel, a different engine and guidance, conventional warhead and other changes. Submarine-launched versions are fired from torpedo tubes in a jettisoned environmental capsule, and all surface-launched models have a tandem boost motor. Land-based Tomahawks would be deployed by USAF Tactical Air Command.

Right: All four versions (submarine, ship, land and air) can have any of three types of warhead.

Below: First launch of AGM-109 air-launched Tomahawk, from a Navy A-6 in March 1976. In 1979 this missile was evaluated against the AGM-86B.

Above: Test launch from underwater tube at San Clemente, Calif.

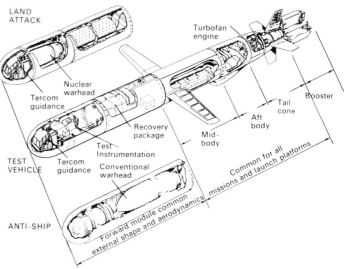

Lockheed UGM-27 Polaris

Origin: Lockheed Missiles & Space Company, Sunnyvale, California.
Type: Submarine-launched ballistic missile.
Dimensions: Length (Polaris A2) 31ft 0in (9·45m), (A3) 31ft 6in (9·60m); body diameter 54in (137cm).
Launch weight: (A2) about 30,000lb (13,600kg), (A3) 35,000lb (15,850kg).
Propulsion: First stage (A2) Aerojet solid motor with jetevator control, (A3) Aerojet motor with glass-fibre case and four rotatable nozzles; second stage (A2) Hercules motor with gimballed nozzle, (A3) Hercules motor with liquid injection.
Guidance: Inertial, developed by MIT, manufactured by GE/Hughes.
Range: (A2) 1,700 miles (2800km), (A3) 2,875 miles (4630km).
Flight speed: (both) about Mach 10 at burnout.
Warhead: (A2) AEC (Lawrence Lab)/Lockheed Mk I, thermonuclear, about 1 MT, (A3) Lockheed Mk 2, three MIRVs, about 200 kT each.

Development of the Polaris weapon system started in 1956, when it became apparent that an advanced solid-propulsion missile could be made compatible with submarine launch tubes, thus carrying it nearer its target and hiding it in the ocean's depths. UGM-27, Polaris A1, became operational on the first FBMS (Fleet Ballistic Missile System) submarine in 1960; in 1962 one impacted on target with a live warhead. None of this version remain in use. UGM-27B, Polaris A2, with increased range resulting from a longer second stage, became operational in 1962; none are in use but many are being used in test programs. UGM-27C, Polaris A3, achieved a 60 per cent increase in range by filling the available space more completely, using a lighter structure and later propellant. Operational since 1964, it remains in use on the ten oldest FBMS vessels, of the SSBN-598 *George Washington* and 608 *Ethan Allen* classes. Each has 16 tubes. (Britain's Royal Navy uses A3 on its four 16-tube submarines, with a different British warhead system.)

Below: A Polaris A3 training shot from a Fleet Ballistic Missile Submarine submerged off Cape Canaveral in April 1966.

Lockheed UGM-73 Poseidon

Origin: Lockheed Missiles & Space Company, Sunnyvale, California.
Type: Submarine-launched ballistic missile.
Dimensions: Length 34ft 0in (10·36m); body diameter 74·0in (188cm).
Launch weight: About 65,000lb (29,500kg).
Propulsion: First stage, advanced solid motor by Thiokol and Hercules with gas-pressurized gimballed nozzle; second stage, Hercules motor with similar nozzle.
Guidance: Inertial, developed by MIT, manufactured by GE and Raytheon.
Range: See "warhead".
Flight speed: At burnout, about Mach 10.
Warhead: AEC (Lawrence Lab)/Lockheed MIRV system carrying ten 50 kT RVs for ultimate range of 3,230 miles (5200 km) or 14 for 2,485 miles (4000km), in each case with full kit of penaids.

Resulting from prolonged studies of the benefits of later technology, Poseidon C3 can be carried by Polaris submarines after the installation of the Mk 88 fire-control system and minor modifications to the launch tubes. Compared with Polaris A3 it has at least equal range, carries double the payload and has roughly twice the accuracy (halved CEP), as well as much improved MIRV and penaid capability. Of the US Navy's 41 FBMS submarines, 31 are operational with Poseidon. Each carries 16 launch tubes. Since 1973 a modification program, completed in 1978, has rectified deficiencies which showed up after initial operational capability was achieved in 1970. More than 40 missiles, withdrawn from submarines after operational patrol, have been fired with excellent results.

Right: Liftoff of a Poseidon C3 from Pad 25C at Cape Kennedy Air Force Station, Cape Canaveral, in May 1970. Development flight testing was completed the following month.

Lockheed UGM-93 Trident

Origin: Navy and Lockheed Missiles & Space Company, Sunnyvale.
Type: Advanced SLBM (submarine-launched ballistic missile).
Dimensions: Length 34ft 0in (10·36m); body diameter 74in (188cm); (Trident D5 same diameter but longer).
Launch weight: 70,000lb (32,000kg); (D5, about 110,000lb, 50,000kg).
Propulsion: Three tandem stages of advanced solid motors each developed jointly by Thiokol and Hercules, with thrust vectoring; studies by Thiokol (first stage), Hercules (second) and CSD (third) for alternative propellants and nozzle systems.
Guidance: Inertial.
Range: (Trident C4) 4,400 miles (7100km), (D5) 6,800 miles (11,000km).
Flight speed: Similar to Minuteman.
Warhead: Eight Mk 4 (100 kT each) MIRVs, with possibility of using Mk 500 Evader MARV (manoeuvring RV) later; (D5) not known.

Up to 30 extremely large submarines are being built to carry this larger longer-range SLBM system (see warships technical section). Each will carry 24 launch tubes. So far four vessels are being built, the first (SSBN-726) being due to reach IOC in late 1979. Flight testing of the Trident I C4 missile has improved after a shaky start, but underwater launches are not due until 1979. By that time Trident C4 is due to begin installation in ten existing Poseidon-armed SSBNs, all ten being converted by 1984. Trident D5, which may be 46ft (14m) long, would have considerably greater throw-weight and/or range, but would be compatible with C4 tubes.

Right: Liftoff of Trident C4X-02 from a flat pad at what is now Cape Canaveral Air Force Station, in February 1977.

Below: This Atlas F, once emplaced as an Air Force ICBM, is seen at liftoff down the Western Test Range from Vandenberg AFB in March 1974 carrying the Trident re-entry vehicle.

Martin LGM-25C Titan II

Origin: Martin Marietta Corporation, Denver (Colorado) Division.
Type: ICBM deployed in hardened silo.
Dimensions: Length 102ft 8½in (31·30m); body diameter 120in (305cm).
Launch weight: 330,000lb (149,690kg).
Propulsion: First stage, Aerojet LR87 twin-chamber engine burning nitrogen tetroxide and Aerozine; second stage Aerojet LR91, similar but one smaller chamber (all chambers gimballed).
Guidance: Inertial, IBM/AC Spark Plug.
Range: 9,300 miles (15,000km).
Flight speed: Over 15,000mph (24,000km/h) at burnout.
Warhead: General Electric Mk 6 RV containing thermonuclear warhead (about 6 MT) and penaids.

By far the biggest and oldest of America's surviving strategic missiles, Titan was begun in the mid-1950s as a later alternative to Atlas with the bold feature of a second stage that had to ignite in space. Titan II, operational since 1963, combined silo emplacement with hypergolic (self-igniting) propellants which reduced reaction time from hours to one minute. There have for 13 years been six squadrons each with nine missiles, and despite their age they remain in business because without them the US would have no missile with anything approaching the power and throw-weight of much larger numbers of Soviet ICBMs. In March 1978 work began on replacing the original guidance by the USGS (Universal Space Guidance System) used on the Titan III space launcher, chiefly to reduce maintenance cost from about $173 million to $101 million per year. This underlines the unlikelihood of early retirement.

Below: Liftoff from Cape Kennedy Air Force Station of an LGM-25C Titan II in January 1964 carrying a special liquid-oxygen converter pod (bulge projecting from second stage). Titan II is America's largest missile, but obsolescent.

ASALM

Origin: Martin Orlando division, and McDonnell Douglas.
Type: Advanced Strategic Air-Launched Missile.
Dimensions: About the same as SRAM, but with fold-out wings.
Launch weight: About 2,700lb (1220kg).
Propulsion: Integral rocket/ramjet.
Guidance: Almost certainly inertial plus Tercom, or active homing.
Range: Several hundred miles.
Flight speed: Highly supersonic.
Warhead: Probably conventional as AAM, nuclear or thermonuclear as ASM.

For ten years is has been recognised that a superior missile propulsion system comprises an integral rocket/ramjet in which the same case and nozzle is used first as a solid-propellant boost rocket and then, after automatic jettisoning of the rocket nozzle and inlet-port covers, as a supersonic air-breathing ramjet for sustainer propulsion. Martin Orlando will begin flight trials in 1979, with a strong industrial team providing airframe, guidance (initially just enough for range safety at White Sands) and propulsion. ASALM could become a prime weapon for the FB-111H, with guidance and warhead tailored either to the destruction of hostile aircraft (especially those of an AWACS nature) or for use against surface targets.

Below: Impression by McDonnell Douglas artist of how his company's ASALM might look. It would have no wings and would rely on body lift at perhaps Mach 4 (2,650mph).

AIR-TO-SURFACE TACTICAL

Hughes AGM-65 Maverick

Origin: Hughes Aircraft, Culver City (production at Tucson, Arizona).
Type: Rocket missile with various forms of guidance (see text).
Dimensions: Length (AGM-65A) 97·0in (246cm); body diameter 12·0in (30·5cm); wing/fin span 28·0in (71cm).
Launch weight: (AGM-65A) 462lb (210kg).
Propulsion: Thiokol TX-481 solid motor (details classified).
Guidance: See text.
Range: Typically (A) 8 miles (13km); (B) 14 miles (22·5km).
Flight speed: Supersonic.
Warhead: Usually 130lb (59kg) shaped charge for maximum penetration.

Aerodynamically derived from the Falcon air-to-air missile family, Maverick is the most important American family of tactical ASMs and has been built in large numbers (so far, in the order of 28,000 missiles). The first 19,000 were of the AGM-65A type with day TV guidance. With this the pilot visually acquires the target, uncages the missile (removing a cover from the glass seeker head), locks the seeker on the target manually, releases the track switch and fires the missile which thereafter homes electro-optically. AGM-65A was used in SE Asia and the Yom Kippur war. AGM-65B has scene-magnification TV and optics, for earlier lock-on and thus the capability of firing at longer range or against smaller targets. AGM-65C has laser guidance, using either an airborne or ground laser designator to home it precisely on targets lacking optical contrast or at night. AGM-65D, the most costly version, has an IIR (Imaging Infra-Red seeker) which, especially when matched with an FLIR (Forward-Looking Infra-Red) in the launch aircraft, can give pinpoint accuracy by day or night despite haze or fog. The US Navy expect to buy a heavier Maverick with the 250lb (113kg) Mk 19 warhead for use against ships and hardened land targets, with laser guidance; this version would be considerably heavier and about 4in (102cm) longer.

M-X

Origin: Studies by Air Force and industry.
Type: Advanced land-based mobile ICBM.
Dimensions: Larger than Minuteman.
Launch weight: Probably to be about 165,000lb (75,000kg).
Propulsion: Three stages of advanced solid motors with vectoring nozzles, plus PBCS and MIRVs.
Guidance: Includes inertial.
Range: Similar to Minuteman III.
Flight speed: Similar to Minuteman III.
Warhead: Advanced package of MIRVs and penaids.

The dramatically increased capability of the Soviet Union to destroy hardened Minuteman silos has prompted urgent work on a new-generation ICBM with higher performance and increased survivability. Instead of being silo-emplaced M-X would be mobile, occupying any of a very large number of shelters, trenches or other readily constructed sites, as well as existing silos for Minuteman or Titan II. Missiles would normally be mounted on a transporter/launcher, as was originally planned for Minuteman; it is not yet known whether these can be road vehicles or rail only. Tests began in 1976 on advanced nozzles, propellants, cases, guidance, re-entry vehicles and hard or semi-hardened installations.

Below: Full-scale mock-up of an MX proposal at Boeing Aerospace Company. An artist's impression of a buried-trench launch system for a mobile MX appears on page 67.

Above: Air launch is another possibility for MX, and this test with a Minuteman package extracted from a C-5A Galaxy in 1974 demonstrated this concept.

MISSILES

Hughes/TI Night Attack Missile

With data similar to those for Maverick (because it uses the same airframe) NAM is guided by a Texas Instruments non-imaging IR seeker, claimed to cost only one-third as much as the IIR. Targets are acquired on the parent aircraft's FLIR or Pave Tack pod, and a correlator automatically slaves the missile to the target. Trials from A-6Es and other aircraft are reported to have been extremely successful.

Above: Standard AGM-65A test round under A-7D Corsair in 1972. Left: New IIR (Imaging Infra-Red) Maverick on F-4E in 1978. This seeker, which is compatible with GBU-15 and Walleye glide bombs, "sees" through darkness, fog and dense smoke.

Far left: A TV-guided AGM-65A about to hit dead-centre on a bunker. The other two photographs are from a high-speed film recording the impact of a laser-guided AGM-65C on an M48 tank target. Hughes claim that over 500 rounds launched in development scored "a record 90 percent direct hits" and that 226 production missiles fired at tank-size targets in operational performance incentive firings have scored 92·2 percent.

Hughes/Martin AGM-62 Walleye

Origin: Naval Ordnance Test Station; production first by Martin Orlando Division and later by Hughes.
Type: Glide bomb with TV guidance.
Dimensions: Length 11ft 3in (3·43m) (Mk II, 13ft 3in, 4·04m); body diameter 15·0in (38cm) (Mk II, 18·0in, 45·7cm).
Launch weight: Walleye I, 1,100lb (499kg); Walleye II, 2,340lb (1061kg).
Propulsion: None.
Guidance: See text.
Range: Depends on launch height, but never over 10 miles (16km).
Flight speed: Mach 0·9.
Warhead: Walleye I, conventional Mk I Mod 0 850lb (385kg); Walleye II, conventional Mk 5 about 2,000lb (907kg).

This glide bomb has cruciform delta wings with trailing-edge controls, a TV camera in the nose and a ram-air turbine to generate electric and hydraulic power. The launch aircraft crew identify the target in their own CRT monitor screen, which "sees" the missile's TV picture. The missile is then locked on manually and released. Production began at Orlando in 1966, with Hughes adding output in 1967–70. Experience in SE Asia confirmed possible high accuracy. Walleye II, a bigger missile for large or very hard targets, was deleted from the budget in 1974, when fully developed, but the ER/DL WE II (extended-range data link Walleye II) is now in use with larger wings for greater range and with the ability to lock-on at greater range and/or pass control to a second, following, aircraft.

Above: An early Martin-built Walleye mounted under the wing of an A-3 Skywarrior trials aircraft before firing at the Naval Missile Center at Point Mugu, California, in 1967.

Martin/Maxson AGM-12 Bullpup

Origin: Martin Orlando and Maxson Electronics.
Type: Radio command rocket missile family.
Dimensions: Various.
Launch weight: Varies from 550lb (249kg) to about 1,800lb (816kg).
Propulsion: Various prepackaged liquid rockets.
Guidance: Bright flares tracked visually by launch-aircraft crew who steer missile via radio command link.
Range: Varies from 6 to 10·5 miles (10 to 17km).

Flight speed: Typically Mach 1·8 to 2·0.
Warhead: (AGM-12A) 250lb (113kg); (-12C) 1,000lb (454kg); (-12E) anti-personnel.

Developed in 1954–55, this was the pioneer American tactical ASM. Large numbers were supplied in three major and many minor versions, some having nuclear warheads and others being for training. Production in the US ceased a decade ago but large stocks are being used for training.

Below: An unusual sight near Edwards AFB, California, in October 1964, was a series of firings of AGM-12B from an F-5A Freedom Fighter undergoing evaluation by the USAF.

Rockwell International Hellfire

Origin: Rockwell Missile Systems, Columbus, Ohio.
Type: Laser-guided "fire and forget" missile for use against tanks and other hard targets.
Dimensions: Not disclosed.
Launch weight: About 90lb (41kg).
Propulsion: Not disclosed.
Guidance: Laser homing from air or ground designator (see text).
Range: Up to "several kilometres".
Flight speed: Transonic.
Warhead: Hollow-charge.

Rockwell have managed several major tactical missile programmes using closely similar airframes, among them Hornet, ADSM (Air-Defense Suppression Missile) and Hellfire. The last-named, now in full development, is likely to be the most numerous Army and Air Force battlefield missile for use from helicopters and the A-10A. Since 1974 many trial firings, mainly from AH-1G Cobras, have yielded encouraging results, one trick being to ripple

two or more missiles at about 0·25-sec intervals during the brief pop-up period of an anti-tank helicopter from behind its cover. Each Hellfire is coded to lock-on to a separate laser beam, so that all travel to their own targets, the helicopter meanwhile having returned to cover. The usual laser is the Tri-Service (Maverick C) type, but Hellfire is being developed with various other laser, RF and IR seekers, and with the Hughes ATVS (Advanced TV Seeker) for low-cost daytime use.

Below: Development firing of an early Hellfire (HELicopter-Launched, FIRE and forget) from an AH-1G Cobra in July 1975.

Rockwell GBU-15 Hobos

Origin: Rockwell International, Missile Systems Division.
Type: Family of guided bombs.
Dimensions: Varies with bomb but usually very close to 148in (375cm); body diameter (Mk 84) 18in (46cm), (M118) 24in (61cm); span (Mk 84) 44in (112cm), (M118) 52in (132cm). Planar-wing (folding-wings) models have much greater span.
Launch weight: (Mk 84) 2,240lb (1016kg), (M118) 3,404lb (1544kg).
Propulsion: None.
Guidance: Various, see text.
Range: Short (free-fall bomb), except MGGB, see text.
Flight speed: Subsonic.
Warhead: Unchanged from original bombs.

Used in considerable numbers in the closing stages of the war in SE Asia, the Hobos family (Homing Bomb System) comprise the Mk 84 2,000lb bomb or M118 3,000lb bomb to which have been added a new nose, lateral strakes and tail section. The forward guidance section is usually a KMU-353 or -390 EO (electro-optical) unit with TV camera or target-seeker optics. Alternative guidance units use IR seeker cells, laser receivers or the Maverick type IIR (imaging IR) seeker, in each case with DME as an optional all-weather addition. CEP is said to be within about 1m. A derived weapon was the MGGB (modular guided glide bomb) with fold-out wings for gliding in from a safe stand-off distance, and a data-link for command guidance. An alternative payload is the SUU-54 dispenser.

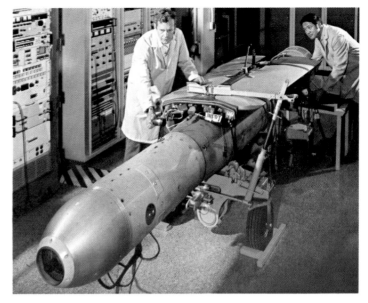

Above: First PWW (Planar-Wing Weapon) with wings folded in checkout at Hughes who provided the seeker head and data link.

Texas Instruments AGM-45 Shrike

Origin: Texas Instruments and Sperry Rand Univac.
Type: Passive homing anti-radiation missile.
Dimensions: Length 120in (305cm); body diameter 8·0in (20·3cm); wing span 36in (91·4cm).
Launch weight: 390lb (177kg).
Propulsion: Solid motor, Rocketdyne Mk 39 Mod 7 or Aerojet Mk 53 Mod 2 or Mod 3.
Guidance: TI passive EM-radiation seeker.
Range: 8 to 10 miles (13–16km).
Flight speed: About Mach 2.
Warhead: HE plus fragmentation, 145lb (66kg).

Developed by the Naval Weapons Center at China Lake, Shrike was derived from the Sparrow AAM and uses some similar parts but with different tail fins and with passive-homing TI/Univac guidance. Production began in 1963 and, following disappointing results in Vietnam, a large family of improved Shrikes were developed each tailored to particular frequency bands. It is believed that different frequency bands can be covered by exchanging guidance heads, even after the missile is on an aircraft. So far the Navy has bought about 11,500 of all models, deployed by all its tactical aircraft. The USAF began buying Shrike in 1965 and have acquired about 12,600, with a small batch in FY78 funds. Main carriers of late USAF models are the EF-4E (F-4G) Wild Weasel and (planned) EF-111A. The successor to Shrike is HARM.

Above: Shrike firing by an F-4C of the 57th Fighter Weapons Wing at Nellis AFB, Nevada, for EF-4E (F-4G) demonstration.

Below: Production AGM-45A Shrike ready for flight on an A-7E Corsair at Naval Weapons Center, China Lake, in October 1972. By this time Shrike was working well, and usually effective.

Texas Instruments AGM-88A HARM

Origin: Texas Instruments, Dallas.
Type: High-speed anti-radiation missile.
Dimensions: Length 13ft 8¼in (4·17m); body diameter 9·5in (24cm); wing span 44·5in (113cm).
Launch weight: 772lb (350kg).
Propulsion: Thiokol advanced solid motor.
Guidance: Passive homing on EM radiation.
Range: Over 10 miles (16km).
Flight speed: Mach 4.
Warhead: Advanced conventional.

This is the planned successor to Shrike (by the same prime contractor) and Standard ARM, with much higher flight performance, faster and cleverer electronics and ECCM, and enhanced lethality. First contracts were awarded in 1972 and numerous test firings had in 1978 progressed to the definitive Thiokol-powered weapon. At least 5,000 rounds will be in the initial Navy batch, reportedly for the A-4, A-6, A-7, F-4, F-14, P-3, S-3 and E-2C, and the USAF will use HARM as the standard weapon on the EF-4E (F-4G) Wild Weasel and EF-111A.

Above: **Impression of HARM in action, by an artist from the US Naval Weapons Center at China Lake, California.**

Paveway "smart bombs"

Origin: USAF and Texas Instruments, Dallas.
Type: Laser-guided conventional bombs.
Dimensions: Varies with bomb; Mk 84 is 168in (427cm) long.
Launch weight: Varies with bomb, see text.
Propulsion: None.
Guidance: Laser homing.
Range: Typically within 3 miles (5km), depending on launch height.
Flight speed: Free-fall bomb.
Warhead: Conventional bombs, see text.

Texas Instruments achieved a dramatic cost/effectiveness breakthrough around 1970 by perfecting an add-on pinpoint guidance system for many free-fall bombs. Unit price was in the order of $2,500, not including the laser designator (which can be carried in the launch aircraft, in an accompanying aircraft or on the ground). The most common Paveway bombs are the 500lb Mk 82, 750lb M117, 1,000lb Mk 83, 2,000lb Mk 84, 3,000lb M118 and cluster munitions such as SUU-54, Rockeye and LGDM (laser-guided dispenser munition). Actual weights of USAF bombs are typically 10 per cent greater than nominal, and the guidance head adds a few pounds extra. Each head comprises a streamlined nose carrying at the front a bullet-shaped seeker mounted on gimbals and with a ring tail. This is always aligned by the airstream with the direction of bomb motion. Its silicon seeker cells detect the laser light from the target and drive four canard guidance fins to control trajectory towards the laser light source. When fitted with the

guidance unit, and the short tailfins, the bomb becomes a guided missile with its own designation; thus, the Mk 84 becomes GBU-10 (Guided Bomb Unit). Paveway weapons proved extremely effective in Vietnam, and are now a primary tactical weapon family of the Air Force, Navy and Marines, using a wide range of designators.

Right: Two grossly dissimilar "smart" weapons used by Tactical Air Command: an EO-guided Mk 84 (upper, on F-111) and a laser-guided Paveway bomb (lower, dropped from diving F-15 Eagle).

ANTI-SHIP MISSILES

General Dynamics AGM-78D/ RGM-66D Standard ARM

Origin: General Dynamics, Pomona (California).
Type: Anti-radar missile (AGM, air-launched; RGM, ship-launched).
Dimensions: Length 15ft 0in (4·57m); body diameter 13·5in (34·3cm); fin span 42·9in (109cm).
Launch weight: Basic 1,356lb (615kg), Mod 1 1,800lb (816kg).
Propulsion: Aerojet Mk 27 Mod 4 dual-thrust solid motor.
Guidance: Passive radar seeker by Maxson and GD/Pomona.
Range: 15 miles (25km).
Flight speed: Over Mach 2.
Warhead: Conventional, impact/prox fuze.

Announced in 1966, Standard ARM is a development of the Standard ship-to-air SAM. The first model used the TI seeker head of the Shrike ARM but improved guidance is now fitted. This missile has augmented, and is now replacing, Shrike in US Navy A-6 squadrons and USAF units flying the F-105, F-4 and possibly other aircraft such as the A-10; it has also been reported as carried by the Navy EA-6B Prowler EW aircraft and the E-2C Hawkeye AEW platform. Carrier aircraft can be fitted with TIAS (Target Identification and Acquisition System) to help the missile strike home despite the enemy radar being intermittently or permanently switched off; in the USAF Standard ARM is linked with the Wild Weasel system and would probably be carried by the EF-4E (F-4G) and EF-111A. (See HARM.) RGM-66D is an interim US Navy ship-to-ship missile which can hit radar-emitting targets beyond the horizon. It is fitted to two patrol gunboats (in stern box launcher) and is being installed on six DDGs and six FFGs.

Above: **AGM-78A Standard ARM loaded on an F-105F electronic-warfare Thunderchief at Holloman AFB, New Mexico, in 1967. Following disappointing results with early Shrike ARMs in SE Asia this weapon was urgently undertaken to provide more assured capability against intelligently managed hostile radars.**

McDonnell Douglas ISSSMD

Origin: McDonnell Douglas Astronautics (Eastern), St Louis.
Type: All-weather ship-to-ship missile.
Dimensions: Not disclosed, but similar to RGM-84A Harpoon (body diameter and wingspan identical).
Launch weight: Very close to RGM-84A.
Propulsion: Teledyne CAE J402-CA-400 single-shaft turbojet rated at 660lb (300kg) static thrust, plus launch boost motor by Aerojet-General, solid rocket MX(TBD)B446-2.
Guidance: Pre-launch, parent platform position data and target location, with IBM computer mid-course, lear-Siegler strapdown platform radar altimeter; terminal, EO (Electro-optical) imaging seeker.
Range: Similar to RGM-84A.
Flight speed: Similar to RGM-84A.
Warhead: Probably same as RGM-84A.

In February 1978 McDonnell Douglas shipped the first of four prototype ISSSMD missiles for testing by the US Navy (probably at the Point Mugu missile range). These weapons have been built under US Navy contract, but no service DoD designation had been assigned as this book went to press in mid-1978. Called ISSSMD, from Imaging-Seeker Surface-to-Surface Missile Demonstration, this programme integrates the airframe of the Harpoon ship-launched missile with the EO seeker head of the defunct Condor air-to-surface missile and the data-link of the Walleye II glide bomb. The first ISSSMD was flown aboard a carrier aircraft (not released) to give a ship crew control experience; the next three were to be ship-launched under Naval Sea Systems Command control to verify the missile's ability to detect, identify and hit close and OTH (over the horizon) targets.

Below: One of four prototype ISSSMD missiles using the Harpoon airframe under test at McDonnell Douglas, St Louis.

McDonnell Douglas AGM/RGM-84A Harpoon

Origin: McDonnell Douglas Astronautics, Huntington Beach.
Type: All-weather anti-ship missile (AGM, air-launched; RGM, ship- or submarine-launched).
Dimensions: Length (AGM) 12ft 7in (3·84m), (RGM) 15ft 2in (4·58m); body diameter 13·5in (34·1cm); span 36·0in (91·4cm).
Launch weight: (AGM) 1,160lb (526kg), (RGM) 1,460lb to 1,530lb (662 to 694kg).
Propulsion: Teledyne CAE J402-CA-400 single-shaft turbojet rated at 660lb (300kg) static thrust; (RGM) in addition, Aerojet MX(TBD)B446-2 tandem solid boost motor for launch and acceleration to Mach 0·75.
Guidance: Pre-launch, parent platform target data and IBM computer; mid-course, Lear Siegler strapdown platform and radar altimeter; terminal, TI active radar seeker.
Range: Up to 70 miles (113km).
Flight speed: About Mach 0·85, 645mph.
Warhead: Naval Weapons Center 500lb (227kg) blast type.

This important anti-ship missile became operational in 1977—78 after extended development. The simplest form is AGM-84A, launched by such aircraft as the A-6E Intruder, A-7E Corsair II, P-3 Orion and S-3 Viking (and Norwegian F-16s). RGM-84A can be fired from surface-vessel Tartar/Terrier/Standard or Asroc launchers, or from a four-round lightweight canister for high-speed craft or a buoyant capsule fired from a submarine torpedo tube. After launch the missile turns toward its target, zooming down to sea-skimming cruise height, finally locking-on with terminal radar and climbing in the last seconds to dive on to the target.

Top: Launch of RGM-84A from PCH-1 hydrofoil High Point in January 1974 test of prototype canister launching system.
Sequence, from top left: An air-to-ship test of AGM-84A from an A-7C Corsair II from China Lake. The target was the destroyer DD-585 Haraden, and the devastation caused by the explosion of the warhead after penetration of the hull is seen in the final picture.

ANTI-SUBMARINE WARFARE MISSILES

Goodyear UUM-44A Subroc

Origin: Goodyear Aerospace, Akron.
Type: Submarine-to-submarine rocket.
Dimensions: Length 20ft 5in (6·25m); body diameter (boost motor) 21·0in (53·3cm); span, no fins or wings.
Launch weight: 4,086lb (1853kg).
Propulsion: Thiokol TE-260G solid tandem boost motor with four jetevator nozzles.
Guidance: Kearfott SD-510 inertial system.
Range: Up to 35 miles (56km).
Flight speed: Supersonic.
Warhead: Nuclear, hydrostatic fuze, about 4 miles (6·4km) radius.

Standard ASW weapon of US Navy attack submarines, Subroc is launched from a 21in torpedo tube in the conventional way. The missile arches up through the water and at a safe distance the rocket ignites, guiding the weapon towards its target both before and after breaking the ocean surface. Steering is accomplished by the jetevators during powered flight. At motor cutoff the warhead vehicle is separated and continues to its target guided by aerodynamic fins. Entry to the water is cushioned, after which the warhead sinks to the correct depth before detonating. Subroc has been operational since 1965. Attack submarines usually carry four to six missiles each. Production is expected to terminate in 1978.

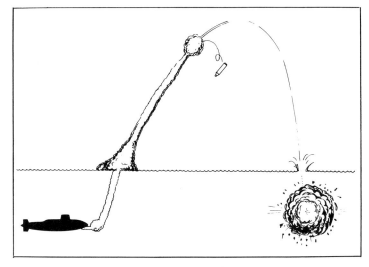

Above: Diagrammatic representation of Subroc mission, as described in the text. After cutoff of rocket propulsion the nuclear warhead is explosively separated and falls unguided.

SURFACE-TO-SURFACE TACTICAL MISSILES

GSRS

Origin: Various competing hardware or proposals being evaluated.
Type: General Support Rocket System.

In 1976 the Army awarded contracts to a number of US and foreign companies to supply concept-definition studies for an artillery rocket system having high mobility, high rate of fire and acceptable accuracy. The possibility of adapting an existing system would be attractive. No decision had been taken in 1977–78 on whether or not to incorporate mid-course guidance or use a TGSM (Terminally Guided Sub-Missile) for increased accuracy.

Below: First launch of the Vought GSRS in December 1977, less than three months after that company was selected as one of the two finalists. The firing was at White Sands.

Martin XM712 Copperhead

Origin: Martin Marietta.
Type: Cannon-launched guided projectile.
Dimensions: 155mm shell.

Without doubt, the tank is the dominant threat facing NATO forces in Europe today. NATO has deployed large numbers of ATGW's (including the HOT, Milan, TOW, Dragon and Swingfire) to meet this threat, but it was realized some years ago that ATGW's and tanks alone could not hope to halt a determined thrust by Warsaw Pact forces. Conventional artillery, when being used in the indirect fire role, has a 1-in-2,500 chance of killing a tank. Several years ago, the US Army started a high-risk program to develop a projectile which could be fired from a standard 155mm weapon (for example, the M109A1 self-propelled gun or the M198 towed howitzer) and hit targets over 12km away.

One of the problems was designing the electronics, as these would have to stand up to 7000g when being fired. Basic research, however, proved that the project was possible and contracts were awarded to Texas Instruments and Martin Marietta. Each company built a small number of projectiles (or Cannon Launched Guided Projectiles as they are called) which were tested at the White Sands Missile Range. The Martin Marietta CLGP scored direct hits on both stationary and moving tanks at ranges of 8 to 12km. The projectile hit the target despite deliberate aiming errors of several hundred metres. In September, 1975, a CLGP hit a stationary M48 tank 8km away while the target was being illuminated by a laser carried in a Praeire IIA RPV. The RPV located the target with a TV camera, focusing on the target and signaled the artillery to fire a CLGP. As a result of these trials, Martin Marietta were awarded a contract for full scale development of the CLGP. This contract is worth some $45 million and calls for the delivery of some 350 CLGP's. Once the CLGP is in volume production it is expected to cost about $5000 per round.

The basic idea is that a forward observer sees an enemy tank approaching. He then radios its approximate position to the artillery and one weapon fires a CLGP in the general direction of the target. Once the CLGP is on its way the forward observer illuminates the target with his Ground Laser Locator Designator (or GLLD), the CLGP senses the reflected laser energy and, by applying commands to its control fins, flies into the laser spot on the target. The CLGP is handled like a normal round of ammunition and the weapon requires no special modifications to fire the round. Future projectiles will have mid-body wings to increase their range to about 20km. A dual mode seeker (eg, either laser or infra-red) will probably be developed so that the projectile can also home onto enemy radars.

Once the CLGP has been fielded, every 155mm artillery piece will have the capability to "kill" armor at long range. The Navy is also developing CLGPs in both 5in and 8in calibres for both surface-to-surface and surface-to-air applications and Congress is trying to get the Navy and the Army to co-operate on CLGPs. It would appear, however, that the Navy requires only 6,000 CLGPs, while the Army wants over 100,000.

Right: Two frames from a high-speed film recording the impact on an M48 target tank of a CLGP Copperhead. In many Copperhead anti-tank trials the weapon has been inert, but this example probably had a warhead. It impacted the top of the turret about two feet above the painted-on aiming mark.

Honeywell RUR-5A Asroc

Origin: Honeywell Aerospace and Defense Group, Minneapolis.
Type: Anti-submarine rocket.
Dimensions: Length 181in (4·6m); body diameter 12·8in (32·5cm); span 33·25in (84·5in).
Launch weight: 960lb (435kg).
Propulsion: Naval Propellant Plant solid tandem boost motor; basic missile is torpedo.
Guidance: Ballistic in flight.
Range: 6 miles (10 km).
Flight speed: Transonic.
Warhead: Standard Mk 44/46 torpedo.

Operational since 1961, this elementary all-weather ASW weapon used sonar and fire-control computer to slew and elevate the launcher (Mk 46 or Mk 10 Terrier/Standard/Asroc launcher). The Asroc flies a ballistic trajectory to the vicinity of the target. The rocket is jettisoned after burnout, and a parachute decelerates the torpedo for a safe water entry, thereafter homing on the target in the usual way. As an alternative, the payload can be a nuclear depth charge, likewise lowered by parachute.

Right: Launch of Asroc from USS *Brooke*, a guided-missile escort. The missile is operational on many US Navy ships.

Above: A GLLD (Ground Laser Locator/Designator) prototype by Hughes Aircraft (builder of the world's first laser) on field test in 1976. This 48lb pack has guided Copperhead.

Above: An early test launch of Copperhead, then called CLGP, from an M109 SP 155mm gun at White Sands Missile Range in July 1975. This weapon could revolutionise artillery.

Martin MGM-31A Pershing

Origin: Martin Orlando Division.
Type: Mobile tactical ballistic missile system.
Dimensions: Length 34ft 6in (10·51m); body diameter 40in (1·01m); fin span about 80in (2·02m).
Launch weight: About 10,150lb (4600kg).
Propulsion: Two Thiokol solid motors in tandem, first stage XM105, second stage XM106.
Guidance: Army-developed inertial made by Eclipse-Pioneer (Bendix).
Range: 100 to 520 miles (160–840km).
Flight speed: Mach 8 at burnout.
Warhead: Nuclear, usually approximately 400 kT.

Originally deployed in 1962 on XM474 tracked vehicles as Pershing 1, the standard US Army long-range missile system has now been modified to 1A standard, carried on four vehicles based on the M656 five-ton truck. All are transportable in a C-130. In 1976 the four battalions with the US 7th Army in Europe were updated with the ARS (Azimuth Reference System) allowing them quickly to use unsurveyed launch sites, and the SLA (Sequential Launch Adapter) allowing one launch control centre easily to fire three missiles. Pershing II is a proposed further improvement, using the same missiles, in which addition of Goodyear Radag (Radar Area-correlation Guidance) will give terminal homing by using on-board radar to compare the approaching target with previously stored radar pictures of it. This will allow the warhead to be made smaller and less destructive.

Right: Launch at Cape Canaveral in May 1974 of a Pershing 1A, the type at present in service. Apart from France's Pluton, this is the West's only long-range army missile.

Below: Pershing 1A dual launch. CEP (circular error probability) of this weapon is about 1,200ft; Pershing II may beat 120ft.

ANTI-TANK MISSILES
Ford Aerospace MGM-51C Shillelagh

Origin: Ford Aeronutronic Division, Newport Beach.
Type: Gun-launched guided missile.
Dimensions: Length 45in (114cm); body diameter 5·95in (15·2cm); fin span 11·4in (29·0cm).
Launch weight: About 60lb (27kg).
Propulsion: Amoco single-stage solid with hot-jet jetevators.
Guidance: Optical tracking and IR command link.
Range: Up to about three miles (4500m).
Flight speed: High subsonic.
Warhead: Octol shaped charge 15lb (6·8kg).

Very large numbers of these advanced anti-tank missiles were supplied to the US Army in 1966–70, for firing from the 152mm dual purpose gun fitted to the General Sheridan AFV and M60A2 main battle tank. The gunner, who can fire a missile or a conventional round depending on the target, has only to keep the target centred in optical cross-hairs for the IR guidance to keep the missile centred on the line of sight. Firings were carried out from UH-1 helicopters, but an air-launched version is not in use. In 1976–78 trials were in hand on a proposed new guidance system using laser designators (either at the launch point or elsewhere) with a view to modifying the existing missiles.

Right: Early trials-firing of Shillelagh at White Sands Missile Range, when there were numerous systems difficulties.

Far right: Launch of a production missile from an M551 General Sheridan, a lightweight AFV which took several years to mature. The missile is also fired by the M60A2 battle tank.

Vought MGM-52C Lance

Origin: Vought Corporation, Michigan Division.
Type: Mobile tactical guided missile.
Dimensions: Length 20ft 3in (6·17m); body diameter 22in (56cm).
Launch weight: 2,833 to 3,367lb (1285–1527kg) depending on warhead.
Propulsion: Rocketdyne P8E-9 storable-liquid two-part motor with infinitely throttleable sustainer portion.
Guidance: Simplified inertial.
Range: 45 to 75 miles (70–120km) depending on warhead.
Flight speed: Mach 3.
Warhead: Usually M234 nuclear (468lb, 212kg) 10 kT, or Honeywell XM251 (1,000lb, 454kg) HE cluster.

In service since 1972, this neat rocket replaced the earlier Honest John rocket and Sergeant ballistic missile, with very great gains in reduced system weight, cost and bulk and increases in accuracy and mobility. Usual vehicle is the M752 (M113 family) amphibious tracked launcher, with the M688 carrying two extra missiles and a loading hoist. For air-dropped operations a lightweight towed launcher can be used. In-flight guidance accuracy, with the precisely controlled sustainer and spin-stabilization, is already highly satisfactory, but a future Lance 2 could have DME (Distance Measuring Equipment) command guidance. The US Army has eight battalions, six of which are normally deployed in Europe.

Right: Trials-launch of a Lance development missile from the M752 at White Sands, with black smoke spewing from the canted rocket-motor vents that spin the missile for stabilization.

Above: An inert troop-training Lance ready on its M752 during a tropical test at Fort Sherman, Panama Canal Zone.

Left: Launch sequence of a Lance development missile, showing how the lateral nozzles impart spin which is afterwards maintained by the four slightly canted tail fins.

Hughes BGM-71 Tow

Origin: Hughes Aircraft Company, Culver City.
Type: Heavy anti-tank missile system for vehicles or aircraft.
Dimensions: Length 46in (117cm); body diameter 5·8in (14·7cm); span 13·4in (34cm).
Launch weight: Typically 42lb (19kg).
Propulsion: Quad boost motor for recoilless launch in tube, then brief coast after tube exit followed by sustainer ignition.
Guidance: Optical sighting and trailing-wire guidance working tail controls.
Range: 200 to 12,250ft (65–3750m).
Flight speed: About 620mph (1000km/h).
Warhead: Shaped charge containing 5·3lb (2·4kg) of HE.

In service since 1970, Tow is by far the most widely used anti-tank missile in the world, and is deployed by the US Army and Marine Corps from almost every kind of battlefield vehicle and helicopter. It is the standard missile for the AH-1J, -1Q and -1S TowCobra attack helicopter, will be deployed on the Hughes AH-64 and is compatible with the OH-6A. Special Tow-vehicles include the Army MICV and the new Emerson ITV (Improved Tow Vehicle) which, like the latest MICV, will be fully armoured and fitted with day/night sight systems. Future sights include IIR (Imaging IR) and laser designators.

Right: Interesting trials vehicle, with M113 chassis, seen at Redstone Arsenal in 1972 with twin Tow launchers on high elevating pillar together with day and night sight systems.

Below right: The infantry launcher weighs 172lb without a missile, and this one is further burdened by infra-red night sighting. It breaks down into five man-portable parts.

Below: Marines firing at dusk from a Jeep-mounted launcher without infra-red sight. Optical magnification helps.

SURFACE-TO-AIR MISSILES/ANTI-BALLISTIC MISSILES

Bendix RIM-8 Talos

Origin: Bendix Aerospace Systems Division, Mishawaka, Indiana.
Type: Long-range ship-to-air or ship-to-ship weapon system.
Dimensions: Length 31ft 3in (9·53m); body diameter 30in (76cm); span 114in (290cm).
Launch weight: 7,000lb (3175kg).
Propulsion: Booster, Allegheny Ballistics tandem solid rocket; sustainer, integral ramjet burning kerosine/naphtha.
Guidance: Mid-course, beam rider; terminal, CW interferometer semi-active homing (RIM-8H, passive radiation seeker).
Range: Varies with height up to beyond 75 miles (120km).
Flight speed: Mach 2·5.
Warhead: (RIM-2D) nuclear; (most others) large continuous-rod HE.

One of the longest-lifed missile programmes in history, Talos began with the Navy Bumblebee project in 1944 to defeat Kamikaze attacks and will remain in major service in the 1980s. RIM-8D has a nuclear warhead which can be fitted to other versions; -8E is a common basic variant; -8F has improved guidance for extreme range and altitude; -8G has improved terminal homing; -8H is an anti-radiation surface-to-surface version; and -8J is an undisclosed current variant. Talos is aboard at least seven large cruisers, one of which shot down two MiGs in Vietnam from over 65 miles' (105km) range.

Right: Two action photographs showing Talos launches from US Navy cruisers, USS *Columbus* (CG-12) on this page and USS *Little Rock* (CLG-4) at far right. No successor is imminent.

232

McDonnell Douglas FGM-77A (M47) Dragon

Origin: McDonnell Douglas Astronautics (second-source production by Raytheon and Kollsman).
Type: Infantry anti-tank/assault missile.
Dimensions: Length 29·3in (74cm); body diameter 5·0in (12·7cm); fin span 13in (33cm).
Launch weight: 13·5lb (6·12kg).
Propulsion: Recoilless gas-generator thruster in launch tube; sustain propulsion by 60 small side thrusters fired in pairs upon tracker demand.
Guidance: See text.
Range: 200 to 3,300ft (60–1000m).
Flight speed: About 225mph (360km/h).
Warhead: Linear shaped charge, 5·4lb (2·45kg).

In service since 1971, Dragon comes sealed in a glass-fibre launch tube with a fat rear end containing the launch charge. The operator attaches this to his tracker comprising telescopic sight, IR sensor and electronics box. When the missile is fired its three curved fins flick open and start the missile spinning. The operator holds the sight on the target and the tracker automatically commands the missile to the line of sight by firing appropriate pairs of side thrusters. The launch tube is thrown away and a fresh one attached to the tracker. The Army and Marine Corps use the basic Dragon, while developments involve night sights and laser guidance.

Below: Flame, debris and a fine smoke ring accompany this launch by a Dragon team of the 509th Infantry at Vicenza, Italy, the first US Army unit overseas to receive the missile.

Above: Demonstration firing of the Dragon weapon system at Redstone Arsenal, Alabama. According to the book, no harm can come to the operator, but it looks highly impressive.

Euromissile/Hughes-Boeing Roland 2

Origin: Developed by Euromissile (Aérospatiale, France; MBB, West Germany) and Americanized and manufactured by Hughes Aircraft, with major participation by Boeing Aerospace and others.
Type: Lofaads/Shorads (Lo-level forward-area air-defense system, Short-range air-defense system).
Dimensions: Length 94·5in (240cm); body diameter 6·3in (16cm); span 19·7in (50cm).
Launch weight: 143lb (65kg).
Propulsion: internal boost and sustain solid motors.
Guidance: Initial IR gathering followed by semi-active radar command to line-of-sight.
Range: Up to 4·3 miles (7km).
Flight speed: Burnout velocity Mach 1·6.
Warhead: 14·3lb (6·5kg), contains 65 shaped charges each with lethal radius of 20ft (6m); prox fuze.

Originally developed as a mobile battlefield system with plain optical (clear-weather) guidance, Roland has from 1969 onwards been further developed as Roland 2 with blindfire radar guidance. The missile has folding wings and is fired from a launch tube on a tracked vehicle, the US Army carrier being the M109. Decision to buy Roland was taken in 1974, but the introduction to Army service has been affected by prolonged technical difficulties and cost overruns, and no American Roland was fired until the end of 1977. In early 1977 it was estimated the US development bill would be at least $265 million, with further overruns predicted. A decision on quantity production was to be taken in October 1978.

Right: The first American-built Roland missile at last gets into final inspection at Hughes Aircraft at Tucson in November 1977. An initial trials batch of 100 are being made.

Facing page: Test launch of a European-built Roland from a "breadboard" converted M109 at White Sands in March 1976. By that time many of the interface problems had surfaced.

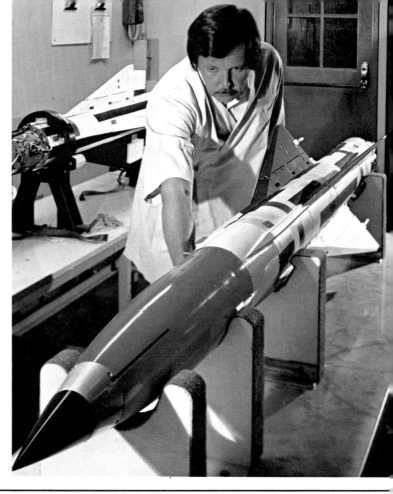

Aeronutronic Ford MIM-72 Chaparral

Origin: Aeronutronic Ford, Newport Beach.
Type: Mobile surface-to-air guided missile system.
Dimensions: Length 114·5in (2·91m); body diameter 5·0in (12·7cm); span 25in (64cm).
Launch weight: 185lb (84kg).
Propulsion: Rocketdyne Mk 36 Mod 5 single-stage solid motor.
Guidance: Initial optical aiming, IR homing to target heat emitter.
Range: About 2·5 miles (4km).
Flight speed: About Mach 2·5.
Warhead: (MIM-72A) 11lb (5kg) HE-frag with pre-formed splinters; (MIM-72C) M-250 (Picatinny Arsenal) blast-frag.

When the purpose-designed Mauler missile was abandoned this weapon was substituted as a makeshift stop-gap, the missile being the original Sidewinder 1C modified for ground launch. A fire unit has four missiles on a manually tracked launcher, carried on an M730 (modified M548) tracked vehicle, with a further eight rounds on board ready to be loaded by hand. Due to the severe delay with the Americanized Roland, Chaparral has continued to fill the gap, and is now widely used by the Army and Marine Corps, usually with an equal number of Vulcan air-defense gun systems. The missile now in production is MIM-72C, which not only carries the better warhead noted above but also has improved DAW-1 all-aspect guidance and the Harry Diamond Labs M-817 prox fuze. To help tide the Army over until Roland is ready, further work on Chaparral involves a smokeless motor, anti-glint canopy, new IFF and resistance to IRCM.

Below: The Chaparral system works in good weather, but needs all-weather radar. Studies are in hand to meet this need.

General Dynamics FIM-43A Redeye

Origin: General Dynamics/Pomona.
Type: Shoulder-fired infantry surface-to-air missile.
Dimensions: Length 48in (122cm); body diameter 2·75in (7cm); span 5·5in (14cm).
Launch weight: 18lb (8·2kg); whole package weighs 29lb (13kg).
Propulsion: Atlantic Research dual-thrust solid.
Guidance: Initial optical aiming, IR homing.
Range: Up to about 2 miles (3·3km).
Flight speed: Low supersonic.
Warhead: Smooth-case frag.

The first infantry SAM in the world, Redeye entered US Army service in 1964 and probably 1000,000 have been delivered to the Army and Marine Corps. It has severe limitations. It has to wait until aircraft have attacked and then fire at their departing tailpipes; there is no IFF. Flight speed is only just enough to catch modern attack aircraft and the guidance is vulnerable to IRCM. Engagement depends on correct identification by the operator of the nature of the target aircraft. He has to wait until the aircraft has passed, aim on a pursuit course, listen for the IR lock-on buzzer, fire the missile and then select a fresh tube. The seeker cell needs a cooling unit, three of which are packed with each missile tube.

Below: Capt Hain, chief of Redeye Test Branch at White Sands, watches a master sergeant sight Redeye on a target. This missile was unsatisfactory, but very much better than nothing.

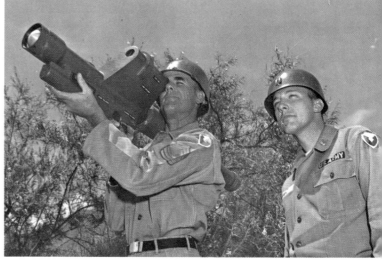

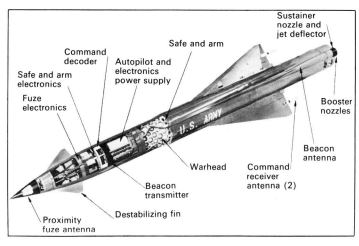

Above: Simplified Roland cutaway showing the costly warhead with multiple shaped charges. The wings unfold after launch.

Above: An American fire unit carried on the M109 chassis and prototype US radar. Three vehicles had been built by early 1978.

General Dynamics XFIM-92A Stinger

Origin: General Dynamics/Pomona.
Type: Shoulder-fired infantry surface-to-air missile.
Dimensions: Length 60in (152cm); body diameter 2·75in (7cm); span 5·5in (14cm).
Launch weight: About 22lb (10kg); whole package weighs about 31lb (14kg).
Propulsion: Atlantic Research dual-thrust solid.
Guidance: Passive IR homing (see text).
Range: Probably about 3 miles (5km).
Flight speed: Supersonic.
Warhead: Smooth-case frag.

Developed since the mid-1960s as a much-needed replacement for Redeye, Stinger has had a long and troubled development but is at last beginning to come into low-rate production with the prospect of inventory delivery to the Army and Marines in 1978–79. An improved IR seeker gives all-aspect guidance, the wavelength of less than 4·4 microns being matched to an exhaust plume rather than hot metal, though there is no indication of whether IFF is incorporated (so the operator may have to rely on correct visual identification of oncoming supersonic aircraft). It is hoped that about three-quarters of future rounds will have a new guidance system using a "two colour" seeker, one part sensitive to IR and the other to UV and thus defeating IRCM or optical countermeasures. Alternate Stinger, a laser-guided beam-rider, was terminated in 1976.

Above: R. Jones of the 3rd Armored Cavalry at Fort Bliss looks highly exposed as he sights Stinger on a very low-flier.

Left: Alternate Stinger, with laser-beam guidance, ready for firing at White Sands a few weeks before termination in 1976.

General Dynamics RIM-66/67 Standard

Origin: General Dynamics/Pomona (California).
Type: Ship-to-air missile; also surface-to-surface, see text.
Dimensions: Length (MR) 15ft 0in (4·57m), (ER) 27ft 0in (8·23m); body diameter 13·8in (35·0cm); fin span (MR) 42in (107cm), (ER) 62in (157cm).
Launch weight: (MR) about 1,300lb (590kg), (ER) about 2,350lb (1060kg).
Propulsion: (MR) dual-thrust solid, Aerojet/Hercules Mk 56 Mod 0; (ER) boost, Atlantic Research Mk 30 Mod 2, sustainer, Naval Propellant Plant Mk 12 Mod 1.
Guidance: Semi-active radar homing, varies with ship installation.
Range: (SM-1, MR) about 15 miles (24km), (SM-2, MR) about 30 miles (48·5km), (SM-1, ER) 35 miles (56km), (SM-2, ER) 60 miles (96km).
Flight speed: (MR) about Mach 2·5, (ER) over Mach 2·5.
Warhead: (SM-1) Usually Mk 90 (about 6,000 fragments, plus blast and incendiary) with Mk 45 proximity fuze.

RIM-66A (SM-1 MR) and RIM-67A (SM-2 ER) are Standard Missile 1 Medium Range and Extended Range, and were respectively developed to replace Tartar and Terrier as standard US Navy ship-to-air weapons. RGM-66D is a horizon-limited surface-to-surface version. Both are in US Navy use, and the same weapon was the basis of AGM-78 and RGM-66D Standard ARM described separately. RIM-66C, SM-2 (Standard Missile 2), is also being developed in MR and ER forms, the latter having a tandem boost motor as in the ER version of SM-1. SM-2 is a similar airframe but has totally different guidance and augmented propulsion, and forms part of the complex Aegis ship-defence system having capability against missiles and multiple threats. Guidance includes a new two-way link for mid-course command and terminal homing with higher ECM resistance. The Aegis system is in intensive development and should become operational in January 1982.

Right: March 1977 launch of Standard Missile-2 Extended Range from USS *Wainwright* (DLG-28). An RPV was intercepted at 50 miles.

Below: Aegis system structural test from USS *Norton Sound*.

Raytheon MIM-23 Hawk

Origin: Raytheon Company, Missile Systems Division.
Type: Transportable surface-to-air missile system.
Dimensions: Length 16ft 6in (5·03m) or 16ft 9½in (5·12m); body diameter 14in (36cm); span 47·5in (122cm).
Launch weight: (23A) 1,295lb (587kg), (23B) 2,835lb (625kg).
Propulsion: (23A) Aerojet XM22E-8 dual thrust solid, (23B) Aerojet XM112 dual-thrust solid.
Guidance: CW semi-active homing.
Range: (23A) 18 miles (30km), (23B) 25 miles (40km).
Flight speed: (both) Mach 2·5.
Warhead: (23A) 100lb (45kg) blast/preformed-splinter frag, (23B) similar but about 120lb (54kg).

Hawk (Homing All-the-Way Killer) was the world's first missile with CW guidance. When developed in the 1950s it looked a good system, but by modern standards it is cumbersome, each battery having a pulse acquisition radar, a CW illuminating radar, a range-only radar, two illuminator radars, battery control centre, six three-missile launchers and a tracked loader, the whole weighing many tons. An SP version has ground-support items on wheels and towed by tracked launchers or loaders. Hawk became operational in August 1960 and is deployed widely throughout the Army and Marine Corps and 17 other nations. Improved Hawk (MIM-23B) has a better guidance system, larger warhead, improved motor and semi-automatic ground systems ("certified rounds" are loaded on launchers without the need for further attention). Further development is attempting to improve CW radar reliability and improve pulse-acquisition speed by allowing automated threat-ordering of all targets that could be of importance. Since the early 1970s Hawk has been planned to be replaced by Patriot.

Above: Self-propelled Hawk vehicle with XM727 carrier bringing up triple-round unit for reloading on launcher.

Right: A 1975 firing of Improved Hawk at White Sands. The triplet of missiles was on the original towed launcher and this round was fired against MQM-34D Firebee RPV targets.

Raytheon RIM-7 Sea Sparrow

Origin: Raytheon Company, Missile Systems Division.
Type: Semi-active homing ship-to-air missile.
Dimensions: Length 144in (3·66m); body diameter 8·0in (20·3cm); span 40in (1·02m).
Launch weight: About 500lb (227kg).
Propulsion: Aerojet Mk 53 Mod 2, Mk 65 or Hercules Mk 58 dual-thrust solid.
Guidance: CW semi-active homing.
Range: (7E) about 5 miles (8km), (7H) about 8 miles (13km).
Flight speed: At burnout, about Mach 3.
Warhead: (7E) 60lb (27kg) conventional, (7H) 66lb (30kg) continuous rod.

AIM-7E (see air-to-air section) is used almost unchanged as RIM-7E, the missile in the US Navy BPDMS (Basic Point-Defense Missile System), which became operational in 1969. It is used on many classes of surface vessel, including the attack carriers, fired from a modified eight-box Asroc launcher. The later RIM-7H has a higher performance and folding fins to fit a smaller launcher box. It is part of IPDMS (Improved PDMS) which also includes new radar and IR sensors. Because of basically limited performance the Sea Sparrow is scheduled to be augmented or replaced by ASMD or SIRCS.

Right: Firing an RIM-7E Sea Sparrow from the nuclear-powered super-carrier USS *Enterprise* (CVN-65), in August 1976.

Raytheon/Martin XMIM-104A Patriot

Origin: Raytheon Missile Systems Division and Martin Orlando Division.
Type: Advanced mobile battlefield SAM system.
Dimensions: Length 204in (518cm); body diameter 16in (40·6cm); span 36in (92cm).
Launch weight: Not disclosed, but about 1,500lb (680kg).
Propulsion: Thiokol TX-486 single-thrust solid motor.
Guidance: Phased-array radar command and semi-active homing.
Range: About 30 miles (48km).
Flight speed: About Mach 3.
Warhead: Choice of nuclear or conventional blast/frag.

Originally known as SAM-D, this planned successor to Nike-Hercules and Hawk has had an extremely lengthy gestation but in 1978 was beginning to look as if it would see service. Indeed, it was once styled AADS-70s, signifying Army Air-Defense System for the 1970s, but in fact it will not be in use before the 1980s, after development which has taken almost 20 years and cost an estimated $1,728 million. Key element in the Patriot system is a phased-array radar which performs all the functions of surveillance, acquisition, track/engage and missile guidance. The launcher carries four missiles each in its shipping container, from which it blasts upon launch. Launchers, spare missile boxes, radars, computers, power supplies and other items can be towed or self-propelled. Patriot is claimed to be effective against all aircraft or attack missiles even in the presence of clutter or intense jamming or other ECM.

Above: Dramatic firing of a Patriot development missile from the standard four-round launching unit. Survivability of the launcher box is immaterial in so costly a weapon system.

SIRCS and ASMD

Origin: Navy; industrial team yet to be selected (1978).
Type: Shipboard Intermediate-Range Combat System.

After several large study programmes, including ASMD (Anti-Ship Missile Defense), the Navy has finally rationalized its requirement for a new weapon system to defend all vessels of 1,000 tons upwards against all kinds of anti-ship missile. The weapon would also be effective against close-range aircraft and would be able to function in an anti-ship or shore-bombardment role. By far the most difficult of the challenging list of requirements is the capability to deal with from four (on small ships) to 14 missiles arriving at roughly the same time. Three teams accepted study contracts: RCA/Martin, Raytheon/Univac/Lockheed and Sperry/McDonnell Douglas. The last-named has worked in partnership with British Aerospace, whose Seawolf is the only existing system that comes anywhere near meeting the SIRCS specification. In-service date could be 1979 if Seawolf were used, or about 1983 for an all-new system.

ASMD continues with the collaboration of West Germany in four versions with different ship systems and with or without Sea Sparrow (p. 237). The main objective is to defeat cruise missiles, backed up by the close-range Sea Sparrow and the Phalanx CIWS (Close-In Weapon System) using the 20mm Vulcan gun. In 1978 there was pressure to standardise on a SIRCS, using the same missile airframe as AMRAAM of the Air Force.

Right: Launch of General Dynamics/Pomona ASMD with 5-in calibre rolling airframe and dual RF/IR terminal guidance. It thus relies on signals from the attacking anti-ship missile.

AIR-TO-AIR MISSILES

AIM-9 Sidewinder

Origin: Developed at the Naval Ordnance Test Station (now Naval Weapons Center) at China Lake, and mass-produced by Philco-Ford (AIM-9B), GE (9B), Motorola (9C), Raytheon (9D), Aeronutronic Ford (9E), Ford Aerospace (9G/H/J) and Raytheon (9L).
Type: Close-range air-to-air missile with IR or SAR homing guidance.
Dimensions: Length 111·5 to 114·5in (283–291cm); body diameter 5·0in (12·7cm); span 22 to 25in (56·64cm).
Launch weight: 165 to 190lb (75–86kg).
Propulsion: Rocketdyne, Thiokol, Bermite or Naval Propellant Plant single-grain solid (Mks 17, 36 or 86).
Guidance: See text.
Range: Early models up to 2 miles (3·2km), latest about 6 miles (10km).
Flight speed: Early, Mach 2; latest about Mach 2·5.
Warhead: Most, 22–24lb (10–11kg) continuous-rod/blast, with prox fuze; (9L) WDU-17B annular blast/frag, with active optical fuze.

Most cost/effective missile programme in history, Sidewinder was rapidly developed on a shoestring budget and fired in 1953. AIM-9B with IR homing became operational in 1956 and over 60,000 were delivered. 9C has semi-active radar (or it can home on radar in the target aircraft). 9D has improved IR. 9E has an improved IR head and better low-altitude performance (thus designated Sidewinder LAP). 9G has the SEAM (Sidewinder Expanded Acquisition Mode) guidance for greater lead-acquisition. 9H has SEAM plus solid-state electronics. 9J has the 9E guidance but a high-power servo system driving long-span canard controls. 9L is a completely new missile with IR conical-scan head with AM/FM and internally cooled seeker cell, new warhead and fuze, and dramatically increased control power with long-span double-delta fins. 9L can attack targets from all angles. It is standard on Navy, Air Force and Marines combat aircraft, and will remain in production (possibly with further motor and fuze improvements) for several years.

Right upper: The USAF AIM-9J, here carried by an F-4E, is being modified to J-1 standard with new motor and rate bias.

Right: A pair of J-1 Sidewinders carried by an F-16. The version planned for this aircraft is the all-aspect AIM-9L.

Below: 1963 (Mk 30) model of the original Navy AIM-9B.

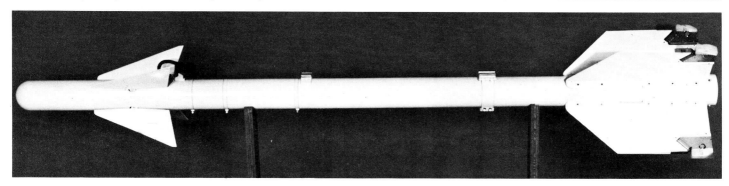

Western Electric MIM-14B Nike Hercules

Origin: Western Electric Company, Burlington, NC.
Type: Large surface-to-air missile system for fixed emplacement.
Dimensions: Length 500in (41ft 8in, 1270cm); body diameter 34·6in (88cm); span 105in (266cm).
Launch weight: 10,712lb (4858kg).
Propulsion: Tandem boost motor, quad cluster with solid propellant; sustainer, internal solid motor.
Guidance: Radar command.
Range: Out to 93 miles (150km).
Flight speed: Mach 3·5.
Warhead: Blast/preformed-splinter frag (usual) or nuclear, with command detonation.

An outgrowth of the Nike Ajax, Nike Hercules became operational with the US Army in 1958. It uses a large high-performance missile and an extensive array of ground installations which detect, interrogate and track the target, track the launched missile, drive the two into coincidence and detonate the large warhead. US Army batteries were deactivated by 1974 except for a few in Alaska, southern Florida and Fort Sill (for training US and many foreign operating personnel). The replacement has for ten years been planned to be Patriot.

Right: Launch of a NORAD (N. American Air Defense Command) Nike Hercules in 1960. This physically large SAM system is still important, mainly to America's allies.

Raytheon AIM-7 Sparrow

Origin: Developed by Sperry and US Navy; later versions developed and produced by Raytheon Company, Missile Systems Division, with (1978) second-source production by General Dynamics.
Type: Radar-guided air-to-air missile.
Dimensions: Length (current versions) 144in (366cm); body diameter 8in (20·3cm); span (wings) 40·0in (103cm), (tail) 32in (82cm).
Launch weight: (7E) 450lb (204kg), (7F) 500lb (227kg).
Propulsion: (E) Rocketdyne Mk 38 Mod 4 or Aerojet Mk 52 Mod 2 single-thrust solid; (F) Hercules Mk 48 Mod 0 or Aerojet Mk 65 Mod O dual-thrust solid.
Guidance: CW semi-active homing (F has PD receiver).
Range: (E) 15 miles (25km), (F) 28 miles (44km).
Flight speed: Mach 3·7.
Warhead: (Prior to E), conventional HE blast/frag, (E) 66lb (30kg) continuous-rod, (F) 88lb (40kg) continuous-rod.

Unique in having spawned land-based and ship-based versions, Sparrow was originally planned at the end of World War II and began trials in 1949. After Sparrow I had seen service a much more advanced Sparrow III entered service in 1958, and advanced versions of this include today's AIM-7E and -7F and the Sea Sparrow RIM-7H. Most of the Sparrows in use, as standard AAMs on the F-4, F-14 and F-15, are of the AIM-7E type or the improved E-2 with plug-in fins and increased manoeuvrability. Production has since 1976 centred on the -7F version, with increased range, maneuver capability against 7g targets, solid-state guidance with PD capability and lock-on in up to 10 dB clutter in the look-down mode, bigger warhead and higher reliability. A new monopulse seeker is needed (such as in production in Britain on Skyflash).

Right: Launch sequence (0·6 sec between frames) of AIM-7F launch from F-16 at Mach 1·05 at 17,600ft. There is no plan to use Sparrow on the F-16, but the capability is provided.

Below right: AIM-7F production checkout at GD/Pomona division.

Below: Compatibility test of Raytheon-built AIM-7F from F-15.

Hughes AIM-4 and -26 Falcon

Origin: Hughes Aircraft, Culver City (production was at Tucson).
Type: Air-to-air guided missiles, various guidance.
Dimensions: Length (4D) 79·1in (201cm), (26B) 81·5in (207cm); body diameter (4D) 6·4in (16·2cm), (26B) 11·4in (29cm); span (4D) 20in (50·1cm), (26B) 24·5in (62cm).
Launch weight: (4D) 134·5lb (61kg), (26B) 254lb (115kg).
Propulsion: (4D) Thiokol TX-58 (M58) single-stage solid, (26B) Thiokol TX-60 (M60) solid.
Guidance: (4D) passive IR homing, (26B) semi-active radar homing.
Range: (4D) 6 miles (10km), (26B) 7 miles (11km).
Flight speed: (4D) Mach 4, (26B) Mach 3.
Warhead: Proximity-fuzed blast/frag (much larger in 26B).

Development of the Hughes Falcon air-to-air missile family began in 1947, and the first IR-homing model became operational in 1954. Extremely large numbers of many versions were subsequently produced, and some remain in USAF and Air National Guard service. The AIM-4D, used by ANG F-102, TF-102 and F-101B aircraft, is one of the smaller versions; in fact many were produced by rebuilding earlier small models such as the 4A and 4C. It has the IR seeker nose of the AIM-4G Super Falcon. The AIM-26B has all-aspect radar guidance, and needs a much larger warhead, the -26A being nuclear. The -26B is used by all aircraft (mostly F-106A and B) of Aerospace Defense Command.

Above: The AIM-26B Nuclear Falcon was introduced in 1960 as the GAR-11 on the F-102A (rear), since replaced by the F-106.

Left: AIM-4H, seen here on an F-4D in 1970, is a -4D with new warhead and active optical (laser-beam) proximity fuze.

Hughes AIM-54A Phoenix

Origin: Hughes Aircraft, Culver City (production at Tucson).
Type: Long-range air-to-air missile.
Dimensions: Length 156in (396cm); body diameter 15in (38cm); span 36in (91·4cm).
Launch weight: 985lb (447kg).
Propulsion: Rocketdyne Mk 47 Mod 0 or Aerojet Mk 60 Mod 0 long-burn solid motor.
Guidance: Cruise, AWG-9 semi-active homing with PD; terminal (said to be final 10 miles/16km) active PD-radar homing.
Range: Over 130 miles (210km).
Flight speed: In excess of Mach 4.
Warhead: Large continuous-rod with Mk 334 prox and Bendix IR fuzes.

Largest and most powerful AAM in the West, and far longer-ranged than the bigger Soviet "Acrid", Phoenix was developed for the F-111B but was finally put into service, with the partner AWG-9 radar, in the F-14A Tomcat. At present the F-14 is the only carrier of Phoenix, which in 1978 continues in low-rate production in an improved AIM-54B form. This has a simpler airframe, solid-state digital electronics and non-liquid conditioning and power systems, for improved reliability and reduced cost. The Sea Phoenix is a proposed ship-to-air or ship-to-ship system using AWG-9, with a range of about 50 miles (80km) but not against targets below the horizon.

Above: Six Phoenix flying on an F-14A, another of which is seen (right) with Hughes AWG-9 radar and planar scanner exposed. Chief drawback of this weapon system is high cost.

Below: A complete Phoenix with, in front, the active terminal radar, guidance and flight-control electronics and (extreme right) one of the control surfaces with its power unit.

Above: Early AIM-4A Falcons mounted on their swinging-link arms in the weapon bay of an F-102A at Holloman AFB.

Below: Launch of an early Falcon (out of picture, probably an AIM-4A) by an F-102A. A second missile awaits launch.

US Reserves and National Guard

Dr Roy A. Werner, Legislative Assistant to Senator John Glenn; staff member US Senate Foreign Relations Committee.

The question of readiness and value of reserve forces is again a major question in US strategic doctrine, which currently calls for reservists "to be the initial and primary source for augmentation of the active forces". But with a small volunteer military, reserve forces are the only means of quickly expanding manpower in an emergency. Thus, to be useful, the 820,000 personnel in selected US reserve units must be ready. If reserve personnel cannot readily deploy, the doctrine is faulty and changes are necessary.

The necessity for rapidly deployable reserve units is clear given the dismantling of the Selective Service System and the possibility of brief, high-intensity wars. Seven months, however, would be necessary to select and train draftee replacements. Moreover, even immediate enlistments would require two to three months of training. Hence, reservists are the sole source of additional manpower for the first ninety days of any future conflict.

But is this concept viable? Unless reserve units are combat ready and capable of meeting exacting deployment schedules, the strategic doctrine fails. Evidence suggests that currently many US reserve units cannot meet the probable schedules. Thus, restructuring is necessary to develop capable reserve forces. If such revamping is opposed, the reserves at their present levels are not a "national security bargain" and should not be perpetuated.

The Planning Process

Logically the planning process for arriving at an optimum defense force structure begins with an appreciation of the threat, then proceeds to structure forces and missions to counter the perceived threat. However, gaps inevitably arise between the "ideal force" and budgetary constraints. This fiscal reality and the desire to maintain an "insurance" factor, leads to reliance upon reserve forces. Although optimizing for a specific conflict is recommended, forces are not always substitutable between potential scenarios. It is easier, of course, to adjust reserve forces to wage a sustained war of attrition than to cope effectively with a *blitzkrieg*. Yet, because the likely adversary of the United States has a maneuver doctrine, the reserve structure and doctrine may be inadequate.

Despite noticeable alterations in foreign policy, defense strategies, weapons technology, and active force levels, the structure and missions of US reserve forces have remained nearly constant. A re-evaluation is long overdue.

Missions which can be performed only by active forces and those for which an active-reserve mix is both prudent and economical must be distinguished. Obviously the level, duration, and intensity of possible conflicts are crucial factors. For example, prospects of a prolonged low-intensity conflict seem remote. Moreover, because of political consequences and lethal new weapons, the probability of a lengthy high-intensity war seem equally remote. Therefore, the most probable conflict is a short, intense war—possibly designed for only limited goals. In such a case what then are reserve force missions? If deterrence fails, reserves must defeat aggression by means

sufficient to serve political objectives. Thus, reserve combat elements should be deployable between within 1 to 30 days, and a training and logistical base sufficient to expand the military services should a prolonged conflict develop. Clearly then, higher priorities must be assigned to deploying units early with a low priority being given to sustaining support personnel and units. The many men on active duty in the USSR help to maintain a vast reserve pool of nearly nine million personnel over current five year intervals and in association with Warsaw Pact allies outproduce NATO in most categories of equipment for conventional warfare.

Force Structure

Force structures and strategy reflect past political and military decisions (or non-decisions). Presently, US reserves are ill-prepared to fight and win a high-intensity, short duration, war in Europe. Yet, many authorities anticipate precisely such a "short intense war."[1] Current strategy which assumes a three week warning of Soviet attack and up to sixty days for reinforcements to arrive[2] is dubious. If we remember Czechoslovakia in 1968 and consider the deployment pattern of Soviet forces, these assumptions become debatable propositions.

Obviously, the partial shifting of initial defensive burdens to the reserves because NATO members are unwilling to sustain sufficient active forces has important consequences. First, reserve reinforcements must be deployable immediately given the Soviet doctrinal emphasis on shock and speed and armor assets. But reserve units require more time to prepare for overseas deployment and US stockpiles still need rebuilding. Moreover, if these re-supply and staging areas were overrun early in a conflict, equipment would be lost. Second, nine of the Army's eleven active divisions based in the United States rely upon reservists to fill their wartime manning levels, hence these divisions will be less effective if deployed within the initial weeks of combat. Third, while ignoring categories of reserve effectiveness, it is obvious that the Warsaw Pact alliance can field more reservists and enjoys shorter logistical lines. Thus, the need for NATO superiority in weapons technology and planning is crucial. A Soviet attack launched in bad weather, utilizing smoke, electronic warfare and chemicals, might well achieve a breakthrough given comparative strengths and still mal-deployed NATO forces. When the weather clears, air power can be fully utilized but it may be too late. NATO must then declare either to gain territory through conventional warfare or to threaten escalation to nuclear warfare. If a conventional role is decided upon, NATO is dependent upon reserves. Is such reliance justified?

If reserve units are incapable of both rapid deployment and mission success, NATO must either accept a *fait accompli* or escalate. Thus, adequate reserves can support deterrence. However, reserve force structure may not be sending out such a positive signal. Only the Air Force has basically altered its force structure since pre-Vietnam days. A decreased emphasis upon air defense interceptor roles and a sharper

Reserve forces are crucial to the Western Alliance, but only a few could be effective within days and some could not reach a crisis point inside three weeks. Infantry, such as the Army reservist laying a mine, rely on personal skills that can be kept honed to a fine edge in peacetime. But hardware, such as the ''Mothball Fleet'' (San Diego Group illustrated) and the ''Boneyard'' of aircraft at Davis-Monthan AFB (below) are of limited value in the suddenly-flaring crisis that can hit today's world. Conscription gives the Warsaw Pact a vast advantage over the United States in possibly vital fast-recall reserve forces.

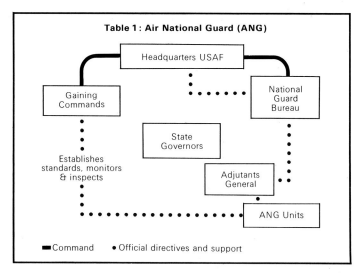

Table 1: Air National Guard (ANG)

Headquarters USAF

Gaining Commands

National Guard Bureau

State Governors

Adjutants General

Establishes standards, monitors & inspects

ANG Units

■ Command ● Official directives and support

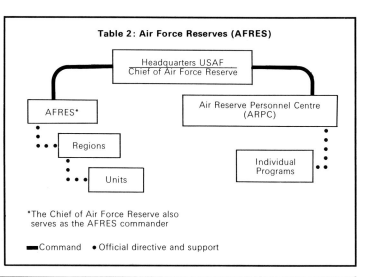

Table 2: Air Force Reserves (AFRES)

Headquarters USAF
Chief of Air Force Reserve

AFRES*

Air Reserve Personnel Centre (ARPC)

Regions

Units

Individual Programs

*The Chief of Air Force Reserve also serves as the AFRES commander

■ Command ● Official directive and support

focus on tactical fighters, air refueling and airlift capabilities by the Air Force reflect both missions and reserve training capabilities. Table 3 reveals the scope of these changes. An even better indication of the Air Force modernization of its force structure is provided by examining the inter-meshing of regular and reserve units (Table 4). More significantly, Air Force reserve units probably receive the best training of any reserve component.

Modern equipment, however, is not present in the Naval reserve inventory. The Navy has passed on to the reserves modernized World War II destroyers (Gearing class) that lack fully modern sensors and helicopters for ASW purposes. Such ships obviously have little capability against Soviet nuclear submarines. Nor are these destroyers very effective against modern diesel powered submarines which, when submerged and running on batteries, are more difficult to detect than nuclear boats. These vessels are also vulnerable to Soviet surface combatants that can kill US ships with anti-ship missiles at a distance beyond the destroyer gun ranges. Adequate shipboard training for inland naval reservists remains a problem despite occasional "fly-ins" for sea duty. More fundamentally, sea control will be difficult in the early stages of NATO conflict given the vulnerability of surface vessels to anti-ship missiles, submarines and Soviet naval aircraft. These factors thus combine to assert a need for structural reform. A Korean War type reactivation would be of limited use, even if 549 mothballed

Table 3: Air Force Reserve and Air National Guard Flying Squadrons

	1960	1967	1974	1976
Wing Headquarters:	39	36	36	36
Fighter Interceptor Squadrons	42	22	21	11
Tactical Fighter Squadrons	24	23	33	38
Tactical Reconnaissance Squadrons	16	12	7	8
Air Commando/SOF	0	4	3	0
Tactical Airlift Squadrons	46	22	36	37
Military Airlift Squadrons	6	44	20	17
Aeromedical Airlift Squadrons	5	0	1	1
Air Refueling Squadrons	0	5	9	12
Tactical Air Support Squadrons	0	0	5	7
Tactical Electronic Warfare Squadrons	0	0	2	4
Special Operations Squadrons	0	0	6	2
Air Rescue and Recovery Squadrons	5	5	4	6
Weather	0	0	0	1

Sources: Congressional Testimony, *Air Force Magazine*, and Department of the Air Force data.

ships were available again. The latest weapons, vessel speeds, and surveillance capabilities make the reserve fleet obsolete. Because any future naval conflict is likely to be a war of platform attrition, surface effect ships, V/STOL carriers and hydrofoils—in large numbers—are the most useful ships. It is time to realize that merely continuing the past force structure will not suffice. The US surface naval reserve, if it is to contribute, must find new approaches to force composition simultaneously with new technology and vessels.

The composition of the Navy's active-reserve mix is found in Table 5 and clearly reveals the limited reserve capabilities. Meanwhile the Army, like the Navy, has been slow to modernize

its reserve elements. Although excessive divisions headquarters with understrength units have been reduced, the Army's mission capabilities are much the same. A high intensity war generally demands armor and mechanized units. Yet, the present structure of 19 active Army and Marine divisions has nine light infantry divisions. Thus, almost half of the US ground com-

Below: Gray smoke pours from the starter exhaust of an old "Hun" (Rockwell F-100 Super Sabre) of the 180th Tac Ftr Group, Ohio Air National Guard. Now replaced by the F-4 and other types, the F-100 is still occasionally flown by ANG jocks.

bat strength is primarily designed for low-intensity operations—not the primary threat identified earlier. While it is true that some general capabilities must be maintained and that no scenario can hope to respond to all possible threats, the imbalance seems striking if rapid NATO reinforcements are needed. Of course, to a degree, it is more sensible to retain light infantry in the reserves to respond to the need for manpower above the active duty numbers. Further, with additional training and equipment, light infantry can assume other roles. But such shifts require time which only lower priority reserve units can spare. It would therefore seem reasonable to enact a proposal under evaluation by the Training and Doctrine Command (TRADOC) to make some of these units anti-tank formations. Such an assignment would more clearly relate to potential conflicts in Europe, in Korea, or in the Middle East.

Another difficulty with the ground combat elements is that the US is deficient in lift capacities for high and mid-intensity wars. Capacity and time frame are the critical elements in such conflicts, wherever they may occur. Yet, there is insufficient sealift to move immediately the armor and mechanized divisions and US air-mobile forces appear not to be suitably equipped. Moreover, light infantry delivered via air transport could find stockpiles captured and some airfields closed. When readiness is also evaluated, it is not surprising that one analyst concluded that it may take the six National Guard divisions designated as NATO combat replacements eight or more weeks after M-day (Mobilization Day) to arrive in Europe.[3]

Without revisions of reserve force structure, it may well be that neither the Army or Navy reserves will make significant contributions to a brief, high-intensity war. Another methodology for examining force structure as related to military doctrine is to analyse mission percentages between reserve and active forces. Table 6 presents such a comparison as of 1977.

Whether one anticipates a brief or prolonged war, logic demands that planners maximize funding and training for early deploying units. The first step in that process is to identify priority and non-priority units. The elimination of some units may also be desirable. Such units include Navy Seabees, Army military police hospital guard units, and a host of other personnel, finance, engineer support, legal, public information and historical units. All these are job specialities for which civilian skills are easily transferable. In the event of mobilization for a longer conflict, these slots will be readily filled. The savings from these unnecessary units could then be directed to modernize equipment, improve training and tailor reserve units to specific missions. If such deletions are not made, existing reserve force levels will require even more money to become combat ready. But, given fiscal realities, more money is unlikely and there is no alternative to pruning.

Readiness

Even if the reserve force structure had the ideal combination of units to respond to both short and prolonged war, the crucial issue is readiness. In October, 1961, three "high priority" Army divisions (2 infantry and 1 training) were mobilized for the Berlin crisis. But, the two priority combat divisions required nine months to achieve combat readiness.[4] In comparison it took only three more months to start from the beginning—form a cadre, basic training, individual proficiency and unit training—and to deploy the Ninth Infantry Division in 1965. Thus, even if we accept as valid the "insurance requirement" for both training and logistical support units for a prolonged war, it may be

Right: Rows of B-52s at Davis-Monthan look like impressive air power, but each lacks engines, weapons, radar and other vital parts, and to refurbish one for combat duty would cost millions.

Table 4: Air Force Flying Squadrons Functional Mix

	Active	Reserve
Wing Headquarters:	68	36
Fighter Interceptor Squadrons	6	11
Tactical Fighter Squadrons	74	38
Tactical Reconnaissance Squadrons	9	8
Tactical Airlift Squadrons	15	37
Military Airlift Squadrons	17	17
Aeromedical Airlift Squadrons	3	1
Air Refueling Squadrons	35	12
Tactical Air Support Squadrons	9	7
Tactical Electronic Warfare Squadrons	1	4
Special Operation Squadrons	5	2
Air Rescue and Recovery Squadrons	6	6
Weather Squadrons	2	1
Bomber Squadrons	25	0
Strategic Reconnaissance Squadrons	2	0

Sources: Adapted from Air Force Reserve, Air National Guard data and *Air Force Magazine*.

asked whether hundreds of thousands of reservists are necessary if they are not deployable much faster than volunteers and draftees. Are possible months of delay, perhaps even defeat, acceptable given the $5.5 billion spent annually on reserves?

Clearly a huge reservoir of partially trained manpower, not readily deployable, is wasteful. The case for reserve organizations must rest upon these forces being deployable to combat theaters within the first month for high priority units and within two to three months for the lower priority sustaining units. Yet, in an exchange between Senator John Culver and then Secretary of Defense, James Schlesinger, the Senator stated, "What you are saying . . . is that it is hard to envision any real combat role within a ninety-day period?" Schlesinger responded, "I would not want to exclude it, but I think it is lower down on a probability scale."[5]

Another major disadvantage for the US, unlike European nations which can emphasize a territorial home defense role, is that US reserves must be capable of complex mobile warfare. Therefore, the training of maneuver battalions and elements to interact in battle is crucial, yet few and often inadequate field exercises at such levels are a common feature of US reserve forces.

This persistent doubt about the early deployment of reserve forces was also evident at a recent Army Operations Research symposium. An analysis of post-mobilization training at the battalion level only led Major Thomas A. Wilson, II (Hq. Force Command) and Dr. John R. Chiarini (Litton Systems) to estimate that two weeks would be required between the altering and the onset of active training and another seven weeks for post-mobilization training.[6] Even more time would be necessary if the units were to deploy as brigades or divisions—some four to six months. These discouraging estimates confirm earlier studies completed by the Army War College Strategic Studies Institute.

It may therefore be unrealistic to expect a reserve component maneuver unit, except for aviation elements, to deploy within thirty days. Armor units, for example, fire only once a year and cannot complete two of the eight gunnery tables without additional post-mobilization training. Thus, reserve units possessing generally only 39 training days a year (15 days active duty and 48 drill periods of four hours each), are hard pressed to meet their readiness criteria. As former Defense Secretary Schlesinger said, "We should stop pretending that we can use all of them as full substitutes for active duty ground forces."[7]

Other reserve elements experience poor training. Air defense units seldom train in, or experience, electronic warfare environments. Engineer, artillery, signal units, and naval surface crews all require extensive teamwork. Such units seldom receive the necessary collective training. A naval reservist recently noted that except for the Naval Reserve Force destroyers and other small reserve ships . . . "the surface reserve sailor gets little practical shipboard-type training."[8]

The single service reasonably ready is the US Air Force. Its reserve elements have visible missions, participate alongside active forces, have generally the same equipment as active components, and possess significantly higher percentages of full-time personnel. The USAF tactical fighter reserve squadrons deployed in the January and May, 1968, mobilizations attained the highest performance ratings in their respective four wings. The results show. Naval aviation learned the importance of training on the same aircraft they will fly when mobilized in 1968. Six squadrons were delayed in that mobilization because of re-equipping and re-training requirements necessary to convert the crews to new aircraft.

After the aviation elements in readiness comes the Fourth Marine Division. The Marines possess many of the same advantages as the Air Force reserves, especially active duty involvement and guidance. Probably only in such a fashion can reservists assume the awesome

Table 5: Naval Ships, Functional Mix[1]	Active	Reserve	Custody[2]
Sea Control (Surface Warfare, ASW, etc)			
Destroyers	73	29	8
Cruisers	23	0	7
Frigates	64	0	0
Minesweepers	3	22	0
Submarines, Attack[3]	74	0	3
Projection			
Amphibious[4]	65	3	17
Battleships	0	0	4
Carriers	13	0	6
Submarines, SSBN	41	0	0
Other			
Patrol	26	5	0
Command	0	0	2
Auxiliary	129	0	34

Source: Department of the Navy, 1976.
1. This table excludes the seventh reserve component, the Coast Guard and the forty-two vessels assigned to the Military Sealift Command.
2. This category includes mothball ships held by the Navy and the Maritime Administration vessels already identified for Navy utilization.
3. Sixty-five are nuclear powered.
4. Assumes a primary role of naval gunfire support for land combat operations (as in Vietnam). Obviously, in an era of ship-to-ship missiles, these vessels are unlikely to engage other ships.

burden of national defense while providing significant cost savings.

Another problem is the growing technological disparity between the regular and the reservist. Equipment is becoming increasingly complex and a reservist who does not train regularly on laser guided weapons, for example, is going to be less proficient. Obviously this disparity will be greater for radar and sonar operators as compared to infantrymen. Moreover, even effective training on outdated equipment, regardless of enthusiasm, is of little value if that equipment cannot be deployable or if stockpiles contain different gear.

The problems are thus centered in the Army's reserve components and naval crews. The Office of the Secretary of Defense conducted a Reserve Component Test Program between 1972 and 1974 of Army divisions and separate brigades. The majority of these units did not attain company level (basic combat unit) proficiency. Recent reforms stressing "hands-on", mission-essential training have somewhat improved the situation. In essence, although defense policy prescribes missions for reserve units, there is scepticism that these units could successfully accomplish their missions without extensive post-mobilization training.

Personnel
The ever-present problem of reserve personnel strength is illustrated by the fact that the then

Major Dwight D. Eisenhower wrote his 1928 Army War College research topic on "An Enlisted Reserve for the Regular Army". Personnel problems continue to plague selected reserve forces: In April, 1977, the percentage of their authorized strength were:

	Percent
Army National Guard	91.7
Army Reserve	89.2
Air Force Reserve	91.4
Air National Guard	99.6
Naval Reserve	97.6
Marine Corps Reserve	89.2
Coast Guard Reserve	100.0

Moreover, authorized strength levels had been reduced the previous year with the Army Guard dropping from 400,000 to 390,000 in 1977 and the Army Reserve dropping from 219,000 to 212,400

Right: Of these four great US Navy carriers seen a few years ago on the West Coast only nuclear-powered *Enterprise* (left) is in commission; *Hancock* (No 3) has been stricken, but *Oriskany* (CVA-34) and *Coral Sea* (CVA-43) are in reserve and in emergency could become operational.

Below: AFRES (Air Force Reserve) pilot on pre-flight check of an A-37A Dragonfly of 434th Tac Ftr Wing.

in 1977. Yet, the adverse trend of declining strength is continuing.

Personnel problems, however, may doom any reform of the reserve forces that does not shrink force levels. The Reserve Forces Policy Board, a mixture of civilian and military advisors, in a November 1976 statement warned that an economic recovery "will intensify the recruiting and retention problem." Recent statistics show the combined reserve shortfall to be about 80,000 personnel. Even more disturbing is the failure of Army reserve components to retain more than half of their enlisted personnel. Moreover, it is not certain that enacting a variety of financial benefits will solve the recruitment and retention problems. If the root of the problem is attitudinal in nature, such incentives will have little effect. The adequacy of individual ready reservists (IRR) is also dubious. This massive manpower pool formerly had no realistic training requirements. More importantly, volunteer military forces are constantly shrinking these numbers. The Army, for example, had more than a million personnel in the pool a few years ago. But projections are that the pool will shrink to 75,000 in the near future. In addition, without proper training the value of this manpower is questionable. In 1974, the Army trained only 13 percent of the IRR pool (39,000) for two weeks; the Navy trained 2,900 volunteers for two weeks. Thus, the reserve personnel system neither delivers a continuing flow of manpower nor adequately trains and retains what manpower it does recruit.

Yet another difficulty in personnel is the buddy-system of officer appointments made possible by geographical dispersion. An innovative approach to opening these closed shops has been made by the 97th US Army Reserve Command (ARCOM). Utilizing senior officers from subordinate commands, the officer career management board publicizes widely all 0–5 and 0–6 positions, interviews interested parties and makes recommendations to the Commander. In the words of one general officer member, the problem is to "identify the qualified, ambitious, effective" officer as well as the "ineffective officers" and place them both "where they belong".[9] An additional aid for the Army reserve components will be the recent changes in AR 140–10 which limit key command and staff slots to three year tours.

Yet another issue is what mix of prior service (generally ex-active duty) and non-prior service personnel is desirable. Obviously, if a trained individual can be acquired, efficiency and readiness should be enhanced. Since Vietnam reserve units have relied on prior service, short-term enlistments to fill the ranks. Although veterans minimize shortfalls, they increase turbulence, grade and longevity, and result in higher personnel costs. Hence, more inexperienced personnel are desirable given cost, retention, and age efficiencies. The one advantage of "veterans" is that they are generally qualified in their respective job skills. Table 7 shows the percentage of "qualified enlisted reservists" in the various services.

Another personnel problem is the mobilization process itself. After readiness, mobilization speed is probably the most significant issue in reserve policy considerations. Israeli and South Korea forces mobilize within 72 hours (many sooner). Both these systems thus signal potential adversaries and probably aid deterrence. Yet, aside from the Berlin 1961 mobilization and the limited call-up in 1968, no full scale US mobilization exercises have been conducted. Ideally, units should be tested within a reasonable time period by alerting them and then moving the unit out for two weeks of annual training. Such an evaluation might impose some hardships, but it would present a more complete picture of the system's capabilities to include possible "no shows" due to health standards, one of today's unknowns. Another option is the unannounced Marine Corps Mobilization Operational Test. These exercises check personnel and mobilization time, equipment, and unit proficiency. Until such realistic tests are conducted, planners cannot be confident of reserve personnel capabilities.

An argument is made, however, that regardless of readiness, political and diplomatic factors will determine any future mobilization decision. Certainly, political authorities have

recently been reluctant to call up more than a minimum of reserve forces in a crisis. Recent crises—Berlin, Vietnam, the Pueblo Incident of 1968—have seen small numbers of reservists called up to dramatize US resolve. However, the demise of conscription and a recent statute granting the President authority to activate 50,000 reservists without declaring a national emergency suggest reserve activation is indeed policy. More importantly, reserve forces perceived as capable of early battlefield deployment aid both deterrence and crisis management by expanding readily deployable military forces.

A major problem, however, will occur by 1980 regarding mobilization requirements. The Army will naturally need manpower to augment the active forces in the event of war. Yet, when the Army calculated active personnel strength, augmented by available personnel from the Selected Reserve, the Individual Ready Reserve (IRR), the Standby Reserve, and the Retired Reserve, and analyzed their manpower needs under the most demanding wartime contingency, a shortfall of about 250,000 personnel in the initial months of an intensive conflict in Europe was found to exist by 1980. This shortfall projected for 1980 did not exist previously because the turnover of draftees possessing reserve obligations meant that more than a million personnel would be available. However, the greatly reduced residual military obligations inherent in a volunteer military have curtailed the supply.

Equipment

Shortages of modern equipment continue to plague reserve forces and degrade readiness. Army reserve components shortfalls of "modern" gear include:

	Percent
Tanks (M60, M60A1, M48A5)	27
Eight-inch SP Howitzers	20
155mm SP Howitzers	19
M113 Personnel Carriers	41
Electrical and Communications (Radios, Radars, ECOM items)	63

Corrective measures in the near term include

Above: Few military duties are outside the scope of reservists. Here a stick of paratroopers board a de Havilland Canada C-7A Caribou with the AFRES in the continental United States. Such training mirrors that of regular troops.

Table 6: Selected Reserve Forces as a percentage of the Department of Defense functional mix

	Per cent
Navy Coastal Riverine Forces	100
Navy Minesweepers	88
Army Combat Engineer Battalions	65
Naval Intelligence	65
Air Force Tactical Airlift Aircraft	61
Air Force Air Defense Interceptors	60
Army Artillery Battalions	58
Army Special Forces	57
Army Infantry and Armor Battalions	52
Air Force Special Operations Groups	50
Navy Cargo Handling Capacity	50
Army Aviation	45
Marine Corps Armor	40
Army Medical	35
Navy ASW Patrol Squadrons	35
Marine Corps Artillery	33
Air Force Tactical Fighter Aircraft	31
Navy Surface Combatants	16
Air Force Strategic Jet Tankers	16

Table 7: Enlisted Personnel Qualified, 1977

Service	Percentage
Air Force Reserve	95
Air Force National Guard	NA
Army Reserve	80
Army National Guard	70.8
Marine Reserve	95.2
Naval Reserve	95.5

issuing the M60 main battle tank to all early deploying roundout or affiliate units (those completing active forces wartime manning tables). The Air Force is accelerating transfer of one hundred and twenty-eight KC-135 tankers to its reserve components. But, modernization of fighter aircraft will extend into the 1980s with F-4s, A-10s, and A-7s. The new F-16 aircraft will not enter reserve units until the mid-1980s. Naval reserve aviation fares better, with P-3A/B ASW aircraft (FY 1977) and the A-7 A/B attack aircraft (FY 1978) already delivered. Yet, these positive examples nevertheless reveal a budgetary constraint. Because the cost of equipping both active and reserve forces with fully modern equipment is so high, as older major stock items are phased out of active forces, they are transferred to reserve components.

Many units are not, however, combat ready because of equipment shortfalls. Table 8 illustrates those units not at their highest stage of readiness. Further, when equipment is short, costs rise and readiness decreases. At the start of FY 1976, the Army National Guard had an equipment mobilization requirement of $6 billion (FY76), a training requirement of $4.5 billion (FY76), but had on hand only $3.5 billion of equipment (FY76). At the same time 18 of the 91 Air National Guard squadrons were equipped with obsolete F-100 fighters. Other reserve components were in similar positions. Over many years various equipment programs have been promulgated that historically do not succeed. The Army told Congress that all Army Reserve units would be at or near authorized equipment levels by FY 1977 in the FY 1973 hearings[10] yet reserve units were still quite short. These shortages degrade mission cap-

Table 8: Percentage of units not at C-1 readiness with equipment shortages as a factor

Air Force	Army	Marines	Navy
6% (AFR)[1]	Classified	1%	43.6% (Air)
Unknown (ANG)			40.0% (Ships)

Source: Adapted from DOD data as of August 1976.
1. Both these AFR units are undergoing conversion to new aircraft.

Above: Veterans of World War II are to be found sprinkled through all the US reserve forces. These "Vets" seen in an amphibious exercise with the Maryland Army National Guard, at Little Creek, Virginia, all hit the beaches at Anzio, Italy, in January 1944.

Left: Reservists are not all former regulars. Some, like this grenade-thrower, are without experience.

abilities. While granting that budget dollars, production line schedules and some foreign military sales all adversely affect the reserves, corrective action is necessary. "We simply cannot afford to spend $5.5 billion annually on a force oriented solely toward a lengthy mobilization of the type envisioned in the past," the Assistant Secretary of Defense for Manpower Reserve Affairs told Congress in 1975.[11]

Emerging Issues

The Laird decision in 1970 to return to traditional policy and rely upon reservists, not conscripts, as the initial reinforcement was accompanied by increased reserve budgets and a focusing on reserve problems by senior defense officials. Obviously, however, reform of reserve units to reflect viable policy options has not been accomplished. The United States can no longer endure the luxury of ill-prepared reservists on M-day (Mobilization Day). Therefore changes are mandatory. The starting point is to ask why the aviation components excel? One of the principal reasons for their success is a full-time manning level of about 20 percent. These levels were designed to provide maintenance care and to enable the units to conduct missions alongside regular units. Obviously not all reserve units can assist active forces. But all reserve units could increase their full-time personnel.[12] The Marines also gain from such augmentation and these active duty personnel may be assigned to the unit upon mobilization. Such methods are one way of infusing recent experience into reserve units.

A crucial immediate issue is, of course, whether reserve units can overcome their manpower shortfalls. Recently some civilian political and military officials have called for a return to conscription. In December 1976, Major General Henry Mohr, Chief of the Army Reserve, for example, argued that the only way reserve manpower needs will "be solved with any degree of effectiveness is with some sort of restoration of the draft". Such a judgment, however, ignores political realities. Nor would a "reserve only" draft produce viable fighting units with conscripts manning the platoons. It was exactly such attitudinal and generational conflict that recently plagued the active military. In prosperous societies the military is seldom popular and reserve units are no exception. Finally, in view of the declining demographic rates in the 1980s for persons of entry level age into military service, it is unlikely that existing reserve force levels can be maintained. Alternative manning tables and re-examination of missions will be necessary. Hence, test programs restructuring units and analysis of reserve missions are essential.

The problem of inadequate collective training has been mentioned. The establishment of Maneuver Commands to assist Army reserve components in group, brigade and division command post exercises was a useful first step. But, these units also need field exercises. Where would the American Army of World War II have been without Louisiana maneuvers? Another source would be greater inclusion in active force missions of rotating volunteer personnel.

The most innovative reserve training concept is the Marines VOTEC, a vocational education program which maximizes teaching by existing civilian instructional centers at low contract costs, thereby eliminating overhead. Examples of this arrangement include the maintenance and overhaul of diesel engines taught by a Texas technical institute and interpreter qualification training at a major university's language facility. The low costs per student hour were $2.75 in FY 1977 and are probably much lower than military skill center courses.

Obviously some improvements such as modern equipment require tax dollars. Further, substantial increases in reserve funding are unlikely. Therefore, planners must consider cuts to transfer funds. A possible starting point is the $1.4 billion (1974 dollars) savings to be gained through consolidation and the elimination of 300,000 excess paid reservists.[13] Such a policy would also narrow the equipment shortage gap. The basic features of that proposal were:

1 Merge training, recruiting and headquarters facilities of the Army Reserve with the Army National Guard and the Air Force Reserve with the Air National Guard.

2 Integrate reserve components into active force structures thereby somewhat reducing active duty manpower requirements.

3 Reduce IRR personnel and selected reserve units that could reasonably be expected to acquire skilled civilian personnel with transferable skills after mobilization began.

4 Alter the base year of retirement benefits from the year in which the annuity is drawn to the year in which the individual actually retires.

Refinements are possible. Although previous Guard-Reserve mergers have failed, the desirability of integrating the chain of command during peacetime cannot be denied. This option faces political problems even if President Carter were to back such moves. However, recognizing the desire of states to retain emergency forces, a possible solution is underway in California. An intensely trained emergency reaction force (like California's) could be left in state control with the remaining reserve and guard units being absorbed in a new Federal structure. Many states have para-military organizations—aside from the reserve units—such as state police forces or home guards that are available whenever the National Guard is employed elsewhere. Another option is to give Chiefs of Staff direct control over reserve policy decisions and reduce the duplication inherent in the National Guard Bureau and reserve Pentagon offices. Small, essentially policy staffs, could still represent "reserve opinions" to the Chiefs without the excess overhead. The premise is simple: an integrated staff for the "Total Force". Further, an internal emphasis on mission-oriented budgeting would sharpen the analytical focus of reserve assets. Dual basing of all mixed active-reserve units is desirable. Where a policy of dual basing is possible, this is the cheapest method.

Other cost savings come to mind. The "magic 48" drill periods could also be reduced for some units and personnel. The Army Reserve presently allows some medical doctors to drill as little as twelve assemblies and the Navy has units that drill twenty-four times annually. Certainly where the unit reflects civilian skills that are directly transferable—medical, building construction, legal, civil affairs, finance, some communication skills—a strong case exists that proficiency can be retained with fewer than 48 drills.

Personnel policy changes could also be advantageous. Reserve units frequently have senior commanders lacking active duty experience at their command level, and junior officers, who because they are ROTC graduates or State National Guard OCS graduates, lacking sufficient training. Senior officers would benefit from a lateral entry scheme that would emplace

them in key operational slots for a year with active forces. Such an in-out program would incur minimal costs and richly reward participants through enhanced professionalism while also educating active duty personnel about reserve components. The Army recently reduced branch qualification courses for state OCS graduates from twelve to four weeks. While granting that more officers can attend such reduced training, they are certainly less competent platoon leaders. One solution is to adopt a modification of the Marine platoon leader program and establish urban centers utilizing advisor personnel and mobile training teams to provide instruction for a year prior to the young officer returning to his unit.

Deeper analysis about possible contingencies and the appropriate force structure and readiness is necessary. As a recent Congressional Budget Office staff working paper on the Army noted:[14] "The force structure that is evolving ... is less well manned, less prepared for sustained combat and substantially more reliant on reserve component units than before."

Is this reliance sound? A recent report of the Defense Manpower Commission took note of a 1973 Secretary of Defense directive which said the "Total force is no longer a 'concept'. It is now the Total Force Policy ..." But the Commission concluded that the policy "is still far from a reality".[15] This is the precarious state in which US defense policy rests. As threats and strategies change, organizational forms must also change.

Footnotes

1. Jeffrey Record, *Sizing Up the Soviet Army* (Washington: The Brookings Institute, 1975) p. 47, and Professor John Erickson, "Soviet Ground forces and the Conventional Modes of Operations," *Journal of the Royal United Services Institute for Defence Studies*, June, 1976, pp. 45–59.
2. *The Washington Post*, 15 November 1976, p. 8.
3. Abbott A. Brayton, "The Transformation of US Mobilization Policies: Implications for NATO," *Journal of the Royal United Services Institute for Defence Studies*, March, 1975.
4. *Hearings: Merger of the Army Reserve Components*, 89th Congress, 1st Session (Washington: Government Printing Office, 1965).
5. *Hearings on S. 2115*, before the Senate Armed Services Subcommittee on Manpower and Personnel, 30 July, 1975.
6. William V. Kennedy, "Army to Revamp Its Reserve Components," *Armed Forces Journal International*, February, 1974, p. 26.
7. *Annual Defense Department Report, FY 1976 and FY 1977* (Washington: Government Printing Office, 1976) p. III–14.
8. Commander A. Babunek, USNR, "Fleet Observations from the Fleet," *US Naval Institute Proceedings* v. 102, n. 4 (April, 1976) p. 86.
9. BG Edwin I. Dosek, "Senior Officer Career Management Problems," *The Officer*, November, 1975, p. 18.
10. *Hearings: Fiscal 1973 Authorization for Military Procurement*, Part 3, p. 1623.
11. William K. Brehm, *Hearings on S. 2115* before the Senate Armed Services Subcommittee on Manpower and Personnel, 30 July 1975.
12. Legal complications arise in the National Guard and would require legislative changes or exempting full-time Federal personnel from state missions.
13. Martin Binkin, *US Reserve Forces: The Problem of the Weekend Warrior* (Washington, DC: The Brookings Institute, 1974).
14. Edwin A. Deagle, Jr., *US Army Force Design: Alternatives for Fiscal Years 1977–1981* (Washington, DC: Congressional Budget Office, 1976) p. ix.
15. *Defense Manpower: The Keystone of National Security*, (Washington, DC: Government Printing Office, 1976) p. 98.

Left: Owing to being often literally on the spot, reserve forces play a major role in saving life and property in major disasters. Here men of the 107th Armored Cavalry, W. Virginia Army National Guard, clear up after a flood.

Facing page: Reserve forces, such as the 1st Battalion, 23rd Marines, were given up to a month's notice that they would take part in the NATO Exercise Display Determination in the Aegean and European Turkey in 1977. Three other NATO countries took part in the exercise which demonstrated, among other things, how quickly US reserve forces have to blend with regular units (of US and friendly forces), on foreign shores if necessary. They may not be given so much notice in actual conflict.

The War Machine Evaluated

Dr. James E. Dornan, Jr., former Associate Professor and Chairman, Department of Politics, Catholic University of America, and Senior Political Science Scientist, Strategic Studies Center, Stanford Research Institute International, Washington D.C.

The previous chapters in this volume have delineated US military capabilities in terms of numbers of personnel, ships, aircraft, armor, and the like. In many respects the picture presented is an imposing one: in the sheer diversity of its capabilities, in the technological sophistication of its weapons systems, and in its potential for sustaining at least limited operations anywhere in the world, the US military machine is today unsurpassed.

The military power of a nation, however, cannot be properly measured in the abstract. Power is relative, and the adequacy of a state's capacity for making war is a function not only of the armed forces which it has at its disposal, but also of such factors as the nature and extent of the obligations which it has assumed and the interests which it must protect, and of the capabilities of its adversaries, real and potential, who might threaten those interests. The key question, in short, is what the United States can do with the power it possesses, as measured against what it would like to be able to do. Applying that question to the circumstances in which the United States currently finds itself, several specific questions follow. How does the power of the United States today compare with that which it wielded a decade ago? Have United States interests, obligations and influence abroad expanded or contracted during that period? Are the changes which occurred and are occurring in America's international power and influence the product of design, or of the expanding power of America's adversaries, or of both? Are the adversaries of the United States less numerous and powerful than a decade ago, or is the opposite the case? What are the trends in the US–USSR military balance? Considered in the light of these and related questions the United States military machine assumes a considerably less imposing aspect.

The Strategic Balance

It is worth noting at the outset that there are a number of intrinsic difficulties which inhibit the ability to measure and especially to compare strategic power. Analysts customarily employ several standards, such as numbers of strategic delivery vehicles, numbers of warheads or force loadings, megatonnage (or perhaps equivalent megatonnage), throw-weight, and such characteristics of strategic weapons as warhead yield, accuracy, and launcher survivability. Each of these indicators has advantages and disadvantages as a measure of strategic power. The number of launchers for strategic delivery vehicles in a nation's arsenal, for instance, in some respects the most obvious measure, is actually useful for little except for comparing force size, since it may tell us nothing about force effectiveness. The number of re-entry vehicles is a somewhat more useful measure since it indicates the number of targets which can be attacked, but re-entry vehicles vary greatly in capability, making comparisons between two opposing strategic forces on this basis alone extremely difficult. Hard information concerning the characteristics of re-entry vehicles is in any case difficult to acquire. And if, in addition to comparing offensive capabilities, we also try to evaluate other dimensions of the

strategic balance, such as the active and passive defensive capabilities of both sides and how they may affect deterrence now and in the future, our task becomes more difficult still.

With these perspectives in mind it is possible to examine the state of the contemporary strategic balance between the US and the USSR. Fairly precise information is available concerning the strategic delivery vehicles in the hands of each superpower (although it must be noted that the Soviet Union has never confirmed American intelligence estimates concerning the size of the Soviet strategic force). At present, the USSR deploys approximately 1,477 ICBMs to 1,054 for the United States, and 909 SLBMs in 81 submarines, to 656 in 41 submarines for the United States. This should be compared with the situation which existed as recently as 1966, when the US led 904 to 292 in ICBMs and 592 to 107 in SLBMs. In strategic bombers the United States retains its traditional advantage, 396 to 215; up to 234 of these are equipped to carry the SRAM (short-range attack missile). In overall totals of strategic delivery vehicles, then, the Soviets possess a significant advantage, approximately 2,600 to 2,092 for the United States.

It should be noted as well that the Soviet missile force is an extremely versatile one, in several significant respects far more versatile than that of the United States. The SS-13 light ICBM and its replacement missiles, the SS-16 and SS-20, are solid-fueled and suitable for deployment in a mobile mode, and thus could complicate verification of a future arms control agreement. The medium-sized SS-11 "Sego", which has constituted the backbone of the Soviet ICBM force for at least a decade, is now being replaced by the larger and more accurate SS-17 and SS-19 models, which deploy four and six multiple independently targeted re-entry vehicles (MIRVs), respectively. The SS-17, moreover, is a so-called zero-stage or cold-launch missile, meaning that it is ejected from its silo by a compressed gas technique, leaving the silo available for re-load and re-fire. Finally, the USSR has more than 300 silos suitable for launching very heavy missiles, of the SS-9 and SS-18 variety. More than 250 of the former have been deployed, many with a warhead estimated at 18-plus megatons, while the Mod. 2 version of the latter, now believed ready for deployment, appears capable of carrying 8 to 10 MIRVs in the 2-megaton class. This missile also has a cold-launch capability. Thus the Soviet ICBM force contains a very large countercity component along with newer missiles with considerable counterforce capabilities. Up to a dozen new missile systems, moreover, are in the development stage, and at least four of these are believed nearly ready for testing.

While it is therefore true that the United States possesses a considerable advantage over the Soviet Union at present in numbers of warheads deployed on missiles—6,342 to 3,556 for the USSR—and while it is also true that the accuracy of the American re-entry vehicles is considerably higher than that of their Soviet counterparts, too much should not be made of this advantage in comparing the capabilities of the two superpowers. Due to the larger size of

The evaluation of a "war machine" must take into account all of the armed forces—from foot soldiers through surface combatant ships to cruise missiles, and all the other weapons described elsewhere in this book. But these are merely the outward appearances. What about the soldier's training, skills, guts and, above all, motivation and morale? How does one assess in military terms the national industrial strength, economy and, most important, national will and national morale? Such evaluation is also only valid when compared with the capabilities of potential enemies.

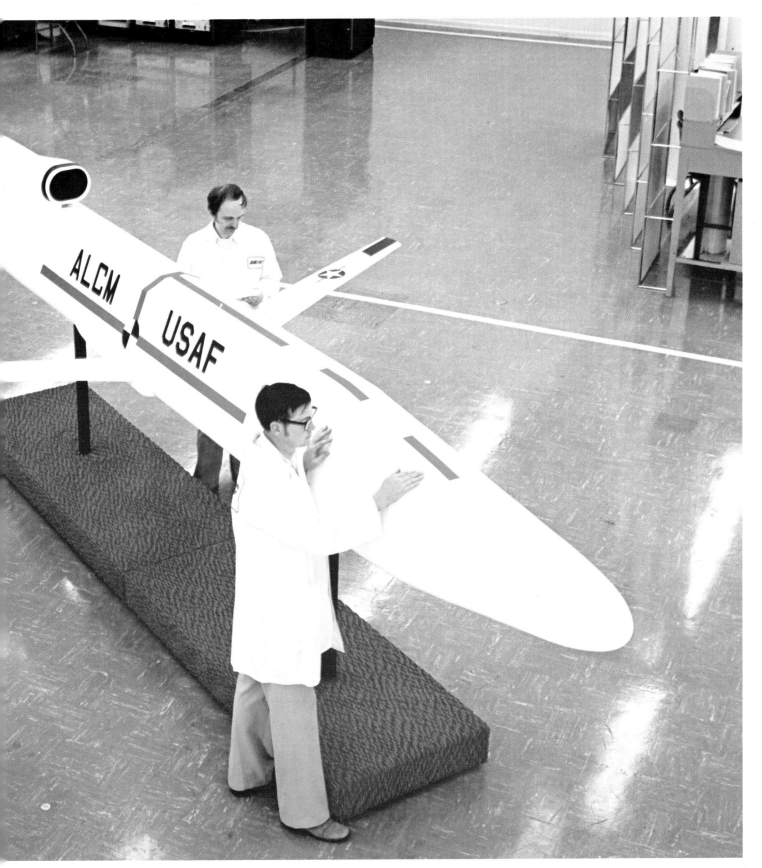

the new generation of Soviet missiles and their substantially greater throw-weight,[1] the Soviet Union will be able to deploy a substantially larger number of MIRVed warheads on land-based missiles than will the United States within a very short period of time. (The USSR already has nearly three times as many warheads on ICBMs as the total number of US ICBM silos.) Moreover, these warheads will be larger than their American counterparts, thus compensating in considerable measure for their relative lack of accuracy. Almost 70 percent of the warheads on American missiles have an explosive yield of less than 50 kilotons, while 70 percent of the Soviet warheads are in the megaton class and a further 10 percent are super-heavy warheads with yields of approximately 20 megatons.[2] As noted above, the SS-18 alone can carry up to ten 2-megaton warheads, while the American Minuteman, by way of contrast, carries only three warheads of 170 kiloton apiece. With its rated accuracy of .25 nautical miles CEP, an SS-18 warhead would have a 60 percent probability of destroying a target hardened to 1,000 per square inch overpressure, or a 90 percent probability of destroying a 300psi target. With slight improvements in accuracy to, e.g., 2.0nm CEP, the probabilities increase to 75 percent and 92 percent respectively. The US *Minuteman III*, by way of contrast, has only a 24 percent probability of destroying a 1,000psi target even with its greater accuracy (usually estimated at .2nm CEP).[3]

Much the same pattern emerges when one analyzes the capabilities of the sea-launched ballistic missile forces deployed by the two superpowers. Early US SLBMs were distinctly superior to initially deployed Soviet models, but this situation is steadily changing. The SS-N-8, first deployed by the Soviet Union in 1973, has a range of 4,800 miles, far greater than that of the US Poseidon, and a substantially greater throw-weight as well. The SS-N-8, however, has been deployed with only a single warhead. In late 1976 the Soviets began testing an additional new SLBM, the SS-N-18, with MIRVs and a range of 5,800 miles. In this area, too, the US technological lead is thus evanescing. The new US sea-launched ballistic missile, the Trident C-4, is scheduled for initial deployment in 1979 on the *Ohio* class submarine, but its range will be only 4,000 miles.

So too with strategic bombers. While the US bomber force has been steadily declining in size, the USSR has been building its new Tu-26 Backfire. Much larger than a non-strategic bomber, but not quite large enough to be unambiguously identified as a full-sized intercontinental aircraft, the Backfire in any case is

capable of reaching most American targets, if only because the United States presently has no effective air defenses. At current production rates, sometime in the early 1980s, the Soviets will for the first time have more strategic bombers than the United States. The Soviet Union during the SALT negotiations has resisted American demands that the Backfire be counted against the total weapons ceiling which a new agreement is to impose; and a considerable debate has developed within and without the government as to the precise military role which the Soviets intend for the Backfire. Controversy over the Backfire, however, illustrates perfectly the strategic irrelevance of much of the arms control process. Even if the SALT negotiators finally agree that the Backfire is nonstrategic, this will not cause it to disappear. If the Backfire is not targeted against the continental US, it will of course be targeted against Europe and perhaps against China. Scepticism is clearly warranted concerning a negotiating strategy that goes to extreme pains to find a way of reconciling Soviet deployment of the Backfire bomber with a SALT agreement, if the only consequence is to give the Soviets a free hand to deploy that formidable aircraft against those whose security is inseparable from that of the United States.

Also important to evaluating the strategic balance between the superpowers are the so-called gray-area weapons deployed by both sides. These include the so-called forward-based systems deployed in Europe, primarily F-111 and F-4 fighter bombers based in Germany and England and A-6 and A-7 attack aircraft deployed on American aircraft carriers in the Mediterranean. These weapons are all vulnerable to a Soviet first strike, however; and only the F-111s constitute at all a serious threat against targets in the western-most extremity of the USSR. The A-6s and A-7s are no longer assigned to strategic missions as their primary role; they would be marginally effective at best against Soviet air defenses in any case. Despite the claims of Soviet negotiators in SALT, therefore, these systems add little to the strategic power of the United States.

The Soviets also deploy an intermediate class of nuclear weapons of substantially greater potency than US forward-based systems, although only some of these weapons would be usable against the United States homeland. These include approximately 500 Tu-16 Badgers and Tu-22 Blinders in service with the Soviet Air Force, as well as 600 IRBMs and MRBMs with ranges up to 1,400 miles. All of these weapons are deployed against targets in Western Europe and Asia. The Russians also have more

Table 1: Numbers of Nuclear Delivery Vehicles

Source: Adapted from *Military Balance, 1977–78,* US Department of Defense, *Annual Defense Department Report, FY 1978,* and John M. Collins, *American and Soviet Military Strength: Contemporary Trends Compared, 1970–1976,* published in *Congressional Record,* August 5, 1977, pp. S 14064–104.

than 600 sea-launched cruise missiles of varying degrees of effectiveness and with varying ranges, the most important of which are the SS-N-3 Shaddock and the newer SS-N-12. Range estimates of the latter two weapons vary considerably, but in no case are they less than 250 nautical miles. Given the preference of Americans for coastal living, if used as part of a strike against the United States, Soviet cruise missiles could destroy about 50 percent of the US population and a large portion of American industry as well. The US answer to the Soviet sea-launched cruise missile, the Navy's Tomahawk, is still in the testing and development state, and in any case the United States may surrender the right to deploy it as part of a follow-on SALT agreement.

The relevant question, of course, is what if any conclusions concerning American security can be extracted from this maze of data, much of it contradictory. Several points seem clear. First, at the moment, there is a kind of rough strategic parity between the superpowers, as those who take an unworried view of the military balance are quick to assert. At the moment, both sides appear to have nuclear forces of sufficient size and composition to deter a direct attack on their homelands.

Equally important, however, is the long-term future of the US deterrent. The Soviet stress on heavy missiles and relatively large warheads is obviously intended in part to compensate for the relative inaccuracy of Soviet re-entry vehicles. Since highly accurate warheads are not necessary for a countercity deterrence strategy, however, the design of the Soviet strategic force suggests that they are seeking the capability to attack and destroy US hardened military targets in the event of war. This analysis appears to be confirmed by Soviet strategic doctrine, which postulates both that nuclear war is possible and that the USSR should be prepared to fight and win if it occurs. Soviet views on nuclear war also appear to explain the attention given to civil defense in the USSR in recent years. As William Van Cleave has emphasized elsewhere in this volume, on the other hand, US strategic doctrine stresses the deterrence mission of nuclear forces virtually to the exclusion of all else. US forces—which up to now have deployed small re-entry vehicles—are designed for countercity deterrence and assured

Facing page upper: The Soviet Union's 2,500-mile range SS-14 Scapegoat, many hundreds of which are on mobile launchers. US reconnaissance satellites have reportedly spotted them on the Chinese border.
Right: Discounting 54 obsolescent Titans, the US land-based missile deterrent is made up of one type of missile, Minuteman (photo shows Minuteman II launch in 1969). It is relatively small.

Table 2: US and USSR ICBMs: Comparative Data

Missile	Number Deployed	Number of Warheads	Warhead Yield	Throw-weight in 1,000lb	CEP (nautical miles)	PK‡ (against 1,000psi)
United States						
Titan II	54	1	10 MT	7.5	0.8	25%
Minuteman II	450	1	1 MT	1.5	.3	33%
Minuteman III	550	3	170 KT	1.5	.2	24%
USSR						
SS-7 Saddler	109	1	5 MT	3.0	1.5	5%
SS-8 Sasin		1	5 MT	3.0	1.5	5%
SS-9 Scarp (Mod. 1 and 2)	238	1	18–25 MT	12.0	.7	40%
SS-9 Scarp (Mod. 4)		3 MRV	5 MT	12.0	.35	58%
SS-11 Sego (Mod. 1 and 2)	774	1	1–2 MT	1.5	.55	15%
SS-11 Sego (Mod. 3)	66	3 MRV	500 KT	1.5	.50	8%
SS-13 Savage	60	1	1 MT	1.0	.70	7%
SS-14	n.a.*	1	1 MT	n.a.*	1+	n.a.*
SS-16	n.a.*	1	n.a.*	2.0	n.a.*	n.a.*
SS-17	40	4 MIRV	200 KT	4.5	.30	12%
SS-18 (Mod. 1)	50	1	18–25 MT	15.0+	.30	98%
SS-18 (Mod. 2)	n.a.*	8–10 MIRV	2 MT	15.0+	.25	61%
SS-19	140	6 MIRV	340 KT	7.0	.25	23%

*Not available.
‡PK here refers to the single-shot probability of "kill" against a silo hardened to 1,000psi. PK values were calculated using the Vulnerability Assessment Calculator developed by Boeing Aerospace Co.

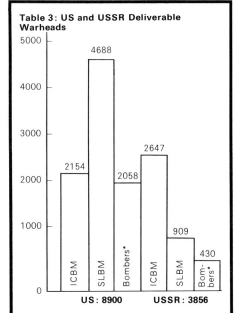

Table 3: US and USSR Deliverable Warheads

US: 8900   USSR: 3856

ICBM 2154
SLBM 4688
Bombers* 2058
ICBM 2647
SLBM 909
Bombers* 430

* Total for bombers includes both warheads delivered by air-to-surface missiles deployed on bombers and gravity bombs. Assumes an average of six warheads and/or bombs delivered by FB-111s, four by B-52s and two by Soviet aircraft.
Source: Adapted from *Military Balance, 1977–78*, US Department of Defense, *Annual Defense Department Report, FY 1978*, and John M. Collins, *American and Soviet Military Strength: Contemporary Trends Compared, 1970–1976*, published in *Congressional Record*, August 5, 1977, pp. S 14064–104.

Below: Probably the only bright spot in US land-based airpower actually available is the McDonnell Douglas F-15 Eagle, over 320 of which have been delivered. Even this excellent aircraft is so expensive it makes a big dent in the budget.

destruction missions against population centers and other soft targets.

Should deterrence fail, this assymetry of doctrine and disparity in capabilities would leave the US in a precarious position indeed. While there is considerable disagreement among pessimists, such as Rudolf Rummel, Edward Luttwak and Paul Nitze, and optimists such as Professor John Steinbrunner and Admiral Gene LaRoque,[4] over current and near-term Soviet counterforce capabilities, a careful analysis of available data indicates that, even given conservative estimates of likely improvements in the accuracy of Soviet missiles, by no later than the mid-1980s the Soviet Union will be able to destroy all but a small percentage of the US ICBM force in a preemptive strike using only a small fraction of its own missile force and holding the remainder in reserve.[5] Defense Secretary Harold Brown recently conceded that even the present generation of Soviet missiles is accurate enough to pose "substantial threat to our ICBMs in the early 1980s".[6] Should the Soviet Union mount such an attack, a US retaliatory strike at Soviet cities would be an act of suicide, since it would be insufficient to win the nuclear war and would merely ensure that American cities would be destroyed in return.

The seriousness of this threat, of course, should not be exaggerated, because even under the best of circumstances the attacker would run enormous risks. He would need tremendous confidence in the reliability of his weapons, in the precision of his strike, and in the restraint and rationality of the enemy. Such restraint and rationality in turn would depend on reasonably low levels of civilian casualties, lack of panic by decisionmakers, and other factors.

Nonetheless the threat is real, and growing. There is little or no possibility that the SALT process will result in a reduced Soviet counter-

Table 4: US and USSR Missile Throw-weight (in millions of pounds)

USSR   7.8   9.1
ICBM   SLBM

US   2.2   3.3
ICBM SLBM

1 2 3 4 5 6 7 8 9 10

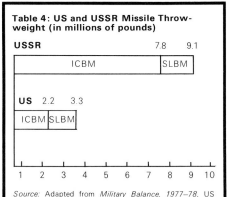

Source: Adapted from *Military Balance, 1977–78*, US Department of Defense, *Annual Defense Department Report, FY 1978*, and John M. Collins, *American and Soviet Military Strength: Contemporary Trends Compared, 1970–1976*, published in *Congressional Record*, August 5, 1977, pp. S 14064–104.

force capability; SALT II, on the contrary, is certain merely to ratify on-going Soviet procurement plans.[7] The United States therefore should proceed with its own force improvement program, and in particular with its planned expansion of its own counterforce capability.

Should a Soviet counterforce attack be launched on military targets on American soil, the US would clearly require a capability to respond not with an assault on Soviet cities, but with an attack on military targets in the Soviet Union. The possession of such an option by the US would of course reduce the likelihood that the attack will occur, since the result of a counterforce exchange might be (*inter alia!*) a standoff at the strategic level, which in turn might set in motion a long war of distinctly uncertain outcome—clearly not a low-risk venture for the USSR.

The possession of improved counterforce

capabilities might be important for the United States for other reasons as well. US strategic weapons have traditionally been assigned roles well beyond the mere requirement to deter a Soviet attack on the United States. These roles are sometimes subsumed under the term "extended deterrence", which can have both a narrow military meaning, ie, the deterrence of attacks on US forward-based systems in Europe, or a broader meaning, such as the deterrence of Soviet attacks on American allies in Western Europe or in Northeast Asia. Traditionally it was assumed that the viability of "extended deterrence" depended upon a US first-strike capability against the Soviet Union, ie, the power to attack the Soviet heartland with such force that the Soviet Union could not mount an effective retaliatory blow against the United States in return. The Soviet acquisition of an assured destruction capability of its own, beginning in the middle '60s weakened, if it did not totally destroy, the credibility of the US first-strike threat, and thus undermined the US nuclear guarantee to Europe. More recently it has been argued by a number of analysts, including former Defense Secretary Schlesinger, that the capability to strike effectively and accurately at military targets in the Soviet Union in the event of a Soviet invasion of the West might serve to deter such an attack, thus reviving extended deterrence in a new form. This posture calls for a range of US weapons and targeting options which considerably exceed those demanded by the minimum or even by the finite deterrence strategies.

Such considerations explain recent US programs designed to improve the hard-target capabilities of the US Minuteman force. Ongoing improvements in the computer software associated with the NS-20 guidance system of Minuteman III are expected to improve re-entry vehicle accuracy to 600 CEP. If, in addition, the MK-12A warhead is deployed on Minuteman III, the hard target kill probability of the system would improve to 80 percent.[8] The so-called M-X, the larger throw-weight missile being considered as a late 1980s successor to Minute-

man, would be more counterforce-capable still. If all these systems are deployed in sufficient numbers, the "counterforce gap" in favor of the USSR which is now expected to exist by the early 1980s will eventually disappear, assuming that the Soviet Union does not develop and deploy new systems beyond those now contemplated. If they are not, the strategic balance will continue to tilt steadily in favor of the USSR.

Strategic Power and Political Behavior

Many participants in the debate over the adequacy of current US military capabilities argue that the US continues to possess strength adequate to deter both nuclear war and direct military threats to its vital interests. Such analysts are generally unconcerned about the numerical advantages which the Soviets have achieved in various categories of strategic weapons. Whatever the accuracy of their assessments of the actual military balance, however, these analysts appear to overlook the fact that even the appearance of military superiority on the part of one superpower over another may have important consequences for world politics. While it is extraordinarily difficult to measure the political consequences of various strategic states—indeed, startlingly little research of a serious nature has been done on the question—certain facts seem clear. The nature of international politics has not decisively been altered by the onset of the nuclear era, nor have the perceptions of most world political leaders concerning the importance of military power undergone substantial change. Leaders of nations large and small continue to evaluate their own position on the power scale relative to that of others; whether their estimates are right or wrong, technically correct or based on ignorance and misinformation, such estimates seemingly continue to influence their conduct. As Edward Luttwak has observed, it is thus through the uncertain medium of others' perceptions that strategic arsenals generate political power. To the extent that American strategy and force deployments evoke positive responses in others, they produce a beneficial

Above: The interceptor version of the Foxbat, believed to be designated MiG-25S (top) and the swing-wing Flogger family of MiG-23 and -27 versions (in Federation of Arab Republics insignia above) are formidable and comprehensively equipped combat aircraft. Western planners dare not overlook the fact that both were in service eight years ago, and on the drawing board in the early 1960s.

political return for the United States; to the extent that US forces do not suffice to negate the image of power generated by the strategy and weapons deployments of the Soviet Union, then the United States may pay a serious political price for allowing the Soviet Union to achieve real or apparent strategic superiority.[9] It is in this sense that strategic deterrence is only part of a much broader phenomenon: the political application of military force, sometimes called armed suasion.

In analyzing this complex of issues, American scholars normally stress the possible reactions of allies and neutral states to the US/USSR military balance. Of equal — and perhaps greater—importance, however, are the possible reactions of Soviet and American leaders themselves to the military balance between their states. Armed suasion is a result, at least in part, of perceptions. Military capability, along with the other elements of national power, contributes to the perceptions that nations have of themselves and which other nations have of them. Military power, moreover, clearly contributes to the self-confidence with which nations deal with adversaries in times of crisis or confrontation. That is why Clausewitz insisted not only that war is a continuation of politics by other means, but also that the acquisition and deployment of military forces in peacetime are—or should be—primarily governed by political considerations. The Soviet view of such matters appears to be essentially Clausewitzean. In recent years Soviet leaders have quite openly called attention to the political

257

Above: Camouflaged M109 SP howitzers
of the 83rd Field Artillery, USA, look fine.
But, while there are enough for small
exercises, there are nothing like enough
(of anything) to fight a defensive war.

purposes which inspire the USSR's military buildup, informing us that the correlation of forces has shifted irrevocably in the direction of the socialist world; the United State's retreat from Vietnam, the abortive US response to the Cuban activities in Angola and the American acceptance of Soviet numerical superiority in the SALT I accords all prove quite conclusively, they have asserted, that the United States is in the process of accommodating itself to an emergent international order in which the Soviet Union is the preeminent power.

American leaders from Kissinger to Carter, of course, have argued that the Soviet leaders are wrong, and that the United States is still second to none in the influence it wields in world politics. In analyzing who has the better of this debate, it is worth reflecting upon the attitudes and behavior of American decision-makers during two of the most important international crises of the postwar period, the Hungarian Revolution and its aftermath in 1956 and the Cuban missile affair of 1962. During both crises, despite the overwhelming strategic superiority that the United States enjoyed over the Soviet Union, US decision-makers proceeded with considerable circumspection, fearful that vigorous US action might set off World War III—a war which under then-prevailing circumstances the United States could not possibly have lost. Is the United States likely to behave even this boldly in a future crisis after the strategic advantage has passed—or appears to have passed—to the Soviet Union?

To be sure, some commentators have suggested

that the Soviet Union is likely to behave as circumspectly as did the United States when it possessed the strategic advantage, and for the same reasons: the leaders of the USSR are no more anxious than those of the US to set off a nuclear holocaust. Moreover, it is argued, the Soviets have proceeded quite cautiously in the past in their efforts to translate military power into political advantage, and can be expected to behave similarly in the future. These arguments appear singularly unpersuasive. There is no reason to believe that the Soviet leaders think about nuclear war or about the relationship between military force and foreign policy in the manner of most American defense intellectuals. Even more significant is the fact that until recently the Soviet Union has been distinctly inferior to the West in strategic power. The world has no experience with a Soviet Union which possesses substantial military advantages over the United States, and it would be dangerous in the extreme to assume that her growing military power will have little or no impact on Soviet behavior in international relations. Indeed, the extent of Soviet cautiousness in the past should not be exaggerated: even while their nuclear forces and local theater capabilities were drastically inferior to those of the United States, the Soviets precipitated the Cuban missile crisis in 1962 and belligerently refused to retreat until the eleventh hour.

In any case, the attention given by American analysts to possible reactions by allies and neutrals to recent changes in the US/USSR military balance is by no means misplaced, for the future of the American-Soviet competition will clearly be affected by more than the outcomes of the direct confrontations between them. How others perceive the emerging international order will clearly have a significant impact upon the shape of that order.

In attempting to measure that impact pre-

cisely, the analyst again confronts considerable difficulty, for it is impossible to determine with any precision how the leaders of America's allies and of lesser nations evaluate and compare military power. It seems clear, however, that the quantitative dimensions of the military balance play a considerable role in the shaping of perceptions. In fact, the less sophisticated the observer the more likely he is to see numerical indicators as the primary measure of military power. The reactions in Europe and elsewhere to the first SALT agreement are illustrative: since 1972, media analyses and polls of public opinion reveal a growing image of the USSR as a power on the ascendant, and the United States as a power in decline; the numerical advantages which the USSR has achieved over the United States in various categories of strategic weaponry appear to constitute the foundation for such perceptions. [0] In many quarters of Europe, in fact, prospects for "Finlandization", as recently as two years ago widely considered by most Western European commentators to be a fantasy of American pessimists, are now being discussed. The meaning of "Finlandization", of course is clear: it refers to the prospect that some or all of the states of Europe, incapable of defending themselves in the face of overwhelming Soviet military superiority, will gradually modify their international behavior and even their internal political systems to suit the convenience and desires of the Soviet Union, as has the nation of Finland during the postwar period.[11] Observing the colossus to the east with which she shares an 800-mile frontier, Finland has come in modern times to measure her security in terms of the friendship which exists between her and the Soviet Union. An important part of Finnish policy, foreign and domestic, takes the form of a careful assessment of Soviet interests and an accommodation to them. Of late the very fabric of Finland's political order itself has been affected by a desire to accommodate the USSR: the scheduled presidential election of 1974 was cancelled when the Soviet Union vigorously expressed its unhappiness at the prospective outcome. Once again it is worth reflecting on future possibilities. How would a communist-governed Italy behave in the face of similar Soviet pressure, or for that matter a socialist–communist coalition in France? No one in the West should view the prospects with equanimity.

Conventional Military Power and American Interests

In general, although there are certain areas in which the US is preeminent, the conventional military balance appears if anything even more unfavorable for the United States than does the strategic balance. That of course should surprise no one, since the conventional balance in many respects has overwhelmingly favored the Soviet Union since the end of World War II.

One important measure of military strength is total men under arms. The United States currently has just over 2 million men in its armed forces, while the Soviet Union has nearly 5 million. There are 8 million men in the Soviet ground forces, compared with 978,000 in the US Army and Marine Corps. To be sure, military personnel in the USSR perform a variety of tasks which in the US are handled by civilians; nevertheless, the gap is startling. A more specific indicator of the conventional balance is the number of combat divisions in the armed forces of each superpower. The US now has 19 divisions, including the Marines, while the Soviet Union has 170—two more than in 1976. While it is true the Soviet divisions are smaller than their US counterparts, the disparity is nonetheless a useful indicator of comparative conventional strength. During the past decade, the Soviets have added about one million men to their force

Left: A shore-based Lockheed P-3 Orion
of the US Navy flies past a Soviet *Kynda*-
class cruiser. Growth of the Soviet Navy
into a global force of great power has
completely upset previous equations.

A similar situation obtains in the area of tactical air power. Not counting approximately 3,000 trainer aircraft and the 2,700 fighters assigned to the air defense forces, the tactical air inventory of the Soviet Union—including fighters, attack aircraft, intermediate range bombers and reconnaissance aircraft—now numbers more than 5,000 planes. Moreover, the quality of Soviet tactical aircraft has improved markedly in recent years. Until the early 1970s, the USSR's tactical air force was notably deficient in range, payload, avionics and electronic countermeasures capabilities. These deficiencies are rapidly being remedied, as new aircraft such as the Su-19 Fencer and improved versions of the MiG-23 Flogger and the Fitter series are deployed in large numbers.

When one moves from the aggregate levels of manpower and military equipment in the hands of the superpowers to the military forces which each has deployed in regions of the world where their interests clash, the precise dimensions of the military problem which the United States would confront in the event of war becomes clear. The European Central Front, of course, is the area which receives most attention. As Stephen P. Gilbert has pointed out elsewhere in this volume, the maintenance of a free Western Europe has for several decades been considered vital to American national security. If the industrial capacity of Western Europe were put to the service of the international objectives of the Soviet state, the United States might well, in the words of one scholar, "be reduced to a fortress America in a world in which we had become largely irrelevant".[13]

It is sobering to realize, therefore, that the military problems confronting the United States in Europe are serious indeed. The balance of

The T-72 Soviet battle tank is dramatically superior to anything in the US Army. Its gun is even bigger than that of Britain's Chieftain at 125mm calibre, and its road speed is 62mph (100kph).

structure. They have, moreover, in recent years increased the size of their divisions by nearly 3,000 men, the density of tanks deployed with each division by at least 50 percent and in some cases even 100 percent.[12] As a result, 20 Soviet divisions today are the equivalent of 25 to 27 divisions of ten years ago. It is worth noting that the United States has a total of 11,600 tanks in active service, while the Soviet Union has at least 45,500. A similar picture obtains in armored

personnel carriers, reflecting Soviet preparations for high-speed mechanized offensive operations in the event of war. The Soviets have deployed 38,000 apc's to 11,245 for the US. New assault and attack-type helicopters (particularly the Mi-24 Hind equipped with 57mm rockets and Sagger anti-tank missiles), improved infantry combat vehicles, self-propelled artillery, mobile rocket launchers, precision-guided anti-tank weapons, and T-72 (T-64) main battle tanks are all presently being deployed by the USSR in large numbers. More than 2,000 T-72s have been added to the Soviet inventory during the past year. The Soviets' traditional shortcomings in logistics are rapidly being overcome; their river-bridging capabilities are unequalled.

Below: The Boeing E-3A (AWACS) typifies modern weaponry, which offers fantastic capability at a cost few can afford.
Iran is buying some, but Western Europe has so far been unable to agree funding.

	NATO	Warsaw Pact
Manpower	630,000	945,000 (including 640,000 USSR)
Divisions		
Armored	10	32 (including 22 USSR)
Infantry and Mechanized	17	38 (including 23 USSR)
Total Divisions	27	70
Main battle tanks	7,000	20,500
Tactical Aircraft	2,150	4,075
	(including 400 interceptors)	(including 2,100 interceptors)

Source: Adapted from Military Balance, 1977–78, US Department of Defense, Annual Defense Department Report, FY 1978, and John M. Collins, American and Soviet Military Strength: Contemporary Trends Compared, 1970–1976, published in Congressional Record, August 5, 1977, pp. S 14064–104.

conventional military power on the European Continent has favored the Soviet Union and its allies since the end of World War II. The Eastern bloc has for many years possessed a substantial margin in military manpower deployed in the region, a 2 to 1 advantage in tactical aircraft, and a 3 to 1 advantage in tanks.

Soviet and Warsaw Pact forces are geared for an off-the-mark, high-speed offensive, relying on heavy concentrations of armor and mechanized infantry forces supported by superior firepower. Soviet artillery not only outnumbers that of the West by a 2 to 1 margin in quantity of tubes deployed, but out-ranges it and has higher rates of fire as well. A Soviet Motor Rifle Division, for example, deploys 110 artillery pieces to 76 for a US infantry division and 66 for US armored and mechanized divisions. The European theater has always received the newest and most effective equipment assigned to the Soviet armed forces; this pattern has not altered in recent years. At least 700 T-72B main battle tanks have lately been assigned to Soviet forces in Germany. There has been an increase in the number of ground-to-ground rocket systems — FROGs, Scuds, and Scaleboards — deployed with Soviet divisions in the region, and SS-20 MIRVed missiles, which have been tested both on tracked and wheeled vehicles and which have a range estimated at 5,000 kilometers and a CEP of 0.4 nautical miles, are believed ready for deployment. The SS-20s will presumably over time replace the present theater missile force of 600 SS-4 Sandal and SS-5 Skean launchers. Nuclear-capable shells have been developed for the 152mm and the 202mm artillery pieces, and possibly for the 152mm and 122mm SPGs as well.

Soviet airpower in the forward area has also increased somewhat over the past decade as well; there are now more than 3,000 tactical combat aircraft in the forward area of the Pact nations, with another 1,000 in the western regions of the USSR within striking distance of the front. But the big improvement in the Pact's tactical air capability in recent years has been qualitative, as suggested earlier. The swing-wing Su-19 Fencer, the first postwar Soviet aircraft designed for ground attack missions, can reach all NATO targets within the European theater. The MiG-23 Flogger and the improved Flogger, the MiG-27, can also be operated from protected positions in the USSR due to their increased range. This provides Soviet air commanders with employment opportunities which they have never before possessed. Finally, the traditional Soviet superiority in CBW (chemical, biological warfare) capabilities has in recent years substantially widened.

To be sure, certain significant weaknesses remain in the Pact's capabilities. It is not clear how long the present Soviet logistics system could sustain high-speed combined arms operations of the sort called for by Soviet theater doctrine. The reliability of the Soviet Union's Eastern European allies remains uncertain, and while the qualitative improvements which have taken place in Soviet and Pact tactical air capabilities in recent years are impressive, the changeover to new aircraft is really just beginning, and the new systems are presently deployed in only relatively small numbers. Finally, Soviet theater nuclear forces remain inferior to those of the West both qualitatively and quantitatively.

NATO strategy in the event of war on the Central Front is based on the principle of forward defense, which calls upon the armed forces of the Western states to contain and repel a Warsaw Pact attack as close to the eastern frontier as possible, relying at least initially on conventional forces; NATO's nuclear weapons are to be held in reserve, to be used as a last resort. The strategy of forward defense itself, were it to be literally followed, would create substantial difficulties for the Alliance, since it would deny NATO forces the option of trading space for time. But NATO confronts problems even more serious than this one. Its supply lines are parallel to the front, and thus in danger of being cut by penetrating Warsaw Pact armored columns. Due to population distribution patterns and the location of industrial installations, the bulk of allied ground forces in the Central Region are not deployed forward in defensive positions. In fact, one of the Alliance's most important components, the United States Seventh Army, is for historical regions largely stationed in southern Germany, facing the important Fulda Gap invasion corridor but far from the North German Plain, across which the principal Warsaw Pact thrust in the event of war would most likely come. The deficiencies in NATO's supply and logistics system are legendary; each nation basically supplies its own forces. While some limited progress has been made toward weapons standardization in recent years, by all accounts there is still a long way to go. Every significant military target in Europe is within easy reach of the Pact's air arm and theater nuclear systems.

Moreover, the United States lacks the airlift and sealift capability for rapid and massive reinforcement of the European nuclear theater as well. There are insufficient numbers of C-5As (only 70 in the entire inventory) and the C-141s are not efficiently designed for the movement of heavy equipment and outsized cargo. One estimate suggests that the movement of one airborne division to the Middle East from Fort Bragg, North Carolina, with accompanying armor and supplies for five days would take 700 C-141 sorties.[14] While, given enough time, significant sealift capabilities could be mobilized, it is not clear that the time would be available. Finally, most analysts doubt the military relevance of the Alliance's current strategy for the employment of tactical nuclear weapons. If utilized as presently planned—late in the game, only after substantial Pact breakthrough through NATO defense lines—currently deployed systems would cause extremely high levels of civilian casualties in West Germany and would not necessarily save NATO's military position. The initial use of nuclear weapons by the Soviet Union, on the other hand, could have a devastating impact on NATO's capability for an effective defense, particularly if the weapons were used against NATO's own storage facilities for tactical nuclear weapons and against airfields and ports which would be vital for the Alliance's reinforcement effort.

In recent years, of course, the United States has developed a formidable array of new equipment based on sophisticated technology which, if deployed in sufficient quantity, could significantly improve NATO's prospects for a successful defense. In antitank guided weapons, for instance, the United States has an enormous advantage over the USSR, in the region of 10 to 1. Much of that new US equipment, however, is coming on line very slowly. The A-10 antitank aircraft program has been considerably stretched out by Congress; only 20 or so are now on hand, and the Air Force's request for purchase of 240 in fiscal year 1978 has been halved. F-15 Eagle interceptor aircraft have also reached the European theater thus far in small numbers.

It is such consideration as these which have led many observers to question whether NATO

Facing page upper: Called Hind D by NATO, these helicopters are relatively large gunships packed with sensors and electronic devices. This is a field in which the United States previously had few problems.

Right: An AH-1Q Tow-Cobra (left) and OH-58A Kiowa, both Bell products, working as a team during Tow tests at White Sands Missile Range in 1974. The Tow, carried by the AH-1Q, is vital to NATO.

Left: Most Tow missiles are fired from surface launchers, either by infantry or, as here, from vehicles. This mass-produced and effective weapon offers at least a hope of stopping Soviet armor.

possesses sufficient military strength to deal successfully with a Pact offensive in the event of war, especially if pre-attack warning time is held to a week or less. In fact, many commentators believe that should the USSR and its allies, having achieved a reasonable degree of tactical surprise. launch an attack across the Central Front, they would overwhelm NATO defenses and occupy all of West Germany and the Benelux nations within a fortnight. As noted above, in the past the West could rely upon its strategic superiority over the USSR to deter such an attack; that superiority no longer exists.

Elsewhere in the NATO region the military balance appears equally unpromising. In the Northern Region a massive concentration of Soviet ground, air and naval forces on the Kola Peninsula face a single Norwegian brigade. On the southern flank the direct military threat appears somewhat less serious, since geographic constraints would make it difficult for the Pact to concentrate the ground forces necessary for a coordinated attack on Turkey, Greece and Italy. In this area, of course, the naval balance between the two superpower becomes particularly critical, and here too Soviet power has been growing steadily relative to that of the United States. Ten years

ago the Soviets had no missile-carrying cruisers; today they have 22. Ten years ago they had 12 missile-carrying destroyers and destroyer-like vessels; today they have more than 40. Ten years ago the Soviet Union had 45 nuclear-powered submarines; today they have more than 130. Finally, after a decade of determined shipbuilding effort, the Soviets have deployed their first true aircraft carrier and have under construction at least three more. Recent reports indicate that they are building a new giant submarine capable of carrying perhaps two dozen SLBMs. So significant has the capability of the Soviet Navy become that the recently retired Chief of US Naval Operations, Admiral Elmo Zumwalt, today doubts whether the US Mediterranean fleet could successfully deal with its Soviet counterpart in the event of war in Europe. In an especially alarmist appraisal, General George Keegan, recently retired chief of Air Force Intelligence, asserts that in the event of war 75 percent of the free world's surface fleets would be destroyed by Soviet forces, naval and air, within a matter of hours. The chart depicts the current naval balance between the superpowers.

While, as the chapter by Bruce Powers in the present volume observes, too much should not

Table 6: US and USSR Naval General Purpose Forces, 1977		
	US	USSR
Aircraft carriers	13	1
Helicopter carriers	7	2
Cruisers	26	31
Destroyers	72	87
Frigates	71	107
Missile patrol boats	1	137
Conventional submarines	10	176
Nuclear submarines	68	78
Amphibious ships	55	82
Minesweepers	3	365
Other (support vessels, etc.)	110	255
Total vessels	**436**	**1321***

*Does not include 391 minor combatants.
Source: Adapted from *Military Balance, 1977–78,* US Department of Defense, *Annual Defense Department Report, FY 1978,* and John M. Collins, *American and Soviet Military Strength: Contemporary Trends Compared, 1970–1976,* published in *Congressional Record,* August 5, 1977, pp. S 14064–104.

be made of differences in the size and composition of the Soviet and American fleets since they were designed with quite different purposes and missions in mind, it is nevertheless clear that the Soviet position relative to that of the United States is substantially stronger than it was a decade ago. It is worth recalling that seapower is far more important to the US than to the USSR. The United States depends on overseas sources for vital natural resources, particularly oil but also key minerals. Open sea lanes therefor become for the United States a vital national objective. In this context the threat both to naval and merchant ships implicit in the Soviet attack submarine force, their 300-plane landbased naval air arm (including at least 30 Backfires), and several dozen surface ships armed with cruise missiles assumes its proper perspective. The 75 United States submarines equipped for ASW would in the event of war be seeking to neutralize at least three times that number of Soviet submarines. The American capacity to escort merchant shipping across the Atlantic or around the Horn of Africa with surface-borne escort vessels is clearly limited. Soviet surface vessels possess limited range and restricted storage capacities, and moreover would be subject to interdiction attacks at key naval choke points leading from the Black Sea, the Sea of Japan, the Barents Sea, and the Baltic. But it is no longer clear that the US, even when its forces are supplemented by those of its allies, possess sufficient naval strength to bottle up successfully the numerically superior Soviet navy.

In Northeast Asia the Soviet military threat and that posed by its allies, principally North Korea, has also been growing, even as the United States gratuitously reduces its military strength in the region. Any attempt to assess the military balance in Northeast Asia must of course take into account the political complexities in the region; it can be argued that so long as political tensions between the USSR and the Peoples Republic of China remain high, the risk of military adventurism by either power will remain low. Nonetheless the military balance in the region bears examination. The Soviets have deployed large numbers of ground forces in Asia during the last decade, but these are stationed principally along the Sino-Soviet

Left: *Kiev,* first of a series of Kuril-class ships classed as anti-submarine cruisers but equipped with a diversity of sensors and weapons. Far larger than most modern warships, they are yet much smaller than the gigantic US carriers.

Right: Totally different from the Kuril class, *Nimitz* (CVN-68) is the world's largest warship, and first of three new super-carriers with nuclear drive. Unlike virtually all Soviet surface combat ships the CVAs are merely carriers of air power, without SSMs, sonar or even guns. At $2 billion each they are questionable.

USAF F-4s, further backed up by 138 USAF F-4s in Japan and the Philippines plus a Marine air wing in Japan. In 1978, however, the US will begin pulling its ground forces out of South Korea; whether the planned improvements in the South Korean armed forces during the period of withdrawal, which is scheduled to be completed in 1981, will compensate for the US troop drawdown is considered doubtful by many observers, particularly since the bulk of US tactical nuclear weapons will doubtless be withdrawn along with the ground forces. The North Koreans currently possess a 2 to 1 advantage in tanks and in artillery and rocket launchers over the ROK, the DPRK's naval and air forces are superior to those of the South, and the South lacks ample reserves of munitions and other war materiel. It therefore remains to be seen what impact the US troop withdrawal from Korea will have upon the stability and security within the region.[15]

Elsewhere in the world, there is no longer any question concerning the Soviet ability to contest the American presence—with varying degrees of effectiveness—in most places. The Soviet military buildup of the past decade has radically altered the nature of the USSR's military strength, transforming what was once essentially a continental force into one of global capabilities, able to support effectively Soviet foreign policy all over the world and of intervening directly if necessary from Central Africa to the Caribbean.

Should the military trends outlined above long continue, the US will lose its ability to protect its vital interests abroad; ultimately doubts are certain to arise concerning the capacity of the United States to protect even its own security.

frontier. Although only 13 of the 43 Soviet divisions are first-line units, Soviet forces in Asia have recently received increasing flows of new equipment, including BMPs, T-62 battle tanks, self-propelled guns, and new aircraft. The Soviet Pacific fleet now deploys 70 submarines and 60 major surface combatants, supplemented by a large contingent of naval infantry and growing numbers of land-based naval aircraft. The US surface fleet in the Pacific, by way of contrast, is down to 21 ships, including two carriers, supplemented by a Marine amphibious unit. Japanese ground, air and naval forces are qualitatively and quantitatively inferior to Soviet forces in Asia in every salient respect; although these forces could make a limited contribution to a US-led effort to contain Soviet military activity in the area, it is clear that the Japanese self-defense forces could not

Above: An A-7E Corsair of VA-27 is towed down the vast deck of *Enterprise* (CVN-65) past protective EA-6B Prowler electronic-warfare carriers, during the 1976 exercise Valiant Heritage. Seaborne air power has repeatedly been proved vital; but is it cost/effective against a modern foe?

defend Hokkaido against a determined Soviet assault. Once again it is worth recalling that traditionally US strategic superiority was said to compensate for any conventional military deficiencies of the US and its allies.

On the Korean peninsula it is usually argued that an uneasy balance presently exists between the North Korean armed forces and those of South Korea, the latter buttressed by the presence of 33,000 US ground troops and 60

Footnotes
1. The SS-11 Sego has an estimated volume of 69 cubic meters and an estimated payload of 1,500 pounds; the SS-19, by way of contrast, has an estimated volume of 110 cubic meters and a payload of 7,000 pounds.
2. See the analysis in Edward N. Luttwak, "Defense Reconsidered", in *Commentary*, March 1977, p. 52.
3. Single-shot kill probabilities were developed by the author using the Vulnerability Assessment Calculator of the Boeing Aerospace Company. See table showing ICBM comparative data.
4. For the pessimists' position, see R. J. Rummel, "Will the Soviet Union Soon Have a First-Strike Capability?", *Orbis*, XX (Fall, 1976), pp. 579–94; for a more optimistic analysis, see John D. Steinbrunner and Thomas M. Garwin, "Strategic Vulnerability: The Balance Between Prudence and Paranoia", *International Security*, I (Summer, 1976), pp. 138–81.
5. See, e.g., the analysis in Luttwak, *The Strategic Balance 1972*, Washington Papers No. 3 (Washington, DC: Center for Strategic and International Studies, 1972), and *idem, Strategic Power: Military Capabilities and Political Utility*, Washington Papers No. 38 (Washington, DC: Center for Strategic and International Studies, 1976).
6. For a report on Secretary Brown's speech, see *Defense-Space Daily*, October 5, 1977 p. 162.
7. For a discussion of the Vladivostok Accord (which will by all accounts constitute the basic framework for the SALT II agreement expected to be signed in 1978) from this perspective, see James E. Dornan, Jr., "The Vladivostok Accord and the Future of Arms Control", *Brassey's Defense Yearbook*, *1975-76* (London: Brassey's, 1976), pp. 97–118.
8. For a discussion of the significance of the guidance improvements for the Minuteman III and of the counterforce capabilities of the MK-12A, see *Science*, June 10, 1977, pp. 1185–86.
9. See the analysis in Luttwak, *The Missing Dimension of U.S. Defense Policy: Force, Perceptions and Power* (Washington: The Essex Corporation, 1976).
10. For an analysis see Dornan, *An Assessment of European Attitudes on Tactical Nuclear Force Modernization* (Washington, DC: Strategic Studies Center of SRI International, 1977).
11. See the discussion in Dornan, "The Decline of America as a World Power", *Imprimis*, July 1977.
12. See the analysis by NATO commander Haig, quoted in "NATO's New Challenge: Conventional Force Buildup Emphasized", *Aviation Week and Space Technology* (August 15, 1977), p. 49.
13. Henry A. Kissinger, *The Necessity for Choice* (New York: Harper & Brothers, 1961), p. 1.
14. See John M. Collins, *American and Soviet Military Strength: Contemporary Trends Compared, 1970–1976* (Washington, DC: Congressional Reference Service, 1977), reprinted in *Congressional Record*, August 5, 1977, p. 14092.
15. For an excellent discussion of the military balance in the Korean peninsula, see Richard G. Stilwell, "The Need for US Ground Forces in Korea", *Korea and World Affairs*, I (Summer, 1977), pp. 140–60.

Appendices

US Military Strength Figures for July 31, 1977

Total numerical strength of the Armed Forces on July 31, 1977, based on preliminary reports was 2,079,354. This represents an increase of 4,544 from June 30, 1977, combined strength of 2,074,810. July strength figures for each service, with month-ago and year-ago figures for comparison, follow:

	July 31, 1977 preliminary	June 30, 1977	July 31, 1976
Total DoD	2,079,354	2,074,810	2,086,944
Army	783,355	779,265	779,798
Navy	526,745	524,875	528,211
Marine Corps	190,855	189,714	192,089
Air Force	578,399	580,956	586,846

The figures represent full time military personnel comprising both regulars and reserves on continuous active duty and officer candidates including cadets at the Military and Air Academies and midshipmen at the Naval Academy.

US Military Personnel Strengths by Regional Area and by Country†

	Army	Air Force	Navy	Marine Corps	Total
Total Personnel	778,547	581,236	526,527	188,845	2,075,155
Ashore	778,547	581,236	312,995	183,495	1,856,273
Afloat	—	—	213,532	5,350	218,882
US Territory and					
Special Locations	537,390	479,529	445,693	159,388	1,622,000
Continental US	480,374	438,930	243,098	138,693	1,301,095
Alaska	9,606	11,290	2,100	156	23,152
Hawaii	18,034	6,104	10,808	10,005	44,951
Guam	87	3,664	4,656	417	8,824
Johnston Island	83	41	—	—	124
Marshall Islands	—	1	—	—	1
Midway Island	—	—	806	—	806
Panama Canal Zone	7,314	1,876	324	130	9,644
Puerto Rico	356	60	3,213	361	3,990
Samoa (American)	1	1	—	—	2
Trust Terr. of Pacific	1	—	—	—	1
Virgin Islands (US)	4	1	—	—	5
Wake Island	—	4	—	—	4
Transients	21,530	17,557	13,513	7,891	60,491
Afloat	—	—	167,175	1,735	168,910
Total Foreign					
Countries	241,157	101,707	80,834	29,457	453,155
Ashore	241,157	101,707	34,477	25,842	403,183
Afloat	—	—	46,357	3,615	49,972
Western and					
Southern Europe	202,319	69,322	32,199	2,914	306,754
Austria	8	2	1	20	31
Belgium*	1,296	603	110	28	2,037
Cyprus	3	1	—	15	19

	Army	Air Force	Navy	Marine Corps	Total
Denmark*	4	17	12	9	42
Finland	6	2	2	10	20
France*	12	13	11	35	71
Germany (Fed. Rep. West Berlin)*	194,278	31,850	280	81	226,489
Greece*	722	2,462	502	11	3,697
Greenland*	—	313	—	—	313
Iceland*	3	1,005	1,901	138	3,047
Ireland	2	8	—	6	16
Italy*	4,029	3,933	3,423	201	11,586
Luxembourg*	—	—	—	6	6
Malta	2	—	3	—	5
Netherlands*	637	1,438	25	10	2,110
Norway*	36	122	35	24	217
Portugal*	67	960	692	10	1,729
Spain	30	4,977	3,502	184	8,693
Sweden	1	6	2	6	15
Switzerland	6	6	1	24	37
Turkey*	1,015	3,730	46	25	4,816
United Kingdom*	162	17,874	2,360	271	20,667
Afloat	—	—	19,291	1,800	21,091
*European NATO	202,261	64,320	9,397	849	276,827
East Asia and Pacific	37,760	31,184	38,661	25,165	132,770
Australia	8	257	409	5	679
Burma	3	3	1	5	12
Hong Kong	6	6	15	14	41
Indonesia	26	29	20	6	81
Japan	3,711	5,625	4,755	4,512	18,603
Okinawa	—	8,657	3,408	16,462	28,527
Laos	—	—	—	4	4
Malaysia	7	2	—	3	12
New Zealand	2	10	54	3	69
Philippines	39	8,832	5,207	2,180	16,258
Singapore	4	1	11	6	22
South Korea	33,507	7,245	253	331	41,336
Taiwan	358	460	338	9	1,165
Thailand	89	57	29	15	190
Afloat	—	—	24,161	1,610	25,771
Africa, Near East and South Asia	849	656	3,125	629	5,259
Afghanistan	5	4	—	2	11
Ascension Island	—	1	—	—	1
Bahrain	3	—	90	—	93
Cameroon	—	—	—	3	3
Chad	3	—	—	—	3
Diego Garcia	—	—	1,150	—	1,150
Egypt	2	4	27	17	50
Ethiopia	29	21	31	26	107
Gabon	—	—	—	5	5
Ghana	3	—	—	3	6
India	3	2	7	17	29
Iran	507	451	121	7	1,086
Israel	24	11	8	20	63
Ivory Coast	4	—	—	5	9
Jordan	9	5	—	7	21
Kenya	2	—	—	10	12
Kuwait	3	—	—	7	10
Lebanon	1	5	—	16	22
Liberia	8	2	3	6	19
Madagascar	—	—	1	6	7
Malawi	2	—	—	—	2
Mali	—	—	—	5	5
Morocco	9	12	640	172	833
Nepal	2	—	—	4	6

	Army	Air Force	Navy	Marine Corps	Total
Nigeria	3	2	—	8	13
Pakistan	6	12	3	13	34
Saudi Arabia	194	107	27	7	335
Senegal	—	—	2	9	11
Seychelles	—	5	—	—	5
Somalia	—	—	—	6	6
South Africa	2	7	3	12	24
Sri Lanka	—	—	3	1	4
Sudan	—	—	—	7	7
Syria	2	—	—	4	6
Tanzania	—	—	—	5	5
Tunisia	8	1	3	6	18
Yemen	2	—	—	3	5
Zaire	13	4	—	5	22
Afloat	—	—	1,006	205	1,211
Western Hemisphere	159	386	5,761	691	6,997
Antigua	—	1	116	—	117
Argentina	6	10	6	15	37
Bahamas	—	2	186	4	192
Barbados	—	—	118	5	123
Bermuda	—	—	1,568	82	1,650
Boliva	18	13	2	9	42
Brazil	23	23	17	18	81
Canada	9	259	422	11	701
Chile	6	6	10	8	30
Colombia	11	9	7	12	39
Costa Rica	2	—	—	4	6
Cuba (Guantanamo)	—	3	2,066	410	2,479
Dominican Republic	6	2	4	8	20
Ecuador	6	7	1	3	17
El Salvador	9	2	—	4	15
Guatemala	7	5	1	7	20
Guyana	—	—	—	6	6
Haiti	3	—	—	6	9
Honduras	5	8	—	6	19
Jamaica	1	—	—	9	10
Mexico	7	5	2	15	29
Nicaragua	11	1	1	4	17
Panama (Republic)	6	2	—	13	21
Paraguay	3	1	1	5	10
Peru	4	9	6	8	27
Turks Island	—	—	124	—	124
Uruguay	4	2	2	7	15
Venezuela	12	16	14	12	54
Afloat	—	—	1,087	—	1,087
Antarctica	—	—	69	—	69
Eastern Europe	70	20	3	56	149
Bulgaria	2	2	—	2	6
Czechoslovakia	1	3	—	6	10
Germany (Dem. Rep)	47	—	—	5	52
Hungary	4	1	—	5	10
Poland	3	1	—	6	10
Romania	3	1	—	6	10
USSR (Soviet Union)	8	8	3	18	37
Yugoslavia	2	4	—	8	14
Undistributed	—	139	1,016	2	1,157

Ashore includes temporarily shore-based.
Army figures for Okinawa not available.
†As of March 31, 1977.   *Source: Department of Defense.*

US Department of Defense Budget FY 1978

By Program, Component and Budget Title (Total Obligational Authority—In Millions of Dollars).

	February 1978
DoD Program	
Strategic Forces	10,619
General Purpose Forces	42,035
Intelligence and Communications	8,239
Airlift and Sealift	8,239
Airlift and Sealift	1,657
Guard and Reserve Forces	7,112
Research and Development	10,816
Central Supply and Maintenance	12,016
Training, Medical, Other Gen Per Act	24,386
Administration and Assoc Activities	2,235
Support of Other Nations	1,257
Total Direct Program (TOA)	**120,373**
DoD Component	
Department of the Army	29,595
Department of the Navy	40,132
Department of the Air Force	34,729
Defense Agencies, OSD and JCS	4,231
Defense-wide	10,568
Civil Preparedness, DCPA	91
Military Functions	**119,345**
Military Assistance Program	1,028
Total Direct Program (TOA)	**120,373**
DoD Budget Title	
Military Personnel	27,586
Retired Pay	9,056
Operation and Maintenance	35,140
Procurement	32,209
Research, Development, Test, Evaluation	11,875
Special Foreign Currency Program	2
Military Construction	1,795
Family Housing and Homeowners Asst Prog	1,420
Civil Preparedness, DCPA	91
Revolving and Management Funds	171
Military Functions	**119,345**
Military Assistance Program	1,028
Total Direct Program (TOA)	**120,373**

Note: Amounts for military and civilian pay increases and other proposed legislation are distributed. Details may not add to totals due to rounding.

Appendices continued

Department of Defense FY 1978 Budget Program Acquisition Costs
(Dollars in Millions)

AIRCRAFT

Army

		FY '77	FY '78	FY '79
AH-1S	Cobra Tow Attack Helicopter	131.3	144.5	151.5
UH-60A Blackhawk	Helicopter	215.4	273.8	379.9
C-12A	Cargo Aircraft	16.9	17.2	—
CH-47C	Helicopter	—	—	78.4
UV-18A	Twin Otter Aircraft	—	2.6	—

Navy

		FY '77	FY '78	FY '79
A-4M	Skyhawk	87.1	9.1	116.9
A-6E	Intruder	96.7	184.8	201.3
A-7E	Corsair II	224.7	126.5	27.2
AH-1T	Sea Cobra	64.3	31.2	—
CH-53E	Sea Stallion	110.4	18.5	183.2
CTX	Cargo Aircraft	—	21.6	27.4
E-2C	Hawkeye	156.5	196.6	208.5
EA-6B	Prowler	135.5	141.8	172.5
EC-130Q	Tacamo IV	—	—	32.5
F-5F	Tactical Fighter	13.9	—	—
F-14A	Tomcat	712.3	890.8	674.4
F-18	Hornet	341.6	654.4	864.8
P-3C	Orion	239.2	323.6	347.1
S-3A	Viking	22.1	59.6	—
T-34C	Mentor	13.7	18.6	1.3
T-44A	Advanced Multi-engined Trainer	15.5	17.7	.8
UH-1N	Iroquois	18.8	—	—

Air Force

		FY '77	FY '78	FY '79
A-10	Attack Aircraft	605.6	831.9	924.9
KC-10A	Advanced Tanker/Cargo Aircraft (ATCA)	28.8	—	156.8
B-1	Bomber	1,555.7	443.4	105.5
C-130	Hercules	—	62.0	—
E-3A	Advanced Warning and Control System (AWACS)	564.1	372.9	304.1
EF-111A	Tactical Aircraft	44.4	52.3	197.6
F-15	Eagle	1,495.3	1,666.7	1,415.7
F-16	Air Combat Fighter	510.7	1,685.3	1,594.5
TR-1	Reconnaissance Aircraft	—	—	10.2

MISSILES

Army

		FY '77	FY '78	FY '79
Chaparral	Air Defense Missile	68.1	34.9	31.9
Dragon[1]	Anti-Tank Missile	76.7	97.3	.6
Hawk[1]	Air Defense Missile	107.5	111.2	75.4
Lance	Surface-Surface Missile	75.3	81.7	70.2
Patriot	Air Defense Missile	180.0	216.4	307.1
Pershing	Surface-Surface Missile	36.3	48.3	75.7
Roland	Air Defense Missile	85.0	131.1	225.4
Stinger[1]	Air Defense Missile	27.4	50.6	149.9
Tow[2]	Anti-Tank Missile	102.9	80.0	54.1
AN/TSO-73	Command and Control System	44.1	39.8	—

Navy

		FY '77	FY '78	FY '79
Poseidon	Strategic Missile	17.7	20.2	24.4
Trident I	Strategic Missile	1,542.1	1,504.6	1,129.7
Harpoon	Anti-Ship Missile	150.4	132.5	133.4
Phoenix	Air-Air Missile	95.8	95.9	114.0
Shrike[3]	Anti-Radar Missile	47.3	41.0	31.4
Sidewinder[3]	Air-Air Missile	93.1	150.3	141.1
Sparrow[3]	Air-Air Missile	169.2	177.8	195.0
Standard ER	Air Defense Missile	58.6	66.1	102.4
Standard MR	Air Defense Missile	61.5	107.9	109.2

Air Force

		FY '77	FY '78	FY '79
ALCM	Air Launched Cruise Missile	79.2	381.5	416.1
GLCM	Ground Launched Cruise Missile	—	18.7	74.1
Minuteman	Strategic Missile	768.5	333.4	122.8
Maverick (E/O)	Air-Surface Missile	4.9	8.3	34.5
Maverick (Laser)[4]	Air-Surface Missile	14.6	59.7	7.9
Target Drones[5]		93.9	99.3	130.0

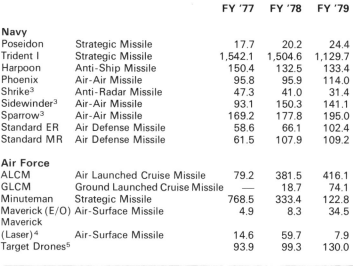

NAVY VESSELS

		FY '77	FY '78	FY '79
AD	Destroyer Tender	300.5	2.6	322.6
AO	Fleet Oiler	102.7	327.2	7.7
CGN-42	Cruiser (Aegis)	29.4	209.9	19.4
CV SLEP	Carrier Modernization	1.6	36.7	36.7
DD-963	Destroyer	186.9	383.5	57.8
DDG-2	Guided Missile Destroyer Modernization	—	102.5	155.0
DDG-47	Destroyer (Aegis)	14.3	938.6	10.2
FFG	Guided Missile Frigate	1,235.0	1,217.6	1,547.9
SSN-688	Nuclear Attack Submarine	1,302.0	310.6	474.4
T-AFT	Fleet Ocean Tug	1.7	53.8	4.8
T-AGOS	Ocean Surveillance Ship	.6	1.2	98.4
T-ARC	Cable Repair Ship	1.5	4.5	192.1
Trident	Ballistic Missile System	1,275.7	1,930.1	1,659.2

TRACKED COMBAT VEHICLES

Army

		FY '77	FY '78	FY '79
M60 Series[1]	Tanks	506.9	532.7	411.7
M88A1[1]	Recovery Vehicle, FT, Medium	80.2	24.8	51.5
M109A1/A2/A3	Howitzer, Medium SP, FT, 155mm	41.9	118.8	64.6
M110A2	Howitzer, Heavy, SP, FT, 8in	—	109.3	—
M113A1	Carrier, Personnel, FT, Armored	84.5	72.3	74.8
M125A1	Carrier, 81mm Mortar	9.9	—	—
M548	Carrier, Logistics	—	—	18.9
M577A1	Carrier, Command Post	—	51.2	—
M578	Recovery Vehicle	18.5	—	—
XM-1	Tank, Combat, FT, 105mm Gun	119.9	274.7	497.0

OTHER PROCUREMENT PROGRAMS

Army

		FY '77	FY '78	FY '79
L16A2	Mortar, 81mm	—	3.0	8.0
M198[1]	Howitzer, Medium, Towed, 155mm	20.6	1.5	53.4
M240	Armor Machine Gun, 7.62mm	14.4	6.3	7.5
—[1]	Lightweight Company Mortar	1.9	4.0	15.4

		FY '77	FY '78	FY '79
Navy				
MK-15	Close-In Weapon System (Phalanx)	38.8	81.8	113.2
MK-30	Mobile Target	2.9	22.0	20.7
MK-38	Mini Mobile Target	1.3	1.4	1.4
MK-46	Torpedo	7.5	1.5	90.7
MK-48	Torpedo	139.2	162.8	113.6
MK-60	Captor ASW Mine	65.9	77.6	17.7
MK-71	Major Caliber Lightweight Gun	42.0	2.8	1.9
MK-75	76mm Gun Mount	4.9	7.3	2.8
FLTSATCOM	Fleet Satellite Communications	78.6	76.1	26.8
Air Force				
GAU-5	Machine Gun	—	—	.3

PROGRAMS IN R & D ONLY

	FY '77	FY '78	FY '79
Army			
Advanced Attack Helicopter (AAH)	130.8	164.9	177.4
Ballistic Missile Defense Advanced Technology Program	102.7	107.3	113.5
Ballistic Missile Defense Systems Technology Program	100.0	106.2	114.0
CH-47 Modernization	25.9	32.0	19.5
Division Air Defense Gun	2.2	17.0	75.7
Hellfire Heliborne Missile	19.2	50.5	65.1
Remotely Piloted Vehicles (RPVs)	5.5	9.2	24.2
Surface-to-Surface Missile Rocket System	6.9	46.4	70.8
Navy			
Advanced ASW Torpedo	25.4	25.0	44.3
Aegis Surface-Air Missile System	28.2	34.5	14.4
AV-8B V/STOL Aircraft	33.6	59.8	85.6
CSEDS Combat System Engineering Development Site	82.8	35.5	37.2
ELF Communications (Seafarer)	14.8	15.0	40.5

		FY '77	FY '78	FY '79
HARM	Air-Surface Missile	30.0	29.7	43.4
LAMPS	Helicopter	72.1	107.3	124.5
MARCORPS	Marine Corps Data System	8.7	14.6	11.8
TACTAS	Tactical Towed Array Sonar	18.2	15.3	25.2
Tomahawk	Cruise Missile	119.4	210.3	152.1
V/STOL	Aircraft Developments	12.4	22.5	52.5
Wide Aperture Array Sonar		8.0	17.0	37.4
Air Force				
CASWS	Close Air Support Weapon System	18.9	10.1	50.6
C-5	Airlift Squadrons (Wing Mod)	18.0	38.1	37.2
E-4	Advanced Airborne Command Post	88.7	65.8	32.0
Joint Tactical Communications (TRI-TAC)[6]		92.9	105.7	98.7
KC-135	Squadrons	6.2	3.8	1.5
M-X	Strategic Missile	69.0	134.4	158.2
NATO	Airborne Early Warning and Control Aircraft	4.6	15.7	10.0
NAVSTAR	Global Positioning System[6]	80.5	86.7	129.0
PLSS	Precision Location Strike System	16.3	31.4	86.8
Within Visual Range Air-Air Missile[4]		—	—	12.2

Footnotes:
[1] Includes Marine Corps Procurement.
[2] Includes Navy and Marine Corps Procurement.
[3] Includes Air Force Procurement.
[4] Includes Navy RDT&E funding.
[5] Includes Army and Navy Procurement.
[6] Includes Army and Navy RDT&E funding.

Index

All figures in bold type represent subjects mentioned in captions.

A

A3D-2 Skywarrior see Douglas
A-4 Skyhawk see McDonnell Douglas
A-6 Intruder and Prowler see Grumman
A-7 Corsair II see Vought
A-9 see Northrop
A-10A see Fairchild Republic
A-11 see Lockheed SR-71
A-37 Dragonfly see Cessna
AAA-4 infra-red detector, **195**
AABNCP see Advanced Airborne National Command Post
ABM see Anti-ballistic missile systems
ABM limitation treaty, 56
Abrams tank see XM1
Acheson Secretary of State Dean, 20
ACIS (Amphibious, Command Information System), 136
Acme (modified Agile) class ocean minesweepers, **134**
Acrid air-to-air missile (Soviet), 240
Active duty military personnel, tabulation, 19
AD see 'Assured Destruction' defence strategy
ADA see Air Defense Artillery
ADM see Atomic Demolition Munitions
ADP see Automated Data Processing
Advanced Airborne National Command Post, **44**, 50, **63**, 165
Advanced Medium Short Take Off and Land (AMST), 158
Advanced Radar Processing System, **182**
Advanced Radar Processing System see also OL-93 Radar Data Processor
Advanced Tanker/Cargo aircraft (ATCA), **157**
Aegis ship defense system, 113, 115, 122, 131, **236**
Aerial reconnaissance, **47**, **53**, **55**
Aeronutronic Ford MIM-72 Chaparral, 72, 91, **234**
Aerospace Defense Command (DOD) 40, 169
AEW see Airborne Early-Warning systems
AFSATCOM see Air Force satellite Communcations System
AG see Experimental ships
Agile class (MSO) ocean minesweepers, 134
AGM-12 see Martin/Maxson
AGM-45 see Texas Instruments
AGM-62 see Hughes/Martin
AGM-65 see Hughes
AGM-69A SRAM see Boeing
AGM-78D see General Dynamics
AGM-86A see Boeing
AGM-88 see Texas Instruments
AH-1 Huey Cobra attack helicopter ordnance loads and capability, 73-80; -IG 73, 78, 224
AH-IS Tow Cobra attack helicopter, 73
AH-64 helicopter see Hughes
AIM-4 see Hughes
AIM-SA Phoenix see Hughes
AIM-7 Sparrow see Raytheon
AIM-9 Sidewinder, 152, 238; -9B 107, **238**; -9D improved IR guidance, 238; -9E LAP (low altitude performance), 238; -9G **180**, 238; -9H **206**, 238; -9J **200**, **238**; -9L **238**
AIM-26 see Hughes
Air Assault infantry, 73
Air cavalry squadron, 73
Air cavalry troop, 73
Air Defense Artillery Units, 72
Air Force Communications Service, 158
Air Force Logistics Command, 158
Air Force Reserves (AFRES)
  flying squadrons, '60, '67, '74 and '76 compared, 244
  organization, 244
Air Force Satellite Communications System, 50
Air Force Security Service, 158
Air Force Systems Command, 158
Air Launched Cruise Missiles, **63**, 66, 67
Air National Guard (ANG)
  flying squadrons, '60, '67, '74 and '76 compared, 244
  organization, 244
Air Tactical Data System, 108
Air-to-Surface Missiles, 223, 224
Air Training Command, 158
Air University, 158
Airborne Early-Warning systems (AEW), 182
Airborne infantry, 73
Airborne Tactical Data System, 182
Airborne Warning and Control system see AWACS
Aircraft carriers
  angled flight deck, 121
  armored flight deck, 122
  lift arrangements, **118**, 119
  steam catapult, 121
Alaskan Air Command, 151, 152
Albacore (AGSS) submarine, 130
Albany (CA-123, later CG-10) cruiser, 124
Albany class cruisers, 124
ALCM see Air Launched Cruise Missiles
Alexander, Army Secretary, Clifford L. jnr, **38**
Allen M. Sumner class destroyers, 131
Allison 501 gas-turbine/electric generator, **108**
Alternate National Military Command Center, **44**
Alternate Stinger see General Dynamics XFIM-92A
America (CV-66) aircraft carrier, 119, **131**
American Civil War, 13, 18, 146
American Revolution, War of, 12
American–Soviet relations, 20, 257
Amphibious Assault Ships (LPH) (LHA), 136, 137
Amphibious Cargo Ships (AKA), **140**
Amphibious Transports Dock (LPD), 137
AMST see Advanced Medium Short Take Off and Land
Anchorage class assault transports, 138
ANMCC see Alternate National Military Command Center
Antelope (PG) patrol gunboat, **134**
Anti-ballistic Missile systems, 63
Anti-radar missile (ARM), 226
Anti-submarine mines CAPTOR, 113. 145
Anti-submarine warfare missiles, 83, 127, 128, 228, 229
Antietam (CV-36) aircraft carrier, 121
AO see Fleet Oilers
Arab-Israel policies, 24
Arcadia class destroyer tenders, 142
ARM see Anti-radar missile
Armed Services Committees
  budget authorization hearings, 42
  Melvin Price questions cancellations, Oct '77, 67
Armored cavalry squadron, 73
Army Air Corps, 146
Army Air Service, 146
Army Re-organization Act, 1920, 146
Army War College Strategic Studies Institute, 246
ARPS see Advanced Radar Processing system
ASALM (Advanced Strategic Air-Launched Missile) see McDonnell Douglas
Ashville class (PG) patrol gunboats **134**, **144**
Asia
  US political and military policies 23, 262, 263
ASM see Air-to-Surface Missiles
ASMD (Anti-Ship Missile Defense) **239**
ASQ-151 EVS electro-optical viewing system, **162**, 163
Asroc see Honeywell RUR-SA
Assistant Secretary of Defense (Comptroller), 42
Assistant Secretary of Defense for International Affairs (OSD), 32
'Assured Destruction' defense strategy, 61, 62, 64
ASTOR, 83, 133
ATCA see Advanced Tanker/Cargo Aircraft
ATDS see Airborne Tactical Data System
Atlantic Command (DOD), 38
Atlas ICBM, 60
Atomic Demolition Munitions, 83
Austin class assault transports, 137
Automated Data Processing, 44
Automatic Data Processing (OJCS), 35
AV-8A see British Aerospace
AV-8B see McDonnell Douglas
Avenger gun see GAU-8A
AWACS (airborne warning and control system) see Boeing E-3A

B

B-1 see Rockwell
B-29 see Boeing
B-36 see Boeing
B-47 see Boeing
B-50 see Boeing B-29
B-52 see Boeing
B-52F see Boeing
B-58 see General Dynamics (Convair)
B-70 project, 60, 61
Backfire see Tupolev Tu-26
Badger see Tupolev Tu-16
Bainbridge (CGN-25) Cruiser, 103, 123, 124
Balloons
  military application, 146
Baltimore class heavy cruisers, 124
Barbel class submarines, **130**
Barney (DDG) destroyer, **132**
Barnstable County USS, **27**
Begin, Menachem, Israeli Prime Minister, **24**
Belknap (CG-26) cruiser, **124**
Belknap class cruisers, 124
Bell Aerosystems ACV (air cushion vehicle), **217**
Bell
  Huey (UH-1 Iroquois), 137, 160, **161**, 230
  Kiowa and Jet Ranger helicopters, **162**, **260**
  209 Huey Cobra, **160**; AH-IJ Sea Cobra 160, 232; AH-IS Tow Cobra 73, 160, 232
Bell SES-100B surface effect ship, **135**
Bell UH-1 Iroquois helicopter see Bell Huey (UH-1 Iroquois)
Bendix RIM-8 Talos, 107, 123, **232**
  -8D nuclear warhead, 83, 232
  -8E variant, 232
  -8F, 232
  -8G improved terminal homing, 232
  -8H anti-radar SSm, 232
  -8J, 232
Benjamin Franklin (SSBN-640) improved Lafayette class SSBN, 60, 126
BGM-71 see Hughes
BGM-109 Tomahawk
  ALCM, 67, 114, 116, **220**
  SLCM, **220**
Biddle (DDG-5) renamed Claude V. Ricketts, 132
Bigelow USS, **117**
Black Hawk see Sikorsky UH-60A
Blackbird see Lockheed SR-71
Blinder see Tupolev Tu-22
Blue Ridge class command ships, **136**
BMP-1 Soviet MICV, 94
Boeing AGM-69A SRAM (Short Range Attack Missile), **219**
Boeing AGM-86 SCAD (Subsonic Cruise Armed Decoy), 218
Boeing AGM-86A ALCM (Air-Launched Cruise Missile, **63**, **218**
Boeing B-29, 58
Boeing B-36, 58
Boeing B-47, 58, 61
Boeing B-52 Stratofortress, 58, 61, 66, 82, 152, 156, 162, **245**; -52D, 163; -52F 19, 58, **163**; -52G, **158**, **163**, **218**; -52H, **59**, **162**, **218**, **219**
Boeing C-135 Stratolifter, 164
Boeing C-135
  KC-135 Stratotanker **44**, 52, 157, **164**, **195**, 248
Boeing E-3A (AWACS) Sentry, 152, 154, **156**, **166**, **167**, **259**
Boeing E-4A, **63**, **164**; -4B, **44**, 164, **219**
Boeing KC-135 see Boeing C-135
Boeing LGM-30 Minuteman ICBM, 58, 60, 61, **67**; -30B Minuteman I, 60; -30F Minuteman II, 61, 66, **219**, **254**; -30G Minuteman III, **59**, 63, 66, **219**, **223**, 254
Boeing NB-52G, **63**
Boeing 707 military versions, 165
Boeing 747 military version, 164
Boeing-Vertol H-46 helicopters
  CH-46, A, D, E, and F Sea Knight, 136, **137**, 140, **141**, **168**, **211**
Boeing Vertol CH-47, A, B and C Chinook helicopter, 95, **164**
Bombs
  B-61 variable yield, 83
  MK82, **23**, **174**, 226
  MK83 2000lb Paveway, 226
  MK84 2000lb Hobo, 225; Paveway, 226
  MK84 see also GBU-10
  M117 750lb Paveway, 226
  M118 3000lb Hobo, 225; Paveway, 226
Bombs see also Hughes/Martin AGM-62 and KMU-421/B Paveway
'Boneyard' aircraft, Davis Monthan AF Base, **243**
Boston (CA-69, later CAG-1) cruiser, 124
BQM-34B see Teledyne-Ryan
Bradley, General Omar N, 19, 82
Brewer see Yakovlev Yak-28
British Aerospace AV-8A Harrier, **113**, 115, **192**, **193**, **209**, 212
Bronstein class frigates, **132**, 133, see also Knox
Brooke USS frigate, **229**
Brooke class frigates, 133, see also Knox
Brown, Secretary of Defense, Harold, 24, **35**, **41**, 66, 256
Browning M2 heavy machine gun see 0.50 Calibre Browning
Brzezinski, Dr. Zbigniew, National Security Adviser, **35**
Bullpup B see Martin/Maxson AGM-12
Bullpup B see also Warheads, SLCM
Buried trench launch system, **67**, 223
Byrnes, Secretary of State, 20

C

C-2A Greyhound see Grumman E-2 Hawkeye
C-5A Galaxy see Lockheed
C-7A see De Havilland Canada
C-9 see McDonnell Douglas
C-130 see Lockheed
C-135 see Boeing
C-141 see Lockheed
CAINS see Carrier aircraft inertial navigation system
California (CGN-36) cruiser, **123**
California class cruisers, 122, **123**
  California (CGN-36), 123
  South Carolina (CGN-37), 123
Canberra (ex Pittsburgh CA-70, later CAG-2), 124
Cannon-launched Guided Projectiles see Martin XM712 Copperhead
Canopus submarine tender, 142
CAPTOR see Anti-submarine mines also Torpedoes MK46 Mod 0
Caribou see De Havilland Canada C-7A
Carl Vinson (CVN-70) aircraft carrier, 118
Carrier aircraft inertial navigation system, 188
Carter, President Jimmy, 23, **28**, **35**, 66
Cayuse helicopter see Hughes OH-6
CBU Rockeye area weapon, 154, 226
Central Intelligence Agency (CIA), **36**, 49, 56
Central Security Service see National Security Agency
CEP see Circular Error Probability
Cessna A-37 Dragonfly
  -37A and -37B (model 318E), 154, **168**, **246**
Cessna O-2A, 154
CEV, 72
CEWI see Combat Electronic Warfare Intelligence
CGN see Nuclear Powered Guided Missile Cruisers
CH-46A see Boeing
CH-47 see Boeing
CH-53A see Sikorsky S-65
Chaparral see Aeronutronic Ford MIM-72
Charles F. Adams (DDG) class destroyers, 131, 132
Charleston class (AKA) amphibious cargo ships, **140**
Chehalis (former PG) research vessel, 134
Chemical warfare
  Soviet capability, 260
Chiarini, Dr. John R., 246
Chicago (CA-136, later CG-11) cruiser, 124
Chief of Naval Operations (CNO), 32, 110, 208, 262
Chief of Staff of the Air Force (JCS), 32
Chief of Staff of the Army (JCS), 32
China. Peoples Republic of
  ICBM development, 64
  US diplomacy 1971/2, 23
Chinook see Boeing CH-47
'Chobham' laminated armour, 88, **89**
Churchill, Winston, 18
CIA see Central Intelligence Agency
CINPAC see Commander in Chief, Pacific
Circular Error Probability, **65**, 254
Civil Reserve Air Fleet (CRAF), 157
CIWS see Close-in Weapon System
Claud Jones class frigates, 133
Claude V. Ricketts (DDG-5) formerly Biddle, 132
Cleveland assault transport, **137**
Clifford, Secretary of Defence Clark, 83
Clements, William, Deputy Secretary of Defense 1972–77, 32
Close-in Weapon System, **117**, see also Vulcan/Phalanx
CNO see Chief of Naval Operations
Cobra see McDonnell Douglas/ Northrop F-18
Colt Commando see 5.56mm M16A1 Rifle
Columbus (CA-74, later CG-12) cruiser, 124, **232**
Combat Electronic Warfare Intelligence (CEWI), 81
Combat Stores Ship (AFS), 140
Command Data Buffer System, ICBMs, 219
Commandant of the Marine Corps, 34, 208
Commander in Chief, Pacific (CINPAC), 151
Commander in Chief, US European Command (USINCEUR), 152
Compass Island class (AG) experimental ships, 144
Congressional Budget Control and Impoundment Act, 1974, 42
Constellation (CV-64) aircraft carrier, 119, **182**
Continental Army of the Revolution, 16
Coontz class destroyers, 130
Coontz frigate (DLG) re-rated Guided Missile Destroyer (DDG), **130**
Copperhead see Martin XM712
Coral Sea (CV-43) aircraft carrier **122**, **206**, **246**
Coronado USS, **28**
Corsair II see Vought A-7
Counterforce capability and CEP, **65**, 254
Courtney class frigates, 133
CRAF see Civil Reserve Air Fleet
Critical Communications, 53
CRITICOM see Critical Communications
Crusader see Vought F-8
Cuban crisis, 1962
  Marine Corps back-up, 211
Curtiss J-1 and JN-4 Jennies, 146

D

Daniel Webster (SSBN-626) submarine, 60, 126
DARPA see Defense Advanced Research Projects Agency
Dash ocean minesweeper, **134**
DASH Drone AS helicopter, 132, 133
DC-10-30F see McDonnell Douglas
DC-130H, **158**
DCA see Defense Communications Agency
DCAA see Defense Contract Audit Agency
DCPA see Defense Civil Preparedness Agency
De Havilland Canada C-7A Caribou, **248**
De Havilland DH-4, 146
Dealey class frigates, 133
Decatur (DDG), formerly Forrest Sherman (DD) class destroyers, 132
Defender helicopter see Hughes OH-6
Defense Advanced Research Projects Agency (DOD), 36, 38
Defense agencies, 36
Defense Civil Preparedness Agency 36, 38
Defense Communications Agency (DOD), 36, 38
Defense Contract Audit Agency (DOD), 36, 38
Defense Intelligence Agency (JCS), 35, 36, 38, 57
Defense Investigative Service (DOD), 36, 38
Defense Mapping Agency (DOD), 36, 38
Defense Nuclear Agency (DOD), 36, 38
Defense Reorganization Act 1958, 36, 40
Defense Satellite Communications System II, **47**; System III, **50** see also USAF Satellite Control Facility
Defense Security Assistance Agency (DOD), 36, 38
Defense Supply Agency (DOD), 36, 38
Delta class SSBN (Soviet Union), 125
Delta Dagger see Gensral Dynamics F-102A
Delta Dart see General Dynamics F-106
Department of Defense (DOD), 32, 34
  budget, fiscal year 1978, 265
  budget legislative course, 42
  budget program acquisition costs FY 1978
    aircraft, 266
    miscellaneous procurement programs, 266
    missiles, 266
    Navy vessels, 266
    research and development, 267
    tracked combat vehicles, 266
  budgetary procedures, 40ff
  command, control and communications systems, 44
  optimal changes in organization, 45
Department of the Air Force (DOD), 35
Department of the Army (DOD), 35
  organization, 70
Department of the Navy (DOD), 35
  organization, 104
Detente, basis of American concept, 20
DH-4 see De Havilland
DIA see Defense Intelligence Agency
Diad strategic offensive forces, 58
DIANE see Digital Integrated Attack Navigation System
Digital Integrated Attack Navigation System, 179
Director of Defense Research and Engineering (OSD), 32
Director of Intelligence, 52
Director of Telecommunications and Command and Control Systems (OSD), 32
DIS see Defensive Investigative Service
Division of Military Aeronautics see US Army
Dixie class destroyer tenders, **142**
Dixon submarine tender, **142**
DMA see Defense Mapping Agency
DNA see Defense Nuclear Agency
DOD see Department of Defense
Dominican Republic intervention 1965, 211
Douglas
  A3D-2 Skywarrior, **224**
  EA-1 early warning aircraft, 166
DPPG see Draft or Tentative Planning and Programming Guidance
Draft or Tentative Planning and Programming Guidance, 40
Dragon see McDonnell Douglas FGM-77A
Dragonfly see Cessna A-37
DSA see Defense Supply Agency
DSAA see Defense Security Assistance Agency
DSCSII see Defense Satellite Communications System II
Dwight D. Eisenhower (CVN-69) aircraft carrier, 118

E

E-1B see Grumman
E-2 see Grumman E-2 Hawkeye
E-3A (AWACS) see Boeing
E-4B see Boeing
EA-1 see Douglas
EA-6A and B see Grumman A-6
Eagle see McDonnell Douglas F-15
Edenton class (ATS) salvage and rescue ships, 144
Edenton salvage and rescue ship, **144**
Egypt, 28
8in nuclear projectile, 83
8in self-propelled howitzer see M110
81mm M29 mortar, **98**, **211**, 212
Eilath, Israeli destroyer, 104, 111
Eisenhower, General Dwight D, 19, 246
Electro-optical viewing system (EVS), **162**, **163**
Electronic intelligence, 54
ELINT see Electronic intelligence
Elliot (DDG) Spruance class destroyer, **131**
Ellsworth, Robert, Deputy Secretary of Defense, 32
Emerson ITV (Improved Tow Vehicle), 232

Energy Department
  contribution to intelligence pool, 52
Engines, aero
  Allison T56 turboprop, 186, 187
  General Electric F101-100, 202; F-103-100 turbofans, 164; F404-400 turbofans, 198; J79-2, -4, -8, -15, -17 turbojets, 194, 203; J85-17A, 168; T-58, T58-8F turboshaft, 184, 204; T700 turboshaft, 183; 205; TF-34-2, 188; TF-34-100 turbofan, 169; TF39-1 turbofans, 184.
  Pratt and Whitney F100-PW-100 turbofan, 172, 196; F-105-100 turbofans, 164; F401-400 turbofans, 180, 201; J52-8A, 178; J52-6, and -8A, 191; J52-408, 178; J-57 series turbojet, 162, 190, 194, 198, 206; J-58, 190; J75 series turbojet, 190, 201; TF30-412A turbofans, 180, 206; TF-33 turbofan, 163, **164**, 166, 186
  Rolls-Royce Pegasus vectored-thrust turbofan, 192; Rolls-Royce Sapphire see Wright, J65-16A; Rolls-Royce Spey turbofan, 194
  Wright J65-16A turbojet, 191
Enhanced radiation warhead, 84, **85**
Enterprise (CVN-65) aircraft carrier, **103**, 118, **120**, **121**, 123, **206**, **246**, **263**
ER see Enhanced Radiation
Essex class aircraft carriers, 118, 122
  Antietam (CV-36), 121
Ethan Allen (SSBN-608) submarine, 60, 126
Ethan Allen class missile submarine, 126
Euromissile/Hughes Boeing Roland, 2, **81**, **234**, **235**
European Command (DOD), 38, 41
EV-1 see Grumman Ov-1A to D
EVS see Electro-optical viewing system
Exercise Avon Express, Nov '77, **40**
Exercise Bead Chevron, **211**
Exercise Carte Blanche, 1955, 82
Exercise Display Determination, 1977, **92**, **250**
Exercise Reforger, Aug '76, **73**, **78**
Exercise Valiant Heritage, **263**
Experimental Ships (AG), 144

F
F-4 Phantom II see McDonnell Douglas F-4
F-5 see Northrop
F-5E see Northrop
F-8 see Vought
F-14 see Grumman
F-15 see McDonnell Douglas
F-16 see General Dynamics
F-18 see McDonnell Douglas
F-80C Shooting Star see Lockheed
F-86 see North American
F-100 see North American (Rockwell)
F-102A see General Dynamics
F-105 see Republic (Fairchild)
F-106 see General Dynamics
F-111 see General Dynamics F-111
Fairchild Republic A-10A, **147**, **152**, 154, **169**, **170–171**, 224, 248, 260
Falcon see Hughes AIM-4 and 26
Farragut (DDG) guided missile destroyer, **130**
FAST (fuel and sensor, tactical) pack, 197
FBI see Federal Bureau of Investigation
Federal Bureau of Investigation counter-intelligence function, 52
Fencer see Sukhoi Su-19
FGM-77A see McDonnell Douglas
FIM-43A see General Dynamics
Finletter Commission on airpower, 149
Fire control systems
  BQG-4 PUFFS, 128
  Hughes Ground Laser Locator/Designator, **229**
  Hughes MA-1, 169
  Praerie II A RPV, 228
Firebee RPV see Teledyne-Ryan BQM-34B
Fishbed see Mikoyan Gurevich MiG-21
500M helicopter see Hughes OH-6
511-1152 series tank landing ships, **139**
5in 38 calibre gun, 132, **133**, 142, 143
5in 54 calibre Mk45 guns, **108**, 130, 131, **132**
5.56mm M16A1 Rifle, **101**
Five Year Defense Plan, 40
Fleet Oilers (AO), **144**
Fleet Satellite Communications, **51**
Fletcher class destroyers, 131
'Flexible Response' defense strategy, 61, 149
Flight refuelling
  Boeing Flying Boom system, **165**
  Douglas ARB (Aerial Refuelling Boom), 192
  probe/drogue system, **212**
Flogger see Mikoyan Gurevich MiG-23
FLTSATCOM see Fleet Satellite Communications
FMS see Foreign Military Sales
FMS Credit Program, 30
Ford, President Gerald, 23
Ford Aerospace MGM-51C Shillelagh, 71, **77**, **230**
Foreign Military Sales (FMS), 30
Forest Sherman (DD) class destroyers, 132
Forrestal (CV-59) aircraft carrier **116**, **120**, 121
Forrestal class aircraft carriers, 119, 120
  Forrestal (CV-59), **120**, 121
  Independence (CV-62), 121
  Ranger (CV-61), **121**
  Saratoga (CV-60), 121
40mm M79 Grenade Launcher, **98**
4.2m mortar, 71
Fox (Belknap class) cruiser, **124**
Foxbat see Mikoyan Gurevich MiG-25
Franklin D. Roosevelt (CV-42) aircraft carrier, 115, 122
Freedom Fighter see Northrop F-5
Fulton class submarine tenders, 143
Fulton submarine tender, **143**
FYDP see Five Year Defense Plan

G
Galaxy see Lockheed C-5A
Gama Goat vehicle see M561
Garcia class frigates, **133**, see also Knox
Gates, Secretary of Defense, 36
Gatling gun, **174**
GAU-8A Avenger cannon, **169**, **170**
GBU-10 guided bomb, **226**
GBU-15 see Rockwell
Gearing class destroyers, 131, 132, 244
General Counsel (OSD), 32
General Dynamics AGM-78D Standard ARM, 154, 195, 226; -78A, **226**
General Dynamics FIM-43A Redeye, 71, 72, 214, **215**, **234**
General Dynamics RGM-66D Standard ARM, 226
General Dynamics
  F-16, 83, 152, 154, **238**, **239**, 248; -16A, 172, **173**; -16B, 154, 170, 172; Model 401, 172; YF-16, **172**, **173**, **174**
  F-102A Delta Dagger PQM-102 RPV target, **154**, **241**
  F-106A and B Delta Dart, 152, 156, **169**, 240
  F-111 'TFX', A-F, EF-111A and FB-111A, 23, **57**, 83, **154**, 174, **176**, 240, 254; -A, **176**, **177**; -E, **177**; EF-111A, 226; -F, **23**, **151**; FB111, 152, 218, **226**; -H, **66**, **176**, 219
  RIM-66/67 Standard Standard II-66C, 122, 130, **236**; Standard I -66A, -67A, **134**, 236
  XFIM-92A Stinger **215**, 235
  (Convair) B-58, 60, 61
  Pomona ASMD, **239**
General Purpose Force, 68
General Support Rocket System see GSRS
George Washington (SSBN-598) submarine, 60, 61, 126
George Washington class missile submarines, 126, **127**
Gettysburg 1–3 July 1864, **11**
Glenaid P. Lipscomb (SSN-685) submarine, 127
Goodyear UUM-44A Subroc, 83, 127, 128, **228**
Grant, Gen. U. S., 13
Grayback class submarines, 127
Greyhound see Grumman E-2 Hawkeye C-2A
Grumman
  A-6 Intruder and Prowler, 83, 111, **121**; **122**, 254; AO6A, 212; A-6E, **179**, 212, 227; EA-6 A and B ECM fit, **179**, 226, **263**
  E-1B early warning aircraft, 166
  E-2 Hawkeye, 108, **120**, **121**; C-2A Greyhound, 182; -2C, **182**, 226
  F-14 Tomcat, 108, 111, 113, **121**, 122, 180; -A, **29**, **117**, **180**, **181**, 240; -B, 181
  OV-1A to D, EV-1, JOV, RV Mohawk, **182**, **183**
GSRS (General Support Rocket System), 228
Guam (LPH-9) Interim Sea Control Ship conversion, 137
Guidance systems
  DAW-1, 234
  Goodyear Radag (Radar Area-correlation Guidance), 230
  Laser 'fire and forget', 224
  NS-20 on Minuteman, 219, 257
  Sidewinder Expanded Acquisition Mode (SEAM), 238
  USGS (Universal Space Guidance System), 222
Guitarro (SSN-665) submarine, 128
Gun turrets, helicopter
  Minigun, 185
Gun turrets, tank
  M60-type, **86**
  Tow/Bushmaster armored Turret, **94**

H
Haig, General Alexander M. Supreme Allied Commander Europe, **35**, **40**
Halleck, Henry Wager, 18
Halibut (SSB-587) submarine, 127, 128, **129**
Halsey, Admiral William F., 10
Hancock (No 3) aircraft carrier, **246**
Haraden (DD-585) destroyer, **227**
HARM see Texas Instruments AGM-88A
Harpoon see McDonnell Douglas
Harrier see British Aerospace AV-8A
HASP-U-2 see Lockheed U-2
Haven (AH) hospital ship, **145**
Hawk see Raytheon MIM-23
Hawkeye see Grumman E-2
Hedgehog AS weapon, 132
Hellfire (Helicopter fire and forget) missile see Rockwell
Hercules see Lockheed C-130
Hermitage (LSD) assault transport, **138**
High Point (PCH-1) hydrofoil, **227**
Hind see Mil Mi-24
Hobos see Rockwell GBU-15
Holland submarine tender, 143
Holloway, Admiral James L. Chief of Naval Operations, **35**, 115
'Honest John' MGRIB missile, 82, 83
Honeywell RUR-5A Asroc, 83, **108**, 122, **123**, **125**, 130, 131, 132, **133**, **229**
Hornet see McDonnell Douglas/Northrop F-18
Hound Dog air-to-ground missile, 162
House and Senate Appropriations Committees defense budget hearings, 43
Howard W. Gilmore (ex Neptune) submarine tender, **143**
Hughes AGM-65 A, B, C and D Maverick ASM, 154, **170**, **186**, **195**, **223**
Hughes AH-64 helicopter, **183**, 232
Hughes AIM-4 and 26 Falcon, **240**
Hughes AIM-4 and 26 Falcon -4A, **241**; -4C, 240; -4D, **240**; -4G Super Falcon, 240; -4H, **240**; -26A, 240; -26B, **240**
Hughes AIM-47A air-to-air missile, 190
Hughes AIM-54A Phoenix, **240**; -54B, 108, **180**, **181**, 240
Hughes BGM-71 Tow, **38**, 71, 72, **80**, 214, **232**, **260**
Hughes OH-6 Cayuse helicopter **184**, 232
Hughes/Martin, AGM-62 Walleye glide bomb, **117**, **223**, **224**
Hughes/TI, Night Attack Missile, 223
Hull (DD-945) destroyer, 132
Hunley class submarine tenders, 143
Hunley submarine tender, **143**
Hussein, King of Jordan, **28**

I
ICBMs see Intercontinental Ballistic Missiles
IFV see Infantry Fighting Vehicle
Illustrious class aircraft carriers (R.N), 122
Imaging Seeker Surface/Surface Missile Demonstration see McDonnell Douglas ISSSMD
Independence (CV-62) aircraft carrier, **121**
Indian wars 1607–1890, 12, 146
Infantry Fighting Vehicle (IFV), 72
Infra-red night vision equipment, **71**, **87**
  FLIR (Forward-Looking Infra-Red), 222
  IIR (Imaging Infra-Red Seeker), 222, 223
INR see State Department: intelligence function
Intelligence
  military attaches abroad, 50
Intelligence Directorate (J-2), 36
Intercontinental Ballistic Missiles, 58, **59**, 252
  Buried Trench concept, **67**, 223
  US/USSR comparative data, 254
Intermediate Range Ballistic Missiles, 60, 254
International Military Education and Training Program (MAP)
Intruder see Grumman A-6
Iran
  US arms sales, 30
IRBMs see Intermediate Range Ballistic Missiles
Iroquois helicopter see Bell UH-1
Isfahan helicopter see Bell Huey
ISSSMD see McDonnell Douglas
Iwo Jima class (LPH) amphibious assault ships, 136, **137**

J
J-2 see Intelligence Directorate
Jack (SSN-605) submarine, 128
Japan
  US defense commitment, 24
JATO see Jet Assisted Take-Off rockets
JCS see Joint Chiefs of Staff
Jeep see M151 A1
Jefferson, President Thomas, 18
Jennies (J-1 and JN-4) see Curtiss
Jet Assisted Take-Off rockets, **187**
Jet Ranger see Bell Kiowa and Jet Ranger
JFM see Joint Force Memorandum
John Adams (SSBN-620) submarine, 60, **126**
John F. Kennedy (CV-67-67) aircraft carrier, **111**, 118, 119, 124, **189**
Johnston, Gen. Joseph E., 13
Joint Chiefs of Staff (JCS), 32, 40, 208
  recommendation against withdrawal from Korea, 20
Joint Force Memorandum, 42
Joint Strategic Objectives Plan, 40
Jones, General David C., Air Force Chief of Staff, **35**
Joseph Jewes class frigates, 133
JOV see Grumman OV-1A to D
JSOP see Joint Strategic Objectives Plan
Jupiter IRBM, 60, 127

K
Kaimalino (Small Waterplane Twin Hull), 135
Kaman SH-2 Sea Sprite helicopter -2D, 123, 132, **133**; -2F, **105**, **184**, **185**; UH-2, 184; -2C, 136
KC-10A see McDonnell Douglas
KC-16 see McDonnell Douglas DC-10-30F
KC-130F see Lockheed C-130 Hercules
KC-135 see Boeing C-135
Keegan, General George, 262
Kelln, A. L., 66
Kerwin, General Walter T. jr., **38**
Kiev aircraft carrier (Soviet), **262**
Kilanea class (AE) ammunition ships, **141**
King, Ernest J., 19
King (DLG-10, later DDG-41) guided missile destroyer, 130
Kissinger, Secretary of State Henry, 22, 23
Kitty Hawk (CV-63) aircraft carrier, **119**
Kitty Hawk class aircraft carriers
  America (CV-66), 119
  Constellation (CV-64), 119
  John F. Kennedy (CV-67), 119
  Kitty Hawk (CV-63), **119**, **206**
KMU-421/B Paveway laser guided 'smart' bomb, **169**
Knox class frigates, 132, **133**
Korea, South
  US military presence, 23
  US 2nd Division, 23, 24
Korean War
  US re-armament, 58, 120, 149
  US units participation, **17**, 156

L
La Berge, Under Secretary Walter P., **38**
La Roque, Admiral Gene, 256
La Salle (AGF-3) assault ship, 137
Lafayette class missile submarines, **126**
Laird, Secretary of Defense, 36, 249
LAMPS (Light Airborne Multi-Purpose System), **105**, 112, 114
Lance see Vought MGM-52C
Landing Vehicle Tracked Personnel see LVTP
LARC see Low Altitude Ride Control
Law of the Sea (OJCS), 35
LCM 6 landing craft, 137
LCM 8 landing craft, 137, 138
LCU landing craft, **216**
LCVP landing craft, 137
Leahy class cruisers, 124, 125, 130
Lee, General Robert E., 13, 15
Lexington class aircraft carriers, 121
LGDM (Laser Guided Dispenser Munition), 226
LHA amphibious force craft, 114, 215
Lincoln, President Abraham, **13**
Little Rock (CLG-4) cruiser, **232**
Lockheed C-5A Galaxy, **21**, **30**, **67**, **67**, **72**, **152**, 157, **185**, 205, **223**, 260
Lockheed C-130 Hercules and variants, 152, **158**, **186**, **187**, 205, 230
  KC-130F, **212**
Lockheed C-141 A and B Starlifter, 152, 157, **186**, 260
Lockheed F-80C Shooting Star, **17**
Lockheed P-3 Orion, 227, 248
  -3C update II, **106**, 108, 110, **186**, **187**, **258**
Lockheed S-3A Viking, **186**, 188, **189**, 227
Lockheed SR-71 A, B and C Blackbird, **47**, **190**
Lockheed U-2, 48, **52**, 55, **190**
Lockheed UGM-27 Polaris SLBM A1, 61, 127, 220; -A2, 61, 126, 220; -A3, **59**, 66, 126, 127, **220**
Lockheed UGM-73 Poseidon SLBM, 58, 63, 104, 125, 254; C-3, 66, 126, **221**
Lockheed UGM-93 Trident SLBM, **62**, 66, 103, 112, 221; I (c-4), 66, 125, 126, **221**, 254; II (D-5), 66, 125, 221
Lockheed YF-12, 169
Lockwood (DE 1064) destroyer, **109**
Long Beach (CGN-9) cruiser, **103**, 120, **123**
Long Ranger see Bell Kiowa
Los Angeles class (SSN) submarines, 127, **142**
Low Altitude Ride Control (LARC), 202
LPH-10, **209**
LSD dock landing ship, **216**
LSU-1643 US Navy, **28**
Luttwak, Edward, 256, 257
LVTP-7 amphibious assault vehicle, **92**, **93**, 212, **213**; C- command version, 93; R- repair version, 93
L.Y. Spear submarine tender, **142**

M
M2 heavy machine gun see 0.50 calibre Browning
M7 Priest self-propelled howitzer, 96
M7A1-6 flame thrower, **86**
M16A1 Rifle see 5.56mm M16A1
M29 Mortar see 81mm M29 Mortar
M37 truck, 99
M47 see McDonnell Douglas FGM-77A
M48 medium tank, 86, **223**; A, 86; A1, 86; A2, 86; A2C, 86; A3, **18**, 86; A5, **86**, 248; AVLB (Armored Vehicle-Launched Bridge), 86
M60 Main battle tank, **72**, **87**, **161**, 248; A1, 71, 72, **73**, **87**, 212, 214, 248; A2, **71**, 72, **77**, **87**, **230**; A3, 71, 87; AVLB (Armored Vehicle-Launched Bridge), 87; M728 CEV (Combat Engineer Vehicle), 87
M60 General purpose machine gun see 7.62mm M60
M67 medium tank, 86; A1, **86**; A2, 86
M67 Recoilless rifle see 90mm M67
M72 Light anti-tank weapon see 66mm M72
M79 Grenade launcher see 40mm M79 and 5.56mm M16A1 Rifle
M88 Medium armored recovery vehicle, **97**
M106 see M113 Armored personnel carrier
M107 Self-propelled gun, 92, **93**
M109 Self-propelled howitzer, **93** 212, **229**, 248, **258**; A1, 73, 93; A2. **93**, 228
M109 R AFV, **81**, **234**, **235**
M110 self-propelled howitzer, 72, 73, **83**, 92, 212, 248
  A1 muzzle-brake, 92; E2, 92
M113 armored personnel carrier, 72, **76**, **91**, **186**, 234, 248; A1, 72, 91
M123A1 self-propelled howitzer see 155mm M114 Howitzer
M125 81mm mortar carrier see M113
M132 see M113 Armored personnel carrier
M151A1 Jeep, 214
M163 and variants see M113 Armored personnel carrier
M163 Vulcan self-propelled see 20mm Vulcan
M167 Vulcan towed see 20mm Vulcan
M203 Grenade launcher see 5.56mm M16A1 Rifle
M224 Lightweight company mortar see 60mm M224
M548 tracked cargo carrier see M113
M551 Sheridan light tank, 72, 73, **87**, **90**
M557 A1 command vehicle, **76**, 91
M561 Gama Goat vehicle, 96
M578 Light armored recovery vehicle, **97**
M656 five-ton truck, 230
M688 spare missile carrier see M113
M715 truck, 99
M727 Hawk carrier see M113
M730 Chaparral carrier see M113
M752 Lance carrier, 72, 91, **231**
M752 Lance carrier see also M113
M806A1 recovery vehicle see M113
M1911 A1 Pistol see 0.45 calibre
MAB see Mobile Assault Bridge
MacArthur, General Douglas, 19
McAuliffe, Eugene, Assistant Secretary of Defense, **41**
McClellan, George B., 18
McCormack-Curtis Amendment see Defense Reorganization Act 1958
McDonnell Douglas
  A-4 A to S and TA-4 Skyhawk, **191**, 212
  AGM-84A Harpoon, 179, **227**
  ASALM project, **222**
  AV-8B, **192**
  C-9, 152
  DC-10-30F ATCA, **157**
  F-4 Phantom II, 152, **154**, 156, 212, 248, 254, 263; EF-4, 194; EF-4E Wild Weasel, 195, 225, 226; F-4A to F-4S, 194; F-4B, **11**, 83; F-4D, **159**, **195**, **240**; F-4E, **149**, **156**, **165**, **194**, **195**; F-4J, **25**, 107, 111, 113, 115, **116**, **119**, **212**; F-4M (UK designation FGR.2), **194**; QF-4, 194; RF-4, 194; RF-4C, 154, **225**
  F-15 Eagle, **24**, **147**, 152, **154**, **156**, **226**, **239**, **256**, 260; F-15A, **196**, **197**; TF-15A, 196
  Northrop F-18 Hornet and Cobra, 113, **116**, 198; F-18A and A-18, **198**, **199**; Northrop YF-17, **198**
  F-101 Voodoo, 194; F-101 A, B and C, 194; RF-101 A to H, 194; RF-101C, **194**; RF-101H, **195**
  FGM-77A (M74) Dragon, 71, 72, 73, **75**, 212, 214, **233**
  ISSSMD ship-to-ship missile, 227
  KC-10A, **192**
  RGM-84A Harpoon, 107, **109**, 114, 116, 122, 127, 128, 133, 135
McNamara Secretary of Defense, 36, 61, 63, 83
MAD see 'Mutual Assured Destruction' defense strategy
Mahan, Prof. Dennis Hart, 18
Mahan, Rear Admiral Alfred Thayer, 15
Mahan (DLF-11, later DDG-42) guided missile destroyer, **130**
Manufacturers
  Aerojet, **115**; Avco Lycoming, 89; Bell Aircraft Corporation, **115**; Bettis Atomic Power Laboratory, 120; Bowen-

McLaughlin-York, 97; Cadillac Gage, 89; Chrysler, 86, 87, 88; Colt Firearms, 101; Control Data Corporation, 89; Detroit Diesel Allison DonGM, 89, 90; Detroit Tank Arsenal, 86, 87; FMC 91, 92, 94; Gould 145; Hesse Eastern Company, 99; Hughes Aircraft Company, 89; Ithaca, 101; Kaiser, 172; Kollmorgan Corporation, 89; Lockheed, **115**; Marconi-Elliott, 172; Maremart Corporation, 100; Martin Marietta, 228; Northrop, 145; Oto Melara (Italy), 91; Pacific Car and Foundry Co., Washington, 92, 97; Philco-Ford Corporation, 90, 238; Faufoss (Norway), 99; Remington, 101; Rock Island Arsenal, 95, 96; Singer-Kearfott, 89, 174; Texas Instruments, 228; Watervliet Arsenal, 98; Westinghouse, 145, 172

MAP see Military Assistance Program

Marine Corps
 2nd Batt. 3rd Division Vietnam 1968, **18**

Marine Corps Memorial, Arlington, **11**

Mars class (AFS) combat stores ship, **140**

Marshall, Col. (later General) George C., 19

Martin LGM-25C Titan II ICBM, 58, **60**, 61, 66, **222**

Martin MGM-31A Pershing, **82**, 83, **230**

Martin XM712 Copperhead, 95, **228**, **229**

Martin/Maxson AGM-12 Bullpup BASM, **224**

'Massive Retaliation' defense strategy, 61

Meade, Maj.Gen. George G., 13

Medium Range Ballistic Missiles, 254

MEECN see Minimum Essential Emergency Communications Network

Mexico, war 1846–1848, 13, 146

MGM 29A see Sergeant

MGM 31A see Martin

MGM-51C see Ford Aerospace

MGM 52C see Vought

MGR1B see Honest John

Mi-24 see Mil

Michigan (SSBN-727) submarine, 125, 221

MICV see XM723 mechanized infantry combat vehicle

Middle East
 US policy goals, 24

Midway (CV-41) aircraft carrier, **122**

Midway class aircraft carriers
 Coral Sea (CV-43), **122**
 Franklin D. Roosevelt (CV-42), 115, 122
 Midway (CV-41), **122**

MiG-21 see Mikoyan Gurevich

MiG-23 see Mikoyan Gurevich

MiG-25 see Mikoyan Gurevich

Mikoyan Gurevich MiG-21 Fishbed, **159**

Mikoyan Gurevich MiG-23 Flogger, **156**, **257**, 259, 260

Mikoyan Gurevich MiG-25 Foxbat, 154, **257**

Mil Mi-24 Hind helicopter (Soviet), 259, **260**

Military Airlift Command (DOD), 40, 157

Military Assistance Program (MAP), 30

MIM-14B see Western Electric

MIM-23 see Raytheon

MIM-72 see Aeronutronic Ford

Minimum Essential Emergency Communications Network, 44

Minuteman ICBM see Boeing LGM-30

MIRV see Multiple Independently Re-Targeted Vehicle

Missile motors
 Aerojet LR87 twin-chamber, 222; LR91 twin-chamber 222; Mk27 Mod 4 solid fuel 226; Mk52 Mod 2 Solid Fuel, 239; Mk53 Mod 2/3 solid fuel, 225, 237; Mk60 Mod 0 solid fuel, 240; General MX (TBD) B446-2 solid fuel, 227; Hercules Mk56 Mod 0, 236
 Allegheny Ballistics solid fuel, 232
 Amoco solid fuel, 230
 Atlantic Research solid fuel, 234; Mk30 Mod 2, 236
 Hercules, 220, 221, 237, 239
 Integral rocket/ramjet McD.D. project ASALM. 222
 LPC-415 re-startable two-pulse solid fuel, 219
 Naval Propellant Plant Mk12 Mod 1, 236
 Rocketdyne Mk36 Mod 5 solid fuel, 234
 Rocketdyne Mk37 Mod 0 solid fuel, 240
 Rocketdyne Mk38 Mod 4 solid fuel, 239
 Rocketdyne Mk39 Mod 7 solid fuel, 225
 Rocketdyne P8E-9 liquid, 231
 Teledyne CAE J402 turbojet, 220, 227
 Thiokol, 221, 226; TE-260G solid fuel, 228; TX-58 solid fuel, 240; TX-481 solid fuel, 222; TX-486 solid fuel, 237; XM 105/6 solid fuel, 230
 Williams Research F107-WR-100 turbofan, 218, 220

Mississinewa (AO-144) fleet oiler, **111**

Mississippi (ex BB-41) Terrier SAM trials, 124

Missouri USS, **16**

Mitchell, General Billy US Army Air Corps., 146

Mitscher class destroyers, **131**

Mk26 combined SAM/ASM/SSM twin launcher, 122, 131

Mk32 torpedo tubes, **108**, 132, 133

Mk71 8in (203mm) gun, 132

Mobile Assault Bridge (MAB), **79**

Mohawk see Grumman OV-IA-D

Mohr, Major General Henry, 250

Mondale, Vice President Walter, 20, 23

'Mothball Fleet' San Diego, **243**

Mount McKinley class command ships, 136

Mount Whitney LCC-20, **114**

MRBMs see Medium Range Ballistic Missiles

Multiple Independently Re-Targeted Vehicle, 63, 252, 254

Mutual and Balanced Force Reduction (OJCS), 35

'Mutual Assured Destruction' defense strategy, 61, 62

M-X ICBM, 66, **67**, **223**, 257

N

Narwhal (SSN-671) submarine, 128

National Command Authorities, 44

National Emergency Airborne Command Post, 44

National Guard
 M48AS medium tank, **86**

National Military Command Center, 44

National Military Command System, 44

National Photographic Interpretation Center, 55

National Security
 areas of possible military conflict 20

National Security Act 1947, 32, 40, 49, 208

National Security Agency (DOD), 36, 37, 53

National Security Council, **33**, 40
 Report (NSC-68) 1950, 58

NATO (North Atlantic Treaty Organization)
 American views, 20, 22, 23, 68, 75, 82, 105, 159
 Claude V. Ricketts mixed manning, 132
 reservist factor in defense strategy, 242
 strategy in the event of war, 260
 US Air Force close air support, 149
 US Tactical Nuclear weapons, 83
 Warsaw Pact/NATO military balance, 260

NATO III communications satellite, **50**, **51**

Nautilus (SSN-571) submarine, 128

Navy Tactical Data System (NTDS), 108, 136, 182

NB-52G see Boeing

NCA see National Command Authorities

NEACP see National Emergency Airborne Command Post

Neosho class (AO) fleet oilers, **144**

Neutron bomb see Enhanced radiation warhead

Newport class tank landing ships, **139**

Nike Hercules see Western Electric MIM-14B

Nimitz, Admiral Chester A., 19

Nimitz class aircraft carriers
 Carl Vinson (CVN-70), 118
 Dwight D. Eisenhower (CVN-69), 118
 Nimitz (CVN-68), **111**, **118**, **262**

90mm M67 Recoilless rifle, **100**

NIPS (Naval Intelligence Processing System), 136

Nitro class (AE) ammunition ships, 141

Nitze, Paul, 256

Nixon, President Richard, 22, 23
 'Safeguard' ABM deployment plan, 64

NMCC see National Military Command Center

NMCS see National Military Command System

Norfolk (DL-1) destroyer leader, 131

Normandy landings, 1944, 14

North American (Rockwell) F-100 Super Sabre, **154**, **244**, 248; DF-100F, 198; F-100A to -100F, 198, 199; F-100C, **199**

North-South issues, 31

Northampton (CC-1) command ship, 136

Northrop A-9, 154
 F-5 Freedom Fighter and Tiger II, 152, **200**; F-5A, B, E and F, 200; F-5A Freedom Fighter, **200**, **224**; F-5E Tiger II, **159**, **200**; CF-5A and D, 200; NF-5A and B, 200; RF-5A, E and G, 200; SF-FA and B, 200
 P.530, 172
 T-38 Talon, **21**
 YF-17 see McDonnell Douglas/Northrop F-18

NPIC see National Photographic Interpretation Center

NSA see National Security Agency

NTDS see Navy Tactical Data System

Nuclear Attack Submarine (SSN), 142

Nuclear Ballistic Missile Submarine (SSBN), 52, 125, 142, 221

Nuclear delivery vehicles US/USSR, 254

Nuclear power plant, naval
 A4W/AIG reactors, 118
 D2G reactors, 122, 123, 124, 127
 S3W reactor, 128
 S4W reactor, 128
 S5G free-circulation reactor, 128
 S5W2 reactor, 128
 General Electric S8G reactor, 125
 Westinghouse CIW reactors, 123
 Westinghouse S5W reactor, 126 128

Nuclear-Powered Guided Missile Cruisers, 122

Nuclear weapons and capabilities, 82, 254

O

O-2 see Cessna

Observation Island (AG) experimental ship, **144**

Office of Management and Budget, 42

Office of the Joint Chiefs of Staff (OJCS), 35

Office of the Secretary of Defense (OSD), 32, 42, 246

Office of the Secretary of the Air Force, 148

OH-4A see Bell Kiowa

OH-58A see Bell Kiowa

Ohio (SSBN-726) submarine, **103**, 125, 221, 254

Ohio class missile submarines, **125**, 126

Oil
 US Strategy and economics, 27

OJCS see Office of the Joint Chiefs of Staff

Okinawa (LPH) amphibious assault ship, **137**

OL-93 radar data processor, 182

Oliver Hazard Perry class frigate, **114**, **133**

OMB see Office of Management and Budget

Omega global navigation system, 197

105mm gun (M60A1 tank), 71, **86**

105mm M101 A1 Howitzer, 75, **96**

105mm M102 Light Howitzer, **96**, 212

106mm recoilless rifle, 212, 214

152mm gun M60A2 tank, 71, 230
 M551 light armor vehicle, 73, **230**

155mm M114 Howitzer, 72, 75, 83, **95**

155mm M114 Howitzer
 M123A1 self-propelled version, 95

155mm M198 Towed howitzer, **95**, 212, 228

155mm self-propelled howitzer, see M109

155mm nuclear projectile, 83

175mm SP gun, **72**, 212

Operation Sea Orbit, 1964, 123

Oregon City converted to Northampton (CC-1), 136

Oregon City class heavy cruisers, 124

Organization of the Joint Chief of Staff (OJCS) see Office of the Joint Chiefs of Staff (OJCS)

Orion see Lockheed P.-3

Oriskany (CVA-34, later CV-34) aircraft carrier, 130, **246**

OSD see Office of the Secretary of Defense

OV-1 A to D see Grumman

OV-10 see Rockwell

P

P-3 Orion see Lockheed

P.530 see Northrop

Pacific Air Forces, 151

Pacific Command (DOD), 38

Packard, David, Deputy Secretary of Defense 1969–72, 32

Paigo (SSN) submarine, **145**

Paris, Treaties of 1763 and 1783, 12

Park, President (Republic of Korea), 23

Patriot see Raytheon/Martin XMIM-104A

Pave Penny laser pod, **170**

Pave Spike TV/laser pods, 195

Pave Strike GBU-15 glide bomb, 163, **223**

Pave Tack FLIR/laser pods, 195

Paveway 'smart' bombs, **226** see also KMU-421/B

PBD see Program Budget Decisions

PDM see Program Decision Memorandum

Pegasus class (PHM) patrol hydrofoils, **135**

Pegasus (PHM-1) hydrofoil, **135**

Penkovsky, Colonel Oleg, 56

Pentagon, **33**

Permit class (SSN) submarines, 128

Pershing, General John J., 10, 14

Pershing see Martin MGM-31A

Phalanx gun system, **108**, 113, 115, 130

Phantom II see McDonnell Douglas F-4

Philadelphia (Los Angeles class) SSN submarine, **127**

Philippines
 129th Reg't, 37th Division, **15**

Phoenix see Hughes AIM-5A

Piedmont destroyer tender, **142**

Pigeon class (ASR) submarine rescue ships, **143**

Planning Programming and Budgeting System, 40

Planning Programming Guidance Memorandum, 40

'Pluton' missiles, 83, **230**

Pogy (SSN-647) submarine, 128

0.45 Calibre M1911 A1 pistol, **101**

0.50 Calibre Browning M2 Heavy machine gun, **100**

Polaris SLBM see Lockheed UGM-27.

Polk, President James K., 13

POM see Program Objective Memoranda

Poseidon SLBM see Lockheed UGM-73

PPBS see Planning Programming and Budgetary System

PPGM see Planning Programming Guidance Memorandum

Prebble (DDG) guided missile destroyer, **130**

Priest self-propelled howitzer see M7

Program Budget Decisions, 42

Program Decision Memorandum, 42

Program Objective Memoranda, 41

Prowler see Grumman EA-6A

Puget Sound destroyer tender, 141

Q

Quadrad Strategic offensive forces, 58

Quailes, Secretary of the Air Force strategic doctrine of sufficiency, 61

R

RA-5C see Rockwell

Radar
 APQ-100, -109, 195
 APS-94 side-looking, **183**
 APS-96 long-range, 182
 APS-116, 188
 APS-120, 182
 Hughes APG-63, **196**
 Hughes ASG-18 pulse doppler, 190
 Hughes AWG-9, 180, **240**
 Hughes AWG-10 pulse-doppler, 195
 Nasarr monopulse, 201
 Norden multi-mode, 185
 SPG-55 missile control, **125**
 SPG-60 pulse doppler air track, **108**
 SPQ-9A surface track, **108**
 SPS-32/33 118, **120**, 123
 SPS-40B air surveillance, **108**
 SPS-48, **118**
 TFR (terrain following radar), **174**
 Westinghouse APY-1, **154**, 166

Raleigh (LPD-1) assault transport, **137**

Raleigh class (LPD) assault transports, 137

RAND Corporation defense strategy studies, 61

Ranger (CV-61) aircraft carrier, **121**

Ranger infantry, 73

Raytheon AIM-7 Sparrow, **239**; -7E, -7E2, 107, **116**, 152, **194**; -7F, **180**, **239**

Raytheon MIM-23 Hawk 91, 214, **236**

Raytheon RIM-7 Sea Sparrow, 108; -7E, 119, 120, 136, **137**, 140, 141, **237**, 239

Raytheon/Martin XMIM-104A Patriot, **237**

Readiness Command (DOD), 38

Realists
 concept of American-Soviet position, 22

Redeye see General Dynamics FIM-43A

Re-entry vehicles
 Mk11C on Minuteman II, 219
 Mk12 on Minuteman III, **64**, 219
 Trident on Atlas launcher, **221**

Regulus 1 SSM, 127

'Regulus' II SSM, 82, 123, 128, **129**

Republic (Fairchild) F-105 Thunderchief
 F-105 B, D, F and G, **154**, 201
 -105F, **226**; F-105G Wild Weasel, **156**, **201**, 226

Reserve Component Test Program 1972–4, 246

RF-4C see McDonnell Douglas F-4 Phantom II

RGM-66D see General Dynamics

Richmond K. Turner (DLG-20) frigate, **113**

Rickover, Admiral, USN, 130

RIM-7 see Raytheon

RIM-8 see Bendix

RIM-66/67 see General Dynamics

Ripley, Eleazar Wheelock, 10

Roanoke (AOR) replenishment oiler, **140**

Rockeye area weapon see CBU

Rockwell
 B-1, **66**, 67, 150, 163, **202**
 GBU-15 Hobos guided bomb, 163, **223**, 225
 Hellfire missile, **224**,
 OV-10; -10A, 154
 RA-5C Vigilante, **121**, 203; A-5A, 203; A-5B, 203
 XFV-12 (NR-356), 201; -12A, 201

Rogers, General Bernard W., **38**

Roland 2, short-range air defense system see Euromissile/Hughes Boeing

'Round Out' reserve units, 81

Rummel, Rudolf, 256

RVR-5A Asroc see Honeywell

RV see Grumman OV-1A to D

S

S-3A see Lockheed

SA-2 SAM, **55**

Sabre see North American F-86

SACEUR see Supreme Allied Command Europe

Sadat, President of Egypt, **29**

SAGE see Semi-Automatic Ground Environment defense system

Sagger anti-tank missile (Soviet), 259

SALT see Strategic Arms Limitation Talks

SAM see Surface-to-Air Missiles

Sampson (DDG) destroyer, **132**

Sanctuary (AH) hospital ship, 145

Sandal see SS-4

Santa Barbara (AE) ammunition ship, **141**

Samuel Gompers destroyer tenders, **141**

Saratoga (CV-60) aircraft carrier, 121, **189**

Sargo (SSN-583) submarine, 128

Satellite orbits, **52**, 55

Saudi Arabia
 US arms sales, 29

SCAD (Subsonic Cruise Armed Decoy) see Boeing AGM-86

Scapegoat see SS-14

Schlesinger, Secretary of Defense James R., 23, 65, 83, 172, 246, 257

Schriever, General Bernard, USAF, 60

Scorpion (launched George Washington SSBN-598) submarine, 127

Scorpion tank, **40**

Scott, Winfield, 10

Sea King helicopters see Sikorsky S-61

Sea Knight helicopter see Boeing Vertol CH-46A

Sea Mauler short range SAM, 133

Sea Phoenix see Hughes AIM-54A Phoenix

Sea Ranger see Bell Kiowa

Sea Sparrow see Raytheon RIM-7

Sea Sprite helicopter see Kaman SH-2D

Sea Stallion helicopter see Sikorsky S-65

Seadragon (SSN-584) submarine, 128

Sea-launched Cruise Missile (SLCM), **220**

Seawolf TH-IL helicopter see Bell Huey

Security Supporting Assistance, 30

Sego see SS-11

Seismic detector, US Army, **56**

Semi-Automatic Ground Environment (SAGE) defense system, 169

Sensors, air-dropped, **57**

Sentry see Boeing E-3A

Sergeant MGM-29A missile, 83

SES see Surface Effect Ship

7.62mm M60 General purpose machine gun, **100**, 212

Shaddock SLCM see SS-N-3

Shah of Iran, **28**

Sheridan, Maj. Gen. Philip, 13

Sheridan light tank see M551

Sherman, Maj. Gen. William Tecumseh, 13

Shillelagh see Ford Aerospace MGM-51C

Shinano, Japanese aircraft carrier, 121

Shipyards
 Avondale Shipyards, Westwego, 133
 Litton Industries, **115**, 136
 Newport News Shipbuilding and Dry Dock Co., 118

Shooting Star see Lockheed F-80

SHORADS see Short-range air-defense system

Short-range air-defense system, **81**

Short Range Attack Missiles (SRAM), **177**, **218**, **219**, 252

Shrike see Texas Instruments AGM-45

Sidewinder see AIM-9

Sikorsky
 S-61 helicopter, 204
  HH-3A, 204
  RH-3A and variants, 204
  SH-3A and -3D Sea King, **121**, **204**
 S-64 helicopter, 203
  CH-54A Tarke, **203**
  CH-54B Tarke, 203
 S-65 helicopter, 204
  CH-53A Sea Stallion, 136, **137**, **204**
  CH-53D Sea Stallion, **204**, **209**, **217**
  CH-53E, 204
  HH-53, 204
  RH-53 and variants, 204
 UH-60A, helicopter, **205**
  S-70, 205
  SH-60B, **205**

Simon Lake class submarine tenders, 141, **142**

SIOP see Strategic Integrated Operations Plan

SIRCS (Shipboard Intermediate Range Combat System), 239

1610 class LCU, 136, 138

60mm M224 Lightweight company mortar, **98**, 212

66mm M72 Light Anti-tank weapon, 99; A2, **99**

Skate class (SSN) submarines, 128

Skean see SS-5

Skipjack class (SSN) submarines, 127

Skyhawk see McDonnell Douglas A-4

Skywarrior see Douglas A3D-2

SLBMs see Submarine Launched Ballistic Missiles

SLCM see Sea-Launched Cruise Missile
Somers (DDG) destroyer, **132**
SONAR, 56
BQQ-2, 128
BQQ-5 hull-mounted, 113, 127, 128
SQS-14 mine detector, 134
SQS-23, 132
SQS-26, 107, 132
SQS-53, 108
SONAR communications
WQS-2, 108
Sonobuoys, **106**
South Africa, **27**
South Carolina (CGN-37) cruiser, 123
Southern Command (DOD), 38
Soviet Union
ABM program, 1960s, 63
anti-submarine warfare capability, 66
chemical warfare capability, 81
ICBM capability, 252
Naval expansion and deployments, 108
Western Europe force structure and doctrine, 75
Spaatz, Carl A., 19
Spain, war 1898, 14
Sparrow see Raytheon AIM-7
Spear class submarine tenders, 141, 142
Specified commands (DOD), 38, 40
Spruance (DD-963/DDG-47) class destroyers, **108**, 114, **131**
Sputnik satellites, 60
SR-71 see Lockheed
SRAM see Short Range Attack Missiles
SS-4 Sandal missiles (Soviet), 260
SS-5 Skean missiles (Soviet), 260
SS-9 ICBM (Soviet), 252
SS-11 'Sego' ICBM (Soviet), 252
SS-14 Scapegoat IRBM (Soviet), **254**
SS-16 ICBM (Soviet), 252
SS-17 ICBM (Soviet), 252
SS-18 ICBM (Soviet), 252
SS-19 ICBM (Soviet), 252
SS-20 ICBM (Soviet), 252, 260
SSBN see Nuclear Ballistic Missile submarine
SSBN-726/7 Trident armed nuclear submarines, 125, 221
SSN see Nuclear Attack Submarine
SS-N-3 Shaddock SLCM (Soviet), 254
SS-N-4 Snark SLBM (Soviet), 127
SS-N-8 SLBM (Soviet), 125, 254
SS-N-12 SLBM (Soviet), 254
SS-N-19 SLBM (Soviet), 254
Standard I and II see General Dynamics RIM-66/67
Standard ARM AGM-78D/RGM-66D see General Dynamics
Starlifter see Lockheed C-141
State Department
intelligence function, 49, 52, 57
Steinbrunner, Prof. John, 256
Stetson, John, Air Force Secretary, **35**
Steuben, Baron von, 10
Stinger see General Dynamics XFIM-92A
Strategic Air Command (DOD), 40, 58, 61, 66, 150
Strategic Arms Limitation (OJCS), 35
Strategic Arms Limitation Talks (SALT), 22, 56, 63, 64, 125, 254, 256
Strategic Integrated Operations Plan, 44
Stratofortress see Boeing B-52
Stratolifter see Boeing C-135
Stratotanker see Boeing C-135
Strausz-Hupe, Robert, **41**
Sturgeon class (SSN) submarines, **128**, **145**
Su-19 see Sukhoi
Submarine Launched Ballistic Missiles, 58, **59**, 60, 61, 104, 123, 125, 228, 252, 254
Submarines, USN
Polaris/Poseidon armed, 60, 66
Subroc see Goodyear UUM-44A
Subsonic Cruise Armed Decoy see Boeing AGM-86 SCAD
'Sufficiency' strategic defense doctrine, 62, 64, 65
Suffolk County class tank landing ships, **140**
Sukhoi Su-19 Fencer (Soviet), 259, 260
Super Sabre see North American F-100
Supreme Allied Command Europe (SACEUR), 152
Surface Effect Ship, **115**, **135**
Surface-to-Air Missiles, 63
Suribachi class (AE) ammunition ships, 141
SUU-54 cluster munition, 226
Swordfish (SSN-579) submarine, 128
Systems Analaysis Division (OSD), 32

T

T-38 Talon see Northrop
T-55 tank, **55**
T-62 battle tanks (Soviet), 263
T-72 battle tank (Soviet), **259**, 260
TA-4 see McDonnell Douglas A-4
TACAN, 136
Tactical Air Command, US Air Force, 151, 152
Tactical Operations System (TOS), 81
Taft, Senator, 20
Talon see Northrop T-38
Talos see Bendix RIM-8
Tang class submarines, 130
Tank Landing Ships (LST), **139**
Tarawa class (LHS) amphibious assault ships, **136**, 127, **215**
Tarke see Sikorsky S-64
Tartar SAM, 107
Mk11 twin launcher, **132**
Mk13 single launcher, 131, **132**, 133
TAV-8A see British Aerospace AV-8A Harrier
Taylor, General Maxwell, US Army, 61
Teledyne Ryan BQM-34B (Firebee RPV), **186**, **236**
'Terrier' surface-to-air missile, 83, 107, 119, 120, 123, **125**, 130
Texas Instruments AGM-45 Shrike, 152, **191**, **195**, **225**
Texas Instruments AGM-88A HARM, 154, 195, **226**
TH-IL Seawolf helicopter see Bell Huey
TH-57A Sea Ranger see Bell Kiowa
Thayer, Superintendent Sylvanus, 18
Thermonuclear weapons
Mk28, 219 see also Warheads
30mm cannon, 80
37mm anti-tank gun, **15**
Thomaston class assault transports, **138**, **144**
Thor IRBM, 60
3in. (76mm) gun mountings, **137**, **138**, 139, 140, 143, 144
Thresher (SSN-593) submarine, 128
Thunderchief see Republic (Fairchild) F-105
Thunderstick all-weather blind attack system, **201**
Tiger II see Northrop F-5E
Titan II ICBM see Martin LGM-25C
Tomahawk see BGM-109
Tomcat see Grumman F-14
Torpedo propulsion systems, 145
Torpedoes
Mk16 Mod 8 ship and submarine, 145
Mk30 Mod 1 training, 145
Mk37 Mod 0 submarine, 145
Mk37 Mod 1 submarine, 145
Mk37C submarine, **145**
Mk43 Mod 1 aircraft and ship, 145
Mk44 Mod 0 aircraft and ship, 145, 185
Mk46 Mod 0 general purpose, 108, 145, 185
Mk48 Mod 1 ship and submarine, **145**
TOS see Tactical Operations System
Total Ship Procurement Package, 131, 133
Tow see Hughes BGM-71
Training and Doctrine Command (TRADOC), 245
Treasury Department
contribution to intelligence pool, 52
Trenton assault transport, **137**
'Triad' strategic offensive forces, 58, 64, 66
Trident SLBM see Lockheed UGM-93
Triton (SSN-586) submarine, 128
Truman, President Harry S., 20, 37
Truxton (CGN-35) cruiser, **103**, **124**
Tu-16 see Tupolev
Tu-22 see Tupolev
Tu-26 see Tupolev
Tube-launched, Optically-tracked, Wire-guided anti-tank missile see TOW
Tucumcari (PGH-2) hydrofoil, 135
Tullibee (SSN-597) submarine, **128**
Tupolev
Tu-16 Badger, 254
Tu-22 Blinder, **25**, 254
Tu-26 Backfire, 254
20mm cannon, IFV, 72
20mm Vulcan Air Defense System, 72, 91, 99, **117**, 130; M163 self-propelled version, 99; M167 towed version, **99**
206-B, -L Long Ranger see Bell Kiowa
208mm 'atomic cannon', 82
2.75in aerial rocket, 80
Type XXI submarine (Germany), 130

U

U2 see Lockheed
UH-1 see Bell
UH-4 see Boeing Vertol
Unified commands (DOD), 38
United States
civilian element in reserves, 245
equipment levels of reserve forces, 248
limitations of deterrence strategy, 256
military personnel strengths by Area/Country, 264
military strength, July 31, 1977, 264
political implications of military strength, 258
reserve forces' readiness, 242
reserve % of DOD functional mix, 248
reserve personnel problems, 247
reserves budgetary authorizations, 248
reservist role in disaster situation, **250**
Selective Service System, 242
Soviet/US battalion weaponry types compared, 214
Soviet/US strategic balance, 252, 259
Strategic Intelligence, 48
United States Air Forces in Europe, 151
United States (CVA-58) aircraft carrier, 120, 121
United States intelligence agencies, 49
United States Security Assistance, 30
Upton, Brevet. Maj. Gen. Emory, 15
US Air Force
air commands, 150
aircraft types and flying hours FYs '68, '77, '78, 156
aircraft types and numbers, active duty squadrons, 152
command, control and communications, 149
flying squadrons functional mix, active and reserve, 245
installations FYs '68, '77 compared, 150
Reserve Forces component, 150, 154, 244, 245
reservists' training situation, 246
squadron strength FYs '68, '74, '76, '77, '78, 154
9th Strategic Air Reconnaissance Wing, 190
support elements, 158
1st Tactical Fighter Wing, 197
20th Tactical Fighter Wing, **177**
35th Tactical Fighter Wing, **149**
36th Tactical Fighter Wing, **197**
354th Tactical Fighter Wing, **152**
US Army
active defense tactics, W. Europe, 76
82nd Airborne Division, **75**, 96
101st Airborne Division, **73**, 96
Armored and Mechanized Infantry Divisions, Europe, 72
Armored Battalion organization, 71
1st Armored Division, **79**
Battalion maneuver units, 68, 71
Brigade formation, 68
deployment factors, W. Europe, 79
Division formation and function, 68
Division of Military Aeronautics, 146
Infantry Battalion structure, 72
Maneuver forces units and locations, 79
Mechanized Infantry Battalion structure, 72
offensive tactics, W. Europe, 77
reservists' training situation, 246
10th Special Forces Group, **80**
tactical doctrine, 75
weapons and tactical developments, 80
USINCEUR see Commander-in-Chief, US European Command
US Marine Corps
air wings, 212
anti-aircraft weapons, 214
anti-tank weapons, 214
beach assault function, **209**, 214
current strength and deployment, 210
Marine Amphibious Unit (MAU), 211, 212, 214
Mobilization Operational Tests, 247
organization and weapons, 212
reservists readiness, 246
statutory definition of function, 208, 210
task organization and tactics, 212, 215
US/Soviet 'type' battalion weapons compared, 214
Vocational Education (VOTEC) program, 250
US Navy
amphibious elements, 104, 106, 111
ASW developments, 113
bases and 'homeporting', 107
building program, 1978–82, 112
composition, 1978, 108
fleet co-ordination, 108
fleet deployment and organization, 1978, 109
function in NATO war, 105, 114
nuclear fuel and weapons debate, 116
objectives, 102
operational patterns and capabilities, 102, 104, 110, 114
peacetime deployment, 105
shipborne technological improvements, 107
ships, functional mix active/reserve, 246
6th Fleet
Fast Combat Support Ship (AOE), **105**
Suda Bay, Crete, **131**
UHF radio communications, 114, 115
wartime functions, 105
US Signal Corps, Aeronautical Division, 146
US-Soviet trade and technological exchange, **23**
USAF Satellite Control Facility, **49**
UUM-44A Subroc see Goodyear
Uzushio class submarines (Japan), 130

V

Vance, Secretary of State, Cyrus, 20
Vancouver (LPD-2) assault transport, 137
Vandenburg, Senator, 20
Vietnam War (c1965–73), 68, 150
B-52F bombing mission, **19**
1st Infantry Dvn. Jan '66, **18**
2nd Batt. 3rd Dvn. Marine Corps, **18**
Vigilante see Rockwell RA-5C
Viking see Lockheed S-3A
Virginia (CGN) class cruisers, **122**
Visual display units, **55**
Vought
A-7 Corsair II, 83, 111, 113, **120**, **121**, **154**, 248, 254; A-7A, **206**; A-7A to E, 206; A-7C, **227**; A-7D, **152**, 154, **223**; A-7E, **206**, **225**, 227, 263; TA-7C, 206
F-8 Crusader, **119**; DF-8, 206, 207; F-8A to -8J, 206; F-8E, 207; F-8J, **207**; F-8L, **206**; QF-8, 206, 207; RF-8, 206
GSRS (General Support Rocket System), **228**
MGM-52C Lance, 83, 91, **231**
Vulcan air defense system see 20mm Vulcan

W

W70-3 ER warhead, 85
W70-9 ER projectile, 85
Wacker, Fred P., A.Sec. Def. (Comptroller), **43**
Waddell (DDG) destroyer, **132**
Wahkiakum County LST-1162, **114**
Wainwright (DLG-28) destroyer, **236**
Wallace, Vice President Henry, 20
Walleye glide bomb see Hughes/Martin AGM-62
Warheads
enhanced radiation, 84, **85**
Soviet/US capability, 254, 256
Soviet/US throw-weights compared, 254
Warheads, ICBM
W-62, 200 kT in Mk12 vehicle, **64**
W-78, 350 kT in Mk12A vehicle, 219, 257
Warheads, SLCM
Bullpup B on Tomahawk, **220**
Washington, General George, 10, 46
Water jet propulsion, **92**
Weapon Able AS rocket launcher, 131
Weizman, Ezer, Israeli Defense Minister, **35**
West Point Military Academy, 10, 18
Western Electric MIM-14B Nike Hercules, 83, **241**
White House, **37**, 42
Wichita class (AOR) replenishment oilers, 140
William Tell weapons meet, Nellis, 1977, **154**
Wilson, General Louis H. jr., Marine Commandant, **35**, **38**
Wilson, Major Thomas A., 246
Wilson, President Woodrow, 14
World War I
43rd Balloon Company USA, **14**
Marine Corps., Bellcan Wood action, 208
Worldwide Military Command and Control System, 44
Wright (CC-2) command ship, 136
WU-2 see Lockheed U-2
WWMCCS see Worldwide Military Command and Control System
Wyoming massacre, July 1778, **12**

X

Xenon searchlight, **86**
XFIM-92A see General Dynamics
XMI Abrams main battle tank, **88**
XMIM-104A see Raytheon/Martin
XM198 Towed howitzer see 155mm M198 Towed Howitzer
XM474 tracked vehicle, 230
XM-712 see Martin
XM723 Mechanized infantry combat vehicle, **94**, 232
XM-727 Hawk reload carrier, **236**
XQM-103 RPV, **158**

Y

Yak-28 see Yakovlev
Yakovlev Yak-28 Brewer, **156**
Yankee class (SSBN) submarines, (Soviet Union), 127
YF-12A and C see Lockheed SR-71
YF-17 see McDonnell Douglas/Northrop F-18
Yun Po-son, former ROK president, 23

Z

Zaire
C-5A airlifts US supplies, **30**
Zulu class submarine (Soviet Union), 127
Zumwalt, Admiral Elmo ret'd, 262

Picture Credits

The publishers would like to thank wholeheartedly all the organizations, agencies, companies and the many individuals who have scoured their collections and so helped us to illustrate this book in the best manner possible.

Most of the photographs published in this book are official US Defense Department photographs supplied by the audio-visual services of the United States Air Force, Navy, Army and Marine Corps, and of the Department of Defense Office of Public Affairs. In addition, the Photograph Libraries of the State Department and The White House also provided photographs. Many of the photographs which appear in the weaponry sections (and elsewhere) were supplied by the manufacturers of the weapons and systems involved. Certain photographic agencies, professional periodicals and other organizations also supplied photographs, as follows: pages **10-11** (bottom): Gettysburg National Military Park (via Weidenfeld and Nicolson): **12**: Orbis Picture Library; **13**: Radio Times Hulton Picture Library; **14** (top): Robert Hunt Library; **21** (top, right): Popperfoto; **24**: Popperfoto; **46-47**: NASA; **255** (top): Educational and Television Films Ltd.; **257** (top): *Flight International*; **257** (bottom): Interinfo; **259** (top): *International Defense Review*; **261** (top): Soviet Studies Centre, RMA Sandhurst; **262**: British Ministry of Defence.

 Turnhout (Belgium)

PRINTED IN BELGIUM

Picture Credits

The publishers would like to thank wholeheartedly all the organizations, agencies, companies and the many individuals who have scoured their collections and so helped us to illustrate this book in the best manner possible.

Most of the photographs published in this book are official US Defense Department photographs supplied by the audio-visual services of the United States Air Force, Navy, Army and Marine Corps, and of the Department of Defense Office of Public Affairs. In addition, the Photograph Libraries of the State Department and The White House also provided photographs. Many of the photographs which appear in the weaponry sections (and elsewhere) were supplied by the manufacturers of the weapons and systems involved. Certain photographic agencies, professional periodicals and other organizations also supplied photographs, as follows: pages **10-11** (bottom): Gettysburg National Military Park (via Weidenfeld and Nicolson); **12**: Orbis Picture Library; **13**: Radio Times Hulton Picture Library; **14** (top): Robert Hunt Library; **21** (top, right): Popperfoto; **24**: Popperfoto; **46-47**: NASA; **255** (top): Educational and Television Films Ltd.; **257** (top): *Flight International*; **257** (bottom): Interinfo; **259** (top): *International Defense Review*; **261** (top): Soviet Studies Centre, RMA Sandhurst; **262**: British Ministry of Defence.